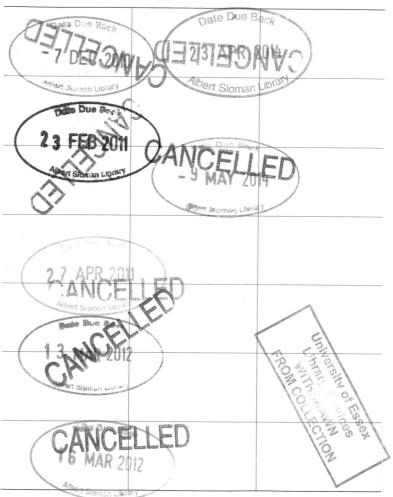

BUTTERWORTHS CORE TEXT SERIES

The Law of Trusts

Fourth Edition

J E Penner
Reader in Law, London School of Economics

Series Editor

Nicola Padfield
Fitzwilliam College, Cambridge

 LexisNexis™ UK

Members of the LexisNexis Group worldwide

United Kingdom	LexisNexis UK, a Division of Reed Elsevier (UK) Ltd, Halsbury House, 35 Chancery Lane, LONDON, WC2A 1EL, and 4 Hill Street, EDINBURGH EH2 3JZ
Argentina	LexisNexis Argentina, BUENOS AIRES
Australia	LexisNexis Butterworths, CHATSWOOD, New South Wales
Austria	LexisNexis Verlag ARD Orac GmbH & Co KG, VIENNA
Canada	LexisNexis Butterworths, MARKHAM, Ontario
Chile	LexisNexis Chile Ltda, SANTIAGO DE CHILE
Czech Republic	Nakladatelství Orac sro, PRAGUE
France	Editions du Juris-Classeur SA, PARIS
Germany	LexisNexis Deutschland GmbH, FRANKFURT, M
Hong Kong	LexisNexis Butterworths, HONG KONG
Hungary	HVG-Orac, BUDAPEST
India	LexisNexis Butterworths, NEW DELHI
Ireland	LexisNexis, DUBLIN
Italy	Giuffrè Editore, MILAN
Malaysia	Malayan Law Journal Sdn Bhd, KUALA LUMPUR
New Zealand	LexisNexis Butterworths, WELLINGTON
Poland	Wydawnictwo Prawnicze LexisNexis, WARSAW
Singapore	LexisNexis Butterworths, SINGAPORE
South Africa	LexisNexis Butterworths, DURBAN
Switzerland	Stämpfli Verlag AG, BERNE
USA	LexisNexis, DAYTON, Ohio

© Reed Elsevier (UK) Ltd 2004
Published by LexisNexis UK

A CIP Catalogue record for this book is available from the British Library.

ISBN 0 406 97364 4

Printed and bound in Great Britain by William Clowes Limited, Beccles and London

Visit LexisNexis UK at www.lexisnexis.co.uk

Preface

Trusts is a gripping subject; unfortunately it grips most students with anxiety. There is good reason for this: it is difficult. Almost every topic in the law of trusts is complicated by demanding intellectual problems, about the correct solutions to which academics and judges alike disagree. The consequence is that a 'Trusts Made Easy' book is like a 'Physical Chemistry Made Easy' book, a book for fools or the gullible. This is a 'Trusts Made Possible' book. It is a shorter text which explains from first principles what trusts is about, so that by the end of the book you should be 'up to speed' not only on the law, but on the important academic controversies surrounding it, which will be of assistance to readers wishing to do well on a typical LLB exam on the subject. I do not presume that you are already an expert on any area of law. Thus I have tried in the introduction and elsewhere to provide the legal and conceptual building blocks of the subject, even if they are also taught (one hopes they are taught) in other subjects on the standard LLB syllabus. For that reason, if you are only interested in the law of trusts, and not reading for a law degree — say you've just been made a beneficiary under a trust, or your general reading tastes run to the peculiar — this book is also for you.

The law of trusts is judge-made (though it has, of course, been amended here and there by Parliament). That is, it was created by judges over time deciding actual cases, building up the body of rules and principles we today recognise as trusts law. For that reason, if you want to write a really good exam script in the subject, ie get a first, you will simply have to read some cases and not rely entirely on this book, or on any other book for that matter. Any textbook is just the author's interpretation of the law, whereas the law itself is found in the cases. To do well you must read them and interpret them by your own lights (taking into account, of course, the views of others mentioned in this book and elsewhere). And if you really want to plumb the depths and soar the heights of trusts law, feel it in your bones and exude it from your pores, reading the cases is a must. (I include a list of 'must read' cases at the end of each chapter.) Making sense out of the body of cases will try every brain cell at your command, so if you fancy yourself a true 'common lawyer', someone who is able to integrate the case decisions in an area of law while at the same time interpreting them to be humane and rational, then this is the subject for you.

Finally, trusts is not a subject you can swot up the evening before an exam. The old saw, 'You can't fatten a hog the night before slaughter', applies here in spades. Read and think; read and pause. Learn to recognise when your brain is full, and stop. Like a box of breakfast cereal your brain will have room for more once the contents have settled. If you start to experience overload, stop, have a cup of tea and do something else for 15 minutes. Then return, and before going on re-read what you were on before. This book proceeds pretty much step-by-step, and at the end of the day, all should be reasonably clear. The only textbook that will ever make perfect sense on first reading is the one you write yourself (and often not even that one). Remember also that the different topics are all part of the same subject, so you will understand each of them better the more you understand all the others. As Wittgenstein said, light dawns gradually over the whole.

I abbreviate the House of Lords to HL, the Privy Council to PC, and the Court of Appeal to CA throughout.

Once again, thanks for ever and ever to my brothers in trust, Tim Akkouh, Richard Barton, Sean Pettit, Tom Prendergast, Bill Swadling, and Charlie Webb, each of whom has made writing and revising this book much more stimulating than it otherwise would have been. Thanks also to Caroline Hardy and Simon Blackett for inspiring me in the first place, and as ever, to everyone at Butterworths.

J E Penner
London School of Economics

Contents

Chapter Eleven   Breach of Trust   335

Chapter Twelve   The Law Governing Fiduciaries   445

Table of statutes

References in **bold** indicate where an Act is set out in part or in full.

Table of cases

PARA

G

V

W

CHAPTER ONE

The Historical Origins of the Trust

SUMMARY

The Court of Chancery and the origin of equity

The relationship between equity and the common law

Equity's creation of the trust

The Court of Chancery and the origin of equity

1.1 The law of trusts is the offspring of a certain English legal creature known as 'equity'. The historical development of English law is marked by the existence of a series of different judicial institutions over time; the most significant of these for the modern student are the Courts of Common Law and the Court of Chancery. The Courts of Common Law developed the basic rules and principles which we now recognise as the law of torts (civil wrongs), much of the law of contract, much of the law of restitution, and much of the law of property. The Court of Chancery generated its own rules and principles, which as a body of law are collectively known as 'equity'. Chancery developed the law of trusts, the law governing fiduciaries, also much of the law of property, of company and commercial law and, very importantly, a variety of legal remedies, such as the injunction, which the Courts of Common Law were unwilling or unable to provide.

1.2 The term 'equity' does not contrast with 'common law' when the latter is understood to distinguish judge-made law from legislation by Parliament. From that perspective, both equity and the common law are creations of 'common law', bodies of rules and principles developed over time as judges gave reasons for their decisions in actual cases.

1.3 The common law was developed and administered in the royal courts, those courts established by the king, in contrast to local manorial courts which were the province of local nobles and which applied local customary law. It was called the 'common' law of England because in theory it applied universally. The origins of equity are much murkier. Equity arose out of the administrative power of the medieval Chancellor, who was at the time the king's most powerful minister. Since the king was regarded as the fount of justice, it was appropriate for him to hear pleas by his subjects concerning injustices, and kings being kings, they eventually delegated the task to their chancellors. Since the Chancellor was to begin with usually an ecclesiastic, he felt able to concern himself with men's immortal souls, and thus their consciences; thus it was on the basis of 'conscience' that he exercised this royal power to remedy injustice, by ordering individuals to act in accordance with good conscience despite what their legal rights might be. In order to appreciate the character of this jurisdiction, and how it came to be in some sense opposed to the common law, certain considerations must be borne in mind.

1.4 The first is that equity, fairness, or justice was never absent from the common law courts. The difference was that from the mid-fourteenth century the complaints that the common law courts would hear became static (the categories of writs, or different forms of action, were closed) as did the procedures of the court as to pleading and evidence. Baker (1990, 118) illustrates the sort of problem that could arise:

> [T]he growing strength of the substantive law could also work injustice, because the judges preferred to suffer hardship in individual cases than to make exceptions to clear rules. The stock example was that of the debtor who gave his creditor a sealed bond [a paper document recording the obligation to pay the debt], but did not ensure that it was cancelled when he paid up. The law regarded the bond as incontrovertible evidence of the debt, and so payment was no defence. Here the debtor would suffer an obvious hardship if he was made to pay twice; but the mischief was a result of his own foolishness, and the law did not bend to protect fools. ... Again, if someone granted land to others on trust to carry out his wishes, he would find that at law the grantees were absolute owners who could not be compelled to obey him. Now it was not that the common law held that a debt was due twice, or that a promise or trust could be broken; such propositions would have been dismissed as absurd. Yet those were the results which followed from observing strict rules

of evidence, rules which might exclude the merits of the case from consideration but which could not be relaxed without destroying certainty and condoning carelessness.

1.5 These characteristics of the common law reflect, in part, the fact that the royal courts were 'courts of record', that is, courts whose decisions were recorded and were treated by lawyers and judges as statements of the law, ie of general rules applying to all. The Chancellor's decisions, by contrast, were not recorded. (However, from the early centuries of chancery onward there are substantial records of the bills of complaint made by applicants to him; thus the task of recreating the principles applied by the early chancellors is a matter of inference from the sort of complaints that were brought to him and the way they were framed.) His decisions were basically regarded as ad hoc exercises of his power to do justice in individual cases — he was not regarded as constructing a body of rules. In contrast to the procedures at common law, the Chancellor had the power of subpoena, ie the power to make litigants appear in person before him and suffer his interrogation of them, which obviously allowed him to treat his decrees as orders directed to individuals to ensure that they acted according to good conscience in the particular circumstances of the case. This is one meaning of the phrase that 'equity acts in personam': equity does not determine rights under law, whether to land or anything else; rather, equity requires particular individuals to act according to conscience.

1.6 Secondly, the jurisdiction of the Chancellor, and his 'court of conscience', must be understood taking account of the nature of government at the time it developed. As Murphy (1991) has pointed out, throughout most of English legal history all forms of government were 'adjudicative' in the sense that governing bodies of all kinds, whether councils or courts or individual officials, basically rendered decisions to do justice in cases of conflict which came before them. One should also bear in mind,

> ... the multitude of forms of mediation and arbitration that existed in medieval society and Chancery's transcendence of them. Disputes in the community were resolved for both private satisfaction and public peace by the expedient of deference, wherein a cause was put by one party or both parties to a common superior executive, including the jurisdiction of a lord or a community in the manor, the hundred, and the county [all medieval units of jurisdiction of one kind or another]. Guilds also

3

exercised mediatory functions, and at a high level the authority of a magnate might be invoked to arbitrate (Haskett (1996)).

It was in response to perceived injustices arising from the decisions of any of the myriad adjudicators, arbitrators or mediators in the medieval world that recourse to the Chancellor might be had, for his review of such decisions would have the force of the central department of state. Thus the conscience-based 'jurisdiction' of the Chancellor was not restricted to countering perceived injustices of the common law courts, but of all adjudicators of the medieval realm.

1.7 The Chancellor's conscience-based corrective role narrowed over the centuries. In time the Chancellor came to exercise a quasi-judicial function, in the Court of Chancery, which by and large was restricted to matters which were in some way covered by rules of the common law. Cases called 'suits', as opposed to 'actions' at common law, could be brought before him, the suitor appealing to the Chancellor on the basis that the rigid application of the common law rules caused injustice in his particular case. In response, the Chancellor could order a person not to act upon his common law rights if in good conscience he ought not to do so, in effect overturning the rules of common law. In theory, however, the common law was regarded as unchanged; the Chancellor merely decreed that the parties could not act upon it.

1.8 As might be expected, however, continual correction of decisions generated by a rule-based system will give rise to rules or principles of correction. It would not be conscionable for the Chancellor to give relief to one suitor unjustly dealt with by the common law, but deny it to the next whose suit was based on substantially the same facts. One of the most fundamental principles of justice, after all, is that like cases be decided alike. The doctrine, ie the body of rules and principles, which arose from the decisions of the Court of Chancery that tempered the harsh or rigid application of common law rules became known as 'equity', reflecting their origin both in the conscience-based administrative jurisdiction of the Chancellor, and in principles of 'equity' found in the Roman and ecclesiastical law in which many early chancellors were learned. Indeed, the widely-perceived contrast between the rigid rules of the common law and the flexible conscience-based fairness of equity was a highly misleading caricature by the end of the eighteenth century. By then the rules of equity were fast becoming as rigid and technical as any in the common law. Equity, which was once said to vary with the length of the Chancellor's foot to emphasise the personal character of the Chancellor's intervention, ie intervention on the basis of what he personally understood to be good conscience, had become a second body of law.

The maxims of equity

1.9 Although Equity developed its own definite rules covering various matters, it also produced a series of 'maxims' or broad principles which manifested equity's general approach to the solution of legal problems. An example of such a maxim is, 'Equity looks to intent, not form'. If, for example, two parties executed documents which characterised a land transaction as a sale of the land, though in substance the transaction amounted to a mortgage of the land, the court of equity would look beyond the form of the documents, which might be decisive at common law, and treat the transaction as a mortgage. We will encounter various of these maxims as we go along. Like any general legal principles, the maxims of equity have been encrusted with judicial interpretation over the centuries, so it would be a great mistake to treat these maxims nowadays as anything more than devices which assist the interpretation and organisation of particular equitable doctrines and help explain their historical development.

The relationship between equity and the common law

Equity as a 'gloss' on the common law

1.10 Equity and the common law were not separate but equal systems of rules covering the same matters only differently. Equity has always relied on the existence of the common law, being essentially, in the terms of Maitland (a great equity scholar), a 'gloss on the law'. If you peeled away all the rules of equity, the common law could still stand alone as a comprehensive body of rules covering tort, contract, property, etc. If you peeled away the common law from equity however, you would not have anything like a comprehensive body of rules – equity, was, and remains, a kind of patchwork overlay modifying particular common law rules.

1.11 The two exceptions to this are the subjects of this book, the law of trusts and the law governing fiduciaries. Now, a legal system can do without trusts (civilian jurisdictions typically have no law of trusts or, to the extent they do, as in Scotland, they are imports from the common law) or the sort of law of fiduciaries found in English and commonwealth legal systems and so could English law. So in that sense trusts and fiduciary law are, like the other creations of equity, not strictly speaking necessary for a modern legal system. Peel them away and you could still have a working body of law. Nevertheless, as we shall see, they are now a vital part of English private law as a whole, and it would amount to a legal revolution if they were abolished.

Strife between equity and the common law

1.12 Equity largely worked through the issuance of 'common injunctions,' by which a plaintiff at common law could be enjoined, ie stopped, by a decree of the Court of Chancery, from proceeding with his case, or restrained from enforcing the result. As one might imagine, from the point of view of the common law judges this was tantamount to the Chancellor's denying claimants access to justice. After several attempts by the common law judges to assert the dominance of the common law over the power of the Chancery, and some consequential political strife, it became settled by the end of the seventeenth century that the decrees of Chancery would prevail. Equity was here to stay. So, for about two centuries, England had a true dual system of courts with two different finely-developed bodies of law.

Remedies at common law and equity

1.13 Different remedies were available from the common law courts and the court of equity. A common law court could order a losing defendant to pay damages, a money sum, to the plaintiff, and in cases concerning land could order a defendant to get off the land so that the plaintiff could take possession. If the defendant refused to pay damages, the Court would empower a sheriff to come round, seize his possessions, and either hold them until he paid or sell them to raise the plaintiff's damages. Similarly, if a defendant refused to get off the land, the sheriff would come round and clear him out. Thus the common law courts had, essentially, only one means of enforcing their decisions: they could separate a person from property. Chancery had a much more sweeping power, which provided scope for a variety of equitable remedies. The Court of Chancery could throw anybody who disobeyed its orders into gaol, for contempt of court. This was not a criminal sentence, where if you served your time you got out. If you refused to carry out an order of Chancery, you rotted in gaol until you decided to comply. (Nowadays, imprisonment for contempt of court is regulated by the Contempt of Court Act 1981, and the court also has powers to act in place of the defendant in certain instances, for example by executing documents, or by appointing others to act in his place; s 39, Ord 45, r 8.) This gives another meaning to the phrase 'equity acts in personam'; equity acts on your body. Equity has the power to make you do something, or to stop doing something, because if you refuse, you lose your liberty for as long as it takes. Thus injunctions have their origin in equity. Equity can also rescind contracts, ie tell people to act as if a contract was never formed, and can rectify documents, that is, tell people to carry on as if the document had different terms. As a result, in many cases litigants whose substantive rights lay at common law would seek the remedial support of Chancery – so, for example, one suffering the smoke of a neighbour's brickworks and unsatisfied with money damages would apply to Chancery for an injunction to shut the brickworks down; or a contracting party would seek an order from Chancery for the specific performance of the contract in a case where money damages for breach would inadequately compensate.

The Judicature Acts

1.14 The administrative inconvenience of a dual system of courts which dealt in different fashions with the same factual issues is apparent, and by the Judicature Acts 1873-75 Parliament abolished the institutional division between the Courts of Common Law and the Court of Chancery. One High Court was established, the judges of which were henceforth to apply the rules of both common law and equity, where appropriate, in the cases before it; where the rules conflicted, the rules of equity were to prevail. What counts as equity today, therefore, is the body of rules and principles which derive from those applied in the Court of Chancery until 1875; judge-made law is a living thing, and so equity has developed since then, in just the same way as has the common law of contract or tort. Despite the abolition of the separate courts, there remain distinct traces of this institutional history which bear directly on the current state of English law.

The fusion of law and equity

1.15 Since 1875 judges apply both common law and equity in the same court at the same time. It remains an open question to what extent the rules and principles of the common law and of equity have been fashioned into one coherent, principled body of law, whether that is, the common law and equity have 'fused'. The fusion question can be framed in this way: Although judges and lawyers now deal with whatever rules of equity and common law apply to the case before them, in what sense should they maintain the distinct historical and intellectual origins of these rules in their heads? Maintaining such a notional distinction will have consequences in so far as the mere fact that a rule arose in the common law or in equity will have consequences for its application. Consider the following old chestnut of the fusion debate: because equity arose in a 'court of conscience' it is said that, as a matter of unalterable principle, all equitable relief is discretionary. For example, if a plaintiff seeking the equitable remedy of specific performance of a contract has acted unconscionably in some way himself, then equity will refuse to help him, leaving him to his remedies at common law. The maxim (**1.9**) framing this rule is 'He who seeks Equity must come with clean hands'. By contrast, it is said, common law remedies lie 'as of right', the court having no similar discretion. So we now pose the question: should it still matter which court originally devised a particular remedy when judges come to decide how they should apply it nowadays? Surely not. If it remains true that some remedies that arose in equity should only be granted on a discretionary basis (and there may be good grounds for this), this must be justified as a matter of principle which fits into a coherent rationale which explains the remedial rules in that particular area of law. This coherent rationale must, of course, also explain the various restrictions and limitations that exist today upon remedies originally given at common law. Even if an explanation is based upon concerns about justice which were originally given voice by Chancery, that does not entail that the rule must henceforth be identified as an equitable one, any more than we would identify a modern rule of the law of wills as ecclesiastical, because the law of wills was originally the province of the ecclesiastical courts. Nevertheless, this particular version of the 'history is destiny' fallacy lingers. It lingers in part almost certainly because of the theoretical difficulties that have arisen in accommodating the most important single development of equity, the law of trusts, into one coherent law of property. Fusion may seem somewhat straightforward when directed towards remedies, but the idea of ironing out the differences between the common law and equity in property law, is, as we shall see (**2.54**), a different kettle of fish.

Equity's creation of the trust

1.16 The most important development of the preceding institutional history is the law of trusts. Trusts is the only branch of law that LL B students study which arose purely in the Court of Chancery. The law of trusts is worthwhile studying separately from the rest of equity for two reasons. First, the rest of equity is best studied in combination with the common law rules which govern the different substantive areas of law to which these other equitable rules apply. For example, equitable remedies are best examined in the context of studying the various substantive actions, like breach of contract, where they are given; or, if remedies per se are the focus of inquiry, it is silly to restrict one's attention to equitable remedies, missing the important points of comparison with common law and statutory remedies. Land law courses necessarily include the substantive development by equity of the land law, and the substantive equitable wrong of breach of confidence happily fits within the study of torts generally or the law relating to industrial property. Second, matters of pedagogical convenience aside, the law of trusts is worthwhile studying in its own right because the 'trust' – equity's imposition of stringent personal obligations upon a legal owner to hold property for the benefit of another, with the result that he is no longer able to treat the property as his own – may be regarded as the paradigm case of equity's interference with common law rights in pursuit of justice.

The use

1.17 The historical roots of the trust lie in a medieval property device, the 'use'. The history of the land law in the first centuries following the Conquest can be described as the process by which true property or ownership in land arose, as the influence of the social and political structure of feudalism waned. Under feudalism, rights in land basically amounted to rights in a complex hierarchical system of social and political authority and agricultural wealth distribution. This hierarchy was maintained through a system of 'tenures' of land, under which different 'tenants' had rights in the same land. At the top of this ladder was the king, at the bottom the person actually in possession of the land, and in between there might be any number of 'mesne (pronounced 'mean') lords'. It was essentially a system of taxation. Each tenant, starting with the one in possession who, via the labours of his serfs, would produce agricultural goods, passed the wealth of the land upward by doing 'rent-service' of various kinds to the lord immediately above him, and so on up to the king. Thus although a person might have an 'estate', an ownership interest, in some piece of land, this estate was as likely to be a 'seigneury', ie the right to a rent from a tenant immediately below on the feudal ladder, as it was to be an estate giving possession of the land itself. Different kinds of rights and duties defined the different kinds of tenure by which land could be held, such as knight service, the obligation to provide knights or money for arms, or socage, the obligation to provide agricultural products. The use arose as a means of avoiding some of the more disgruntling rules of the tenurial feudal system. Land could not be left by will, but could only be inherited according to the rules of primogeniture, the general effect of which was that the entirety of a man's rights in land passed to his eldest son. This preserved large estates in land, but it meant that a man could not take advantage of his landed wealth to provide for all of his children on his death. Another problem arose if one wanted to benefit certain religious orders. For various reasons it was difficult if not impossible to provide for them by conveying land to them. Among nobles, there was also the problem that the English crown was often bloodily contested over long periods of time, in particular during the War of the Roses. If a landowner were in the position of having backed the wrong claimant to the crown, not only would he lose his life, being condemned as a traitorous felon by the victor, but all his lands would be forfeit to the crown, ruining his family. Finally, certain legal incidents of feudal land-holding could themselves become very oppressive. In particular, if land held in knight-service passed to a minor heir, the lord immediately above on the feudal ladder acquired the 'right of wardship', the right to manage the estate and take all the profits of the land until the heir reached maturity. These elements (amongst others) of land tenure inspired medieval lawyers to avoid them. The avoidance mechanism was the use.

1.18 Although land could not be left by will, there were no similar restrictions on *inter vivos* dispositions, ie dispositions while the tenant was alive. Thus A, a feudal tenant, could convey his property to X, Y, and Z as co-owners. Of course, a straightforward conveyance like this would not do A any good to realise any plans for his land: by conveying the land in this way he would give up all claims to it; rather, the property was conveyed *on use*; the conveyance was written to X, Y, and Z to the use of some person or persons who A wanted to benefit, called the 'cestui(s) que use'. (These are terms of old 'law French' – England was conquered by the Normans, after all. The way they are pronounced today would not meet with the approval of the Parisian on the street. 'Cestui(s) que use' is pronounced 'settee(s) key use'.). In general, A could benefit whoever he wanted, in however complicated a fashion he wished: thus A could convey the property to the use of an order of Franciscan monks, or to his own use for his life and then to the use of his widow for her life, and then to the use of all of his children in equal shares. The common law completely ignored the words 'to the use of'. As far as it was concerned, X, Y and Z were the owners by conveyance, subject to all the feudal duties of their estate, and could do whatever they liked with the land, regardless of the wishes of A, for A no longer held the legal estate to the lands; X, Y and Z did.

1.19 The conveyance was made to X, Y and Z as co-owners to exploit a particular technical common law rule. The form of co-ownership that was invariably employed was the joint tenancy. Joint tenancy has the significant feature of the right of survivorship (in latin, the *jus accrescendi*), by which upon the death of any joint tenant, his interest disappears – it does not pass to his heir – with the result that there is just one fewer co-owner. Thus if X died, his heir would not inherit a share of the property; his interest just disappears; Y and Z now together own the property as joint tenants. (The other common form of co-ownership is 'tenancy in common'. Here, in contrast, the tenant in common possesses an ownership share which passes to his heir.) As joint tenants of the legal title to the land, X, Y, and Z would be liable to comply with the feudal duties, but importantly, because of the right of survivorship, the particular worry of a minor heir inheriting the land could be completely avoided. The danger of inheritance would only arise if following a series of deaths only one of the original joint tenants remained, who would then be the sole owner. If he then died, his heir would inherit. But that could easily be avoided, for after the death of X, for example, Y and Z could convey the land to themselves and V and W, on the same use as A originally did. In this way, whenever the number of joint tenants dropped to a low number, a simple reconveyance to another group of joint tenants ensured that the property was never inherited, and so a wardship would never arise.

1.20   The use, therefore, could be employed to avoid all of the rules of feudal tenure mentioned. The benefit of land could be passed to others than those who would inherit under the rules of primogeniture. It could be passed to those who were legally disentitled from holding property, eg religious orders and minors, and A could convey his lands to a neutral party so that if A went to the block for treason, he could do so with the comfort he had not ruined his family dynasty —not being legal owner of his lands, they would not be forfeit to the crown, and so his wife and children would not be destitute — the legal owners would continue to hold for them upon use. Finally the use could be used to ensure a minor never inherited.

1.21   The attentive reader may have noticeed one rather gaping potential flaw in these schemes employing the use. What could the cestuis que use do if X, Y and Z refused to honour the use? As we have seen, the common law did not recognise the use; X, Y and Z were the full legal owners, and so A's cestuis would get no relief in a court of common law. Here enters the Chancellor and his conscience-based power to remedy injustices. It would be unfair to allow X, Y and Z to take the benefit of the land themselves, for they only got it in order to benefit the cestuis que use. The Chancellor would enforce the use at the suit of the cestuis, ensuring that X, Y, and Z held the land according to the use A dictated.

1.22   Now it is sometimes thought that this failure of the common law to recognise the use is indicative of the harshness or rigidity of the common law, a harshness and rigidity so severe that it would deprive A, his wife, and children of their rights in land, thwarting the clear agreement between A and X, Y, and Z. But this is a profound misunderstanding. The common law's blindness to the use was essential for the benefits of the use to be achieved. It was only because the cestuis had no legal title to the land that the various schemes to avoid the incidents of feudal land-holding would work. If the common law were to recognise a new kind of seigneury or legal estate in the use, then it would not have put the cestuis' interests in the land beyond the reach of the very legal rules the use was engineered to avoid. It was the very rigidity of the common law in refusing to recognise a legal estate in the use which made the use effective. The common law was not hostile to the use; undoubtedly a large number of common law judges and lawyers held land to uses and/ or were cestuis que use themselves. The problem of enforcing uses against legal title-holders was a real, but secondary problem, which appears to have been met differently as time went on. It seems that when the use originated, it was understood by all that the legal title holders were bound in honour and conscience, not law, to give effect to the use, the very extra-legality of the obligation permitting the device to be effective. The non-legal sanctions for failing to comply with such an obligation cannot be discounted. Failure to meet one's conscientious obligations could and did result in social obloquy, or church-directed penance or even ex-communication. And it is natural that as the social bonds of feudalism declined in importance failures to perform uses would come before the Chancellor in greater numbers, so that his jurisdiction became the normal, then exclusive means of enforcement, ultimately leading to the rules governing uses and trusts that make up such a large part of equity doctrine.

1.23 How should we characterise the use? One way is this: a use is a kind of 'structured gift'. A conveys property to X, Y and Z to the use of someone to whom he wants to give the property but which for various reasons he cannot do under the common law rules of property; an obstacle in feudal times, as we have seen, was the rule of primogeniture. The use can also be characterised as a kind of feudal tax-avoidance mechanism. Transferring the benefit of land by way of use enabled feudal tenants to enhance the value of their land, by disengaging it in part from its feudal incidents, particularly those that operated upon inheritance.

The origin of the trust

1.24 This book is about the law of trusts, not the law of uses, so what happened? Very briefly: Henry VIII wanted money, and set about getting some by prosecuting with a vengeance his ancient feudal rights as the man at the top of the feudal pyramid. He even had a special court set up, the Court of Wards, to help him do so. Because by this time feudalism was essentially anachronistic, his efforts were branded 'fiscal feudalism'. Vexed at being deprived of the feudal revenues he would otherwise have got but for the employment of uses by his noble tenants, he managed to get Parliament to pass the Statute of Uses in 1535. This statute 'executed the uses': a conveyance from A to X, Y and Z to the use of B was after the Act treated as a conveyance from A to B directly. The title passed from A to X, Y and Z, and then to B as the use was automatically 'executed', cutting out X, Y and Z. It was thenceforth impossible for someone holding the legal title to be bound to benefit another, since there was no longer any use by which he could be bound. How the trust arose in the next century and a half to replicate the use in all but name is an interesting bit of history, but not, alas, to be gone into here. Suffice it to say that by the turn of the eighteenth century, where a legal title holder X, now called the trustee, held property to the benefit of B, now rendered as 'in trust for B' rather than 'to the use of B', (B was consequently renamed the 'cestui que trust', and now generally called the 'beneficiary'), Chancery would require X to hold the land for the benefit of B, just as if he had formerly held it to B's use.

1.25 Since the incidents of feudalism are now abolished, you might ask why anyone would want to give a 'structured gift' today. Why do people set up trusts? For most private trusts, the basic reason is the same as in medieval times, to provide for loved ones in a way one cannot do, or it would be unwise to do, simply by transferring legal title. One cannot give minors land, so if one wants a minor to have Blackacre ('Blackacre' is the name common lawyers always give to a hypothetical piece of land), it must be held on trust for him by someone else. One may be worried that one's son is a spendthrift, and so give money for his living expenses to a trustee to dispense, on condition that the benefit will pass to someone else if that son goes bankrupt. One may want someone to have the dividends, ie the income, from shares, and someone else to have the capital. One cannot fragment the legal title to shares to accomplish that. In certain circumstances, the law of taxation also favours giving property by way of trust when one is alive over leaving property to others in one's will, so many trusts are essentially tax-avoidance devices.

1.26 Note that the structured gift and tax-avoidance functions of the use/trust work in essentially opposite ways. To the extent that the use/trust avoids feudal incidents or taxes, it frees property from restrictions which reduce its value to an owner. On the other hand, the structured gift burdens property, and the structure of benefits under a trust can be very complicated indeed. If the feudal use worked to free land from the institution of feudalism, its modern counterpart, the trust, also ties up property with bonds quite as tight to different social institutions, such as the family, or the workplace as in the case of pension fund trusts.

Further reading

Baker (1990), chapters 6,12,13,14,16; Simpson (1986) chapters I, VIII,
   IX; Haskett (1996); Burrows (2002a)

Self-test questions

1. What features distinguish equity from the common law?

2. What does it mean to say that 'equity acts *in personam*'?

3. What does 'fusion' refer to?

4. What was a 'use', what purposes did it serve, how did it work, and
   how is it related to the trust?

CHAPTER TWO

Property, Obligations and Trusts

SUMMARY

Equitable title

The express trust

Fiduciary obligations

The personal and proprietary nature of the trust

The context of insolvency

Testamentary gifts

Equitable title

2.1 In chapter 1 we operated with the rather vague notion that a trustee 'holds property on trust' for the beneficiaries. It is now time to make this notion explicit and precise. The first concept to be grasped is that of *equitable title*. Equitable title exists whenever equity will require the legal owner of property to hold the property for the benefit of some other person or group of persons (which group may include the legal owner himself). In the eyes of Equity, those for whom the property is held are the real owners of the property, and they are therefore said to have 'equitable title' in it. However, note the unusual quality of this ownership. While equity regards the equitable title-holders as being the true owners, equity does not *disturb* the legal owner's title to or possession of the property. Rather, the legal title holder is *obliged* to hold the property for the benefit of the equitable title holders. And this gives rise to the notion of the trust. The trust is the particular obligation under which the legal title holder is to hold the property for the benefit of the equitable title holders. And this obligation is owed *to* the equitable title holders, so they are the ones entitled to enforce the trust obligation. So the 'equitable ownership' of the trust property is a special kind of ownership: so long as the trust is in existence, the equitable title holders take the benefit of their rights of ownership not by dealing with the trust property directly, as if they were legal owners, but indirectly, by enforcing the terms of the trust obligation against the legal owner.

The express trust

2.2   The express trust can be regarded as the central or core instance of the trust. An express trust is a trust which is intentionally set up. Say that I wish to put away some money for my two minor daughters. While this is a nice thing to do, there are obvious problems in just transferring the legal title to property to a 10- and a 13-year-old. What I will do, therefore, is to create a trust in their favour. As the original legal owner of the property, I am called the 'settlor', for I 'settle' the property upon my daughters under the trust. (Confusingly, not all express trusts are nowadays properly called 'settlements'; settlements are trusts, usually family trusts, in which there are *successive* interests (**3.20**).) There are essentially two ways in which I can do this. I can simply declare that I now hold such and such property, say 1,000 shares of ABC plc, 'on trust' for my daughters. Or I can transfer the shares to someone else, my brother, say, to hold on trust for my daughters. In the former case, called a 'self-declaration' of trust, I become the *trustee*, the holder of the legal title of the shares who must deal with the property according to the terms of the trust; in the latter case my brother does. In both cases I am the settlor, and my daughters are the *cestuis que trust*, or *beneficiaries*. Most express trusts are created in writing, and the document which contains the *terms* of the trust, ie the detailed provisions which structure the way the property is to be held by the trustee for the benefit of the beneficiaries, is normally called the *trust instrument*. Sometimes this document can also work to transfer the legal title of the property from the settlor to the trustee, but legal title in the property must be transferred to the trustee according to the correct transfer procedures for that kind of property, whether land or shares or whatever other kind of property is to be held on trust.

2.3   Since, as we have just seen, a settlor can declare himself trustee of property for someone, the settlor and the trustee can be the same person.

A settlor can also convey property to a trustee on trust for himself, so the settlor and beneficiary can be the same person. A trustee can also be one of several beneficiaries, as would result from a transfer to B on trust for B and C in equal shares. But what cannot exist is a lone trustee who is also a lone beneficiary. The law does not recognise a division of the individual self so that you would have an obligation to hold property for yourself in a defined way, an obligation which you could enforce against yourself.

Beneficial title

2.4　The impossibility of a legal owner being a trustee for himself alone shows that it is incorrect to think that the outright owner of a piece of property, that is, the legal owner of property which is not subject to any trust, has both legal and equitable title; he has the legal title *simpliciter*, and there is no equitable title at all. This is not to say that equity is blind to the legal ownership of property; equity is perfectly aware that a legal owner of property subject to no trust has the benefit of the property himself, having no obligation to hold it for another. 'Beneficial' is the compendious term: a legal owner of property is the beneficial owner if the property is not subject to any trust; where property is held on trust, the beneficiary under the trust is the beneficial owner. In determining the rights of individuals to property under the law of trusts, the pertinent question is always whether equity recognises a distinct beneficial interest in the property, ie an equitable title, which displaces the legal owner's beneficial interest. The mistake is to think that because a legal owner has the beneficial interest, he has both a legal and an equitable title to the property.

Exercising powers to create an express trust

2.5　You should think of express trusts as the creations of the settlor; an express trust is created when a settlor *effectively exercises his powers of ownership* to do so. Understanding the significance of this will involve a brief digression.

Powers

2.6　A power is the capacity to change or create rights, duties, and other powers. One has the power to enter into contracts; if you and I agree that I will pay you £5 for washing my car, then we give birth to a new legal relationship: we both have rights and duties we did not have before. I have the right that you wash my car and the duty to pay you £5 for doing so, and you have, correspondingly, the duty to wash it and the right to be paid £5 for doing so. Owners of property have, simply by virtue of their ownership, all sorts of associated powers. If I own Blackacre I can exercise my powers over it to lease it, to give it away, to license you to come onto it to have dinner with me, and so on. One of the other things I can do if I own Blackacre is create a trust of it in your favour, either by self-declaration or by transferring Blackacre to a trustee to hold on trust. In the former case, I have imposed a duty upon myself to hold Blackacre for your benefit, and have conferred a right upon you to the benefit of Blackacre. In the latter case, the trustee will have undertaken a duty to hold Blackacre for your benefit, and you will have the corresponding right that he does so. Express trusts can be created by the settlor's exercise of his power gratuitously, or because he is obliged to do so under a contract. For example, occupational pension funds are held in trust and arise in fulfilment of the duties generated by employment contracts.

Operations of law

2.7 New rights, duties, and powers are not only created by individuals exercising their legal powers, but may also arise 'by operation of law'. Consider the case of a tortious injury, ie an injury which occurs because someone has committed a civil wrong (a 'tort'). If I negligently run you down with my car, you now have the right to sue me for 'damages', ie money compensation. But it would be a dreadful mistake to think that because I was the one who ran you down, I thereby exercised a power of mine to confer upon you a right to sue me for damages. The law only recognises capacities to create new rights, duties, or powers where the law wishes to provide a facility to do things in particular ways: the law recognises a power to enter contracts, or declare trusts, or make a will, because the law is in favour of those things. The law is not in favour of my running people down, so I have no legal powers attached to that capacity. The right to sue someone for damages arises *by operation of law* on the occurrence of your negligently-caused injury because the law regards it as just that you should be able to sue for compensation.

2.8 The distinction between rights, duties, or powers that an individual creates when he exercises a power, and those which arise by operation of law, is of great significance in the law of trusts: while express trusts are created by a settlor through the exercise of his powers of ownership, other trusts, constructive and resulting trusts, may arise by operation of law on the basis of particular facts. Sometimes it is difficult to tell them apart as we shall see, but telling them apart is crucial, because, in general, the terms (**2.2**) of a constructive or resulting trust are minimal, whereas the terms of an intentional, express trust, are rarely so. Thus whether a trust arises by operation of law or intentionally is usually a vital factor in determining the scope and nature of the legal title holder's obligations to the equitable title holder.

Revocability

2.9   A settlor may be able to revoke the trust, that is, bring it to an end and get the trust property back, and it is important to understand the legal basis for revoking a trust where it is possible. Trusts are normally created by the settlor transferring property to a trustee while at the same time declaring the terms of the trust, thereby creating the equitable title of the beneficiaries. And just like any other transfer or creation of an interest in property, once the act of transfer or creation is complete, the interest in the property belongs to the recipient, and that is the end of it as far as the transferor is concerned. Thus the settlor cannot think of the trust property as still 'really his'. He cannot get it back, for he is legally out of the picture. In the same way that a donor of an outright gift has nothing to say about what the 'donee' (ie the recipient) does with the property once the gift is made, neither has the settlor anything to say about the trust, the way it is administered, etc after the trust is created. The equitable interests under the trust belong to the beneficiaries, and they, and only they, may enforce the terms of the trust against the trustee. That is the 'default' position. But in setting out the terms of the trust the settlor may grant himself powers under it. He can give himself a power to bring the trust to an end, that is, to revoke it. He can also give himself lesser powers, such as the power to replace the trustees, or the power to decide the shares of the property that the beneficiaries will take, and so on. But the point to realise is this: if the settlor has a power to revoke the trust or to appoint new trustees, that power must be an express or implied power in the terms of the trust itself; the power derives from the trust terms, not from the settlor's position as the one who originally owned the property. Indeed, under the terms of the trust the settlor may give such powers to anyone he

21

chooses. Particularly for trusts that are administered in foreign, or 'offshore' jurisdictions (often places which offer tax advantages for holding property in trust there, such as Jersey or the Bahamas), a settlor may give a range of powers to individuals who have come to be called 'protectors'. These individuals monitor the trust, and by using these sorts of powers it is hoped they can 'protect' the trust, ie ensure its administration by the trustees is to the expected standard and coincides with the settlor's original purposes for setting it up (**3.18**).

Fiduciary obligations

2.10 As we have just seen, a trustee is under an equitable obligation to hold the property for the benefit of the beneficiaries. What kind of obligation, or obligations, does he have? Consider first the case of the express trust. There is an obvious similarity to the kind of obligations that a party to a contract has — the trustee *agrees* to undertake the trust, so his obligations are voluntarily undertaken. Secondly, his obligations are spelt out by the declaration of trust more or less explicitly, as in a contract: the trustee will be required to do various things with the trust property, eg invest it, pay over the income to X for his life, pay over the capital to Y if she attains the age of 30, and so on. Nevertheless the common law of contract has never enforced the trustee's obligations (as we will see, this tells us something about the nature of the trust (**2.48**)); it has remained the province of equity. And typically, though not necessarily, equity will regard the trustee as having, further to his explicit obligations under the terms of the trust, a special kind of over-arching obligation to the beneficiaries, a *fiduciary* obligation, which has characteristics which are very different from any contractual obligations recognised at common law. Fiduciary obligations are obligations owed to another person to act with *loyalty* and *good faith* in dealings which affect that person. A person who owes a fiduciary obligation is called a fiduciary, and the person to whom he owes the duty is generically called a principal. Although the trustee-beneficiary relationship is the classic example of the fiduciary-principal relationship, it must be clearly understood that the law governing fiduciaries is conceptually distinct from the general law of trusts governing trustees. Agents and company directors are both examples of fiduciaries, and as we shall see in Chapter 12 when we examine the law governing fiduciaries in detail, many, if not most, of the cases we will look at concern non-trustee fiduciaries, in particular company directors. The reason why we will look at fiduciary law in detail is that most trustees do have fiduciary obligations, and these obligations can extensively shape the way a trustee must act when carrying out the terms of the trust.

2.11 The fiduciary obligation to act with loyalty and good faith means more than that the fiduciary must act honestly and fairly. What it especially imports is the idea that the fiduciary *must act solely with the interests of his principal in mind*: the fiduciary must act to secure his principal's best interests, and must not allow his own self-interests, or the interests of others, to govern his behaviour in any way that would conflict with the principal's best interests. Fiduciary law is thus the origin in modern society of the legal notion of 'conflict of interest'. The fiduciary must not only act so as not to favour his own or others' interests over his principal's, but must also avoid putting himself in positions of conflict of interest. (It must be noted, however, that in the same way as a trustee can also be a beneficiary and therefore someone whose own interests 'count' under the trust, it is clear from the cases that specific fiduciary duties, eg the duty not to purchase the trust property (**12.59** et seq), which would normally apply to a trustee can be removed by the settlor (see *Sargeant v National Westminster Bank plc* (1990) and *Hayim v Citibank NA* (1987), such that the trustee can favour his own interests.)

2.12 The fiduciary obligation just described is thus very different from that of contracting parties to one another. While contracting parties must comply with their contractual obligations, of course, any leeway they have in the performance of those obligations amounts to a freedom to act in their own best interests; in general, contracting parties are not required to act 'selflessly' when they decide precisely how they will comply with their contract, to secure the best interests of their opposite number — what they owe the other party is strictly a matter of what rights that other has secured in negotiating the terms of the contract. (Possibly this picture of contractual obligations may have shifted. There is much talk about recognising a general obligation of 'good faith' in contractual performance. But certainly the traditional common law never imposed any such standard.)

2.13 The preceding reference to some 'leeway' in complying with a contract has an essential parallel in fiduciary relationships. Fiduciary relationships, at least in their core sense, are relationships in which the fiduciary has a *discretion* in the way he chooses to meet his obligations to his principal. Strictly defined, a fiduciary relationship exists when one person, the fiduciary, has agreed to undertake *legal* powers to affect the *legal* position, ie *the legal rights, duties or powers*, of another, the fiduciary's principal, and the fiduciary has a discretion in the way he will exercise those legal powers (*legal* here meaning 'recognised by law', so *legal and/ or equitable* powers). The two central cases are that of trustee and beneficiary, and agent and principal. A trustee has the legal title to the trust property, and therefore has the legal power to affect the position of the beneficiary. He buys and sells trust property in the course of making investments of the trust fund; he may have a discretion under the trust instrument to pay one beneficiary more than another; he may have the power to appoint successor trustees. In exercising those powers, he must bear only the beneficiaries' interests in mind. He should not buy company shares as an investment because he has an interest in the company and thinks it needs more capital; he should not exercise his discretion to give beneficiary X a great deal and beneficiary Y nothing because he is in love with beneficiary X; he should not appoint his brother as his successor trustee because the latter is down on his luck and could do with the trustee's fees.

2.14 Similarly, an agent is someone who is empowered to make contracts for his principal with third parties, and must similarly act in consideration only of the best interests of his principal. He should not, for example, sell his principal's goods to a third party because the third party is willing to 'kick back' part of the purchase price to him. Business partners are also generally fiduciaries to each other. Under a partnership, the partners work together to bear the costs of a business and share in the profits and, in consequence, third parties are allowed to sue an entire partnership, or firm, for breach of contract, etc. Obviously, then, a partner's individual use of his legal powers to contract will affect the legal position of all of the other partners, and therefore they are treated as fiduciaries one to another. Similarly, company directors are fiduciaries to their companies. Their direction of the company's business clearly affects the company's legal position vis-a-vis its employees and third parties, so they must act only with the company's best interests in mind. The crucial point in all these cases is that a fiduciary is one who voluntarily undertakes to act as a *decision-maker* for someone else: the fiduciary is empowered to make decisions (legally *binding* decisions) for his principal's benefit (decisions which, therefore, alter the principal's *legal* position).

The personal and proprietary nature of the trust

The personal duties of the trustee

2.15   Since the trustee has legal title to the property in question, the trustee has all the legal rights and powers associated with the property. If land held on trust is occupied by squatters, then it is the trustee who has the right to evict them. It is the trustee who has the power to buy and sell the trust property, so he is the one who makes the trust investments. The trustee must, however, act upon these rights and exercise those powers in accordance with his *personal* obligation to exercise his ownership of the property for the benefit of the beneficiaries. In general, then, the beneficiaries' rights in respect of the property are legally protected by the trustee's enforcement of his legal rights to the trust property. Third parties owe their duties in respect of the property, for example to keep off it, and the trustee enforces those rights in his own name to protect the beneficiaries' equitable interests. But the beneficiaries do not have any power to enforce those legal rights themselves; the trustee must, for the simple reason that he is the one who has those legal rights (see *MCC Proceeds Inc v Lehman Bros* (1998)). If the trustee fails to do so, the beneficiaries may launch a legal action against third parties, *joining the trustee*, ie suing the trustee as well so as to make him participate and enforce his legal rights to the property for the benefit of the beneficiaries. (See *Parker-Tweedale v Dunbar Bank plc* (1991).)

2.16   The trustee's obligations under the trust are often sub-categorised into duties of two kinds: 'administrative' and 'dispositive' duties. Roughly, administrative duties govern the trustee's power to make contracts and his powers of ownership to maintain the value of the trust property, which is also called the 'trust corpus' or 'trust fund'. Trustees have the duty to invest the trust property safely and so that it makes a reasonable return. A legal owner of property not subject to a trust has all the same powers, but not the duties. He can invest it, or not, as he chooses, and may engage in dangerously speculative investments. A trustee must invest the trust property and must not do so in a dangerously speculative way. Where appropriate, trustees must also insure the trust property, against fire, for example, if the trust property is a house.

2.17 Dispositive duties are those which require the trustee to dispose of the trust property to the beneficiaries according to the terms of the trust. These are the duties compliance with which delivers to the beneficiaries the particular benefits the settlor intended. In short, they govern the trustee's power as a legal owner to give the property away. For example, the trustee may have a duty to pay one beneficiary the income of shares for ten years, and then transfer title to the shares to another beneficiary. The trustee is not free to benefit whom he would like, like any other legal owner. His duty to exercise his power to give away the property only according to its terms is the essence of any trust.

A trustee contracts in his own name

2.18 In the same way that the trustee is the trust's legal face to the world because of his legal ownership of the property, the same goes for the contractual obligations the trustee enters into in the course of carrying out the trust. When, for example, a trustee sells some company shares he holds on trust and buys others in the course of his investment of the trust fund, he makes these contracts to buy and sell in his own name. The trust itself has no legal personality like a company, on behalf of which agents of the company make contracts which bind the company as a legal person itself. Having no legal personality, one cannot sue a trust for breach of contract; one sues the trustee for his own breach of contract, even though the breach was of a contractual obligation he undertook to benefit the trust. In general, trustees are 'indemnified', have an 'indemnity' for any liabilities they incur in properly carrying out the terms of a trust, which means that he may use the funds of the trust to meet any contractual obligations he incurs in carrying out the trust according to its terms.

2.19 In the case of a typical trust where the contracts the trustee enters into are those of investment and seeking the advice of solicitors and financial advisors, this indemnity is generally a perfectly adequate mechanism for protecting the trustee. However, a group of late nineteenth century cases reveal the obvious dangers for a trustee who, for example, carries on a business for the benefit of a trust in his own name. You can imagine that a trustee might run such a business so badly or unluckily that it goes bankrupt; in other words, all the funds of the trust may be lost. Because the trustee is liable for the business's debts himself, he will be personally liable to the creditors, and there being no remaining trust funds, his indemnity against the trust funds will be worthless. In that case, he will have to dig into his own pocket to meet the claims of the creditors. Only a mad trustee would nowadays run a trust business in his own name — if a business was settled on trust, then a trustee would insist that the business was incorporated, the trust owning the shares of the business. Then, if the business went bankrupt, the trust might lose all its value (ie the value of the shares would drop to nothing), but the trustee would not himself be personally liable to the business's creditors. (Recently the Trust Law Committee, a body of judges, lawyers, and academics interested in trust law reform, has proposed a general reform of the rights of creditors of trustees (Trust Law Committee (1997, 1999)); however the arguments for and against the reforms cannot be gone into here.)

2.20   Although the trust has no separate personality like a company does, notice the parallel 'limited liability' of shareholders and beneficiaries. If a company goes bankrupt, shareholders are not required to cough up to the company's creditors — their liability is limited to the value of their shares. If the company goes bankrupt, they will be worth nothing, but they will not have to reach into their pockets to cover the company's debts. (In the past, some company shareholders did have this liability, to pay 'calls' on their shares to keep a company solvent.) The position of beneficiaries is similar, in that they are not generally bound to indemnify a trustee for the debts he may incur in carrying out the trust business — the trustee has an indemnity out of the trust fund, but to the extent that is insufficient, he cannot go after the beneficiaries themselves to make up the shortfall.

2.21   Now, you may ask, if the law, via the trust, has produced a device for providing individuals with limited liability in this way, why do people use the legislated corporate form to carry out businesses with limited liability for investors? Why are there not as many businesses organised as trusts, where the trust fund is made up of contributions by investors, who 'settle' money as a trust fund for themselves as beneficiaries, the fund being used by the trustee to run a business, the investor/beneficiaries participating in the profits of the trust business according to the trust terms in proportion to the amounts they put in, just as a subscriber to company shares does? Briefly, the reason is that the law looked through this arrangement and regarded the investors as more than beneficiaries: as joint venturers in a business enterprise, the law regarded the trustee as not only their trustee, but also as their agent, carrying out their business for them. Thus the trustee was their agent, and they were jointly the agent's principal. Thus they were all *personally* liable under the contracts their agent, the trustee, made for them, and so the trust arrangement did not provide them with limited liability. In consequence, limited liability for business enterprises did require legislation, for the common law (including equity) did not provide it, though the trust device might appear to offer just that promise. (See Flannigan (1984, 1986); Cullity (1985, 1986); Ford and Hardingham (1987).)

2.22 The reader may find the discussion in the preceding paragraph all a little *recherche*, of at most historical interest. The reader would be mistaken. The main point to draw from it is that while the trust relationship and the agency relationship are different relationships, *nothing stops them from occurring together*. It would be rare in a family trust, where property is held by a trustee for a settlor's spouse and children, for the trustee to be the spouse and children's agent as well. Normally, the trustee would not take any directions from the beneficiaries, eg entering into particular contracts concerning the trust property because they said so or running a business held by the trust at their direction. The trustee carries out the settlor's wishes as expressed in the trust terms, and the spouse and kids take what they get. This is important: in the normal family trust the trustee is not an agent of the beneficiaries, and this is a good thing from the beneficiaries' perspective, because it means they are not personally liable for the trustee's acts. But trusts are used outside the family context, including where there is an agency relationship. For example, if you are an airline, in certain cases it may make sense for a ticket agent of yours to hold the money he receives on the sale of your airline tickets on trust for you. But though he is, in this respect, your trustee, he is still acting as your agent, and as his principal you will still be liable for his acts as your agent, for example under any contracts he makes on your behalf. This sort of situation came up in the Canadian case of *Trident Holdings Ltd v Danand Investments Ltd* (1988, Ontario CA). Danand was the legal owner of land for six equitable co-owners who wished to develop it. Trident contracted to install electrics, but claiming a breach of contract, brought an action against Danand and the six equitable owners of the land. The six argued that as beneficiaries of a trust of the land, they were not directly liable to Trident. The court noted, however, that the only terms of the trust concerning the land were that Danand as 'bare nominee and trustee' (**2.23**) had to follow the directions of the six. The court therefore quite properly found that the six directed Danand — Danand was their agent, and therefore as principals, they were each personally liable to Trident under the contract. The fact that Danand held property on trust for the six did not alter the fact that Danand was also their agent.

Bare trusts

2.23   Under a bare trust, as in *Trident*, a trustee holds property for a beneficiary on no specific trust terms besides the requirement to do with the property as the beneficiary dictates. Bare trustees are often called *nominees*, to indicate that their role is to do little more than hold the property in their names and do the beneficiary's bidding. Since there are no specific trust terms, there is no structure imposed on the benefit the beneficiary is to receive; in consequence, in equity it is fully and absolutely his without any restriction, and indeed, the beneficiary has the right to compel the trustee to transfer the legal title to him at any time, collapsing the trust. Another common way of putting the situation is to say that the nominee or bare trustee holds the trust property 'to the order' of the beneficiary. Perhaps the most common example of a trust of this kind is the trust upon which a solicitor holds his client's purchase moneys prior to completion of the sale of land. The solicitor holds the money in his client trust account, and the solicitor can only disburse the money according to his client's instructions and, in the case of a sale of land, this will be the instruction to transfer the money to the vendor for transfer of title to the land.

Legal and equitable title compared

2.24   You will often hear the rights and powers the trustee and beneficiary have in respect of the trust property spoken of in terms of split ownership, expressed as *legal title* and *equitable title* respectively. The idea behind this is that the trustee is the owner at law, and has legal title, while the beneficiary is the owner in equity, and has equitable title. One must, however, take care in the use of the word 'title' here, because it might suggest that the trustee and beneficiary have identical rights, the only difference being that the legal owner's are enforced by the common law, while the beneficial owner's are enforced in equity. Thinking so is a bad mistake, however, for this reason: legal title normally comprises the full panoply of ownership powers, but equitable title rarely does. The legal owner of property, even if he is a trustee, has, in law, all these powers, but only in the limiting case of the bare trust or nomineeship does the owner in equity, ie the beneficiary. In that particular case, it is reasonable to say that the trustee is the owner of the property in law, and the beneficiary the owner in equity, because the trustee in such a case must do whatever the beneficiary says with it. Here it makes sense to say the trustee and beneficiary have essentially identical ownership powers, the trustee having legal powers and the beneficiary powers in equity, powers the beneficiary exercises through his directions to the trustee.

2.25 But this is the limiting case, and it is not by any means the typical case of a trust. In the vast majority of trusts the benefit the beneficiaries receive from the trust property is defined, and therefore limited, by the terms of the trust; beneficiaries under most trusts have essentially none of the powers normally associated with ownership or title. They get the benefit of the property as defined by the terms of the trust, such as it is. That is, of course, the main reason settlors benefit people through trusts in the first place, so that *they* can decide what the beneficiaries will get out of the property, in other words, to give them a specified benefit from the property *without giving them ownership*.

2.26 Hence the mere existence of 'equitable title' indicates nothing whatsoever about the content of rights and duties between the legal title holder and the equitable title holder. In particular, the fact that equity recognises such a divided title does not entail that the legal title holder should be regarded as owing the same sort of obligations to the equitable title holder as does a trustee under an express trust. While the 'paradigm' case of the trust is the intentionally set-up express trust, trusts can also arise by operation of law. These trusts, of which two kinds are traditionally recognised, ie resulting and constructive trusts, will be discussed in detail in chapters 4 and 5. For now, it suffices to say that one of the complicating factors of these trusts is that what the operation of law often gives rise to is merely an equitable title, ie a beneficiary's equitable proprietary right to some property.

2.27 For example, a much discussed case from land law is the constructive trust of the family home (**5.7** et seq); in certain circumstances, a legal title holder of land may be required by law to hold the land on trust for himself and, typically, his wife or partner, in equal shares because although the spouse's name was not put on the title when the property was acquired, her detrimental reliance on a common understanding that the property should be shared would make it unconscionable for him to have the full beneficial interest in the land. This holder of the legal title to this property, while properly named, I suppose, a constructive 'trustee', never undertook to hold the property on trust for anyone, and is unlikely to think, much less know, that an equitable title in the property exists; partly because of this, he often has no particular duties whatsoever towards the equitable title holder, as would an express trustee to his beneficiary; rather, he is generally in the position of a bare trustee, who essentially holds the property to the order of the equitable titleholder to the extent of the latter's interest. Thus, when a constructive 'trustee' finds out he holds the legal title for the benefit of a constructive 'beneficiary', his only duty is to transfer the legal title to the equitable owner forthwith or, as in the example, if the equitable title-holder's interest is more complicated, such as an ownership share in the property, to give effect to that interest forthwith. (On this distinction between being a legal owner subject to someone else's equitable interest and being a 'full-blown' trustee with trust duties, see also *Westdeutsche Landesbank Girozentrale v Islington London Borough Council* (1996) per Lord Browne-Wilkinson.)

The nature of the beneficiary's right

2.28 It is now time to consider the beneficiary's right from his perspective. For simplicity we shall assume that there is only one beneficiary. The beneficiary has the personal right that the trustee comply with his duties, and as a fiduciary he must exercise all his powers over the property with the best interests of the beneficiary in mind. Obviously, the net result of the trustee's compliance with his duties is that the beneficiary will receive whatever benefit the terms of the trust dictate. If he is an income beneficiary, for example, he has the right to receive payments when the trust investments generate income. He holds this right against the trustee, who has the correlative duty to pay the beneficiary that income. In this respect, the beneficiary has a right that the trustee pay him an amount of property at a particular time, and therefore he has a right which is very much like the right to be paid a debt, and he can transfer this right by assigning it to a third party.

2.29 Asssignable personal rights of this kind, like debts, are a kind of property right. The way to see this most easily is to look at what happens if the assignor of a debt, or a beneficiary of a trust who assigns his equitable interest under the trust, goes bankrupt. If the contract of assignment were regarded merely as a personal obligation on the part of the assignor to transfer the benefit of the personal right (debt or trust interest) to the assignee, then if the assignor went bankrupt, the assignee would be in the position of an unsecured creditor (**2.57** et seq), who would be forced to make a claim against the assignor's 'trustee in bankruptcy' (the person who takes charge of a bankrupt's property and pays his debts to the extent there are assets available to do this (**2.57**)) for the amount which he was promised, just like all the other people who are owed money from the assignor. The point is that the assignee would not 'own' the right to the debt or equitable interest from the outset, so that he could demand it directly from the debtor or the trustee as the case may be. Rather, he would have to claim it 'through' the assignor; and since any payment made to a bankrupt assignor would go first to his trustee in bankruptcy, it would be pooled with the rest of the assignor's assets, and the assignee could only receive, as any creditor could, a pro rata distribution of money based on the total amount of assets the bankrupt had as against the total amount of claims against him. But happily, for the assignee, this is not the case. In the case of a true assignment of an assignable right, and an interest under a trust *is* an assignable right, the assignee is entitled to claim that he 'owns' the right already, ie that he 'steps into the shoes' of the assignor and holds the personal right against the debtor or trustee himself directly. This makes it his property already and therefore it does not go into the bankrupt assignor's pool of assets available for all his creditors generally. In short, the assignee becomes the new owner of the assignor's personal right, and the assignor drops out of the picture completely; thus the assignee's interest is not affected in the least by the assignor's bankruptcy.

2.30 But the beneficiary's right is more than just an assignable personal right against the trustee to be paid his benefit according to the trust terms, for equity regards the beneficiary as being the owner of the trust property itself. The beneficiary's right is proprietary in so far as it is a right in the trust property itself, ie, in so far as its fate is tied up with the fate of the trust property. One indication of its proprietary character is that it lasts only so long as the trust property does, that is, will only be effective so long as he is able to find or identify the trust property. If the trust property is stolen through no fault of the trustee and the property cannot be found, or is destroyed through no fault of the trustee, then the trust essentially evaporates, for there is no property to which the beneficiary's rights under a trust can attach (*Morley v Morley* (1678)). As a consequence of this theft or destruction the trustee's personal duty to dispose of the property in accordance with the terms of the trust likewise disappears, for he is no longer an owner of any trust property. Thus, if the property disappears, then so does the trust, and so does the beneficiary's right. There is a sharp difference between the right of the beneficiary in this respect and the right of the buyer under a contract of sale to be delivered the goods, or the right of a creditor. If the goods which the seller is bound to deliver are lost or stolen before title passes, then the buyer does not lose his contractual right to the seller's delivery of them; he may bring an action for damages for their full value. Similarly, if a debtor is robbed it is no skin off his creditor's nose – a debt does not attach to any specific property of the debtor, and thus not specifically to any property of his that is stolen, and the debtor cannot use the robbery as an excuse for not paying in full. In the case of the beneficiary, however, he is the one who loses if the trust property is lost or stolen, since equity regards his rights as being dependent upon his continuing equitable title, which attaches to the trust property from the outset of the trust.

2.31 Note, however, that the trustee's liability for a *breach of trust* committed while the trust is up and running continues even if the breach caused the total loss of the trust property. For example, if the trustee commits a breach of trust by investing the trust fund improperly so that all the money is lost, the trustee is liable to reconstitute the trust by restoring property of the same value as what was lost.

2.32 Another important aspect of the proprietary nature of the beneficiary's interest in the trust is that, in most cases, the interest is an interest in a trust *fund*. In law, a fund is a collection or set of properties in which an owner retains the same title although the individual items of property in it change. In the typical trust, the trustee has the power to change the individual items of property, typically so that the trustee can manage the trust for the benefit of the beneficiaries, by changing the trust investments from time to time. Although the particular shares or bonds that the trust holds change from time to time, the beneficiaries' title to the property of the trust does not. The beneficiary does not have a particular right to any of the particular items in the trust fund. That is why, when a beneficiary assigns his interest under a typical trust, he does not need to specify that he is assigning his interest in each and every particular item of trust property which happens to be in the trust at the time. He assigns his interest in the fund, whatever happens to be in it at the time, and whatever happens to be in it in the future.

2.33 Because trusts are founded upon a special arrangement in which the legal title to property, and therefore all the legal powers to deal with it, is held by someone who is not permitted to act as if he owns it for his own benefit, they create an obvious danger: if the trustee is an incompetent or a rogue, he is in the position drastically to harm the beneficiary's interest by transferring the trust property to a non-beneficiary. All may not be lost, however; since the beneficiary's right is proprietary he can, where possible, follow the trust property into the hands of a person to whom the trustee wrongly transferred it, and demand that this new owner hold the property on trust for him – in other words he can assert his equitable title in the property against a subsequent holder of the legal title to the property, just as if that person were the original trustee himself. The only problem is that he cannot claim his rights against every subsequent holder of the legal title, and so the proprietary nature of the beneficiary's right is limited.

Claiming equitable title against third parties

2.34 Historically, the law concerning which subsequent holders of the legal title to trust property would be required by equity to hold the property on trust for the beneficiary developed piecemeal. Roughly, equity held first that a purchaser for value who had notice of the trust, ie knew he was buying property that the trustee held on trust for another, was obliged to give effect to the beneficiary's rights; then the trust obligation was extended to those who inherited the property from the trustee; then, to a donee (the recipient of a gift) with or without notice of the trust; then to creditors of the trustee who had seized the trust property in order to realise the debts owed them (roughly the equivalent of a trustee's trustee in bankruptcy (**2.57**)). So the development of the beneficiary's right to follow the property was conceived in equity as the transfer of the personal duty of the trustee to others where the circumstances were such that they ought, in good conscience, to hold the property for the beneficiary. Thus this aspect of the proprietary character of the beneficiary's right grew out of equity's willingness to shift personal trust obligations onto subsequent takers of the legal title to the trust property. But this shifting stopped at the door of the *bona fide purchaser of a legal interest in the trust property without notice, whether actual, constructive, or imputed, of the trust*, a person sometimes called 'equity's darling'.

The bona fide purchaser

2.35 If the trustee transfers the legal title to the trust property to someone who has:

- given good 'consideration' for it, ie has given money or money's worth in exchange for it; and who

- has no actual notice, ie knowledge, of the beneficiary's rights; and

- has no 'constructive' notice of them either, ie knowledge of those interests which he would have acquired if he had made all usual and reasonable investigations when purchasing that kind of property; and

- has no 'imputed notice' either, ie any agents working for him in making the purchase have no actual or constructive notice either,

then this purchaser takes the property with good legal title free of any trust obligations, and the beneficiary loses his equitable title in the trust property. The beneficiary's equitable title is extinguished, and he cannot demand the property back from the bona fide purchaser, nor can he demand that the bona fide purchaser act like a trustee and deliver his benefits under the trust as if it still applied to that property.

2.36 We can then, divide recipients of trust property into two classes; first, we have *volunteers*, the term given to persons who receive property but do not give valuable consideration for it — for these recipients, their knowledge of the trust is irrelevant, for they will be liable to hold the property on trust in any case; secondly, those who have given consideration — these people can acquire beneficial ownership of the property free and clear of the trust, so long as they can establish they had no knowledge of it.

2.37 There are a few points worth noting. First, the rule applies to the bona fide purchaser of any legal *interest*, not just a *legal title* in the property which someone may acquire. An example is a legal security interest (**2.59**). Where a person who bona fide and without notice lends money to the trustee and the trustee, in breach of trust, 'charges' some trust property to secure the repayment of the loan, the lender takes an interest which is not subject to the beneficiary's rights. The practical upshot in this situation would be that if the trustee failed to pay back the loan, then the lender could 'realise' his security by taking possession of the secured trust property and selling it to pay off the debt. As a bona fide purchaser of this legal charge, he would prevail over the beneficiary's equitable title to the property.

Bona fide purchasers of equitable interests

2.38 Second, notice that the rule only applies to the case where the purchaser acquires a *legal* interest. If, for example, the trustee in breach of trust grants an *equitable* security interest in the trust property, that is a security interest which equity will enforce but which is not recognised at common law, then the lender will take subject to the rights of the beneficiary even if he is a bona fide purchaser for value of this interest with no actual, constructive, or imputed notice of the beneficiary's rights. The bona fide purchase rule only applies in a contest between a legal interest holder and an equitable interest holder. In a contest between two equitable interest holders, like the beneficiary and the lender in this case, the general rule of equity is that the interest which was created first in time prevails. Why is there this difference? It appears to have arisen as a kind of 'jurisdictional' curiosity. The beneficiary and the honest purchaser who has paid good value for his interest stand essentially on an equal footing with respect to their moral claims to the property. The rogue trustee has dealt dishonestly with both, selling the property out from under the beneficiary, and selling a flawed title (because impressed with a trust) to the purchaser. We have the classic case of a rogue and two innocents, and the court is faced with a choice as to whose claim should prevail. However, because the purchaser of an equitable interest was already within the jurisdiction of equity, ie his interest was equitable, equity had to deal with their competitive claims, and adopted the 'first in time' rule. On the other hand, equity did not weigh up the competing claims of the beneficiary and the bona fide purchaser of a *legal* interest. Only if that purchaser's conscience was affected could he be subject to the 'conscience'-based jurisdiction of equity; since it was not — he had done nothing unconscionable — equity regarded itself as having no power to intervene against him (see *Pilcher v Rawlins* (1872)), and this is the origin of the expression 'equity's darling'. Thus the bona fide purchaser of a legal interest got his legal title free and clear of the trust because of a sort of 'default' rule about the 'conscience'-based jurisdiction of equity.

Equitable interests as trust property

2.39   In the foregoing it was assumed for the sake of simplicity that the trustee always holds the *legal* title to the trust property, but as we have seen (**2.28**), a beneficiary's equitable interest is itself a valuable right which can be assigned; such a right can therefore form part of a trust corpus itself. Thus a beneficiary can declare a trust of it, which is called a 'sub-trust'. Here the trustee of the legal property holds it on trust for the beneficiary, who in turn holds his right to it under the sub-trust for the sub-beneficiary. Equitable property can take many forms besides a traditional beneficial interest under a trust, in particular with respect to land. Equitable interests in land, such as equitable mortgages, leases, or easements, are well-known proprietary rights in land, and now are protectable under various registration systems. If registered, they will bind everyone who takes the legal title, *including* a bona fide purchaser. For that reason, certain equitable rights in land are nowadays as secure as legal rights. If rights of this kind are held on trust we again have a case where the trustee holds equitable, not legal title to trust property, and although it would be unusual to regard the trustee's holding of equitable interests in land as 'rights held under a sub-trust', this is technically correct.

2.40   But though the rule can be understood as having arisen because of the jurisdictional separation between law and equity, and equity's understanding of its own jurisdiction (ie, as conscience-based) in the context of that division, are there good, practical reasons of *justice* for having a bona fide purchaser rule? There is such a rule, called the 'holder in due course' rule, which applies to negotiable instruments and money. The essence of the rule is that a person who in good faith gives good value for money (eg sells goods taking money in return) or for negotiable paper — commercial rights 'reified' or 'materialised' in paper documents, like cheques — gets good title to them even if it turns out that, for example, the money was stolen, or a previous transfer of the negotiable instrument was achieved by fraud. The general justification for this is that in some contexts, eg the world of commerce, it is better for the law to favour *security of receipt* over *security of title*. That is, in order to aid the practical workings of commerce the law holds that innocent purchasers of commercial paper, for example, should be protected even if that would mean someone who has suffered by the acts of a thief or fraudster loses their title. Why? The concern is that if the bona fide recipient, the holder in due course, were the loser in this situation, individuals, to be sure they got a good title, would have to spend a great deal of time inquiring into the validity of the title of the seller, which in these contexts would be very difficult. In consequence, some transactions might not go ahead at all, and the others would be made more costly. So instead the law allows for ease of transactions, and throws the risk on the titleholder. Also, it might be more sensible for the risk of theft or fraud, say, to lie with the original owner. As the owner, he's in the best position to prevent the theft of his goods, not the bona fide purchaser from the thief or someone further down the line in a chain of transactions.

2.41 Of course, the law does not take this attitude with respect to all kinds of property. In the case of chattels, ie things like chairs and chocolate bars, the law favours security of title over security of receipt. Here, the rule *nemo dat quod non habet* applies. Roughly translated, 'one cannot give what one hasn't got', and in the case of chattels, precisely what the thief has not got is good title to the goods, so he cannot pass a good title to anyone who buys them from him, no matter how innocent they are. So if you buy a 'hot' television from a friend of a friend, no matter how innocently, the true owner can bring an action against you for 'conversion', ie for converting *his* goods to *your* use, and you will pay him damages for the full value of the TV.

2.42 We are thus faced with this question: on what side of this line ought the beneficiary's right in the trust property fall? We know from above that the rule is already established — the bona fide purchaser takes free of the beneficiary's interest — but is there a sound reason for this in justice? The author shall not press his views on the bona fide reader for value, but will only say that no one is ever forced to put their property on trust, and putting one's property on trust, by the very nature of the device, puts one's property in a situation which presents it misleadingly to the world. We expect the legal owners of property to do with it what they want. We do not expect an owner to be bound to deal with this property only according to an obligation to benefit someone else. Trusts are entirely private (they are not, for example, recorded by the state in some central registry), and no one can tell just by looking at a piece of property or its owner that it is held on trust. Thus in creating a trust, one does expose it to the risk that one's trustee is an incompetent or a rogue who will deal with it in ways which to the rest of the world look perfectly legitimate, but are, in truth, not. Perhaps, since a settlor creates this risk, the results of things going wrong when the risk materialises should fall on the beneficiaries rather than on third parties who have acquired the trust property innocently *and* paid good value for it, ie bona fide purchasers.

'Notice' in different contexts

2.43   Finally, about the formulation of the rule: the rule as stated refers to the bona fide purchaser's having 'notice of the trust'. This formulation accurately describes the working of the rule in the context of its historical development, where land was transferred by deed. These transfers were carried out according to a standard conveyancing practice. For example, in the case of the sale of the fee simple of Blackacre, the buyer's solicitor would inspect the past title deeds and the property itself to discover any proprietary interests in Blackacre held by third parties. For example, the neighbouring owner of Whiteacre might have an easement, such as a right of way, over Blackacre. If it were a *legal* interest, this easement would most probably have been created by deed and the solicitor should discover it when inspecting the deeds. Nevertheless, being a legal interest, the rule was that it would bind the purchaser of Blackacre whether his solicitor was able to discover it or not. (Of course, following the purchase, he could sue the seller for damages for not disclosing that Blackacre was subject to this easement.) Blackacre might also be subject to some equitable proprietary interests. For example, the owner of Blackacre might have granted another of his neighbours an equitable right called a 'restrictive covenant' preventing him from using Blackacre in a particular way, as a knacker's yard, say. Such an *equitable* right would only bind the purchaser if his solicitor actually discovered it or ought to have discovered it by making the proper investigations, and if so, then the purchaser would take Blackacre subject to this equitable right. In essence, then, the extent of notice in this context defined the extent of the rights in the land the purchaser acquired; his legal estate was limited by or subject to all the valid legal interests in the land and all the valid equitable interests in the land of which he had actual, constructive, or imputed notice – if he wanted to buy the land free of those interests, he had to deal with those interest-holders themselves, to buy them out, as it were. On the other hand, those equitable rights not caught by actual, constructive or imputed notice did not bind him at all. So the doctrine of notice here was not so much being caught out by unknown trusts of the property, but determining exactly how extensive or how limited was the property one was getting.

2.44 The rule's operation is quite different in the case of other property. There is no standard 'conveyancing' practice for the sale of other property, like chattels, or shares. Individuals are not expected to investigate the title as they would do if they were buying land, for the simple reason that third parties do not generally have a variety of interests in chattels or shares. Therefore the practical effect of the rule in most circumstances is that the purchaser is only bound if he has actual, constructive, or imputed notice that he is dealing with a trustee of the property who is selling the property in *breach* of trust. For example, brokers who buy shares from pension trustees will know, of course, that the shares are the property of the pension fund. But that does not mean that they take these shares bound by the rights of the beneficiaries, just because they know they are dealing with trust property. Having actual notice of the trust in this case does not require them to hold any shares they buy from the pension fund trustees on trust for the pension fund beneficiaries. They will only take the shares bound by the equitable rights of the pension beneficiaries if they have notice that the trustees are selling the shares in a way inconsistent with the beneficiaries' rights, ie in breach of trust.

2.45 For that reason, in the case of sales of most trust property, like shares or other investments, with respect to the issue of notice you should think of the rule as follows: a bona fide purchaser for value of the legal title without actual, constructive, or imputed notice that the transaction is made in *breach of trust* will take free of the beneficiary's interests. (Prior to the legislative property law reforms of the late 19th century and 1925, a purchaser from the trust would have to inquire into the terms of the trust to make sure that there was no breach by the trustees, and make sure the trustees applied the purchase money properly as part of the trust fund; nowadays there are no such duties; A purchaser from a trustee is entitled to assume that he is complying with the trust unless he has knowledge otherwise; see Swadling (1987); Harpum (1990)).

Tracing trust property

2.46   Although the beneficiary's proprietary right *in the original trust property* is obliterated by its sale to a bona fide purchaser, all is not necessarily lost, for the beneficiary may acquire a substitute proprietary right by operation of law, the availability of which depends upon what are called 'tracing rules'. If my rogue trustee sells the trust property, say shares, to a bona fide purchaser for £1,000, my equitable title to the shares is extinguished. But since it is clear that the trustee has received the £1,000 in exchange for the shares, the law will trace the value of the shares into the £1,000. The law will keep track of that value if it shifts again, for example into a car which the trustee buys with that money, or into any other property which is exchanged for the proceeds, tracing through one exchange substitution after another. Tracing will only stop when either the property into which I trace that value is lost or destroyed, or the evidence of what substitutions were made runs out, or the property is exchanged for non-property, for example where the trustee blows the trust money on a holiday. The rules of tracing will be discussed in detail in chapter 11. The great thing about tracing value in this way is that it gives the law a basis for giving the beneficiary new rights, in particular proprietary rights (though, as we shall see when we discuss breach of trust in chapter 11 personal rights may depend upon tracing as well). For example, because my value from the shares can be traced into the £1,000, I may be able to claim that I have an equitable title in that money, or if there are subsequent exchanges, I may be able to claim an equitable title in the later exchange products.

Personal remedies for breach of trust against third parties

2.47   Second, all may not be lost even though the beneficiary's proprietary rights run out because the original trust property disappears through loss, theft, or destruction, or can no longer be followed because acquired by a bona fide purchaser, or its value can no longer be traced into substitute property – the beneficiary will still have *personal* rights against the original trustee, who is strictly liable for breach of trust, and must pay out of his own pocket the full value necessary to restore what was lost to the trust; the beneficiary may also be able to make similar personal claims against others. We shall discuss these rights in chapter 11; in general they arise against any one who dishonestly participates in a breach of trust, and against anyone who receives trust property or its traceable proceeds in the knowledge that it comes to him as the result of a breach of trust.

The nature of equitable 'title' – property and obligations

2.48   Recall from **2.10** that the trust can be regarded as a binding agreement between the settlor and the trustee, the essence of the agreement being that the trustee undertakes an obligation to hold property in a certain way; but recall also that the common law never enforced this agreement as a contract. Without going into the historical reasons for that, it is important to understand that the result is that English law appears to give effect to two very different kinds of voluntarily undertaken obligation, ie obligations a person consents to undertake; the first kind, of course, is the contractual obligation. I consent to bind myself under a contract, and the law will enforce my contractual obligations at the behest of the other party; the second kind is the trust undertaking. No person is ever forced to undertake a trust; one does so voluntarily. The difference between the two is crucial, and to understand why this is so, we must take a look at two aspects of equitable title.

2.49   Recall that a beneficiary is regarded as having proprietary rights in the trust property itself, and so when trust property is transferred in breach of trust, the beneficiary can enforce his *continuing* equitable title in the property against anyone who acquires legal title to it (except for equity's darling). Thus one can easily conceive of the beneficiary's equitable 'title' as a proprietary right in the trust property. But one can also conceive of it in a different way, which emphasises the personal obligation aspect of the trust relationship. In the typical express trust, while it is up and running, the beneficiaries have no rights to the actual property in the trust fund; rather, their interest is only their interest in being paid out whatever property they are to receive under the trust at the correct time according to its terms. On this view, the 'trust' is the trustee's obligation to carry out the trust terms properly. Clearly the trust relies upon both the proprietary and obligational elements to work, for when a trust is up and running, it depends upon the trustee meeting his personal obligations to the beneficiaries to deliver them the intended benefits of the trust, but it also depends upon the proprietary aspect for, as we have seen (**2.30**), the trust obligations only exist so long as there is specific property upon which they can 'bite'. In light of this dependence of the trust obligation on the continuing existence of the property to which the beneficiary has equitable title, and in view of the fact that the beneficiary can maintain his equitable title in the trust property against third parties into whose hands it comes (save for equity's darling), it seems clear that the law has essentially taken the view that the trust is, fundamentally, proprietary; that is, the obligations by which the beneficiaries are entitled to the benefit of the property attach not just to the trustee for the time being, but 'run' with the property.

2.50   The law did not have to develop so as to create a 'proprietary' trust of this kind (there is no equivalent legal device in civilian legal systems), but as a matter of fact it has. In consequence, the creation of a trust is fundamentally regarded not merely as the voluntary undertaking of an obligation, but as a *transfer* of the beneficial title to property, from the settlor, who has the legal beneficial title, to the beneficiaries, who together take an equitable beneficial title. Thus the expansion of the personal liability of subsequent takers of trust property to include all but equity's darling (**2.34** et seq) is the consequence of the law's deciding to treat the trust property, despite the interposition of the trustee, as really the property of the beneficiaries; thus the imposition of the personal obligation on subsequent takers merely reflects the fact that the beneficiaries' proprietary interest is realised via a trust, and so in order to give effect to the kind of proprietary interest it is, the subsequent taker must be placed under a 'trust' obligation to hold it for their benefit. The case of equity's darling is, on this view, a justifiable (**2.42**) exception to the general *nemo dat* principle (**2.41**) that protects security of title.

2.51   It further follows from this proprietary perspective that, even though the trustee's undertaking his trust obligation is necessary for the device to work, this voluntary undertaking of an obligation is not regarded as the essence of the transaction. Indeed, so strong is the proprietary orientation that the creation of a trust is regarded as the unilateral act of the settlor giving his property away, rather than the bilateral act of making an agreement with a trustee, with the consequence that 'a trust will not fail for want of a trustee'. Thus, for example, if a person in his will gives property to Fred to hold on trust for Anna, and Fred refuses to take the property on trust, the court will appoint someone else to be trustee (**10.51**). Think how strongly that contrasts with the law of contract. Imagine declaring that one will perform one's own version of 'Stairway to Heaven' on zither and cymbals for Prince Charles for £1m, and upon Prince Charles's (naturally) declining the offer, the court finding someone else to be the other party to the contract. But this willingness of equity to find a replacement trustee makes perfect sense if the settlor's creation of a trust is regarded as merely his exercising the powers of ownership (**2.6**) to make a structured gift (**1.23**, **1.26**), for gifts are unilateral transactions. (A donee can, of course, refuse a gift, and so also a beneficiary can disclaim any interest given to him under a trust, but the existence of these rights of refusal do not turn the making of a gift into a bilateral agreement (see Penner (1996a)).

2.52 The 'transfer of property' conception of the trust is further reflected in the fact that while the parties to the trust agreement are the settlor and the trustee, it is not the settlor who is entitled to enforce the agreement against the trustee as would be the case if the agreement were contractual, but the beneficiaries (**2.9**), and this is perfectly appropriate given that they are now the beneficial owners of the trust property — their property rights are second-order in the sense that they only receive them via the trustee's meeting his trust obligations, but they are nonetheless rights to the very trust property. Thus, given the joint 'proprietary right' and 'personal obligations' nature of the trust, the law might have favoured the personal obligations aspect, by which the trust is the obligation on the trustee, which may by operation of law be imposed on third parties who receive the trust property, so as to prevent any unjust enrichment they would otherwise get by receiving the property obligation-free. It did not, though different scholars (in particular Maitland (1909)) have tried to explain the trust in something like this way.

2.53 Unfortunately this view still occasionally raises its bewildered head to confuse and annoy, most recently in the European Court of Justice in *Webb v Webb* (1994); the facts alleged were that a father had provided his son with money to buy a holiday flat for him in France, the son to hold the legal title on trust for the father. The son denied the existence of the trust, and the problem was that while the father's equitable interest would be enforced were the property in England, equitable interests in land are not recognised by the civilian law of France. There were possible ways of getting around this problem which might have entitled the father to succeed (see Birks (1994)), but for our purposes here we need only observe that the means chosen by the court was to hold that the father's right to his interest in the property was merely a personal right against the son — he was not regarded as having a proprietary interest in the land itself.

> The father does not claim that he already enjoys rights directly relating to the property which are enforceable against the whole world, but seeks only to assert rights as against the son.

But, as we have seen, this is a misunderstanding of the notion of equitable title. The beneficiary can only claim against third party recipients of trust property *because* his title is regarded as continuing and enforceable against the whole world save the exception of equity's darling. As Birks (1994) points out, the only reason the court was able to reach this result was by focussing on the fact that the son, not the father, held the legal title to the flat:

> ...the [father] had not got that legal estate and could not get it or be given it except by the act of the [son]. ...[But] the father sought a declaration that the son held the flat on trust for him. A declaration does not create an interest. It states what is already the case. To focus on the son's legal title and his obligation to convey is to miss the true reason why the son might be compellable to make the conveyance and, by doing so, avoid any analysis of the equitable interest which the [father] claimed to be already vested in him. The [son] was not a [trustee] unless in the circumstances the [father] already had an equitable beneficial interest in the flat. The [father] was not entitled to a conveyance unless he had the entire equitable beneficial interest in the flat.

Thus by treating the father's rights as merely 'obligational', that is rights only against the son to fulfill an obligation, the court denied the specifically proprietary nature of the trust.

Trusts and the fusion of law and equity

2.54   We are now in a position to see why the trust poses a problem for the fusion of law and equity (**1.15**). The trust appears to depend upon maintaining a clear distinction between legal and equitable title, and so would appear to require that the rules of law and the rules of equity stay unfused. This, it is humbly submitted, is a pernicious non-sequitur. For it appears to entail that the law of property depends for its intellectual cogency on a kind of blind adherence to the labels we use to refer to proprietary interests, rather than to the actual character of those interests themselves. The trust is, certainly, a very particular (perhaps peculiar) property device. It depends upon dividing *the powers of ownership* (the right to transfer the property, to possess it, and so on) which remain with the legal owner, *from the rights to the benefit of the property* that in usual circumstances would follow naturally from the possession of those powers (that is, if one has the powers of ownership one can use those powers to benefit from the property in the way that one wants, one can sun oneself in one's garden, invite friends over, eat one's food, and so on). The rights to the benefit of the property go to the equitable title holders, somewhat differently depending upon whether things are going as planned or whether things have gone wrong. When the trust is up and running and working fine, the equitable title holders achieve their benefits because the trustee is meeting his personal trust obligations to deliver the beneficiaries their rights as intended. But if things go awry, they then depend on their personal rights to sue the trustee for breach (or any third party accessory to the breach of trust) or on their proprietary rights to the trust property itself to chase it into the hands of third party recipients (so long as they are not equity's darlings) or pursue the traceable proceeds of it. The point, however, is that characterising the nature of the trust in this way does not depend upon using the terms 'legal' and 'equitable', though of course these are convenient labels. It depends upon properly elaborating the various personal and proprietary rights, powers, and duties that make up this relationship. There is no reason on earth to think that it is impossible to do this without maintaining two divided 'systems' of property law or property rights. Again, this is not a diatribe against the use of a term like 'equitable title'. Such a term is perfectly convenient, and it is valuable for a legal term to convey something of its historical origin. But it is one thing to consciously retain a particular term, and quite another to be blinded by it. The continuing reference to 'equitable' interests should not be regarded as a licence to say that English property law need forever be conceived as (read conceptually hampered by) separate systems of rules which cannot be made to work together as a single, coherent whole.

2.55 There is a further reason, if that was not enough, to regard any continuing resistance to the progress of ironing out the rules of property into a coherent and justifiable system as pernicious. As was pointed out in the first chapter with respect to the application of common law and equitable remedies, it can easily underwrite the 'history is destiny' fallacy (**1.15**) that, because equitable interests arose in the court of chancery, their nature will forever be foreign to the perspective of the common law, and therefore in dealing with them, one must make reference to the peculiar conscience-based jurisdiction of equity, rather than the rights-based jurisdiction of the common law. Besides being historically dubious (**1.8**) and something of an insult to judges and lawyers in both jurisdictions, it simply presumes (but gives no reason for doing so) that the two bodies of law are divided by untranslatable intellectual foundations. Now, no one said fusion was going to be easy, and it is by no means complete a century and quarter after the Judicature Acts (**1.14**). Of course it requires a great deal of work over time, dealing with actual cases before the court, to 'translate' between the terms and perspectives of these bodies of doctrine one to the other, so that one finally achieves a perspective which draws as much as possible on the particular genius of each for achieving justice in particular cases. But it is no less possible than the equally important job of ironing out the difficulties between particular areas of doctrine *within* the common law or *within* equity.

2.56   Finally, your author must be allowed to make a plea on the behalf of trusts law examiners everywhere. Do not, explicitly relying on equity's historical origin (and implicitly relying on the current state of incomplete fusion), defend your answer in an exam by saying something fatuous like 'Equity is a court of conscience ...' and continue by favouring one side of the argument or another because the result seems 'fair' to you. A court of conscience equity may have been, and certainly equitable doctrine reflects good conscience, but it is good conscience *according to law*, ie good conscience which has been made more or less explicit and precise in past decisions, and is now reflected in the current set of rules. In the same way one might say that the common law seeks to do justice, but again, justice according to law. Just because equitable doctrine is called equity does not let you off the hook of writing an appropriate, legally framed, answer.

The context of insolvency

2.57   One of the main reasons why proprietary rights are valuable is

47

that people and companies can become insolvent. One is insolvent if one has insufficient assets to meet one's liabilities – in other words, one has not enough financial resources to meet the demands of all one's creditors. In the case of individuals, the legal device of bankruptcy allows the insolvent individual to get out of this mess and start again afresh. It works roughly as follows: all of the property of the bankrupt, including any rights to be paid any debts owing to him or any interests he has under trusts, becomes the property of his trustee in bankruptcy, whose job it is to distribute these assets, the bankrupt's 'estate in bankruptcy', in proportionate shares to the bankrupt's creditors. Thus, if the bankrupt's estate is worth £10,000, and his total debts are £100,000, each creditor will receive 10 pence in the pound for the debt he is owed. Following this distribution, and after a period of time, eg three years, the bankrupt is 'discharged' from all his debts, and can begin economic life again, albeit without much in the way of assets. (Certain assets of the bankrupt remain his, and are not used to pay off his creditors: roughly, the property personally required by him in the pursuit of his employment or business and such property as is required to meet his and his family's basic domestic needs.) The analogous process with respect to a company is called liquidation; in essence, the liquidator distributes all of the assets of the company to its creditors on a proportionate basis. Following this distribution the company no longer exists. There is no compendious term which covers both the trustee in bankruptcy and the liquidator of a company, so henceforth when the term 'trustee in bankruptcy' is used it will, for our purposes, comprise them both.

2.58 Proprietary rights become very important in the case of insolvency. If a bankrupt owes you £100, then you are likely to see little money, for as a general creditor you will only be paid a proportionate share of the bankrupt's assets. You might be lucky to see any money at all. To the extent, however, that your rights against the bankrupt are proprietary, then you are in a much stronger position – an asset of the bankrupt which is subject to the proprietary right of someone else is, to the extent of that right, not the bankrupt's own property, and therefore not part of his estate in bankruptcy to be used for distribution to his general creditors – it belongs to the person with the proprietary right. The beneficiary's *equitable* rights to property held on trust stand on the same footing as legal title in this respect in the case of insolvency. The trustee has no beneficial interest in the property he holds on trust, and so neither can his trustee in bankruptcy who acquires title to all the trustee's legal assets should he become bankrupt; thus the property is not available to the trustee's trustee in bankruptcy for distribution to the trustee's own creditors. In short, a beneficiary's equitable rights bind a trustee in bankruptcy. Obviously then, personal rights to be paid sums of money, for example a claim for money damages for breach of contract, are not as valuable in a bankruptcy as proprietary rights, for they give the right-holder no special claim on any particular asset of the bankrupt. For this reason, plaintiffs who have a claim for money against a bankrupt will often try to claim that their past dealings with him created a trust over some of the bankrupt's property, for then they can simply withdraw this property from the bankrupt's estate.

Security interests

2.59 A beneficiary's equitable title is functionally similar to a 'security interest' in the context of insolvency. A security interest is a right that a creditor holds in particular property of his debtor. The classic example is a mortgage over land. In return for providing money, the lender (the 'mortgagee') makes sure that the borrower (the 'mortgagor') grants him a mortgage over the borrower's land. (Contrary to common parlance, it is the lender, then, who gets a mortgage.) A mortgage is a right that the lender has in the land of the borrower, and it has the effect of securing payment of the loan. If the borrower defaults on his contractual repayments of the loan, then (roughly) the lender has the right to take possession of the land and sell it to pay off the loan (plus whatever interest or other costs are specified by the loan contract). All security interests work in essentially the same way. They entitle the creditor who has one, called a 'secured' creditor, to sell the property in question if the borrower defaults on his repayments. Because security interests 'charge' the property with the repayment of a loan in this way, they are often just called 'charges'. The vital point about charges is that they are proprietary rights. They attach to the property itself. If the property passes out of the hands of the borrower into the hands of his trustee in bankruptcy, the lender will still be able to 'realise' his security, ie sell the property to pay off the debt, even though it is no longer held by the borrower. Any of the money proceeds of sale which are not required to pay off the outstanding debt belong, of course, to the trustee in bankruptcy – in other words, the security interest only charges the property to the extent of the sum owed. Security interests are not only created by two parties to a loan agreement. A court can make a 'charging order' against a defendant's property, which gives the plaintiff a charge over the property to secure the payment of an award of damages.

2.60 The justice (or lack thereof) of the beneficiary's right to withdraw his property from the bankrupt's estate should be judged in view of the fact that a trust, like a contract, is a private arrangement. While it is working, more or less, the beneficiary enforces his rights against the trustee, like a contracting party pressing for performance against the other contracting party. When things go badly wrong because the trust property is transferred away in breach of trust, the beneficiary, in a sense, takes the trust public, and tries to get the property back from third parties. You can make an analogy here with a secured loan. The loan contract is private, but when the borrower goes into bankruptcy, the lender goes public with the contract and claims the actual property itself back from the trustee in bankruptcy, disappointing all those other creditors. You can see why, in these circumstances, Parliament has tried to make things as fair as possible by putting in place public registration systems both for many equitable proprietary rights in land and for security interests, to protect third parties who would otherwise be hurt if caught out by the proprietary effect of these private arrangements. But there is no registration system as such for interests under trusts; they remain private. Thus in order to avoid surprising innocent third parties, the law must be judicious in accepting claims by those who would argue that their past dealings with a bankrupt gave rise to a trust over some of his property in their favour, as this will effectively give the claimant a priority over other creditors which may, in the circumstances, be quite unfair.

Testamentary gifts

2.61 A *testamentary* trust is one created as a gift under a will. (Trusts created by living settlors are called *inter vivos* trusts.) Many trusts are created in this way, so a passing familiarity with the rudiments of the law of wills and of intestate succession is very useful. The property of a dead person is called the 'deceased's estate', and it passes to the living in one of two ways: either according to the deceased's will, or if he has no valid will, that is, if he dies 'intestate', then according to the rules of intestate succession. The rules of intestate succession are essentially 'default' rules which distribute the property in the way that most people would have distributed it had they made a will; to their spouse first, then to their children; if there are no spouse or children, then to their parents, siblings, and finally to more distant relations. The person who makes a will is a 'testator', and in his will he nominates one or more 'executors' who will 'prove' the will, ie have the will declared valid by a Court of Probate. The property of the deceased goes to the executors who will pay off the deceased's debts, and then distribute the deceased's estate to those to whom he has given it under his will. In the case of intestacy, there is no will to execute; the court will instead appoint one or more 'administrators' who will, like executors, clear up the deceased's affairs by paying his debts, and then distribute the estate according to the rules of intestate succession. Both executors and administrators are called the 'personal representatives' of the deceased.

2.62 For historical reasons, different terms apply to testamentary gifts of different kinds of property. Land is 'devised' by will, and therefore the gift is called a 'devise' and the donees 'devisees'. Generally, personalty is 'bequeathed', but gifts of sums of money are called 'legacies' and their recipients 'legatees'. 'Gifts' will suffice for a compendious term. The gifts under a will do not take effect from the time it is made, but only when it comes into operation on the testator's death. Thus if one of the intended recipients dies before ('predeceases') the testator, his gift 'lapses'. With respect to that piece of property, it is as if the testator made no specific gift of it at all. Intended testamentary gifts, including intended trusts which are to take effect on the testator's death, may fail for a number of reasons. The testator may have failed sufficiently to specify either the recipient or the property to be given, for example. Because intended gifts under wills fail, a very important clause in any will is the one in which the testator gives 'the rest and residue' of his estate; this 'residuary' clause gives all the property left over after the specific gifts, of Blackacre to A, of 500 shares in X plc on trust to C for life and then to D absolutely, and so on, are distributed. The recipients under this clause, the 'residuary legatees' (so called whatever kind of property they get) will get more to the extent that any of the specific gifts fail. If there is no residuary gift or for some reason it fails, for example because the named residuary legatees have predeceased the testator, then any property not disposed of by specific gifts in the will will be distributed as if the testator made no will at all, ie under the rules of intestate succession. Thus it is apparent that there is always an incentive for a good fight over the validity of specific gifts in the will – the residuary legatees or, failing them, the intestate successors, will always look carefully at their validity, because they will take the property if a specific gift fails. This applies just as much to specific testamentary gifts which are trusts; indeed, most of the cases concerning the validity of trusts concern testamentary trusts.

2.63   The 'formal' requirements of wills, principally that a will be signed by the testator and attested by two witnesses, are prescribed to ensure that the will truly represents the testator's intentions and, in general, the law will allow no departures from this method. If an entire will is invalid for not being correctly formally made, the deceased's estate is distributed under the rules of intestate succession, no matter how obvious it might be that this was contrary to his actual intentions. Here again is an opportunity for a good fight. Those who would take as intestate successors, if not well provided for in the will, have the incentive to press every reasonable argument that the will is invalid.

2.64   While the main function of a will is to dispose of the testator's property, so that the power to make a will is essentially a legal power of ownership, a testator may (conditionally) impose obligations under a will, otherwise he could never create trusts, which require the creation of the duties of trusteeship. The reason why the testator can only *conditionally* impose trust obligations is that no one is ever required to take up the role of trustee; a trustee must undertake these obligations voluntarily. On the other hand, it is a principle of equity that a trust will never fail for want of a trustee, and so the court will find someone who will take on the trust (**10.51**); so although the testator's imposition of trust obligations is in theory dependent upon their acceptance by someone, as a practical matter they will be accepted so he can impose as he likes. A testator may also direct his executors or trustees to enter into contractual obligations with respect to his property, for example, to sell some of it or to give an interest free loan to his brother-in-law. What a testator cannot do by his will, of course, is to enter into a contract, ie undertake contractual obligations himself, for when the will takes effect he is, of course, dead.

2.65   The deceased's personal representatives are not trustees for the people who will take the property under the will or on intestate succession (*Stamp Duties Comr (Queensland) v Livingston* (1965)). They are the full legal owners of the deceased's property, though they are under stringent obligations to dispose of his property properly, and for this reason, their role is very trustee-like. Furthermore, prospective beneficiaries under a will or under the rules of intestate succession, although they do not have an interest in the deceased's estate itself as a beneficiary does in the property of a trust, have a right against the personal representatives to administer the estate properly, and this right, like the beneficiary's right to his interest under a trust, can be assigned or bequeathed (*Re Leigh's Will Trusts* (1970)). Executors are often appointed to be the trustees of the testamentary trusts which a testator specifies in his will.

Further reading

Matthews (1996); Hayton (1996b); Swadling (1997); Brownbill (1992, Parts I-III); Scott (1917); Weinrib (1975); Birks (2002); Hackney (1987), ch 5; Penner (2002)

Self-test questions

1. What is equitable title?

2. What are fiduciary obligations?

3. What is the significance of 'equity's darling'?

4. How does the trust work as a combination of personal and proprietary rights, duties and powers?

5. What is a security interest, and in what respects is it comparable to a trust?

6. Explain the role of a deceased's personal representatives; in what respects are they like trustees?

CHAPTER THREE

Express Trusts

SUMMARY

Fixed trusts, discretionary trusts, and powers of appointment

Beneficial interests under fixed trusts

The principle in *Saunders v Vautier*

The rule against perpetuities

The enforcement of discretionary trusts and powers of appointment

Administrative duties and powers

Beneficial interests under discretionary trusts and powers of appointment

Protective trusts

3.1 Express trusts are very flexible devices for structuring the benefits which property can provide, in particular in ways which are impossible or inconvenient to do simply by making an outright gift. Essentially three ways of doing so can be employed – fixed trusts, discretionary trusts, and powers of appointment.

Fixed trusts, discretionary trusts, and powers of appointment

Fixed trusts

3.2 The beneficial interests under a fixed trust are, as the name implies, fixed, which means that the *share* of the value of the trust property the beneficiary will receive is defined by the terms of the trust. This does not mean that the actual monetary value the beneficiary will receive can be determined from the outset. For example, company shares may be held on trust to pay the income (ie the dividends) to B for his life, and then to transfer legal title to the shares to C. Both B and C know what their interests are, though the particular amounts of income which B may receive from the trust property will vary with the amounts of the dividends paid on the shares. Nevertheless, any income will be certain as soon as it comes into existence when a dividend is declared.

Discretionary trusts

3.3 In contrast, the terms of a discretionary trust give the trustee a *dispositive* (**2.16-17**) discretion. The trustee may have a discretion as to the particular amounts any beneficiary may receive, a discretion as to whether certain individuals receive anything at all, or both. A typical trust of this kind is one in which a testator leaves money in trust for his children 'in such portions as the trustees shall in their absolute discretion see fit'. The main reason for giving the trustee a discretion of this kind is that it allows the trustee to respond to changing circumstances. If one child gets married and has children of his own, it may be sensible to give that child more money. If one of the children decides to become a 'trustafarian' or 'trust babe', ie forego education, refuse employment, and live off what he can prise out of the trustees, it may be sensible to cut him off for a time. Under a discretionary trust, no individual who is in the class of possible beneficiaries, ie in whose favour the trustee may exercise his discretion, has any individual interest, any individual 'equitable title', in the trust property, until the trustee actually exercises his discretion and declares that such and such a share or amount will go to that individual. The possible beneficiaries have only a hope, or expectancy, of receiving the testator's bounty. However, the fact that the trustee has a discretion does not mean he can do anything he wants – he still has the obligation to carry out the terms of the trust, and therefore he *must* exercise his discretion within the trust terms and distribute the trust property.

3.4   The result of the trustee's having a discretion to select only some of the possible beneficiaries means, of course, that some might not receive any money at all, in which case they will not really be 'beneficiaries' of the trust. For this reason, the term 'objects' is used, and the group of objects among whom the trustee may select is called the 'class of objects'. This is a compendious term which covers beneficiaries under a fixed trust, possible beneficiaries under a discretionary trust, and possible recipients under a power of appointment, to which we now turn.

Powers of appointment

3.5   A power of appointment under a trust allows the power-holder to 'appoint', ie give, property to individuals, free of the trust. Consider the following trust term: '£100,000 on trust to pay the income to A for life, and then to my nieces and nephews in equal shares, with power to A to appoint by deed such of the capital to such of my nieces and nephews and in such shares as he shall in his absolute discretion see fit'. This starts out as a trust, but A is given a power of appointment to transfer as much of the £100,000 as he wants at any time to the settlor's nieces and nephews before his death. If A exercises the power, he will simply take the property right out of the trust and give it to someone in the class of objects (the nieces and nephews). Because a power of appointment is a power to give away property, it is a power of ownership, although limited by the trust terms. Because powers to appoint property are given to individuals, power-holders are often called 'donees of the power', or 'donees' for short; this terminology is obviously confusing because one naturally thinks of the person *to whom* property is appointed as the donee, not the one who does the appointing. In any case, beware of this term when you read the cases.

3.6   Where does the property which the power entitles the trustee to appoint come from? From the assets of the trust, of course. Powers usually specify whether they allow the power-holder to appoint income or capital. In the example above, the power is to appoint the capital of the trust itself. Notice also who loses out when the appointment is made. In this case, if A exercises the power, he will reduce the capital base from which income is earned, so it will cost him in income, and by appointing to such nieces and nephews as he chooses, he takes capital away which would otherwise go to them all in equal shares on his death. The people whose interests diminish when the property is appointed are called those 'who take in default of appointment'.

3.7   Powers are generally restricted, essentially in the same ways that discretionary trusts are limited. The settlor can restrict the power so that the power-holder can only appoint to a certain class of objects, the amounts that any object receives can be limited, and so on. A power to appoint to anyone in the world, including the power-holder himself, is called a 'general' power. Such a power essentially amounts to absolute ownership, though a power to appoint to anyone which can only be exercised by will, which obviously cuts out the power-holder himself, is still considered a general power. A 'special' power is a power to appoint to a restricted class of persons, eg the testator's children, even if that class includes the power-holder. A 'hybrid' or 'intermediate' power is a power to appoint to anyone *except for* a restricted class, eg anyone except the settlor or his spouse or children (see, eg, *Re Park* (1932); *Re Beatty* (1990)). Powers of appointment can be classified in a number of different ways (see Thomas (1998) ch.1), but this classification of powers into general, special, and intermediate will do for our purposes.

Fixed trusts, discretionary trusts, and powers compared

3.8　Fixed trusts and discretionary trusts are alike because, being trust obligations, the trustee is under a duty to distribute the property. This is obviously not the case with powers, though (as we shall see) there may be various duties which govern the power holder's exercise of the power. On the other hand, discretionary trusts and powers are alike, and different from fixed trusts, because the discretionary trustee and the power holder both have a discretion, in the case of the discretionary trustee, a discretion as to whom he will distribute the property, in the case of the power-holder, generally that discretion as well (not always — one can have a 'fixed' power, where the power-holder, if he chooses to exercise it, must appoint only to one individual or to specific individuals in defined shares) but always a discretion as to whether he appoints at all. Clearly, then, in the case of the discretionary trust and the power of appointment, there may be fiduciary duties which may apply to the persons who operate them, and this complicates things quite a bit, as we shall now consider.

Duties and powers virtute officii (powers given to office holders), personal powers (powers nominatum), powers 'in the nature of a trust', fiduciary powers, bare and mere powers

3.9　There are any number of ways in which a person can be instructed by the terms of a trust to transfer property in some way. The first point to emphasise here is that such instructions can be given both to the trustees of a settlement, ie the titleholders of the property who are in charge of seeing to the proper administration of the trust, or to others, just particular individuals the settlor chooses. Although these particular individuals do not have title to the trust property, the trustee must comply with the terms of the trust, and so if such a power holder chooses to exercise the power and appoint property (usually by executing a deed which is delivered to the trustee), the trustee must follow his instructions and give the property away as he directs. The second point is that both of these sorts of operators of instructions under the trust may be under fiduciary obligations to the objects of the powers or duties they have. We can list the various options as follows:

3.10 A. Cases where there is a duty to distribute trust property

(i) Duties virtute officii: these are the general run of the mill duties to distribute property given to the trustees of the trust, whether fixed trusts or discretionary trusts. They are called duties 'virtute officii' because they are held by a person in virtue of his holding an office, ie the office of trustee. They are, therefore, imposed upon whomever happens to be the trustee(s) of the trust for the time being. Because the office here is the office of a trustee, such trustees will have fiduciary obligations to the objects of these trust duties to the extent they have any discretion in carrying them out. There is an important practical consequence of giving a power under a trust to 'the trustee' or 'the trustees'; the power is exercisable by whomever are the trustees for the time being, ie not only by whatever particular individuals are the trustees at the outset but by any successor trustees appointed to replace them. Always remember that trustees may die, retire from the trust, or be removed, and then replaced by others (**10.48** et seq). So a settlor must beware of relying upon the special knowledge or particular moral integrity of the trustees he initially chooses, giving them extensive discretion because he trusts they will exercise it in a way of which he would approve; they might all be hit by a bus, and the successor trustees may not have these same attractions.

(ii) Powers 'in the nature of a trust': these are 'powers' given to individuals by name ('nominatum'), rather than to trustees, but on the true construction of the terms of the trust the individual holder of the 'power' is under a duty to exercise the power. For example, a testator may give his brother a power to appoint property by his (the brother's) will, where in the circumstances it is clear that the testator intends to oblige the brother to make that appointment. Thus the brother is under a duty to exercise the power – he must exercise it. Just like a trustee of a trust he must act, though unlike the trustee he is not the legal owner of the trust property. If he fails to act, the court will act for him, in the same way as the court will enforce a trust should the trustees themselves fail to act (*Brown v Higgs* (1803)). And, just like a trustee, if there is a discretion as to whom he selects as the object of the power, he will have a fiduciary obligation to exercise this power taking only the best interests of the objects into account. Thus such an individual is a kind of 'one-off' trustee, a trustee not of the whole settlement but only of his own particular right under the trust.

3.11 B. Cases where there is no duty to distribute trust property

(iii) Powers virtute officii: If a power of appointment is given to a trustee, he is given a discretion whether to appoint the property at all, and typically a further discretion to appoint in such amounts to such objects within the class of objects as he sees fit. Unless otherwise specified, and this would be rare, a trustee who is given a discretion is bound to exercise that discretion in keeping with his fiduciary obligation to consider only the best interests of the objects. This has three important consequences. The first is that the trustee may not release the power, ie surrender it. It was given by the terms of the trust for the benefit of its objects, and it would be a breach of fiduciary obligation to release it, for that would clearly be an act against their interests. Second, the trustee, although not being bound to exercise the power, must consider using it from time to time. Finally, in exercising the power, the trustees must consider not only the best interests of the objects of the power, but the interests of those beneficiaries of the trust who would take in default of appointment, for to appoint the property to the objects of the power is to take it away from them. It is sometimes said that the trustee only owes fiduciary obligations to, ie must only take into account the interests of, those who take in default of appointment, for they are beneficiaries of the trust, whereas the objects of the power are just that, objects of a power not objects of the trust (see Smith, 2004). But this seems wrong in principle, for under the terms of the trust the objects of fixed trusts, discretionary trusts, and powers of appointment are all equally contemplated as objects of the settlor's bounty, and although as we move from fixed trusts to powers of appointment their likelihood of receiving an actual benefit may diminish in theory, *to the extent they are capable of benefiting under the trust, to that extent their interests should govern any exercise of the trustee's discretion.*

(iv) Personal fiduciary powers: In the same way as a named individual who is not a trustee may be given trust duties, he may be given powers of appointment nominatum, and in the same way that a trust obligation to distribute property may be imposed upon him (ii above), the trust instrument on its true construction may also impose fiduciary obligations upon him in his exercise of the power. In that case, he is in the same position as the trustee who has powers of appointment virtute officii – he cannot release the power, must consider using it, and must exercise it only with the objects and those who take in default in mind, but analogously with (ii), he is a 'one-off' fiduciary power-holder.

(v) Pure personal powers: These are powers of appointment given nominatum where no obligations of whatever kind are imposed under the terms of the trust. Here the individual power holder may ignore the power or release it (ie inform the trustees in writing that he surrenders his right to exercise the power), and if the power confers a discretion upon him to appoint to only one or some of a class of objects, he may exercise the power in any way that suits him, favouring one object over another as he likes. Thus the absence of any fiduciary obligations to the objects means that he has no obligation to the objects to benefit, or even consider benefiting, them in any way.

3.12   Cases (iii) and (iv) are sometimes distinguished from (v) by referring to the former as 'fiduciary' and the latter as 'bare' powers. While these terms are accurate as far as they go, one should bear in mind that in the case of a trustee the imposition of the fiduciary obligation turns not on the trust instrument specifically defining the character of the power as such, but because it is a power *held* by a trustee in virtue of his office, and so like any discretion he has it is willy-nilly subject to fiduciary obligations in its exercise. Irrespective of whether fiduciary obligations apply to the exercise of a power, powers of appointment, where there is no duty to appoint, are sometimes distinguished from discretionary trusts (aka 'trust powers') and 'powers in the nature of a trust', where there is such a duty, by being called 'mere' powers, 'mere' indicating the absence of any duty to distribute the trust property. Finally, note that there is nothing preventing the settlor from giving a pure personal power to a trustee, ie not *virtute officii*, but in his own name, although for obvious reasons this will have to be clearly spelled out.

3.13 Because there is no duty upon a power holder to appoint, he might well not, and so there will always be those who will take the property if no appointment is made, who will, in the standard terminology, 'take in default of appointment'. As the provision for A and his nieces and nephews in the example above (**3.5**) illustrates, one whole 'trust' can combine the different devices of the fixed trust, the discretionary trust, and the power of appointment, and given, as we have just seen, the various ways of distributing duties, fiduciary powers, and pure personal powers, the terms of a trust can be very complicated, involving many different actors. Trust instruments are therefore capable of giving rise to troublesome interpretive difficulties in determining whether what might on one reading be a discretionary trust is really just a fiduciary power of appointment, or whether a power conferred *nominatum* is accompanied with an obligation to exercise it, or only a fiduciary obligation to exercise it in good faith if exercised at all, or is a purely personal power.

Administrative duties and powers

3.14 Besides dispositive duties and powers, any number of administrative duties (**2.16**) and powers are necessary to keep the trust running while it is in existence. And just as is the case with dispositive duties and powers, there can be fixed and discretionary administrative duties, and fiduciary and personal administrative powers. For example, trustees have a fixed duty to keep the trust accounts, ie the records of trust dealings. They have a discretionary duty to invest the trust fund so as to earn a reasonable rate of return, where the discretion as to how they invest is, of course, fiduciary, so they must choose their investments with only the best interests of the beneficiaries in mind. Trustees have a power to retire from the trust, and may have a power to appoint new trustees; as they receive these powers *virtute officii* they are fiduciary powers.

3.15 But administrative powers may also be given to individuals *nominatum*, and again, they may be accompanied by duties to exercise them, or may be mere powers which might be fiduciary or might be purely personal. Although rare, a named individual (eg a 'protector' (**3.18**)) might have a duty, ie be under a trust obligation, to consider and either give or refuse consent to certain actions taken by a trustee under his powers under the trust (eg a power to 'export' the trust, ie change the jurisdiction in which the trust is administered). A named individual may be given the power to replace the trustees — this is a popular power for settlors to confer upon themselves in *inter vivos* trusts. This power may be fiduciary, in which case it may only be exercised in the best interests of the beneficiaries, or purely personal, in which case the holder may exercise it as he likes. Now, given that administrative powers given to named individuals are *administrative*, ie they concern the proper running of the trust, there must be a strong initial presumption that they are fiduciary, because the purpose of a trust is to provide for and protect the interests of the beneficiaries, and so any power to enhance the trust's proper working would presumably be similarly oriented (see Hayton (1999)).

3.16 However, this might not always be the case. Assume an *inter vivos* trust of which the bulk of the trust fund is a majority shareholding in the settlor's private company, and assume the trust instrument confers upon the settlor a power to refuse consent to the trustees' voting him off the board of directors of the company. Such a provision may not be inserted in order to protect the best interests of the beneficiaries, but to protect the settlor's own position. Whether an administrative power is fiduciary in such a case will depend upon the true construction of the terms of the trust. Settlors have what might be called a very broad 'freedom of trust', and the courts are generally assiduous in trying to read a trust instrument to give effect to their intentions. How a trust instrument is read in terms of the imposition of duties and the conferral of powers is very important of course, and in certain cases fine distinctions must be drawn.

3.17 Consider the following: a trust allows the trustees a discretion in dealing with the income of the trust as it arises: they may either pay it directly to the income beneficiaries (**3.19**), or may 'accumulate' it (**3.21**), ie retain the income for later distribution. Now at first glance, it may not appear important whether this is framed as a duty to distribute income as it arises with a power to depart from that duty and accumulate, or as a duty to accumulate with a power to depart from that duty and distribute, since the exercise of the power entails departure from the duty, and vice versa. On either reading, then, it appears the trustee has the same freedom of choice, so how can it matter how it's put? Here is how it matters: because trustees must comply with their duties, which task is framed as the duty sets the 'default' position from which we proceed if there is a problem of some kind. Roughly, powers are options whereas duties must be carried out. Thus in order to exercise a power to depart from a duty, trustees must agree unanimously to do so; in the absence of agreement there is no question but that they comply with their duties. So, if on the true construction of the trust instrument we have a duty to distribute income and a power to accumulate, and the trustees cannot agree to exercise the power, they must distribute the income. And conversely, they must carry out a duty to accumulate if they could not agree to exercise their power to distribute. So such fine distinctions can have significant practical consequences. Finally, in interpreting different trust instruments the different circumstances of different trusts, whether they are family trusts, pension fund trusts, or commercial trusts will obviously colour the initial presumptions one might apply to determining whether duties are imposed or powers conferred, and whether powers are fiduciary or personal.

Extensive power and duty holding by non-trustees: protectors

3.18 There is nothing in theory to prevent a settlor from giving extensive dispositive and administrative duties and powers to non-trustees, but for obvious reasons this is a dangerous thing to do if they are given to named individuals. Those named individuals may perish, or be otherwise unco-operative, and so a settlement which only runs smoothly if named third parties do their job is a precarious one. This, in general, is why most of the powers and duties needed to make the trust run are given to office holders, ie the trustees. However, in the last few decades, a new animal has appeared called the 'protector', a non-trustee who under the trust is sometimes given extensive powers, in particular powers to give or refuse consent to the trustee's exercise of various of their powers and discretions. Protectors originally arose in the 'offshore' trust industry; an English settlor, often with tax planning in mind, would create a trust in, say, the Bahamas. Because the trustee in this case is far away, as a comfort the settlor would give to himself or to someone else he trusted like his solicitor or his old friend the job of keeping an eye on the trustee (almost always a company specialising in trust business), and giving them sufficient powers to keep the trustee in check if it seemed the trustee might not act in the way a settlor intended. The question which now vexes trust lawyers, and some courts in offshore jurisdictions, is precisely how to treat the giving of such powers, and sometimes duties. Is the protector a 'quasi-trustee', who is a fiduciary toward the beneficiaries? Or is his role a personal one? Or, indeed, is he a fiduciary to the settlor, who must exercise his powers in the settlor's best interests (which raises the interesting question whether this makes the settlor a beneficiary of some kind (and what kind?) under the trust). If there are provisions for a replacement protector, should the protectorship be regarded as a fiduciary office like that of a trustee? In some jurisdictions the trust legislation itself contains provisions concerning protectors (eg Bahamas Trustee Act 1998, ss 2, 81-83), but where this is not the case, as in England, the effect of the grant of such powers and possibly duties must be determined by the court interpreting the terms of the trust. It will be interesting to see whether, in the next few decades, the role of protector becomes a common feature of trusts and, secondly, what the courts will eventually make of it, if they make much of it at all. It is not possible to say how extensive the use of protectors is in UK trusts; there is, as far as I know, no English case which has considered the role or duties or powers of a 'protector' under that description .

Beneficial interests under fixed trusts

Capital and income interests

3.19 Under a trust, the beneficial interests in the trust property can be carved up pretty much any way the settlor wishes. However, there are standard ways of doing so which we shall encounter again and again, in particular dividing the property between 'income' and 'capital' beneficiaries. Consider the following gift: 'To A for life and then to X, Y and Z in equal shares'. A will receive the benefit of the property during his lifetime, but what determines the extent of his benefit? Can he insist that the trustee transfer as much of the property as he wants to him, so that X, Y, and Z will only get what he has not used up before he dies? No. A is entitled only to the income of the property, and the income he receives will depend upon the kind of property in the trust. Income on shares consists of the dividends that are paid, on bonds or other-interest bearing investments the interest payments, on land rent. During A's life X, Y, and Z will get nothing. They are the capital beneficiaries; after A's death they are entitled to the property itself, free of any trust, in equal shares. The value of their interest will fluctuate with the market sale price of the trust property.

Successive interests

3.20 Where there are income and capital beneficiaries there are 'successive' interests. Successive interests are interests in the same property which take effect one after another, usually following the successive deaths of the beneficiaries. In the example above, A will get the benefit for the time being, and only later will the capital beneficiaries X, Y, and Z get any value from the trust property. Traditionally successive interest trusts, called 'settlements', were the province of dynastic families, and were used to define each successive generation's beneficial interest in a family's landed estates with a view to preserving them for subsequent generations. Because land was the subject matter of settlements, successive interests were framed in terms of two freehold estates in land, the life interest and the fee simple. A life interest, unsurprisingly, lasts for the lifetime of an individual, and a fee simple estate is unlimited in time, and therefore a gift of a fee simple amounts to absolute ownership. So a typical gift might be to Fred for life, then to Beatrix for life, then to Albert in fee simple. Fred will enjoy the benefit or income of the property for his life; when he dies Beatrix will get the income for as long as she lives, and when she expires Albert will take the absolute ownership. Due to the significance of the land settlement, the income beneficiary for life of a trust of any kind of property is often called the 'life tenant', the traditional land law term for the present holder of a life estate, and the capital beneficiary the 'remainderman', the corresponding term for one who took the fee simple following a life estate. Successive interests are not, however, restricted to time periods equivalent to the life estate and fee simple. One might make a gift of the income of shares to Richard until he attains the age of 21, and then to Tom for 10 years, and then to Mary absolutely.

Exhaustive and non-exhaustive trusts of income

3.21 Trusts of the income of property can be cut down by giving the trustees a 'power to accumulate', that is, a power to save the income as it arises rather than distributing it to beneficiaries. The accumulations can be directed to go either to the capital beneficiary or to accumulation funds which can later be paid over to the income beneficiaries. Trusts with a power to accumulate are called 'non-exhaustive', for when the power is exercised the distributions to the beneficiaries do not exhaust all of the income. Trusts of income with no power to accumulate are called 'exhaustive'.

Conditional and defeasible interests

3.22 Complicating matters somewhat, there may also be conditional and defeasible interests in property held under a trust. Conditions may be of two kinds, conditions precedent and conditions subsequent. A condition precedent is a condition which must be fulfilled for a gift to take effect, eg 'Blackacre to A in fee simple, on condition that he marries before the year 2010'. A condition subsequent is a condition of defeasance – the gift will come to an end if the condition occurs, eg 'Blackacre to A in fee simple, but if he should become a barrister, then to B in fee simple': if A becomes a barrister, then B will become entitled to Blackacre. Finally, a determinable interest is one which, while similar to a gift defeasible upon condition subsequent, is conceptually different. A gift defeasible upon condition subsequent is regarded as a full gift, of a life interest for example, which might come to an end before running its normal course, ie until the death of the life tenant. A determinable interest is regarded as being a gift of property for a lesser period than an estate like a life interest, this lesser interest being framed by the event by which the interest comes to an end; however, as things turn out its actual duration may extend to the full period of a normal estate, eg a full life interest, if the determining event does not occur. Thus a life interest determinable upon X's marriage will 'ripen' into a complete life interest if X never marries. The very subtle conceptual distinction between determinable interests and interests defeasible upon condition subsequent, so that the legal effect of a gift 'to Mathilda for life, but if she remarries, to Betty' (a life interest defeasible upon condition subsequent) differs from one 'to Mathilda during her widowhood' (a determinable life interest), has been much criticised for being 'extremely artificial' (Pennycuick V-C, *Re Sharp's Settlement Trusts* (1973)).

Vested, absolute, and contingent interests

3.23 Because interests can be defeasible or conditional, the interest can shift from one person to another. A person's interests are 'vested' if he is entitled to receive the benefits of the property as matters stand at the present. Thus, where there is a gift 'to A for life, remainder to B', A and B both have vested interests, since as things stand right now the property will go to them. It is not to the point that B has only a future interest. His capital interest is still vested, because he is in line to receive it and no one else is. Because this gift is not subject to any condition of defeasance or determining event (the capital will go to B and only B (or his heirs) when A dies, and A must die sometime), B's interest is also 'absolute'. An absolute interest is one which cannot be defeated. An example of a person with a vested interest which is not absolute is the unmarried widow Mathilda in the example above (**3.22**) – the income interest is vested in her and she receives the income, but it is not absolute, for if she remarries she will lose it. Another example is the person who will take property in default of appointment before any appointment is made. Until appointment, he is in line to receive the property, but he is clearly not absolutely entitled for his interest will be defeated by an appointment. Those who have vested, but defeasible interests, have counterparts in those persons who will get a vested interest if the former's are defeated. Thus, if a gift is 'Blackacre to Harry for life, but if he publishes the photographs of my 40th birthday party, then to Jane for life', then Jane has a *contingent* interest in Blackacre, which will vest if Harry publishes those photographs.

3.24 Although the trust device allows a settlor to distribute his bounty in a variety of ways over a period of time, the law does put limitations on this power. In particular, the law limits his ability to keep the property in the trust and out of the hands of the beneficiaries whom equity regards as the true owners of the property. The two principal means of doing so are the principle in *Saunders v Vautier* and the rule against perpetuities.

The principle in *Saunders v Vautier*

3.25 Although named after the case of *Saunders v Vautier* (1841), the principle is actually of much longer standing, and may be stated as follows: wherever a beneficiary with an absolute interest under a trust is *sui juris*, ie of full age and sound mind, he may call for the trust property which represents that interest, and the trustees are obliged to transfer the legal title of it to him; if he is a sole beneficiary, this will result in the complete collapse of the trust. For example, if a settlor creates a trust under which his son A is to receive the income of property until he is thirty, at which time he is to receive the capital, that son can demand the legal title as soon as he reaches 18.

3.26   This represents a significant limitation upon the settlor's 'freedom of trust', but it can be justified in two ways. First, there might be something of an 'anti-trust' justification, as follows: while it is fine to empower owners to create structured gifts of property where this is essentially the only means of giving the benefits of property, as for example when money is provided for minor children, this power should not be used to allow an owner to control his beneficiaries when they are fully competent to look after themselves. If you give property to someone, you naturally take the risk that they will use that property in ways which are foolish or which otherwise might defeat your hopes. But that is the price of treating people, including donees of property, as autonomous individuals. The law of trusts should not, therefore, allow settlors to treat sane adults as children, and so the principle of *Saunders v Vautier* reflects the law's desire that all individuals, once *sui juris*, should be treated as capable of running their own affairs, including their rights over property.

3.27   The second justification is related, and concerns the idea of equitable ownership. In the eyes of equity, the beneficiaries are the owners of the trust property, not the settlor. They have the rights against the trustee, and must enforce the trust themselves. When they reach full age, in essence the trust is in their hands. They can enforce their rights against the trustee or not, may consent to the trustees acting outside the terms of the trust, ie doing what would otherwise be a breach of trust (**11.47** et seq), and may 'vary' (ie alter) the terms of the trust as they wish (**10.66** et seq). The settlor has no say in any of this. Thus they are (in theory) in full control of the property via the office of the trustee. But if that is so, why cannot they do with their property what they like, as can any other full owners, and in particular, take the property out of the trust completely if they so desire? It is important to note, however, that the principle allows the beneficiaries to collapse the trust, *not* to 'micro-manage' the trust by telling the trustee how to exercise his powers and discretions. For example, in *Re Brockbank* (1948), the court stated that while *sui juris* beneficiaries could collapse the trust and re-settle the fund on new trustees, they were not entitled to direct the present trustee to exercise his power to appoint a replacement trustee (**10.48** et seq) as they wished. In short, the principle in *Saunders v Vautier* does not turn all trustees into the *agents* of their beneficiaries (**2.19-22**). Although statute has recently conferred a power upon *sui juris* beneficiaries to replace their trustee (**10.54**), this does not alter the general principle that beneficiaries have no right to micro-manage the trust.

3.28 The operation of the principle varies according to the type of trust. Under fixed trusts, *sui juris* beneficiaries may in principle demand that the trustee transfer the legal title to whatever share of the trust property is theirs, but this is subject to a general limitation that such a transfer must not result in the devaluation of the other beneficiaries' shares. In *Stephenson v Barclays Bank Trust Co Ltd* (1975), Walton J said:

> In general, the [individual *sui juris* beneficiary] is entitled to have transferred to him... an aliquot share of each and every asset of the trust fund which presents no difficulty so far as division is concerned. This will apply to such items as cash, money at the bank or an unsecured loan, Stock Exchange securities and the like. However, as regards land, certainly, in all cases, as regards shares in a private company in very special circumstances...the situation is not so simple, and even a person with a vested interest in possession in an aliquot share of the trust fund may have to wait until the land is sold, and so forth, before being able to call upon the trustees as of right to account to him for his share of the assets.

3.29 More recently, in *Lloyds Bank plc v Duker* (1987), the court refused the request of one beneficiary for the transfer of his proportionate interest in shares of a private company held on trust; the transfer would have given him a controlling block of shares in the company, and as a result his shares would be worth more per share on the open market than the remaining shares in the trust. The judge ordered the sale of all the trust shares on the open market, which, since it would give control of the company, would attract for the whole block of shares a higher price; the beneficiary could then claim his proportionate share of the proceeds of sale. It is important to note that the beneficiary acquired the large proportionate interest in the shares both because certain of the gifts in the original will which disposed of the shares lapsed and through a subsequent bequest. Where a testator or settlor specifically gave one beneficiary a majority interest in a trust of shares, it might also be inferred that he intended that beneficiary to take the market value benefit of a controlling interest, in which case the principle of *Saunders v Vautier* should allow him to withdraw his shares.

3.30   The application of the principle in the case of discretionary trusts is stated in *Re Smith* (1928) by Romer J:

> What is to happen where the trustees have a discretion whether they will apply the whole or only a portion of the fund for the benefit of one person, but are obliged to pay the rest of the fund, so far as not applied for the benefit of the first named person, to or for the benefit of a second named person? There, two people are the sole objects of the discretionary trust and, between them, are entitled to have the whole fund applied to them or for their benefit. It has been laid down by the Court of Appeal in *In re Nelson* (1918) that, in such a case as that you treat all the people put together just as though they formed one person, for whose benefit the trustees were directed to apply the whole fund.

Therefore, such beneficiaries may together call upon the trustees to transfer the trust property to them as co-owners. If the discretionary trust is one to pay the income only, they can demand the trustee pay the Income, as it arises, to them directly as co-owners of it all.

The rule against perpetuities

3.31   As the name implies, the rule against perpetuities prevents settlors from creating perpetual trusts. The rule requires that the beneficiaries of the trust property must get those shares, that is, their rights to the trust property must vest in interest, ie vest absolutely, within a certain period from the time the trust came into effect. The absolute vesting of interests means that the various beneficiaries are all identified and their interests definitely determined to be theirs, and so they may individually or together require the trustees to transfer the trust property to them under the rule in *Saunders v Vautier*. The rule does not mean that by the end of the perpetuity period the trust must collapse, all legal title to trust property being transferred to individual beneficiaries. The trust must simply be in the position where this can happen.

3.32   The reason for the rule is straightforward: it prevents individuals from directing the use of their property from their grave long after they are dead. The rule ensures that within a certain time after the trust comes into effect, the full beneficial ownership of the property gets into the hands of living persons. A detailed examination of the rule is unwarranted here but an outline of its operation is useful, as the effect of the rule will come into play now and again.

3.33 Applying the modern (ie post-seventeenth century) common law rule against perpetuities was a most difficult and complex process, both because of the way the time limit was calculated, and because of the way it took into account the possibility of events occurring which might make a gift fail. The time period of the rule was framed to allow testators to make gifts to their grandchildren that would not vest until the children reached the age of majority, which was 21 when the rule was devised. The rule was devised to make that possible, but also to make sure that this was the limit of what a testator could do to extend the time before his gifts actually vested; in consequence, the allowable time period was framed in a particular way, in reference to 'lives in being' plus a further period of 21 years. The way in which this limit worked is best explained by an example. If I leave property in my will to be divided equally between all my grandchildren who attain the age of 21, under the rule we calculate the time period within which the beneficiaries will become entitled to their shares of the property as follows: If I have any living grandchildren when I die their shares will vest when they each turn 21, and so, being alive at my death, they must turn 21 within 21 years following my death. But I may end up having more grandchildren than them, because my living children may have more kids. My own children who are alive at my death are lives in being for the purpose of the rule. (If my wife is pregnant with my child, a child *en ventre sa mere*, as the expression goes, that child counts as a child living at my death, thus a life in being for the purpose of the rule.) The rule now works as follows: obviously, any child born to my children must be conceived before my children die; therefore, the last grandchild of mine which could possibly be born will be conceived no later than the death of my last living child; therefore that last grandchild will turn 21 (ignoring periods of gestation) no later than 21 years after the death of the last life in being. Thus a gift to any or all of my grandchildren who attain their age of majority, 21, must vest, if it vests at all (all of my grandchildren may, as it turns out, die before 21 – that makes the gift fail, but not for perpetuity), within the period determined by the lifetime of the last surviving life in being plus 21 years. Thus the rule can be stated as follows: a gift upon trust is valid if the interests in the trust property of those who are intended to benefit must vest, if they vest at all, within 21 years following the death of the last surviving life in being. The following examples will show why there were complexities and difficulties applying the rule.

3.34 Say that I have three daughters, all of whom are over 60. They're not going to have any more children, so I'm not going to have any more grandchildren. So if in my will I leave a sum of money to be divided equally amongst my *great* grandchildren who attain the age of 21, that gift will vest within a period determined by lives in being plus 21 years. The relevant lives in being here are my grandchildren. I will have no more, and the last great grandchild of mine will come into existence (if only in the womb of his mother) no later than the death of my last surviving grandchild. And so none of my great grandchildren will attain the age of 21 (again discounting periods of gestation) later than 21 years following the death of the last surviving life in being. Nevertheless, this gift is void for perpetuity. The courts reasoned that only death prevented anyone from having another child, and so, my daughters being alive, they might yet have another child after my death, although each was over 60 (this was taken to be a matter of 'logical' possibility — the seventeenth century judiciary was not anticipating advances in reproductive technology). Such a grandchild would not be alive at my death, so would not be a life in being, and this grandchild could have a child after the death of the last surviving grandchild of mine who was alive at my death, thus after the death of the last surviving life in being. That great grandchild's share would vest more than 21 years after the death of the last life in being. Thus, the gift fails because the rule was applied on the basis of what *could* happen, however unlikely something might be, not on the basis of what was likely to happen or actually happened over time. A famous trap is that of the 'unborn' widow. Consider this testamentary gift: 'Blackacre to my son A for life, then to A's widow for life, then to A's eldest child then living absolutely.' A is already alive, so is a life in being for the purpose of the rule. The problem is that A might marry someone who is not alive at my death, ie someone yet to be born when I die. After growing up and marrying A, she might outlive A (and anyone else alive at my death) by more that 21 years. So the gift to A's eldest son might vest more than 21 years after the death of the last life in being, so the gift is void.

3.35 The Perpetuities and Accumulations Act 1964 changed the rules somewhat. In particular it introduced the notion of 'wait and see', by which a gift is valid if it turns out that it vests in the perpetuity period, even though it might not if some possible event or other actually occurs. Secondly, it created a provision by which a settlor can select any period of up to 80 years as the period for his gift, rather than relying on lives in being plus 21 years.

3.36 The rule applies not only to the vesting of fixed interests, but also to interests which arise under discretionary trusts and the exercise of powers of appointment. Special powers of appointment must be exercised, if they are exercised at all, within the perpetuity period, and by parity of reasoning, distributions under discretionary trusts must occur within the perpetuity period as well. By contrast, since general powers are akin to ownership, the rule requires only that the power is acquired during the perpetuity period, since this acquisition in effect vests the interest in the property. It is not clear how hybrid powers are to be treated under the common law rule, though under s 7 of the 1964 Act it appears that any power which does not allow a person to appoint to himself without the consent of anyone else (a general power for the purposes of the Act) will be treated as a special power.

3.37 Finally, as the title of the 1964 Act indicates, statutory rules have been introduced to limit the period in which a settlor can direct that the income of trust property may be accumulated, generally to no longer than 21 years. The details are not important here.

The enforcement of discretionary trusts and powers of appointment

The enforcement of discretions generally

3.38 The objects of a trust or a power have *locus standi*, or standing in court, to sue trustees or other duty or power holders under a trust to ensure the latter do not violate the terms of the trust by which these duties or powers are granted and defined. Duty holders, whether trustees or other individuals, may act wrongly either by *nonfeasance*, ie not carrying out their duty, or *misfeasance*, ie exercising their duty but doing so incorrectly. Because there is no duty to exercise mere powers, mere power holders can only be brought to court for misfeasance, using the power innappropriately, not for failing to use it at all (generally speaking, see **3.54**). Of course, fixed duties, whether dispositive or administrative, pose no problem in this regard. If a trustee or other fixed duty-ower fails to carry out a fixed trust obligation, the court will either make him do it or will order whatever is to be done itself. The difficulties lie in controlling trustees and other power holders in the exercise of their discretions.

3.39   The court's control of trustee's discretions is a difficult and complex subject (see Cullity (1975)), but the following points outline the general position:

(1) in determining what sort of bounds exist upon the trustee's or other power holder's discretion, the first thing to be done is to construe the terms of the trust. In the leading case of *Gisborne v Gisborne* (1877), the HL refused to intervene on behalf of a beneficiary where the trustees had exercised their 'uncontrollable authority' under the trust instrument to pay her less from the fund than they might have done.

(2) Where the discretion is held by a trustee, or by an individual but the power is fiduciary, the discretion must be exercised in good faith in the best interests of the beneficiaries, though it is fair to point out that it is often very difficult to prove that a particular decision, within the scope of the trustee or power holder's discretion, was taken *mala fide* or not in consideration of the best interests of the beneficiaries; different persons will appreciate the best interests of the beneficiaries differently.

(3) Even where there is no fiduciary obligation attached to the exercise of a discretion, one should generally be able to determine from the trust instrument some *purpose* for which the power or discretion was conferred, so that an exercise of discretion for an ulterior purpose will be found to be wrongful. This standard by which to judge the exercise of a power or discretion underlies the doctrine of 'fraud on a power', which we will discuss in a little detail below (3.55-56).

(4) Under the *Re Hastings-Bass* (1975) principle the exercise of a power may be treated as void or voidable, or the non-exercise of a power by a trustee may be overturned and the court will treat the power as having been exercised, where it can be shown that the trustee would not have acted/failed to act as he did if he either had taken considerations into account which he ought to have done, or not taken considerations into account which he ought not have done. Recently, for example, in *Abacus Trust Co (Isle of Man) Ltd v NSPCC* (2001) the court declared void the exercise of a power of appointment which, having been exercised three days too soon, exposed the beneficiaries of the trust to an avoidable tax liability of £1.2m. On the other hand, in *Breadner v Granville-Grossman* (2001), Park J refused

to apply the principle so as to retrospectively hold that a power of appointment which the trustees failed to exercise before its expiry had been exercised.

(5) Most recently, but so far only in the context of pension funds, judges have assessed the validity of a trustee's exercise of discretion on the public/administrative law 'Wednesbury principle' (*Associated Provincial Picture House Ltd v Wednesbury Corpn* (1948)); for example in *Edge v Pensions Ombudsman* (1998), Scott V-C said a judge should refuse to interfere unless the trustee took into account improper, irrelevant, or irrational considerations, or otherwise the trustee's decision could be shown to be one that no reasonable body of trustees could have made.

The enforcement of dispositive discretions: discretionary trusts and powers of appointment

3.40 Up until the decision of the HL in *McPhail v Doulton* (1971) it was a fairly simple matter to distinguish between the way in which the court would enforce the trustees' compliance with a discretionary trust and the way in which it would oversee the exercise of powers of appointment. In the case of both, any distribution in violation of the terms of the trust or power, ie any misfeasance, would be invalid. The chief difference lay in the effects of nonfeasance. With respect to discretionary trusts, if the trustees failed to exercise their discretion and distribute the property, the court would order a distribution. Before *Kemp v Kemp* (1795) the court would, in rare cases, exercise the trustees' discretion itself to distribute the property unequally to the objects, but following that decision the practice became to apply the maxim 'equality is equity' and distribute the property equally amongst them. In the case of powers, by contrast, the case of nonfeasance presented no problem. There was no duty for the court to enforce.

Certainty of objects

3.41 What changed in *McPhail* was the test of certainty which applied to the objects of discretionary trusts. Normally much of what follows is covered in trust books in the chapter on 'Certainty' (in this book, chapter 7), but being a radical thinker I propose to include it here because it concerns the enforceability of discretionary trusts and powers, and the rights of the objects under them, more than it does certainty *per se*.

Certainty of objects is a requirement of both trusts and powers, and means nothing more than that the terms of the trust or power have to indicate with sufficient precision who is in the class of objects.

The 'complete list' test and the 'is or is not test'

3.42   The historical test for certainty of objects for trusts, whether fixed or discretionary, was that for a trust to be valid, one had to be able to draw up a complete list of the objects. In a discretionary trust for the settlor's children, for example, this could be easily accomplished since it was clear that the class of objects comprised the settlor's children and no one else. Whether or not the 'complete list' test was applicable to mere powers of appointment fell to be decided in *Re Gestetner Settlement* (1953). The power in question was a power to appoint property to a large and fluctuating group of objects including the settlor's former employees and their surviving spouses. It was held that the power was valid even though a complete list of the possible objects of the power could not be drawn up at any one time. Harman J stated:

> [T]he document on its face shows that there is no obligation on the trustees to do more than consider – from time to time, I suppose – the merits of such persons of the specified class as are known to them and, if they think fit, to give them something... I cannot see [that] such a duty [makes] it essential for these trustees, before parting with any income or capital, to survey the whole field, and to consider whether A is more deserving of bounty than B ... there is no difficulty ... in ascertaining whether any given postulant is a member of the specified class. Of course, if that could not be ascertained the matter would be quite different, but of John Doe or Richard Roe it can be postulated easily enough whether he is or is not eligible to receive the settlor's bounty.

3.43   Thus was born the 'is or is not' test for certainty of objects: since the power holder has no duty to distribute the property, all that matters is misfeasance, ie if he appoints property at all, he must be sure to appoint only to those within the class of objects and not those outside it; all he need know with certainty is whether any particular person is within the class or not; in particular he does not need a complete list of all objects who are eligible to receive the trust property.

3.44   In *IRC v Broadway Cottages Trust* (1955), the CA had to decide whether the same test should apply to a *discretionary trust* for a similarly large and fluctuating class including the settlor's employees and their wives and widows. In summary, the arguments against the 'is or is not' test, and in favour of the complete list test, were these: Starting from the principle stated by Lord Eldon in *Morice v Bishop of Durham* (1805), that in order to be valid, a trust must be one which the court can control and execute, various factors made the court's control and execution of such a trust impossible:

- In the absence of a complete list only a subset of the whole class can be identified; such a subset cannot 'claim execution of the trust' or call for the trust property under the principle in *Saunders v Vautier* because the trustees have no duty to distribute to any subset of the whole class; as a result, where the whole class of objects cannot be identified the trustees' duties are 'illusory'.

- Since no complete list can be made, it is impossible to infer that the testator intended a trust for the entire class in equal shares in default of distribution, so the court is unable to deal with a failure of the trustees to distribute by ordering such a division; the court could not order a particular unequal division, for that would be exercising a dispositive discretion, and that discretion is the trustee's alone.

- The court's ability to execute a trust must be judged in reference to what might happen, not in reference to what is likely to happen. It must be assumed that the trustees might, for some reason, refuse to distribute, and the court be required to carry out the trust by order. This must be assumed also of new trustees replacing old ones who proved recalcitrant. Replacing one set of trustees after another is not execution of the trust by the court.

- The trustee must know or be able to ascertain all the objects whom he might select, otherwise he is merely selecting from *some* members of the class, in which case he is not carrying out the terms of the trust, ie to exercise his discretion to select from amongst *all* of the objects.

- Similarly, the court cannot mend the invalidity of a trust of this kind by imposing an arbitrary distribution amongst some only of the whole unascertainable class; to create a certain class to replace the uncertain one chosen by the settlor would amount to imposing a different trust.

3.45 The essence of the argument in favour of the 'is or is not' test was that no difficulty in practice in effectively controlling the execution of the trust would arise:

- Having undertaken the trust, the trustees can be assumed to be willing and able to carry it out.

- With respect to malfeasance by the trustees: the 'is or is not' test allows the trustees to ensure that only qualified beneficiaries take benefits, and so the trustees can distribute within the terms of the trust. Conversely, distribution to non-objects can be determined with certainty, and could be restrained by the court on the suit of any qualified member of the class.

- With respect to nonfeasance by the trustees: At the suit of any qualified member, recalcitrant trustees could be replaced, and this process could be repeated. 'The possibility that not only the original trustees but every set of trustees appointed in their place would fail or refuse to do this is so remote that it can for practical purposes be disregarded.' In the unlikely event of its becoming necessary, the court could declare a trust in default of distribution for a modified class of whose members a complete list could be made.

3.46 The trust failed. Jenkins LJ had this to say:

> We confess to some sympathy for the appellants' argument, which has an attractive air of common sense, but we do not think that it can be allowed to prevail. We think the submissions... to the effect that the trust is not one which the court could control or execute, and that this objection cannot be met by urging the improbability of assistance by the court ever becoming necessary, are well founded. We also agree that... the court would not be executing the trust merely by ordering a change in trusteeship.

At this time, then, one important distinction between discretionary trusts and powers of appointment was their respective tests for certainty of objects, which directly reflected the court's consideration that discretionary trusts, being trusts, required possibilities of precise enforcement in the case of nonfeasance which did not apply to powers of appointment.

McPhail v Doulton

3.47 Thus the matter stood until *McPhail v Doulton* (1971), which concerned a discretionary trust for a large class comprising employees and ex-employees of a large company and their dependents and relations. Although about a year before the HL in *Re Gulbenkian's Settlement Trusts* (1970) had confirmed *obiter*, that while the 'is or is not test' was appropriate for powers, the complete list test remained the appropriate test for discretionary trusts, a different panel of their Lordships in *McPhail v Doulton* decided 3:2 that the 'is or is not test' was appropriate for discretionary trusts as well. The majority decision, given by Lord Wilberforce, essentially recognised the 'common sense' arguments put in *Broadway Cottages Trusts*, accepting that in practice trusts for large classes of beneficiaries could be adequately enforced.

3.48 Lord Wilberforce emphasised that the difference between the practical tasks facing trustees who held a mere power of appointment and those of trustees who held property on a discretionary basis was a matter of degree:

Any trustee [holding a mere power] would surely make it his duty to know what is the permissible area of selection and then consider responsibly, in individual cases, whether a contemplated beneficiary was within the power and whether, in relation to other possible claimants, a particular grant was appropriate. Correspondingly a trustee with a duty to distribute, particularly among a potentially very large class, would surely never require the preparation of a complete list of names, which anyhow would tell him little that he needs to know. He would examine the field, by class and category; might indeed make diligent and careful inquiries, depending on how much money he had to give away and the means at his disposal, as to the composition and needs of particular categories and of individuals within them; decide on certain priorities or proportions, and then select individuals according to their needs or qualifications. If he acts in this manner, can it really be said that he is not carrying out the trust? ... Such distinction as there is would seem to lie in the extent of the survey which the trustee is required to carry out; if he has to distribute the whole of the trust fund's income, he must necessarily make a wider and more systematic survey than if his duty is expressed in terms of a power to make grants. But just as, in the case of a power, it is possible to underestimate the fiduciary obligation of the trustee to whom it is given, so, in the case of a trust (trust power), the danger lies in overstating what the trustee requires to know or to enquire into before he can properly execute his trust. The difference may be one of degree rather than of principle ...

3.49   It is not correct, however, that the difference between the trustee's exercise of his discretion to appoint under a discretionary trust and a mere power is only one of degree, of the extent of the survey undertaken, for in the case of the latter the interests of the objects of the power must be weighed against those who would take in default of appointment (**3.11**).

3.50   As regards the court's enforcement of the trust, Lord Wilberforce thought that no conclusions could be drawn from the fact that in large trusts of this kind, equal division was not a possible means of enforcement:

> As a matter of reason, to hold a principle of equal division applies to trusts such as the present is certainly paradoxical. Equal division is surely the last thing the settlor ever intended; equal division among all may, and probably would, produce a result beneficial to no one.

Rather, enforcement should be tailored to the particular trust or power, and the practicalities of the situation must be borne in mind:

> Assimilation of the validity test does not involve the complete assimilation of trust powers with powers. As to powers ... although the trustees may, and normally will, be under a fiduciary duty to consider whether or in what way they should exercise the power, the court will not normally compel its exercise. It will intervene if the trustees exceed their powers, and possibly if they are proved to have exercised it capriciously. But in the case of a trust power, if the trustees do not exercise it, the court will; ... the court, if called on to execute the trust power, will do so in the manner best calculated to give effect to the settlor's or testator's intentions. It may do so by appointing new trustees, or by authorising or directing representative persons of the classes of beneficiaries to prepare a scheme of distribution, or even, should the proper basis for distribution appear, by itself directing the trustees so to distribute.

3.51   It should be borne in mind that *McPhail* does not appear to alter the traditional enforcement of discretionary trusts where the class of objects is small: if there are no clear indications as to how the trustee ought to exercise his discretion, the court will order an equal division amongst all the objects.

3.52   In the case of both powers and discretionary trusts, the distribution of property must be within the terms of the power or trust. Normally, the objects of the power or trust will enforce the trust to prevent misfeasance of this kind, by bringing the trustee to court. They have every incentive to do so, of course, for any property distributed outside the proper bounds is property not available for distribution to them. In the case of a power, however, this enforcement is more likely to be undertaken by those entitled upon default of exercise. They hope the power is not exercised at all in the given time period, for any unappointed property is theirs. They are therefore likely to be astute to discover and object to any appointments outside the proper class of objects.

3.53 Besides appointing outside the class of objects, a purported exercise of a power will be invalid if the power holders never truly applied their minds to what they were doing, as in *Turner v Turner* (1984) where the power holders blindly followed the directions of the settlor without appreciating they had a discretion to exercise.

3.54 In the case of nonfeasance, it is clear that the court must enforce the trust by one of the ways mentioned by Lord Wilberforce (**3.50**), according to the nature of the trust. An illustration is found in *Re Locker's Settlement Trusts* (1978). There trustees of a discretionary trust applied to the court for its approval when they sought to distribute income which had arisen over a three-year period some eight years before, but which they had failed to distribute at the time as they ought to have done. It was argued that, having failed to comply with their duty at the relevant time, the trustees were disabled from distributing the income on a discretionary basis among the objects now, and that the court must give effect to the trust by ordering an equal division among all the objects. Goulding J disagreed. Although, following *McPhail*, the court had ample power to execute a discretionary trust upon the failure of the trustees to do so, trustees intent upon making good their past failure by subsequently exercising their discretion should be encouraged to do so, as this was more in keeping with the settlor's intention than execution by the court, though in such circumstances the court should 'readily listen' to any misgivings of such a course where the trustees have failed to listen or act upon the beneficiaries' requests for distribution; in such a case the ample powers of the court to execute the trust might justifiably be invoked. Furthermore, a distinction may be drawn between powers of appointment and discretionary trusts in this regard. Failure to exercise a power of appointment results in the property going to those who take in default of appointment, so a power holder's failure to act normally raises no issue of this kind. Goulding J did not specifically consider the case of a failure of a trustee or other fiduciary power holder to act in a timely fashion. One presumes that the court might have to engage in some remedial measures if it was shown that property went to someone who took in default of appointment and the trustee or other fiduciary power holder did not even consider exercising his power of appointment as his duty requires. Indeed, in certain cases, the courts will control mere powers to the extent of requiring their exercise. Thus in *Klug v Klug* (1918) the court felt under a duty to direct a transfer of funds (under a power of advancement, 10.41 et seq) 'when one trustee very properly desires to exercise his discretion ... and his co-trustee [who refused to do so because she disapproved of the beneficiary's marriage] will not.' And in the case of pension fund trusts, the beneficiaries who have earned their rights may have legitimate expectations that mere powers held by trustees to augment the benefits to which they are strictly entitled under the trust will be exercised in their favour (*Mettoy Pension Trustees Ltd v Evans* (1991); see also Nobles (1992)).

'Fraud' on a power

3.55 A purported exercise of a power will also be invalid if it constitutes a 'fraud' on the power. A fraud occurs when the appointment is made to a person who is properly with the class of objects, with the purpose, however, of benefiting someone who is not a proper object, where, for example, a power holder who could only appoint to members of her family appointed to her sister believing and intending that the sister would apply most of the funds for the benefit of a couple with whom she had lived (*Re Dick* (1953)).

3.56 The leading case is the PC decision in *Vatcher v Paull* (1915) which outlines the basic principles: 'Fraud' does not denote conscious immoral or dishonest wrongdoing, but merely that the power has been exercised with the intention to benefit someone outside the class of objects. Typically, this will be done under a bargain between the appointer and appointee, under which the latter will upon receipt of the property secure the benefit for someone not properly within the class, typically the appointer himself when he is a non-object, though a bargain of this kind is not essential for a fraud to occur. The test appears to be that the power holder has deliberately set out to benefit a non-object by making the appointment to a valid object, and it is irrelevant that the appointee might not, as it turned out, have complied with the appointer's wishes (*Re Dick*).

Fraud does not occur simply because the appointer sets conditions on his exercise of the power; only conditions which if fulfilled result in securing the benefit of the appointment for a third party will be bad.

Beneficial interests under discretionary trusts and powers of appointment

3.57 As we have seen (**3.30**), the principle in *Saunders v Vautier* applies to discretionary trusts, but this does not mean that the beneficiaries, if all *sui juris*, are treated as having a vested interest, either individually or together; only if they exercise their *Saunders v Vautier* rights and demand the income or trust property from the trustees do they acquire indefeasible interests *(Vestey v IRC (No 2)* (1979)). Indeed, rather than 'co-owners' or 'group-owners', until such time as each object has his own individual right to retain whatever income is appointed to him, their individual interests are essentially in competition with each other (Lord Reid, *Gartside v IRC* (1968)). It is worthwhile noticing that one party in many of these cases is the IRC, the Inland Revenue Commissioners. Whether or not an object has a vested interest has been important for purposes of taxation law. (See, eg *Pearson v IRC* (1981); *Re Trafford's Settlement* (1985).)

3.58 In the case of general or hybrid powers, the objects have no rights whatsoever, since the class of objects amounts, essentially, to the whole world, or in the case of hybrid powers, the whole world minus a few. Those entitled in default of appointment will have the only rights to ensure that the power is not improperly exercised. Objects of special powers are in a similar position to objects of a discretionary trust individually, but not collectively. Individually, they may of course retain what is appointed to them, and they can enforce the power by ensuring no invalid appointments are made, and where the powerholder is under fiduciary obligations (**3.11**), can insist upon the powerholder properly considering its exercise, though they cannot, of course, insist upon any appointments (*Re Gulbenkian*). But because there is no duty to appoint at all, the objects have no *Saunders v Vautier* rights at all. Their interests are in competition not only with each other, but primarily with those entitled in default of appointment, who are generally regarded not only as the primary objects of the settlor's bounty (*Vatcher v Paull* (1915)), but are regarded as the persons in whom the property is vested, subject, of course, to defeat by the exercise of the power of appointment (*Re Brooks' Settlement Trusts* (1939)).

3.59 The decision in *McPhail* poses some conceptual difficulties. As Hayton (1996) has said, one of the irreducible core elements of a trust is an obligation owed by the trustee to the beneficiaries. In a *McPhail*-type trust, however, the beneficiaries appear to be little more than postulants, seeking the trustees' largesse but having no enforceable right to it, and perhaps more to the point, little incentive to pursue the remedies which the HL made available to have the court replace the trustees or help devise a scheme of distribution. Since there is no clear likelihood that pursuing such remedies will result in a favourable distribution (ie one that includes oneself), who would bother seeking them? Although Lord Wilberforce was keen to forge rules to reflect the practical, common sense realities of the situation, did he not disregard the rather obvious point that the object of a large discretionary trust may have little more real incentive to enforce the trust than does the object of the mere power? Lord Wilberforce expounds the various approaches the court, 'if called on', might make to enforce the trust in a practical fashion, without considering whether, in reality, these 'practical' remedies are likely ever to be asserted by the objects. Remember that in the case of a mere power to appoint to such a large class, there will always be those who take in default of appointment who have an interest in monitoring the trustees for mis-use of the power. There is no one with a similar interest in property held under a large discretionary trust. For this reason, such trusts may in practice be trusts of 'imperfect obligation' (**9.18**), depending on the likelihood that the trustees' duties will be enforced. Remember that trusts are private. Should the law create an exception in these cases and require trustees of a *McPhail*-type trust to publicise its existence, in order to increase the chances of enforcement? Should such an obligation extend to powers to appoint to large classes of this kind?

3.60 Besides enforcement, there is also the issue of *Saunders v Vautier* rights and equitable ownership. Whatever such rights discretionary objects have under a *McPhail*-type trust in theory, they are clearly impossible to exercise if the class of beneficiaries cannot combine together because it is unascertainable on the complete list test. Perhaps the most suitable analogy for the *McPhail* situation is the case of the executor of a will and those who will take under it. Recall (**2.65**) that executors are the legal owners of the deceased's estate, but not trustees for the likely recipients, and until such time as the estate is actually distributed, a recipient has only a right to compel the executor to carry out his duties; a recipient has no rights, even equitable rights, in the property itself.

The situation under a *McPhail*-type trust seems essentially similar. The objects do not have together, nor individually, any right in the property whatsoever, but merely have a right to the enforcement of the trust. The trustees, for their part, appear to be legal owners subject to the equitable rights of enforcement of the beneficiaries (See Harris (1971); Grbich (1974)). The practical differences, however, are quite important. To become effective, a will must be admitted to probate, which makes the will public. No publicity is equally required for the *McPhail*-type trust, although one presumes that in many cases trusts of this kind will be testamentary. The more striking feature, however, is that wills must be executed in a fairly short time and the expectant recipients are likely to follow the trustee's actions fairly closely, since the will will tell them what benefits they are intended to receive, and this will make surveillance of the trustees worthwhile. Thus we are faced with the question whether the courts should, as the HL in *McPhail* seemed happy to do, allow settlors to create equitable obligations where the practical likelihood of enforcement appears so much lower than in any other previously recognised trust situation. In *Broadway Cottages* Jenkins LJ refuse to 'spell a valid power out of an invalid trust', ie validate the settlor's gift by allowing the trustees to exercise the trust as if it were a power (see also **7.6- 7.7**). Might this not have been a preferable route to take to give effect to the settlor's wishes? Perhaps the test for whether we should recognise a trust is an 'equitable *ownership/Saunders v Vautier*' test: if there is no person or group who can reasonably be said to have equitable title or at the minimum, practically exercisable *Saunders v Vautier* rights, then it is difficult to hold that the 'trustees' are in reality subject to 'trust' obligations.

Protective trusts

3.61   A beneficiary under a fixed trust, such as a life tenant, has a vested interest in the trust property, which can be assigned, or given as security on a loan, and most significantly, will go into the beneficiary's estate in bankruptcy if he becomes insolvent. A settlor may be happy to give a beneficiary an interest under a trust, but may like to avoid that entitlement going to pay his creditors if he becomes bankrupt. A protective trust is a device which combines a determinable life interest with a discretionary trust to protect trust assets from just this occurrence.

A determinable life interest followed by a discretionary trust

3.62 The protective trust works as follows. There are two trusts: first there is a gift of a determinable life interest in favour of the person the settlor wishes primarily to benefit, for example his son, who is known as the 'principal beneficiary'; on the occurrence of a determining event the trust property is then to be held on a second trust, which is a discretionary trust in favour of a class of objects, which may include the principal beneficiary himself. The determining events always include the situation in which the principal beneficiary's right to income is assigned to anyone else or goes to his trustee in bankruptcy, but typically also includes any case where the beneficiary's interest becomes charged, or more vaguely, 'payable' to anyone else. On the determining event the secondary, discretionary, trust kicks in by operation of law, for the determinable interest automatically terminates when a defeating event occurs – no exercise of any power of revocation is necessary. The situation will now be that the income is distributable at the trustees' discretion to the objects of the secondary trust, 'the secondary objects'. Since an individual object of a discretionary trust has no vested interest in the trust property (**3.57**) neither can his creditors or trustee in bankruptcy, and thus the trust property is kept out of their hands so long as the trustee chooses not to give the bankrupt object any, which he obviously will not.

3.63 It is absolutely essential that the first gift is a determinable life interest and not a life interest defeasible upon a condition subsequent, for any one of three reasons, otherwise the protective trust will not work. The chief reason is that as a matter of historical concepts of property, conditions which prevent the alienation of property, that is the assignment, charging, or transfer by operation of law of property, are absolutely void, whereas determinable interests which determine upon an alienation are not (Burn (1994), 345). Second, and less crucially, a condition subsequent is strictly construed, and if uncertain, eg too vague, the condition is struck down but the gift remains; thus if the condition were struck down in this way the principal beneficiary would take an absolute life interest which would not be protected. Finally, and least importantly, gifts defeasible upon condition subsequent do not end automatically when the condition arises; rather, the happening of the condition gives the secondary donee a right to bring the principal gift to an end; therefore the secondary donee must act. For example, in the case of land, the secondary donee acquires a right to re-enter the land if the defeating condition occurred, but the primary donee's rightful possession of the land lasts until the secondary donee actually re-enters. With respect to the protected life interest in income, at least one of the secondary objects is required to demand that the trustees henceforth apply the property under the secondary trust. Presumably, this would be no more than an inconvenience in most cases; nevertheless, if protective trusts could be framed in terms of conditions subsequent the primary beneficiary's life interest would remain following a forfeiting event, and the trustee would be required to apply the benefits to, for example, a trustee in bankruptcy, until a secondary object acted.

No protective trust for oneself

3.64 Although technically the protective trust works just as well for a settlor who wishes to transfer his own property on protective trusts to avoid the consequences of his own bankruptcy, this is not allowed (*Re Brewer's Settlement* (1896)). The justification is roughly as follows: A may give B a gift structured or limited in whatever ways he wishes, so if he wants B to have an interest, but not B's trustee in bankruptcy should B become insolvent, that's OK. As a donee from A, B cannot expect any particular gift, or any gift at all, and neither can his creditors; if the latter are therefore deprived of A's bounty, they have no just cause to complain. On the other hand, A may not escape his liability to his own creditors by purporting to 'give' his property to himself in the same way. His own property is absolutely his, and must retain the normal 'incident', ie conceptual attribute, of property, of being available to pay his debts.

3.65 On the other hand, a person may put his property on trust for himself, determinable on the event that he assigns or charges or otherwise alienates it – the policy is only against avoiding the effects of bankruptcy. If a settlor includes as one of the events his becoming bankrupt anyway, that provision will be ineffective against his trustee in bankruptcy in accordance with the general policy, but does not make the other events ineffective. So, in *Re Detmold* (1889), the occurrence of one of the other operating events terminated the trust, and so the settlor no longer had an interest which could pass into his estate in bankruptcy when he later became bankrupt. What happens, however, if the settlor becomes bankrupt, so that the life interest passes as one of his assets into the hands of his trustee in bankruptcy, and then another defeating condition occurs? Is the life estate subsequently defeated by the later terminating event? The secondary objects will obviously argue 'yes', since they will claim that their rights against the primary beneficiary must remain against his 'successor in title', ie anyone who takes the life estate from him. The answer, however, is 'no': Peterson J nicely reasons it out in *Re Burroughs-Fowler* (1916):

> It is said that the result may be that the trustee in bankruptcy will be in a position to dispose of more than was vested in the bankrupt himself. That would be so in any case, because, so far as the trustee is concerned, the provisions for terminating the protected life interest upon bankruptcy are void. It seems to me that the true view is that, so far as the trustee in bankruptcy is concerned, the provisions as to bankruptcy and insolvency must be excluded from the settlement, and the trustee is therefore in a position to deal with the interest of the [bankrupt] ... as if those provisions were excluded. So far, however, as the [secondary object] is concerned the forfeiture by reason of the bankruptcy has already taken place, and, therefore, it is no longer possible for the [bankrupt] hereafter to do or suffer something which would determine his interest. The result is that the trustee in bankruptcy is in possession of the life interest of the bankrupt, which is now incapable of being effected by any subsequent forfeiture.

The s 33 protective trust

3.66 Protective trusts can be expressly stated in a trust instrument, but may also be created by directing the trustees to hold property for X 'on protective trusts', which automatically invokes the particular protective trust formulated in s 33(1) of the Trustee Act 1925:

> **33.**– (1) Where any income, including an annuity or other periodical income payment, is directed to be held on protective trusts for the benefit of any person (in this section called 'the principal beneficiary') for the period of his life or for any less period, then, during that period (in this section called the 'trust period') the said income shall, without prejudice to any prior interest, be held upon the following trusts, namely:–
> (i) Upon trust for the principal beneficiary during the trust period or until he, **whether before or after the termination of any prior interest, does or attempts to do or suffers any act or thing, or until any event happens, other than an advance under any statutory or express power, whereby, if the said income were payable during the trust period to the principal beneficiary absolutely during that period, he would be deprived of the**

right to receive the same or any part thereof, in any of which cases, as well as on the termination of the trust period, whichever happens first, this trust of the said income shall fail or determine;

(ii) If the trust aforesaid fails or determines during the subsistence of the trust period, then, during the residue of that period, the said income shall be held upon trust for the application thereof for the maintenance and support, or otherwise for the benefit, of all or any one or more exclusively of the other or others of the following persons (that is to say)–

(a) the principal beneficiary and his wife or husband, if any, and his or her children or more remote issue, if any; or

(b) if there is no wife or husband or issue of the principal beneficiary in existence, the principal beneficiary and the persons who would, if he were actually dead, be entitled to the trust property or the income thereof or the annuity fund, if any, or arrears of the annuity, as the case may be;

as the trustees in their absolute discretion, without being liable to account for the exercise of such discretion, think fit.

3.67 As the s 33 formulation of the events giving rise to forfeiture (in bold above) shows, forfeiture clauses are generally very widely framed so as to apply to any circumstance which might defeat the principal beneficiary's receipt of the benefit of the trust. Notice the initial phrase in bold: 'whether before or after the termination of any prior interest', which indicates that if the trust initially takes effect in circumstances where a determining event has taken place (eg any income the primary beneficiary received would be payable to a third party), then there will be a forfeiture at the outset. This occurred in *Re Walker* (1939): the person who would become a principal beneficiary under a testamentary protective trust was a bankrupt who had applied for his discharge from bankruptcy. The court granted the discharge, but suspended it for one month, and in this period the testator died. Bad timing. Because he was still a bankrupt when the trust came into effect on the testator's death, the interest was forfeit.

3.68 If there is a doubt as to the interpretation of a forfeiture clause, whether the s 33 formulation or an express clause, it is resolved in favour of the principal beneficiary, not primarily because he is the first object of the settlor's bounty – the settlor obviously considered the secondary objects to be worthy of a benefit as well (*Re Sartoris' Estate* (1892)) – but for the mundane reason that those who wish to assert their rights based upon a forfeiture have the burden of showing that a forfeiture has occurred (*Re Baring's Settlement Trusts* (1940)).

3.69 The actual words of the clause are all-important, as shown by the pair of cases, *Re Gourju's Will Trusts* (1943) and *Re Hall* (1944). In both cases the principal beneficiaries' income became payable to the Custodian of Enemy Property under the Trading with the Enemy Act 1939 by virtue of their residence in France during the second world war. In effect, if there was no forfeiture, the Custodian would hold the income on behalf of the principal beneficiaries until the war was over or they could return to England to claim it, so it was to the beneficiaries' advantage if there were no forfeiture. In *Gourju*, the will creating the trust incorporated the statutory provision, by which the life interest can terminate upon the happening of any event; Simonds J concluded that the happening of the events made the income payable to the Custodian, so the forfeiture occurred:

> It was urged upon me by counsel for Madame Gourju that the result of such a decision is a forfeiture by reason of an event which can never have been contemplated by the testator, an event, moreover, of a wholly different character from any event fairly within his contemplation. With that I cannot but agree, but the words of the clause are too strong for me, and I can only express the earnest hope that in the welter of legislation that peace will bring, the hard case will not be forgotten of a beneficiary who, like Madame Gourju, suffers an undeserved forfeiture of her income.

3.70 By contrast, in *Hall* the forfeiture clause was an express provision which did not refer to the happening of events, though it did comprise the principal beneficiary's 'suffer[ing] any act or thing' whereby the property would become payable to someone else. Uthwatt J construed it this way:

> Reading the clause as a whole, it seems to me that it is directed to the forfeiture of the annuity in the event of the annuitant personally doing certain classes of things, such as alienating or charging it, or permitting an act to be done whereby she is deprived of her annuity. It appears not to be directed to a case where the annuity is subject to an alienation which is not the result of the countess's own act. ...She was in France, the normal place for a French national, when her property became subject to the provisions of the Act, and I fail to see how the fact that she was

there and remained there can be said to amount to the doing of an act of the kind which is contemplated by the clause. The question whether she has 'suffered' anything is, perhaps, more open. The word 'suffer' is capable of more meanings than one. I have come to the conclusion that it is proper to attribute to the word in this clause the meaning 'permit'. It is clear that the annuitant has not permitted anything to be done.

3.71 Section 33 of the Act expressly exempts the exercise of a power of advancement from being a cause of forfeiture, and this applies to any trust which incorporates the statutory provision. A power of advancement allows the trustee to advance, or pay, capital to the income beneficiary (**10.41**); the obvious effect of doing so is to reduce his right to income, since as a result there is less capital upon which income can arise, and so, but for the exemption, the advancement could be seen to work a forfeiture. The exemption appears to apply to express protective trusts as well (*Re Rees* (1954)), and may simply be a matter of common sense not requiring any statutory exemption (*Re Hodgson* (1913); *Re Shaw's Settlement* (1951)) – advancements simply secure the benefit of the trust property to the beneficiary by another means, not deprive him of his entitlement to it. Whether the exercise of any other power which affects the principal beneficiary's right to income, such as a power to appoint capital to a third party, causes a forfeiture, is a matter of interpretation of the instrument.

3.72 Under the Trustee Act 1925, s 57 the court may by order 'vary', ie modify, the terms of a trust (**10.72**), and such orders, though they may affect the life tenant's right to income, do not effect a forfeiture:

> If and when the Court sanctions an arrangement or transaction under s 57, it must be taken to have done it as though the power which is brought into operation has been inserted in the trust instrument as an overriding power. (Farwell J, *Re Mair* (1935))

Orders affecting a life tenant's right to income made under the court's divorce jurisdiction to distribute property likewise do not effect a forfeiture (*General Accident Fire and Life Assurance Corpn Ltd v IRC* (1963), CA), and where the court order extinguishes one spouse's protected life interest entirely, this extinguishes the secondary discretionary trust as well – it does not arise as if the extinction of the primary trust counted as a forfeiture (*Re Allsopp's Marriage Settlement Trusts* (1959)). *Re Richardson's Will Trusts* (1958) is an anomalous exception. The case concerned a protective trust which was to operate until the principal beneficiary attained the age of 35, at which time his interest became absolute. On 3 June 1955, the court ordered that a payment of £50 per annum to his ex-wife be charged on his life interest; on 24 October 1955, he turned 35, and on 27 August 1956, he was declared bankrupt. Dankwerts J held that the court order effected a forfeiture. It is difficult not to believe that the result was motivated by the fact that, without the forfeiture, the trustee in bankruptcy would have acquired the interest in the income subject to the wife's charge, leaving the principal beneficiary nothing. Instead, under the discretionary trust upon forfeiture, the former principal beneficiary was entitled to discretionary payments, which it appears had in fact been made before his bankruptcy.

3.73   It is clear that a forfeiture should occur whenever the principal beneficiary's right to receive the income is transferred or charged either by the beneficiary himself or by operation of law or by another's exercise of his rights, as in *Re Balfour's Settlement* (1938) where by reason of the beneficiary's instigation of a breach of trust the trustees were entitled to impound the income (**11.49**). More difficult is the case of forfeiture upon the condition that the income becomes 'payable to' someone other than the principal beneficiary. In *Re Baring's Settlement Trusts* (1940) it was held that 'payable to' covers a broader range of cases than those where the principal beneficiary's property interest vests in a third party by reason of an assignment or charge. But a forfeiture cannot arise simply because the principal beneficiary has debts of sufficient size that he must devote some of his trust income to paying them off. The income remains payable to him, and he only has the personal duty to pay these debts out of all of his property. In order for a forfeiture to arise under the 'payable to' provision, some third party must be able to demand that the trustee must pay the trust income to him directly, and such circumstances should generally involve the state, as in the cases above concerning the Custodian of Enemy Property and court orders upon divorce. In *Re Baring's Settlement Trusts* an order of sequestration, which allowed third parties to demand payment of the principal beneficiary's income to enforce another order of the court was held to forfeit the life interest. However the cases also appear to indicate that 'payable to' will be construed narrowly, ie to the case where the third party may demand payment of the income as it arises, ie as the trustee receives it or can claim it, eg when dividends are paid on shares or rent on land falls due; a third party's right to demand income which has *already accrued* under the trust, ie funds that were already in the trustee's hands, does not effect a forfeiture (Re Greenwood (1901)). Furthermore, a forfeiture does not occur where a third party did acquire the right to demand payment of the income as it arose, but that right ended before any income actually accrued, on the basis that until any income arose none was actually 'payable' (Re Longman (1955). See also Re Salting (1932).) A trustee's right to require payment from the income for his charges and expenses as attorney to the principal beneficiary causes no forfeiture; it is akin to the appointment of an agent to collect one's rents who has the right to deduct his commission before paying the remainder to the beneficiary (Re Tancred's Settlement (1903)). In Re Westby's Settlement (1950), Lord Evershed MR held that even if such a right to be paid expenses was effective to create a charge over the income, the interest would not be forfeited; a forfeiture clause is directed to protect the beneficiary's net income from the trust after any proper expenses are incurred.

3.74 Following a principal beneficiary's bankruptcy and consequent forfeiture, he may be an object under the secondary discretionary trust, and will be if the s 33 provision is invoked. Following his discharge in bankruptcy, he may be paid income at the trustees' discretion. While still a bankrupt, the trustees may apply income for his benefit, by, for example, providing him with services such as meals or accommodation, but only to the extent that this is for his 'mere support' (Re Ashby (1892)). Any money that is paid directly to him may be claimed by his trustee in bankruptcy, but to the extent that he receives no property in his own right, as when the trustee, at his discretion, pays third parties for services, the trustee in bankruptcy has no claim, for the bankrupt receives no property (Re Coleman (1888); Re Smith (1928)). Unless the trustee has the power to accumulate income, however, he may not retain accrued income in order to pay it to the former principal beneficiary upon his discharge from bankruptcy; the trustee must distribute the income within a reasonable time following its accrual (Re Gourju's Will Trusts (1943)).

Further reading

Thomas (1998), ch 1; Waters (1996); Hayton (1996, 1999); Harris (1971); Grbich (1974); Cullity (1975)

Must read cases: *Stephenson v Barclay's Bank Trust Co Ltd* (1974); *Re*

Trafford's Settlement (1984); *Lloyds Bank plc v Duker* (1987); *IRC v Broadway Cottages Trust* (1955); *Re Gulbenkian Settlement* (1968); *McPhail v Doulton* (1970); *Vatcher v Paull* (1914); *Re Locker's Settlement* (1977); *Re Baring's Settlement Trusts* (1940); *Re Coleman* (1888); *Re Gourju's Will Trusts* (1942); *Re Westby's Settlement* (1950).

Self-test questions

1. What is a bare trust (review **2.23** et seq), a fixed trust, a discretionary trust, and a power of appointment, and how do the interests of the objects of each differ?

2. Acting as the settlor, write several provisions in a trust instrument giving dispositive and administrative discretions to trustees, to individuals nominatum, and to an individual nominatum who is also described as the 'protector of the settlement'. Then elaborate how you think the court would determine whether these discretions must be exercised, were 'mere' powers but fiduciary powers, or were pure personal powers.

3. What are income interests, capital interests, successive interests, defeasible interests, absolute interests, vested interests, and contingent interests? Give examples of each.

4. Following *McPhail v Doulton* (1970) the distinction between discretionary trusts and powers of appointment held by trustees is only one of degree. Discuss.

5. How does a protective trust achieve its purpose?

6. Eric transferred a block of flats to trustees to hold for him on trust for life or until he 'does or attempts to do or suffers any act or thing, or until any event happens whereby Eric would be deprived of the right to receive the rental income or any part thereof', upon the happening of which they were to hold it on trust for his wife. The rent from the apartment house is collected by agents who deduct a commission. Eric is declared bankrupt, and the next day he assigns his interest under the trust to his brother Philip. Advise Eric's trustee in bankruptcy.

CHAPTER FOUR

Resulting Trusts

SUMMARY

Intentional trusts and trusts which arise by operation of law (TABOLs)

Presumed intention resulting trusts (PIRTs)

Automatic resulting trusts (ARTs)

The nature of resulting trusts and resulting trusteeship

Intentional trusts and trusts which arise by operation of law (TABOLs)

4.1   In the last chapter we considered express trusts, and there I advised that the way to understand express trusts is to think of them as trusts made by the settlor himself when he *effectively exercises his powers of ownership to create a trust.* These trusts might be called 'intentional trusts', because the settlor by effectively exercising his powers to create a trust has produced what he intended. However there are also trusts which arise by operation of law (TABOLs, for short). The law itself imposes trusts in certain circumstances, which is to say that the law itself creates an equitable title for beneficiaries in the property of a legal owner. Resulting trusts, as we shall see, may be either intentional trusts or TABOLs.

Automatic resulting trusts (ARTs)

4.2   Resulting trusts characteristically arise in two situations. In the first, a resulting trust will arise where an express trust fails, or fails in part, for some reason. For example, a settlor may transfer Blackacre to trustees on trust for Barbara for life and then for her children in equal shares. As it turns out, Barbara dies without children. In consequence, the beneficial remainder interest 'results', or springs back, to the settlor, and the trustees will hold Blackacre on bare trust for the settlor (or his successors if he has died in the meantime). Because these trusts arise automatically upon the failure of the intended disposition, these are generally called *automatic resulting trusts*, or ARTs.

Presumed Intention Resulting Trusts (PIRTs)

4.3 Second, there are *presumed intention resulting trusts*, PIRTs. (These trusts are also called, simply, 'presumed resulting trusts', but since presumed *intention* resulting trust is more accurate, that usage will be employed.) There are two categories, purchase money PIRTs and gratuitous transfer PIRTs. If two or more persons put their money together to buy property equity will normally hold that they share the equitable title to the property in proportion to the amount of money each put in regardless of the way the legal title is held, whether in both of their names, in one of their names, or in the name of a third party. Whoever the legal title holders are, they will hold the property on bare trust for them both in proportionate equitable shares. Similarly, if A pays the whole purchase price of property, but the title is put in B's name, B will hold the property on bare trust for A. These are both cases of *purchase money PIRTs*.

4.4 If A, however, simply transfers property he already owns to B *gratuitously*, ie receiving no payment in return – no 'consideration' as lawyers say – B will likewise hold the property on bare trust for A under a *gratuitous transfer PIRT*.

4.5 In all these cases, the holder(s) of a legal title will hold the property on bare trust for those who put the value in. The recognition of these trusts is founded upon an evidentiary presumption: in the absence of evidence, equity will presume that someone putting money into the purchase of an asset intends to take a proportionate share, up to the entire value if he pays the full price; or when someone transfers legal title gratuitously to someone equity presumes he intends to create a bare trust in his favour; hence the term 'presumed intention' resulting trust. This presumption, and thus the trust, will be defeated by actual evidence of any contrary intentions of the parties regarding their shares of the beneficial ownership (*Westdeutsche Landesbank Girozentrale v Islington*

London Borough Council (1996); Swadling, (1996)), and of course, an express declaration of trust made by the donor or the joint contributors will displace the operation of a gratuitous transfer or purchase money PIRT, respectively (*Pettitt v Pettitt* (1970) per Lord Upjohn; *Goodman v Gallant* (1986)). Because the law presumes that a gratuitous contribution or transfer *implies* an intention to create a trust, PIRTs are also sometimes called 'implied' trusts.

4.6 The explicit terminological distinction between 'automatic' and 'presumed' resulting trusts was originally drawn by Megarry J in *Re Vandervell (No 2)* (1974) as follows (though it was clearly foreshadowed by Lord Upjohn in *Vandervell v IRC* (1967)). PIRTs are intentional trusts, created by the settlor's exercise of his powers of ownership to create a trust. Because however, the law presumes the settlor's intentions, he need do nothing to prove, by a written document or otherwise, any declaration of trust accompanying the transfer of the legal title to his property, either the trust property itself in the case of a gratuitous transfer PIRT, or his money in the case of a purchase money PIRT. This evidentiary presumption may, however, be rebutted by evidence that the settlor did not intend to create a trust, eg intended instead to make a gift to the transferee. In contrast, the ART arises by operation of law automatically on the failure of an express trust, independently of any intentions of the settlor (though see **4.30** et seq). ARTs arise by what is sometimes called the application of 'proprietary arithmetic': if the settlor transfers property to be held on trust, but for some reason the trust fails to be effectively established in whole or in part, then by subtraction, whatever is left effectively undisposed of results to him.

Presumed intention resulting trusts

Law of Property Act 1925, s 60(3)

4.7 The evidentiary presumption underlying voluntary transfer PIRTs applied equally to transfers of land and personal property ('personalty') like chattels or company shares before 1926. Before 1926, if a gift of land was intended it was necessary to expressly state in the deed of conveyance that the land was conveyed to the use and benefit of the donee in order to displace the presumption. Section 60(3) of the Law of Property Act 1925 provides, however, that a resulting trust is not to be implied merely because there is no express statement of this kind. Does this section effectively abolish voluntary conveyance PIRTs of land? In *Lohia v Lohia* (2000) Nicholas Strauss QC decided that the section did abolish voluntary conveyance PIRTs of land (see Chambers (2001)), but the CA (2001) refused to endorse that view on appeal, disposing of the case on other grounds; more recently, in *Ali v Khan* (2002) Morritt V-C, giving the judgment of the CA, said that *Lohia* established the s 60(3) did abolish the presumption (see also Chambers (1997), 16-19; Chambers (2001)).

4.8 Regarding personalty, the presumption still technically applies. Since, however, most gratuitous transfers are intended to be gifts, the presumption should give way to the slightest contrary evidence, including evidence of the surrounding circumstances and commonsense inferences to be drawn therefrom – the presumption fully applies when it is my round and I buy you a pint, but no judge in his right mind would say that you hold that pint on trust for me. Nevertheless, *Fowkes v Pascoe* (1875) and *Re Vinogradoff* (1935) nicely contrast the wildly varying effects that can result when different judges apply the presumption. In *Fowkes*, a woman of substantial means purchased stock in the name of a son of her former daughter-in-law; the only evidence of the woman's intentions were the surrounding circumstances; since there was no conceivable reason for her transferring the stock to him to hold as her nominee, she must have intended to give it to him; thus the presumption of resulting trust was rebutted.

4.9 In contrast, *Re Vinogradoff* is an atrocity of a decision. There a woman had transferred £800 of War Loan stock into the joint names of herself and her four-year-old granddaughter. Following her death, it was claimed that the child held the stock on resulting trust, there being no evidence to establish an intention to make a gift. Given that her granddaughter was four, the probability that the donor intended to make her a gift, not make her her trustee, is about as close to one as probabilities get in this life. Furthermore, any express attempt to have made her a trustee have been ineffective, since under the Law of Property Act 1925 an infant (ie a person under the age of majority) can not be a trustee. Undaunted, Farwell J held that the granddaughter held the stock on resulting trust, so the executors of the grandmother's estate were entitled to it. The idea that sensible inferences may be drawn from all the circumstances is the approach taken nowadays.

In reality the so-called presumption of a resulting trust is no more than a long stop to provide the answer when the relevant facts and circumstances fail to yield a solution. (*Vandervell v IRC* (1967) per Lord Upjohn; see also *Pettitt v Pettitt* (1970); *McGrath v Wallis* (1995))

4.10 The presumption is applied much more regularly in the case of purchase money PIRTs, and is of particular importance where the property in question is land. Why? As shall be discussed in some detail in chapter 6, certain transactions concerning trusts are required by statute to be in writing or at least evidenced in writing to be valid or enforceable. And declarations of trusts of land are burdened by such a writing requirement. However, resulting trusts and constructive trusts (**Ch 5**) are valid even if there is no writing. In consequence, people who nowadays (foolishly, it must be said) acquire ownership shares in land on the basis of an informal understanding will need to rely upon being able to claim that the property is held on a PIRT or constructive trust. The PIRT allows one to make a more straightforward claim, for the only evidence one needs to take advantage of the evidentiary presumption is evidence that one contributed to the purchase price of property; in the case of constructive trusts, as we shall see (**5.12** et seq), one has to prove considerably more, and usually with greater difficulty. So, although in many of these cases the court is able to find what the parties genuinely intended on the basis of the evidence, and so no reliance on the evidentiary presumption is required, because the cases have been pleaded as cases of resulting trust the courts proceed to declare the equitable interests based on the parties' intentions, without noticing they are giving effect to trusts over land which do not meet the requirements of writing. Or perhaps they do notice, but play this game with lawyers anyway in order to give effect to informal trusts of land without appearing to thwart the requirements of the statute.

4.11 In the case of PIRTs, 'purchase money' should be read as 'purchase contribution in money or money's worth'. In *Springette v Defoe* (1992) the sitting tenant of a house was entitled to a discount from the market price; when she purchased the property with her cohabitee the value of the discount was treated as a contribution she made to the purchase price in determining her equitable share. In the case of land purchased with the aid of a mortgage, the person(s) raising money on a mortgage, and therefore liable to repay the loan, will be credited with a corresponding contribution. For example, assume A and B purchase a house in their joint names for £50,000, A contributing £10,000 in cash, the remaining £40,000 coming from a mortgage loan under which both A and B are liable. A will therefore have an equitable share of (10 + 20 (half the loan))/50 = 60%, and B a 20/50 = 40% share. Note that one's equitable share is determined by the share of one's *liability to repay the loan*, not by the value of the money one actually repays (*Cowcher v Cowcher* (1972); *Re Gorman* (1990)). The result of this is that if the house A and B bought doubles in value in a year to £100,000, and they sell, B will acquire a much better return on the money he has actually paid than A (but note, this 'leveraging' or 'gearing up' effect is the general (and usually intended) effect of borrowing to purchase a successful investment). Assume that following the sale and the repayment of the outstanding mortgage, the profit comes to £40,000: A will receive a 60% share, £24,000, in return for a £10,000 deposit and paying half the mortgage premiums for a year, while B will receive a 40% share, £16,000, for having only paid half the premiums. It may not even be the case that A and B have split the premium payments in half; even if A had paid all the premiums, B would acquire the same £16,000 share, since it is his joint mortgage liability that determines his contribution under the PIRT.

4.12 Since this may appear to lead to an unjust result, the courts have on occasion varied the parties' shares via a constructive trust (**5.9** et seq), but it is important to keep these two kinds of trust separate. To determine the shares acquired under a purchase money PIRT one must precisely follow the movement of a person's beneficial ownership of money or right to value (eg a sitting tenant's discount, or the right under a mortgage agreement to have money applied to a purchase of a property in one's name) into the purchase price paid for the acquisition of the resulting trustee's title to the property. Wherever a trust is ultimately determined which strays from this strict accounting, we are in the realm either of constructive trusts (**4.18, 4.20, Ch 5**) or backwards tracing (**5.16, 11.110** et seq). In *Goodman v Carlton* (2002) the CA denied a resulting trust share arising from the defendant's joint liability under a mortgage loan providing most of the purchase money for a house on the basis that there was never any intention on the part of either her or the other borrower under the mortgage loan that she would ever repay any part of the loan; her intention either rebutted the resulting trust in her favour, or the parties' common intention served as a basis for reducing her share to zero.

4.13 The fictitious reliance on the presumption we noticed in **4.10**

can lead lawyers and judges to rely upon the presumption as a problem solver where it has no application. This happened in *Abrahams v Abraham's Trustee in Bankruptcy* (1999). A couple were both members of a syndicate, each paying a pound a week to buy lottery tickets and share the winnings. Following their break-up, the wife continued to contribute two pounds a week, initially out of habit to cover the membership shares of both her and her husband, but later with no such intention. When the syndicate had a big win, the wife took a double share of the winnings in proportion to her contributions, and the husband's trustee in bankruptcy claimed one of the shares. The court decided that since the wife contributed the money, she held the right to the husband's share on resulting trust, he being unable to prove that the wife had intended to pay one of the weekly one-pound contributions for his benefit. But the presumption of resulting trust was simply not relevant here. The question simply could not turn on whether she held her second share *against him* under a purchase money PIRT, for he had no legal title to the tickets or winnings at all. The only proper way to have framed the question was: given that the wife was entitled to two shares in the syndicate's winnings, could the husband establish that the wife had gratuitously made contributions for the second share on his behalf. And it was clear that by the time of the win, she had no such intention. The husband, in other words, simply failed to establish an intentional trust on his behalf. Resulting trusts do not come into it. Perhaps the court confused itself because the wife's right to the proceeds was itself equitable (a right to her share of the winnings, legal title to which was held by the 'treasurer' for the syndicate), and so, once ensconced in the consideration of equitable rights, it hastily reached for the presumption. But the husband's claim would have been the same if the wife and husband had regularly purchased second hand books for their joint collection, and following their break-up the wife had bought some more, one of which turned out to be a rare first edition worth £500K . She would not defend her legal ownership of that book by claiming she held it for herself in equity under a purchase money PIRT. She would just say she bought it for herself, and would put her husband to the strict proof of any supposed trust of the book under which he had an interest.

The presumption of advancement

4.14 The presumption of a resulting trust does not operate in all cases of gratuitous transactions. As Freud might have said, sometimes a gift is just a gift. In these circumstances, it is said that a 'presumption of advancement' or a presumption of gift operates. The circumstances are where A gratuitously transfers property to, or contributes money to property put in the name of, his wife or his child or to someone to whom he stands *in loco parentis*, ie someone for whom he feels an obligation to provide as would a parent (*Re Paradise Motor Co Ltd* (1968)). However, the terminology 'presumption of advancement' is misleading:

> Though normally referred to as a presumption of advancement it is no more than a circumstance of evidence which may rebut the presumption of resulting trust. (*Pettitt* per Lord Upjohn).

4.15 In other words, if the recipient is a man's wife or child, this fact counts as evidence which may be, and normally is, sufficient evidence to meet the evidentiary hurdle posed by the presumption of resulting trust. In view of that, in these cases if the father wishes to show that the property was not a gift but was intended to be held on trust, then it will be necessary for him to lead evidence which establishes this trust. According to this view, then, the presumption of advancement works on the basis of a standard inference from the facts where it applies; the courts, without any more evidence before them, will infer that the man is making a gift, and does so on the basis that equity recognises an obligation upon a man to provide for his wife and children (*Bennet v Bennet* (1879)). Seen in this way, the presumption of advancement is as much an evidentiary presumption as is the presumption of resulting trust.

4.16 However, there are two ways of understanding the relationship between the presumptions. On the first, the presumption of advancement is both historically and conceptually dependent upon the existence of the presumption of resulting trust; it serves as a 'second step' exception to the general presumption of resulting trust, which *first* applies to *any* case where contributions are made to a purchase in the name of another. The importance of conceiving the relationship between the presumptions in this way is as follows. Recall again the formalities issue (**4.10**). Normally, trusts of land must be evidenced in writing to be enforceable, but there is a statutory exception for resulting (and constructive) trusts. Therefore, by tagging the presumption of advancement on to the presumption of resulting trust as a second order presumption, the reasoning can proceed in this fashion: where the father leads evidence to overcome the presumption of advancement, the presumption of resulting trust, which applied but whose operation was suspended while the presumption of advancement operated, now falls back into place. He may then simply rely upon the fact that he contributed to the purchase price to establish his beneficial ownership share under a *resulting* trust, and therefore avoids the disabling effect of the formality statute.

4.17 The other way of regarding the presumption of advancement is this: all the 'presumption of advancement' means is that there is no presumption of resulting trust in cases where it applies. On this view, there are certain cases where contributions to the purchase in the name of another attracts the presumption of resulting trust, and others where it does not. On this understanding, where a father leads evidence to 'rebut' the presumption of advancement, he has more difficulty avoiding the effect of the formality statute. Because no presumptions operate at all, what the father does when he leads evidence of the trust is to try to establish an intentional, or express, but *informal* trust. And the statutory formality requirements would defeat his interest under such a trust. However, the father's not dead yet; though he cannot establish a resulting trust, he may be able to succeed by establishing that his share is validly held under a *constructive* trust. To establish a constructive trust further facts must be proven, roughly, that the father relied to his detriment on the trust and so therefore it would be fraudulent or unconscionable for the legal title holder to refuse to honour the trust.

4.18 Which of these views is right is actually rather difficult to determine, because having paid over his contribution to the purchase price on the understanding that he would acquire an ownership share in it is probably the best sort of evidence that one relied to one's detriment on the understanding (one paid over real money — is there any more obvious detriment than that?), so it would be unconscionable or fraudulent for the legal title holder to refuse to honour his share in equity. In other words, given the sort of facts these cases involve, the result from applying the constructive trust analysis would almost always mimic the result of applying the resulting trust analysis. This might explain, in part, the occasional statements by judges that it is unnecessary to distinguish between resulting and constructive trusts in deciding certain cases of this kind (eg Lord Diplock in *Gissing v Gissing* (1971)). On the other hand, we can be certain that a court is applying a constructive trust analysis wherever the ownership shares the court declares are *not* in proportion to the contributions to the purchase price, or the court considers whether proportionate shares actually reflect the intentions of the parties; for in those cases the court must be assuming that, or considering whether, the parties did not intend a proportionate shares trust, and a resulting trust can only be a proportionate shares trust. Once it has moved beyond the straightforward assignment of interests in proportionate shares, the court is in the world of constructive trusts, giving effect to the actual, *informal* expressions of the parties' intentions.

4.19 Founding an evidentiary inference on the theory that, in general, a husband intends to make gifts to his wife but not *vice versa*, and that, in general, fathers, but not mothers, intend gifts to their children, today seems exorbitantly sexist (although the court in *Bennet* did hold it was easier to prove that a mother intended a gift than that a stranger did, ie that the presumption of resulting trust imposed an even weaker evidential burden in her case). In *Pettitt* a majority of their Lordships clearly felt the presumption of advancement was a creature of the nineteenth century which was largely out of date. Lord Upjohn, while willing to apply the presumption said:

> These presumptions or circumstances of evidence are readily rebutted by comparatively slight evidence.

While the opinions in *Pettitt* might have suggested the judicial reform or even abolition of the presumptions of advancement, it has not happened (in England) yet. (In Australia the presumption now applies equally to gifts from mother to child: *Nelson v Nelson* (1995).) It may be, as Hayton ((2001b), 335) says:

> ... easier for courts to pay lip-service to the old case law whilst being satisfied on flimsy evidence that the old- fashioned presumption has been rebutted.

4.20 For example, in *McGrath v Wallis* (1995), the weak presumption of advancement of a share in a family house between father and son who both contributed to the purchase price of a house in the son's name was rebutted and a trust in favour of a father was established, on the basis, first, that putting the house in the son's name alone could be explained because it allowed the purchase to be assisted with a mortgage; secondly, that at one stage a declaration of trust formally expressing the father's and son's ownership shares in proportion to their contributions was drawn up by the father's solicitors, and though it was never executed there was no evidence that he had later given his solicitors contrary instructions; and finally, as the father was only 63 and in good health, there was no obvious reason to make a gift to his son of an 80 per cent share in the house where he would himself live. However, once the court determined that the father had not intended a gift, it did not declare that the property was held on trust by the son for himself and his father in shares proportionate to their contribution to the purchase price; it did not, in other words, declare a purchase money PIRT. Rather, the court looked at the overall intentions of the parties as to what their respective shares should be, and declared a trust in those proportions (as it happened, these intentions did coincide with the shares they would have received under a straight purchase money PIRT, but that's not the point). What this shows is that, in cases of PIRTs, the evidence led may not only confirm or upset the presumptions of resulting trust or advancement, but may be sufficient for the court to look more closely at the parties' actual intentions and find their respective interests to be determined by a constructive trust.

4.21 In the case of a purchase money PIRT, it should be remembered that a gift or a trust are not the only kinds of transactions which may be found on the evidence: A may give B money as a loan, which B then spends to purchase property. Obviously, evidence of such a loan would displace any claim A might make to a purchase money PIRT of the property (Re Sharpe (1980)).

Illegality

4.22 Unfortunately, whether a presumption of resulting trust applies or not has been shown to be of crucial significance recently in the case of illegal property transfers. In general, neither the common law nor equity will allow a plaintiff to establish a claim on the basis of evidence which implicates him in an illegal purpose; thus, the equitable maxim, 'he who comes to equity must come with clean hands'. The obvious problem with such a rule is that, as often as not, the defendant to the action, who prays in aid this maxim, has hands just as filthy as the plaintiff, so as between the parties at least, the rule can appear to have unfair consequences.

4.23 Such a case faced the HL in *Tinsley v Milligan* (1994). Two women who cohabited as a lesbian couple agreed to put the house in the name of one of them in order that the other could misrepresent her assets to the benefits agency, and thus claim benefits to their joint economic advantage. Both were therefore parties to the fraud. They subsequently fell out and Tinsley, the legal title-holder, sought to evict Milligan, who adduced evidence of her contributions to the purchase price to establish a share in the house under a purchase money PIRT. A bare majority of the HL found for Milligan. They reasoned that (1) because Milligan had the advantage of the evidentiary presumption of resulting trust, therefore (2) in order to establish her interest under such a trust the only evidence she needed to adduce was of her contribution to the purchase price, and (3) she therefore did not need to say *why* she contributed the money, and so she did not need to adduce any evidence of her fraud, and so (4) she escaped the operation of the clean hands principle. The dissenting Lords Goff and Keith would have applied the principle in its more traditional formulation, ie that where evidence of the plaintiff's illegal behaviour which was relevant to the matter came before the court, equity would refuse its assistance, and therefore Milligan's equitable share in the property would not be enforced against Tinsley; as a result, Tinsley would have been able to evict her.

4.24 While the majority decision is understandable in light of the fact that Milligan had since admitted her fraud to the Department of Social Services, and that if Milligan had lost her co-fraudster Tinsley would end up with an undeserved windfall, the majority can be criticised for reaching its decision in this technical way. The upshot is that where the evidentiary presumption of resulting trust operates, the fraudster who transfers his property to another, say to defraud his creditors when bankruptcy looms, can retrieve the property when the coast is clear (ie when discharged from bankruptcy or having settled with his creditors who are unaware of the transferred assets) simply by adducing evidence of the transfer.

4.25 Note that Milligan's later confession was not the ground of the decision, so the case provides no basis for distinguishing between a plaintiff who succeeds in his fraud and one who does not. But where the presumption of advancement applies, for example where the fraudster transfers the property to his wife, the fraudster must lead evidence to show that he intended a trust, and so must rely upon evidence of his true intentions for the transfer; since these of course were fraudulent, in his case his unclean hands will deny him his interest under the trust. So we have the nice situation that a male fraudster who stashes his property with his son will come a cropper, but a female fraudster doing the same will retrieve her ill-hidden assets.

4.26　The CA recently dealt with the former situation in *Tribe v Tribe* (1996). A man, worried that his liabilities under two leases would be his financial ruin, transferred his shares in the family company to his son in order to safeguard his assets. As it turned out, he sorted out his liabilities under the leases without having to resort to the fraudulent deception. He sought a declaration of trust from the court when his son refused to re-convey the shares. Reviewing past authorities in which the rule was not applied where the intending fraudster had 'repented' and withdrawn from his fraudulent scheme, the court applied this exception, holding that the elder Tribe was entitled to establish a trust on the evidence of his fraudulent intentions, since the scheme had not been acted upon.

4.27　This case is more interesting because of a different reason. In the course of his judgment Millett LJ said this:

> A resulting trust... rests on a presumption which is rebuttable by evidence.... The transferor does not need to allege or prove the purpose for which property was transferred into the name of the transferee; in equity he can rely on the presumption that no gift was intended. But the transferee cannot be prevented from rebutting the presumption by leading evidence of the transferor's subsequent conduct to show that it was inconsistent with any intention to retain a beneficial interest. Suppose, for example, that a man transfers property to his nephew in order to conceal it from his creditors, and suppose that he afterwards settles with his creditors on the footing that he has no interest in the property. Is it seriously suggested that he can recover the property? I think not. The transferor's own conduct would be inconsistent with the retention of any beneficial interest in the property.

But if this is the law, then *Tinsley* is wrongly decided, for Tinsley led evidence that Milligan had successfully defrauded the DSS on the basis that she had no beneficial interest in the property – remember, the fact that she later confessed to the DSS was not the basis of the decision. Milligan's subsequent conduct was clearly 'inconsistent with the retention of any beneficial interest in the property'. Though Millett LJ, purports to explain the ambit of *Tinsley* in this passage, the result is that he fundamentally undermines its *ratio*.

4.28 Two final points: first, while all rules which deny a plaintiff the assistance of the court where his claim discloses an illegality may appear to unjustifiably favour a defendant, the working of the evidentiary presumptions for and against a resulting trust appear to make the operation of a rule more of a lottery than can possibly be justified: always remember, the presumptions are mere evidentiary presumptions as to intentions – evidence of actual intentions should always be relevant, regardless of which party raises them. And this raises an odd aspect of Lord Browne-Wilkinson's reasoning for the majority in *Tinsley*. In a spirit of fusion (**1.15**), he wished to bring equity's view of illegality more in line with that of the common law, where it seems that A's ownership of property will not be disturbed even if the transaction which gave rise to A's ownership, typically a contract of sale, was itself illegal. Thus, since Milligan's ownership share under the resulting trust was her property even though the transaction in which she got it was tainted with illegality, following the common law she should be able to retain it. This is all well and good, except that using the technical evidentiary presumptions to achieve this result ensures that equity *will not follow the common law* when the case is one where the presumption of advancement applies; this is queer fusion indeed, for a father who owns a share under a purchase money resulting trust where the trustee is his wife or child has an interest in the property just as much as would a wife or mother, and his ownership is tainted by illegality in just the same way; to follow the common law in one case and not the other in this way is to distort the process of fusion by embedding in the 'fused doctrine' one of the most anachronistic and generally unjustifiable rules in all of equity. (I told you that achieving fusion was not easy.) The broad application of the 'clean hands' rule, as favoured by Lords Goff and Keith, yet tempered by a similarly broad but well-defined set of exceptions based on the plaintiff's prior withdrawal from the scheme, later confession and reparation, and so on, would be preferable (see Rose (1996)), although the reasoning of the HL will undoubtedly be followed until it looks at the issue again, as it was by the CA in *Lowson v Coombes* (1999).

4.29 Second, recall (**4.10**) that there are many cases where the courts invoke the presumptions, and find interests under 'resulting trusts', where there is no need to invoke the presumptions at all, because there is ample evidence as to the parties' intentions. The same is true in these illegality cases. All the parties were alive and testified, and the court decided whether there was a trust interest on the basis of all the evidence. The presumptions are artificially employed here to manipulate the illegality rules.

Automatic resulting trusts

The relevance of intentions to ARTs

4.30 As we have seen, Megarry J distinguished ARTs and PIRTs partly on the basis that the former arose by operation of law independently of the settlor's intention. Recently, Lord Browne-Wilkinson doubted this in *Westdeutsche Landesbank Girozentrale v Islington London Borough Council* (1996):

> Megarry J ... suggests that [such a trust] does not depend on intention but operates automatically. I am not convinced this is right. If the settlor has expressly, or by necessary implication, abandoned any beneficial interest in the trust property, there is in my view no resulting trust; the undisposed-of equitable interest vests in the Crown as *bona vacantia* [ie goods without an owner]...

4.31 There are two ways of understanding this. The first is that, despite appearances, in the vast majority of cases where resulting trusts arise on the failure of an express trust to dispose in whole or in part of the beneficial interest in the trust property, the court really does inquire into and assess whether the settlor intended a resulting trust to arise, and finds that he did. This seems fanciful, since courts appear not to make any such inquiry and it seems unlikely that settlors have any actual intentions in this regard at all. If they did, one presumes that they would express them. On the other hand, Lord Browne-Wilkinson may only be saying that despite the normal, 'intention-independent', automatic operation of the resulting trust in these circumstances, there are cases where (1) the facts show that the settlor did actually intend to abandon any interest in the trust property if the trust failed, and (2) he did not *express* this intention *as a term* of the trust he created, ie he did not declare as he did the other terms of the trust that if the trust failed in whole or in part that he abandoned his interest, but (3), nevertheless, because of these 'collateral' intentions to abandon the court treats the undisposed of trust property as *bona vacantia*. This does not upset Megarry J's characterisation, but only modifies it in a very minor way as follows: the ART is not wholly 'intention-independent' in that it may be *displaced* by a settlor's actual intentions to abandon to the Crown all interest in the trust property which might otherwise result to him. This surely occurs in a vanishingly small fraction of trusts, and it is not clear that there have ever been any cases of this kind (**9.92**).

4.32 The complicated way in which an ART can arise is shown by the attempt of a rich industrialist, one Guy Anthony Vandervell, to endow a chair of pharmacology in the Royal College of Surgeons. The facts of the case are somewhat convoluted, but the essential points are clear enough. There were three players: Vandervell himself, who controlled and owned most of the shares of a private engineering company he had founded; the Royal College of Surgeons (RCS); and Vandervell Trustees Ltd. (the trust company), a company which administered two separate trusts, one for Vandervell's children, and one a retirement, profit-sharing and savings fund for Vandervell's employees. The plan to endow the chair in the RCS (as devised by Vandervell's accountant to avoid tax) was to get shares of Vandervell's company into the hands of the RCS, and then Vandervell, using his control over his company, would have the company declare dividends on the shares sufficient to fund the chair; as part of the scheme, the RCS would grant an option to the trust company to purchase the shares, so that once the dividends were paid the shares could be retrieved from the RCS.

4.33 Vandervell duly instructed a bank which held some of the company shares on bare trust for him to transfer the shares to the RCS, and RCS in turn granted an option to purchase the shares for £5,000 to the trust company. The evidence was fragmentary, but at a minimum it was clear that the option was not to be granted to Vandervell himself because he did not want the beneficial ownership of the shares, which would increase his tax liability. Dividends sufficient to fund the chair were declared. In *Vandervell v IRC* (1967) a majority in the HL decided that because the option was essentially an interest in the shares that Vandervell had himself created by the arrangement, he had a beneficial interest in it; therefore, though the option was granted to the trust company, it held the option on resulting trust for Vandervell. Since he held the beneficial interest in the option under a resulting trust, he had retained a beneficial interest in the shares, for by exercising the option he could regain ownership of them. So although the RCS clearly had a beneficial interest in the shares, so did Vandervell under the option. Under the rules of taxation prevailing at the time, this beneficial interest in the shares entitled the Inland

Revenue to charge Vandervell large amounts of surtax on the dividends, so as it turned out, the grant of the option proved hugely costly to him.

4.34 Given the relative simplicity of the facts, it is startling how difficult the different judges in the CA and the HL found it adequately to characterise the transaction in which the RCS received the shares and granted the option to the trust company in a way which explains their finding a resulting trust to Vandervell. In *Re Vandervell (No 2)* (1974), where he closely analysed *Vandervell v IRC*, Megarry J gives the gist of what the judges appeared to think:

> [Quite] apart from mechanism or motive, there is the fact, of paramount importance in relation to any concept of resulting or implied trust, that it was Mr. Vandervell alone who was providing the property in question. The option was an option over shares of which Mr. Vandervell was the sole beneficial owner. If Mr. Vandervell disposed of those shares in such a way that he brought about the vesting of a major benefit in the college and a minor benefit in the defendant company, then it seems to me that Mr Vandervell was providing both those benefits, even if his provision of the minor benefit was indirect and not made under compulsion.

4.35 Now, when a judge in a trust case says things like 'Quite apart from mechanism or motive', start to worry, for if the law of trusts is about anything, it is about mechanism and motive – in other words it concerns whether or not individuals have effectively exercised various powers of ownership, and the consequences of having done so or having failed to do so. That is what this case concerned, and so mechanism and motive are all-important. And, perhaps surprisingly, (at least) five legal mechanisms might account for the transaction in *Vandervell*:

(1) There were two entirely separate gratuitous transactions – Vandervell gave the RCS some shares, and RCS gratuitously granted the trust company an option;

(2) Vandervell made a binding contract with the RCS;

(3) Vandervell made a gift of the shares with a 'legal condition';

(4) Vandervell made a gift of the shares upon an equitable condition; or

(5) Vandervell transferred the shares to the RCS on trust to (a) set up a chair in pharmacology and (b) grant an option to the trust company.

4.36 We can dismiss (1) from the outset. While Vandervell certainly had an independent reason to grant the RCS the shares – it was how he intended to endow the chair – the RCS had no independent reason to give the trust company anything; furthermore as a charity, the RCS could not just give rights to its property away; thus (1) is simply implausible on the facts. (2) is more likely. The contract would be one whereby, in return for instructing his bank to transfer the legal title to the shares it held on bare trust for him to the RCS and subsequently declaring dividends upon them, the RCS would use the dividends to found a chair of pharmacology in Vandervell's name, and grant the option to the trust company. (3) and (4) are also possible: Vandervell made a gift of the shares (again by instructing his bank to transfer the legal title of the shares to the RCS) on condition the option was granted to the trust company. This condition would more likely be regarded as equitable (4) than legal (3). While conditional gifts of land were both perfectly valid at law and common prior to 1926, no similar facility for conditional legal gifts of personalty was ever developed. (See Bell (1989), pp 225-226.) To the extent a gift could be made 'conditional' at law, the 'condition' did not attach to the *property*, but was treated as a conditional *obligation* on the donee. Thus a gift of personalty upon a condition which failed neither revived the donor's title in the property nor gave him any other proprietary right in it (eg a right to re-possess akin to a 'right to re-enter' land). Rather, upon failure of the condition the donee would have a personal restitutionary obligation to repay the value of the gift, so that he would not be unjustly enriched (*Re Garnett* (1905)). However, conditional gifts of any kind of property are perfectly valid in equity (**3.22**). Finally, (5) is also possible. Vandervell instructed the bank to transfer the shares to RCS, RCS agreeing to hold them on a trust which had two main terms, to found a chair in pharmacology with any dividends received and to grant an option to the trust company.

4.37 Interpreting the transaction as (3) is probably unsustainable. If RCS breached the condition to grant the option, they would be liable only to repay the value of the shares to Vandervell, for, as just mentioned, the restitutionary obligation to repay the value would be personal, and would not require the return of the shares. Since it was clear that Vandervell wanted to have the shares themselves in the hands of the trustee company (in order to facilitate a possible public flotation of the company), it seems implausible that he would have entered into a transaction where if things went wrong he would have no right to the return of the shares, but only a money payment for a remedy.

4.38 (2), (4), and (5) are all plausible, for if the RCS failed to grant the option in each of these cases, Vandervell could enforce their obligation and get the shares into the hands of the trust company. On (2), Vandervell would sue for breach of contract. Now, as stated, the grant was to be to the trust company, not Vandervell himself, and Vandervell sought no benefit from the shares. The general rule of the law of contract is that a person is only allowed damages to compensate him for his own loss, not for the losses suffered by any third party (here, the trust company to whom the option was to be granted), and so Vandervell would himself have suffered no loss under the contract, and so he would only be awarded nominal damages in an action brought against the RCS. However, because the contract involved unique property, private company shares, the court would award specific performance (**5.3**), and Vandervell could get specific performance so that the RCS would have to grant the option to the trust company, even though the grant was not to Vandervell's personal benefit (*Beswick v Beswick* (1968)); indeed, the RCS would be regarded as already holding the shares on contractual constructive trust subject to the option (**5.3**). The problem with (2) is simply that the transaction does not particularly look like a contract. The 'consideration' that the RCS would provide would be the funding of the chair in Vandervell's name, but that seems a rather strained interpretation. The RCS clearly wanted the chair as much as Vandervell, and so the whole thing looks much more like a gift than an enforceable contract.

4.39 There is a difficulty interpreting the transaction as (4) as well. While under (4), the RCS's failure to meet the condition by granting the option would result in the retrieval of the shares, the problem is that on the failure of the condition the shares would revert in equity to the transferor, ie to the bank to hold once again on bare trust for Vandervell; again, since Vandervell intended to get the shares into the hands of the trust company, this seems an inappropriate mechanism in the circumstances. (The condition *could* have been framed such that, on failure of RCS to grant the option, they would then hold the shares on trust for the trust company, ie so the shares would not revert to the transferor, but that seems overly convoluted, and essentially equivalent to (5)).

4.40 (5) probably best captures the transaction, ie that Vandervell had the legal title of the shares transferred to RCS on trust (a) to hold any dividends on trust to found the chair, and (b) to grant an option to the trust company to purchase them. Upon granting the option, RCS then held the shares either absolutely (subject of course to the option), or on charitable trust to further fund the chair should the option not be exercised.

4.41 This examination of the possible mechanisms for the transaction is not intended to be a mere exercise (or pointless romp) in legal technicalities. It may not be easy to adequately crystallise Vandervell's motives and acts into a workable legal transaction, but it is necessary to do so, for his motives and acts *did have legal consequences*, so *some* legal mechanism achieving those consequences must be discerned, or the case is simply unexplained.

4.42 Now, here's the crucial point that arises from this examination. On either (2) or (4) or (5), using strict 'follow the value' PIRT principles, Vandervell gave value to RCS to endow the trust company with a valuable right, the option — he either purchased it for the trust company under the contract (2), or made it an equitable condition in its favour under the grant (4), or gave it to the trust company under a trust (5) — and in the absence of any evidence of Vandervell's actual intentions the trust company would hold that option on a purchase money PIRT for him. In other words, Vandervell provided value in the form of shares to the RCS and 'purchased', either by way of contract, equitable condition, or trust, the grant of the option to the trust company.

4.43 There was, however, evidence of Vandervell's intentions to displace the PIRT. Apparently, the main rationale for requiring the RCS to grant the option was simply to ensure that the shares could be retrieved from the RCS to forestall problems in pursuing a public flotation of Vandervell's company. It was not clear that Vandervell entertained any specific intentions as to who should have the beneficial interest in the option the trustee company was to acquire, except that he did not want to retain or re-acquire any interest for himself in the shares. Save for Lords Reid and Donovan, all the judges found it inconceivable that Vandervell intended the trust company to take the option beneficially – in other words, he must have intended that the trust company was to hold the option on trust for somebody. But what trust? The majority found that the intended trust was simply too vague and undefined to be valid. Now, the court might appear a wee bit mean in their unwillingness to draw inferences from the surrounding circumstances. Both the CA and Lords Upjohn and Donovan considered the possibility that the option was transferred upon trust for the children's or employees' trust in such proportions as the settlor or the trustee company might declare, in other words a discretionary trust.

4.44　The result was an ART, in this rather unusual way: the PIRT was not displaced by evidence that Vandervell intended a gift or a loan to the recipient, the trust company, which is usually the way a PIRT is displaced – there was no such evidence and most of the judges found such an intention inconceivable; the PIRT was rather displaced by evidence which disclosed that Vandervell had an intention to create a trust for someone else, specifically *not himself* as provider of the value, the intention which is presumed in the case of a PIRT. To be sure, it was an imprecise trust on the court's view – to hold the property for, well, someone, but at any rate not for himself. Nevertheless this intention was sufficient to displace the operation of the PIRT. This express trust failed, since the objects (**3.4**) were not sufficiently 'certain', ie specified (**7.2**, **7.35** et seq), and therefore the beneficial interest resulted to Vandervell *under an ART*. Most ARTs arise when the settlor transfers property directly to the trustee on trusts which fail to dispose of the beneficial interest, not in the rather complicated way in which Vandervell provided the option for the trust company. Because of that, the judgments in the HL can be confusing, and Megarry J's review of them in his judgment in *Re Vandervell (No 2)*, while somewhat tedious, is preferable.

4.45　One rule of law which comes out clearly in *Vandervell v IRC* is that simply having a positive intention not to retain any beneficial ownership in property transferred to another, as Vandervell had, will not prevent the transferor from ending up with the beneficial title under an ART, since if the transferor not only has that intention but has also the intention that the transferee is to hold on trust, and the trust fails, then the only possible result is an undefined express trust, which leads to an ART (see also *Re Flower's Settlement Trusts* (1957)). As Plowman J said in *Vandervell* at first instance,

> As I see it, a man does not cease to own property simply by saying 'I don't want it'. If he tries to give it away the question must always be, has he succeeded in doing so or not?

This was cited with approval by Lord Upjohn in the HL's decision, and more recently by Lord Millett giving the advice of the PC in *Air Jamaica Ltd v Charlton* (1999).

4.46 In recent years the question of how and whether ARTs should arise in the context of pension fund trusts has arisen. *Davis v Richards and Wallington Industries Ltd* (1991) made matters less clear. There Scott J held *obiter* that in the case of a pension trust which had a surplus, ie more funds than necessary on actuarial principles to pay the various existing and future pensions, the proportion of the surplus deriving from the employer's contributions would be held on ART for the employer. As regards the proportion deriving from the employees' contributions, however, such funds were to be treated as *bona vacantia*, ie goods without an owner which can be claimed by the Crown. One reason Scott J gave for this result was the difficulties that would arise in working out the respective shares of the employees to the money held on ART: different members who have historically contributed the same amount would be entitled under the scheme to different benefits through the formula for determining pensions (the difference in factors such as length of service and salary on retirement can bring about this result) and those who take a refund of contributions instead of a pension generally receive less value. This seems quite unjustifiable; the shares of individuals to the surplus could be divided either on a past contributions basis or on a defined benefit basis as things stood when the surplus was to be distributed. That such a choice must be made is surely not so grave a problem that the money must be declared *bona vacantia*. As to the members claiming a refund, if they are in the scheme (ie have not taken their refund) when the actuary declares the surplus, they should take on whatever basis the others do; if they have already exited, they may justifiably be excluded. This aspect of Scott J's decision has recently been disapproved by the PC in *Air Jamaica Ltd v Charlton* (1999), where the court devised a scheme to allocate the funds held on ART (see **9.89-9.92** for circumstances in which inconvenience in the distribution of funds held on ART justifies treating them as *bona vacantia*.).

4.47 ARTs will come up again in chapter 9, when we discuss trusts which may 'fail' for two particular reasons, where a trust 'purpose' is accomplished or becomes impossible, and on the dissolution of an unincorporated association which defines a trust's class of beneficiaries. Since it is not clear that these cases really are instances of the failure of a trust giving rise to an ART, it is better to discuss those matters there.

The nature of resulting trusts and resulting trusteeship

Trusts 'resulting in pattern'

4.48 PIRTs and ARTs are both resulting trusts in that they are 'resulting in pattern', which is to say that the beneficial interest in the property 'results', ie goes back, to the person from whom it came. Patterns of this kind can be used to classify all trusts. In contrast to resulting trusts, there are 'prosulting' trusts (a term I borrow from Birks), ie trusts where the beneficial interest goes forward, to someone other than the person whence the value came. If pattern alone is the only criterion used to identify resulting trusts, then the category of resulting trusts would include many more trusts than just PIRTs and ARTs. Any express bare trust in which the settlor transferred property to a trustee in trust for himself is properly called a 'resulting' trust on this basis. Indeed, any trust in which the settlor receives any benefit whatsoever by whatever means would be a resulting trust. So, for example, if a settlor put property on trust for himself and his wife and children in such shares as the trustee should in his absolute discretion see fit, then if the trustee exercises his discretion in the settlor's favour and gave him a share, he would receive this share under a resulting trust, since he provided the trust property in the first place, and now it has come back, or 'resulted' to him. The usefulness of classifying all trusts which are 'resulting in pattern' in this way is doubtful; in particular it does not tell us *why* the beneficial interest 'resulted', whether because of the settlor's intention or by operation of law (**4.49**), or the basis upon which the person to whom the value returns receives it, that is, as a settlor or as a beneficiary (**4.50**).

Resulting trusts as intentional trusts and TABOLs

4.49 The paradigm example of an intentional trust is the express trust. However PIRTs fit in this category as well, for remember, PIRTs operate by way of an evidentiary presumption as to what the settlor's intentions were, ie as to whether he created a trust or not; the traditional view is that the law does not impose such a trust on the parties by operation of law. The PIRT is simply an intentional trust which is resulting in pattern, whose recognition by the court is made easier because the settlor benefits from the evidentiary presumption by not having to prove his intention to create a trust, eg by pointing to an oral or written declaration of trust, unless evidence is led by the transferee which tends to show that he actually intended a gift. In other words, while the evidentiary presumption affects the burden of proof, it does not change the nature of the trust as one created by the settlor himself. By contrast, in the case of ARTs, (assuming that Megarry J was right and Lord Browne-Wilkinson's remarks are to be interpreted as I said they should (**4.30-31**)), a paradigm example of a TABOL is the ART, for it arises on the failure of an express trust to dispose of the entire beneficial interest in the trust property irrespective of the settlor's intentions, and even, as *Vandervell* shows, where a resulting trust is the last thing the settlor intended or wanted.

The role in which the 'resulting beneficiary' takes

4.50 The distinction between the PIRT and the express trust as intentional trusts and the ART as a TABOL is sharpened by looking at the role or capacity in which someone who has provided value receives a benefit to himself under a trust, ie in cases where a trust is 'resulting' in pattern. Under an express trust or a PIRT, the benefit of the property goes to the person intended to take under the trust, that is, it goes to the person who originally provided the value not because he was the *settlor*, but because he is a *beneficiary under the intentional trust*. In this sense, the express trust for oneself and the PIRT, though superficially 'resulting' in pattern, are truly 'prosulting' in pattern, because the benefit of the property goes forward from the settlor to the intended beneficiary. Even though these two roles are filled by the same individual, this individual has rights under the trust because he was the intended beneficiary, not because he was the settlor. An individual can, after all, be both settlor *and* beneficiary under a trust (**2.3**), and there seems no reason to adopt a scheme of classification which obscures this. By contrast, the benefit an individual gets under an ART arises precisely because he was the settlor, absolutely irrespective of whether he was intended as a beneficiary. The ART is a new trust imposed by the law in the settlor's favour, under which he is newly a beneficiary, because of the logic of proprietary arithmetic (**4.6**) – that which he fails to dispose of by his express trust goes back to him.

Resulting trusteeship

4.51 Both the PIRT and the ART are bare trusts, so the legal title holder has essentially only one duty: to do with the property what the resulting beneficiary directs. This is obvious in the case of the ART. In the case of the PIRT, this is so because the evidentiary presumption only goes so far as to presume the location of the beneficial ownership – no other trust terms are presumed. Any further terms of an intentional trust must be proved without the benefit of the presumption. If they are, the trust will not properly be called a PIRT, for the proof of that more complex trust will amount to the proof of an informal, express, trust.

A new theory of resulting trusts

4.52 Recently, a new, more expansive role for resulting trusts has been suggested by Birks (1992) and Chambers (1997), based on a re-formulation of the underlying theory of resulting trusts which merges PIRTs and ARTs. According to this thesis, a resulting trust arises whenever a person transfers property or contributes value to a purchase for no consideration and *without the intention to give the beneficial ownership of it* to the recipient; the law gives rise to a trust to prevent the *unjust enrichment* of the recipient, ie if the transferor or contributor did not intend the recipient to take beneficially, the law deems it unjust for him to do so, and makes him hold the property on resulting trust.

4.53 On this theory, a profound change from the traditional view of the resulting trust is proposed; rather than being part of the rules of *title* governing the law of trusts – evidentiary rules for establishing an equitable title in the case of PIRTs, and a rule establishing the consequences of failed attempts to create equitable interests, ie equitable titles, in the case of ARTs – the Birks/Chambers thesis regards the resulting trust as a restitutionary trust – a trust which arises by operation of law in all circumstances, and which does so as an application by equity of unjust enrichment principles, using the trust device to anticipate and reverse what would otherwise be an unjust enrichment.

4.54 The unjust enrichment is that of the recipient of the gift in the case of a gratuitous transfer PIRT, or the recipient of the beneficial legal title in the case of a purchase money PIRT; in the case of an ART, the trustee-recipient of the legal title would be unjustly enriched if not for the resulting trust. Because 'no gift of the property to the recipient was intended' in any of these cases, each recipient would be unjustly enriched but for the law's imposition of a trust.

4.55 There are two main attractions of the theory, if it is right. The first is that it unifies the PIRT and ART. Based on this restitutionary reasoning, PIRTs and ARTs are displayed as variations on the same theme. Equity will impose a trust whenever property passes from a transferor in circumstances where he did not intend to make a gift of it to the recipient. The second is that it reveals the application of restitutionary reasoning in a branch of law, the law of trusts, where hitherto it had been obscured. It properly situates the law of resulting trusts in the realm of remedies for unjust enrichment, rather than leaving it as a bit of untheorised doctrine in the law of trusts.

4.56   The theory is, however, subject to criticisms. First, although PIRTs and ARTs both share the term 'resulting trusts', if there are reasons to think they effect different rules of law and are conceptually distinct, it is no theoretical advantage to 'unify' them under one theory. They do seem to fulfil a quite different function. For example, PIRTs seem to operate rarely, depend upon an evidentiary presumption, and could be abolished tomorrow. If the presumption of resulting trust were abolished, it would merely alter the burden of proof in cases where a claimant wished to establish the existence of a trust. One could not simply abolish the ART in the same way. The law must give some answer where a person transfers title to property to a trustee on trusts, where all or some of the intended beneficial interests fail. One could allow the trustee to keep the property on the basis that a recipient of property is bound only by whatever *effective* trusts the transferor managed to create. (A similar rule used to govern wills; any property remaining not disposed of by the testator's gifts went to the executors; the rule was changed by the Executors Act 1830.) The law could hold the property abandoned, to go to the crown as bona vacantia. Think of your own rule. The point is that there must be a rule of some kind, like the ART, where there is no similar need for a rule like the PIRT rule, and that suggests that these two resulting trusts do not have the same function or rationale.

4.57   Furthermore, the theory only achieves its unification of the law of trusts by depending very heavily on the way in which resulting trusts are *described*. On the traditional view, an ART arises irrespective of the settlor's intention. It does not refer to the settlor's intention at all. Mr Vandervell (**4.43**) certainly did not intend the right in the option to come back to him. It was the last thing he wanted. By contrast, PIRTs arise because the settlor is presumed that the property is to be held on trust for him. The presumption is an evidentiary one, displaced by contrary evidence. On the Birks/Chambers theory, however, all resulting trusts arise where there is an *absence* of intention, the absence of intention to make a gift (**4.52**, **4.54**). But the law typically looks to the parties' actual intentions in deciding what is just in the circumstances, not to things absent to their mind, intentions they did not have. It is obviously preferable to base the finding of a PIRT on the presumption as to what a party really intended, ie that the recipient was to hold the transferred property on trust, rather than on a rule of law which is essentially a prejudice against gifts, ie in the absence of proof of an intention to give, the law will impose a trust on the recipient. (It is also worth pointing out that one idea lying behind the theory, ie that equity disapproves of gifts, is subject to challenge, for most trusts are gifts, *structured* gifts (**1.23**), and equity happily enforces them, and the use arose because the Chancellor was willing to enforce gratuitous uses against the legal title holders.)

4.58 If correct, the Birks/Chambers theory would result in many more resulting trusts imposed by law. Take this case: I mistakenly pay my gas bill a second time, simply forgetting that I had done so already. Assume for simplicity I pay in cash. The gas company acquires legal title to the money when I pass it to one of its employees, though I do so under a mistake, because I voluntarily hand it over intending title to pass. At common law I am entitled to a restitutionary personal claim against the gas company for the amount I mistakenly paid. The Birks/Chambers thesis, however, steps in to give me more: although I intended to pay the money to meet a contractual debt to the gas company, the transfer was in fact for no consideration since having paid for my gas once, I received no value in return for my second payment; but clearly I did not intend to make a gift of the money to the gas company; therefore the gas company is a recipient of a gratuitous transfer where I, the transferor, intended no gift, and so according to Birks and Chambers the gas company should hold the money they received on resulting trust for me. Obviously, I will be very happy about acquiring this equitable proprietary right if, following my mistaken payment, the gas company becomes insolvent (**2.57** et seq). If Birks and Chambers are right, many common law personal restitutionary claims may be elevated to equitable proprietary rights via this restitutionary resulting trust, for it makes any recipient who winds up with the transferor's property without paying for it, and cannot prove the transferor intended to make a gift of it to him, a trustee. This result occurred in *Chase Manhatten Bank v Israel-British Bank* (1981). Goulding

J held that the plaintiff bank, who mistakenly paid the defendant bank $2m, not only had the normal common law restitutionary personal claim against the recipient of a mistaken payment; in addition, immediately upon receiving the money the recipient bank incurred a *fiduciary* obligation to return that very money; therefore the recipient bank held it on trust for the paying bank. Accordingly the paying bank could claim any traceable proceeds acquired with the money as his in equity, thus withdrawing the proceeds from the pool of assets on the recipient's insolvency.

4.59 Swadling (1996) has opposed this view, arguing that a presumed resulting trust depends not on the absence of intention to make a gift, but only on a presumption that there was a genuine intention to create a trust – thus the presumption of resulting trust is displaced by evidence of *any* intention contrary to the intention to create a trust – the transferee does *not* have to prove that the transferor intended to make him a gift; therefore, in the case of the mistaken payment, since my intention was to transfer the money to the gas company as outright legal owner – how else could I pay the debt I thought I owed? – the intention to create a trust is displaced, and therefore a presumed intention resulting trust does not arise. In *Westdeutsche Landesbank* the HL unanimously adopted Swadling's view (although Chambers's book-length treatment of the issues was not yet published and so was unavailable to the court). More recently Chambers's analysis has received the support of Lord Millett both in his extra-judicial writing (Millett 2000) and in *Air Jamaica* and in *Twinsectra v Yardley* (2002), although it is not clear that he would apply the theory in exactly the same way as would Birks and Chambers (eg he has stated extra-judicially (Millett (1998)) that *Chase Manhattan was* wrongly decided; see also the discussion of *Twinsectra*, **9.56** et seq). The issue, therefore, remains a live one, and it has now probably become essential exam preparation to be aware of, and be able to discuss, the Birks/Chambers thesis.

Further reading

Birks (1996b); Chambers (1997), especially ch 1; Swadling (1996a); Rose (1996).

Must read cases: *Vandervell v IRC* (1966); *Re Vandervell (No 2)* (1974); *Pettitt v Pettitt* (1971); *Cowcher v Cowcher* (1971); *Westdeutsche Landesbank v Islington London Borough Council* (1996); *Tinsley v Milligan* (1993); *Tribe v Tribe* (1995); *Air Jamaica v Charlton* (1999).

Self-test questions

1. What are presumed intention resulting trusts (PIRTs) and automatic resulting trusts (ARTs), and what distinguishes them?

2. Mark and Fiona run a business together, and are afraid that they are about to go bankrupt. They each own 25,000 shares of ABC plc, which they transfer to their son Damian to avoid losing them to their creditors. Mark then receives a legacy, which he uses to clear their debts. Mark and Fiona now seek the return of their shares, but Damian refuses. Discuss.

3. What is the difference between an intentional trust and a trust arising by operation of law (TABOL), and the difference between a trust 'resulting' and 'prosulting' in pattern? Do these distinctions illuminate the nature of resulting trusts?

4. 'The automatic resulting trust is a necessary feature of any legal system that recognises transfers of property on trust, but the recognition of presumed intention resulting trusts is inessential, and in the case of English law the presumed intention resulting trust has outlived any possible usefulness it might once have had and should be abolished.' Discuss.

5. Owing to a serious computer error, the London School of Econometrics mistakenly directs its bank to pay £1,500 into several hundred its employees' bank accounts with the payment reference 'performance bonus'. Is there any basis in law for the School to claim that these employees hold these mistaken payments on trust for it?

CHAPTER FIVE

Constructive Trusts

SUMMARY

Varieties of constructive trust

Trusts of the family home

The nature of the constructive trust

Varieties of constructive trust

5.1 All constructive trusts arise by operation of law, ie are TABOLs (**4.1**), but beyond this common characteristic, there is little that binds the various examples of constructive trusts together as a category. This chapter will very much serve as an introduction to constructive trusts, not a thorough examination, for reasons which will become apparent as we proceed. We will only examine one kind in detail here, the constructive trust of the family home.

5.2 For our purposes we can identify three broad categories of constructive trust: (1) those that arise through the application of the maxim 'Equity looks upon that as done which ought to be done' to give enhanced rights to parties to specifically enforceable contracts; (2) those which preserve a beneficiary's equitable proprietary rights when there has been a breach of trust; and (3) those in which individuals acquire for the first time an interest in another's property because of their past dealings or relationship with the legal owner.

5.3 As to (1), the maxim 'Equity looks upon that as done which ought to be done' reflects the approach of equity when it deals with certain property transactions which typically have two stages. When one buys land, one normally enters into a binding contract of sale, which is later followed by the execution of the documents which transfer title. Whenever the property being sold is unique in the eyes of equity, equity will allow the buyer specifically to enforce the contract of sale; that is, if the vendor refuses to carry out the contract and transfer the title, the buyer is not left to his common law right to sue for damages; equity will order the vendor to transfer the property itself. This is the general position with contracts for the sale of land, because, in the eyes of equity, all land is unique. But moreover, because 'Equity looks upon that as done which ought to be done', equity will treat the vendor *as having transferred* the title to the land to the buyer the moment the contract is agreed. The vendor, then, will hold the land on a constructive trust for the buyer until he transfers the legal title. We shall not examine this sort of constructive trust in any detail, though it will arise now and again, so you must be aware of its existence.

5.4 As to (2), if a trustee should transfer legal title to property in breach of trust to a third party recipient who is not a bona fide purchaser, then the equitable title will remain the beneficiary's (**2.34** et seq). How should this recipient who is bound by the beneficiary's continuing equitable title be described? What kind of 'trustee' is he? He was never intended to hold the property – he holds it because of a breach of trust, after all – and so he cannot be an express trustee; not being an express trustee, he is generally called a 'constructive trustee'. However, it is best to describe him more fully, if you're going to describe him as a trustee at all, as a 'constructive trustee of an express trust interest'; that is, the equitable interest in the property remains throughout, and so retains its characteristic as one created by an express trust, but the trustee is not appointed a trustee of the express trust; rather his 'trusteeship' is constructive, imposed by law, so that the beneficiary can claim his equitable interest against him. It is also worthwhile remarking that referring to this use of 'constructive trust' may be misleading on the view of the matter expressed by Lord Browne-Wilkinson in *Westdeutsche Landesbank* (1996), that is, that no true trust arises until the recipient title-holder of property subject to an equitable beneficial interest is aware of, and thus his conscience is affected by, it. While one must not push this thought too far, it does helpfully point out that in these cases the beneficiary's fundamental right is essentially a proprietary ownership interest, albeit an equitable one, in some specific property. This proprietary interest continues so long as the rules of title which govern it (ie govern how title to it can be transferred, lost, and so on) indicate that the beneficiary retains the equitable title. And if and when the recipient's conscience is affected by his knowledge of the trust, he is not in any way expected to *carry out* the original express trust as an express trustee must; rather, when he is informed of the trust he is merely required to hold the trust property to the order of the beneficiaries, ie to give it back to them. Therefore it may be wise to refer to the recipient of property subject to a trust merely as a legal title-holder subject to an equitable ownership interest; that may well be preferable to calling him a 'constructive trustee'.

Personal liability as constructive trusteeship

5.5   Where a breach of trust occurs the trustee is personally liable to the beneficiary to make up the loss; that is, the beneficiary has a personal money claim against the trustee for whatever losses were caused by the breach. This remedy is particularly important where the trust property was transferred away in breach of trust and it can neither be followed nor traced. Others besides the trustee, however, may be personally liable for breach of trust. Where a person dishonestly assists in a breach of trust, or where a person receives or deals with trust property as his own knowing it was transferred to him in breach of trust, the beneficiary will have a personal claim against such a person to make good the loss caused by the breach (**11.77** et seq; **11.164** et seq). Unfortunately, the traditional terminology for describing such a person's liability is to say he becomes 'liable to account as a *constructive* trustee', because he acquires the same personal liability as the trustee for the breach of trust. But, as Lord Millett says,

> ... he is not in fact a trustee at all, even though he may be liable to account as if he were. He never claims to assume the position of trustee on behalf of others, and he may be liable without ever receiving or handling the trust property. If he receives the trust property at all he receives it adversely to the claimant. He is not a fiduciary or subject to fiduciary obligations... I think we should now discard the words 'accountable as a constructive trustee' in this context and substitute the words 'accountable in equity'. (*Dubai Aluminium Co. Ltd. v Salaam* (2003))

5.6   (3) is a problematic category, for the power of equity to create property rights, ie equitable title, for one individual in the property of another, in order to do justice because of his past dealings or relationship with the legal owner, has not been informed by entirely coherent principles. As an introduction a few examples will suffice. Those familiar with land law will be aware of what are called 'constructive trusts of the family home'. If P and Q, who is usually P's spouse, come to an informal agreement or arrangement that Q is to share in the ownership of the property in which they live, the legal title to which is in P's name alone, and Q then relies on the arrangement to his detriment, Q will acquire an equitable share in the property under a constructive trust. The second example arises in a completely different context; it has been held that an employee standing in a fiduciary relationship to his employer who accepts a bribe to breach his fiduciary duties will hold the bribe money on constructive trust for his employer. Although they do not have any informal agreement to this effect as in the case of P and Q and the family home, the fiduciary relationship, it has been argued, is sufficient to give the employer an equitable title in his ill-gotten gains. This case will be examined in detail in Chapter 12. A third example is the 'Pallant v Morgan (1953) equity': roughly, where A and B have an arrangement or understanding (not necessarily contractually binding) that A will act to acquire property for them jointly, but A then acquires the property for himself, A will be held to hold the property on constructive trust for both of them (see Banner Homes v Luff Developments (2000)). A final example is provided by the case of 'mutual wills'; roughly, where two people make wills on the understanding the survivor will not alter his will (eg assume a husband and wife both leave all their property to each other first and then all their property to their children), in order to prevent any 'fraud' that might arise if the survivor were to alter his or her will (eg say the husband survived, taking all of his wife's property under her will, but then decided to alter his will to give half the property to charity rather than all to their children), the survivor will be regarded as holding his property on constructive trust to give effect to the terms of the mutual will (Dufour v Pereira (1769)). The only constructive trust we shall examine in detail in this chapter is the constructive trust of the family home.

Trusts of the family home

5.7 Broadly speaking, what concerns us here are the circumstances under which it is just for the law to vary the property rights between individuals in what is usually the most significant asset either one of them owns (or both of them co-own), because of their relationship to each other or their past dealings together. While traditionally the typical relationship was that between husband and wife where the husband was the sole legal owner of the matrimonial home, in principle and practice the relationship or dealings can be between any two or more individuals: between unmarried cohabitees, whether straight or gay, parents and (adult) children, or any others (*Cooke v Head* (1972)). Indeed, the significance of this law is now much reduced for married couples than for others, for disputes over beneficial ownership typically arise on the breakdown of a relationship, and the courts are empowered to vary the property rights of spouses upon divorce (Matrimonial Causes Act 1973, s 24; Matrimonial Property and Proceedings Act 1970, s 37). The court has no similar jurisdiction to vary the property rights of other cohabitees. Nevertheless, determining the beneficial interests in the family home under these rules remains important even for married couples in cases where third parties are involved. For example, if one of the couple becomes bankrupt, only that person's share will be available to his trustee in bankruptcy for distribution to creditors; therefore, regardless of the situation between the cohabitees themselves, if an informal arrangement gives rise to ownership shares not easily detected by third parties dealing with one or both cohabitees, this can have important effects on those third parties' rights.

5.8 Different common law jurisdictions have taken different theoretical approaches to the basis upon which equitable property rights arise in these circumstances. For example, in New Zealand, the courts have emphasised the reasonable expectations of the party claiming an equitable share in the property; thus a wife who in all the circumstances can reasonably claim to have expected a share in the family home given the parties' conduct, and who has relied upon those expectations, will be successful (*Gillies v Keogh* (1989)). In Canada the courts have emphasised the unjust enrichment that the defendant would obtain if the plaintiff were to receive no share in the property; thus, for example, a husband who has benefited throughout the marriage by his wife's raising their children and domestic work will hold the legal title upon constructive trust for himself and his wife in appropriate shares (*Pettkus v Becker* (1980); *Sorochan v Sorochan* (1986); *Peter v Beblow* (1993)). In England, the foundational HL decisions in *Pettitt v Pettitt* (1970) and *Gissing v Gissing* (1971) laid down the 'common intention' approach.

5.9 *Pettitt* can in one sense be regarded as the negative side of the coin, and *Gissing* the positive. In *Pettitt* their Lordships were unanimously concerned to refute the proposition that the courts had a general jurisdiction to rearrange the property rights of cohabitees on the breakdown of their relationship in whatever way seemed 'fair and just in all the circumstances'. They revealed, however, a variety of opinions as to the circumstances in which the court could find that one party had acquired a beneficial equitable interest in the property of another. *Gissing*, in particular the speech by Lord Diplock, provided that basis: where the parties had a common intention that the beneficial interest in the property was to be shared, the best evidence of which being an actual agreement, and that common intention was acted upon by the plaintiff to his detriment, then the defendant would hold the property on constructive trust for them both in the intended shares.

The requirement that the plaintiff act to his detriment

5.10 Why, if a common intention to share the property is proved or inferred from all the evidence, does this not operate as an effective declaration of trust, albeit an informal one? Why must the plaintiff also show that he acted to his detriment on the parties' arrangement? The problem is the existence of a statutory requirement, s 53(1)(b), which provides that an oral declaration of trust of land is unenforceable. (Formality requirements will be discussed in detail in chapter 6.) Equity will therefore not enforce a purely voluntary informal trust of land.

5.11 So, while a common intention is necessary, it is not sufficient to establish a constructive trust. The plaintiff must also show he acted to his detriment in reliance on the agreement or understanding (*Midland Bank plc v Dobson* (1986)). The extent and quality of reliance should match what was expected under the parties' common understanding, but in many cases this is unclear. In *Grant v Edwards* (1986) Browne-Wilkinson VC said:

> In many cases of the present sort, it is impossible to say whether or not the claimant would have done the acts relied on as a detriment even if she thought she had no interest in the house. Setting up a house together, having a baby, making payments to general housekeeping expenses ... may all be referable to the mutual love and affection of the parties and not specifically referable to the claimant's belief that she has an interest in the house. As at present advised, once it has been shown that there was a common intention that the claimant should have an interest in the

house, any act done by her to her detriment relating to the joint lives of the parties is, in my judgment, sufficient detriment to qualify ... Accordingly, in the absence of evidence to the contrary, the right inference is that the claimant acted in reliance [on the common intention] and the burden lies on the legal owner to show that she did not do so.

Where both a common intention and detrimental reliance is proven, then, as Hayton ((1996), 366) puts it:

Equity acts *in personam* to prevent [the defendant] pleading the lack of formalities, so [the plaintiff] gets what was agreed. [The plaintiff's] interest should date from the time she commences to act to her detriment in the contemplated manner so that it is then inequitable for [the defendant] to deny her an interest.

5.12 Following a wealth of case law interpreting *Pettitt* and *Gissing*, the HL again spoke in 1990. In *Lloyds Bank plc v Rosset* (1991) Lord Bridge, giving the only judgment of a unanimous House, provided what is now the authoritative enunciation of the basic principles:

The first and fundamental question which must always be resolved is whether, independently of any inference to be drawn from the conduct of the parties in the course of sharing the house as their home and managing their joint affairs, there has at any time prior to acquisition, or exceptionally at some later date, been any agreement, arrangement, or understanding reached between them that the property is to be shared beneficially. The finding of an agreement or arrangement to share in this sense can only, I think, be based on evidence of express discussions between the partners, however imperfectly remembered and however imprecise their terms may have been. Once a finding to this effect has been made it will only be necessary for the partner asserting a claim to a beneficial interest against the partner entitled to the legal estate to show that he or she has acted to his or her detriment or significantly altered his or her position in reliance on the agreement in order to give rise to a constructive trust or proprietary estoppel.

In sharp contrast with this situation is the very different one where there is no evidence to support a finding of an agreement or an arrangement to share, however reasonable it might have been for the parties to reach such an agreement if they had applied their minds to the question, and where the court must rely entirely on the conduct of the parties both as the basis from which to infer a common intention to share the property beneficially and as the conduct relied on to give rise to the constructive trust. In this situation direct contributions to the purchase price by the partner who is not the legal owner, whether initially or by payment of mortgage instalments, will readily justify the inference necessary to the creation of a constructive trust. But, as I read the authorities, it is at least extremely doubtful whether anything less will do.

Evidence of a common intention is to be read objectively, as a reasonable person would do, from the statements or conduct of the parties. In particular, a dishonest actual intention of the legal owner will not defeat an agreement or understanding objectively viewed, as for instance, where the legal owner makes an excuse for putting the title in his name alone, as in *Eves v Eves* (1975) where the excuse was that the female partner was too young to own property, or in *Grant v Edwards* (1986) where the legal owner said placing the female partner's name on the title would prejudice her in her divorce proceedings.

5.13 The common intention may be one in which the parties decide on their respective beneficial shares from the outset, or may be one in which the parties decide that each should get a 'fair' share according to the contributions each had made directly or indirectly to the acquisition of the property, in which case the court will obviously have leeway in determining the extent of the beneficial interests (*Gissing v Gissing; Midland Bank plc v Cooke* (1995)). In *Huntingford v Hobbs* (1993) the female partner paid about 61% of the purchase price of the property, and with the male partner jointly undertook to repay the mortgage which funded the remainder. On the facts, however, it appeared that there was a common intention that the male partner would pay all the mortgage instalments, and so in determining their respective shares, the CA credited him with the full value of the mortgage loan contribution to the purchase; by the same token, however, on the sale of the property the value of outstanding mortgage debt was debited entirely from his share of the proceeds. (See also *Carlton v Goodman* (2002) where on the CA's analysis, a common intention displaced the interest which otherwise would have been found under a PIRT where two parties were jointly liable under a mortgage loan.)

5.14 *Rosset* makes clear that the limits within which a common intention can be inferred merely from conduct are narrow. The activities of a husband (doing odd jobs about the house to keep it in repair and minor renovations and improvements) and of a wife (cooking, cleaning, and looking after the kids) doing what husbands and wives 'normally' do were regarded as wholly insufficient evidence of a common intention to share the property beneficially (*Pettitt*; *Gissing*; *Burns v Burns* (1984)). The requirement of direct contributions to the purchase price 'initially or by payment of mortgage instalments' seems to confuse constructive trusts with purchase money PIRTs. Contributions to the initial purchase price will give rise to a PIRT unless made by the husband to a purchase in the sole name of his wife; however payments of mortgage instalments do not give rise to a resulting trust (*Cowcher v Cowcher* (1972)), unless the court is tacitly applying 'backwards tracing' to such payments. 'Backwards tracing' is tracing value through the payment of a debt. If my rogue trustee uses £5,000 of trust money to pay off a bank loan, then I trace into the product he purchased with the loan money; if he purchased a car with the loan money, I trace the value of the trust money into that, and claim equitable title to the car, even though he acquired title to the car *before* he misapplied my money to pay off his debt, hence the term 'backwards' tracing. Similarly, one backwards traces when one allocates shares in the ownership of a house on the basis of the payment of instalments under a mortgage loan. It would be perfectly sensible to apply a backward tracing purchase money PIRT analysis to the payment of mortgage instalments, but the courts have never said that that was what they were doing. The orthodox view, therefore, must be that the mortgage instalments are contributions referable to the acquisition of the property under a common intention constructive trust, a constructive trust inferred, however, from nothing more than the very paying of the instalments. Query whether this does not amount to a backward tracing purchase money PIRT under different terminology.

5.15 The decision by the CA in *Midland Bank plc v Cooke* (1995) represents something of a departure from these principles. A house was purchased in Mr Cooke's name alone, with his savings, a mortgage taken out by him, and a wedding present from his parents. Mr and Mrs Cooke testified under oath that they had made no agreement concerning the beneficial interest in the house. The CA decided that the wedding present was a gift to both Mr and Mrs Cooke, and therefore, since the money was half hers, Mrs Cooke acquired an interest in the house under a purchase money PIRT. If resulting trust principles were to define their respective shares, Mrs Cooke would have an interest of approximately 7 per cent due to her share of the wedding gift. The CA decided her share was 50 per cent. It declined to adopt the view that where a party's interest is defined purely by their contribution to the purchase price, no common intention being proved, all other conduct is irrelevant to determining that party's beneficial interest. Where one party has successfully asserted a beneficial interest in the property, the court should undertake a survey of the entire course of conduct between the parties to determine their respective beneficial shares; furthermore, Waite LJ said:

> ... positive evidence that the parties neither discussed nor intended any agreement as to the proportions of their beneficial interests does not preclude the court, on general equitable principles, from inferring one.

This statement must be doubted in view of the HL's reasonably clear statements in *Gissing* and *Rosset* that a common intention constructive trust can only arise on the basis of a real common intention.

The constructive trustee is a bare trustee

5.16 The legal owner holding the family home under a constructive trust is just a bare trustee vis-à-vis the equitable owner of a share. There are no other 'terms' of the trust with which he has fiduciary obligations to comply. The plaintiff and defendant are merely co-owners in equity to the extent of their respective shares.

Third parties and insolvency

5.17 The plaintiff's equitable proprietary interest under the constructive trust will be capable of binding third parties who deal with the legal title-holding defendant (eg *Williams & Glyn's Bank Ltd v Boland* (1981, HL); *Kingsnorth Trust Ltd v Tizard* (1986)), though it will not do so in all cases (eg *City of London Building Society v Flegg* (1988)); the details will not be considered here. The standard practice of purchasers or mortgagees of land is to make such inquiries as to avoid being caught by the plaintiff's interest. Of greater concern, perhaps, is the position of third parties where the legal title holder, usually the husband, goes bankrupt. For example, a wife who acquires an equitable share of the property under a constructive trust will take the value of that share free of the claims of her husband's creditors. Given how common it is these days for title to the family home to be shared, it is perhaps somewhat precious to manifest much concern for the unsecured creditors in these circumstances, since it is not very plausible that *they*, as opposed perhaps to a mortgagee, advanced money to the husband relying on a belief that he owned the whole of, rather than co-owned, his family home. The sale of the property now 'co-owned' by the husband's trustee in bankruptcy, who wants to realise the husband's share in money, and the wife, who generally wishes to remain in occupation, will not be postponed for more than a year in most circumstances (*Re Citro* (1991)), so the trustee can get the money out of the house quite smartly.

Proprietary estoppel

5.18 Notice that in the passage from Lord Bridge's decision in *Rosset* he mentions the constructive trust and 'proprietary estoppel' in the same breath. While proprietary estoppel in its various forms is a much older doctrine than the common intention constructive trust, they are similar. Where a defendant represents by his words or conduct that the plaintiff will acquire some entitlement to his land, and the plaintiff acts to his detriment in reliance upon the representation, the defendant may be 'estopped', ie stopped, from standing on his strict legal rights to the land in order to withdraw the entitlement. The two main differences between the common intention constructive trust and proprietary estoppel are first, that the former relies upon some common understanding or agreement, while the latter is based upon the defendant's representations, and second, that the only result of the operation of common intention is a constructive trust, whereas in the case of a proprietary estoppel the plaintiff will acquire the 'minimum equity to do justice' (*Crabb v Arun District Council* (1976); *Pascoe v Turner* (1979)); instead of awarding an equitable interest in the property, the court may award more appropriate lesser interests, such as a licence to occupy or a charge on the property for money expended. In this respect, proprietary estoppel is a more flexible doctrine. Hayton ((1996a), 373 et seq) argues that the distinction between common intention constructive trusts and proprietary estoppels is illusory, and that the courts should draw upon their experience of applying both doctrines to reach the equitable result, an approach suggested by Browne-Wilkinson VC in *Grant*. A full examination of proprietary estoppel and a comparison with the constructive trust is beyond our purposes, but even the brief comparison above is suggestive – how different in most cases will an informal 'common' understanding be from an informal representation by the defendant legal owner which is reasonably acted upon by the plaintiff? Recently, the CA in *Yaxley v Gotts* (2000) held that a builder who converted the defendant's house into flats on the assurance that in return he would acquire the ground floor flat was entitled to a 99-year lease of the ground floor rent-free equally under a common intention constructive trust and by way of proprietary estoppel. (See also *Banner Homes Group plc v Luff Developments Ltd* (2000).)

The nature of the constructive trust

5.19 All trusts arising by operation of law may, at first glance, appear to have a 'remedial' nature: if a right is created by the law, then surely it must be an application of the principles of justice in response to a fact situation demanding it. Thus the constructive trust arises because it would be unconscionable for the legal title holder to deny his cohabitee the equitable interest they agreed the latter should have, so the law provides one. But *all* legal rules are intended to express the principles of justice, and indeed, learning the law is in part finding out what justice means. The term 'remedial' means something different: a remedial equitable interest is one which is *awarded by a court* following the trial of a legal action; such a trust does not pre-exist the court award (although parties may anticipate what a court will award and act accordingly, as when a negligent driver (or rather, his insurance company) pays compensation to the person he injured so avoiding an expensive legal action). Are there remedial constructive trusts of this kind?

5.20 The issue basically turns on the court's discretion: is the constructive trust that a court finds in a particular case more like a court order which is shaped by the court's discretion in response to the particular facts of the case, or is the constructive trust more 'institutional', as it is called, a trust which arises because of the rules of title governing the acquisition of equitable interests in property, which the court has really no choice in declaring once the facts of the case are proven at trial? The vendor's constructive trust and the 'constructive' trust under which a recipient who is not a bona fide purchaser holds trust property clearly arise more or less automatically on the facts as does the ART (**4.30** et seq). Arising as they do in this automatic way, they are clearly institutional, and should be treated as rules of title, ie rules which govern the acquisition or loss of interests in property. In contrast, a common intention constructive trust or a proprietary estoppel is more like an equitable mushroom that arises from the legal mycelium whenever the conditions are right, not so much by the operation of rules governing title transactions, but as a remedy which is afforded on the basis of the parties' ongoing behaviour, with particular reference to expectation and detrimental reliance. The distinction is not watertight, of course, because any rule by which a title is transferred or a new title arises can be considered a rule of title, no matter how nebulous the rule actually is. Nevertheless, it is fair to say that the rule giving rise to a vendor's constructive trust or an ART looks more like an 'automatic' rule of title, whereas the rules, such as they are, governing common intention constructive trusts, look a lot more like considerations taken into account by the court when deciding to 'award', as it were, an equitable interest (see *Muschinski v Dodds* (1985) per Deane J). This remedial kind of constructive trust appears to be accepted at least theoretically in other jurisdictions (in particular the US (American Law Institute, *Restatement of Restitution*, para 60) and Canada (*Rawluk v Rawluk* (1990) and see Chambers (2001-02)); such a trust is understood to come into existence only when the court declares it, but has effect retroactively to the time when the facts which justify the award occurred.

5.21 In English law the constructive trust, even in cases of constructive trusts of the family home, must be regarded as institutional, not remedial for the very good reason that there is something fishy and apparently unjust about declaring a property interest with retroactive effect, for proprietary rights bind third parties. It is fishy because if I acquire a property from X in which the law regards Y as having no interest, it is not clear how simply by owning the property I could become subject to Y's rights which arise by virtue of a later court order against X – it seems illegitimately to mix up personal and proprietary rights, since once X has sold me the property, it is no longer connected to him personally any more than it is to anyone besides its current owner, ie me. It tends towards injustice, for if Y has no right against X when I buy the property (since the court has not by then made the remedial order), there is no way that I can protect myself from Y's right. I cannot even be a bona fide purchaser without notice, since there is nothing in existence of which I can take notice. Even if the courts may minimise the effect of the award on third parties by setting particular conditions on the trust, for example that it be subject to particular third party rights, this requires the court to be vigilant in protecting the rights, possibly unknown, of parties not before the court, and in any case seems *ad hoc*.

5.22 Whatever one's views about the theoretical merits or demerits, as a matter of authority, in *Polly Peck International plc (No. 2)* (1998) the CA put paid to the remedial constructive trust in England following a thorough review of the cases and the academic literature. As Nourse LJ put it: 'It is not that you need an Act of Parliament to prohibit a variation of proprietary rights. You need one to permit it: see the Variation of Trusts Act 1958 [10.70] and the Matrimonial Causes Act 1973 [5.9].' So unless the HL decides to reverse the CA on this, it would appear that the remedial constructive trust is a dead letter in England.

5.23   On reading the cases you might think that in reality the law of trusts gives judges such discretion that their 'finding' a constructive trust on the facts virtually amounts to 'awarding' the plaintiff a retrospectively effective equitable interest. Nevertheless the HL in *Pettitt* certainly denied that the courts should have such a discretion. The more interesting question is whether the courts should have a discretion to award a plaintiff an equitable interest which takes effect only from the date of the court order, along the lines favoured by Hayton ((2001b), 398 et seq). Such an equitable title would automatically be subject to the rights of innocent third parties in the property acquired before the award. Such a prospective constructive trust, ie one operating from the date of the court award, will not assist the plaintiff if the defendant is bankrupt, but will protect the plaintiff if the defendant goes bankrupt before the plaintiff gets his share out of the property, and will entitle the plaintiff to the actual property, which will be worthwhile if the property itself, rather than just its value, has significance for the plaintiff. Such a prospective constructive trust has never been awarded under English law, though in *Muschinski v Dodds* (1985) the High Court of Australia made just such an order.

Are common intention trusts of the family home really intentional trusts rather than TABOLs?

5.24   Are common intention trusts of the family home truly *intentional* trusts, ie informal *express* trusts, which are enforced in order to do justice (or at least prevent injustice) *despite* the fact that such trusts are *prima facie* unenforceable because of s 53(1)(b) LPA 1925, *or*, are they rather trusts which arise by operation of law (TABOLs) which reflect, but do not depend upon or exactly match the intentions of the parties? On the first view, the trust the court enforces is precisely the trust the parties informally agreed upon or understood, taking the view that a statutory provision cannot be allowed to let the legal title-holder 'commit' a fraud by denying the equitable beneficial interest of his cohabitee that was the subject of their common intention (**6.9** et seq). If this is correct, then the common intention trust of the family home is *not*, as it has so far been labelled, a constructive trust. For such a trust is not a TABOL, and constructive trusts are TABOLs. The contrary view is that these are TABOLs, and the constructive trust that arises *reflects* the intentions of the parties, but is not, as it were, created by the parties expressing those intentions. The practical consequence of the distinction is obviously that if common intention trusts of the home are intentional trusts, then the courts cannot depart from the parties' intentions in their declaration of what rights each of them have. Whereas on the latter view, the parties' intentions are one, but only one, factor to be taken into account in determining the character of the trust, in particular the size of the claiming party's beneficial share of the ownership. Clearly, if *Midland Bank* (**5.17**) was rightly decided, then the latter view prevails, since the court awarded equal shares despite the fact that the parties had no common intention as to their beneficial ownership at all. The problem is, that following *Gissing* and *Rosset* strictly, it would appear that this sort of departure is not permitted and, if so, the former view looks to be correct. But on the other hand, the association of the common intention trust with the doctrine of proprietary estoppel tips the balance back toward the constructive trust, for it seems clear that the law (or the court's) giving an interest to provide 'minimum equity' to satisfy the plaintiff's legitimate expectation of an interest in the property need not coincide with whatever interest the plaintiff expected, nor whatever interest the defendant felt he was denying by standing on his strict legal rights. The prevailing view is that the common intention trust is a constructive trust, a TABOL, which is why it is discussed in this chapter of the book. But it is worthwhile keeping the alternative interpretation in mind. It may be that in some cases, the very trust informally agreed upon by the parties is the one enforced, reflecting the former view, whereas in other cases such intentions only form one part of the picture, so that only the constructive trust perspective is explanatory.

Further reading

Gardner (1993); Birks (ed) (1994, Vol II, Part IV); Birks (2000b); Rickett (1999); Chambers (2001-02)

Must read cases: *Pettitt v Pettitt* (1969); *Gissing v Gissing* (1970); *Grant v*

Edwards (1986); *Lloyds Bank plc v Rosset* (1990); *Midland Bank plc v Cooke* (1995); *Polly Peck International plc (No 2)* (1998)

Self-test questions

1. What are some examples of constructive trusts? Do they have any common features?

2. Phillippa and Paul purchase Whiteacre together for £50,000. Phillippa contributes £10,000, Paul £1,000, and the remainder is raised by way of a mortgage on Whiteacre, for the repayment of which Paul is solely liable. Paul loses his job and Phillippa pays all the mortgage instalments. Paul starts a business which fails, and has been declared bankrupt. The house is now worth £100,000. Discuss.

3 What is the difference between the 'remedial' and 'institutional' views of constructive trusts?

4. 'The first, and absolutely essential, point that must be grasped to fully understand the 'constructive trust of the family home' cases is that this whole area of law has arisen principally because it concerns *informal* understandings or arrangements to do with beneficial interests in *land*. Because declarations of trusts of land must be evidenced in writing or are unenforceable under s 53(1)(b) LPA 1925, the law's initial attitude to these informal arrangements must be that they cannot be enforced as they fail to meet the requirements for the creation of such interests as laid down by Parliament.' Discuss.

5. On your reading of the cases, does the 'intentional trust enforced despite s 53(1)(b)' interpretation or the constructive trust interpretation better account for the court's recognition of the common intention trust of the family home?

CHAPTER SIX

Formalities and Secret Trusts

SUMMARY

The purpose of formalities

Declarations of trusts in land: s 53(1)(b) of the Law of Property Act 1925

The doctrine of *Rochefoucauld v Boustead*

Dispositions of subsisting equitable interests: s 53(1)(c)

Formal requirements on testamentary gifts: s 9 of the Wills Act 1837

Informal testamentary trusts: secret and half secret trusts

The purpose of formalities

6.1 The law sometimes imposes a requirement on the *form* of legal transactions before it will regard those transactions as effective, typically a requirement that the transaction be made or recorded in writing. The law may impose formalities for different purposes, but three are of particular relevance to transactions which create or transfer equitable interests in property.

As a cautionary measure

6.2 Property rights, including equitable interests under a trust, are very valuable rights. They should not be effectively dealt with in a casual or informal way, just in case the transferor did not seriously consider the consequences of his act. The formality of writing, in particular the requirement that the transferor signs his name, is suited to this purpose, because these days even the most benighted rube understands that when he signs his name to a document which is not a personal letter he is generally doing something of legal consequence.

For evidential purposes – I

6.3 Writing requirements provide documentary evidence which make frauds more difficult on the presumption that it is easier to get away with lying to the court about what someone said than it is successfully to forge documents and lie to the court about their origin.

For evidential purposes – II

6.4 Documentary evidence also prevents the administrative problems that might arise when the memory of oral transactions has faded. Also, when transactions are complicated, the writing down helps the parties to be clear about what they intend. Finally, in the case of trusts, the writings are useful simply as a paper record for the trustee which ensures that he does not commit an inadvertent breach of trust by, say, paying income to a former beneficiary who has since assigned his equitable right to the income to someone else.

6.5 It is a maxim of equity that 'equity looks to intent not form'; equity has never itself insisted on formal requirements for any transactions (which undoubtedly has something to do with the fact that the Chancellor could subpoena parties and interrogate them in person (**1.5**)). Parliament however, by statute, has imposed formal requirements on the creation and transfer of equitable interests, and equity must take due regard of them. Here we will be concerned, first, with the formalities for creating a trust, that is bringing into existence equitable rights, and then formalities for the transfer, or assignment, or disposition of already existing equitable interests, that is, the existing rights of beneficiaries under a trust.

Declarations of trusts in land: s 53(1)(b) of the Law of Property Act 1925

6.6 Section 53(1)(b) of the Law of Property Act 1925 provides:

> A declaration of trust respecting any land or any interest therein must be manifested and proved by some writing signed by some person who is able to declare such trust or by his will;

Section 53(1)(b) applies only to land. There is no similar provision with respect to personalty: therefore there is no formal requirement for the declaration of a trust of personalty. Thus you can orally declare that you hold your copy of this book on trust for your mother, and if you mean it, then you do.

6.7 Section 53(2) of the Act provides:

> This section does not affect the creation or operation of resulting, implied or constructive trusts.

To the extent that resulting, implied, and constructive trusts arise by operation of law, this provision is strictly speaking unnecessary, or inserted ex *abundante cautela* (out of an abundance of caution), for there can be no formality requirements for trusts which arise by operation of law. The clause does save PIRTs, however, since these are intentional trusts, not TABOLs (**4.49**).

6.8 The person 'able to declare such trust' under s 53(1)(b) will normally be the settlor, of course. This is plain where the trust is self-declared, ie the legal owner of land declares that he shall himself hold the land on trust. A somewhat complicated example is the case of *Rochefoucauld v Boustead* (1897), which turned on the failure to declare a trust in writing. The plaintiff, the Comtesse de la Rochefoucauld, had mortgaged her estates in Ceylon, and the mortgagee demanded payment of the mortgage debt. She had insufficient funds following her divorce, and her friend Boustead orally agreed to buy the estates from the mortgagee at a price sufficient to cover the mortgage debt and expenses, and hold the estates on trust for her, subject to her paying off the purchase price and further expenses. Since Boustead purchased the beneficial title from the mortgagee which he impressed with the trust in the plaintiff's favour, he should have signed the necessary writing. Where A transfers land to B to hold on trust for C, A has the beneficial title before the transfer of the land to B, so is the one able to declare the trust. If he transfers the title but fails to declare the trust in writing, A should remain the appropriate signatory if anyone is, simply because it is A's intentional trust which we are concerned about. It seems doubtful, though, whether A's later writing should be effective to allow C to enforce the trust against B, since the whole point of the section is to make oral declarations of trust unenforceable, and the declaration which matters must be the one A makes prior to or at the time legal title is transferred to B, ie when he still has the beneficial interest. Youdan (1984) argues that B, the legal owner, may sign the writing as the one who would be beneficial owner if there were no trust. Where B is willing to do so, his production of the writing is, however, better regarded as his own self-declaration of trust in favour of C giving effect to A's wishes. In *Gardner v Rowe* (1828) an oral express trust was enforced against the trustee (so as to avoid claims by his creditors in bankruptcy); though the trust was evidenced by a post-transfer writing of the trustee, the case turned on the doctrine enunciated in *Rochefoucauld v Boustead*, not on the writing point, so it does not decide the issue.

The doctrine of *Rochefoucauld v Boustead*

6.9 Section 53(1)(b) uses the words 'manifested and proved by some writing', which have been interpreted to indicate *not* that a purported declaration of trust is void without such a writing, but that it is *not enforceable* in law; the express trust exists and binds the parties, but the beneficiary cannot invoke the assistance of the court to make the trustee carry it out. In *Rochefoucauld v Boustead* (1897), however, the CA did enforce the oral express trust, because it would be a fraud for a person taking the land as a trustee to plead the statute and keep the land for himself. 'Equity will not allow a statute enacted to prevent fraud to be used as an instrument of fraud', and so the court will allow parol (ie oral) evidence to prove the express trust, despite s 53(1)(b).

6.10 In *Bannister v Bannister* (1948) an elderly woman conveyed two cottages to her brother-in-law at a below market price on the understanding that she should be able to live rent-free in one of them for the rest of her days. When he tried to evict her, the CA declared that he held one of the cottages on trust to give effect to the agreement. It did not matter that the brother-in-law had no fraudulent intent when the property was transferred; the fraud consisted of relying upon the absence of writing when the sister-in-law tried to enforce her beneficial interest. Scott LJ described the trust as a constructive trust, without however giving any reasons for this classification. The constructive trust analysis may appear to be preferable to the express trust analysis simply because it gives an identical result without appearing to disregard the statute, since constructive trusts are specifically exempted from formality requirements by s 53(2).

6.11 *Rochefoucauld* and *Bannister* were both two party cases. How should the doctrine apply in the three party case, ie where A transfers land to B upon trust for C? If one adopts the constructive trust approach, the law may impose the result most justified in the circumstances – in some cases the constructive trust should be a bare trust for A, which merely prevents B's unjust enrichment; in others it should reflect the terms of the unenforceable express trust, so carrying out A's intention. In general in the three party case a bare trust in favour of A is preferable because it gives due weight to the statute, for the express trust is not enforced, yet at the same time B's fraud is prevented. Moreover, the cautionary purpose is served: if A still wishes to carry out his intentions, he can declare the trust again; if he does not, then the statute has properly saved him from the effect of his oral declaration. Moreover, C can hardly complain that a *fraud* has been perpetrated against him simply because he has not received a gratuitous benefit from A. A constructive trust in favour of C should only be found where C relied to his detriment either because of a representation by A or because B has acted to carry out the trust, or perhaps, where A is no longer able to declare a trust in C's favour afresh, for example because he is dead, a case we shall consider when we look at secret trusts (**6.43** et seq).

6.12 These considerations apply with even greater force to the case where A makes a self-declaration of trust in favour of C, for A cannot defraud himself, and appear to justify the result in *Rochefoucauld*, a self-declaration case. Boustead gratuitously promised the plaintiff to buy the estates for her benefit; thus he was the settlor of the trust, and the cautionary purpose should normally counsel the court to find no trust at all and allow him to renege, for it would be no fraud if Rochefoucauld did not receive this gratuitous benefit. The court's analysis of the facts is not well reported, but Boustead had, apparently, been giving effect to the express trust, upon which the plaintiff might have relied, and so in all the circumstances the decision was probably correct.

Disposition of subsisting equitable interests: Law of Property Act 1925, s 53(1)(c)

6.13 Section 53(1)(c) of the Law of Property Act 1925 provides:

A disposition of an equitable interest or trust subsisting at the time of the disposition must be in writing signed by the person disposing of the same, or by his agent thereunto lawfully authorised in writing or by his will.

The section refers to a 'disposition' of an existing equitable interest. We shall be concerned almost entirely with what counts as a disposition for purposes of the section. 'Equitable interest or trust' refers to equitable interests in both land and personalty (*Grey v IRC* (1960)). Notice also that by this section, unlike s 53(1)(b), a disposition must *be in* writing – if not in writing it is absolutely void, not merely unenforceable.

6.14 The section might be interpreted either broadly or narrowly. The predecessor section in the Statute of Frauds 1677 upon which it was based required writing for 'grants and assignments' of equitable interests; if that were taken as the intended meaning of 'disposition', then the section would have a fairly narrow compass. It would not apply to surrenders or releases of one's equitable interest, for there the beneficiary merely gives up his interest; he does not grant it to another. Similarly, a beneficiary's declaration of trust over his interest in favour of someone else would not be caught, since he does not assign or grant his equitable interest but retains it in order to give effect to the sub-trust. In *Grey v IRC* (1960) the HL unanimously held that that 'disposition' was to be given its natural meaning, which would appear to cover *every* transaction (not being an operation of law) by which any individual deals with his equitable interest under the trust. It has been the object of some criticism of this decision that the definition sections of the LPA 1925, which give a broad meaning to 'disposition' (s 205(1)(ii), but which defines 'equitable interest' in terms of interests in land only (s 205(1)(x)), were neither cited to the court or referred to in their Lordships' judgments. But as to 'disposition', the court did give a broad meaning to the section anyway, and as to the equation of equitable interest with an interest in land, the better view is that s 53(1)(c) should not be restricted to land in any case, for the interest in a trust is an interest in a fund (**2.32**), not in whatever properties constitute it. And as many trusts contain both land and personalty as investments, it would be silly to make the application of s 53(1)(c) depend upon whether, at the time any assignment is made, there happened to be some investment of the trust in land, such that an assignment would be invalid on 24 June, the day before the trustee sold an investment in land, but valid if it were made on 26 June, the day after. Beneficiaries are not expected to track the trustee's investments from day to day, after all.

6.15 How broad is broad? One could attempt to apply s 53(1)(c) not only to every act of the beneficiary by which he somehow deals with his interest, but also to the exercise by anyone of any power, such as discretion to distribute property under a discretionary trust, or the exercise of a power of appointment, which might affect the beneficiary's 'equitable interest'. So, for example, where a trustee exercised his discretion under a discretionary trust either to distribute property to Fred, or to give him nothing and all to Mabel, his sister, such an act such an act would be a disposition of Fred's and Mabel's equitable interests, and therefore subject to s 53(1)(c). Such a wide meaning would also presumably capture a decision of the trustee in the course of exercising his discretion to invest the trust property, for by investing in one way or another he would inevitably be to some degree enhancing the interests of the income beneficiaries over the capital beneficiaries, or *vice versa* (**10.3**).

6.16 This wider meaning of disposition is misconceived, practically and conceptually. It is misconceived as a matter of practice because it would subject to the rigours of s 53(1)(c) — remember, a transaction which does not comply with it is absolutely void — almost every exercise of any discretion by the trustee. Trustees must, of course, keep the trust accounts and therefore must record their decisions in any case, but to render void, perhaps years afterward, perfectly sound decisions made in the course of administering the trust for failure to be put in writing, where the writing down of the particular transaction itself provides no further assistance in determining whether the trust was properly carried out than do the trust accounts (recording payments of money and so on) seems to be a recipe for injustice. Take another rather horrible practical example, one which clearly points to why this wide reading is bad. Consider a gift 'Blackacre to Maria for life but if she takes up residence in the US, then to Priscilla'. By acting to take up residence in the US, Maria defeats her equitable interest in Blackacre, and so her act 'disposes' of her subsisting equitable interest. So in order for her disposition not to be void under s 53(1)(c), she must take up residence in the US *in writing*. Eh? Something has gone wrong conceptually for, obviously, not every act that an individual can take under the terms of a trust which will affect the interests, ie the overall position, of the beneficiaries under the trust, can even be done 'in writing'.

6.17 Consider again the section. It refers to a disposition of a *subsisting* equitable interest or trust. It therefore must refer to an existing interest under a trust. It therefore must refer to an existing interest under the specific trust under which it exists, which contours the interest in whatever ways it does. The interest, in other words, is defined by the trust, and so the interest is itself subject to whatever effects, whether positive or negative, it may be subject to under the terms of the trust. In short, the interest is whatever interest it is under the trust, warts and all. Therefore any acts by individuals rightly taken under the terms of the trust which affect a particular beneficiary's position do not *dispose* of his interest. They are actions which *give effect* to his interest, even if they put him in a worse position, for those possible negative effects are part and parcel of the interest he has. Thus a person who takes in default of appointment who loses any chance of taking because the power is exercised has not had his interest disposed of; having a defeasible interest under the terms of the trust, the possibility was realised and it was defeated. His interest, such as it was, was *fulfilled* in one of the ways it might have been, and the fact that it's hard cheese on him that it was fulfilled to his detriment does not alter that. Similarly with a trustee's exercise of any of his discretions under the trust in ways which will affect the beneficiaries' positions. The effects of these exercises of discretion are part and parcel of having a discretionary interest. By exercising these discretions, the interest is given effect to, not disposed of. And this proper interpretation must logically extend to the possible defeat of the beneficiary's interest, either because the interest is defeasible, as with Maria's life interest in Blackacre, or because the interest is subject to a power, such as a power of appointment. Indeed, a trustee may have the power under the trust to add or delete beneficiaries *tout court*, and any beneficiaries subject to this power of deletion must likewise regard the effect of the power as part and parcel of their interest.

6.18 Thus the better interpretation of the section is this: A 'disposition' of an equitable interest must refer to the act of someone who is capable of disposing of the interest as it is under the terms of the trust, that is, as a property right of a particular kind. The only person who can generally do that is the owner of the property right, or as the section contemplates, his agent. Thus the section applies to any dealing by the beneficiary with his interest under the trust. Not only does the cautionary purpose apply in any such case, but the purpose called 'evidential II' (**6.4**) does also: trusts can be extremely complicated, and a paper record of various transactions concerning the equitable interests is vitally important, so important that it would be justified if the law insisted upon writing as the price of their validity (see Green (1984)); the point here is that, since the beneficiary's interest is his own, he can deal with it without any consultation or even notice to the trustee, and the trustee's being able to insist upon seeing a writing before treating a beneficiary's assignee as now entitled to the interest is a secondary valuable consequence of the section's application. The cases, however, do not reveal such a straightforward approach, ie applying the section to any dealing by the beneficiary with his interest. We shall consider the different possible transactions in turn.

Assignment to a third party

6.19   Assignments are clearly caught by s 53(1)(c): if A, for example, holds an equitable income interest in shares under a trust, and wishes to assign it to X, he must do so in writing; a purported oral assignment is absolutely void.

Declaration of trust

6.20   It is generally accepted that where a beneficiary declares a trust of his equitable interest, creating a sub-trust, s 53(1)(c) does not apply. If the equitable interest is in land, any trust must be evidenced in writing by s 53(1)(b), but if the equitable interest is in personalty, such as a trust of company shares, an oral declaration of sub-trust appears to be valid. The rationale for the exception is that, while the declaration of the sub-trust does have the effect of extinguishing the beneficiary's *beneficial* interest in the trust, either in whole ('I declare that I hold my income interest on trust for Tim, Tom, and Tammy, in such proportions as I see fit') or in part ('I declare that I hold my income interest on trust for Trevor for life and then for myself absolutely'), and so in that sense is a disposition, it is not a disposition given that the beneficiary must *retain* his entire equitable title in order to give effect to the sub-trust. Thus, in the same way that a legal owner of property does not dispose of some 'pre-existing' equitable interest of his when declaring a trust (**2.4**), neither does the equitable owner dispose of any pre-existing equitable sub-trust interest when he declares a sub-trust. Thus the distinction is the difference between the *creation* of a new equitable interest over something one already has and must retain, and the *transfer* of something one has and which one thereby loses. Of course, when either a legal beneficial owner or an owner of an equitable interest declares a (sub-)trust they do shift, and thereby dispose of, their *beneficial* interest in the property concerned. But, and this cannot be repeated enough, a 'beneficial' interest is not equivalent to an 'equitable' interest (**2.4**), and it is to the latter that s 53(1)(c) refers. By creating the new trust interest both the legal owner and the equitable interest owner retain their original interest — they do not dispose of it, and to repeat the point, each must retain this pre-existing interest for it is on that property right that the new trust 'bites'.

6.21 An exception to the rule that s 53(1)(c) does not apply to declarations of trust is, however, widely accepted in the academic literature, to wit: if the beneficiary declares a *bare* sub-trust, ie 'I declare that I hold my life interest upon trust for Ted absolutely', then the declaration is void unless in writing. The idea is that the beneficiary is now a mere conduit between the trustee and the sub-beneficiary. The sub-beneficiary, it is said, should approach the trustee directly for his benefits, since it is pointless for the trustee to pay the beneficiary/sub-trustee and for him immediately to turn around and pay the sub-beneficiary. If this is right, then the declaration of a bare sub-trust amounts to an assignment of his equitable title and should count as a disposition under s 53(1)(c). Certain nineteenth-century cases, *Onslow v Wallis* (1849), *Re Lashmar* (1891), and *Grainge v Wilberforce* (1889), seem to suggest that the beneficiary/sub-trustee drops out of the picture in this way, although their authority for this proposition is disputed (Green (1984)). Where the trust is not a bare one, the sub-trustee will have to carry out the trust he creates, and he is said to have some 'active duties' to perform under the trust, such as the sub-trustee's discretion in the Tim, Tom, and Tammy example above. Thus, not being a mere conduit, he does not drop out of the picture, and therefore the sub-trust is not in essence an assignment, and so an active duty sub-trust is valid without writing.

6.22 The bare trust/active duties distinction seems a slender reed upon which to rest a difference in the requirement of writing. The idea seems to be that, because the beneficiary drops out of the picture when he creates a bare, or no active duties, sub-trust, he has effectively assigned his interest. But even if those nineteenth century authorities apply, it would seem that the beneficiary/sub-trustee drops out not by virtue of his own declaration of the sub-trust, but either by operation of law, which collapses the sub-trust giving the sub-beneficiary rights against the trustee automatically (the case law for which proposition, as noted above, is disputed), or because the sub-beneficiary leaps over his head to the trustee, taking his beneficial rights to the source, as it were, under the principle of *Saunders v Vautier* (**3.25**). But this seems wrong in principle. The beneficiary/sub-trustee could not himself insist on quitting the scene; the trustee could always choose to pay him and let him deal with his own sub-trust. After all, the trustee has no obligations under the sub-trust and so no duties to his beneficiary's sub-beneficiary. No solicitor in his right mind would advise the trustee to take over the trust of his sub-beneficiary on his own initiative; he would essentially be 'intermeddling' in a trust to which he was not appointed as a trustee, an act which would make him personally liable as a 'trustee de son tort' (**11.75**). If this is right then the beneficiary/sub-trustee does not, indeed cannot, drop out of the picture simply by declaring the sub-trust. In any case, distinguishing between these sub-trusts to alter writing requirements seems unmotivated in light of the various purposes for which formalities are imposed. Feel free, therefore, to argue that no sub-trusts should require writing, or that all should (as does Green (1984)) on the policy basis that any disposition of one's *beneficial* interest under the trust should require writing for the reasons given in **6.2-4**. Be careful, however, to mention these distinctions in an exam answer before you go on to dispute them, since they will have attached themselves limpet-like to the brain of the typical trusts law examiner.

Directions to the trustee to hold the equitable interest for another

6.23 If A directs his trustee to hold his equitable interest for a third party, it is generally accepted that this requires writing. This is in effect an assignment achieved, not by dealing with the third party directly, but by instructing the trustee henceforth to treat the third party as the beneficiary. *Grey v IRC* is usually cited as authority for this proposition, although as we shall see it actually concerned a different transaction. Nevertheless, the rationale for the application of s 53(1)(c) is straightforward. The beneficiary here, by his own direction, extinguishes his own equitable interest in favour of another, and so there is little to distinguish this from an assignment.

Directions to the trustee to hold the equitable interest on new trusts for another, and variations

6.24 Now we will discuss the 'big three' cases of this topic, *Grey v IRC*,

Vandervell v IRC (1967), and *Re Vandervell (No 2)* (1974). The courts made something of a hash of all of them, so it is difficult to say exactly what each decided, hence the 'and variations' above.

6.25   *Grey* involved an attempt to avoid paying *ad valorem* stamp duty on the setting up of a trust. *Ad valorem* stamp duty is a tax charged on documents which transfer the *beneficial* interest in property. For example when you transfer title to a house, *ad valorem* stamp duty is payable, '*ad valorem*' indicating that the amount of the duty is a percentage of the value of the property. At the time *Grey* was decided, stamp duty was payable on the transfer of shares. So, for example, if you transferred shares to Theresa on trust for Ben, the beneficial interest passed from you to Ben, and so *ad valorem* stamp duty was chargeable on the share transfer document. If by some means you could get the shares into a trust for Ben without having to use a document that transferred the beneficial title, then you could avoid paying *ad valorem* stamp duty. Furthermore, any transfer document which did not transfer a *beneficial* interest only attracted a fixed stamp duty of 50p. So a transfer of shares from one trustee to another, eg when a trustee retired, only cost 50p stamp duty, since the beneficial interest remained with the beneficiary throughout. Say you wanted to transfer shares to Theresa on trust for Ben, but avoid *ad valorem* stamp duty. Here's how you could do it: declare that you hold the shares on trust for Ben. Shares are personalty, so you can declare such a trust orally: no document, so no stamp duty. Now retire from the trust in favour of a new trustee, Theresa, and transfer the legal title in the shares to her. The share transfer will be stampable at 50p, not *ad valorem*, because it does not transfer the beneficial interest, which already lies with Ben. (The only catch in this scheme is that if you write a document recording your declaration of trust too soon after your oral declaration, the Revenue will regard the writing as a document which transfers the beneficial interest to Ben, and you will pay *ad valorem* stamp duty on it (*Cohen and Moore v IRC* (1933))). By this means, then, you could transfer the shares to Theresa on trust for Ben paying only 50p in stamp duty. The settlor in *Grey* was not so lucky.

6.26   In *Grey*, the settlor owned 18,000 company shares, which he desired to transfer in equal amounts into six trusts for his grandchildren which he had already set up. He transferred the shares to the two trustees of the grandchildren's trusts, but to hold the shares on bare trust for himself, and so, since the beneficial interest remained with him, the transfer document only attracted 50p stamp duty. He then orally directed the trustees to hold the shares in six separate and equal blocks upon the pre-existing grandchildren's trusts. Five weeks later the trustees executed a document declaring that they held the shares on the children's trusts. The Revenue argued that this document was stampable *ad valorem* because it transferred the beneficial interest in the shares from the settlor to the grandchildren. The trustees argued that the settlor's oral direction did so, and that such a direction did not require writing under s 53(1)(c) to be valid. As we have seen (**6.14**), the HL read 'disposition' broadly and unanimously decided that such a direction was a disposition within s 53(1)(c) and so needed to be in writing; therefore the oral direction was void. Somewhat strangely, the later writing in which the trustees stated that they held the shares on the grandchildren's trusts was regarded as validly transferring the settlor's interest; the case therefore also appears to stand for the proposition that a later writing may retroactively validate an invalid oral disposition. Although the settlor was not expressed as a party to the deed declaring the trusts, he did sign it, and so the participation of the beneficiary is necessary for this to work.

6.27 What precisely does the case decide? The settlor's direction was clearly not a direction to the trustees to hold his equitable interest for his grandchildren in equal shares. That would simply have made them equitable co-owners of the shares under the same bare trust. Neither was it a self-declaration of trust, in which he declared that he would henceforth hold the shares on trust for the grandchildren on trusts identical to the ones he had already set up for them with the trustees. Rather, he directed his trustees in their nominee capacity to divide the shares into equal lots and thereafter hold the lots as trustees of the grandchildren's trusts, each trust to receive one lot. The important point is that the trustees were not to continue to hold the shares as nominee trustees for new beneficiaries, but to hold the shares in their quite separate capacity as trustees of the grandchildren's trusts. Because the trustees of the grandchildren's settlement were the same two persons who were the settlor's nominee trustees, the legal title did not have to be transferred, but this should not obscure the point. A trustee is a separate trustee to each of the trusts he administers, and must keep the property of the different settlements separate. For example, in this case, the trustees would be required either to divide the share certificates equally into six lots, or use the share serial numbers, to allocate particular lots to each of the different grandchildren's settlements (see Green (1984)). At a minimum, therefore, the case decides that an oral direction to bare trustees to hold the trust property on different trusts which they also administer is void unless in writing, though a later writing may be effective as a 'belt and braces' device to cure a prior invalid oral direction. However Green (1984) is clearly right to argue that the case must also be authority for the proposition that a direction to bare trustees to transfer the property to other trustees on different trusts is similarly void unless in writing, since the situations are identical except for the fact that in the former the trustees of both trusts happen to be the same persons, and this is no reason to distinguish between the two. However, in *Vandervell v IRC* the HL unanimously decided that an oral direction to a trustee to transfer the legal title to shares to different trustees on new trusts was valid. The HL did not, apparently, realise they were deciding this, but they did.

6.28 Review the facts of *Vandervell v IRC* (**4.32-33**). The Revenue's first argument was that the first part of the transaction, the transfer of the shares held on bare trust for Vandervell by the Bank to the RCS on Vandervell's oral direction failed because this amounted to a disposition of his equitable interest under the bare trust, and therefore it needed to be in writing under s 53(1)(c). The point their Lordships thought they were deciding was this: Is A's oral direction to his trustee to transfer the legal title to shares held on bare trust to a third party absolutely, ie so the third party acquires the beneficial legal title to them, valid, or must it be in writing under s 53(1)(c)? They all decided that s 53(1)(c) did not apply and so the oral direction was valid.

6.29 The reasoning of their various Lordships was brief and does not repay intense scrutiny (see Green (1984)). For his part, Lord Upjohn said this:

> [I]f the intention of the beneficial owner in directing the trustee to transfer the legal estate to X is that X should be the beneficial owner I can see no reason for any further document or further words in the document assigning the legal estate also expressly transferring the beneficial interest; the greater includes the less. X may be wise to secure some evidence that the beneficial owner intended him to take the beneficial interest in case his beneficial title is challenged at a later date but it certainly cannot, in my opinion, be a statutory requirement that to effect its passing there must be writing under section 53(1)(c).

To the extent that Lord Upjohn is satisfied because the transfer of a legal title involves a document anyway, and so a 'further' document seems superfluous, he has forgotten that the rule of law he has just propounded will apply equally to chattels, which can be transferred out of the trust by delivery – the result is that a trustee may give away trust property on the basis of an oral direction with no writing whatsoever. Second, the point is not whether a legal transfer normally includes the beneficial interest – of course it does; the question is whether it does in this case, where the beneficiary has not expressed in writing his intention to give up the beneficial interest. Without any writing, why should we not presume that when the trustee, T, transfers the legal title to X, that X takes the legal title because he has been appointed as a new trustee to replace T, in which case the beneficiary's interest would, of course, remain attached to the property? Lord Upjohn's concern that X, the recipient, might want some sort of writing is interesting, since it indicates he is somewhat aware of the kind of trouble that oral dispositions can cause, not only the X's of the world, but beneficiaries, who might be defrauded on the basis of supposed oral directions, and trustees, who may later have to prove oral directions to show that their actions were not in breach of trust. (Lords Pearce and Donovan took the same line. Lord Wilberforce, in an interesting departure, decided that s 53(1)(c) did not apply on the basis of a quite different reading of the facts, roughly that the bank had effectively transferred the legal title to the shares to Vandervell before the transaction with the college, and so it was Vandervell himself, through his agent, who assigned the legal title to the college, not the bank as his trustee.)

6.30   You will recall, however, that their Lordships unanimously decided that the grant of the option from RCS to the trust company was Vandervell's own doing, somehow part of the arrangement he set in motion, which on any plausible version of the transaction gave rise to the shares being held by the RCS on trust to grant the option to the trust company or on equitable condition to grant the option to the trust company. That was why on the failure of the express trust of the trust company's interest in the option Vandervell was found to have the beneficial interest in it under an ART (**4.35** et seq). But if this is true, which it must be because that is the decision of the case, then the transfer by the bank of the shares was a transfer subject to some kind of equitable obligation or condition, that is, *subject to some trust*. In consequence, their Lordships' decision that the oral direction by Vandervell was valid

157

is authority for the proposition that an oral direction to a trustee to transfer property held on bare trust to another person *on trust* for a third party, is valid. This of course directly contradicts the broader basis of decision that Green (1984) argues is the right interpretation of *Grey*.

6.31 Most commentators, however, take Lord Upjohn at his word and it is textbook gospel to say that *Vandervell v IRC* decides only that an oral direction to a bare trustee to transfer the trust property to a third party absolutely for his own benefit is a valid disposition. This decision is commercially convenient, it is said, because it allows nominee trustees of shares, like brokers, to sell them on the oral directions of their beneficiaries. This justification is specious: the buying and selling of shares amounts to the trustee's exercise of his power of investment (**10.2**), and in general trustees never have to get the written direction of the beneficiaries to manage the trust property in this way, that is, s 53(1)(c) does not apply, because these 'dispositions' of the trust property are not the disposition of anyone's equitable interest, but merely dealings with the trust corpus in which those equitable interests lie. Such a transaction with the trust property is made by exercising an *administrative* power or discretion, not a *dispositive* one (**2.16**). The only difference the trust's being a bare trust makes is that the beneficiary has the right to tell the trustee how to exercise any of the powers he has in virtue of being the legal owner of the trust property, including the power to exchange trust property for other property. The exercise of this administrative power, then, has nothing whatever to do with the trustee's defeating or extinguishing a beneficiary's interest by *giving* the trust property away, or extinguishing part or all of the beneficiary's entitlement under the trust (whatever its specific property) on the basis of oral instructions. (For a contrary view, see Nolan (2002), who thinks oral instructions of both the administrative and dispositive kind should be treated alike in the case of a bare trust). As with the bare sub-trust/non-bare sub-trust distinction above, feel free to make these points, but in an exam recite the accepted catechism to begin with.

6.32 The Vandervell saga continued in *Re Vandervell (No 2)*. Once the Revenue made its claim for the surtax, Vandervell and the trust company decided to exercise the option. The trustees used £5,000 from the children's trust and purchased the shares. The trustees wrote to the Revenue informing it that the shares were now held under the children's trust. As he had done for the RCS, Vandervell then exercised his control over his company and had various dividends declared on the shares over the next few years, amounting to more than a million pounds; in doing so he intended to provide for his children, and subsequently wrote a will leaving them nothing more. After his death, the executors of his will claimed that none of the preceding transactions had worked to displace Vandervell's beneficial interest in the option, nor therefore in the shares purchased through its exercise; thus the dividends declared on those shares were his property in equity as well; hence the executors claimed that the trust company held the shares on trust for Vandervell's estate.

6.33 The CA decided that a valid trust had been declared in favour of the children, and so the dividends properly belonged in the children's trust. The CA gave a number of reasons, most of which are insupportable. The only plausible one, and pertinent to our discussion, is in this passage from Lord Denning MR's decision:

> A resulting trust for the settlor is born and dies without writing at all. It comes into existence whenever there is a gap in the beneficial ownership. It ceases to exist whenever that gap is filled by someone becoming beneficially entitled. As soon as the gap is filled by the creation or declaration of a valid trust, the resulting trust comes to an end. In this case, before the option was exercised, there was a gap in the beneficial ownership. So there was a resulting trust for Mr Vandervell. But, as soon as the option was exercised and the shares registered in the trustee's name, there was created a valid trust of the shares in favour of the children's settlement. Not being a trust of land, it could be created without any writing. A trust of personalty can be created without writing.

6.34 Hayton ((2001b), 86) and Green (1984) both assume that what makes Lord Denning's decision even possibly correct is a finding on the facts (however erroneous) that the trust company had the power to declare trusts of the option or shares purchased with it; by exercising the option and holding the shares on trust for the children the trust company declared a trust that 'filled the gap' in the beneficial interest, which declaration the CA found did not attract the requirements of s 53(1)(c). On this view the case has a tinily narrow ambit, to wit: where a trustee holds property upon an almost bare trust for a settlor, but there is (oddly, it must be said) one term of the trust that gives the trustee the power to declare new trusts of the property, his exercise of that power need not be in writing.

6.35 But this interpretation cannot stand with the facts of *Vandervell v IRC*, nor with Lord Denning's own words: Vandervell held under an *ART*, an automatic resulting trust – a trust which simply cannot contain any special powers of this kind for the trustees or anyone else. An ART is the barest of bare trusts. So even if on the facts the express trust Vandervell had intended the trustee company to hold the option under gave the trustee company the power to declare new trusts, that trust failed for uncertainty, and nothing of it lingered in the ART that arose upon its failure. Rather, the CA decision, per Lord Denning MR at least, appears to be that because Vandervell was fully aware of and assented to the trustee company's exercise of the option to hold the shares on the children's trust, his assent amounted to an oral declaration of trust. So the case is authority for the proposition that where a settlor transfers personal property on trust, yet fails to make an effective oral declaration of trust, so that an ART in his favour arises, his subsequent oral declaration of trust is valid, his beneficial interest under the ART not requiring to be disposed of in writing under s 53(1)(c). This decision is not in conflict with *Grey*, since there the settlor intentionally transferred property on *express* bare trust for himself. In *Re Vandervell (No 2)*, by contrast, Vandervell had tried to do what was perfectly legitimate, ie transfer personalty to a trustee on orally declared trusts, only the oral declaration failed for uncertainty. If the settlor remedies the situation by declaring trusts which are certain, why should that declaration require writing when the first did not? This, indeed, would appear to be the one case where an exception to s 53(1)(c) is justified, since one might say that the second, valid, declaration is part and parcel of one transaction in which the holder of legal title to personal property (or the equivalent, assuming that Vandervell had the right to transfer the legal title to shares by orally directing the bare trustee bank to do so, ie that *Vandervell v IRC* is rightly decided) transfers it on trust – and that, of course, is the one case of an oral declaration of trust which is perfectly valid, there being no equivalent to s 53(1)(b) which applies to personalty. This view is fortified by the analysis at **4.50**. One receives the beneficial interest under an ART not as a beneficiary — the interest does not 'prosult' to one as someone intended to take as a beneficiary — it truly 'results' to one *as settlor*. Therefore it makes sense to think that one deals with this interest as the settlor, ie declaring the trust, hopefully successfully this time, not 'disposing' of one's beneficial interest as an interest properly established under a trust, in which case, the formality requirements for declaring a trust of personalty should apply, ie none.

Releases, surrenders, and disclaimers

6.36 A release and a surrender are the same thing. A beneficiary surrenders his interest when he clearly indicates that he no longer wishes to benefit under the trust. If the beneficiary has a vested interest, for example a life interest in shares, what follows is an ART in favour of the settlor, if the trust is *inter vivos*, or in favour of the residuary legatees, if the trust is testamentary. If the beneficiary has only a contingent interest, eg he is the object of a discretionary trust or power of appointment, then his surrender just removes his name from the list of possible objects; there is no ART because he has no vested interest in any property upon which it could operate. Section 53(1)(c) should apply to surrenders or releases, since they clearly amount to the beneficiary's disposing of his entire equitable interest in favour of others, even if he does not know or care who will benefit under the trust by his surrender. There is, however, no good authority on the point, almost certainly because any careful trustee will insist that a beneficiary surrendering his interest will do so in writing. *IRC v Buchanan* (1958) is perhaps of some small assistance. There the CA interpreted 'disposition' as used in the Finance Act 1943 to include the exercise by a beneficiary of a special power under a trust to surrender her life interest in favour of her children.

6.37 A person *disclaims* an interest under a trust when he refuses any beneficial interest from the outset. The only authority for the application of s 53(1)(c) to disclaimers is *Re Paradise Motor Co Ltd* (1968). The CA held that 'a disclaimer operates by way of avoidance, and not by way of disposition'. A person disclaiming 'avoids', that is, never obtains any equitable interest, and therefore never acquires anything to dispose of: s 53(1)(c) has no application. This characterisation of disclaimers seemed entirely *ad hoc*, to avoid one more complication in a case in which the beneficial ownership to shares had to be determined on vague and ill-remembered oral testimony, and the authority the court referred to (*Re Stratton's Disclaimer* (1958), CA) actually takes the *opposite* line: that a beneficiary takes the benefit of an equitable interest from the moment the gift becomes effective in his favour, and therefore his disclaimer *does* amount to a disposition extinguishing a right he presently enjoys. Little weight, then, should be given to the decision. Certainly the purposes behind the section apply just as much to disclaimers as to other dispositions, and 'disposition' under s 205(1)(2) LPA comprises a disclaimer.

Agreements to assign or vary equitable interests for consideration

6.38 As we have seen (**5.3**), in the case of specifically enforceable contracts for the transfer or creation of rights in property, equity will impose a contractual constructive trust on the grantor of the interest. This doctrine operates just the same in the case of assignments of equitable interests where the interest is 'unique' in the sense that a failure to receive it under the contract cannot be adequately compensated by money damages. *Always* remember (some judges do not, eg Lord Wilberforce in *Chinn v Collins* (1981)) that this constructive trust depends on the availability of specific enforcement of the contract, and this in turn depends on whether the property is unique in this way. For example, private company shares are, since they cannot be freely purchased on the open market, but public company shares are not.

6.39 In the case of an agreement to assign equitable interests under a trust, the contractual constructive trust that arises is a constructive sub-trust. The beneficiary holds his equitable interest on constructive sub-trust for the purchaser, subject to the right to retain the interest until the purchaser pays up; until he does, the beneficiary can refuse to assign the underlying equitable title. When the purchaser does pay up, the beneficiary holds his equitable interest on bare sub-trust for him. If you believe in the view that a bare sub-trustee drops out of the picture (**6.21-6.22**), then this sub-trust collapses, and the equitable interest moves without any assignment by the beneficiary. If you demur from this view (as you should), the purchaser can insist upon the beneficiary assigning the equitable interest to him in writing. In either case, once the purchaser pays for the interest, he is the full beneficial owner of it and may enforce this interest with the full weight of equity behind him.

6.40 In *Oughtred v IRC* (1960) the contractual constructive trust was employed in an attempt to avoid stamp duty. Mrs Oughtred and her son Peter both held interests in a trust of private company shares. They agreed to vary their equitable interests, as a result of which Mrs Oughtred would acquire the entire beneficial interest in the shares under a bare trust; in return she would transfer a separate block of shares to Peter. Following the agreement, Mrs Oughtred and Peter executed a deed which declared that Mrs Oughtred now had the entire beneficial interest in the shares. The trustees then formally transferred the legal title to the shares to her absolutely. The question before the court was whether the formal share transfer attracted *ad valorem* stamp duty, or only a 50p duty because by virtue of the constructive trust, she already beneficially owned the shares in equity. The HL majority held that the formal share transfer attracted *ad valorem* stamp duty, but largely on what might be called the 'principles of stamp duty law'. Lord Jenkins held that while the purchaser under a specifically enforceable agreement has a proprietary interest of some sort, that does not prevent the subsequent transfer of the property which completes the transaction from being stampable *ad valorem*. After all, *ad valorem* stamp duty was payable (and remains payable) on documents transferring title to land even though the purchaser acquires the beneficial interest when the contract is agreed under the paradigm example of a contractual constructive trust. Lord Radcliffe dissented, accepting that upon the agreement being made Mrs Oughtred became the absolute owner in equity, and so felt that the share transfer did not transfer any beneficial interest.

6.41 The view that the constructive trust arising on the specifically enforceable agreement is sufficient to create an enforceable equitable interest has been endorsed since, outside the stamp duty context, by Megarry J in *Re Holt's Settlement* (1969), where there was an agreement to vary the interests under a trust, and by a majority of the CA in *DHN Food Distributors Ltd v Tower Hamlets London Borough Council* (1976) where the interest in question was in land. Most recently, the CA in *Neville v Wilson* (1997) held that the equitable interest in private company shares could pass by virtue of a contractual constructive trust arising on a specifically enforceable, though oral, agreement. In that case the equitable interest in certain shares was held by a company — the legal title in them was vested in two nominees purely for the purpose of qualifying them as directors. The company was subsequently wound up, but though the equitable interest in these shares was clearly an asset of the company it was never dealt with according to the shareholders' winding-up agreement — indeed, the nominee trustees were thereafter treated by all concerned as the beneficial owners of the shares, taking the dividends for themselves, and so on. Nevertheless, trustees they were, and so the trial judge concluded that the equitable title, as an asset of the company never transferred, remained with the company, which was of course now defunct having been wound up. Since by the time of trial the defunct company could not be re-instated as a legal entity, the result was that no one owned the equitable interest in the shares, and so it passed as bona vacantia to the crown. On appeal it was argued that the shareholders' winding-up agreement gave rise to a constructive trust over the shares in favour of the shareholders. After reviewing the decisions in *Oughtred*, the CA agreed, reasoning that:

> So far as it is material to the present case, what subsection (2) says is that subsection (1)(c) does not affect the creation or operation of implied or constructive trusts. Just as in *Oughtred v IRC* the son's oral agreement created a constructive trust in favour of the mother, so here each shareholder's oral or implied agreement created an implied or constructive trust in favour of the other shareholders. Why then should subsection (2) not apply? No convincing reason was suggested in argument and none has occurred to us since. Moreover, to deny its application in this case would be to restrict the effect of general words when no restriction is called for, and to lay the ground for fine distinctions in the future. With all the respect which is due to those who have thought to the contrary, we hold that subsection (2) applies to an agreement such as we have in this case.

Reform of s 53(1)(c)

6.42 The preceding look at the cases suggests that a statutory reform making clear those dispositions to which a writing requirement should apply is a good idea. It might also be suggested that, in analogy with s 136 LPA (the assignment of debts), for an assignment of an equitable interest to be valid notice of the assignment must be given, in writing, to the trustee.

Testamentary trusts: Wills Act 1837, s 9

6.43 Section 9 of the Wills Act 1837 provides:

> 9. No will shall be valid unless —
> (a) it is in writing, and signed by the testator, or by some other person in his presence and by his direction; and
> (b) it appears that the testator intended by his signature to give effect to the will; and
> (c) the signature is made or acknowledged by the testator in the presence of two or more witnesses present at the same time; and
> (d) each witness either —
> (i) attests and signs the will; or
> (ii) acknowledges his signature,
> in the presence of the testator (but not necessarily in the presence of any other witness),
> but no form of attestation shall be necessary.

The section applies to any testamentary gift, including testamentary trusts. Unless properly signed and attested, an intended testamentary gift fails. Formalities are of obvious importance here, as a will takes effect when the testator is dead, so we will not hear any oral evidence from him as to his intentions. (It is worthwhile reviewing **2.61-65** at this point.)

Non-testamentary gifts giving an interest on death

6.44   Not every gift by which the donee takes an interest on the donor's death is testamentary. For example, I can declare that I hold Blackacre on trust for myself for life, and then for you. My personal representatives will hold Blackacre for you from my death. This *inter vivos* trust immediately vests in you a future interest in Blackacre. For a gift to be testamentary it must be *revocable* and *ambulatory*. A valid testamentary gift, ie one in a will, can be revoked or amended by the testator any time before his death, though he must do so in writing in compliance with s 9. A document which amends a will in part is called a 'codicil' and becomes part of the testator's whole will.

6.45   'Ambulatory' means that a will, while valid when properly made, just walks along without immediate effect, only operating when the testator dies. Thus gifts which would have been valid had they been made *inter vivos* when the testator made his will may fail at the time of his death, because in the interval things may happen to his legatees, to him, or to his property. A gift 'lapses' if the intended legatee predeceases the testator; the property goes back into the deceased's estate, and from there either to the residuary legatees or intestate successors. When a testator makes a will, he may leave specific gifts, eg of his car to X or his house to Y, or pecuniary legacies, eg £10,000 to Z. The testator might be rich when he makes his will, but bankrupt when he dies. Before any property is distributed under a will, all of the testator's creditors must be paid, and some of his property might have to be sold to do this. Thus the particular items of property and the total wealth distributable under the will can never be ascertained until his estate is administered. A specific gift *adeems*, ie fails, if the testator's estate does not include the specific property; if for example, he sold his car then any specific gift of the car in his will fails. A gift *abates* when a legatee's gift is proportionately reduced because there is insufficient property to satisfy all the testator's gifts. Thus a pecuniary legacy may abate anywhere down to zero if the testator is not as rich at his death as he thought he would be when he made his will.

6.46 Even if the *inter vivos* trust of Blackacre above is made revocable, it is not truly ambulatory since until revoked it cannot lapse by reason of your pre-deceasing me – if you die first then your successors will take the fee simple in Blackacre when I die. Nor will the gift adeem or abate if it turns out that I am deeply in debt when I die – the beneficial interest in Blackacre has been disposed of *inter vivos*, and cannot form part of my estate.

6.47 Besides *inter vivos* trusts giving an interest which vests on the death of a settlor, property can 'go' to others on one's death by operation of the right of survivorship on jointly held property (**1.19**). Thus if I transfer Blackacre to you and me as joint owners, or set up a joint bank account in our names, and I then die before you, you become the sole owner as my joint interest just disappears on my death. I can also take out a life insurance policy naming you as the beneficiary; the policy will pay out to you on my death. In *Re Danish Bacon Co Ltd Staff Pension Fund* (1971) Megarry J held that the right of an employee to nominate someone who will receive death in service benefits under a pension fund was not testamentary and therefore not subject to s 9 requirements. Megarry J also held that such nominations do not require writing under s 53(1)(c), since the nominator is not disposing of any subsisting equitable interest – the benefit only arises on his death. (See also *Baird v Baird* (1990).)

Informal testamentary trusts: secret and half secret trusts

6.48 Secret and half secret trusts are testamentary trusts which fail to comply with the Wills Act because they are not disclosed or disclosed fully in a valid will. Typically, a fully secret trust (FST) arises when T appears to take an absolute gift under A's will, but T has informally agreed with A to hold the property on trust for B. Secret trusts, however, can arise when there is no will at all: If T is A's intestate successor, he may also informally agree with A to hold the property he gets on trust for B (*Sellack v Harris* (1708)). After A's death, T, whether a legatee under A's will or A's intestate successor, is in the position to fraudulently deny the informal trust and keep the property for himself .

6.49 A half secret trust (HST) is one in which the existence of the trust is apparent on the face of the will, but the terms of the trust are not disclosed, eg 'I leave Blackacre to X on trusts which I have communicated to him'. Unlike the fully secret trust case, X is not in the position to deny the trust, and so cannot fraudulently take the property himself, for he is clearly a trustee for someone, and of course equity will not allow him to take the property beneficially.

6.50 Why should anyone wish to make informal testamentary trusts of this kind? One possibility in the case of fully secret trusts (FSTs) is simply that the legatee or intestate successor has persuaded the testator to do so, in order to perpetrate a fraud. The legatee might say, 'Don't give your property in a will – that will only lead to a great deal of squabbling in court – leave it all to me and I will do what you wish without fear of legal challenge.' Generally, however, secret trusts are intentionally created by the testator to ensure the secrecy of testamentary gifts. Since wills must be proved in a Court of Probate the contents of a will become public, and any person or member of the tabloid press can buy a copy for a trivial sum. (A brisk business was done in Princess Diana's will.) Testators wishing to provide for their secret lovers or other objects which would embarrass them or rather, harm their posthumous reputations, may instead of leaving them property by will leave property absolutely to a friend who agrees to hold the property on trust secretly for these beneficiaries. If the testator regards the obligation the legatee undertakes as only a moral obligation, and the legatee is trustworthy, then legal enforcement is not required. The imposition of such moral obligations does not interfere with the effect or policy of the Wills Act, for in law the legatee becomes the absolute owner under the will, and moral obligations to the deceased do not upset that. The question is whether and in what circumstances informal promises to a testator should be given legal effect? Should the enforcement be restricted to the case where the testator is truly a victim of an intentional fraud, or should a testator's scheme to create a secret testamentary gift, colluded in by his secret trustee, also be enforced despite the Wills Act? Originally, it appeared that equity would enforce the promise as a trust obligation over the property only in the case of actual fraud. Equity would not allow a fraudulent legatee to plead that the trust was invalid under the Act on the basis 'equity will not allow a statute enacted to prevent fraud to be used as an instrument of fraud'. This is the 'fraud theory' of the enforcement of secret trusts, but the leading nineteenth century case, *McCormick v Grogan* (1869), HL, is ambiguous as to what counts as fraud.

6.51 In *McCormick*, the testator left all his property to his friend Grogan. On his deathbed, he told Grogan that he had left all his property in his will to him, to which Grogan replied, 'Is that right?'. The testator also told him where to find the will and a letter with it. There was no further communication between the testator and Grogan. The letter to Grogan detailed a large number of gifts in pursuit of which he desired Grogan to apply the money, although he left much to Grogan's discretion. Grogan did not make all of the detailed gifts, and one non-recipient, McCormick, sought to have Grogan declared a secret trustee. The HL refused to do so, but their Lordships' conception of the fraud in response to which equity will make the legatee a trustee is ambiguous. Their reasons suggest either that the necessary fraud is (1) a fraudulent scheme on the defendant's part *to induce* the property owner either to make a will in the defendant's favour (or not revoke a will in his favour), or refrain from making a will because the defendant will take on his intestacy, in which the defendant misrepresents his true intentions, falsely promising to carry out the owner's wishes, thereby acquiring the owner's property on his death for his own benefit; or (2) merely the defendant's 'fraudulent' refusal, when he receives the property on the owner's death, to comply with an agreement with the original owner upon which the owner relied in disposing of the property as he did. (1) is obviously much narrower, and amounts to saying that a testator who attempts to make informal testamentary gifts will by operation of the Wills Act fail to do so unless he was fraudulently induced to avoid making a valid testamentary gift by a legatee or intestate successor who benefits from the fraud. (2) essentially allows the testator to opt out of the strictures of the Wills Act; so long as he effectively communicates his testamentary intentions to a legatee or intestate successor, who agrees to carry them out, this joint endeavour to defy the Wills Act will succeed because equity will enforce the agreement against the legatee.

6.52 Whatever the actual state of the authorities in 1869 which led to their Lordships' ambiguous characterisation, (2) is the way the law has developed. As stated by Lord Sterndale MR in *Re Gardner* (1920):

> The obligation upon the [secret trustee] seems to me to arise from this, that he takes the property in accordance with and upon an understanding to abide by the wishes of the testatrix, and if he were to dispose of it in any other way he would be committing a breach of trust, or as it has been called in some of the cases a fraud. I do not think it matters what you call it. The breach of trust or the fraud would arise when he attempted to deal with the money contrary to the terms on which he took it.

6.53 The recent case of *Re Snowden* (1979) provides a good example of the current ambit of the court's willingness to enforce FSTs. There an indecisive testatrix, after making various particular gifts in her will, left the residue of her estate to her brother, he 'knowing her wishes' for the money. Her brother died six days after she did, and the question was whether on very insufficient evidence a trust of the residue was undertaken by him. Megarry VC found that the testatrix had only imposed a moral, not a legal, obligation upon her brother, so there was no secret trust. However, he pointed out that only some cases of secret trust involved the possibility of fraud, and there was none here – the secret trustee could not personally benefit by any fraud, for he had died – the question was whether there was a secret trust which would take the property out of his estate on death. While the burden of proof that a secret trust exists lies on the person who asserts its existence, in cases where there is no fraud the normal civil standard of proof, ie what is more likely on the balance of probabilities, applies.

6.54 The state of the law now is well put by Hayton ((2001b), pp 103-104):

> Testators, today, who do not want their testamentary wishes to become public by admission to probate as part of their will can take advantage of the doctrine of secret trusts to make provision for mistresses, illegitimate children, relatives whom they do not wish to appear to be helping or organisations which they do not wish to appear to be helping. Indecisive, aged testators can also leave everything by will absolutely to their solicitors, from time to time calling upon or phoning their solicitors with their latest wishes.

6.55 Equity's enforcement of secret trusts has, therefore, allowed testators to make informal, even oral, testamentary dispositions in flat defiance of the Wills Act; to opt out of it, as it were. The only 'fraud' necessary is the legatee's refusal to carry out his agreement with the testator, the agreement being to carry out an informal testamentary disposition so that the testator can bypass the provisions of the Wills Act. In its confused appreciation of fraudulent behaviour in this context equity allows a testator to make an informal will just because he uses a human instrument, ie his legatee, to do so. By reposing his informal, even oral, will in this human vessel he can succeed where another testator committing his wishes to an unattested paper cannot, because the unattested paper 'cannot commit fraud', even though the human legatee and the unattested paper are fulfilling exactly the same function. While perhaps a bit extreme, it is perhaps relevant to draw upon the law's traditional view that where property is transferred under an illegal agreement, one should allow the property interest to lie where it falls (**4.28**). A strict application of this principle to the 'illegality' of intentionally avoiding the Wills Act would leave the beneficial title of the property in the hands of the legatee and defeat the testator's intentions.

Fraud and HSTs

6.56   The trustee of an HST can lie about the trust upon which he holds the property, telling the world it was for his own mistress rather than the testator's, for instance, but he cannot deny there is any trust and take the property for himself like the fully secret trustee can, as he is a trustee on the face of the will. As a result, because the court would only get round the Wills Act in the case of fraud, it was not settled until the 1929 HL decision in *Blackwell v Blackwell* whether HSTs should be enforced. The gift in *Blackwell* was as follows: 'I give and bequeath to my friends … the sum of twelve thousand pounds free of all duties upon trust to invest the same as they in their uncontrolled discretion shall think fit and to apply the income and interest arising therefrom yearly and every year for the purposes indicated by me to them …'. The appellants argued that where the trustee was named in the will, there could be no fraud under any version of the fraud theory in *McCormick v Grogan*; the question was merely one of 'for whom is the trust property held'; if there is no further validly expressed intention which specifies the trust terms, then the trust fails and the trustee holds under an ART for the residuary legatees. The HL disagreed, allowing parol evidence to prove the terms of the trust. The HL adopted a new variation on 'fraud'. According to Lord Buckmaster, the defendant's fraud is not falsely to induce the testator to make a gift in the defendant's favour, nor to refuse to comply with his promise to the testator, but to cheat the testator's intended donees of their intended benefits – the fraud is a fraud on the secret beneficiaries.

6.57   This reasoning is circular. As Sheridan (1951) points out, to consider the fraud as a fraud 'on the beneficiaries' begs the question. There is no fraud on an intended beneficiary if a gift intended for him 'fails' for formal invalidity, for if it is an invalid trust, he is not a beneficiary. The question is whether a half-secret trust is a valid or invalid *means of* making someone a beneficiary despite the Wills Act. If it is not, then there is no fraud. By thinking of the intended beneficiaries *as* properly entitled beneficiaries from the outset, is to assume what needs to be shown, ie that failing to enforce a half-secret trust abets a fraud.

The 'dehors the will' theory of HSTs

6.58 Viscount Sumner provided a further reason for the result, articulating what is now conventionally called the '*dehors* (ie outside) the will' theory of secret trusts:

> The limits, beyond which the rules as to unspecified trusts must not be carried, have often been discussed. A testator cannot reserve to himself a power of making future unwitnessed dispositions by merely naming a trustee and leaving the purposes of the trust to be supplied afterwards, nor can a legatee give testamentary validity to an unexecuted codicil by accepting an indefinite trust, never communicated to him in the testator's lifetime. … To hold otherwise would indeed be to 'give the go-by' to the requirement of the Wills Act, because he did not choose to comply with them. It is communication of the purpose to the legatee, coupled with the acquiescence or promise on his part, that removes the matter from the provisions of the Wills Act and brings it within the law of trusts, as applied in this instance to trustees, who happen to be legatees.

Under the '*dehors* the will' theory, secret trusts are regarded as *inter vivos* declarations of trust by the testator; the only atypical feature is that the trusts are not constituted, ie the property is not transferred into the hands of the trustee, until the testator's death, through his will. Therefore secret trusts operate outside the will, and therefore the Wills Act has no application.

6.59 The *dehors* the will theory is fundamentally unsound. In the first place, the theory should be called the '*dehors* the Wills Act' theory to reflect what it means. The argument is that secret trusts are *inter vivos* trusts, therefore not testamentary, therefore not within the ambit of the Wills Act. Of course secret trusts are outside the *will*: wholly in the case of FSTs, partly in the case of HSTs. But that entails nothing whatsoever about the application of the Wills Act – every informal testamentary disposition is outside the will; if it were a formally valid testamentary disposition it would *be* a will, or part of one. So the theory depends upon establishing that secret trusts are not testamentary dispositions at all, so the formality requirements of the Wills Act simply do not apply.

6.60 But, alas, secret trusts *are* testamentary dispositions. They are perfectly revocable by the testator – he can either revoke the trust *per se* by communicating with his secret trustee and cancelling or modifying the arrangement, or more simply, he can execute another will deleting or modifying the gift to his legatee (or by just writing a will if the fully secret trust operates on intestacy), thus ensuring that the 'inter vivos' trust he declared is never constituted. Secondly, and more fundamentally, such a trust simply cannot be an effective inter vivos trust because in order to be effective the testator would be declaring a trust of 'future' property, and such a declaration is invalid, ie creates no trust. Future property just refers to property which does not exist yet. Now you might think that if I own Blackacre, and I tell you that I'm giving it to you in my will to hold on trust for Albert, then what's wrong with that? Blackacre exists doesn't it? The point however is that I'm not declaring a trust over Blackacre now – I could do that, but that would *take Blackacre out of my estate on death.* But I have not done that. I am declaring a trust over property which may or may not be in my estate on death. Even if I do my utmost to ensure that Blackacre will be in my estate, it may turn out that I have to sell it before I die, or I may die in such debt that Blackacre will have to be sold by my executors. This, of course, is even more obvious in the case of a pecuniary legacy, eg a secret trust of £5,000. There is a further problem in the case of an *inter vivos* trust of a pecuniary legacy: unless you actually identify the actual money, ie the very notes and coins, the trust fails for uncertainty of subject matter. A person cannot just say, 'I now hold £5,000 on trust for you', even if he's worth millions; before the trust is valid he must segregate or otherwise identify the money which is the property of the trust (**7.53** et seq). Clearly, there's no way of doing that now with money only identified some indefinite time in the future by executors following their administration of the estate. Therefore a legatee's hope of receiving any property of any kind under a will is considered by the law to be a mere *spes*, Latin for a mere expectancy, which one can never count upon getting. As a testator, I am in no better position in this respect before I die than a legatee. So the fact of the matter is that secret trusts are imposed over property which will only be ascertained upon the administration of the testator's estate, and are subject to ademption and abatement like any other such gifts (for an interesting example, see *Re Maddock* (1902)). They are, therefore, ambulatory, and therefore, testamentary. Of course the Wills Act applies to them. The *dehors* the will theory is just an attempt to cloak the embarrassing jam equity has got itself into with its willingness to flout the Wills Act.

6.61 The theory has also proved to have confused a court in a nearby area. In *Gold v Hill* (1999) the court purported to treat the nomination of a beneficiary under a life insurance policy, the beneficiary having agreed to hold the insurance proceeds on trust for the nominator's wife and child, as a situation analogous to a secret trust. The analogy to, much less the application of, the doctrine of secret trusts is misconceived. The nomination of a beneficiary under a life insurance policy is not a testamentary gift (**6.47**), but akin to the assignment of a contractual right to a benefit. It is therefore not caught by the Wills Act, and any declaration of trust or undertaking of the trust by the nominee concerns the creation of a trust over a right which is personal property, so no formality requirements apply. Therefore, there is no need to import a doctrine whose purpose is to overcome the failure to comply with the *formality* requirements of *testamentary* gifts. The only reason one would apply the doctrine mistakenly in this way would be to assume that all informal undertakings to hold property on trust would normally fail, and so one needs some kind of 'dehors the normal rules' equitable intervention to save the day, which is clearly false. The CA in *Kasperbaur v Griffiths* (1997) stated *obiter*, quite correctly, that the doctrine of secret trusts has no application to nominations of beneficiaries under life insurance policies.

6.62 It is submitted that the true reason for the decision in *Blackwell* has nothing really to do with the court's realising a new 'dehors' justification for secret trusts, but is the obvious *pragmatic* reason, here stated by Viscount Sumner:

> In [both fully and half secret trusts] the testator's wishes are incompletely expressed in his will. Why should equity, over a mere matter of words, give effect to them in one case and frustrate them in the other?

In other words, though there might be a valid *juridical* basis for enforcing FSTs but not HSTs, ie that there's no possibility of fraud in any meaningful sense in the latter, the different rules would be in *pragmatic* conflict, ie, the law would look like an ass. Once equity has sold the Wills Act up the river by allowing testators to give it 'the go-by' with FSTs, it seems rather irrational to stop there and deny equity's enforcement to HSTs, and might well lead to apparent injustice, since from the testator's perspective the decision to use the words 'on trust' in his will can hardly seem to him to be of much consequence; furthermore, it would seem strange if a person who complied with the Wills Act as much as he could while keeping his gifts secret, by declaring in his will that the gift was held on trust, should be in a worse position than one who keeps everything secret. The result is, then, that both FSTs and HSTs, if properly created, are formally invalid testamentary trusts which equity will enforce.

6.63 Although the '*dehors* the will' theory is insupportable, certain decisions appear to depend upon it. In *Re Young* (1951), the testator's chauffeur was to receive a gift under an HST, but he had also attested the will; under s 15 of the Wills Act 1837, gifts to attesting witnesses and their spouses fail (attesting witnesses must be able to give unbiased evidence about the validity of the will's execution, and if a person or their spouse is to receive property under the will, that might bias him in favour of validity). Dankwerts J held that the chauffeur did not take 'under the will', so was able to receive the gift under the HST. Section 15 does not normally apply to trustees in a will for they receive no *beneficial* interest (*Cresswell v Cresswell* (1868)), but presumably, if the *dehors* the will theory applies, s 15 should defeat both an HST and an FST if the trustee attests the will. This may appear a bit odd in the case of the HST, for the trustee is identified as a trustee on the face of the will. But the *dehors* story says that he is not a trustee *under the will*, so s 15 should apply to him as much as to a trustee of an FST. Of course, one might argue that s 15 should not apply to any trustee, secret or not, since none take a beneficial interest, but such a view cannot stand alongside *Re Young*, for that would be to have it both ways.

6.64 If secret trusts are *inter vivos* trusts, then s 53 should apply; in particular, s 53(1)(b) should apply to secret trusts of land. North J accepted *obiter* in *Re Baillie* (1886) that formal requirements would apply to an HST of land; An oral FST of land was found to be valid in *Ottaway v Norman* (1972), although it must be stressed that the formalities point was not raised.

6.65 An alternative version of the '*dehors*' theory was advanced by Romer J in *Re Gardner* (1923), which is that the secret *trustee* is the one that declares an *inter vivos* trust over the property he shall receive under the will; that of course, is even more obviously ineffective as a declaration of trust over a mere *spes*. Such a declaration is at most a declaration of a future intention, and a mere intention will not be enforced by equity. Romer J decided that the interest that was to go to a beneficiary under a secret trust did not lapse when she pre-deceased the testator, because she was a beneficiary not under a testamentary trust, but under the *inter vivos* trust declared by the secret trustee. This logically follows from the finding that the legatee declares himself a secret trustee, but for the reason stated, such a trust is invalid, so the decision should not be followed.

Communication and acceptance

6.66 In order to prove an FST or an HST, the evidence must show (1) the intention of the testator to create a trust; (2) timely communication of that intention to the intended trustee; and (3) timely acceptance by the intended trustee of the trust obligation. The communication may be by the testator's agent (*Moss v Cooper* (1861)), and so long as the secret trustee undertakes the obligation to carry out the trust, he may 'sail under sealed orders', that is, the testator can provide him with an envelope containing the terms of the trust not to be opened until his death (*Re Keen* (1937); *Re Boyes* (1884); *McCormick*). However, the testator must have decided the terms of the trust when the communication is made; 'The devisee or legatee cannot by accepting an indefinite trust enable the testator to make an unattested codicil' (*Re Boyes*). There must be an actual acceptance of or acquiescence in the trust obligation (*McCormick*); the imposition of a merely moral obligation is insufficient (*McCormick; Re Snowden*).

6.67 The orthodoxy governing what counts as timely communication and acceptance of the trust differs for FSTs and HSTs: an FST must be communicated to and accepted by the secret trustee before or after the execution of the will, but before the testator's death (*Moss v Cooper*); the rationale here is that because a will is revocable, he may execute his will and then communicate the trust to the intended secret trustee; if the latter refuses the trust obligation, the testator can make another will revoking the gift and leaving the property to someone else (*Re Gardner*, per Warrington LJ). In contrast, HSTs must be communicated before or at the same time as the making of the will.

6.68 This stricter HST rule for timely communication and acceptance arises for no good juridical reason, since the testator can still revoke the gift in the will if his intended trustee does not agree to undertake the trust just as easily as the testator of an FST can. Commentators almost universally abhor the difference in the communication rules, and, for example, in Ireland (*Re Browne* (1944)) and the US (Restatement of Trusts, para 55(c), (h)), the rule that communication and acceptance may occur any time before the testator's death applies to HSTs as well as FSTs.

6.69 The leading case is the CA decision in *Re Keen* (1937) in which £10,000 was given to two trustees:

> ... to be held upon and disposed of by them among such person, persons, or charities as *may* be notified by me to them or either of them during my lifetime.

The court found that before the execution of the will, one trustee was adequately notified as to the terms of the trust by being given a sealed envelope containing the name of the intended beneficiary; though told not to open it until the testator's death, he understood it to contain the terms of the trust: 'a ship which sails under sealed orders is sailing under orders though the exact terms are not ascertained by the captain till later'. The trust failed, however, for two reasons. The first, which is sometimes referred to as the 'broad' ratio, was that Lord Wright MR found that 'may' (italicised above) referred to future communication of the trusts, ie communication after the execution of the will. Such a clause was bad: because it contemplated future dispositions, the testator was reserving to himself the power to make future unwitnessed dispositions and so giving the 'go-by' to the Wills Act, and it therefore violated the principles laid down by Viscount Sumner in *Blackwell*. Even if the clause could be read to encompass prior communications, so long as it contemplated future ones it must be invalid.

6.70 The 'narrow' ratio was simply that the evidence of the trust, ie a trust communicated prior to the execution of the will, was inconsistent with the clause in the will as Lord Wright MR interpreted it, not necessarily defensibly, ie as encompassing only future declarations of trust. One may argue that the broad ratio was unnecessary for the decision, and therefore strictly speaking, *obiter*, so that the actual rule governing post-execution communications of HSTs remains open.

Nevertheless, the rule invalidating post-execution communications is generally regarded as settled, if wrong. In *Re Bateman's Will Trusts* (1970) the rule was applied as if no doubt could be entertained about it.

6.71 The rule is typically explained as the result of a confusion of the doctrine of HSTs with the rule governing the incorporation by reference of documents into wills. Where a will refers to a document existing when the will is executed, that document becomes part of the properly attested will even though it is not itself properly attested; in other words, it is incorporated into the will. Because the existence of the half secret *trustee* is identified in the will, the courts have confused this with a reference to a *trust declaration* which has been made when the will is executed. For this reason, the courts have seen it somehow appropriate to limit the enforcement of HSTs to those communicated and accepted prior to or contemporaneously with the will's execution. If it were not for this confusion, the argument goes, then surely the FST rule would apply, because as stated above, the FST can give the go-by to the Wills Act by allowing post-execution communications, so why not HSTs?

6.72 Perhaps, however, it is not that the judges have confused the enforcement of HSTs with the incorporation of documents, but have realised the *pragmatic* conflict that would arise between the enforcement of HSTs and the doctrine of incorporation by reference if post-execution communications were allowed. The crucial point is that both HSTs and incorporable documents are clearly referred to in the will. Whatever theory of HSTs you prefer, the proving of the HST looks like an exercise in filling in a gap in the will, much as the incorporation of an outside document does. Indeed, the practical similarities between HSTs and documents incorporated by reference are so apparent that Matthews (1979) argues that the *juridical* basis of HSTs is an expanded doctrine of incorporation by reference, ie to incorporate properly evidenced oral testamentary trusts. In view of this, a more expansive rule for admitting HSTs, ie allowing the proof of HSTs created after the execution of the will, would have the embarrassing consequence, embarrassing, that is, for any jurisdiction which is supposed to operate under the formalities of a Wills Act, of giving a wider ambit to unattested *oral* testamentary dispositions referred to in a will than to unattested *written* ones. As a result, the communication rules for HSTs may best be understood simply as an unprincipled but pragmatic half-way house between the doctrines of FSTs and incorporation by reference, and that it is futile to search for any more theoretically satisfying basis. The corollary is, of course, that the courts find it somewhat less embarrassing to have different communications rules for different secret trusts purely on the basis of the insertion of the words 'on trust' into the document.

Failure of a secret trust to be established

6.73   If the testator intends to create an FST, but fails to communicate it to the intended trustee so that it is not accepted by him before the testator dies, then the gift under the will is not impressed with any trust, and the trustee takes absolutely (*Wallgrave v Tebbs* (1855); *Proby v Landor* (1860)). In general, if only one of two trustees is informed of and accepts the trust before the testator's death, then only he will be bound by the trust; the other receives his property absolutely, having undertaken no trust obligation. However, there appears to be a special rule for the case of trustees who receive the property as joint tenants (as opposed to as tenants in common (see 1.19)) where only one joint tenant has accepted the trust before the testator makes his will; in that case both are bound. In *Re Stead* (1900) Farwell J doubted that any good reason supported this rule, but accepted it as authoritative. Perrins (1972) argues that the uninformed legatee should only be bound by the representation of his co-legatee when that representation induced the testator either to make a gift to the two of them in his will or not revoke a gift to the two of them in his will, on the principle that no one should profit from the fraud of another, and that nothing should turn on whether the legatees take as joint tenants or tenants in common.

6.74   If a legatee is told that he is to hold on trust, but the terms of the trust are never communicated to the trustee within the testator's lifetime, he is still a secret trustee, though on a trust which fails: he will hold the property on ART for residuary beneficiaries or intestate successors (*Re Boyes* (1884)). The trustee will similarly hold on ART if the trust is fully communicated, but the trust fails, like any testamentary trust might fail, for uncertainty (chapter 7) or illegality: thus, in *Moss v Cooper*, the residuary legatees successfully pleaded that the legatees held the property they received on a secret trust for charitable purposes, a trust in violation of the Mortmain and Charitable Uses Act 1736; thus the trust was proven, failed for illegality, and the secret trustees therefore held the property on ART for the residuary legatees.

6.75 No cases have decided what should happen if a fully secret trustee were to renounce the gift or predecease the testator. In *Re Maddock* (1902) Cozens-Hardy LJ opined *obiter* that if the legatee renounced the gift or died during the lifetime of the testator, the secret beneficiaries would get nothing. In *Blackwell*, by contrast, Lord Buckmaster said *obiter* that he 'entertained no doubt' that if an FST were proved on the evidence, the court would not allow it to be defeated by the trustee's renunciation. He did not consider the case of a fully secret trustee who predeceased the testator. This should probably be dealt with as a problem of timing and reliance: does the testator have a realistic opportunity to alter his will? If yes, then the trust should fail if the trustee renounces, or predeceases the testator. If the testator is unable to make a new will, the trust should be proved against the secret trustee or, if he is dead, his personal representative. No such problems arise in the case of HSTs, for the court will not allow a trust to fail for want of a trustee, (assuming the terms of the trust can be proved despite the half secret trustee's death).

6.76 In the case of HSTs, the result of any failure of the testator to specify the trusts will be that the trustee will hold the trust property for the residuary legatees, or if none, for the intestate successors. In *Re Colin Cooper* (1939) the testator made a will in which £5,000 was given to two trustees under an HST, having communicated the trust before the execution of the will. Two days before he died, he revoked the will except for the HST, but he also increased the sum to be held on the HST to £10,000; the increase was not communicated to the trustees, and the CA held (1), that the first £5,000 was to be held on the half secret trusts, for that was the extent of the subject matter communicated; the remainder went on ART into the estate, and (2) the fact that the gift of £5,000 was technically not the one in the first will, ie the will to which the communication of the trust applied, did not matter, as they were in substance the same gift. The general principle of (1), that the trust only binds to the extent communicated, applies to fully secret trusts as well. However, there the question arises, who would get the increase? One might say that, as the increase was not impressed by any communicated trust, then the trustees should take it as an absolute gift. On the other hand, by parity of reasoning with *Re Boyes*, one might argue that once obliged, even the fully secret trustee can only take *as* a trustee, so any increase which fails to get into the trust cannot go to him beneficially, but must be held on ART.

6.77 In the case of HSTs, complications can arise between the directions given in the will and the directions communicated to the trustee – the rule is that the instructions in the will prevail in any conflict. In *Re Huxtable* (1902), £4,000 was given in the will for charitable purposes agreed by the testator and the trustee. Evidence was admissible to prove the charity was for the relief of sick and poor members of the Church of England, but not admissible to prove that only the income on £4,000 was to be spent this way, and that the trustee was to dispose of the capital as he wished on his death, for on the face of the will the whole £4,000 was given to charity, and evidence of the trustee's power to dispose of the capital would contradict the will. *Re Gardner* provides something of a contrast. The testatrix left all her property to her husband for his benefit during his life, 'knowing that he will carry out my wishes'. Thus at first glance this gift of a life estate might appear to be the subject matter of an HST (though the words do not clearly manifest an intention to create a trust; see **7.11-13**), with an intestacy with respect to the remainder, since that was not disposed of by the will. However, in view of the evidence, the CA decided that the testatrix's intention was to give her husband the benefit of the life estate, while he held the remainder which came to him as her intestate successor under a fully secret trust to give it to certain beneficiaries under his will.

6.78 The question also arises whether evidence of the half secret trust can show that the half secret trustee is himself to benefit from the trust. In general a person named as a trustee may only take a beneficial interest if that is clearly indicated, and on the face of the will in an HST, that obviously is not the case, so in that sense evidence proving that the trustee is to take under an HST may be regarded as contradicting the will. In *Re Rees* (1950) the testator left his entire estate to his solicitor and a friend as trustees 'they well knowing my wishes concerning the same'. The friend died shortly after the testator, and the evidence of the solicitor was that the trustees were to make certain payments and keep the surplus. The CA held that the substantial surplus went on intestacy. Lord Evershed, MR said that evidence they were to take a beneficial interest would conflict with the terms of the will, since they were named as trustees. In *Re Tyler's Fund Trusts* (1967), Pennycuick J stated *obiter* that he did not find this reasoning 'easy' and that in principle, evidence is admissible to prove all the terms of a trust, including a trust in favour of a trustee. Evershed MR's decision undoubtedly turned in part on the consideration that:

In the general public interest it seems to me desirable that, if a testator wishes his property to go to his solicitor and the solicitor prepares the will, that intention on the part of the testator should appear plainly in the will and should not be arrived at by the more oblique method of what is sometimes called a secret trust.

6.79 As is apparent from the tone of the foregoing, the present author thinks that equity should not enforce secret trusts and half secret trusts, but should require them to fail as testamentary gifts not complying with the Wills Act, except in rare cases where a feckless testator really has been fraudulently induced to make a gift to the legatee, for example by being told that the law will not allow him to give his intended beneficiary any property under a will. No assistance should be given to any scheme by the testator to avoid the Act. *Inter vivos* trusts, joint tenancy, and insurance policies can all be used to make secret post-mortem gifts by those who cannot come clean about their preferred objects of bounty even after their death. Equity should not provide a further means which so exhorbitantly flouts the policy of the Act.

Further reading

Youdan (1984); Green (1984); Sheridan(1951); Hodge (1980); Matthews (1979); Perrins (1985); Watkin (1981).

Must read cases: *Rochefoucauld v Boustead* (1897); *Grey v IRC* (1959), *Vandervell v IRC* (1966); and *Re Vandervell (No 2)* (1974); *McCormick v Grogan* (1869); *Blackwell v Blackwell* (1929); *Re Keen* (1936).

Self-test questions

1. Explain the operation of s 53(1)(b) of the Law of Property Act 1925 and the doctrine of *Rochefoucauld v Boustead*.

2. What do *Grey v IRC, Vandervell v IRC*, and *Re Vandervell (No 2)* decide?

3. Trustbank plc holds 50,000 shares of Zinc Ltd as nominee trustee for Sam. Sam transfers 150,000 shares of Gold Ltd to Trustbank stating that he wishes to provide for his children.

(i) Sam orally directs Trustbank to hold 50,000 shares of Zinc on trust for his three children, Albert, Jane, and Charlotte, in such shares as Trustbank shall in its absolute discretion appoint. Several months later, for revenue purposes, Trustbank makes a written declaration that it holds the shares on trust for the children.

(ii) Sam orally directs Trustbank to transfer 50,000 Gold shares to Albert absolutely, which it does.

(iii) Sam orally directs Trustbank to hold 50,000 of the Gold shares on trust for Jane. Sam tells Jane that he has done so, and Jane demands that Trustbank transfer the shares to her, which it does.

(iv) Trustbank declares that it holds the remaining 50,000 shares of Gold on trust for Charlotte.

Sam dies, leaving his entire estate to his lover, Fred. Advise Fred.

4. In 1993 Samuel made his will, leaving £50,000 to Tina and Trish, and Blackacre to John 'on trust for such persons as I shall instruct him'. In 1994 Samuel mailed Tina a letter which enclosed a sealed envelope; the letter instructed Tina that the sealed envelope was not to be opened until after Samuel's death. Also in 1994, Samuel had lunch with John and told him that he should hold Blackacre on trust for Margaret, Samuel's mistress; John agreed to do so. Samuel died a couple of weeks ago. Tina opened the sealed envelope to discover that it states that she and Trish are to hold the £50,000 on trust for Samuel's illegitimate daughter, Francesca.

Advise Margaret and Francesca.

5. Is there a theoretical basis for secret trusts which justifies their enforcement?

CHAPTER SEVEN

Certainty

SUMMARY

Certainty of intention: the family gift context

Certainty of intention: the commercial context

Certainty of subject matter and objects: common issues

Certainty of subject matter – particular issues: the 'whatever is left' trust; the identification of specific property out of a larger amount

Certainty of objects – particular issues: outright gifts, fixed trusts, and *Burrough v Philcox* trusts; powers and *McPhail* trusts; conditions precedent defining a class

Administrative unworkability and capriciousness

Effects of uncertainty

7.1 A declaration of trust must be 'certain', which means that a settlor must declare the terms of the trust with sufficient 'certainty' or precision for the trustees to know what they must do, or the intended trust fails.

The three certainties

7.2 The traditional elements of this sufficiency of declaration are known as the 'three certainties', following *Knight v Knight* (1840): certainty of intention, certainty of subject matter, and certainty of objects. The first concerns the question whether what the putative settlor did or said amounts to a declaration of a trust over his property. The second requires that the property which is to form the trust corpus is identifiable. The third requires that the intended beneficiaries, the 'objects' of the trust, are identifiable.

7.3 One should distinguish the certainty of intention from the other two. Certainty of intention is like the 'intention to create legal relations' in contract law; it concerns the question whether the putative settlor really meant to create a trust at all. When we deal with the second and third certainties, we are past that point. We know what the person intended, whether a trust, a power of appointment, or an outright gift: these secondary certainties concern the efficacy of the settlor's expression, or the workability of his intentions: does he provide an instruction that can be carried out? Or is it too vague, or too difficult, or even impossible to implement? A severe difficulty in identifying the subject matter or objects may indicate that no trust was intended: uncertainty of subject matter (*Mussoorie Bank Ltd v Raynor* (1882)) or objects (see, eg *Lambe v Eames* (1871)) has a 'reflex action' which indicates an uncertainty of intention to create a trust.

Certainty of intention: the family gift context

7.4 The maxim 'Equity looks to intent, not form' (**6.5**) fully applies to declarations of trust. No particular formula is necessary, not even the use of the word 'trust'. Neither is it necessary for the settlor to know that, technically, that is what he is doing. In *Paul v Constance* (1977) Mr Constance and Mrs Paul lived together as man and wife though not legally married. He opened a bank account in his own name with money received as compensation for an injury at work. Because of their dealings with the account – they both drew upon it to play bingo and deposited their winnings in it – and because on several occasions Mr Constance declared to Mrs Paul, 'the money is as much yours as mine', the court held him to have declared a trust of the property in equal shares for himself and Mrs Paul. Thus very informal declarations of trust of personalty are possible (as we have seen, writing is required in the case of land (**6.6**)).

7.5 Many trusts are testamentary gifts, so finding a trust will often depend on construing wills to infer the testator's 'intention'. Uncertainty can arise because there are ways in which a testator may deal with his property which might superficially resemble trusts, but are not. Wills sometimes contain gifts subject to charges: for example, 'I give the leasehold interest on my factory to James, my son, absolutely, but subject to his paying £10,000 per annum to my widow, Jane'. The gift has been made subject to a charge, but James is not a trustee for his mother. Wills may also contain conditional gifts, eg 'Blackacre to James on condition he pays £10,000 per annum to my widow for life, and upon his failure to do so, to Claire for life'. If James does not comply with the condition, then the property will go to Claire. But again, James is not a trustee.

Trust or power of appointment?

7.6 It may also be unclear whether a settlor intends to impose a trust on the recipient or intends merely to give him a power of appointment (**3.5-3.7**). Consider: '£100,000 to my trustees for distribution to such of my relations as my trustees shall in their absolute discretion think fit': does 'for distribution' mean 'to be distributed', an imperative direction imposing an obligation upon them to distribute, or is it rather to be interpreted as 'available for distribution', thus creating no obligation but giving the trustees a power which they may exercise if they so choose?

7.7 Several rules of construction may determine whether a trust or a power of appointment is intended:

(1) If there is an explicit 'gift over' in default of appointment, eg 'my shares in X company to my trustees, with power to appoint to my children in such portions as my trustees shall in their absolute discretion decide, *and in default of appointment to the London School of Economics*', there is a power of appointment, for if the settlor provides for the case where the trustees do not appoint, clearly they are under no duty to do so.

(2) The second rule is a specification of the first. In order to find a power on the basis of a gift over, the gift over must specifically arise on default of appointment. For example, a residuary gift (**2.62**) is not a gift over for this purpose. Residuary clauses deal with failures of all kinds; nothing, therefore, can be inferred about any specific gift just because the will contains a residuary clause.

(3) Finally, if there is no gift over in default of appointment, one must determine the true intentions of the testator by construing the will or settlement as a whole. For example if the testator uses words which clearly indicate his intention to create a trust with respect to some of his gifts, but does not in the gift under consideration, the court is apt to conclude that there is no trust – the testator knew what words

to use to create a trust, and in respect of this gift did not (see *Re Weekes' Settlement* (1897)). The settlor's use of the word 'power' is not determinative, but words such as 'shall' or 'to be', as in 'shall distribute' or 'to be divided amongst' seem quite clearly to be imperative, strongly indicating the imposition of a duty, and thus a trust. Finally, where a trust is intended but fails for a reason that would not invalidate a similarly framed power, the court will not save the gift by treating it as a power (*IRC v Broadway Cottages Trust* (1955); *Re Shaw* (1957)).

7.8 Settlors may create a power of appointment 'coupled' with an implied trust in default of appointment. It is perfectly possible to give someone a power to appoint certain property, in default of which appointment the property goes to the objects of the power itself, rather than to another class of objects. In cases where there is a gift over in default to the same people who are the objects of the power of appointment, then the power is, in essence, nothing more than a power to vary the shares that the objects would otherwise receive under the gift over.

7.9 In *Re Weekes' Settlement* (1897) a testatrix left property to her husband with a 'power to dispose of all such property by will amongst our children in accordance with the power granted to him as regards the other property which I have under my marriage settlements'. There was no gift over, so that did not decide the issue. The husband died intestate. The children argued that the testatrix's words indicated *a general intention* that the husband should leave the property in question to all the children in equal shares if he did not appoint particular shares to them, in other words, that he was given a power coupled with an implied trust in default of appointment. Their argument failed. The court did not find it possible to construe from the document that the property should be held on trust for all the children jointly if he did not appoint.

7.10 In *Burrough v Philcox* (1840) the pertinent instruction in the will was as follows:

> ... but in case my son and daughter should both of them die without leaving lawful issue, then for the said estates to be disposed of as shall be hereinafter mentioned, that is to say, the longest liver of my two children shall have the power, by a will, properly attested, in writing, to dispose of all my real and personal estates amongst my nephews and

nieces or their children, either all to one of them, or to as many of them as my surviving child shall think proper.

Here the court found a general intention that the class of nieces and nephews and their children should benefit. Lord Cottenham LC said:

[W]hen there appears a general intention in favour of a class, and a particular intention in favour of individuals of a class to be selected by another person, and the particular intention fails, from that selection not being made, the Court will carry into effect the general intention in favour of the class ... and in such case, the Court will not permit the objects of the power to suffer by the negligence of the donee [of the power], but fastens upon the property a trust for their benefit.

Two problems, one old, one new: precatory words and sham trusts

7.11 'Precatory words' are words of prayer or request in wills, for example, this testator's direction from *Mussoorie Bank Ltd v Raynor* (1882): 'I give to my dearly beloved wife ... the whole of my property ... feeling confident that she will act justly to our children in dividing the same when no longer required by her'. Clearly the testator had in mind that his wife would, following her use of the property, pass it on to his children, but did he intend her to hold the property on trust – for her own use for life, say, and then for their children after her death?

7.12 A run of cases leading up to the middle of the nineteenth century provided authority for a 'doctrine of precatory trusts', by which such expressions were held sufficient to create trust obligations (see *Palmer v Simmonds* (1854)). In *Lambe v Eames* (1871) however, the CA refused to find that a testator's gift of his estate to his widow 'to be at her disposal in any way she may think best, for the benefit of herself and her family' was a trust. James LJ said:

[I]n hearing case after case cited, I could not help feeling that the officious kindness of the Court of Chancery in interposing trusts where in many cases the father of the family never meant to create trusts, must have been a very cruel kindness indeed.

7.13 In *Mussoorie Bank* the same attitude was adopted by the HL, and the 'doctrine' of precatory trusts was effectively abolished. Nevertheless in the proper context words which on their face look merely precatory may establish a trust. In *Comiskey v Bowring-Hanbury* (1905) the words 'in full confidence that ... at her death [my wife] will devise it to such one or more of my nieces' were taken to establish a trust for the persuasive reason that immediately following this direction was a statement to the effect that in the event that the wife failed to devise the property to one or more of the nieces herself, it should be divided equally amongst them. It therefore seemed clear that the testator intended his nieces to take following her death, so the wife really held the property on trust for herself for life, and then for the nieces, with a power to vary the niece's particular shares by her will.

7.14 'Sham' trusts, in the context of our interest in the certainty of intention, are equitable property transactions whose written terms purport to divest the settlor of his interest in the trust property, but in reality do not, because he had no intention to create a trust of the kind that the written terms represent. They typically arise in cases where a rich individual is 'sold' an offshore trust as an investment vehicle offering various advantages. Recall that, in the normal case of a trust, as opposed to the case of a bare trust, the settlor cannot regard the trust property as still 'really his' (**2.9**). In the normal case, because the trust property is no longer beneficially the settlor's, no one having any claims against him or his estate when he dies, such as his creditors, a divorced spouse, or his heirs if the settlor comes from a jurisdiction where heirs or dependants have legal claims against his estate which cannot be defeated by his will, will be able (generally speaking) to claim any share of the property in the trust. This is regarded by some settlors as one of the *inter vivos* trust's chief advantages. But what if the 'settlor' of such a trust is told that it is equivalent to a 'living will', in which he can order the trustees to deal with the property as he orders, during his life and on his death? In that case, whatever the actual terms of the trust say, the settlor's intention was not to create a trust by which he gave up the beneficial interest in the property, but was instead to create a bare trust in which he has the full control and beneficial ownership of the property (see, eg the Jersey case *Rahman v Chase Bank (CI) Trust Co Ltd* (1991)). It is therefore claimable by his creditors, is treated as part of his assets on divorce, and falls into his estate at his death. Cases of this kind, then, raise the issue of certainty of intention in a different way — does the settlor intend, by entering into a transaction (whatever it may be called — remember, the particular words are not decisive (**7.4**)) to lose his hold over the trust assets, or does he believe, especially in consequence of the sales pitch made to him, that he will remain the beneficial owner of them? (See Willoughby (1999).)

7.15   Occasionally it is difficult to tell whether someone intended to declare a trust or merely stated an intention to make a future gift. In *Jones v Lock* (1865) a man on return from a business trip responded to his infant child's nurse's statement that he had 'not brought baby anything' by pressing a cheque made out to him for £900 into the wee child's hand and saying, 'Look you here, I give this to baby'. He later contacted his solicitor, expressing the intention to invest the £900 and more for the benefit of the child, as well as to alter his will in the child's favour. Before doing so he died. Though sympathetic, the court was unwilling to find the father's actions a declaration of trust. He intended to deal with the property in the cheque for the benefit of the son, no doubt, but not as a trustee, but as the full owner until such time as he had made his intended arrangements with his solicitor. The court regarded his 'declaration' as merely a declaration that he was now able to provide for his son and intended to do so.

Certainty of intention: the commercial context

7.16   There are different legal bases upon which property, in particular personalty such as goods for sale or raw materials, can be dealt with in the commercial context to serve different ends, including the trust. Which basis is used will, in general, be determined by the intentions of the parties. Here we will briefly consider bailments and agency, retentions of legal title, and equitable charges, in the case of goods and raw materials, and then consider the 'Quistclose' trust of money.

Bailment and agency

7.17   If A rents machinery to B, B acquires possession of the property, though not legal title. This transfer of possession is called a bailment; A is the bailor, and B the bailee. Although B has duties to A in respect of the property (to return it in good shape, for instance), this is not a trust, since the legal title is never B's. If B is also A's agent with power to sell the property, again, B is not a trustee; he merely has the power to transfer A's legal title to a buyer. As agent B is a fiduciary to A (**2.10**), he must act in A's best interests when dealing with A's property, but he is still not a trustee of it. Normally, when an agent sells property of his principal under his authority to do so, the money proceeds are his own. He is simply in debt to the principal in that amount (minus, usually, his commission). If the money proceeds are stolen, it is his loss; he owes the principal all the same. Sometimes the contract requires the agent to hold the proceeds of sale on trust for the principal, and here there is a trust, even if the agent may, before remitting the proceeds, deduct his commission (see, eg *Royal Brunei Airlines Sdn Bhd v Tan* (1995)).

Retention of legal title

7.18 A number of legal arrangements may underlie A's supplying raw materials to B, a manufacturer. A may just sell the raw materials to B, for cash or on credit. Where A provides the materials to B on credit, A may worry about B's becoming insolvent, and so in the contract of sale A may employ what is called a reservation of title or 'Romalpa' clause (*Aluminium Industrie Vaassen BV v Romalpa Aluminium Ltd* (1976); *Clough Mill Ltd v Martin* (1984)), under which the legal title to the materials remains with A until (1) they are sold by B after they are incorporated into his manufactured products, whereupon the title to them passes to the buyer of the products, or (2) B has paid off all outstanding debts to A, whereupon the title passes to B himself. If B becomes insolvent, A can reclaim all of the materials B has on hand. There is no trust here; the legal title to the goods simply remains with A until either (1) or (2) occur.

Equitable charges

7.19 Alternatively, the legal title to the raw materials may pass to B under the contract, but A may try to establish that he has an equitable charge (**2.59**) on them, which will make him a secured creditor. If B is a company, however, which for obvious reasons is often the case, the equitable charge must be registered or it is void against B's general creditors or his liquidator (Companies Act 1985, s 395). Thus even if A is able to establish, through the interpretation of the contract, that he has an equitable charge over company B's property, this is unlikely to help in company B's insolvency for it is unlikely that A will have registered the charge if its creation was simply a consequence of the proper interpretation of their contract.

A trust of the materials?

7.20 A, however, may have one more string to his bow. If A can claim that he transferred the legal title to the materials to B 'on trust' for himself, so that he, A, becomes the equitable beneficial owner, then A may reclaim the property upon B's insolvency. The leading case is *Re Bond Worth Ltd* (1980). In *Re Bond Worth* the supplier purported to transfer legal title to fibre to a company for its manufacturing purposes, while retaining equitable title for itself, as well as acquiring equitable title to the manufacturer's products incorporating the fibre and to the proceeds of sale of those products. The court held that such an arrangement effectively amounted to an equitable charge on the fibre, the products, and the proceeds. It now appears to be orthodoxy that while legal retention of title clauses with respect to transferred chattels are effective, those that purport to 'retain' equitable title will be treated as charges, but the reasoning is questionable (see Worthington (1996), 15-24). There is a sound policy reason for this position though: the registration requirement for charges against companies means these interests will be publicly ascertainable by prospective creditors.

The Quistclose trust of money

7.21 The position is significantly different in the case of money advanced by A to B to enable B specifically to pay off certain debts (*Barclays Bank Ltd v Quistclose Investments Ltd* (1970); *Carreras Rothmans Ltd v Freeman Mathews Treasure Ltd* (1985)) or to pursue certain projects (*Re EVTR* (1987)). Quistclose (Q) was an investment company that advanced £209,000 to Rolls Razor (RR) in order to allow the latter to pay a dividend which it had already declared. It was accepted by all concerned that if RR had used the money to pay the dividend, then RR would simply have owed Q £209,000 (plus interest); had RR paid the dividend and then gone into liquidation, Q would have been an ordinary creditor. RR was in trouble and did indeed go into liquidation, but before paying the dividend. The HL held that RR held the money on trust to pay the dividend and that, upon their failure to do so, the money was held upon trust for Q.

7.22 Quistclose trusts represent a departure from the 'default' position when money is lent in a commercial context. Normally if A lends money to B, the money immediately becomes B's legal property and A becomes an ordinary creditor; it does not matter that A pays the money to B under certain conditions, eg to spend it only on certain business projects. If B spends the money otherwise, he just commits a breach of contract, but not a breach of trust (the consequence of such a breach of contract may be, eg, that the loan is immediately repayable). Furthermore, it is not obvious what kind of trust this is.

7.23 We will address the nature of this trust in detail in Chapter 9 (**9.46** et seq). While there remains substantial controversy, in the recent HL judgment of Lord Millett in *Twinsectra v Yardley* the trust was explained as a case of a loan arrangement which incorporates a 'bare trust with mandate' (**9.47**). The typical example is the trust under which a solicitor holds his client's funds before completing the purchase of land. If you are buying a house, the transaction normally involves two distinct steps: contract and completion. First you and the seller will enter into a contract for the purchase. The contract will specify a date when you will hand over the money, and the seller will transfer title to the house. Both steps will normally involve the participation of your solicitor or conveyancing agent. Prior to completion, you will transfer the purchase money to your solicitor, who will hold the fund in his client account, ie a trust account. He will hold those funds on bare trust for you, *but* subject to your contractual standing order, or 'mandate', to transfer the funds to the seller on the day of completion in return for acquiring the title to the property. The contractual mandate is a term of your contract with your solicitor to carry out the purchase transaction for you.

7.24 It is important to appreciate the effect of this arrangement. Throughout the time your solicitor holds the funds in his account, he holds them on trust for you. So if your solicitor were to go bankrupt, the funds would still be yours in equity, and so could not be claimed by your solicitor's trustee in bankruptcy for distribution to his general creditors (**2.57**). And if your solicitor used the trust funds in any way inconsistent with your mandate, he would commit a breach of trust, for under a bare trust the trustee holds the funds to your order (**2.23**), and your mandate is your order. When your solicitor transfers the funds to the seller on completion, he carries out your order, your mandate, and thus properly disposes of the funds according to the terms of the trust, and the trust comes to an end.

7.25 In the case of a Quistclose trust, this arrangement is combined with a contract of loan. When the lender (L) transfers the money to the borrower (B), this transfer is on trust, a bare trust with mandate. B holds the money on trust for L until he uses the money for the purpose agreed under the loan contract. Once he does that, fulfilling the terms of the bare trust with mandate, the arrangement turns into a pure loan, with B liable to repay L the money at whatever interest rate is agreed, for there is no longer any money held on trust. But the effect of this arrangement is two-fold. If B spends the money on a purpose outside the agreed loan purpose, this will be a breach of L's mandate, thus a breach of trust, and L can follow and trace this money; secondly, if B goes insolvent before spending the money according to the mandate, as happened in *Quistclose*, L retains the equitable beneficial interest in the money under the trust, and so is safe from B's insolvency.

7.26 Now, to the issue of certainty of intention. The main question will be whether the parties intended the normal loan arrangement, which creates merely a debtor–creditory relationship, or a *Quistclose* trust loan. Loan contracts can, of course, stipulate a *Quistclose* trust, ie require B to hold the loan money on trust until spent properly according to purposes specified in the contract. But as we have seen, a trust can be created without the use of the word 'trust' (**7.4**), and the use of the word 'trust' will not create a trust if that does not represent the parties' true intentions (**7.14**). But every trust must comply with the necessary features of a trust, and here the most significant feature is whether or not L requires, and B understands, that B must keep the loan moneys separate from all of his other moneys. In *Quistclose* and *Carreras Rothmans*, for example, special bank accounts were set up to receive the money. Payment into B's solicitor's client account is sufficient for this purpose, for although a solicitor's client account mixes money from different clients, it is a trust account and there are specific rules by which solicitors track each client's equitable interest in the account (*Twinsectra*). If neither L nor B see anything wrong in paying the loan money into B's current account, this should give rise to a strong presumption that whatever the terms of the loan contract, including the use of the word 'trust', there was no intention to create a *Quistclose* trust.

7.27 For example, in *R v Common Professional Examination Board, ex p Mealing-McCleod* (2000) (**9.53-55**), the contract of loan between the lender and borrower included a provision in the following terms: 'You must use the cash loan for any purpose specified overleaf … You will hold that loan, or any part of it, on trust for us until you have used it for that purpose'. That seems straightforward enough. But one should still look at how the money was advanced. What if the bank, according to its regular practice, merely paid the loan money into its borrower/client's current account? That would strongly raise the suspicion that the contractual provision was mere boilerplate, especially if this was the bank's standard form, probably inserted on solicitor's advice at head office to take advantage of the decision in *Quistclose*, with the local loan officer or bank manager probably having no clue as to its real significance. One can easily imagine if the borrower/client asked what it meant the manager's saying something like 'it means you must spend the loan money on the purpose you told us about in applying for the loan', which of course indicates no intention to create a trust as opposed to a mere contractual obligation.

7.28 *Twinsectra* itself was a very close case on the facts. Carnwath J at first instance found that the lender and the borrower never really considered a trust of the loan moneys, leaving it up to their respective solicitors; for their part, a provision that the loan money was to be used solely for the acquisition of property formed part of the loan documents; but the solicitors never discussed the provision. In this respect the case was far from the typical purchaser's instruction to a solicitor for the release of funds to acquire a specific piece of land in furtherance of a particular contract of sale. Carnwath J decided that the purpose was too vague, and did not really form part of the parties' intentions in concluding the contract. However this decision was overturned in the CA, and the HL agreed. In both places much greater emphasis was placed on the presence of the provision in the loan documents, and it was held that 'the acquisition of property' was a trust obligation certain enough to be enforced. This is almost certainly wrong. Recall (**3.47**) that the test for certainty of objects is the 'is or is not' test. Applied to the case of a mandate or order, this test would require that it is certain whether *any* possible expenditure of the trust money clearly 'is or is not' within the mandate. What does 'property' mean here? Land? Business supplies? A new necklace for the borrower's wife? The CA and the HL got into a muddle over this because the original negotiations for the loan concerned the purchase of a *specific* parcel of land, which is obviously certain, and without thinking seemed to think the certainty of that carried over to the purpose expressed in the actual loan documents.

7.29 It should be noted, as pointed out by Lord Millett in *Twinsectra*, that if the intention to create a trust is clear, then any uncertainty in the

to achieve a purpose while
Learnt
achieving
spending
his money
directly
= QI

purpose or instruction would mean that B would have no right to use the money for any purpose; that is, there would be no instruction on which he could act to dispose of the funds. The point about the vagueness of the purpose here is that if the intention to create a trust *as opposed to a straight loan of funds to B* is in issue, then vagueness, hence uncertainty, about the purported trust has the regular 'reflex action' (**7.3**) of generating a similar uncertainty as to whether a trust was genuinely intended to be part of the loan arrangement at all.

7.30   As regards the line of cases more or less directly leading to *Quistclose*, Millett (1985) gives the best explanation of when loans will be treated as giving rise to *Quistclose* trusts, ie where the intentions of the parties must be gathered from the circumstances as opposed to being expressed explicitly in the loan contract: if you can interpret the arrangement as one in which B is, *in essence, spending L's money to achieve a purpose which L cannot by spending his own money directly*, a Quistclose trust will arise. In *Quistclose* itself, Q was hoping to stave off RR's bankruptcy by ensuring that RR was able to pay its declared dividend. If, however, Q had tried to do that itself, it would have revealed to the world RR's desperate circumstances. So it could only do so by putting the money in RR's hands.

7.31   While this seems a reasonable explanation of *Quistclose* and prior 'staving off bankruptcy' cases, you might well wonder whether the court should give its aid to such schemes by being astute to infer a trust where normally it would only infer a debtor–creditor relationship, a trust which by its very nature will misrepresent to the world, and in particular to prospective creditors, the true financial state of a company. It should also be noted that the prior 'staving off bankruptcy' cases were cases of trusts to pay off the troubled individual's or company's *creditors*, not to pay a *dividend* to a company's *shareholders*, about which we presumably have more mixed feelings. On the other hand, you may think these attempts at rescue praiseworthy, and that those who try them should not suffer unduly if they fail, as they might if rescue funds are treated like any other kind of loan. But there is a more general point here: especially in the commercial context, the law should be wary of imposing trusts willy-nilly. Where the circumstances generate uncertainty as to whether a *Quistclose* trust was intended, it makes sense to expect some reason why the parties would have thought it necessary to use this device rather than a regular loan before inferring that one was created.

'Pre-payment' trusts

7.32 Trusts may also protect prepayments by customers. In *Re Kayford Ltd* (1975) a mail order company unilaterally decided to place all of the money it received as prepayments for goods in a special account, only drawing upon the account when it filled an order. It was held that, upon the company's liquidation, the money in the account was held in trust for the customers even though they were unaware of the arrangement. While there is nothing particularly difficult about inferring or finding such a unilateral declaration of trust by the company, under insolvency law such a declaration appears to be an illegitimate preference of the company favouring some creditors over others. Should the court recognise a company's intentions if they have this result? (For an interesting set of facts upon which a *Re Kayford* type trust failed for uncertainty, leaving the company who tried to declare the trust with the beneficial interest in the fund so that it was available to its creditors, see *Re Challoner Club Ltd* (1997).)

7.33 A more extreme example is found in *Neste Oy v Lloyds Bank plc* (1983). An agent for shipowners received money from them to pay various liabilities they incurred, for example to ports where their ships were berthed. The moneys were paid into the agent's general account, not held separately. One final payment by a shipowner was received by the agent after it had ceased trading. The court held that this last payment was held on *constructive* trust – in other words the court *imposed* a trust despite the actual intentions of both of the parties, on the basis that any honest recipient of the payment in these circumstances would have understood that the sum ought to be repaid immediately. It seems wrong, however, simply to find a kind of *Kayford*-type prepayment trust rather than the ordinary debtor-creditor relationship when neither party makes the slightest gesture to declare a trust, simply because someone is unlucky given the timing of someone's insolvency. There are *always* creditors who advance that unlucky last prepayment or make that unlucky last shipment of goods on credit to a company just before it becomes insolvent.

Reform

7.34 The Law Commission is currently at work on a broad reform, the purpose of which is to create a general registration scheme for all interests which are effectively security interests (**7.18** et seq) in personal property (Law Commission (2003)). If implemented by legislation, then interests under retention of title clauses, charges, *Quistclose* trusts, and 'pre-payment' trusts, will all need to be registered to be effective against third parties, in particular trustees in bankruptcy (see further Glister (2004a)).

Certainty of subject matter and objects: common issues

7.35 Modifying Emery's (1982) classification we can divide up the common sources of uncertainty of subject matter and objects into three categories:

- conceptual uncertainty;

- evidential uncertainty; and

- 'whereabouts' uncertainty.

Conceptual uncertainty concerns the problem of vagueness in the language used by the testator. For example, if a testator gives 'a lot' of his estate to 'my shorter employees' in equal shares, we appear to be faced with a problem. How much is 'a lot', and who, of all his employees, count as the 'shorter' ones.

7.36 Evidential uncertainty may arise because, while the language used to identify the property or persons is precise enough, it seems unlikely or impossible to find the evidence which will allow the trustees to carry out a settlor's, in particular a testator's, instructions. Consider 'the fishing rod which I used to catch a prize salmon on September 7, 1968, I give to the woman I had dinner with that night in celebration'. This bequest is conceptually certain both in subject matter and object – he caught the fish with only one rod, and only one woman dined with him. But determining which of the fishing rods the testator owned at his death is the prize-winning one, and who the lucky woman is, may be impossible simply because there is no reliable evidence.

7.37 Finally, the whereabouts problem; consider this bequest: 'The photograph of me with Winston Churchill I give to my nephew Paul'. On its face, there appears no problem at all. There is no conceptual or evidential uncertainty making it difficult to determine which photo is the right one and who Paul is. But what if it turns out that the testator kept the photo hidden somewhere in his 60-room mansion, Grandacre, and secondly, that Paul emigrated somewhere (no one remembers precisely where) in 1973? It may be just impossible to locate either the photograph or Paul.

Whereabouts uncertainty

7.38 We can start with the whereabouts problem, because it is essentially no problem at all (see *Brown v Gould* (1972), per Megarry VC). No trust ever fails because the whereabouts of the property or the object is presently unknown. The trustees would not be required to pull down Grandacre in order to eliminate every possible hiding place for the photo. The gift is valid, and Paul may be put in possession if and when the photograph ever turns up. In a roughly similar fashion, trustees are required to hold a gift to a person whose whereabouts are presently unknown, and give it to him if and when he ever turns up. In *Re Gulbenkian* (1970) Lord Upjohn opined that, in the case of a beneficiary of a class gift whose whereabouts were uncertain, the trustees could apply to the court for a direction to pay his share into court. In short, the problem is correctly thought of as one confronting the trustees when faced with their duty to *distribute* the trust property, not as a problem concerning the very existence of the trust.

Evidential uncertainty

7.39 Evidential uncertainty of either subject matter or objects defeats an outright gift, a trust for a specified individual, or a fixed trust. The reasoning is straightforward: if the settlor expresses his gift in such a way that evidence must be adduced to identify the property or the person and that evidence is not available, then the gift or trust simply cannot be executed according to its terms. This does not mean that any requirement of evidence defeats an intended gift. There are rules which govern how evidence can be adduced to give effect to a testator's wishes expressed in his will, the general point of which is to ensure that such evidence only gives effect to the testator's declared wishes but does not serve to change or make ambiguous what the testator put in his will, and similar rules should govern the admission of evidence in the case of trusts generally. Evidential uncertainty of objects causes particular problems in the case of discretionary trusts and powers, which will be discussed below (**7.63** et seq).

Conceptual uncertainty

7.40   Conceptual uncertainty arises from the settlor's use of imprecise or vague language to express his intentions. Vagueness is an ineliminable aspect of language. Vagueness can be understood as the problem of the uncertain boundaries which arise when we try to apply our words to things in the world. For example, the word 'tall' appears to have very uncertain boundaries; 'tall' is not a synonym for '5'10" or over'; it is not that precise. People may disagree whether Jim is tall, and an individual may be in a quandary himself as to whether Jim is tall or not. Jim may be 'on the borderline' for 'tall'. Vague terms will certainly apply in some cases – Paul, who is 7'8" is certainly tall – heavens, he's *very* tall – and certainly not apply in others – to Stephen who is 4'11" – but there will be a range of cases for which the application of the term is indeterminate, or *uncertain*. We can make a rough and ready distinction between two kinds of vagueness. 'Degree' vagueness covers words like 'tall'; 'tall' clearly refers to a scale, height, along which we can place individuals. The second kind of vagueness is 'category' vagueness. An example is 'furniture'. 'Furniture' is a term which applies to certain household objects. A sofa is certainly furniture, and a dinner plate is certainly not. But what about a carpet? Or a refrigerator?

7.41   In everyday communication vagueness is not a problem because, in context, we can draw boundaries which are sufficiently workable to understand what we are up to. When greater precision is wanted, we can stipulate a meaning for a term which provides a more precise boundary for its application. For example, we can stipulate that for our purposes, 'tall' means '5'10" or over', or if we run a department store, we can stipulate that furniture includes carpets if carpets are sold in the 'furniture' department. While these stipulations are arbitrary, that does not mean they are unreasonable. '5'10" or over' is a reasonable stipulation for tall, although reasonable people might choose different measures, but 4'11" is not, since that boundary does not reflect anything like the normal borderline area where 'tall' is thought to be vague.

7.42   In some cases courts are willing to determine a boundary for a vague term, in other cases not. In *Palmer v Simmonds* (1854) the words 'the bulk of my said residuary estate' were held to indicate too uncertain a proportion of the residuary estate to establish a trust. The judge did assume that ' the bulk' meant more than half but that that was still too imprecise to establish the subject matter of the trust. By contrast, in *Re Golay* (1965) the gift of a 'reasonable income', to go along with a life interest in a flat, did not fail for uncertainty. Ungoed-Thomas J said,

> The court is constantly involved in making such objective assessments of what is reasonable and it is not to be deterred from doing so because subjective influences can never be wholly excluded.

In other words, the court was willing to stipulate a meaning for 'reasonable income'. Vague words are not useless, even at the borderline. Their vagueness at the borderline just requires us to do some work, that is, stipulate criteria for a term's application to give a working definition which is precise enough for the task at hand. Did the court have better reason to do this in *Re Golay* than in *Palmer*?

7.43 The same problem arises for certainty of objects. The career of the expression 'my old friends'/'my friends' is particularly interesting. Although 'my old friends' and my 'friends' were held to be conceptually certain in *Re Gibbard* (1966) and *Re Barlow's Will Trusts* (1979) respectively, in the former the court was applying a test for certainty which was later rejected by higher courts (*Re Gulbenkian* (1970)), and the latter concerned a gift subject to a condition precedent, where, apparently, a lower standard for certainty is required (**7.69**). In *Re Barlow's Will Trusts*, Browne- Wilkinson J denied that the meaning of 'friends' was 'too vague to be given legal effect', and he stipulated criteria for its application:

> Without seeking to lay down any exhaustive definition ... it may be helpful if I indicate certain minimum requirements: (a) the relationship must have been a long-standing one; (b) the relationship must have been a social relationship as opposed to a business or professional relationship; (c) although there may have been long periods when circumstances prevented the testatrix and the applicant from meeting, when circumstances did permit they must have met frequently.

In contrast, Lord Upjohn used 'old friend' as a paradigm example of conceptual uncertainty in *Re Gulbenkian* (1970), as did Megarry V-C in *Brown v Gould* (1972):

If there is a trust for 'my old friends,' all concerned are faced with uncertainty as to the concept or idea enshrined in these words. It may not be difficult to resolve that 'old' means not 'aged' but 'of long standing'; but then there is the question how long is 'long.' Friendship, too, is a concept with almost infinite shades of meaning.

7.44   Not surprisingly, in *Re Wright's Will Trusts* (1982) (CA) a trust for 'such people and institutions as [my trustees] think have helped me or my late husband' failed for uncertainty, Blackett-Ord V-C at first instance observing that helping the testatrix 'could mean anything from helping the testatrix across the road to saving her from death, dishonour, or bankruptcy.'

Resolution of uncertainty by outside opinion

7.45   Should a settlor be able to express his directions as precisely as he can, but provide that if there is dispute over their meaning or application, recourse may be had to a living individual who shall settle the matter? In *Re Coxen* (1948), the settlor made a gift of a residence to his widow, which was however to end 'if in the opinion of my trustees she shall have ceased permanently to reside therein'. Jenkins J held:

> If the testator had insufficiently defined the state of affairs on which the trustees were to form their opinion, he would not I think have saved the condition from invalidity on the ground of uncertainty merely by making their opinion the criterion... in my view the testator by making the trustees' opinion the criterion has removed the difficulties [in deciding whether the determining event has occurred, which] may necessarily be a matter of inference involving nice questions of fact and degree.

Re Coxen thus stands for the proposition that an opinion clause cannot cure conceptual uncertainty, but may allow an individual to determine matters of fact as to whether the concept applies in any particular case. Thus Hayton ((2001b), 177) says that opinion clauses may cure evidential, but not conceptual, uncertainty.

7.46   In *Re Leek* (1969) the objects of a trust were 'such other persons as the company may consider to have a moral claim upon' the settlor; Harman LJ said:

> It was argued that ... the trust was too vague ... If the trust were for

such persons as *have* moral claims, I would agree with this view, but this is not the trust. The trustees are made the arbiters and the objects are such persons as they may *consider* to have a moral claim; and I do not see why they should not be able on this footing to make up their minds and arrive at a decision. (italics original)

7.47 In *Re Tuck's Settlement Trusts* (1978) the CA considered a condition on the inheritance of a baronetcy, that the wife of any heir must be of 'Jewish blood' and 'worship according to the Jewish faith'; in the case of doubt the decision of the Chief Rabbi in London was to be conclusive. Lord Denning MR said:

I see no reason why a testator or settlor should not provide that any dispute or doubt should be resolved by his executors or trustees, or even by a third person ... if there is any conceptual uncertainty in the provision of this settlement, it is cured by the Chief Rabbi clause.

7.48 Lord Denning's view does not, however, represent the law, for though all of the judges upheld the settlement, Lord Russell and Eveleigh LJ did so on a different basis. Lord Russell did not consider the Chief Rabbi clause since he did not find the condition to be uncertain. Eveleigh LJ said that the settlor:

... is in effect saying that his definition of Jewish faith is the same as the Chief Rabbi's definition. Different people may have different views or be doubtful as to what is 'Jewish faith', but the Chief Rabbi knows and can say what meaning he attaches to the words ... I therefore do not regard the settlor as leaving it to the Chief Rabbi to discover what the settlor meant or to provide a meaning for the expression used by the settlor when the meaning is in doubt ... The fact is that the Chief Rabbi knows what he means by 'Jewish faith' and the testator has said that he means the same thing.

Thus in Eveleigh LJ's view the Chief Rabbi's opinion is regarded not as determining the meaning of the settlor's words by providing workable criteria for them; the Chief Rabbi's opinion is merely evidence of the settlor's opinion. In practice does this not amount to letting the Chief Rabbi determine the meaning of the settlor's words?

7.49 In *Re Tepper's Will Trusts* (1987) gifts were subject to the condition that the recipients 'shall remain within the Jewish faith and shall not marry outside the Jewish faith'. Scott J, following Eveleigh LJ, held that *Re Tuck's* established the admissibility of evidence to elucidate the meaning of terms like 'the Jewish faith'.

7.50 In general, courts try not to invalidate trusts if a reasonable construction can be placed on the words which will make them valid (*IRC v McMullen* (1981) per Lord Hailsham), but individual judges vary in their willingness to find a 'benignant' construction. As a result, settlors are faced with uncertainty about the extent to which a court will allow the determination of a vague term. Examining vagueness in legal language, Endicott (1997) cites the example of the 'anti-rave' provision in the Criminal Justice and Public Order Act 1994, s 63 by which the police are empowered to shut down sound equipment at a 'gathering' where the music 'by reason of its loudness and duration and the time at which it is played, is likely to cause serious distress to the inhabitants of the locality'. To further assist the judge 'music' is defined to include 'sounds wholly or predominantly characterised by the emission of a succession of repetitive beats' (presumably to capture the essence of the music that ecstasy-users prefer, but alas, unsuccessfully to distinguish it from the sound of a pneumatic drill). While it may be excessive to grant settlors the freedom to create legally binding obligations with the use of language as vague as that employed by Parliament, it may not be churlish to suggest that judges, given as they are to making sense of such statutory provisions, should make some reasonable effort to ensure the validity of trust provisions couched in vague language. Where an opinion clause empowers the trustees or a third party to establish criteria for applying the settlor's words, that does not mean they can choose any criteria at all. As Browne-Wilkinson J's decision in *Re Barlow's* shows, the provision of criteria, while necessarily arbitrary, can be more or less reasonable, and the courts could act if the criteria chosen were irrational or perverse; they need not, therefore, be worried that reference to opinion clauses ousts the jurisdiction of the court to determine whether a provision is conceptually certain. Of course the courts must remain the ultimate arbiters of which clauses are just so vague that any determination of criteria for them would, in effect, be writing the will or the settlement for the settlor. But this cannot be said of opinion clauses of the Chief Rabbi kind which save the courts from having to determine criteria themselves for terms which should be given a determinate meaning, and they should welcome the help.

Certainty of subject matter: particular issues

The 'whatever is left' trust

7.51 In *Sprange v Barnard* (1789) a testatrix left £300 in securities to her husband 'for his sole use; and at his death, the remaining part of what is left, that he does not want for his own wants and use', was to be divided equally amongst three others. The court held that the husband was entitled absolutely, for a trust of what property remained after the husband's use 'would be impossible to be executed'; similar negative attitudes to this kind of 'whatever is left' trust are found in *Lambe v Eames* (1871) and *Mussoorie Bank Ltd v Raynor* (1882).

7.52 More recently, however, *Ottaway v Norman* (1972), the Australian (*Birmingham v Renfrew* (1936)) 'floating' or 'suspended' trust analysis was applied. The son and daughter-in-law of the deceased claimed that he had left his house, its contents, and his money to his housekeeper for her use so long as she lived, but on trust to leave the property to them on her death. Brightman J opined that there was a valid trust of the house and contents (the latter being subject to normal wastage and wear and tear), which he was content to assume was 'in suspense' during the housekeeper's lifetime, attaching to the property only upon her death. It is not clear from this 'floating trust' analysis whether the 'floating trustee' has any obligations to preserve the property during his life. May he spend as much as he wants? Could the housekeeper in *Ottaway* have sold the house and spent the proceeds living on the Costa del Sol? In *Birmingham* the court said that gifts 'calculated to defeat' the trust could not be made, but such an obligation seems so nebulous as to be unenforceable. In *Ottaway v Norman* the trust did not extend to the money the housekeeper received under the will. Such a trust would be 'meaningless and unworkable' unless the money was given with the obligation that it be kept separate from her own money, and there was none.

The identification of specific property out of a larger amount

7.53 In *Boyce v Boyce* (1849) a testator left three houses to his widow, instructing her to give to his daughter Maria whichever one Maria chose and to give the other two houses to his daughter Charlotte. Maria died before choosing any house, and the court held that the gift to Charlotte failed for uncertainty, reasoning that the gift to Charlotte was of the *other* houses that remained following Maria's choice. Since she made none, the ascertainment of such *other* houses became impossible, and so the gift failed.

7.54 While *Boyce* turns on quite unusual facts, it is one instance of a more general problem which has recently arisen as an important issue in the commercial context, that of identifying which specific things, out of a larger class of things, are to be held as the subject matter of a trust. While in *Boyce* the failure turned on Maria's failure to select a property, in the commercial cases the failure generally turns on the failure of a seller of goods to choose particular goods to satisfy the buyer's contract; once identified, but only then, may those goods serve as the subject matter of a trust if one was intended by the parties. In *Re London Wine Co (Shippers) Ltd* (1986) a company which dealt in wines went into receivership. Its customers had purchased wine but left it in the company's possession for storage, and naturally assumed that they could retrieve 'their' wine and that it was not part of the insolvent company's assets. Unfortunately, the customers did not become legal owners of any wine. Although the company represented to them that it held particular cases of wine in storage for them, and even charged them storage fees, in reality the company did not allocate any particular cases of wine to any particular customers, and in general did not ensure that it had on hand sufficient quantities to meet all the customer's purchases should they all have demanded actual delivery of their purchases all at once. Wines were only allocated to any individual customer when he actually took delivery. Under sale of goods law, legal title to goods does not pass under a contract of sale until such time as the seller actually appropriates specific property to the contract. In a thorough review of the case law, Oliver J decided that, for essentially the same reason, the company did not hold any of the wine on trust for the customers: it could not be said with any certainty which wines were the subject matter of a trust for any particular customer.

7.55 *Re London Wine* was approved by the PC in *Re Goldcorp Exchange Ltd* (1995), a case involving similar claims against a dealer in precious metals. While sympathising with the customers, Lord Mustill affirmed that a right in property, whether legal or equitable, cannot exist in the air, hovering over an undifferentiated mass of property; it can only exist in relation to property which is specifically ascertained, ie identified. For fans of fusion (**1.15**), the decision is also right as a matter of policy, for insisting upon one set of 'certainty of subject matter' rules which applies both to the transfer of legal title and to the creation of equitable title. If the common law and equity are ever to produce a rational law of property, they cannot diverge on matters as fundamental as this. In particular, equity should not develop its own 'flexible' notion of certainty of subject matter just in order to provide the sympathetic result in a particular case.

7.56 Unfortunately, before the decision in Re *Goldcorp* was given, the CA delivered its decision in *Hunter v Moss* (1994), which throws this area of law into some turmoil. Mr Moss was the owner of 950 shares of a private company. In order to place his finance director, Mr Hunter, on the same footing as his managing director in respect of their interests in the company, he purported to declare (as the court found) a trust of 50 of those shares. He later sold the 950 shares when the company was taken over by a larger concern, keeping all the proceeds for himself. Hunter claimed a proportionate share of the proceeds of that sale, ie the proportion which would be his in equity if the declaration of trust were valid. There was a problem, however, in that Moss had never done anything to segregate or identify any particular lot of 50 shares out of the whole 950 he was to hold on trust for Hunter. Although the case concerned 'intangible property', ie shares, not goods, there seems no good reason to distinguish the clear rule in *London Wine*, approved in *Goldcorp*, that a trust cannot exist unless and until the property to which it relates is specifically ascertained (although the CA appears to have distinguished *London Wine* on a goods/intangibles distinction without further reasoned argument). In order to have specifically ascertained the property in this case Moss would have needed either to isolate share certificates to the specified amount, or at least indicate the registration numbers of the shares to be held on trust. Nevertheless, Dillon LJ held that the trust was effectively declared. His decision was based on an analogy, to wit: since a testator may validly bequeath 50 of his 950 shares of X Ltd without previously segregating them, Mr Moss should equally be able to create an *inter vivos* trust of 50 of his 950 shares of X Ltd without previously segregating them. But under a will there is no immediate trust of any of the property for any of the intended legatees until the estate is properly dealt with by the executors, paying off the testator's debts and so on (**6.44** et seq). The legatee's proprietary interest in specific items of property, whether shares or shoehorns, only arises when such property is actually identified for distribution. As Hayton (1994) points out, the *inter vivos* situation analogous to the testamentary bequest is the case where A properly transfers legal title of his 950 shares to B to hold on trust to distribute 50 of them to C, not Moss's declaration in this case.

7.57 The decision leads to obvious problems. Assume such a trust. What happens when Moss deals with the 950 shares? Say he sells 100 shares (properly transferring title) to Fred. Whose shares are these? Hunter's or Moss's? If they are Hunter's, Moss has just committed a breach of trust; if they are not Hunter's, he has not. One does want to know whether a breach of trust has occurred. Martin ((1997), 96) suggests that this worry is insubstantial, since the rules of tracing (**2.46, 11.96** et seq) may be notionally employed: thus, we proceed *as if* Moss did segregate 50 shares out of the 950, but then immediately mixed them again with the other 900, so we have a mixture of 950 shares, just like the case where a trustee in breach of trust mixes £50 of trust money in his bank account, raising the balance to £950. Under the rules of tracing, Hunter will be able to trace his value into particular shares in the 950, which particular shares he traces into depending upon the circumstances. But this is a strange way to deal with a certainty problem, that is by assuming that in the very act of declaring a trust a person also makes himself a trustee in breach. The better view is Moss has not properly created a trust at all, and while he might have been contractually *obliged* to do so (under a term of Hunter's employment contract with him), it is conceptually confused to deal with his *failure to make himself* a trustee by treating him *as a trustee in breach*.

7.58 One of the strange aspects of this case was that it was argued as if Hunter was a volunteer, ie Hunter did not argue that Moss was obliged by a term of Hunter's employment contract to transfer 50 of the shares to him or hold 50 shares on trust for him. One can only speculate why; perhaps Hunter felt that he would have a difficult time proving that he had provided any new consideration for Moss's promise of the shares. But as Hayton (1994) points out, and as we shall see in chapter 8, equity does not normally perfect imperfect transactions by creating equitable rights for people who have not paid for them. If Hunter is to be treated as a volunteer here, then he does not suffer any loss if the trust fails, and there are no obvious special factors to compel the court to bend over backwards and find an otherwise uncertain, and therefore invalid, trust valid.

207

7.59 The situation would be different had Hunter actually provided consideration, but the right response in that case is probably not to adopt Martin's tracing approach: Hayton suggests that the court should impose an equitable charge on Moss's shares in favour of Hunter to the value of the 50 shares. An alternative approach would be the imposition of a constructive trust on Moss over the whole 950 shares, to hold them in shares of 1/19 for Hunter and 18/19 for himself, thus creating an equitable co-ownership of the shares until such time as Moss segregated 50 for Hunter. This approach accords with the amendment to the Sale of Goods Act 1979 (Sale of Goods (Amendment) Act 1995) which holds that purchasers of unidentified goods from an identified bulk will obtain legal title to the bulk as co-owners in shares proportionate to their purchases. It seems overly fanciful to adopt a notional segregation and re-mixing and the immediate invocation of the rules of tracing when these other, more straightforward, techniques are available.

Trusts of residue

7.60 One last point on certainty of subject matter, which I stress because students regularly get this wrong in exams: a testamentary gift or trust of the residue under a will is NOT UNCERTAIN. In the course of executing the will, the executors will determine to the very penny the residue of the estate. 'That is certain which can readily be made certain', the saying goes, or 'id certum est quod potest reddi certum', if you prefer Latin.

Certainty of objects: particular issues

Outright gifts, fixed trusts, and Burrough v Philcox trusts

7.61 In these cases, the object or each member of a class of objects must be known with certainty, or the gift or trust will fail. Thus a gift of '£1,000 to Jim' will fail if there is uncertainty as to who Jim is. The same goes for a trust of the income of 1,000 shares of ABC plc for Jim. Similarly, in the case of a gift to or fixed trust for a class, the trust fails unless the entire class can be ascertained with certainty. For example, '£100,000 on trust to pay the income to my children in equal shares' will fail unless each of the settlor's children can be ascertained. Thus the test of certainty in these cases is the 'complete list test' (recall **3.42**). The same test applies to a '*Burrough v Philcox*'-type discretionary trust (**7.10**), because each individual in the class will take an equal share should, for some reason, the trustee fail to appoint the trust property, just as the objects of a fixed trust for a class do.

7.62   A settlor may create a trust for a class whose members may be unborn, as in a trust for his grandchildren. Until they are born, of course, these objects are not ascertained, but that does not invalidate the trust for uncertainty of objects. These objects will be identified with certainty over the course of the trust as long as it is not perpetuitous (**3.31** et seq).

Powers and *McPhail* trusts

7.63   Previously (**3.44** et seq) it was discussed why the 'is or is not' test for certainty of objects was held to apply both to powers and to *McPhail*-type trusts. The *McPhail* case was remitted to the High Court for determination whether the trust was valid under the 'is or is not' test. Thence it went up to the CA as *Re Baden's Deed Trusts (No 2)* (1973). The trust was for, amongst others, employees and their 'dependants' and 'relatives'. 'Dependants' was not regarded as uncertain at all; it had been used in many other deeds and by Parliament to describe individuals financially dependent upon others for their support. 'Relatives', however, led to a difference of opinion. 'Relative' or 'relation' means a descendant from a common ancestor, and so everyone has an indefinite, though undoubtedly large, number of distant relatives about whom they have never heard; if such persons were to be included in the class, then it would be a very large class indeed, and if one thinks in grand historical terms, we may all descend from those original australopithecenes that managed to scrabble out a living in the Olduvai gorge some millions of years ago. There is nothing *conceptually* uncertain about 'descendant from a common ancestor'. The problem turns entirely on proving the connection, ie upon evidential uncertainty.

7.64   Sachs LJ made a clear distinction between conceptual and evidential certainty; the 'is or is not' test applies to the former, and 'the court is never defeated by evidential uncertainty'. It is a question of fact whether 'any individual postulant has on inquiry been proved to be within [the class]; if he is not so proved then he is not in it.' Thus it was perfectly alright that 'relative' means a descendant from a common ancestor. Someone offering sufficient proof of that 'is' within the class; someone unable to do so 'is not'. Sachs LJ did not say who has the onus of proof, though presumably if any postulant must be proved to be within it to take, then the trustees would have to be satisfied so that their decision would stand in the face of a challenge by another beneficiary. Thus although Sachs LJ would not allow evidential uncertainty to defeat the trust, he does rely upon the existence of evidence to define the boundaries of the class.

7.65 Megaw LJ introduced a factor of substantial numbers into the 'is or is not' test: if it could be said with certainty that a substantial number of beneficiaries fell within the class, the class was certain. If this means that only those may take who are within the 'substantial numbers' within the class on the evidence available to trustees at the outset, eg a list of company employees and their spouses and children, then this appears to cut down the class contrary to the settlor's intentions and reintroduce a version of the 'complete list' test. More likely, the 'substantial numbers' merely establishes the validity of the trust. In that case, however, it gives no guidance to the trustee when considering the extent of any survey he must make of the class before distributing (**3.48**), ie the extent of the consideration he must give to distributing to those not within the 'substantial numbers', yet who may fall within the class intended by the settlor.

7.66 Stamp LJ refused to allow evidential certainty to intrude upon or patch up the problems caused by a conceptually certain term: if 'relatives' means descendants of a common ancestor, one either glosses the word or the trust is void for uncertainty; the 'is or is not test' is a test of a class defined by the concepts the settlor used; it cannot be watered down to a test which depends upon a burden of proof, for that makes the test one of evidential certainty, not conceptual certainty, and raises the problem that only one or a few possible objects bring forward the suitable proof:

> [I]t is not enough that trustees should do nothing but distribute the fund among those objects of the trust who happen to be at hand or present themselves.

Rather, the trustees must survey the class of objects and so the test must indicate the scope of this duty, not merely determine the validity of making a payment to a particular individual who presents himself:

> [I]t would in my judgment follow that, treating the word relatives as meaning descendants of a common ancestor, a trust for distribution such as is here in question would not be valid. Any 'survey of the range of the objects or possible beneficiaries' would certainly be incomplete, and I am able to discern no principle on which such a survey could be conducted or where it should start or finish.

However Stamp LJ found authority for interpreting 'relatives' to mean next of kin, and on that basis found the trust valid.

7.67 One notes an important distinction between Stamp LJ's and Sachs LJ's opinions regarding the character of the trustees' duties. Sachs LJ seems concerned only that the trustees are able, with certainty, to distribute the money only to valid recipients, and therefore he focuses the 'is or is not' test on the status of 'any given postulant'. Stamp LJ emphasises the trustees' duty to survey the class, and from this perspective he is surely right that no sensible survey could be made of the employees and all those who have descended from a common ancestor, for that would be like surveying the UK. Almost certainly the trustees will think of 'relatives', when 'surveying the field', as the employees' near relatives. This difference reflects different senses in which a large, discretionary trust is a trust. For Stamp LJ, the whole class of objects really do have the right to be considered, and therefore the trustees must have a sensible picture of them as a whole; there appears a fairly traditional right-duty relationship between the class of beneficiaries and the trustees. For Sachs LJ, the objects are much less like a class, appearing rather as applicants or postulants to a fund for which they might qualify for a distribution, and the trustees are like power holders who may benefit particular individuals; their only duty is to make sure they get on with the job and distribute the funds, and so they need a solid test of whether or not any individual distribution is legitimate.

7.68 Together Sachs and Megaw LJJ found that 'relative' meaning 'descendent of a common ancestor' was not an invalidating term on the 'is or is not' test, though it remains so on the 'complete list' test. Thus a trust for one's 'relatives' in equal shares fails unless 'relatives' is read as next of kin.

Conditions precedent defining a class

7.69 One may make gifts subject to conditions precedent in equity (**3.22**). For example, one might give Blackacre to one's daughter conditional upon her obtaining a 2:1 degree. Notice that the condition does nothing to identify the donee. Here we are concerned with conditions precedent that do. In *Re Barlow's Will Trusts* the testatrix directed her executor to allow any of her friends to buy paintings from her collection at below market value. Thus the condition precedent, friendship, defined *a class* of potential donees, and so the standard of certainty required here makes a useful point of comparison with that for certainty of objects of a trust. Browne-Wilkinson J held that the executor was not required to determine a class of donees defined by the term 'friends', but rather that the direction should be construed as a series of individual gifts to such persons who could satisfy the criteria for 'friendship', on which criteria he gave guidance as we have seen (**7.43**). As a result, the decision in *Re Barlow's Will Trusts* appears to establish that, in the case of gifts with a condition precedent that defines a class, first, an 'is or is not' rather than a 'complete list' test is appropriate and, second, that the court will be liberal in determining criteria for vague terms.

Administrative unworkability and capriciousness

7.70 Not knowing when to stop is a problem that can happen to anyone, even judges. Just before concluding his judgment in *McPhail*, Lord Wilberforce said this:

> There may be a ... case where the meaning of the words used is clear but the definition of beneficiaries is so hopelessly wide as not to form 'anything like a class' so that the trust is administratively unworkable or in Lord Eldon LC's words one that cannot be executed ... I hesitate to give examples for they may prejudice future cases, but perhaps 'all the residents of Greater London' will serve. I do not think that a discretionary trust for 'relatives' even of a living person falls within this category.

Here we will try to give some kind of sensible meaning to this added condition on the validity of trusts, but it may be a hopeless enterprise.

7.71 In the first place, there is some ambiguity in respect of 'so hopelessly wide'; does this refer specifically to the size of the class, so that any discretionary trust for eight million or so would necessarily fail? Would that make sense given the court's willingness to validate the *McPhail* trust, where on broad reading of relative – descendant of a common ancestor – the class was surely huge, certainly in the millions? Why should mere size render the trust administratively unworkable anyway? Large numbers will not entail that the trustees will be stampeded with postulants; indeed, it is more likely that the beneficiaries of a small family trust, having the incentive to harangue the trustees, give trustees more trouble than any trust of the *McPhail* kind would. If the problem is the survey the trustees must undertake, the difficulty of doing that surely has more to do with whether the class or various sub-classes within it are defined in such a way as the trustees can determine the settlor's intentions regarding how they are to distribute within it, than with absolute numbers. Or does 'hopelessly wide' refer, not to the size of the class, but to the class definition; that is what the grammar of Lord Wilberforce's statement suggests. But what is it for a definition to be 'hopelessly wide'. Hopelessly vague? 'All the residents of Greater London' is not vague at all.

7.72   The only reported case in which a trust has failed for administrative unworkability is *R v District Auditor, ex p West Yorkshire Metropolitan County Council* (1986). The council was about to be abolished, and it proposed to transfer its remaining funds, £400,000, on trust for 'any or all or some of the inhabitants of the County of West Yorkshire' in order to benefit them in various ways, amongst which included informing all interested and influential persons of the consequences of its abolition. Lloyd LJ decided:

> A trust with as many as two and a half million potential beneficiaries is, in my judgement, quite simply unworkable. The class is far too large … It seems to me that the present trust comes within the … case to which Lord Wilberforce refers. I hope I am not guilty of being prejudiced by the example which he gave. But it could hardly be more apt, or fit the facts of the present case more precisely.

Lloyd LJ dismissed the idea that anything but the size of the class was at work to invalidate the power, in particular 'capriciousness', ie that the class was 'an accidental conglomeration of persons who had no discernible link with the settlor':

> [T]hat objection could not apply here. The council had every reason for wishing to benefit the inhabitants of West Yorkshire.

213

Yet significantly, he stated:

> What we have here, in a nutshell, is a non-charitable purpose trust.

Such trusts are normally invalid (chapter 9), because a trust for a purpose has no beneficiaries, and thus no one to enforce it. Therefore administrative unworkability may mean that the class of beneficiaries is 'hopelessly wide' because the trust is not really for a class of individuals at all; it is really a trust to carry out a purpose which is masquerading as a valid trust by the inclusion of a bogus class of beneficiaries.

7.73 Further guidance must be gleaned from three cases dealing not with discretionary trusts, but with 'intermediate' powers, ie powers to appoint to anyone in the world except for a specified class: *Blausten v IRC* (1972), *Re Manisty's Settlement* (1974), and *Re Hay's Settlement Trusts* (1981). In *Blausten* Buckley J held that such a power was only valid because under the particular provision in question any appointment by the trustees required the settlor's consent; this set metes and bounds on the exercise of the power. Otherwise it would have been invalid.

7.74 In *Manisty* Templeman J took quite the opposite view. As he saw it, the 'is or is not' test required only that it could be said with certainty whether any individual was an object of the power, and though the class of objects of an intermediate power were unlimited, there was no difficulty determining that. On this point Buckley J in *Blausten,* like Stamp LJ in *Re Baden (No 2),* focused on the duty to survey, while Templeman J, like Sachs LJ, emphasised the validity of any particular appointment. On the question whether a trustee is given any guidance in his exercise of the power in such a case, Templeman J was not perturbed, for the expectations of the settlor are often not difficult to discern; though 'all the beneficiaries are equal some are more equal than others'; while the terms of the power itself may not guide the trustees, that does not mean that they may not sensibly exercise it, which is presumably why the settlor gave them absolute discretion to do so. And it appears that the trustees' duty to survey the entire class of objects is not onerous:

> If a settlor creates a power exercisable in favour of his issue, his relations, and the employees of his company, the trustees may in practice for many years hold regular meetings, study the terms of the power and the other provisions of the settlement, examine the accounts and either decide not to exercise the power or to exercise it only in favour, for example, of the children of the settlor. During that period the existence of the

power may not be disclosed to any relation or employee and the trustees may not seek or receive any information concerning the circumstances of any relation or employee. In my judgment it cannot be said that the trustees in those circumstances have committed a breach of trust and that they ought to have advertised the power or looked beyond the persons who are most likely to be the objects of the bounty of the settlor.

7.75   Significantly, Templeman J directly related the concept of administrative unworkability to the idea of capriciousness by reference to Lord Wilberforce's example:

> The court may also be persuaded to intervene if the trustees act 'capriciously', that is to say, act for reasons which I apprehend could be said to be irrational, perverse, or irrelevant to any sensible expectation of the settlor; for example, if they chose a beneficiary by height or complexion or by the irrelevant fact that he was a resident of Greater London ... The objection to the capricious exercise of a power may well extend to the creation of a capricious power. A power to benefit 'residents of Greater London' is capricious because the terms of the power negative any sensible intention on the part of the settlor. If the settlor intended and expected the trustees would have regard to persons with some claim on his bounty or some interest in an institution favoured by the settlor, or if the settlor had any other sensible intention or expectation, he would not have required the trustees to consider only an accidental conglomeration of persons who have no discernible link with the settlor or any institution. A capricious power negatives a sensible consideration by the trustees of the exercise of the power.

7.76   Here we have another candidate for the meaning of administrative unworkability: the settlor's direction is so capricious that no trustee could discern a sensible way to carry it out. However it is doubtful that there is any real standard for capriciousness that will defeat a trust. In *Bird v Luckie* (1850) Wigram VC said:

> No man is bound to make a will in such a manner as to deserve approbation from the prudent, the wise, or the good. A testator is permitted to be capricious and improvident ...

And the English case generally cited as authority for the court's power to strike down capricious directions is a purpose trust case. In *Brown v Burdett* (1882) the testator's instruction to trustees to block up the rooms of a house for 20 years was struck down.

7.77 In *Hay's* Megarry VC opined that the width of a power *per se* could not invalidate it if it were given to a non-trustee. The difficulty arises when the power is given to a trustee, whose fiduciary position requires him to deal with the power responsibly. He said:

> [T]he duties of a trustee which are specific to a mere power seem to be threefold. Apart from the obvious duty of obeying the trust instrument, and in particular of making no appointment that is not authorised by it, the trustee must, first, consider periodically whether or not he should exercise the power; second, consider the range of objects of the power; and third, consider the appropriateness of individual appointments.

7.78 Megarry VC specifically rejected Buckley J's view that an intermediate power (if not saved by the settlor's consent provision as in *Blausten*) would be invalid as creating a class so wide as not to form a true class:

> I do not see how mere numbers can inhibit the trustees from considering whether or not to exercise the power.

He held the intermediate power valid. With regard to administrative unworkability, he simply pointed out that Lord Wilberforce's words concerning administrative unworkability were directed to discretionary trusts, not powers. With regard to capriciousness, he doubted Templeman J's analysis of a power to benefit 'residents of Greater London':

> In saying that, I do not think the judge had in mind a case in which the settlor was, for instance, a former chairman of the Greater London Council ...

7.79 Unfortunately Megarry VC went on to say this:

> Of course, if there is a real vice in a power, and there are real problems of execution or administration, the court may have to hold the power invalid.

A real vice in a power? Real problems of execution or administration? It is hardly helpful of Megarry VC to conclude a discussion of what makes a power bad or administratively unworkable by throwing out a couple of novel criteria for invalidity which he leaves unexplained.

7.80 Megarry VC did, however, say this regarding discretionary trusts, although the statement is clearly obiter:

I consider that the duties of trustees under a discretionary trust are more stringent than those of trustees under a power of appointment, ... and as at present advised I think that I would, if necessary, hold that an intermediate trust [ie a trust by which the trustees could appoint to anyone save a specified class] is void as being administratively unworkable.

But why? The mere presence of a duty to distribute neither clarifies nor muddies the trustee's task – it just means the trustee must distribute the property. If the task cannot be carried out, it would seem as impossible to carry it out for both powers and trusts, and conversely, if it can be carried out for one, it can be carried out for the other. It seems an inadequate reason to hold an 'intermediate' trust void.

7.81 McKay (1974) considers five possible interpretations of 'administrative unworkability': (1) the beneficiaries of a valid class have no common attributes; (2) the class is too large; (3) the trustees will be unable to perform their administrative duties; (4) the court will be unable to execute the settlor's directions; and (5) the trust is capricious. In view of the past cases in which trusts or powers which have been held by the court to be valid, McKay argues that not only is there no discernible flaw in the trust for 'residents of Greater London' which should render it invalid, but also that:

None of the possible bases upon which [administrative unworkability] could or has been said to rest satisfactorily provides a substantive base for it ... this is principally due to the disruptive influence acceptance of any of those grounds would have on both the decided cases and the presumed spirit and intention of *McPhail v Doulton* itself.

7.81A Swadling (2000) suggests that the test of administrative workability requires there to be a 'core class' of objects within the larger class to which the trustees may primarily devote their survey of objects, eg the employees, not their relatives, in *McPhail*. While this is a useful suggestion, it has not been endorsed by any decision, and it does not follow in any obvious way from Lord Wilberforce's actual words.

7.82 Here's a final suggestion drawn from Lord Reid's opinion in *Re Gulbenkian*, where he said:

I could understand it being held that if the classes of potential beneficiaries were so numerous that it would cost quite disproportionate enquiries and expense to find them all and discover their needs or deserts, then the provision would fail.

Consider the following discretionary trust: '£1,000 on trust to be distributed in such amounts as my trustees shall in their absolute discretion see fit amongst those persons who have given up their seat on a bus to the settlor'. The problem here seems to be that in order to determine which persons are eligible, the trustees will have, at a minimum, to advertise, and will probably have to conduct some investigations of those coming forward to determine the validity of any payments; thus in order to carry out any survey of the objects the trustees will have to deal with evidential difficulties, and £1,000 will not be enough to enable them to do so if the recipients are going to receive any worthwhile amounts. Thus, in line with Lord Wilberforce's view that the equal division of the trust fund amongst all the beneficiaries of the *McPhail* trust would benefit no one, the costs of administering this trust would probably result in no payments being made; thus to carry out the trust would result in its defeat in practice. On that basis, one might well say that the trust is administratively unworkable. And if one does want seriously to argue that the duties of a trustee to survey the field are more onerous than those of the trustee of a mere power, we may, if we interpret administrative unworkability in this way, explain why administrative unworkability only applies to invalidate trusts and not powers: regarding this example, we might allow a power to stand, for if anyone who gave up their seat on the bus to the settlor showed up and proved that he had done so, he could be paid by the trustees. The extent of the power-holder's survey would be simply to take the claims of postulants seriously, rather than having to make some effort to hunt them down. Conversely, the trustee of a discretionary trust *must* carry out some sort of search simply because the trustee *must* distribute the fund and therefore *must* find someone who can be paid, and *ex hypothesi*, that search would exhaust the trust fund.

Effects of uncertainty

7.83 At the risk of stating the obvious: where property is given to a named individual, if there is uncertainty of intention in that it is uncertain as to whether a trust obligation has been imposed, then that individual takes the gift absolutely, free of any trust obligations. If property is given to a trustee *virtute officii,* ie as a trustee, it is assumed the intention was to create a trust, but if the objects or subject matter is uncertain, the trustee will hold the property on an ART (**4.2** et seq), or as part of the residue if the failed trust is testamentary. If there is certainty of intention but uncertainty of subject matter, then there can be no disposition of property to found the trust, and thus the intended trust fails. If there is certainty of intention and subject matter but uncertainty of objects, ie there is no one the court is willing to hold to be beneficiaries or objects of a power, the property is held on an ART, or falls into residue if the failed trust is testamentary.

Further reading

Emery (1982); Hopkins (1971); Grubb (1982); Hayton (1994); McKay (1974); Penner (2004)

Must read cases: *Barclay's Bank v Quistclose Investments* (1970); *Twinsectra v Yardley* (2002); *IRC v Broadway Cottages Trust* (1955); *McPhail v Doulton* (1970); *Re Baden (No 2)* (1973); *Re Tuck's ST* (1978); *Re Goldcorp Exchange* (1995); *Hunter v Moss* (1994); *Re Hay's ST* (1981)

Self-test questions

1. What is uncertainty of intention, and how does it relate to uncertainty of subject matter or objects?

2. What is conceptual uncertainty and what may be done to resolve it?

3. What, if anything, is 'administrative unworkability'?

4. Consider the validity and the effect of the following testamentary gifts:
    (A) £100,000 to Fred for his use in his remaining days, to leave what is left to Tom by will.
    (B) £200,000 on trust for distribution as the trustees shall in their absolute discretion see fit, to persons or dependants of persons who have had coal miners in the family for at least three generations.
    (C) One of my vintage cars to each of my old friends.
    (D) The residue of my estate to my trustees for distribution to such persons and in such proportions as they in their absolute discretion see fit, save that no distribution whatsoever shall be made to my wife or children.

5. Raymond, a builder, borrowed £20,000 from Floyd's Bank. The loan document stated, 'You will hold this money on trust for us until you spend it on the Loan Purpose (see overleaf)' and under 'Loan Purpose' was written 'for business purposes'. The loan was negotiated at his local Floyd's branch and Floyd's Bank paid the money into Raymond's business account at his branch the next day (the bank's standard practice). In the next several weeks Raymond drew cheques on the account (i) to pay £3000 in past parking fines he mostly incurred parking his van near jobsites; (ii) to pay his brother £4000 he owed him, money borrowed to buy his van; (iii) £1000 to his mother as a birthday present. Discuss.

CHAPTER EIGHT

The Constitution of Trusts

SUMMARY

Equity will not assist a volunteer

Perfecting an imperfect gift: I: the *Re Rose* principle; II: the rule in *Strong v Bird*; III: *Donationes mortis causa*; IV: proprietary estoppel

Covenants to settle

The equitable enforcement of covenants to settle

The enforcement of covenants to settle at common law

The trust of the benefit of a promise to settle

Fortuitous vesting

Concluding considerations on covenants

8.1   A trust is fully set up, or constituted, only when the property is in the hands of a person who is properly bound to be a trustee. The issues which arise concerning the constitution of trusts are closely tied up with equity's general principles for dealing with gifts, and so we shall begin by considering gifts in general. A gift is any transaction which benefits an individual who has not paid, ie given any consideration, for it; such an individual is called a 'volunteer'.

8.2   In *Milroy v Lord* (1862) Turner LJ laid down three 'modes' of making a gift:

*   an outright transfer of the legal title to the property (or the outright assignment of an already existing equitable interest);

- a transfer of the legal title of the property to a trustee to hold on trust; or

- a self-declaration of trust.

8.3 In the case of a self-declaration, the constitution of the trust is automatic; the title to the trust property is in the hands of the trustee as soon as the declaration is made because he made the declaration. Where the settlor transfers property to B on trust for C, he must both effectively declare the trust, and effectively transfer the title to the property to B – it is this second step which constitutes the trust.

'Equity will not assist a volunteer'

8.4 The maxim 'equity will not assist a volunteer' describes an important guiding principle of the court of equity. The principle has two main strands:

- equity will not enforce gratuitous promises; and

- equity will not perfect an imperfect gift.

Equity will not enforce gratuitous promises

8.5 If A promises B that he will give him Blackacre, or if A promises B that he will put Blackacre in trust for him, and A refuses to deliver on his promise, equity will not enforce the promise at B's request. As Hackney ((1987), 118) puts it, 'You cannot sue for presents in equity'.

Equity will not perfect an imperfect gift

8.6 In *Milroy v Lord*, Turner LJ said:

> [I]n order to render the settlement [ie the gift] binding, one or other of these modes [**8.2**, above] must, as I understand the law of this Court, be resorted to, for there is no equity in this Court to perfect an imperfect gift. The cases I think go further to this extent, that if the settlement is intended to be effectuated by one of the modes to which I have referred, the Court will not give effect to it by applying another of those modes. If it is intended to take effect by transfer, the Court will not hold the

intended transfer to operate as a declaration of trust, for then every imperfect instrument would be made effectual by being converted into a perfect trust.

Thus the three 'modes' of conferring a benefit are three *mutually exclusive* 'modes'; equity will not treat the intentions of a donor to make an outright gift, where the property for one reason or another fails to pass from the donor to the donee, as a self-declaration of trust. *Jones v Lock* (1865) and *Richards v Delbridge* (1874) are illustrative. In *Jones v Lock*, the 'cheque for baby' case (**7.15**), everything turned on the true intentions of the father. Although he intended to make provision for the infant in various ways, he did not intend to declare a trust of the cheque. As a result, the court found that there was no self-declaration of trust, and the court would not give aid to one claiming the benefit of an imperfect gift. Similarly, in *Richards v Delbridge*, the court would not devise a trust in order to perfect the ineffective legal assignment by Delbridge of the lease to his mill and the stock in trade of his business to his grandson.

8.7   Equity will also not perfect an ineffective transfer of the legal title to property to an intended trustee to constitute a trust by treating the intending settlor as having made a valid self-declaration of trust. If the property fails to get into the hands of the intended trustee, there is no trust. Recently, however, the PC in *T Choithram SA v Pagarani* (2001) generously construed the words of a rich businessman intending to transfer almost the entirely of his wealth on trust shortly before his death. Having just executed a deed of trust establishing a charitable foundation and appointing himself as one of the trustees, he orally indicated that he 'gave' all his wealth to the foundation. He never executed the necessary documents to transfer legal title in his property to the trustees. The PC held that in this context, his words of gift could be interpreted as words of declaration of trust and, being one of the trustees of the foundation, this constituted the trust, although the reasoning can be criticised (see Rickett (2001)).

8.8   But be careful to note what 'equity will not assist a volunteer' does not mean: it does not mean that volunteers who are *already* beneficiaries under an *existing* trust have no rights in a court of equity. As beneficiaries of a constituted trust they are fully entitled to the benefit of the trust, have equitable proprietary rights in the trust property, have the right to sue the trustees to enforce the trust, and so on. It does not matter whether they are volunteers or not at this stage. Indeed, most trusts are for volunteers, since most trusts are created by settlors to benefit family members who have certainly never paid the settlor for their benefits under the trust. Equity is not in the business of dismantling *effectively* transferred gifts, or dismantling *effectively* constituted trusts. In short, equity will not assist volunteers *to become* donees or beneficiaries under a trust, but once a person is a donee or a beneficiary, it matters not one whit whether he paid for the privilege or got it for free (*Ellison v Ellison* (1802); *Paul v Paul* (1882)).

Non-volunteers

8.9 By contrast, by *extreme contrast*, the intended non-volunteer beneficiary of a trust, ie one who has given consideration, may rely on the eager assistance of equity to constitute the trust. Obviously, an intended 'donee' who has given consideration for an 'outright gift' is in a different position as well, which is reflected in a complete change of terminology. A 'donee' who has given consideration is not a donee: he's a buyer under a contract of sale. He will therefore have common law legal rights for damages if the seller refuses to perform, and in the case of land and unique chattels, equity will not only order specific performance if the seller refuses to transfer the property, equity will regard the title to the property as having passed the moment the contract is formed (**5.3**). In the case of a promise to create a trust for which the intended beneficiary has provided consideration, equity will again specifically enforce the promise and find a constructive trust in his favour.

Future property

8.10 Promises to transfer property on trust, or 'promises to settle', often involve 'future property', which we have already encountered (**6.60**); future property is property which someone *might* receive, such as a legacy under a will, or royalties from the sale of a book. It is thus no more than a *spes* (**6.60**) or mere 'expectancy'. The case of future property provides an example of equity's willingness to perfect an imperfect legal transaction where consideration is given. Because future property does not exist, it obviously cannot be transferred. Thus if I execute a deed whereby I purport to assign to you all the royalties from a book not yet published, that deed assigns nothing, for no royalties exist; thus at common law, an assignment of future property is totally ineffective. If the assignment is gratuitous then equity of course will not take any steps to make the intended assignment effective either. If, however, you give consideration for the assignment, then equity will perfect this imperfect transaction: equity will treat the assignment of future property as a contractual obligation to assign the future property if and when it is received (*Tailby v Official Receiver* (1888); *Re Ellenborough* (1903)). On a similar basis, in *Don King Productions Inc v Warren* (1998; affd CA 1999) Lightman J held that partners could hold the benefit of their individual rights under personal contracts on trust for the partnership, even though such rights could not be assigned at law.

The general principle behind all of this is that equity is happy to come to the aid of someone who has given consideration for the benefit of property, but is unwilling to do so on behalf of a volunteer. Nevertheless, there are a number of exceptions to this basic rule.

Perfecting an imperfect gift: I – The *Re Rose* principle

8.11 In *Re Rose* (1952), the CA interpreted *Milroy v Lord* to the effect that, while equity cannot perfect a gift where a donor has not done everything in law which he must do to transfer his title, it will treat as effective an intended transfer where the donor has done everything he is obliged to do to make the gift valid. In *Re Rose* the donor had properly executed a share transfer form and delivered it, with the appropriate share certificate, to the donee. Though the legal title to the shares did not pass until the donee registered the transfer with the company, the court held that, in equity, such a gift is valid from the time that the donor does everything he is obliged to do to transfer the shares. After he has done that, and until such time as the shares are registered in the donee's name, the donor holds the shares as a trustee for the donee. If a dividend were declared in the interim, the donor would accordingly hold the dividend payment upon trust for the donee as well.

8.12 *Re Fry* (1946) may appear to be out of line with this view. In that case a donor of British company shares who was resident in America was required by law to obtain the consent of the British Treasury before he could effectively transfer his legal interest. While the donor had done everything he could, in that he had completed the transfer form in favour of his son and had submitted the necessary forms to the Treasury, he died before the Treasury had given permission for the transfer. Romer J held that the donee had obtained no interest in the shares, and applying *Milroy v Lord*, refused to treat the transaction as having passed the beneficial interest in equity. Romer J thought that it was up to the donor to obtain, not just apply for, Treasury permission, and that furthermore, since the Treasury might have sought further information before granting permission, the donor might well have had an opportunity to scuttle his own gift by failing to provide that information; therefore the donor had not done everything necessary to divest himself of his interest in the shares nor relinquished his power over them.

8.13 *Mascall v Mascall* (1984) is a case applying the *Re Rose* principle to transfers of land. There the court held that the intending donor had made a complete gift in equity by executing the registered land transfer document and handing it, with the land certificate, to the donee. Again, as in *Re Rose,* until registration of title the donor holds the land in trust for the donee.

8.14 The ambit of the rule has been expanded by the recent CA decision in *Pennington v Waine* (2002). There a shareholder properly completed a share transfer form in favour of her nephew, but instead of passing this to the company for registration, delivered it to one of the company's auditors; she also informed her nephew of her intention to transfer the shares. On the strength of this and a statement from the auditor, her nephew became a director of the company, a position which required a shareholding. The shareholder died before the transfer was completed. Clearly, in this case, unlike *Re Rose*, the transferor had not done 'everything in her power' to secure the share transfer. The CA held, however, that the shares were held on trust for the nephew, apparently on the basis that all that is required for the rule to operate is the execution of the transfer form with the intention that the transfer is to have immediate practical effect, in circumstances where it would be 'unconscionable' for the transferor to renege on the transaction. The decision makes the rule now very uncertain, and we can expect all kinds of imperfect transactions to reach the courts on the basis that it would be unconscionable if they were not perfected (see also Garton (2003)).

II – The rule in *Strong v Bird*

8.15 At common law the appointment of a debtor to be one's executor had the effect of cancelling the executor's debts to the estate. This result

*for payment
of debt
of which*

was determined by the application of the following technical reasoning: the executor, on becoming the owner of the testator's property and the successor to all of the testator's rights in action, was placed in the position of having to sue himself to recover the debt; since one cannot have a right of action against oneself, the debt was effectively cancelled. Originally equity prevailed over this rule and made the executor account for the money to the deceased's estate, but in *Strong v Bird* (1874) the court of equity held that the common law rule should prevail, if, and only if, the testator had manifested an intention to forgive the debt in his lifetime and this intent continued up to his death. This is something like the perfecting of a gift, since the debt is regarded as discharged without a formal release of the debt being made.

8.16   The rule was extended in *Re Stewart* (1908) to apply not only to imperfectly released debts, but also to imperfect gifts, again if, and only if, the testator had manifested an intent to give the gift in his lifetime and this intent continued up to his death. Whatever the merits of this extension of the rule, it should be understood that with this extension equity is now positively assisting a volunteer. In *Strong v Bird* itself, the court simply allowed the common law rule to stand in particular cases, ie where the continuing intention of the testator was to release the debt. But there has never been any common law rule whereby an ineffective attempt to make a gift during the testator's life is made effective upon the putative donee's being appointed his executor. Equity is acting off its own bat to assist a volunteer in this case.

8.17   Here are the oft-quoted words of Neville J in *Re Stewart*:

> The reasoning is first that the vesting of the property in the executor at the testator's death completes the imperfect gift made in the lifetime and secondly that the intention of the testator to give the beneficial interest to the executor is sufficient to countervail the equity of the beneficiaries under the will, the testator having vested the legal estate in the executor.

The first leg of this reasoning emphasises the 'fortuitous' vesting of the property: equity will perfect the imperfect gift just because it gets into the hands of the person it was intended for. The second leg appears to state that the rationale for perfecting the gift is that the gift was intended for the donor's executor, as if a donor's appointment of someone to be his executor has special significance in this regard. While one may presume that a testator has faith in the trustworthiness and competence of his executor, it is fanciful to believe that many, or indeed any, testators pick their executors in the knowledge that in doing so they will perfect any invalid gifts or releases of personal debts made to them during their lifetime. The rule seems to work purely on the basis of the 'fortuitous' vesting of the property in the hands of the executors.

8.18   This view supports the extension of the rule in *Re James* (1935) to imperfect gifts made to someone who on the *intestacy* of the donor is appointed one of the administrators of the deceased's estate (**2.61**). This extension was doubted in *Re Gonin* (1979) by Walton J, who would restrict the application of the rule to executors, for they are chosen by the testator, while administrators are chosen by the court, usually from amongst a number of people who might serve. Extending the rule to administrators turned the rule into 'something in the nature of a lottery'. The rule in *Strong v Bird* itself creates an unprincipled lottery however, because one cannot truly suppose that the appointment of a person to be one's executor indicates anything about the testator's intentions to perfect imperfect gifts – how many solicitors, do you think, advise their clients about the rule in *Strong v Bird* when instructed to draw up a will? As a rule by which imperfect gifts are perfected by fortuitous vesting, it applies just as much to the administrator as to the executor. The original reaction of equity to the common law rule regarding the release of executor's debts is the right one; he should account to the estate for the debts he owes it. Once *Strong v Bird* overturned this sensible attitude of equity, then there can be nothing but a lottery in which some individuals will have imperfect gifts perfected, and others not, purely on the basis of who ends up, by hook or by crook, as the personal representative of the deceased. The rule has nothing to recommend it and the HL, which has never affirmed it, should overrule it the first chance it gets.

8.19   Applying the rule depends upon showing the deceased had a 'continuing intention' to release the debt or make the gift. It is important to understand what 'continuing intention' means. In *Re Pink* (1912) Kennedy LJ said:

> [A] continuing intention on the part of the testator means … a continuing intention that the gift should have been given at the time it was given.

Thus the deceased's intention must be that he had made an immediate gift which he thought was effective, and maintained that view up until his death. Thus properly understood, the deceased's intention is better framed as his *continuing belief* that he had released the debt or made an outright gift. The doctrine specifically does not cover an intention to make an *inter vivos* gift in the future, a promise to make a gift, or the intention to give the property at one's death. Hayton ((2001b), 258-59) questions whether the restriction to failed immediate gifts is consistent, since once equity has gone so far as to assist volunteers simply because of fortuitous vesting, why should it not allow the perfection of promises or intentions to give *inter vivos* or testamentary gifts? Kodilinye (1982) points out that the present rule at least reflects the situation as the deceased understood it to be – ie his view was that he had given away the property or released the debt, while the suggested extension would enforce promises that the deceased knew full well that he had not complied with. The point is well taken, but on Hayton's extension of the doctrine it would still have to be proven that the deceased has a continuing intention to carry out the promise; thus in both cases the doctrine would equally give effect to the deceased's wishes, and from that perspective it is difficult to distinguish between the merits of the two situations.

8.20 The rule in *Strong v Bird* requires that the property of a gift to be perfected is specific and identifiable as subject matter which might have been previously transferred in accordance with the deceased's beliefs/intentions. Thus ineffective gifts of or promises to give future property (**8.10**) or sums of money, cannot be perfected by the rule.

8.21 Following *Re Ralli's Will Trusts* (1963), in which Buckley J made reference to the rule in *Strong v Bird* in finding that a trust was constituted when the property fortuitously came into the hands of the trustee, it appears that the rule applies to perfect not only imperfect gifts but unconstituted trusts where the intended trustee becomes the deceased's personal representative. Again, the deceased must have maintained the continuing belief or 'intention' that he had constituted the trust, though in fact the transfer to the trustee was ineffective.

III – *Donationes mortis causa*

8.22 *Donationes mortis causa* (singular *donatio mortis causa*), also called deathbed gifts, are gifts which are made *inter vivos*, but which are conditional, only taking effect on death. If the donor revives and demands the property back, he is entitled to it. Conditional gifts of tangible personal property, like a book or a bicycle, have always been possible at common law; the gift transaction takes place in the normal way by the transfer of possession, but on condition, and on death the condition is perfected and the gift becomes absolute. The intervention of equity is necessary, however, to perfect gifts of things like money in a bank balance or shares, which can not simply be handed over on one's deathbed, but require more to transfer title.

8.23 *Cain v Moon* (1869) laid down the essential requirements for a valid *donatio mortis causa* (DMC):

- The gift must be in contemplation, though not necessarily expectation, of death. All the reported cases deal with a donor suffering from illness, but, for example, going into battle or attempting to climb the Matterhorn should do.

- The donee must in some respect receive the property in question before the death of the donor; what this amounts to turns on the nature of the property; for a chattel, the donee must take possession or acquire the means to do so, eg the key to a box in which it is held. Receiving some clear token of the property will suffice, as in *Woodard v Woodard* (1995) where receiving the keys to a car, though not the logbook, was sufficient. For a bank account balance, some 'indicia of title' must be transferred, such as the deposit book; in case of shares the delivery of share certificates has been held to work (*Dufficy v Mollica* (1968)), and the CA recognised a DMC of land for the first time in *Sen v Headley* (1991) where the indicia of title transferred was the title deeds.

- Finally, the circumstances must show that the property is to revert to the donor if it turns out that he recovers; in other words, the *gift must be made conditional on the donor's impending death*. It is a common error in exams to assume that all imperfect gifts following which the donor soon dies can be perfected as DMCs – only gifts *conditional* on the donor's death may be. A DMC was held valid where the donor died from pneumonia rather than from the incurable disease in contemplation of which the gift was made (*Wilkes v Allington* (1931)); this case is generally understood to stand for the proposition that, so long as the gift is made in contemplation of death, it matters not whether the testator dies in the particular way he expected.

IV – Proprietary estoppel

8.24 In certain cases of proprietary estoppel (**5.20**) the court, to give effect to the plaintiff's 'minimum equity', will do what amounts to perfecting an imperfect gift. In *Pascoe v Turner* (1979) a man declared to the woman with whom he was living as her husband that the house was 'hers and everything in it'. She spent most of her savings on the house. Following their separation he tried to turn her out. The court held that the minimum equity in the case was for the man to transfer the fee simple to the woman.

Covenants to settle

8.25 Covenants are promises formally expressed by being written in a deed; formerly deeds needed to be sealed, typically by a blob of wax or a red wafer affixed to the document; now (Law of Property (Miscellaneous Provisions) Act 1989, s 1) deeds must be signed and witnessed, and seals are no longer required. If the covenantor, the party who makes the promise in a deed, fails to perform what he promised, the covenantee, the party to whom the promise was made, may bring an action at common law for damages. Covenants are very much the product of formal legal thinking: the deed itself was all important. If the seal fell off the deed, then the covenantee could not sue upon it. If after having the covenant enforced against him, the covenantor left the deed undefaced in the covenantee's possession, the covenantee could sue on it and be awarded damages again (**1.4**). Thus, covenants are expressions of voluntarily-undertaken obligations which, because they are expressed in a particular form, can be enforced at common law.

8.26 Covenants must be distinguished from contracts. The modern law of contract developed entirely separately from the law of covenants. The modern law of contract does not require any formal expression of an agreement for it to be legally binding (except in so far as formality requirements have been imposed by statute, eg Law of Property (Miscellaneous Provisions) Act 1989, s 2 requires contracts for the sale of land to be in writing). In the course of its development of contract law the courts developed the doctrine of consideration. Why and how it particularly arose is complicated, but in its modern formulation it essentially requires that in order for a voluntarily-undertaken obligation, roughly, a 'promise', to be legally binding, the person to whom it is made, the promisee, must have given value or 'consideration' for it. The doctrine of consideration has nothing to do with the law of covenants. A covenant is formal means by which the common law allows persons to make legally binding promises, *regardless* of consideration. In view of this, while promises under seal are sometimes called 'specialty' contracts, it is not clear that one should treat covenants as governed by the law of contract *per se*, rather than by their own bespoke law of covenants, which will of course in many respects be similar or identical. This is of some importance, for covenants to settle are arrangements between two parties, the covenantor/settlor and the convanantee/trustee, for the benefit of a third party, the beneficiary. If they are truly contracts, then they will be governed by the Contracts (Rights of Third Parties) Act 1999, which will permit third party beneficiaries of a contract, basically for the first time in modern English legal history, to sue under the contract for their benefit. However, if covenants are not truly contracts, then the Act will not apply. We will see.

8.27 While equity will not assist a volunteer, equity will in many cases assist those who have given consideration, by for example, ordering the specific performance of a contract in certain circumstances. But combine the maxim 'equity looks to intent not form' with 'equity will not assist a volunteer' and it is clear that in equity a gratuitous promise is a gratuitous promise whether in a deed or not, and so equity will not enforce a promise just because it is in a deed even if the common law will. If I make a legally binding contract to buy your Rembrandt, I will have given good consideration, and so not only may I sue you for damages if you fail to deliver the Rembrandt, I may get an order for specific performance from equity (now governed by Sale of Goods Act 1979, s 52) because it is unique and money damages would be inadequate. If, however, you promise to give me the Rembrandt in a covenant, though I can still sue you at common law for money damages if you fail to deliver, I cannot get specific performance from equity, for equity will not assist a volunteer. This marked distinction looks even more odd in light of the fact that neither the common law, nor equity (*Bassett v Nosworthy* (1673); *Midland Bank Trust Co Ltd v Green* (1981)) is concerned about the 'adequacy' of consideration, ie whether the amount paid for the property is substantial or trivial. Thus if I contract with you to provide you with a lease in return for your paying me a peppercorn, equity will specifically enforce that contractual obligation, indeed will treat me as having granted you the lease already (**5.3**), but if I make the same promise in a covenant for no consideration, it will not.

Covenants to settle and marriage settlements

8.28   A 'covenant to settle' is simply a covenant to create a trust, eg 'I, X, hereby covenant with Y that I shall transfer Blackacre to Y on trust for Z'. While X may covenant with Y to transfer property to him on trust for Z in any circumstance, covenants to settle were typical provisions in marriage settlements. A marriage settlement is a trust created by a man and a woman in contemplation of marriage. Normally the property is vested in separate trustees, but in certain cases the husband would be the trustee. Marriage settlements were popular amongst the propertied classes in the nineteenth century, and essentially allowed the wife of the marriage to have control over the property she brought into the marriage, for at common law, a married woman's property became her husband's; it could thus be squandered by a wastrel husband, and if the wife died before her husband without 'issue', ie without having had children, the property brought into the marriage would pass to him and thence to his heirs. Thus the families of wives settled property upon them in trust, first, to allow the woman control over the property she brought into the marriage, for the settlement would give the wife certain powers over it, and secondly, the trust would direct that the property of the wife would be held on trust for her next of kin, ie her own relations, if she should die without issue.

8.29   Typically marriage settlements included covenants with the trustees of the settlement by both the husband and wife to settle 'after-acquired' property on the trusts of the settlement. 'After-acquired property' is simply property acquired after the date of the marriage, and such covenants typically restricted the obligation to property above a certain value. Coming from rich families, both the husband and wife were likely to inherit significant wealth only after the marriage began, and the inclusion of such inherited wealth in the marriage settlement would naturally be 'part of the bargain' which established their position in the dynastic line of both families. Thus both the husband and wife would make a covenant with the trustees to transfer to them, on the trusts of the marriage settlement, any property they would receive over, say, £100 in value. These covenants were not made for any consideration recognised at common law. Equity, by contrast, regarded marriage as 'the most valuable consideration imaginable' (A-G v Jacobs-Smith (1895)), and so though equity would not enforce these promises to settle because they were formalised as covenants, it would enforce them because 'marriage consideration' had been provided. Furthermore, equity regarded the issue of the marriage and their issue, ie the children and grandchildren, to be 'within the marriage consideration', and thus able to enforce the covenants. The doctrine of marriage consideration applies only to marriage settlements, that is settlements made in contemplation of marriage. A husband and wife who are already married who set up a trust for themselves and their children do not create a marriage settlement, and the children are not within any marriage consideration.

The enforcement of covenants to settle by equity

Covenants in marriage settlements

8.30 Because equity recognises marriage consideration, it is willing to enforce covenants to settle in marriage settlements, that is, it will order the covenantor to transfer the property to the trustees of the settlement, thus constituting the trust over the property specified in the covenant. Pullan v Koe (1913) is a typical case. The settlement included the usual covenant by the wife to settle after-acquired property of £100 or more. The wife received £285; she spent part of it and put the rest into bonds in her husband's name. On the husband's death, the trustees of the settlement sued his executors for the transfer of the bonds to them so they could hold them on the marriage settlement trusts. The court held that it was the duty of the trustees to enforce the covenant, and equity would order specific performance of the covenant, as there existed beneficiaries of the marriage settlement who were within the marriage consideration. The court held further that the £285 was impressed with the trust the moment the wife received it, equity looking upon that as done which ought to be done (5.3). Thus not only would equity insist on specific performance of the covenant, but that the trust was constituted by way of constructive trust the minute the covenant could be performed.

8.31 Re Plumptre's Marriage Settlement (1910) is a counterpart case: here, the next of kin, who were to take the property if there were no issue of the marriage, sued to enforce a covenant to settle after-acquired property. Their suit failed. The court would not order specific performance, as they were volunteers, not being within the marriage consideration. Eve J relied upon the unanimous CA decision in *Re D'Angibau* (1879), in which Cotton LJ emphasised the distinction between a fully constituted trust, under which volunteer beneficiaries have just as much right as beneficiaries who have given consideration, and a gratuitous promise to create a trust, which will not be enforced against the promisor at the suit of volunteers.

8.32 What happens if a wife receives after-acquired property (bound by a covenant to settle) at a time when there are children of the marriage, but she never transfers the property to the trustees, and later the children die? Can the next of kin argue that the trust was immediately constituted by way of constructive trust as in *Pullan* when the wife received the property, since at that time the covenant was specifically enforceable, there being children of the marriage within the marriage consideration? Once a trust is constituted, it is constituted for all the beneficiaries, volunteers or not (**8.8**); even if it is constituted as a result of a beneficiary who has given consideration suing to enforce the covenant, once the trust is constituted by the covenantor transferring the property to the trustees, it is constituted for non-volunteer and volunteer beneficiaries alike (*Davenport v Bishopp* (1843)). So if the wife had transferred the property to the trustees, the trust would have been constituted for all the beneficiaries, and if the children died the next of kin would have a perfect right to their benefits under the terms of the settlement. Therefore, does not the application of the maxim 'equity looks upon that as done ...' to constitute the trust immediately via a constructive trust also constitute the trust for the next of kin? Alas, no. Apparently, the trust constituted by the constructive trust becomes unconstituted again, believe it or not, when those within the marriage consideration disappear, because the constructive trust evaporates. According to Eve J in *Re Plumptre's Marriage Settlement*:

> [T]he argument founded on the rule that equity looks on that as done which ought to be done is, in my opinion, met and disposed of by [the view that], this rule, although usually expressed in general terms, is by no means universally true. Where the obligation to do what ought to be done is not an absolute duty, but only an obligation arising from contract, that which ought to be done is only treated as done in favour of some person entitled to enforce the contract as against the person liable to perform it.

So volunteers like the next of kin cannot rely upon any constructive constitution of the trust.

8.33 Although we have specifically looked at promises to settle where the consideration is marriage consideration and the promise is expressed in a covenant, the principle that equity will assist someone who has given consideration for the creation of a trust is of general application. Contracts to create trusts occur all the time in the commercial world, as for example, a contract whereby an agent is obliged to hold proceeds of sale on trust for his principal (**7.17**). Consideration has been given for that promise to 'settle', and equity will not hesitate to enforce it. The proceeds will be regarded as held by the agent on constructive trust when he receives them.

The enforcement of covenants to settle at common law

8.34 So far we have considered the equitable enforcement of promises to settle, and we have seen that where consideration has been given, equity will order the promisor to transfer property to the trustee thereby constituting the trust, and that in the meantime the promisor will hold the property in question upon constructive trust. On the other hand, where the intended beneficiary is a volunteer, equity will not order the constitution of the trust. This is all quite straightforward. So far the fact that these promises to settle have been expressed in covenants has not really mattered; if these promises had been made orally, the results would have been exactly the same. Equity is not concerned with form, and its willingness to enforce promises to settle turns, as we have seen, on whether consideration (including marriage consideration) for the promise has been given, not on the form in which the promise has been expressed. Now, however, the nature of covenants does become important, for these are promises which are enforceable at common law irrespective of whether any consideration had been given.

8.35 Consider the standard covenant to settle. S, the settlor/covenantor, promises to transfer the property to T, the trustee/covenantee, on trust for B, the beneficiary, who is not himself a party of the covenant, and who is a volunteer. The question now is whether T should be able to enforce the covenant *at common law*, and what this would mean. At first glance, there appears no reason why he should not. At common law T is a covenantee, and therefore the promisee of a legally enforceable promise. Can he not therefore bring a common law action for damages for breach of covenant against the covenantor, thereby getting money to the value of the property that ought to have been transferred on trust into his hands, and thereby constitute the trust himself? The answer appears to be 'no', although the cases which establish this have been extensively criticised.

8.36   The principal case is *Re Pryce* (1917), where Eve J held that covenantees/trustees ought not to enforce a covenant to settle in favour of next of kin who were volunteer beneficiaries. Eve J reasoned as follows:

> '[V]olunteers have no right whatever to obtain specific performance of a mere covenant which has remained as a covenant and has never been performed': see per James LJ in *In re D'Angibau*. Nor could damages be awarded either in this Court, or, as I apprehend, at law, where, since the Judicature Acts, the same defences would be available to the defendant as would be raised in an action brought in this Court for specific performance or damages. In these circumstances, seeing that the next of kin could neither maintain an action to enforce the covenant nor for damages for breach of it, and that the settlement is not a declaration of trust constituting the relationship of trustee and cestui que trust between the defendant and the next of kin, in which case effect could be given to the trusts even in favour of volunteers, but is a mere voluntary contract to create a trust, ought the Court now for sole benefit of these volunteers to direct the trustees to take proceedings to enforce the defendant's covenant? I think it ought not; to do so would be to give the next of kin by indirect means what they cannot obtain by any direct procedure, and would in effect be enforcing the settlement as against the defendant's legal right to [the property in question].

8.37   The statement from *Re D'Angibau* (1879) that volunteer beneficiaries may not obtain the *equitable* remedy of specific performance of a covenant, while true, is not obviously relevant; it does not dispose of the question whether a trustee/covenantee may sue on the covenant *at common law*. To the extent that the following statement indicates that damages would not only be unavailable in equity but also at law for breach of covenant following the Judicature Acts, it is just wrong (see Elliot (1960)). If Eve J only means that the volunteer beneficiaries would be unable to get damages in equity (because volunteers) or damages at common law (because not parties to the covenant), then again, this is true, but as with the preceding statement, not obviously relevant. The real heart of the decision lies in the statement that by allowing the trustee/

237

covenantees to sue at common law, the next of kin would achieve by indirect means what they could not achieve directly, and this would in effect, allow the enforcement of the covenant to settle by volunteers, in violation of the general principle. The case is most easily criticised by pointing out that Eve J here seems to have allowed equitable principles to exceed their proper jurisdiction. The general principle, recall, is that 'equity will not assist a volunteer', not 'equity will stand in the way of a volunteer'. By ordering that the trustee/covenantees may not sue, Eve J appears to trench upon the trustee/covenantee's common law rights. What has equity to say about whether a covenantee at common law sues upon his covenant? The covenantee is not seeking the assistance of equity at all; he is not asking for specific performance, but for the common law remedy he is entitled to by his common law right to enforce the covenant. From this perspective, Eve J has no jurisdiction to direct the covenantee one way or another, and so the case is wrongly decided.

8.38 Several authorities go the other way: two, *Fletcher v Fletcher* (1844), *Re Cavendish Browne's Settlement Trusts* (1916), will be discussed below. Most recently the decision in *Cannon v Hartley* (1949) seems to conflict, if not in letter, then in spirit, with *Re Pryce*. In *Cannon* a man, on separating from his wife, covenanted with both his wife and daughter to settle after-acquired property upon them, but did not. The daughter, who had given no consideration but was a party to the covenant, sought to enforce the covenant at common law. Romer J considered that *Re Pryce*, properly understood, was authority only for the proposition that equity would prevent the enforcement of a covenant to settle when the plaintiff was both (1) a volunteer and (2) not a party to the covenant. Romer J awarded the daughter substantial damages for her father's failure to settle the property, stating:

> In the present case the plaintiff, although a volunteer, ... is a direct covenantee under the very covenant upon which she is suing. She does not require the assistance of the court to enforce the covenant for she has a legal right herself to enforce it. She is not asking for equitable relief but for damages at common law for breach of covenant.

8.39 The narrowing of *Re Pryce* on the basis that it only applies to non-parties to covenants seems dubious, for equity is not concerned with the formality of who is a party to the covenant − it is not concerned with covenants at all but the promises they express, whether to parties or non-parties; with respect to the promise itself it is the issue of consideration that matters, and the daughter here was a volunteer. The essence of Romer J's decision, that equity's assistance is not being invoked, for she is suing at common law, and further, that equity will not interfere in her doing so, seems to take the exact opposite approach to that of Eve J in *Re Pryce*.

8.40 *Re Pryce* was followed in *Re Kay's Settlement* (1938) (albeit reluctantly by Simonds J), and the latter was followed in *Re Cook's Settlement Trusts* (1965), so the principle that trustee/covenantees may not sue the covenantor at common law for damages must be regarded as authoritative. Assuming however, that these three first instance decisions may be met, if ever considered by the higher courts, by judges more in sympathy with Romer J's views than Eve J's, we must explore the consequences of allowing a trustee/covenantee to sue upon the covenant at common law.

8.41 If the trustee is allowed to sue upon the covenant, what remedy will he obtain? It seems quite clear that he will not be able specifically to enforce the covenant in favour of the beneficiary, that is, obtain an order that the covenantor transfer the property on trust to him, for an order of specific performance is an equitable remedy, and the trustee is a volunteer. (*Beswick v Beswick* (1968) establishes that a party to a valid contract, ie one who has given consideration, may obtain an order for specific performance which benefits a volunteer third party, but in the case we are considering both the trustee/covenantee and the beneficiary are volunteers, so this equitable remedy is unavailable.)

8.42 If the trustee/covenantee brings an action at common law for breach of covenant, he may recover on either of two bases. First, regarding the action as one particularly for breach of covenant, not breach of contract:

> ... for breach of a covenant to pay a certain sum, the measure of damages (if that is the appropriate expression) is the certain sum. (Elliot (1960))

Even in contract, generally the remedy in an action for an agreed sum is the payment of that sum (see Treitel (2003), 1013). Alternatively, according to the normal rule of common law damages for breach of contract, the damages will be measured by the covenantee's loss. Here again, the covenantee's loss is the value of the promised property. It is sometimes argued that the trustee/covenantee has suffered no real loss himself, for it is the intended beneficiary who has really suffered a loss by the covenantor's breach of covenant; therefore the covenantee's damages will be nominal (**4.38**) unless he can recover damages for the volunteer beneficiary as a third party, and the common law will generally not allow him to do so (*Woodar Investment Development Ltd v Wimpey Construction UK Ltd* (1980), HL). This is misconceived. Though in the deed the covenantee is to hold the property 'on trust for' the beneficiary, the common law, you will recall (**1.18**), has always ignored the words 'on trust for'. It is no answer to a claim in damages for breach of contract at common law that the plaintiff is a trustee who was contracting for others, and the same is true here.

8.43 If this is right, then the trustee/covenantee who is allowed to sue at law will recover the value of the trust property the covenantor promised to transfer. It is here where things start to fall apart, for we must now ask, does the recovery of these substantial damages constitute the trust the settlor/covenantor intended? Another way of putting this is: for whom does the trustee/covenantee hold the damages? The mere receipt of that property does not make the trustee/covenantee a trustee of it unless equity is willing to recognise the trust obligation. Or rather, the intended beneficiary will only be able to enforce a trust over that property against the trustee/covenantee if equity recognises that he holds the damages on trust for him. If this operation of securing the covenanted property is done entirely at common law, then it is still up to equity to decide whether the property is to be held on trust. In order to understand the issues at stake here, we must first make a digression.

The trust of the benefit of a promise to settle

8.44 Most commentators accept that the *Re Pryce* unenforceability problem is avoided where the covenant to settle is a special one which creates an 'immediate binding trust of the promise', perhaps like this: 'I hereby covenant to transfer £1,000 to Fred to hold on trust for Alice, and the benefit of this covenant shall forthwith be held by Fred on trust for Alice.' The idea is that in the case of the normal covenant to settle, the covenantee is not a trustee of anything until he receives the trust property, at which time the trust is constituted and he becomes a trustee. Until that time, he holds his common law rights to enforce the covenant for himself absolutely. This special kind of covenant, however, makes him a trustee at the outset, and the subject matter of the trust is his common law rights under the covenant. This might seem a strange sort of trust property, but it is not at all. The right under the covenant is a personal right, but then so is every contractual right a trustee may acquire on behalf of the trust in administering it, as, for example, the right against a bank to the balance of the trust bank account. All can serve as rights held on trust. That is not the problem with the 'trust of the benefit of the promise idea'.

8.45 The problem is that, according to this idea, in the normal case of a covenant to settle like those in *Re Pryce* and *Re Kay* the covenantee is *not* the trustee of his rights under the covenant for the intended beneficiary. This is entirely implausible. In the normal case, the trustee/covenantee is already a trustee of property under a settlement into which the covenanted property will go if the covenant is performed. Thus when the settlor covenants with the trustee to transfer property to him to hold on trust for the beneficiaries of the settlement, the trustee is immediately constituted trustee of the legal right to sue under the covenant. This is so simply because he undertakes in the covenant to hold the property he will receive under it *as a trustee* for the beneficiaries. As Hackney ((1987), 117) puts it:

> At no stage does the transaction operate at common law alone, giving [the covenantee] any rights under the covenant, since the covenant is made to him as a trustee, any more than would a simple transfer of property to Y on trust for Z give Y beneficial property rights at common law.

8.46 The alternative analysis, that the covenantee covenants for himself, would mean (1) that it is up to the covenantee whether or not to enforce the covenant; since he covenants for his own benefit, it is up to him whether he pursues his rights to become a trustee; and (2) that it is up to the *settlor/covenantor* to enforce the trust against the covenantee when the covenantee receives the trust property, *not* the intended beneficiary, for if, when the covenantee receives the covenanted property, he refuses to hold it on trust for the beneficiary, then he is merely acting in breach of covenant, not breach of trust, for, remember, according to this view there is no trust until the covenantee holds the property (gives effect to the intended trust terms) according to his common law obligation, ie in accord with his covenant. The intended beneficiary is not a beneficiary yet, and not being a party to the covenant himself, he has no rights to enforce it. Therefore to assume that the mere receipt of the intended trust property by the covenantee constitutes the intended trust is to confuse equitable ownership with a common law obligation.

8.47 According to this view, it would be up to the settlor (or following his death, his personal representative) to enforce the covenant and require the covenantee to hold the property on trust, and the settlor would have no obligation to the intended beneficiaries to do so. There is yet a further problem, which becomes apparent if the settlor does try to enforce the covenant. Since the intended trustee is not to hold the property for his own benefit, but as a trustee, the settlor gives him no consideration for holding the property on trust (any remuneration he might receive under the constituted trust comes from the beneficiaries, not from the settlor). Thus equity will not enforce the obligation against the trustee by an order of specific performance, requiring him to hold the property on trust. The settlor is left to his common law remedies; this will either be damages for breach of covenant, which will essentially amount to the value of the trust property, or restitution of the value of the property transferred. The upshot is that if the covenantee does not covenant as a trustee, *neither the settlor/covenantor nor the intended beneficiaries* can enforce the covenant so as *actually to constitute the trust*. These considerations strongly suggest that such covenants, in which the covenantee does not covenant as a trustee, are exceedingly rare.

8.48 The courts, to their credit, have never given any explicit approval of this analysis, and certainly the decisions in *Re Pryce* and *Re Kay* do not in any way seem to depend upon it; indeed, if the judges in those cases thought that, it would be odd that they were willing to hear arguments, because the cases were applications by *trustees* seeking directions of the court as to how they should act *as trustees*. Nevertheless, it is orthodox to say that if in these cases the trustees had held the benefit of the covenant on trust from the outset, their enforcement of the covenants would have been allowed. Support for this proposition is supposedly gleaned from two cases where it is said that covenants were enforced because, exceptionally, there was an immediate binding trust of the covenant, *Davenport v Bishopp* (1843) and *Fletcher v Fletcher* (1844).

8.49 *Davenport* involved a suit by a husband against the heir of his deceased wife for the transfer of property from the heir into the husband's marriage settlement. The heir obtained the property by succession when the wife died, but it was property which the wife, when alive, was bound to transfer to the trustees of the settlement under a typical after-acquired property covenant. The husband was not a volunteer, but since there was no issue of the marriage, a relation who was a volunteer would benefit if the property was transferred into the settlement. The heir argued that while the property should go into the trust so as to give the husband his benefit, the volunteer beneficiary under the settlement should be denied any benefit from the property, having given no consideration. In other words, the heir argued that even where someone who had given consideration wished to enforce the covenant and constitute the trust, he could only constitute it for himself, as it were, not for any volunteer beneficiaries. Not surprisingly, Knight-Bruce VC found such an idea insupportable, affirming the basic principle that a trust, once constituted, is constituted for all the beneficiaries, volunteers or not. In passing, he said:

> The surviving trustee of the settlement, or his representative, may be thought to be a trustee of the covenant for the benefit both of Mr. Davenport and of the heirs of Miss Lucas [volunteers].

Put in context it is clear that Knight-Bruce VC is simply making the same point in a different way, that the trustee, when suing on the covenant on behalf of a non-volunteer, in effect also sues for the volunteers, for by constituting the trust he does so for all the beneficiaries. It is not a statement that the trustee may sue for volunteers in special circumstances where he is a 'trustee of the covenant'. Indeed the decision turns on Knight-Bruce VC's accepting that if there was only a volunteer beneficiary, the trustee could not constitute the trust. The result, then, is that the case re-iterates the *Re Pryce* line of cases – that trustees/covenantees are always trustees of the promise in a covenant, but that does not entail that equity will allow them to enforce a gratuitous covenant to settle.

8.50 In *Fletcher v Fletcher* (1844), a father had covenanted to transfer property upon trust to named persons as trustees for his sons, but did not do so. Wigram VC held that the covenant was enforceable by either the named trustees or the intended beneficiaries. The essence of his judgment on the enforceability point is in these lines:

> According to the authorities I cannot, I admit, do anything to perfect the liability of the author of the trust, if it is not already perfect. This covenant,

however, is already perfect. The covenantor is liable at law, and the Court is not called upon to do any act to perfect it.

What Wigram VC has decided here is simply that a covenantee may sue a covenantor *at common law* for the trust property. In other words, the decision is simply a decision contrary to the ruling in *Re Pryce*. He only then goes on to consider an objection by counsel, that there could not be a trust of the benefit of a covenant. Wigram VC did not think 'there is any difficulty in that'. Therefore, while the case is authority, contrary to *Re Pryce*, that a trustee/covenantee may sue at common law on the covenant, it does not make the right of the trustee/covenantee to do so depend upon finding 'a trust of the benefit of the covenant' as if that were something special. *Fletcher v Fletcher* is not the only authority which contradicts *Re Pryce*. In *Re Cavendish Browne's Settlement Trusts* (1916) Younger J held that trustees were entitled to substantial damages for the breach of a covenant to settle. The case is badly reported. *Fletcher* is one of the cases listed as having been cited to the court, but there is no indication that the case turned on the particular finding of a trust of the benefit of the covenant.

8.51 In *Re Cook's Settlement Trusts* (1965) Buckley J considered an argument that the covenant created an immediate binding trust of the promise, but decided against it on the ground that there cannot be a trust of a promise to transfer future property. This is simply ill-founded. (See, eg *Lloyd's v Harper* (1880)). As a result it is difficult to know what the case stands for, but since there was no analysis of *Fletcher*, one should not draw the conclusion that the case lends weight to the thesis that *Re Pryce* prevents the enforcement of a covenant because the covenantee is not a trustee of the benefit of it.

8.52 We can now return to the question of what *Re Pryce* actually stands for, and the related question for whom would the covenantee hold the damages he was awarded if he were able, *pace Re Pryce*, to sue on the covenant at law. If the preceding consideration of the 'trust of the benefit of the covenant' idea is correct, then virtually all covenantees of covenants to settle are trustees of their rights under the covenant. If that is so, then the decision in *Re Pryce* does not mean that the court is interfering in the enforcement of a covenantee's common law right to make himself a trustee; he is a trustee already. The court is directing a trustee not to use his common law rights to 'get in', or realise a common law claim to, property, purely because the common law right is founded on a voluntary promise. By the same token, *Re Pryce* means that the court will not allow a beneficiary to enforce a common law right held by the trust, if this right is only the benefit of a voluntary promise enforceable at common law. It must be emphasised that this is a perfectly coherent position for equity to take. Equity has jurisdiction over trusts and their constitution, and if equity will not impose new equitable obligations on people who do not presently have them and do not wish to have them for the sake of those who have not paid for them, then that is fully consonant with equity's refusal to interfere against a legal owner whose conscience is not affected, and in the eyes of equity it is not unconscionable to refuse to confer a gift on someone, even if one earlier promised to do so. In short, equity will not allow a trustee or a beneficiary to enforce a voluntary promise to bring property into the trust. It is of no moment, on this analysis, that the promise is one that the law would enforce as far as it can, ie getting property into the covenantee's hands. Equity has charge of trustees and beneficiaries, and if equity will not enforce a trust over property which results from the enforcement of a gratuitous promise, then it will insist that the trustee, who is the promisee of that promise, should not enforce it.

8.53 If this is right, it is simply not clear how equity would respond to the case of a trustee who does somehow manage to enforce his rights at common law to win substantial damages. On one hand, equity might require the trustee to hold the damages on trust for the intended beneficiary, for the covenantee is a trustee after all, and equity's refusal to assist a volunteer ought to be restricted to preventing the enforcement of a voluntary promise to settle when equity's assistance is required, or, perhaps, when its directions are sought — it may be significant that in both *Re Pryce* and *Re Kay* the trustees were seeking the advice of the court as to whether they should enforce the covenant at common law. This view might be strengthened by the attitude of the court to 'fortuitous vesting' (**8.17**), which we turn to shortly. If the court is willing to treat the settlor/covenantee's trust as constituted so long as the property gets into the trustee's hands, then the court may treat the trustee/covenantee's own actions which result in this as equally constituting the trust. Certainly if *Re Pryce* were over- ruled, and trustees were not prevented by equity from suing on covenants, the result would be that they would hold the damages on trust for the intended beneficiaries.

8.54 If, however, *Re Pryce* remains an authority, and a trustee/ covenantee sues and wins damages (ie without having sought the directions of the court first as to whether he might do so) – Hayton ((2001b), 253) argues that equity will step in and make the trustee/ covenantee hold the damages on *resulting trust* for the settlor, ie the covenantor who he has just successfully sued at common law. Why? Since equity will not assist a volunteer, equity will not allow the beneficiary to enforce a trust of the damages against the covenantee/trustee. This would be in line with the preceding analysis of *Re Pryce* but takes it one step further: not only will equity not enforce a constituted trust of the benefit of a promise in the volunteer's favour, but it will not enforce a trust over the proceeds of the enforcement of that promise by a volunteer (at common law) either. But, says Hayton, neither can the trustee/ covenantee keep the damages for himself, because he undertook the covenant as a trustee. Equity will therefore make him hold the damages upon resulting trust for the covenantor, putting them both back in the position they were at the beginning. This, so the argument goes, justifies *Re Pryce*. The court of equity stops the whole pointless process from the outset. Clever, don't you think?

Fortuitous vesting of the trust property

8.55 In *Re Brooks' Settlement Trusts* (1939), Lloyds Bank were trustees of a marriage settlement, under which the wife had a power of appointment. One of her sons created for himself and his wife and children a voluntary settlement, of which Lloyds Bank were also the trustees, to which settlement he assigned all his interest in any property he might receive as a result of his mother's appointing property to him from her marriage settlement. His mother did, by deed, appoint property to her son. Before this appointment, Lloyds Bank held legal title to this property as trustees for the mother; if they carried out the appointment by complying with her exercise of their power of appointment they would transfer the property to the son. But Lloyds Bank had a second role, as trustees of the son's own settlement, and according to this settlement this self-same property was to go into it. So Lloyds Bank held the property either as trustees of the mother's settlement, under which they ought to pay the money out to the son, or they held it as trustees of the son's own settlement, as property which properly belonged in it. The question, then, was whether the son's assignment of any property he might receive by way of his mother's power of appointment, combined with the fact that the trustees had the legal title to the property, amounted to the constitution of the son's settlement. Farwell J decided it did not:

The son had no more than a mere expectancy under the marriage settlement until the appointment was made. That being so, the son, when he assigned his interest under the [marriage] settlement to the trustees of [his own] voluntary settlement, … was assigning, or purporting to assign, something to which he might become entitled *in futuro* – not a contingent interest, but a mere expectancy. It is clear on the authorities that he cannot be compelled to allow the trustees to retain the appointed sum, and that he can call on the trustees to pay it over to him.

8.56   Farwell J said that in the case of an assignment for value, ie where there was consideration, the trustees could hold the property on trust, enforce the convenant as it were, on the principles of *Re Ellenborough* **(8.10)**, ie on the basis that equity would treat the assignment of future property as a promise for consideration to assign the property if and when received. But here, as there was no consideration allowing equity to treat the invalid legal assignment of a mere expectancy as a valid promise to assign, and further that there was clearly no declaration by the son as a trustee himself, Farwell J held that the son retained beneficial ownership of the property appointed, and ordered Lloyds Bank to pay the money to him.

8.57   Farwell J viewed this result as unfortunate, and said that the law:

> … makes it impossible to enforce the [son's] voluntary settlement, even to the extent of permitting the trustees of that settlement to retain, as subject thereto, the money in their hands.

This appears to indicate that Farwell J might have reached the opposite result had the so-called property in question not been a mere expectancy at the time of the son's assignment. In other words, had the property contemplated in the covenant not been future property, the covenant might have been held to bind the son, and the trustees could have devoted the property to the voluntary settlement. But even if that were the case, the son still would not have abided by the covenant and assigned the property into the voluntary settlement. The trustees would still have legal title only because of their multiple roles, not because the son had assigned the property, in other words merely by virtue of the fortuitous vesting of the property. But, as Hayton ((2001b), 254 et seq) argues, given the decision that Farwell J made it was not consistent of him to think there would have been a different result had the son's assignment been for existing property, for the case turns not on the law regarding the effectiveness of legal assignments, but on equity's refusal to assist a volunteer. If there had been consideration for the son's assignment, then equity would have assisted; equity would not have let the fact that this was an assignment for future property stand in its way – equity will treat an assignment of future property as an enforceable promise to assign where consideration is given (8.10). On this interpretation, then, an expansive view of the maxim 'Equity will not assist a volunteer' was taken, giving rise, according to Hayton, to the principle that 'only the settlor (or his agent) can constitute a trust'; a trust should not be regarded as constituted by mere chance, as opposed to by the settlor's own act.

8.58 The counterpart case supporting the validity of fortuitous vesting is *Re Ralli's Will Trusts* (1964). Here a wife covenanted in her marriage settlement to assign property she acquired during the course of her marriage. The after-acquired property in question was a reversionary interest under her father's will, which fell in after her mother died, but which she never assigned. She died, and as it turned out, the sole remaining trustee of the marriage settlement was also the executor of her will, so he became the legal owner of the reversion she ought to have assigned to the marriage settlement when she had first received it. Buckley J decided the case on the terms of the original marriage settlement, holding that under a clause of the settlement the wife declared that she held any existing property on trust for the marriage settlement, and further that the reversionary interest was existing property at the time of the creation of the settlement; therefore, the wife had declared herself a trustee of the reversion on the trusts of the marriage settlement from the outset; consequently her executor held the property on the same trust when he received the legal title to her estate. But Buckley J went on to state, *obiter,* that even if this were not the case, the property became subject to the settlement trusts by the fortuitous circumstance that the trustee of the settlement was the same person as the executor of the will:

> That the [trustee] holds the fund because he was appointed trustee of the will is irrelevant. He is at law the owner of the fund and the means by which he became so have no effect on the quality of his legal ownership. The question is: for whom, if anyone, does he hold the fund in equity? In other words, who can successfully assert in equity against him disentitling him to stand on his legal right?

8.59 Buckley J held that the wife, if she were alive, could not make such an assertion against the executor/trustee (and her legatees under her will could not be in a better position) because in order to assert her right to the fund, she would have to show that the trustee could not conscientiously withhold it from her; but all the trustee had to do was point to the covenant to show that in conscience he *should* withhold it from her. It was the beneficiaries under the covenant who in equity had the superior claim upon his conscience. Buckley J accepted that the constitution of the trust in this case would be fortuitous, and that if the executor of the wife's will had been someone different, so would have been the result. But this naturally turned on the fact that the operation of the maxim 'equity will not assist a volunteer' is in a sense inherently fortuitous, for it only goes so far as to prevent a court assisting a volunteer in transferring property to constitute a trust; it does not compel equity to positively divest volunteers of the benefits once their trustee obtains legal ownership. Such a view is, of course, in direct conflict with the principle that Hayton asserts, that 'only a settlor or his authorised agent can constitute a trust'.

8.60 There is a lurking problem in Buckley J's framing of the principle upon which fortuitous vesting operates, which is this: he says essentially that a trustee as bare legal owner must decide who, in equity, has the best claim upon him. Here the question was: in what capacity did the trustee/executor hold the fund – as trustee of the marriage settlement or as executor of the will? Now it may perhaps be fair to demand that a trustee/executor in the context of a close family arrangement like this one might ask himself such a question and be bound to take cognisance of the answer; if therefore, in this case, the trustee/executor paid out the money to the legatees under the will he could be properly held to be in breach of trust. But is it at all sensible to make this question-posing approach into a general principle determining whether a trustee is in breach of trust? Take the case of Lloyds Bank in *Re Brooks'*, which is undoubtedly the trustee for thousands of separate trusts. *Qua* legal owner, Lloyds Bank owns all that trust property as a single legal owner, and in Buckley J's view, Lloyds merely looks round to the various equitable claims that can be made upon it under those thousands of trusts in order to decide where its duty lies. But in the case of a large trustee like a bank that is a counsel of nonsense. Clearly it must (for accounting purposes at least) segregate the trust property it legally holds into separate accounts relating to the different trusts it administers. Should a bank really be in breach of trust if property is appointed under one trust, and it pays it out without knowing that such property is also subject to a covenant in another trust, which it is administering quite separately? Is a bank or any other professional trustee required to keep a list (if such a list could even be kept) of actual and possible cross references between all the trusts it administers? Can Buckley J really be suggesting that trustees ought to be required to survey all their trusts as a unit, treating themselves as legal owners of a big pile of property, and checking to make sure that none of the provisions overlap?

8.61 Surely not. Trustees have the duty to treat themselves as separate trustees for separate settlements, and to keep the property in separate funds, and consequently they should not be liable for failing to find cross-connections that give rise to fortuitous vesting, at least unless and until a beneficiary whose equitable rights are constituted by the fortuitous vesting notifies them. This problematic aspect of imposing an obligation to cross-check what might be very unrelated trusts surely indicates that Buckley J's *obiter dictum*, if it is correct at all, must be restricted in its operation to cases where the trustees are actually aware of the interlocking connexion between the trusts which work to vest trust property fortuitously.

8.62 A final point: Buckley J based his decision in part on the rule in *Strong v Bird*. Even if the extension of this rule to the perfecting of trusts which the testator intended in his lifetime by the vesting of the trust property in the executor or administrator is correct, its application to the facts in *Re Ralli* is questionable. Buckley J did not refer to any evidence of a continuing intention to constitute the trust, and the requirement of continuing intention is the only thing which keeps that rule within any manageable bounds at all. The application may, perhaps, be explained, by considering the covenant itself to be evidence of a continuing intention where no other evidence is available.

Concluding considerations

8.63 The complications in this area of law arise from a failure of fusion (1.15) of equity and the common law to take place with respect to gratuitous obligations. It should not matter that the recognition of binding but gratuitous promises was first recognised by the common law. If the law (meaning the English legal system, not the common law) provides a means by which gratuitous promises can be made legally binding, then that means should be available for promises of all kinds unless good reason

250

is given otherwise, and no reason is discernible in the cases which would rule out binding, gratuitous promises to settle. 'Equity will not assist a volunteer' is a slogan, not a reason, in this respect.

8.64 Precisely the same point applies to the availability of orders for specific performance. It should not matter that equity devised the remedy of specific performance. It should be employed by the court whenever it is just to do so, and its use or restriction should not depend upon its historical provenance, but upon principled reasons as to why its use is appropriate in one circumstance but not another. While it may well be the case that such principled reasons may be gleaned largely from past decisions of the court of equity, it makes no sense to say that only judges acting as equity judges have a coherent grip on the remedy and that therefore it is not a remedy of the legal system as a whole. It should be available on demand to judges to employ wherever it appears appropriate to do so. If the law treats a gratuitous promise to transfer that Rembrandt as legally binding because expressed in a covenant, then the enforcement of that right should turn on the same principles as apply to a right arising under a contract for consideration, unless there are good reasons why not. Specific performance is given under a contract because the Rembrandt is unique and so money damages would be an inadequate remedy. Therefore specific performance ought to be given to enforce the same obligation expressed in a covenant, though gratuitous, since money damages are just as much an inadequate remedy here and for precisely the same reason.

Further reading

Kodilinye (1982); Elliot (1960); Hackney (1987), 110 et seq; Hornby (1962); McNair (1988); Rickett (2001); Garton (2003).

Must read cases: *Milroy v Lord* (1862); *Re Rose* (1952); *Re Stewart* (1908); *Re Pryce* (1916); *Re Kay's Settlement* (1938); *Cannon v Hartley* (1948); *Re Brook's Settlement Trusts* (1939); *Re Ralli's Will Trusts* (1964).

Self-test questions

1. In 1985 Fred and Barbara created a settlement on their divorce for their then minor children, Claire and Eric. The trustee of the

settlement was Tony, Barbara's brother. The settlement was originally constituted by the transfer of £100,000 to Tony, and in the trust instrument were included covenants by both Fred and Barbara to settle one-half of any property either might thereafter acquire by legacy or inheritance.

In 1987, Fred made a separate covenant with Tony to transfer one half of any royalties on his new book, to be held on the trusts of the settlement. The book earned £50,000, but Fred never transferred any money into the settlement.

In 1988, Barbara received a legacy of £250,000 in shares of G Ltd. She has always paid the dividends to Claire, and said on numerous occasions that she intended to give the shares to Claire. On 10 July 1995, she made an appointment in early August with her solicitor for the purpose of executing the share transfer to Claire.

On 13 July 1995, Fred and Barbara both died from food poisoning after attending Eric's university graduation. Fred left all his property to his brother Stuart, who is also the executor of his will. Barbara died intestate, and Tony and Claire have been appointed administrators of her estate.

Advise Eric.

2. In what circumstances will equity perfect an imperfect gift? Are any reforms in the law indicated?

3. To what extent is this a correct statement of the law: 'Only a settlor can constitute a trust'?

CHAPTER NINE

Trusts and Purposes

SUMMARY

The beneficiary principle and the invalidity of pure purpose trusts

Anomalous valid purpose trusts

Powers for purposes

An enforcer principle?

Valid trusts for persons limited by a purpose: *Re Sanderson* trusts

The bare trust with mandate and *Quistclose* trusts

Gifts to unincorporated associations

The dissolution of unincorporated associations

Less than unincorporated associations: the case of political parties

The rule against perpetuities

9.1 This chapter concerns how the law enables a person to devote their property to the carrying out of purposes, but restricts the ways in which that can be done. Although trusts are typically involved in legal mechanisms by which property is devoted to a purpose, this is almost always part of a mechanism which employs both the trust and a contractual obligation of some kind. In general, the law does not allow you simply to transfer property on trust to carry out a purpose, for example, '£10,000 on trust to oppose UK entry into the common European currency', unless the purpose is charitable, aka 'public'. This 'no private purpose trusts' rule is a corollary of what is know as the 'beneficiary principle'.

The beneficiary principle and the invalidity of pure purpose trusts

9.2 The 'beneficiary principle' can be stated thus: for a trust to be valid, it must be for the benefit of ascertainable individuals, ie specific beneficiaries. The corollary of this rule is, roughly, that equity will not recognise a trust to carry out a purpose, since the benefits of carrying out a purpose cannot be localised to specific individuals. Hence, the principle is also framed as the 'no purpose trusts' rule.

9.3 The two most quoted statements expressing the 'no purpose trusts rule' come from the case of *Morice v Bishop of Durham* (1804, before Sir William Grant MR, 1805 on appeal to Lord Eldon LC). Both emphasise that for a trust to exist (putting charitable trusts to one side), there must be someone who will have standing to bring the trustees to court to enforce the trust obligations against the legal owner. Thus there must be definite objects, ie beneficiaries, who can bring the trustees to court. Sir William Grant MR said:

> There can be no trust, over the exercise of which this Court will not assume a control; for an uncontrollable power of disposition would be ownership, and not trust ... There must be somebody, in whose favour the court can decree performance.

Implicit in this statement is the view that only those who are intended to benefit qua beneficiaries have standing to enforce it. This rule is in essence parallel to the 'privity' rule of contract law; only those who are rightholders under the trust may enforce it, not every Tom, Dick, or Mary who might like to see it carried out.

9.4 From this point of view, the beneficiary principle can be regarded as a corollary of the certainty of objects requirement: if a trust is expressed in terms of a purpose, then it will be impossible to determine any definite objects of the trust, and therefore there are no persons at

254

whose insistence and for whose benefit the Court can order the trustee to carry out the trust. Lord Eldon clearly equates the court's control over the trust with the existence of ascertainable objects and indeed, subject matter:

> As it is a maxim, that the execution of a trust must be under the control of the court, it must be of such a nature, that it can be under that control; so that the administration of it can be reviewed by the court … unless the subject and the objects can be ascertained, upon principles, familiar in other cases, it must be decided, that the court can neither reform maladministration, nor direct a due administration.

9.5 The best statement of the principle, however, is Roxburgh J's in *Re Astor's Settlement Trusts* (1952). In 1945, Viscount Astor made a settlement of most of the shares of 'The Observer Limited'. The income from the trust fund that was set up was to be applied to a number of purposes, including the maintenance of good understanding between nations, the preservation of the independence and integrity of newspapers, editors, and writers, the protection of newspapers from control by combines, and the improvement of newspapers. It was admitted that the purposes were not charitable (see chapter 13).

9.6 Roxburgh J framed the beneficiary principle in this way:

> The typical case of a trust is one in which the legal owner of property is constrained by a court of equity so to deal with it as to give effect to the equitable right of another. These equitable rights have been hammered out in the process of litigation in which a claimant on equitable grounds has successfully asserted rights against a legal owner or other person in control of property. Prima facie, therefore, a trustee would not be expected to be subject to an equitable obligation unless there was somebody who could enforce a correlative equitable right, and the nature and extent of that obligation would be worked out in proceedings for enforcement.

9.7 According to Roxburgh J, either the legal owner of the property is under an equitable obligation or he is not. If he is, then someone else must have corresponding equitable rights against him which can be enforced. If he is not, then he can deal with the property as he wishes because he is the beneficial owner. Roxburgh J sees no ground between these two alternatives, and it is submitted that he is perfectly right. The very existence of a trust turns on their being a trust obligation to someone who, in consequence, has equitable ownership of the trust property. If we take the requirement of equitable ownership seriously, speaking about the need for someone with standing to enforce the trust is a distinctly second-order way of framing the beneficiary principle. The essence of the principle is that for a trust to exist, there must be someone other than the trustee who has the real beneficial ownership of the trust property. If there is no such person, then not only is there no person *to enforce* obligations against the trustee, but more fundamentally, there are *no trust obligations to* enforce, for the legal owner owns it for his own benefit absolutely.

9.8   Since, however, in cases of this kind the settlor has clearly intended to create a trust by transferring the property to a trustee, the trustee cannot keep the property for himself. An ART (**4.2**) arises, because the settlor has failed effectively to dispose of the beneficial interest in the property. In this case he fails to do so because he tries to do the impossible – create a trust without a beneficiary, which for equity is no trust at all.

9.9   There is a well-established exception to this rule in the case of trusts for charitable purposes. The duty to enforce charitable trusts fell on the King as *parens patriae,* and on to the Attorney-General as his legal representative. 'But,' said Roxburgh J:

> ... if the purposes are not charitable, great difficulties arise both in theory and in practice. In theory, because having regard to the historical origins of equity it is difficult to visualise the growth of equitable obligations which nobody can enforce, and in practice, because it is not possible to contemplate with equanimity the creation of large funds devoted to non-charitable purposes which no court and no department of state can control ... If the purposes are valid trusts, the settlors have retained no beneficial interest and could not initiate them. It was suggested that the trustees might proceed ex parte to enforce the trusts against themselves. I doubt that, but at any rate nobody could enforce the trusts against them.

So the trust failed.

9.10   Roxburgh J further decided that the trusts were also void for uncertainty, citing in particular the phrases 'different sections of people in any nation or community', 'constructive policies', and 'integrity of the press'.

256

9.11   In *Re Denley's Trust Deed* (1969) Goff J appeared to narrow the 'no purpose trusts' rule considerably, while at the same time arguing that he was not diminishing the effect of the beneficiary principle, properly understood. The case concerned an *inter vivos* trust of a piece of land,

> ... to be maintained and used as and for the purpose of a recreation or sports ground primarily for the benefit of the employees of the company and secondarily for the benefit of such other person or persons (if any) as the trustees may allow to use the same ....

The gift was properly limited to a perpetuity period. Goff J held that the gift was valid:

> I think that there may be a purpose or object trust, the carrying out of which would benefit an individual or individuals, where the benefit is so indirect or intangible or which is otherwise so framed as not to give those persons any locus standi to apply to the court to enforce the trust, in which case the beneficiary principle would, as it seems to me, apply to invalidate the trust, quite apart from any question of uncertainty or perpetuity ... The present is not, in my judgment, of that character, and it will be seen that ... the trust deed expressly states that, subject to any rules and regulations made by the trustees, the employees of the company shall be entitled to the use and enjoyment of the land ... [I]n my judgment the beneficiary principle of *Re Astor* ... is confined to purpose or object trusts which are abstract or impersonal. The objection is not that the trust is for a purpose or object per se, but that there is no beneficiary or cestui que trust ... Where, then, the trust, though expressed as a purpose, is directly or indirectly for the benefit of an individual or individuals, it seems to me that it is in general outside the mischief of the beneficiary principle.

Goff J held that the class of 'beneficiaries' (it is not clear whether Goff J intended the word in its genuine technical sense, or meant simply people who would benefit *in fact* from the execution of the trust) was ascertainable at any given time, and thus satisfied the certainty of objects requirement on the 'complete list' test. Following *McPhail* one presumes that the class of beneficiaries need only satisfy the 'is or is not' test to be certain.

9.12   What precisely is the effect of a trust for individuals framed in terms of a purpose? While the benefited individuals have standing to enforce the trust, what does this amount to? May they enforce the trust only in order to make the trustees carry out the purpose, or may they

257

combine to defeat the purpose under the principle in *Saunders v Vautier* (**3.25**), insisting that the trustee, for example, lease the land and divide the profits between them? Have they an ownership interest, or just an interest in receiving whatever benefit would come to them through the serving of the purpose? Goff J does not discuss this. His only remarks concerning any disputes while the trust is up and running concern disputes between different groups of benefited individuals, which give no guidance as to how a dispute between the trustees and these individuals is to be resolved, for example had the employees wanted the commercial profits of the land, not its use as a playing field.

9.13 Goff J's decision has received some *obiter* consideration. In *Re Grant's Will Trusts* (1979), Vinelott J said that the case was:

> ... altogether outside the categories of gifts to unincorporated associations and purpose trusts. I can see no distinction in principle between a trust to permit a class defined by reference to employment to use and enjoy land in accordance with rules to be made at the discretion of trustees on the one hand, and, on the other hand, a trust to distribute income at the discretion of trustees among a class, defined by reference to, for example, relationship to the settlor. In both cases the benefit to be taken by any member of the class is at the discretion of the trustees, but any member of the class can apply to the court to compel the trustees to administer the trust in accordance with its terms.

It is not clear whether there really is 'no distinction' between the two classes of cases. In the latter case, the discretionary trust is one in which the *class* of beneficiaries is defined by the individuals' relationship to the settlor, but their *individual* shares are entirely at the trustee's discretion. In such a case the trustees' discretion is wholly dispositive, a matter of who within the class shall benefit at all, and in what amounts. By contrast, in the *Re Denley* case, the mere power of the trustees to make rules governing the enjoyment of the land does not amount to a discretion over who and in what proportion the beneficiaries may benefit from the property. This is a mere administrative discretion, to ensure that all the employees may enjoy the sports ground as much as possible; the trustees would be in breach if they framed rules governing the use of the land which intentionally excluded a particular group of employees. This view cannot stand as an interpretation of *Re Denley* which respects the actual facts and Goff J's decision. Rather, it reads down the case to the point of overturning it in substance.

9.14 *Re Denley* was also considered in *Re Lipinski's Will Trusts* (1976), which we will consider further below. Oliver J adopted the passage quoted from Goff J's decision as being 'in accord with authority and with common sense', but did not discuss precisely how *Re Denley* should be applied to the *Re Lipinski* facts, where a gift expressed to be for the purpose of constructing new buildings was given to an 'unincorporated association' (**9.63** et seq), a group of individuals who together form a society, or club, bound by rules. In particular, finding the gift valid he said the following:

> [I]t seems to me that whether one treats the gift as a 'purpose' trust or as an absolute gift with a superadded direction or ... as a gift where the trustees and the beneficiaries are the same persons, all roads lead to the same conclusion.

The vital point here is that on the latter two treatments of the gift, the testator's expressed purpose may be entirely ignored, either because as a 'superadded direction' it merely expresses a motive for the gift (recall 'precatory words', **7.11**), or on the basis that, the trustees and the beneficiaries being the same persons, ie the members of the club, the property is absolutely owned, and thus on *Saunders v Vautier* principles the beneficiary/trustees may do with the property what they like. This seems at odds with the impression Goff J clearly gives that the trustees are to carry out the purpose.

9.15 Thus both Vinelott J's and Oliver J's interpretations appear to be killing *Re Denley* with kindness. While they are happy to agree that the *Re Denley* trust was valid, in doing so they effectively gut the decision, at least in so far as it expanded the scope of valid purpose trusts. Finally, recall *West Yorkshire Metropolitan County Council* (**7.72**). One of the reasons Lloyd LJ gave for finding that trust for all the residents of West Yorkshire bad was that it amounted to an invalid purpose trust which could not be treated as a case like *Re Denley* because the class being so large, there were no ascertainable beneficiaries.

Anomalous valid purpose trusts

9.16 The most significant exception to the 'no purpose trusts' rule is charitable trusts. Charitable trusts are trusts for purposes 'beneficial to the public' as defined by the law of charities (Chapter 13). The other exceptions are all testamentary trusts. These are trusts for the maintenance of particular animals owned by the testator (a horse, *Pettingall v Pettingall* (1842); horses and hounds, *Re Dean* (1889)) and for the construction and maintenance of graves and funeral monuments (*Mussett v Bingle* (1876); *Re Hooper* (1932)).

9.17 In *Re Endacott* (1960) a testator left his entire residuary estate, which amounted to more than £20,000, 'to the North Tawton Devon Parish Council for the purpose of providing some useful memorial to myself'. The gift was not allowed as an exceptional testamentary trust to construct a monument: Lord Evershed MR said, 'It would go far beyond any fair analogy to those decisions'. There also appears to be a similarly-grounded exception for the saying of private masses for the repose of the testator's relatives' souls (*Bourne v Keane* (1919); *Re Heatherington* (1990)).

9.18 These trusts are sometimes called 'trusts of imperfect obligation', for there are no beneficiaries of these trusts, and thus no obligations to any beneficiaries who may enforce them to carry out the purpose against the 'trustee'. However, this does not mean that the legal holder of the money to be devoted to the purpose may spend the money as he likes. If a testamentary gift is upheld as a purpose trust of this kind, the court will make a '*Pettingall*' order (named after the order made in that case). The trustee must undertake to the court to carry out the purpose, and the 'interested' parties, ie those persons who would take if the trust were to fail and who will take any funds surplus to the requirements of carrying out the purpose, are given leave to apply to the court if the trustee applies the property outside of the intended purpose. Thus the 'enforcement' of these 'trusts' is essentially identical to the enforcement of powers of appointment.

9.19 Two final points on these exceptional trusts, one serious, one trivial. The serious point concerns a case which is regularly cited in the textbooks as a *possible* case of a valid anomalous purpose trust. In *Re Thompson* (1934) a testator left money to a friend in trust for the purpose of promoting fox-hunting. Clauson J decided that he could make a *Pettingall* order because there was a residuary legatee who as an interested party could enforce the trust by applying to the court. But on this basis any purpose trust of whatever kind could be enforced; the *Pettingall* order is devised to deal with a trust of imperfect obligation only if it is already found to fall within the class of exceptions to the general no purpose trust rule in the first place. It is getting things absolutely the wrong way round to find that a purpose trust is valid whenever one can devise a *Pettingall* order.

9.20 The trivial point is simply that leaving property for their maintenance is as much as you can do for your pets after you die. The idea that a millionaire may leave his fortune to his favourite cat is a cartoon fiction having no basis in law, just in case you were wondering. Your animals are your property in law, and you cannot leave property to property. In legal terms, leaving property to your cat, Fred, is no different from leaving property to your toaster; the most you can do is leave a reasonable sum to keep Fred in the condition to which he has become accustomed.

Powers for purposes

9.21 The beneficiary principle applies to trusts, not to powers of appointment. As there is no obligation to exercise powers, there is no similar problem of finding a true beneficiary to enforce their exercise; moreover, those who take in default of appointment are the owners of the property until appointed (**3.5-6**), so a power for a purpose does not generate any ownerless property in equity (**9.7**). The courts have expressed their willingness to uphold powers to devote trust property to purposes. In *Re Douglas* (1887) the court was willing to uphold a power to appoint money to 'such charities, societies, and institutions' as the power-holder should select, even if on the proper construction this allowed the appointment to non-charitable societies or institutions. Although this case concerned a power to appoint property to institutions, not to purposes *per se*, such institutions would themselves apply the property to particular purposes, so the case is cited as evidence of judicial willingness to uphold powers for purposes. In *Re Shaw* (1957), George Bernard Shaw had in his will devoted funds for the purpose of devising a 40-letter alphabet for the English language. Harman J accepted that a power to devote funds to the purpose would have been valid, but having decided that the provision imposed a trust to carry out the purpose, he relied on *IRC v Broadway Cottages Trust* (1955) to hold that a valid power is not to be spelled out of an invalid trust (**7.7**).

9.22 Those who take in default of appointment, while they can ensure that the power-holder does not exercise the power improperly, cannot, however, insist that the power-holder exercise the power; they would be unlikely to insist even if they could, for every such exercise will diminish the amount of property they will receive in default. Thus while a settlor can empower someone to spend the trust property on a purpose, there will be no one who is interested in ensuring that the power is exercised. Therefore a settlor creating a power cannot ensure that the trust property will be applied to the purpose he desires, though, obviously, if he gives the power to someone who is loyal to him and shares his devotion to the purpose, he may be confident that the property will be applied to it despite the absence of any legal means of enforcement.

9.23   The case of powers for purposes raises the interesting question whether such powers can be fiduciary powers, ie whether their holders, typically the trustee of the trust, owes any fiduciary obligations in their exercise. As we have seen (**3.11**), fiduciary power-holders owe fiduciary obligations both to those who take in default of appointment, and to the objects of the power. But here, there are no objects of the power – the power is to carry out a purpose, and a purpose cannot be owed anything. So any proposed *positive* fiduciary duty, say to consider exercising the power from time to time, which is not owed to those who take in default of appointment (their interests are best served if it is not exercised at all), has no corresponding right-holder, no human object. Since there are not private duties without corresponding private rights, there cannot be any fiduciary obligations of this kind.

9.24   On the other hand, a power-holder clearly has duties not to *misuse* the power, a duty which can be enforced by those who take in default of appointment. And to the extent that the fiduciary obligations binding the power holder concern wrongful acts, rather than wrongful omissions, which affect the interests of those who take in default of appointment, then such duties can be enforced. Thus, for example, if the trustee fiduciary power-holder were to carry out the trust purpose, say to devise a 40-letter alphabet for English, by setting up his own company and paying the trust money to it to carry out the purpose, such an expenditure would be made in conflict of interest; those who take in default would have standing to challenge this expenditure, for to the extent that the trustee exercises the power in order to benefit himself, he exercises the power improperly, diminishing their interests under the trust, favouring his own interests over those of these beneficiaries. It would also appear that such a trustee cannot release the power – although a trustee can decide not to exercise the power at all, any purported release would be ineffective and, for example, would not bind any successor trustee. The fiduciary principle works here not because any one has standing to enforce a fiduciary obligation not to release, but because the holder's being a fiduciary extinguishes any valid power to release. Thus it seems that there can be a fiduciary purpose power, although the fiduciary character of the power is limited.

9.25 A power to appoint property to purposes must be expressed with sufficient precision for the power-holder and the court to know with certainty what will count as appointing property to the purpose, in case any person who would take in default of appointment were to challenge a particular expenditure by the power-holder. As we have seen (**7.28**), the 'is or is not' test should apply, which is to say that any power must be expressed with a certainty sufficient to determine whether *any* proposed expenditure is within the power or not. In *Re Astor*, Roxburgh J would have held the trust to fail for uncertainty if not for lack of beneficiaries. Since the capricious creation or exercise of a power may also be invalid (**7.75**), one presumes that a power to appoint property to purposes may founder if capricious.

An enforcer principle?

9.26 Should the law, or on an unconventional view of the case law, *does* the law, allow private purpose trusts? Hayton (2001a; 2001b, 209-212) argues that the cases should be read to reveal not a beneficiary principle, but rather an *enforcer* principle. An enforcer principle would allow a settlor to create a private purpose trust so long as the trust revealed a person or class of persons who could enforce the trust against the trustee, eg the employees who factually benefited from the trust in *Re Denley*, or a particular individual named by the settlor as one who should have standing to enforce the trust.

9.27 While perhaps attractive in theory, there are severe difficulties with this view, in so far as it can be genuinely treated as the creation of a true private purpose trust. Remember that trusts are private, and that the only rights under the trust are those that are given to specific individuals or classes of individuals by the settlor. While the settlor can carve up the beneficial interest in the trust property in any way he likes, does he effectively create a purpose trust by giving the trustee a duty to apply the money to a purpose, and an 'enforcer' a power to enforce that duty? It is difficult to see how. Why cannot the trustee and enforcer agree to split the money between themselves? After all, no one else, no third party or the court, has any independent right to enforce any duties against the trustee (there is no equivalent of the Attorney-General who enforces charitable purpose trusts), and so no one can insist that the enforcer exercise his power to make the trustee apply the money to the purpose. The extent of the trustee's duty is the extent to which that duty will be enforced against him by the enforcer, and if the enforcer has no interest in seeing the purpose carried out, he is perfectly entitled at law to cut a deal with the trustee to split the money between themselves, in the same way that contracting parties can re-negotiate their rights under a contract if they choose to do so, for trusts, like contracts, are purely private arrangements in which there is no public interest, and these private purpose trusts, by *definition*, generate no public interest, not being charitable.

9.28   The upshot is that while it may be perfectly sensible for the law to validate arrangements like *Re Denley* or 'purpose trusts' with named enforcers, the beneficial interest in the trust property does not 'go to the purpose'. It is distributed between the person who has the duty to spend the money on the purpose, usually, one imagines, the trustee, and any person, the 'enforcer', who has the corresponding power to enforce the duty against him. It would not help, of course, to impose a duty upon the enforcer to enforce the purpose trust against the trustee, for one would then just need a third party to enforce that duty against the enforcer, and then another to enforce his duty, ad infinitum. The result is that the 'purpose trust with enforcer' mechanism Hayton describes, while perhaps within the law, does not deliver a true purpose trust, but rather enables the settlor to give his trustee a power to apply property to purposes and a power to another to make him exercise that power.

9.29   True non-charitable purpose trusts can only be created if the law is changed so as to give some public force to the purpose trust, so that the trust property is governed not merely by the private rights of individuals (in which case, it is no longer clear that they can be called 'private' purpose trusts). This, of course, is true of charitable purpose trusts, which are enforced by the Attorney-General. Certain 'off-shore' jurisdictions, to attract trust business, have also, by legislation, created true non-charitable purpose trusts, under which the court has the power to enforce any purpose trust at the application of any interested party ((Bermuda) Trusts (Special Provisions Act) 1989, as amended 1998), or which employ criminal sanctions to ensure that the enforcer enforces the trust ((Cayman Islands) Trust Law 2001, incorporating (Cayman Islands) Special Trusts (Alternative Regime) Law 1997).

Valid trusts for persons 'limited by a purpose': *Re Sanderson* trusts

9.30   Certain trusts which can be thought of as 'purpose trusts' have always been allowed by equity. This is a category of trusts under which the beneficiary is only allowed to take a certain amount which is determined by the costs of carrying out a purpose. Here's an example: '£100,000 to be paid by my trustees to my daughter Barbara in amounts equivalent to those she has expended on her education, the remaining funds to go to my son Peter'. The gift to Barbara is a gift to pay the costs of her education, and on that basis it appears that the settlor (usually in these cases, a testator) has created a trust for the purpose of educating Barbara. Nevertheless, one should not regard this sort of gift as an anomalous valid purpose trust. Consider this gift: '£100,000 on trust to pay Julia £1,000 on each occasion that Chelsea FC wins a match during the regular football season of 2003-2004, all funds remaining to be paid to Timothy'. This trust is perfectly valid, if unusual: the settlor has simply chosen an unusual way of carving up the beneficial interests between the two beneficiaries; it would be odd if such a gift were valid but a gift which limits the amount that a beneficiary receives on the basis of what it costs to educate him were not. That is why it is better to frame such a gift as a 'trust in which the subject matter is apportioned to the beneficiaries in reference to the costs of carrying out a well-defined purpose' rather than as a purpose trust. The purpose in these trusts is not to be regarded as the replacement of the human object of the trust with a purpose; the purpose is part of a device or formula which defines the *subject matter* of the trust for a particular object, an object, ie a beneficiary, who is fully human. True, if the beneficiary does not incur any costs of the required kind, then that beneficiary will take nothing; in that way these gifts may certainly provide an incentive for the beneficiary to achieve the purpose, although not always: consider a trust to pay the rehabilitation expenses of members of a mountaineering society who injure themselves by falling off mountains.

9.31 The leading case concerning such trusts is *Re Sanderson's Trust* (1857). Here a testator left property upon trust to 'pay and apply the whole or any part of the [income] for and towards [the] maintenance, attendance, and comfort', of his imbecile brother for the remainder of his life. At the death of this brother there remained unexpended income, and the question was whether those funds should be held on trust for the residuary legatees under the testator's estate, or whether the money should go into the brother's estate. In other words, the question was whether the gift was limited to such portion of the income as was required to pay for the brother's maintenance, or whether it was an absolute gift of the whole.

9.32 Page-Wood VC distinguished the two possible interpretations of testamentary gifts of this kind as follows:

> In reference to gifts of this description, there are two classes of cases between which the general distinction is sufficiently clear, although the precise line of demarcation is occasionally somewhat difficult to ascertain. If a gross sum be given, or if the whole income of the property is given, and a special purpose assigned for that gift, this Court always regards the gift as absolute, and the purpose merely as the motive of the gift, and therefore holds that the gift takes effect as to the whole sum or the whole income, as the case may be ... [If] an entire fund is given for the maintenance of children or the like, they take the whole fund absolutely, and the maintenance is treated in effect as simply the motive in making the gift; while, on the other hand, if a portion only of the fund is given for maintenance, then they are entitled to draw out so much only as may be necessary for the purpose specified.

9.33 Thus there developed a body of case law directed to determining whether the testator intended that the whole of the trust property should go to the beneficiary, the purpose of maintenance, or education, or whatever, merely indicating the motive of the gift, or whether he was creating a fund out of which money might be distributed only on the basis of meeting the costs or expenses of the purpose. In this case Page-Wood VC decided that the brother was only entitled to such part of the fund as was necessary for his maintenance, attendance, and comfort. Nevertheless, it is clear that the brother, and others who benefit under like trusts when the costs or expenses that the trusts cover are met, are just as much human beneficiaries as persons who are recipients of absolute gifts. In particular, they are not to be regarded as beneficiaries of discretionary trusts, in which the trustees, at their discretion, may or may not spend the money on the particular purpose, ie to pay the particular expenses the testator indicated. The beneficiaries are fully entitled to demand the requisite payments to meet the costs or expenses specified by the trust.

9.34 Settlors, then, may devote property to certain purposes *in the sense* that they may leave property on trust to spend any amount of the property, up to all of it, on certain well-defined expenses of named beneficiaries, and these beneficiaries can enforce these trusts, by demanding whatever amounts fall within the expenses or costs defined by the purpose from the trustees. Any property left when the purpose is accomplished will result either to the settlor or, in the case of a will, to the testator's residuary legatees, unless a specific gift over of the remainder is made.

9.35 The courts in the nineteenth century were well versed in enforcing trusts of this kind, in particular trusts to pay for the maintenance, education, and advancement of children. A trust for maintenance is one which will provide for a person's daily costs of living, a roof over his head and food, clothing, etc; a trust for education is straightforward; a trust for advancement is a trust to pay sums of money to 'advance' someone in the world, usually an infant who is approaching adulthood, by paying the costs of getting him started in his career; a typical example of a payment for advancement in the nineteenth century would be the purchase of a 'living' for a cleric, ie an appointment to an office in the Church of England, or the purchase of a commission in the army. Because the nature of these costs and expenses were so familiar it is possible, and makes sense, to treat such trusts as trusts to pay certain well-defined expenses. It is not clear that other purposes could so easily be treated in this way; indeed, it might even be regarded as a test of the validity of *Sanderson*-type trusts that the 'purpose' can be clearly localised to a particular beneficiary as the payment of a certain share of a fund, that share determined by well-defined expenses which he may incur – in other words, only well-defined costs or expenses will be *certain* enough, although the certainty here is the certainty of subject matter – if the 'purpose' does not provide a reasonably workable determination of the expenses which over the course of the trust will define the share the beneficiary is to receive then the testator has not defined with sufficient precision the subject matter of the trust in that beneficiary's favour.

Because the subject matter is defined via the cost of carrying out a purpose, as with the certainty of other purposes, the 'is or is not test will apply (**7.28; 9.25**). In *Conway v Buckingham* (1711) the life tenant was required to build a mansion house according to the testator's model; the trust was properly seen as a valid *Re Sanderson*-type trust, the effect of the testamentary instruction being to diminish the interest of the life tenant and benefit the remainderman by requiring the capitalisation of the income in a particular way. The dispute in the case between the life tenant and the remainderman was whether the amount spent by the life tenant was sufficient given the vagueness of the testator's 'design' or model, and the court held that it was.

9.36 In cases of this kind it may be difficult to determine whether a testator intended a gift of the whole fund with an attached motive or direction, or a gift of such part of the property as is required to meet the beneficiary's costs of achieving a purpose such as his education. A somewhat unusual case was *Re Skinner's Trusts* (1860). Here the Reverend Skinner left £1,000 in his will for the publication of his own work, 'intitled 'An Analysis of Language, and Symbols of the Worship of the Sun' in two volumes' the profits and copyright of which were to be used to provide his grandson funds for his education. The executors of the will set aside £1,000, and sought advice from an expert and the publisher, both of whom advised against its publication. The question was whether the grandson was entitled to the whole fund, the publication of the manuscript being only a suggested means by which he should benefit, or whether the publication of the manuscript was the essential means by which the grandson was to benefit. On the latter view, it was argued that the trust had failed because the book was unpublishable; it would be equivalent to the case where Julia in the example of **9.30** would get nothing if Chelsea FC were to go bankrupt and cease to play. Page-Wood VC, while regarding the case on the borderline, preferred the former interpretation, thus the whole amount went to the grandson.

9.37 In *Re Bowes* (1896) £5,000 was left upon trust for the purpose of planting trees on an estate. The evidence of foresters indicated that only a fraction of the land would benefit from the planting at a cost of only £800. North J decided that the paramount intention of the gift was to benefit the persons entitled to the estate, and so this intention should prevail over the specific means of planting trees where that means, if carried out, would be actually disadvantageous to the beneficiaries. Thus the owners of the estate were entitled to the £5,000 absolutely.

9.38 The problem of inferring the settlor's intention has been particularly acute in 'appeal' cases, where an appeal has been made to raise funds to provide for individuals who have suffered some misfortune. It is obviously a vexed task to determine whether an amorphous group of often anonymous contributors had one intention or the other, and perhaps these cases should be regarded as in a class of their own. In *Re Abbott Fund Trusts* (1900), one Dr Abbott of Cambridge placed money on trust for the support of his family, including two daughters who were deaf and dumb, but the trustee turned out to be a rogue and the trust money disappeared. Several persons in turn sought subscriptions on behalf of the two daughters, which were held by trustees who made quarterly payments to the two women. On the death of the survivor of the two some £366 remained. The only evidence of the intention of the subscribers was the circular making the appeal for funds, which stated that the fund was to enable the women to reside in Cambridge and to provide for their 'very moderate wants,' and, if the trustees so decided, to purchase annuities for them. Stirling J decided:

> I cannot believe that [the fund] was ever intended to become the absolute property of the ladies so that they should be in the position to demand a transfer of it to themselves, or so that if they became bankrupt the trustee in bankruptcy should be able to claim it. ... I think that the trustee or trustees were intended to have a wide discretion as to whether any, and if any what, part of the fund should be applied for the benefit of the ladies and how the application should be made. That view would not deprive them of any right in the fund, because if the trustees had not done their duty – if they either failed to exercise their discretion or exercised it improperly – the ladies might successfully have applied to the Court to have the fund administered according to the terms of the circular. In the result, therefore, there must be a declaration that there is a resulting trust of the moneys remaining unapplied for the benefit of the subscribers to the Abbott fund.

9.39 In *Re Andrew's Trust* (1905) money was raised by subscription for the children of the Bishop of Jerusalem. Again, the evidence as to the objects of the trust was slim, found in a letter by the now deceased canon who had initiated the appeal, who described the money as having been collected:

> ... for and towards the education of Bishop Barclay's children, ... [and] that it was by no means intended for the exclusive use of any one of them in particular, nor for equal division, but as deemed as necessary to defray the expenses of all, and that solely in the matter of education.

The children's education having been provided for under their father's will, the trustees sought a declaration enabling them to distribute the fund to the children. Kekewich J decided as follows:

> Here the only specified object was the education of the children. But I deem myself entitled to construe 'education' in the broadest possible sense, and not to consider the purpose exhausted because the children have attained such ages that education in the vulgar sense is no longer necessary. Even if it be construed in the narrower sense it is, in Wood VC's language, merely the motive of the gift, and the intention must be taken to provide for the children in the manner (they all then being infants) most useful.

9.40 After reviewing these two decisions in *Re Osoba* (1978), Megarry VC said:

> I think that you have to look at the persons intended to benefit, and be ready, if they still can benefit, to treat the stated method of benefit as merely indicating ... the means of benefit which are to be in the forefront. In short, if a trust is constituted for the assistance of certain persons by certain stated means there is a sharp distinction between cases where the beneficiaries have died and cases where they are still living. If they are dead, the court is willing to hold that there is a resulting trust for the donors; for the major purpose of the trust, that of providing help and benefit for the beneficiaries, comes to an end when the beneficiaries are all dead and so are beyond earthly help, whether by the stated means or otherwise. But if the beneficiaries are still living, the major purpose of providing help and benefit for the beneficiaries can still be carried out even after the stated means have all been accomplished, and so the court will be ready to treat the standard means as being merely indicative and not restrictive.

While there is obvious sense in this, Megarry VC appears to take a dangerously *ex post* view of the interpretation of testamentary gifts. Surely any interpretive strategy should be primarily devoted to figuring out the testator's intention from the outset, when the trustees who are to administer the trust receive the funds. It is then that they must be certain whether the trust is a gift of the whole with a mere motive or a *Re Sanderson* trust only of a part.

9.41 Second, do Megarry VC's words about the means in a gift of the whole, that they 'are intended to be in the forefront', mean that even where the gift is of the whole, the trustees must *first* apply the money according to the motive, to defray the expenses of maintenance or education or whatever, until such time as they are no longer incurred, as when the education of the beneficiary is complete? In other words, does the gift become an absolute one only upon the 'purposes' either being accomplished or no longer capable of fulfilment? (Cf *Re Bowes*.) If so, what happens if before the 'purpose' comes to an end, ie before the trustees distribute the property as an absolute gift, the beneficiaries all die? Whether the gift is a gift of the whole or only a part surely cannot turn simply on the time of the beneficiaries' death, for that would engender a lottery whereby the remaining surplus of a large gift for the education of Albert would go into his estate if he died the day after graduation (the purpose being complete, the gift of the whole would now 'take'), but would go on resulting trust if he died the day before. Megarry VC's guidance on the construction of such gifts should, then, be followed with some care.

9.42   *Re Osoba* (1978, Ch D, 1979, CA) concerned a testamentary trust of residue for the maintenance of the testator's widow and his mother, and for 'the training of my daughter Abiola up to university grade'. There was no gift over which would take effect on the completion of the purposes. The testator's mother had predeceased him, and by the time the case came before the court the testator's widow was dead, and Abiola had finished her university education; the question was whether the surplus funds were to be held on a partial intestacy, all of the trust purposes for the residue now being fulfilled. Megarry VC said he would lean toward construing a gift of residue as an absolute gift, since otherwise any surplus would go on resulting trust to those who would take on intestacy, not an intention one would normally ascribe to a testator. Megarry VC construed the instructions as to how the money should be spent as a mere indication of motive, and decided that the wife and Abiola together became entitled to the whole fund absolutely on the testator's death.

9.43   There are three reasons for having gone into these cases in some detail. The first is simply to make clear that such trusts, which are in a sense a variation on purpose trusts, exist in the law but do not violate the beneficiary principle so long as they are interpreted as 'trusts in which the subject matter is apportioned to beneficiaries in reference to the costs of carrying out a well-defined purpose'.

9.44 Second, however, if the subject matter of a trust can be apportioned in this way, then it is clear that well-defined purposes may be taken into account in determining how a trustee should distribute the trust property, since such purposes indicate clearly how the subject matter may be expended. Thus these trusts raise the question: even in cases where the beneficiaries' interests are not limited by the purpose, should the trustees nevertheless take the settlor's purpose into account? Should they spend the money on the stated purpose first? Should, for example, the trustees have refused to give Abiola the whole trust fund until she was either educated up to University grade, or it became clear that carrying out the purpose was impossible (say Abiola was so thick that no University would admit her)? One might suggest that the courts should at least require the trustees to comply with the settlor's directions, not so as to ultimately limit the extent of the beneficial gift, but to give effect in so far as possible to the means by which the settlor chose to give it. Thus, it might be right to say that until the beneficiaries use their *Saunders v Vautier* rights to vary or collapse the trust, individual beneficiaries should be able to insist that the trustees comply with the settlor's declared means of distribution in so far as it is certain. This view does not detract from the beneficiary principle, because the whole gift would still be to the beneficiaries. It would only properly limit the trustee's discretion through the enforcement of the settlor's intentions by the people who are appropriately entitled to do so, ie the beneficiaries. This view might go some way to rescuing *Re Denley* from death by interpretation (**9.15**) for, if correct, unless and until the beneficiaries exercise their *Saunders v Vautier* rights, the trustees should apply the trust property for their benefit according to the settlor's instructions.

9.45 Third, and finally, *Sanderson* trusts make a nice point of comparison with what might be called 'equitably enforceable property regimes', such as the rules governing the administration of wills and estates (**2.61** et seq) or the bankrupt's estate by his trustee in bankruptcy (**2.57** et seq). The intestate successors or beneficiaries of a will or the bankrupt's creditors have no proprietary interest in these estates of property while they are being administered, though they do have rights to ensure they are properly distributed according to the regime of rules in place. In one sense, then, the executor or administrator or trustee in bankruptcy can be thought of as holding property on 'purpose trust', the eventual effect of the purpose being that the property will be distributed to individuals. By contrast with *Sanderson* trusts, however, while these estates are being administered according to their respective rules the 'beneficiaries' have no *Saunders v Vautier* rights to vary the terms of the 'rules of distribution'. Were English law to recognise true purpose trusts, one would presume that parties interested in the trustee's carrying out such trusts would only have limited rights of enforcement of this kind.

The bare trust with mandate and *Quistclose* trusts

9.46   The bare trust with mandate and the *Quistclose* trust have already been explained in outline (**7.21-7.25**), so re-read those paragraphs now. There are three issues to consider here. The first is to extend our analysis of the bare trust with mandate and look at its operation in some cases. The second is to consider the alternative analyses raised by Lord Millett in *Twinsectra*. First, however, there is an initial basic question raised by Swadling (2004): the *Quistclose* arrangement seems to put the lender in the best of all possible worlds: if the borrower becomes insolvent before spending the money, the lender can rely upon the trust to retrieve the value of the loan; but if the money is lost through no fault of the borrower/ trustee – say the bank where the money is held on trust fails – in which case normally the lender/beneficiary would bear the loss, here the lender can rely upon the loan element of the arrangement, and demand full re-payment. It is submitted that this issue is best dealt with as a matter of construing the loan contract. Nothing in principle prevents a lender from having the best of all possible worlds in this way, for a trustee can, under the terms of the trust, be made an insurer of the trust funds, so that even if the funds are lost through no fault of his own he may be liable to restore their value. But it is submitted that the 'default' construction of the loan arrangement should be as follows: the borrower accepts the liability to pay interest on the loan money from the minute the funds are received, for whatever the delay between receiving the funds and his actual spending of them, the borrower has the use of the funds from the moment received. However the borrower should not be liable for the innocent loss of the funds, eg through a bank failure, unless this is an explicit term of the contract. If such a thing should occur, the contract should be taken to have been frustrated, and come to an end, the lender bearing the loss of the trust funds. This would appear to be the appropriate corollary disadvantage to the lender's advantage of having the beneficial interest in the funds until expended by the borrower. Given that in most cases the lender bank will place the funds in an account the borrower has with the lender itself, this would appear to be the just result, for the loss will only arise when the lender bank itself fails; it would seem harsh if the borrower were made to repay the full amount of the loan to a lender whose own failure made the borrower's obtaining any value from the loan impossible and, as stated, any opposite conclusion should only be found where the terms of the loan arrangement explicitly provide for this.

The mandate imposes a personal obligation

9.47 The basic bare trust with mandate analysis was first explained in detail by Millett (1985). The most important feature of this analysis is that the beneficial interest in the trust property remains with the settlor, A, on bare trust, subject however to the trustee's, B's, power or duty to apply the funds according to the settlor's standing order, or mandate. There are no *trust terms* other than that B should hold the trust property to A's order. A's instructions constitute mandates which A may give, vary and revoke from time to time – they may either impose duties on B positively to do something, or confer powers upon B to deal with the property in certain ways if he so chooses. These mandates impose *personal* obligations upon B. If B distributes the trust property in violation of one of these mandates he certainly commits a breach of trust, but not a breach of trust because the mandate is a term of the trust; he commits a breach of the only trust term there is, the overarching duty to hold the property to A's order or mandate. By distributing the trust property in violation or outside the scope of A's orders, he fails to hold the property to A's order and thus commits a breach of trust.

9.48 In contrast, B commits no *breach of trust* if his failure to comply with a mandate is one of *non-feasance*. In that case B still holds the property to A's order; he simply fails to carry out A's mandate. For example, if I transfer £10,000 on bare trust to my broker to make investments on my behalf, and he fails to carry out my order to invest £5000 in shares of XYZ plc, my the broker will not have committed a breach of trust – he did not violate my property rights in equity – rather, he just failed to fulfil a personal contractual obligation to me, for which he will be liable for damages if I suffer a loss because of it.

9.49 Note that the bare trust with mandate does not work if one treats A's mandate as a specific term of a trust that B undertakes, imposing true trust duties, for to the extent that B is under a duty to apply the trust property in some way, to that extent is A's beneficial interest under the trust *displaced*, ie it is no longer a bare trust in A's favour. Of course, where the mandate was that B should apply the trust property to some purpose, this would be an invalid purpose trust, and so would fail (see further Penner (2004)).

The extent of the mandated purpose for the trust money

9.50   Millett (1985) pointed out that 'The settlor's motives must not be confused with the purposes of the trust; the frustration of the former does not by itself cause the failure of the latter'. The point here is that one's ultimate goal in setting up a *Quistclose* trust may have been thwarted, but that does not mean that the trust did not operate according to its terms. In general, there is only one appropriate point at which to decide whether a trust has been properly carried out according to its terms: when the trustee applies the money by dealing with it with a third party. Thus, a trustee applies trust property according to his investment power when he makes an authorised investment, ie buys an investment like shares from someone. A trustee correctly applies the trust property dispositively when he gives the trust property to a properly entitled beneficiary. The trust over the property, once it is transmitted correctly to the beneficiary, comes to an end, for the transfer fulfils the trust terms. Likewise, a trustee who correctly applies the trust property according to his mandate, disposes of the property correctly according to the terms of the trust (to hold it to the settlor's order), and thus the trust over the property comes to an end.

9.51   Unfortunately, the confusion of ultimate goal with a proper application of the trust property according to the trust terms has dogged recent cases supposedly decided on *Quistclose* principles. In *Re EVTR* (1987) the appellant, who had received a quarter of a million pounds following a premium bonds win, advanced £60,000 to his old employer to enable it to purchase new equipment. The employer then contracted with an equipment supplier and a leasing company, paying over the £60,000. The supplier provided temporary equipment until the new equipment could be delivered. The employer became insolvent before the new equipment arrived, and the supplier and leasing company refunded £48,000 to it. The CA held that, though the funds that had been advanced were paid out, the trust continued to the extent that, when the ultimate purpose failed, the refund was held for the original provider. Dillon LJ said:

> True it is that the £60,000 was paid out by the [employer] with a view to the acquisition of new equipment, but that was only at half-time, and I do not see why the final whistle should be blown at half-time.

9.52 The problem here, of course, is that the employer's payment out of the money appears to be the only appropriate point at which the trust relationship ends and its relationship with the provider of the funds becomes that of debtor and creditor. If that is not full-time, what is? When the equipment has been used for a while? What if it turns out that after a year the equipment turns out not to be much use, and is sold? Are the proceeds of that sale to be held on trust for the original provider? Had the purchase gone ahead so no refund arose, the court could only have dated the transition from the trust relationship to one of debtor and creditor when the money was paid, and so should it here. It is submitted that the CA must have imposed some kind of constructive trust giving the provider an equitable title in the traceable proceeds of his loan money. There was, however, no basis in authority for such a trust, and it seems to give the provider an unjustifiable priority over the company's other creditors. Had it been found, on the true intention of the parties, that the appellant was to retain an equitable interest in the equipment and any traceable proceeds until he was paid back his loan, then the appropriate finding would have been, following *Re Bond Worth Ltd* (**7.20**), that he had an equitable charge, and that this was not a *Quistclose* trust at all. Such a charge would have to have been registered to be valid against the company's creditors or liquidator.

9.53 The second case, *R v Common Professional Examination Board, ex p Mealing-McCleod* (2000), decided by a panel of two in the CA, is a tissue of confusions. A law student, following several court actions against the CPE Board, was liable to them for substantial legal costs. When she pursued a further legal remedy, the Board was awarded an order for security for costs, ie the student had to pay £6,000 into court before the action would proceed. She obtained the £6,000 from her bank, with the provision in the loan agreement quoted at **7.27**. The student paid the money into court, but as she was successful in her action, the money was not required to pay any costs of that action to the Board. The Board, however, claimed the money to defray the earlier costs awards against the student which were still unpaid. Whether or not the Board's claim that money paid into court to cover the possible costs of one action should be available to pay the cost of previous ones was good in law, the basis upon which the CA refused the Board's claim was that the money was held upon a *Quistclose* trust. At trial, Hidden J got it absolutely right. He held that, while there was an express Quistclose trust of the money, the trust element ended when the student paid the money into court; and even if the trust endured beyond this point, the court had no notice of it, so took free of any residual trust.

9.54   The CA, allowing the student's appeal, held that because the express agreement was that the money should only be paid as security for the student's costs in the particular action, and since the funds were not so required, the funds remained bound by the trust and could be demanded from the court by the student who would be bound in trust to return them to the bank. The trust of the money bound the court, irrespective of its notice of the trust, for the court was a volunteer, and 'effectively in the position of a stakeholder' (per Slade LJ). With respect, this reasoning is insupportable. True it is that a *Quistclose* trust only comes to an end when the trust money is properly applied by the trustee/borrower (here the student) for the loan purpose, whereupon the trust disappears and the borrower is only personally bound to repay the money. But the only 'purpose' for such a loan is to make the proper payment under the loan agreement for, once that is done, there is no longer any trust corpus upon which any trust obligation owed to the lender can bite. Here, that purpose was fully accomplished when the student paid the £6,000 into court to provide security for costs. Since that payment was properly made, the trust over the money came to an end. Thus the 'purpose' of the loan which defines the extent of the trust cannot be made to encompass *all the intended consequences which are expected to flow from the proper application of the loan money*. If that were the case, then the very basis of the *Quistclose* trust and the prior staving-off bankruptcy cases would be rendered senseless. On the CA's broad reading of purpose in this way, the money actually paid to creditors under a staving-off bankruptcy trust, or the dividend money had it been paid to the shareholders in *Quistclose* itself, would be held on trust by these payees to return to the lender if it turned out that the bankruptcy or liquidation was not averted. For that was the 'purpose' of the loan broadly speaking. But if the trust attaches to that, not only is the trust an invalid purpose trust, the whole point of the exercise would be useless, for if the creditors or shareholders received their payments, not as theirs beneficially, but subject to a trust which gave them no beneficial interest unless bankruptcy or receivership was averted, then these payments would not satisfy their claims against the company thus allowing it to stave off its bankruptcy or receivership, and would indeed almost certainly precipitate the bankruptcy or receivership. And this applies across the board to such trust/loans. The money is only good to the borrower if he can pay it over beneficially to third parties to accomplish the purpose of the loan. That he holds it in trust himself until he does so cannot alter his power to confer beneficial legal title on his payees if the loan is to have any value to him. Thus the terms of the trust defined by the 'purpose of the loan' must be restricted to the purpose of transferring the beneficial legal title to the money to the proper recipients as defined by the loan agreement.

9.55 Furthermore, putting these objections to one side, even if the bank tried by its loan agreement to bind third party recipients to hold the payments they received from the borrower on trust, it could not do that simply by making it a term of its agreement with its borrower. These third party recipients would only hold the property on trust if they undertook to do so, either to the bank or to its borrower, and in none of the cases are those the facts. Accordingly, the issue of the court or any recipient being a volunteer or having notice is perfectly irrelevant, because if the borrower was entitled under the loan agreement to pay the money to the third party, then full beneficial legal title to the money was properly paid under the loan arrangement in full compliance with its trust provision. A third party could be bound only where the loan money was *improperly* paid, ie paid in breach of the trust in so far as it was specified in the loan agreement (and this happened neither in *Re EVTR* or *R v CPE Board*), the third party being bound either as a volunteer or, having given consideration, having had notice of the breach of trust (**2.34**). Finally, if any more need be said, on the CA's reasoning on payment of the £6,000 into court the court would either itself have been under an obligation to keep that £6,000 separately, as trust money, or be considered a wrongdoer, since according to the CA the money was bound by the trust throughout. Really, however, as in *Re EVTR*, the court was merely imposing a constructive trust because it felt it was the just thing to do in all the circumstances, but with even less justification here, for at least in *Re EVTR* the holder of the property was the borrower/trustee. Here, the constructive trustee, ie the court, was a third party who was transferred the legal title to money in full compliance with the loan/trust agreement with no notice of its provisions.

9.55A   It is submitted that the only conceivable way to bring the decisions in *Re EVTR* and *R v CPE Board* within workable trust law principles is to analyse them along the following lines: consider the case where the borrower transfers money from the separate bank account into which the lender pays the loan moneys to his solicitor, to hold on trust for him in the latter's client account, prior to making a purchase which will carry out the purpose of the loan. Now assume that the borrower becomes insolvent. It would seem appropriate to allow the lender to claim that the borrower's right to the money in his solicitor's client account should be held on trust for the lender, on the basis that the borrower's transfer to his solicitor was merely preparatory to his expending the money on the loan. Notice that the solicitor does not, under this analysis, hold the money on trust for the lender, as the courts in *Re EVTR* or *R v CPE Board* would have it. Rather, the borrower himself holds his right against the solicitor on bare trust for the lender, as an asset which is merely a change in form from his prior right to the money in the separate bank account. On this analysis, the rights the borrower held to the refund in *Re EVTR* and to the repayment of money deposited in court in *R v CPE Board* were held on trust for the lender. Nevertheless, this analysis still requires one to determine at which point the trust moneys are properly expended according to the trust terms, and thus it would still seem that the cases were wrongly decided, as these rights were not rights acquired merely in preparation for carrying out the trust purpose; rather, they were rights which adventitiously arose following the expenditure of the trust moneys in complete fulfilment of the trust purpose.

Alternative interpretations of the Quistclose trust

9.56   The judgment of Lord Wilberforce in *Quistclose* suggested that there was a primary purpose trust to pay a dividend, which purpose failed on RR's liquidation, giving rise to a resulting trust in Q's favour. There are any number of problems with this analysis (for a thorough demolition see Swadling (2004), 9 et seq), not least of which is that, to work, non-charitable purpose trusts must be valid, and they are not. The analysis is not viable, and can be ignored. There are two other analyses of such trusts which prior to the decision in *Twinsectra,* attracted support, Millett's (1985) analysis, the one adopted by this text above, and one by Chambers (Chambers 1997, Chapter 3).

9.57   Chambers's analysis, which draws support from the terms in which judges spoke in deciding these sorts of cases up to the early part of the

20th century, in particular the use of the term 'quasi-trust', is as follows: When the lender, L, pays the loan moneys over to the borrower, B, B does not hold the money on trust for L; rather, under the loan contract which specifies the purpose(s) on which B may spend the money, L acquires an equitable right to require that B spend the money only on those purposes, a right which equity will enforce by injunction. Where it becomes impossible to carry out the purpose of the loan, a resulting trust then arises, ie at this point B holds the funds on trust for L for the first time in the course of events. This resulting trust arises because B was not intended to take the funds beneficially to use as he wishes. (This analysis of the character and relevance of the parties' intentions is in keeping with Chambers's general analysis of resulting trusts; **4.52** et seq.)

9.58 The HL has addressed the issue in *Twinsectra v Yardley* (2002). While the CA (1999) unanimously adopted Potter LJ's analysis, which was in most respects identical to Chambers's, Lord Millett in the HL forcefully rejected this analysis and, not surprisingly, favoured his own, although it departed significantly from his 1985 analysis. Lord Millett was in a minority of one in the case, and his analysis formed part of his dissenting opinion. The leading speech was given by Lord Hutton, who agreed with both Lord Millett's and Lord Hoffmann's analysis of the *Quistclose* trust, and Lords Steyn and Slynn agreed with both Hutton and Hoffmann. So much turns on whether Lord Hoffmann's and Lord Millett's analysis were essentially the same. Unfortunately Lord Hoffmann's analysis was very brief; although it seems to be largely in keeping with Lord Millett's analysis, he nowhere adopts or refers to Lord Millett's analysis.

9.59 In *Twinsectra* Lord Millett stated quite categorically that *Quistclose* trusts are resulting trusts that arise by operation of law. This departed in a serious way from his 1985 view that the *Quistclose* trust was an express trust, ie based on the parties' actual intentions. According to that analysis, there is no 'resulting' trust at all: A's beneficial ownership is intended from the first − he takes that interest as the intended beneficiary under the bare trust with mandate. In *Twinsectra*, however, Lord Millett said that the *Quistclose* trust is:

> an entirely orthodox example of the kind of default trust known as a resulting trust. The lender pays the money to the borrower by way of loan, but he does not part with the entire beneficial interest in the money, and in so far as he does not it is held on resulting trust for the lender from the outset.

9.60   This characterisation of the *Quistclose* trust seems to follow from Lord Millett's approval of Chambers' general theory of the resulting trust, which he endorses in *Twinsectra* as follows:

> The central thesis of Dr Chambers's book is that a resulting trust arises whenever there is a transfer of property in circumstances in which the transferor (or more accurately the person at whose expense the property was provided) did not intend to benefit the recipient. It responds to the absence of an intention on the part of the transferor to pass the entire beneficial interest, not to a positive intention to retain it. Insofar as the transfer does not exhaust the entire beneficial interest, the resulting trust is a default trust which fills the gap and leaves no room for any part to be in suspense. An analysis of the *Quistclose* trust as a resulting trust for the transferor with a mandate to the transferee to apply the money for the stated purpose sits comfortably with Dr. Chambers's thesis ...

9.61   It is not at all clear how this analysis covers *Quistclose* trusts that are express, ie cases where the documents specifically declare that B holds the property on trust for A until properly applied for the specified purpose, for in such cases there is no question that there is merely an absence of intention on A's part that B should take the property beneficially – there is a positive intention that the property is to be held on trust for A. It is possible, of course, to distinguish between express *Quistclose* trusts and ones that arise by operation of law, but it is difficult to see the point. Whether the *Quistclose* trust is express or arises by operation of law, the structure of the trust and its operation is the same. As Lord Millett said in *Twinsectra*:

> I do not think subtle distinctions should be made between 'true' *Quistclose* trusts and trusts which are merely analogous to them. ... There is clearly a range of situations in which the parties enter into a commercial arrangement which permits one party to have a limited use of the other's money for a stated purpose, and must return it if for any reason the purpose cannot be carried out. The arrangement between the purchaser's solicitor and the purchaser's mortgagee is an example of just such an arrangement. All such arrangements should be susceptible to the same analysis.

But the arrangement between the solicitor and his purchaser's mortgagee is express, so Lord Millett's 'resulting trust arising by operation of law' simply cannot apply.

281

9.62 Knowing whether such trusts are express (if sometimes informal) express trusts, or are rather resulting trusts arising by operation of law is a vital question, for that largely determines how the court should properly take into account evidence of the parties' intentions in determining whether a *Quistclose* trust has been created or has arisen. If the trust arises by operation of law in response to the absence of intention, none of the traditional certainties for express trusts, which might otherwise constrain a finding of trust, are relevant, for these concern the intentional creation of trusts, not trusts arising by operation of law. There is a danger that the resulting trust analysis will allow the Court to find trusts in commercial circumstances on flimsy evidence about what might have been *absent* from A's mind, as opposed to determining the true intentions of the parties. It is arguable that this happened in *Twinsectra* itself (see Penner (2004)). It is submitted that first thoughts were best thoughts, and that Lord Millett's 1985 analysis is superior to his *Twinsectra* account, which tries to bend his 1985 analysis to make it work within Chambers's theory of resulting trusts, which he clearly admires. (For a recent case applying *Twinsectra*, see *Patel v London Borough of Brent* (2003).)

Gifts to unincorporated associations

9.63 An unincorporated association is a collective body of individuals, like a student law society, which does not have its own legal personality like a company does, hence the name *unincorporated* association. Unincorporated associations are of interest here because if an individual wishes to devote his money to the carrying out of a purpose, in particular after his death, then one way of doing so is to give money to an unincorporated association whose own purposes are those of the settlor. If the settlor wishes to promote fox-hunting with a testamentary bequest, he might consider making a gift to a local hunt association. What we will be concerned with here is, firstly, the way in which these unincorporated associations hold property, given that they have no legal personality and, secondly, whether a settlor's intention that the association devote the gift to a specific purpose has any legal effect.

9.64 In *Conservative and Unionist Central Office v Burrell* (1982) Lawton LJ stated four criteria for the existence of an unincorporated association: such an association will exist where there are:

[1] two or more persons bound together for one or more common purposes, not being business purposes, [2] by mutual undertakings, each having mutual duties and obligations, [3] in an organisation which has rules which identify in whom control of it and its funds rests and on what terms and [4] which can be joined or left at will.

The existence of mutual undertakings giving rise to mutual duties and obligations is normally read to indicate that the members are bound by a contract *inter se* (ie amongst themselves). Each member is party to a contract that creates the legally binding rules of the association. So, for example, the contract amongst the members of a student law society may set rules about joining or leaving the society, about membership fees, about electing a president or treasurer, and so on. The last requirement Lawton LJ gives, ie that the association can be joined or left at will, is ill-put. Read strictly, it must be doubted, because there may be rules limiting both who can join the association and upon what basis, and similar rules about leaving. The idea underlying this criterion is that any individual enters the contract *inter se* voluntarily.

9.65   The purpose trust rule applies with just the same force to gifts to unincorporated associations as it does to gifts to individuals. The problems are slightly trickier here, however, because though a settlor may give property to an unincorporated association, he may not be giving the property on trust to carry out a particular purpose he chooses or any of the general purposes of the association; rather, he may just be giving the property to the association absolutely, *in the hope* that they will spend it as he wishes. Gifts of the latter kind are perfectly valid, while those of the former are, of course, invalid, as purpose trusts.

9.66   The leading case on the application of the beneficiary principle to gifts to unincorporated associations (UAs) is the PC decision in *Leahy v A-G for New South Wales* (1959). The gift in question was of a large estate called 'Elmslea':

> ... upon trust for such order of nuns of the Catholic Church or the Christian Brothers as my executors and trustees shall select ...

This wide power of selection allowed the trustees to select orders of nuns which were not charitable under the law. This trust was saved by the application of a New South Wales statute which restricted the power of selection to charitable objects. A majority in the High Court of

Australia accepted that the gift would also be valid as a gift to a UA, given to the members 'for the benefit of the community'. Viscount Simonds, giving the decision of the PC, said:

> [A]n unincorporated society ... though it is not a separate entity in law, is yet for many purposes regarded as a continuing entity and, however inaccurately, as something other than an aggregate of its members. In law a gift to such a society simpliciter is nothing else than a gift to its members at the date of the gift as joint tenants or tenants in common. It is for this reason that the prudent conveyancer provides that a receipt by the treasurer or other proper officer of the recipient society for a legacy to the society shall be held a sufficient discharge to executors. If it were not so, the executors could only get a valid discharge by obtaining a receipt from every member ... [But] what is meant when it is said that a gift is made to the individuals comprising the community and the words are added 'it is given to the benefit of the community?' If it is a gift to individuals, each of them is entitled to his distributive share (unless he has previously bound himself by the rules of the society that it shall be devoted to some other purpose). It is difficult to see what is added by the words 'for the benefit of the community'. If they are intended to import a trust, who are the beneficiaries? If the present members are beneficiaries, the words add nothing and are meaningless. If some other persons or purposes are intended, the conclusion cannot be avoided that the gift is void. For it is uncertain and no doubt tends to a perpetuity ... it is to be noted that it is because the gift can be upheld as a gift to the individual members that it is valid, even though it is given for the general purposes of the association. If the words 'for the general purposes of the association' were held to import a trust, the question would have to be asked, what is the trust and who are the beneficiaries? A gift can be made to persons (including a corporation) but it cannot be made to a purpose or to an object ... It is therefore by disregarding the words 'for the purposes of the association' ...and treating the gift as an absolute gift to individuals that it can be sustained.

The testator's words could only be construed as intending a trust for the purposes of the orders that might be selected, not a gift to their individual members, so, but for the statute the gift would have failed.

The contract-holding theory

9.67 In *Neville Estates Ltd v Madden* (1962), Cross J interpreted *Leahy* to hold that there are three possible constructions of a gift to a UA. The first is as a gift to the individual members as co-owners, whereby each may take their own share. Secondly the gift may be to the individual members:

> ... but subject to their respective contractual rights and liabilities towards one another as members of the association. In such a case a member cannot sever his share. It would accrue to the other members on his death or resignation, even though such members include persons who become members after the gift took effect ... Thirdly, the terms or circumstances of the gift or the rules of the association may show that the property in question is not to be at the disposal of the members for the time being, but is to be held in trust for or applied for the purposes of the association as a quasi-corporate entity. In this case the gift will fail unless the association is a charitable body.

9.68   In *Re Recher's Will Trusts* (1972), Brightman J expanded on the nature of the second kind of gift:

> In the absence of words which purport to impose a trust, the legacy is a gift to the members beneficially, not as joint tenants or as tenants in common so as to entitle each member to an immediate distributive share, but as an accretion to the funds which are the subject-matter of the contract which the members have made *inter se*.

This analysis of the way in which unincorporated associations receive gifts and hold property is generally termed the 'contract-holding theory', although it operates through a trust of the association members' money. It is nothing other than the bare trust with mandate mechanism we have already looked at in detail above. The treasurer-trustees of the association hold the association's funds on bare trust for the members of the association, to deal with the funds according to the mandates, or standing orders, which arise from time to time under rules of the association created by the contract of the members *inter se*. Such rules may allow the UA president to require the disbursement of funds for certain purposes, to require that the president and treasurer co-sign cheques for large payments, and so on. A gift which is an 'accretion to the funds' is therefore a gift to the treasurer-trustee of the UA to hold such property on the same trust as he does the other funds of the UA. Thus the given funds become subject to the bare trust with mandate which determines the way the treasurer-trustee deals with the members' funds. (See *Re Bucks Constabulary Widows' and Orphans' Fund Friendly Society (No 2)* (1979), per Walton J.)

9.69 Certain worries have been expressed about this analysis (see eg Matthews (1995a); Gardner (1998)) but the worries may be dispelled. True it is that a person cannot give a gift *subject* to another's contract rights. I cannot by unilaterally giving £10 to you declare that you hold it under some sort of contractual obligation to someone else. But that is not what the doner does here. By making the gift to an association or its members *as* members of the association, he indicates that it is to go to the treasurer-trustee of the association to hold the property under the same trusts as he holds all the other property of the association; thus the settlor simply defines the trust he imposes by reference to a trust which exists already. That this trust is a bare trust with (contractual) mandate, and so the uses to which the property may be put may be varied by changes to the mandate, does not mean that when a settlor transfers property on this trust the terms on which he transfers the property and thus his intention to transfer the property on trust is uncertain, for the trust, being a bare trust, has perfectly certain terms, ie the treasurer is obliged to hold the funds to the order of the members, as expressed in their mandates. At all times the trust terms, what the trustee is entitled to do, are certain.

9.70 Furthermore, there is no perpetuity problem with this trust any more than there is with the trust under which the trustee holds the rest of the association's property. The trust of the association's property is for the members for the time being. As members leave and join they are added to or deleted from the class of beneficiaries under an explicit or implicit power of the trustees or members to add or delete members, ie beneficiaries (see **6.17**). Since at all times the members for the time being are fully entitled to exercise their *Saunders v Vautier* rights and collapse the trust, the trust, while it may last as long as the association does, is not perpetual, for the rights are always fully currently vested (**3.31**); there are no obligations to unascertained future members, for they are not beneficiaries, even contingent ones, under the trust at any time.

9.71 Finally, while it might be thought that this interpretation of the association's trust gives rise to a s 53(1)(c) problem, ie that whenever a member leaves or a new member joins all members of the old class of beneficiaries must, in writing, assign their trust interests under the trust to the new class of member/beneficiaries, this is a mistake which, as we have seen, follows from an mistakenly over-broad interpretation of s 53(1)(c). That section does not apply to powers to add or delete beneficiaries, and every member of a UA understands that under the rules he will lose his interest in the trust property should he leave or be expelled from the association, and so this possibility is part and parcel of his interest (**6.17**).

9.72 The contract-holding theory explains how unincorporated associations may receive gifts which they can devote to their purposes, without such gifts being purpose trusts. That does not mean that a gift to an unincorporated association, properly construed, may not be on trust to carry out a purpose, and therefore invalid. *Re Lipinski's Will Trusts* (1976) concerned a gift to an unincorporated association which could well have been construed as a purpose trust. A testator left half of his residuary estate to 'the Hull Judeans (Maccabi) Association in memory of my late wife to be used solely in the work of constructing the new buildings for the Association and/or improvements to the said buildings.' Interpreting the provision, Oliver J felt that little turned on the fact that the gift was expressed as a memorial to the testators' wife – while that expressed a tribute the testator wished to pay, it did not, by itself, indicate a desire to create a perpetual endowment. Neither did the fact that money was to be available solely for construction or improvements indicate a perpetual purpose, for such money could be spent right away – 'improvements' is different in this respect from 'maintenance', which may well indicate a perpetual purpose trust. Framing the legacy in terms of a sole purpose only ruled out construing the gift as one to the members absolutely in equal shares.

9.73 Oliver J considered that the members of the association for the time being were an ascertainable class of beneficiaries, and given the existence of such a class, could see no reason why the trust should fail:

> If a valid gift may be made to an unincorporated body as a simple accretion to the funds which are the subject-matter of the contract which the members have made inter se ... I do not really see why such a gift, which specifies a purpose which is within the powers of the unincorporated body and of which the members of that body are the beneficiaries, should fail. Why are not the beneficiaries able to enforce the trust or, indeed, in the exercise of their contractual rights, to terminate the trust for their own benefit? Where the donee body is itself the beneficiary of the prescribed purpose, there seems to me to be the strongest argument in common sense for saying that the gift should be an absolute one within the second category, the more so where, if the purpose is carried out, the members can by appropriate action vest the resulting property in themselves, for here the trustees and the beneficiaries are the same person.

9.74 Oliver J argued that this interpretation of the law was at least consistent with *Leahy* as in that case there was no such ascertainable class. Second, there was authority in *Re Turkington* (1937):

> [T]here the gift was to a masonic lodge 'as a fund to build a suitable temple in Stratford'. The members of the lodge being both the trustees and the beneficiaries of the temple, Luxmoore J construed the gift as an absolute one to the members of the lodge for the time being.

9.75 Finally, Goff J's decision in *Re Denley* to uphold a purpose trust where there was such a class was, thought Oliver J, 'directly in point'. He also considered that although the gift was solely for a particular purpose, *Re Bowes*, amongst other cases, was authority for the proposition that where the entire amount of the gift was to go to the beneficiary, the purpose could be overridden as a mere motive or superadded direction. His conclusion, as we have seen (**9.14**), was that the gift was valid as one to the members, though expressed pretty plainly as a purpose.

Inward versus outward looking purposes

9.76 It appears that one criterion for Oliver J's holding was that the 'donee body is itself the beneficiary of the prescribed purpose', in other words that the purpose was 'inward-looking', as a benefit to the members themselves, rather than 'outward-looking', as one which might or would necessarily benefit members of the community outside the association. Such a requirement is very doubtful. On the facts of this case, the objects of the association's constitution were clearly to benefit Anglo-Jewish youth generally, so such a requirement would have made the trust fail in the present case. In *Re Bucks Constabulary Widows' and Ophans' Fund Friendly Society (No 2)* (1979) Walton J said that the analysis of the way in which a UA holds its funds is no different:

> ... whether the purpose for which the members of the association associate are a social club, a sporting club, to establish a widows' and orphans' fund, to obtain a separate Parliament for Cornwall, or to further the advance of alchemy. It matters not. All the assets of the association are held in trust for its members – of course subject to the contractual claims of anybody having a valid contract with the association – save and except to the extent to which valid trusts have otherwise been declared of its property.

As long as the 'purpose' framing the gift is one which the members themselves pursue by spending their own money under the rules of their association, the gift is to their 'inward-looking' benefit, and the court can construe such a gift as an accretion to the association's funds. (See also *Re Recher's Will Trusts* per Brightman J.)

9.77   While requiring a gift framed as a purpose trust to be 'inward-looking' before finding it valid is, therefore, unnecessary in the case of a UA, it may well be necessary if the class of beneficiaries are not members of such an association. Recall that in *Re Denley* the purpose trust was only valid because it was considered to be directly or indirectly for the benefit of the class of ascertainable beneficiaries. If outward-looking purposes could be valid so long as the settlor named a class of beneficiaries, then *Re Astor* is essentially overthrown. For example, by naming a class of beneficiaries consisting of all the employees of national and regional newspapers in the UK, which class is ascertainable on the is or is not test, Viscount Astor could have provided a class which would indirectly benefit from the outward-looking purposes he intended, members of which class would have standing to enforce it but who for all intents and purposes could never get together under the principle in *Saunders v Vautier* to vary or end the trust. Thus, it must be the case that gifts expressed as trusts for outward-looking purposes may be valid if made to unincorporated associations just for the reason that the membership, as the class of ascertainable beneficiaries is, by definition almost, capable of getting together and deciding whether to carry out the purpose or not. This prevents the possibility that a *Re Astor* abstract and impersonal trust will ever actually gain an independent life.

9.78   *Re Lipinski* raises once again the status of the settlor's purpose – as Oliver J makes quite clear, the members of the unincorporated association are free to ignore it completely if they so wish. A prospective Mr Lipinski who wishes above all to see his purpose carried out may be well advised to frame his gift as a *Sanderson*-type trust, eg 'to the Hull Judean (Maccabi) Association in such amounts as equal its expenditure on new buildings' with a clear gift over of any remaining funds, or as a gift on condition. A settlor should bear in mind that the certainty requirements for conditions subsequent, eg 'but if they fail to construct new buildings within five years of my death, then to the Red Cross', are strict, and if uncertain the gift will be treated as absolute (**3.63**), so care

289

must be taken to frame the condition in such a way that it can clearly be applied.

The dissolution of unincorporated associations

9.79 The 'contract-holding' theory of the way in which unincorporated associations hold their property is now generally accepted. It must however, be distinguished from a different 'contractual' theory of UAs, which is of doubtful validity. Under this theory the property of UA's can only be explained as the holding of property on a true purpose trust, which would violate the beneficiary principle. In order to consider the merits of this theory, we must briefly return to the subject of automatic resulting trusts, or ARTs.

9.80 In *Re Gillingham Bus Disaster Fund* (1958) funds were raised on appeal to defray the cost of funerals for those who had been killed when a bus ran into a column of marching cadets, and to care for those who were disabled; any surplus funds were to be devoted to 'other worthy causes'. The gift was a *Sanderson*-type trust for the cadets, but the gift over 'to worthy causes' was void for being a non-charitable purpose trust (**13.35**). The Treasury Solicitor claimed the surplus as *bona vacantia*, ie goods without an owner. Harman J approached the question as follows:

> The general principle must be that where money is held upon trust and the trusts declared do not exhaust the fund it will revert to the donor or settlor under what is called a resulting trust. The reasoning behind this is that the settlor or donor did not part with his money absolutely out and out but only sub modo to the intent that his wishes as declared by the declaration of trust should be carried into effect. When, therefore, this has been done any surplus still belongs to him. This doctrine does not, in my judgment, rest on any evidence of the state of mind of the settlor, for in the vast majority of cases no doubt he does not expect to see his money back: he has created a trust which so far as he can see will absorb the whole of it. The resulting trust arises where that expectation is for some unforeseen reason cheated of fruition, and is an inference of law based on after-knowledge of the event.

9.81 Since here the subscribers' expectations were 'cheated of fruition', an ART of the surplus arose in their favour in the proportions to which they had contributed. However, the resulting trust doctrine in appeal cases of this kind seems somewhat pointless for those who anonymously gave small amounts in collection boxes, for it means that the trustees must pay the money into court, where it will be held, essentially in perpetuity, on the off-chance that one of the anonymous subscribers of small amounts to the fund cares enough to come forward and prove that he had made a donation, hence the suggestion to treat the property as *bona vacantia*. Nevertheless, preferring to rely upon principle over matters of convenience, Harman J held firm on the resulting trust:

> In my judgment the Crown has failed to show that this case should not follow the ordinary rule merely because there was a number of donors who, I assume, are unascertainable. I see no reason myself to suppose that the small giver who is anonymous has any wider intention than the large giver who can be named. They all give for the one object. If they can be found by inquiry the resulting trust can be executed in their favour. If they cannot I do not see how the money could then ... change its destination and become bona vacantia.

9.82   Under the contract-holding theory, it is clear that the members of a UA own the society's property under the terms of their association, and therefore, upon dissolution of the society, the property is clearly not *bona vacantia*, but nor is there need for any resulting trust, for the money is held under a bare trust (in their favour) with mandate. The members have owned it all along, and therefore it is theirs to be distributed amongst themselves upon dissolution. Before this theory was articulated, however, there was a line of cases in which upon the dissolution of a UA the only alternative destinations of surplus funds were thought to be an ART and *bona vacantia*. In *Re Printers and Transferrers Amalgamated Trades Protection Society* (1899) contributions from the society's members funded benefits for the contibutors, in particular strike and lock-out benefits, and in *Re Hobourn Aero Components Ltd's Air Raid Distress Fund* (1946) employees contributed funds to pay benefits to members on war service or those injured in air raids. In both cases, on the dissolution of the associations the court held that there was a resulting trust of the remaining funds in favour of the members in proportion to their contributions. By contrast in *Cunnack v Edwards* (1896), CA, where members contributed to provide widow's benefits, upon dissolution the court reasoned that the members had received all they had contracted for, ie the relevant widow's pensions, and so the surplus was *bona vacantia*.

9.83   *Re West Sussex Constabulary's Widows, Children and Benevolent (1930) Fund Trusts* (1971) falls into this line of cases. In 1968 the West

291

Sussex Constabulary was amalgamated with other police forces, and therefore its benevolent fund, which paid allowances to the widowed mothers, widows, and children of deceased constables who were members, was to be wound up. The forces were amalgamated from 1 January 1968, and the remaining members of the fund held a meeting in June 1968 at which it was decided that the remaining funds, some £35,000, should be used to purchase annuities for those widows, etc, who were receiving benefits, the balance to be distributed to the members.

9.84 Goff J reasoned that the amalgamation of the forces meant that there were no longer any members of the fund by June 1968, since the only persons who could be members were constables of the West Sussex constabulary, which had ceased to exist. Thus the June 1968 decision was invalid and the funds remained undisposed of. Goff J accepted that the members might have devoted the funds in this way had they met before the amalgamation, but they had simply acted too late. Now, if it were true that the contract between the members required that they be constables of the West Sussex force, then the amalgamation of the forces would have put their contract at an end. But that would only mean that the contractual rules of the association, such as a rule that by majority vote they could vary the terms upon which their property was held by the UA treasurers on trust, would no longer be operative. Any mandate to apply the property would have been extinguished, but not the bare trust of the funds. The death of this contract would do nothing to alter the *ownership rights* of the members to the fund, only their *contractual rights and duties* to deal with it in certain ways. Thus if the members were owners of the fund before 1 January 1968 (though bound by contractual mandate to deal with it under the rules), they remained owners afterward (though no longer so bound).

9.85 The former members then argued that they were the beneficial owners of the fund, as with any other UA, but Goff J rejected this argument; the fund simply did not look like a members' club, but was a pensions or dependant relatives fund; thus rather than being for the benefit of the members for the time being, only third parties could benefit.

9.86 The members then argued that there was a resulting trust in their favour. In rejecting this argument, Goff J advanced the 'contractual' basis of the decision in *Cunnack*:

In my judgment the doctrine of resulting trust is clearly inapplicable to the contributions of [the former and surviving members]. Those persons who remained members until their deaths are in any event excluded because they have had all they contracted for, either because their widows and dependants have received or are in receipt of the prescribed funds, or because they did not have a widow or dependants ... they and the surviving members alike are also in my judgment unable to claim under a resulting trust because they put up their money on a contractual basis and not one of trust ...

The only persons who had a claim, therefore, were those surviving members who had dependants who had not received any benefits yet – they might be able to claim against the fund on the basis of total failure of consideration or frustration of the contract. This application of 'contractual' reasoning must be wrong, since it requires that the funds were held on a perpetual pure purpose trust, ie a trust to enter into contracts to provide annuities and so on for the relations of members of a constabulary – in short, a trust to carry out a (non-profit) business, the funds held not for any beneficiaries, but for the purpose of entering into and discharging contractual obligations.

9.87 In *Re Bucks Constabulary Fund*, a case with very similar facts, Walton J found himself 'wholly unable to square [Goff J]'s decision in *West Sussex*] with the relevant principles of law applicable', and applied the modern contract-holding analysis. The member/constables of the *Bucks* fund were entitled to it in equal shares on dissolution of the association.

9.88 There is however, a 'loose end', as Swadling (2000, 376) puts it:

In the case of money subscribed to a movement or campaign via its secretary, it is tolerably clear that any surplus left when the campaign is abandoned or frustrated must be returned as on a failure of consideration. This is a matter for the law of unjust enrichment. It is by no means clear that the same should not apply to property given on the basis that it be subject to the contract between the members [of a UA]. Much must depend on the precise construction of the basis on which the donations were given and, in turn, on the rules of the society. The *Buckinghamshire Constabulary* case certainly decides that the property in such cases belongs to the members, but it does not finally dispose of the question whether in some cases they may not come under an obligation to make restitution of its value to donors.

9.89 However, though on the modern contracting holding theory there should have been no 'surplus' funds to dispose of in *Re West Sussex*, Goff J's treatment of undisposed of funds is regarded as relevant if applied to cases where an ART properly arises, as in a case like *Re Gillingham Bus Disaster Fund*. The surplus is to be notionally divided in proportion to its sources, ie (1) money raised by raffles or entertainments, whereby individuals contract with the association or trustees, the profits of which go into the fund; (2) small anonymous donations, such as those received in collecting boxes; and (3) identifiable donations, such as amounts contributed by cheque and legacies. An ART arises only for the last category. No one in the first category who contributes to the fund incidentally as a function of buying a raffle ticket or attending an entertainment has given money upon trust; he receives his full benefit from the contract; Goff J reasoned that the purchaser may or may not be interested in aiding the cause, so therefore no trust intention can be imputed to him, and secondly, his contribution is indirect, via any profit, that accrues from his purchase.

9.90 This does not seem particularly justifiable. If the trustees engage in commercially viable entertainments or raffles which make profits, which they then donate to the trust, of course the purchasers are out of the picture. But if, as is common, the purchasers 'purchase' entertainment or buy raffle tickets fully realising there is a large gift element, surely the intention to be presumed of such a purchaser is that the profits certain to be made are to be applied to, and only to, the purposes of the appeal. That they doubtless do not expect any money some day to return to them on failure or completion of the purpose of the appeal would put them in the same boat as any other contributor.

9.91 Similarly, Goff J reasoned that the contributors of small anonymous donations must be assumed to have intended to part with their money absolutely in all circumstances. Again, distinguishing between large, identifiable contributors and small contributors or raffle ticket purchasers on the basis of their likely intentions is difficult to sustain. The better basis for the result is simply that the ART solution, though theoretically correct, is so patently pointless in the case of the small contributors and purchasers, none of whom will ever try to prove a valid claim to the money, that the *bona vacantia* solution is simply imposed as the most practical result in the circumstances. As Harman J points out in *Gillingham*, surely the only thing that distinguishes these classes of contributors is the possibility that they might actually be able to claim their money –

there is no reason to believe that they were more or less likely to entertain any 'secondary' intentions governing the proper direction of their money if the primary trust failed. But *pace* Harman J, that fact should not prevent the *West Sussex* result, for practical reasons.

9.92   As it stands then, neither *Gillingham Bus Disaster Fund* nor *West Sussex* disclose any factual settlor's intention which can displace the operation of an ART, and it is difficult to imagine one that realistically is likely to arise. What will displace it, apparently, is the inconvenience of the ART's effect in practice. With respect, it was, therefore, incorrect of Lord Browne-Wilkinson to have cited *West Sussex* as a case where settlors' actual intentions displaced an ART (**4.31**); that the ART there was supplanted by the *bona vacantia* solution is much better explained as a matter of convenience, not because the settlors' intentions so dictated.

Less than unincorporated associations – the case of political parties

9.93   In *Re Grant's Will Trusts* (1979), the testator left his entire real and personal estate to the Chertsey and Walton Constituency Labour Party. Vinelott J held that the gift was one to create a perpetual trust to further the purposes of the local Labour party, and therefore the gift failed. He held that the local Labour party was not an unincorporated association, because its rules were capable of being altered by an outside body, the National Labour party, which could in fact direct the local party to transfer its assets to it. Furthermore, the local members could not:

> ... alter.the rules so as to make the property bequeathed by the testator applicable for some purpose other than that provided by the rules; nor could they direct that property to be divided amongst themselves beneficially.

9.94   It is not clear whether Vinelott J's reasoning on this point is sound. While there is no other case which discusses the issue directly, Cross J in *Neville Estates* proceeded on the assumption that the Catford Synagogue was an unincorporated association though affiliated with the United Synagogue which limited the power of the Catford members to alter their rules; moreover the United Synagogue could require the Catford Synagogue to transfer its real property to the United Synagogue.

9.95 In *Conservative and Unionist Central Office* the CA decided that the national Conservative Party was not an unincorporated association either. The party was an historical political movement, in which the various membership constituencies, the parliamentary party and the constitutency associations, had political but not contractual links. In particular, there were no rules by which the constituencies could control the leader of the party's or the central office's expenditure of the central office funds, and there was no historical point at which any contract between the members *inter se* could be said to have occurred.

9.96 If national political parties, and their local constituency parties, are not unincorporated associations, then how do they hold their property? In *Conservative Central Office* Brightman LJ suggested the 'mandate' theory to explain how *living* subscribers to the party donate their funds. Such funds are given upon an order from the donor, the principal, to the party treasurer, his agent; such an order is a mandate, although not a mandate over funds the treasurer takes on trust; it is a purely personal obligation to deal with property the treasurer takes as full beneficial legal owner; if the treasurer fails to apply the money as the order specifies (here for party purposes) he may be sued to so apply it, and he may be restrained from misapplying it. The mandate becomes irrevocable once the treasurer mixes it with other party funds. Brightman LJ, however, acknowledged that this analysis would not explain testamentary gifts to political parties because:

> ... no agency could be set up at the moment of death between a testator and his chosen agent. A discussion of this problem is outside the scope of this appeal and, although I think that the answer is not difficult to find, I do not wish to prejudge it.

It is, unfortunately, quite difficult to find a way of making a testamentary gift which fits coherently with the mandate theory of *inter vivos* gifts. A better analysis may be that both *inter vivos* and testamentary gifts to political parties are conditional gifts at law or in equity (**4.36**), which would be subject to the unjust enrichment analysis Swadling proposes above (**9.88**).

The rule against perpetuities

9.97   There are two principal cases in which the rule against perpetuities (**3.31** et seq) becomes relevant in the discussion of the beneficiary principle: (i) the cases of the few, anomalous, true purpose trusts, and (ii) in the context of gifts for unincorporated associations. A true purpose trust, such as a trust for the upkeep of a grave, can last forever. Therefore, if the testator does not specifically limit his gift to a perpetuity period, the gift will be void for perpetuity. It may be the case that a testator is not entitled to choose the statutory perpetuity period of 80 years provided by the Perpetuities and Accumulations Act 1964. This turns on technical considerations regarding the interpretation of s 15(4) of the Act and the question whether the rule against perpetuities applies in a distinct way to pure purpose trusts (see Matthews (1996)), and no case has decided the point. A testator may, however, employ a lives-in-being-plus-21-years clause to indicate a perpetuity period. For this purpose a 'royal lives' clause is appropriate, for example, '£10,000 to my trustees on trust to maintain my grave, such trust not to extend beyond the expiry of 21 years following the death of the last surviving descendent of Queen Elizabeth II alive at my death'. Since there are no lives in being which are inherently relevant to the duration of a purpose trust, the testator must choose people whose lives shall count. The purpose of picking the descendants of a king or queen is simply that, being famous, it will be easy for the trustees to determine when the last surviving life in being dies. If the testator does not use a royal lives clause, and wishes to set an exact time period, then, assuming he is not entitled to use the statutory period of 80 years or less, he may only choose a period within the definable portion of the common law rule, ie the portion not determined by the duration of any lives in being, thus periods of 21 years or less. If the testator specifies that his gift is to continue 'for as long as the law allows' or uses some similar phrase, courts have allowed the gift to last for 21 years (*Pirbright v Salwey* (1896); *Re Hooper* (1932)).

9.98   In the case of unincorporated associations, the problems are different. As we have seen, there are no valid pure purpose trusts for the purposes of an unincorporated association. For such gifts to be valid, they must be, or they must be interpreted to be, gifts to the members of the association themselves. But in some circumstances, the gift might properly be interpreted to be for the present and future members of the association, thus a gift to a class which may gain members as long as the association lasts. If the trust were not limited, the shares of any number of future individuals might vest for as long as the association lasts, hence indefinitely. Therefore a settlor who wishes to give a gift in these terms should ensure that it comes to an end within a suitable perpetuity period, either a stated period of eighty years or less, or a period determined by the relevant lives in being for the gift plus 21 years (here the relevant lives in being would be the members of the association at the time the trust takes effect), or a period determined by a royal lives clause. Even if the testator indicates no perpetuity period at all, the gift might possibly be saved by s 4(4) of the 1964 Act, which automatically closes the class of beneficiaries at the end of the period determined by taking the members at the time of the gift as the relevant lives in being, plus 21 years (see Hayton (1996a), 180-181).

Further reading

Gravells (1977); Millett (1985); Rickett (1980); Green (1980); Matthews (1995a); Gardner (1998); Hayton (2000); Penner (2000); Smith (2004); Penner (2004); Swadling (2004); McKnight (2004).

Must read cases: *Re Astor's Settlement Trusts* (1952); *Re Denley* (1968); *Re Grant's Will Trusts* (1979); *Re Lipinski's Will Trusts* (1977); *Re Sanderson's Trust* (1857); *Re Osoba* (1977); *Twinsectra v Yardley* (2002); *Leahy v A-G (NSW)* (1959); *Re Bucks Constabulary Widows' and Ophans' Fund* (1979); *Conservative and Unionist Central Office v Burrell* (1982).

Self-test questions

1. Explain the rationale of the beneficiary principle; is this rationale less persuasive following the decisions in *Re Denley* (1969) and *McPhail v Doulton* (1970)?

2. How may unincorporated associations hold property?

3. Smith dies, leaving £100,000 to the Aylesbury Morris Dancing Society 'for the purpose of building a Morris Dancing Centre as a memorial to myself'. Shortly after Smith's death the club decides to wind up, as most members wish to join another Morris dancing club. The

treasurers report that the Society's current funds are £8,150, which amounts to a share of £163 for each of the 50 members, a figure which does not include the bequest of Smith, of which they have just been advised. Advise the treasurers.

4. Simon is a member of his local branch of the Socialist Workers Party, and is also a member of a Marxist reading group of about 30 people who raise money to buy publications by various means and who have a treasurer who holds the group's funds in a local bank. Simon has found out that he has six months to live. On his death he wants to ensure that his considerable fortune is devoted to the furtherance of Marxist causes. Advise him.

5. Brian, a collector of art, transfers £50,000 to Frances, a dealer, to 'buy antiques for me which have good investment prospects'. Brian tells Frances that she is entitled to 'take a 10% commission' on any purchases she makes. Frances pays the money into her current business account which is in overdraft, raising the balance to £40,000. She then (i) spends £30,000 on 17th century furniture; (ii) draws a cheque on the account for £3,000 as her personal commission which she pays into her personal account; (iii) uses £2,000 to pay for travel and hotel expenses to attend an antiques auction where she buys nothing; (iv) transfers £1,000 to another dealer as a deposit on a future purchase which is not, in the end, completed. With the balance in the account at £4,000, Frances's bank fails. Advise Brian. (It would be worthwhile to review **7.26** et seq.)

CHAPTER TEN

The Trust Up and Running

SUMMARY

The duty of investment

The Trustee Act 2000

The standard of prudence in making trust investments

'Social' or 'ethical' investing

The delegation of trustee functions

The power of maintenance

The power of advancement

Appointment, retirement and removal of trustees

Custodian, nominee, managing, and judicial trustees

Beneficiairies' rights to information

Variation of trusts

10.1   Trustees, as legal owners of the trust property, have all the rights and powers to deal with the trust property as would any other legal owner, though they must, of course, exercise these rights and powers solely in the interests of the beneficiaries. Because they are trustees, however, they have further particular powers and duties arising from their office, the traditionally most important of which are the duty of investment and the powers of maintenance and advancement.

The duty of investment

10.2   The duty of investment has two main aspects: (1) a duty to invest the trust property so as to be 'even-handed' between the different classes

301

of beneficiaries; and (2) a duty to invest so that the fund is preserved from risk yet a reasonable return on capital is made.

Even-handedness between the beneficiaries

10.3 In many trusts the benefit of the property is divided between income and capital beneficiaries (**3.19**). In legal terms, income is whatever property actually arises as a separate payment as a result of holding the capital property. Thus on shares the dividends are the income, on land the rent is income, and so on. The income beneficiary is entitled to whatever income arises. On the other hand, if holding the property yields no new property rights, rental payments or dividends or so forth, there is no income, even if the shares or the land double in value, making a huge economic return on the investment. Some investments produce no income: eg currency, gold, antiques. Conversely, some investments will be 'all' income, what are called 'wasting assets'; an example is a 20-year lease: the rent is income; though in economic terms it also represents the return on the initial capital investment in the lease, in legal terms the capital just slowly reduces to zero as the lease runs its course. Therefore it is obvious that the trustee may favour the income beneficiary at the expense of the capital beneficiary, or *vice versa*, by making particular kinds of investments. The law therefore imposes a duty of even-handedness, which requires the trustee to balance their interests fairly in making his investment decisions. (For a case where the trustees thoroughly failed to do so, see the New Zealand case of *Re Mulligan* (1998); the trustees invested so as to maximise the income of the life tenant, with the result that there was little capital left in the fund on her death.) This is a fiduciary obligation (**2.10, Ch 12**), for only by being even-handed in exercising his discretion as to the trust investments does the trustee act in the best interests of all of the beneficiaries of the trust.

10.4 The two chief characteristics of any investment are risk and return, and they correlate directly. That is, the higher a risk an investment presents, the greater the percentage return on capital any investor will demand. You will (at the time of writing) win a greater sum betting on Scotland to win the next World Cup than on Brazil (alas). Historically, the law has favoured the safety, or non-riskiness of trusts investments over high return. In particular, following the burst of the 'South Sea Bubble' in 1720, an orgy of speculation in shares of the South Sea Company which ended, as one might expect, in tears, equity regarded investment in company shares as a risk quite beyond the pale. Therefore, until this century trustees were restricted to investment in 'consols', fixed-interest government securities.

10.5 Of course, the trust instrument itself may, and invariably does, empower the trustee to invest as the settlor allows, and in general, such investment clauses are very wide. Originally, again out of concern for the safety of the trust property, investment clauses were interpreted restrictively, but now are given their plain meaning (*Re Harari's Settlement Trusts* (1949)). If there is no express investment clause, the statutory regime provided by the Trustee Act 2000 governs the trustee's investments.

The Trustee Act 2000

10.6 Prior to 1 February 2001, the Trustee Investments Act 1961 governed the trustee's duty of investment unless the trust instrument specifically provided an investment clause. The Act was one embodiment of an approach to regulating trustee investments which is generally called the 'legal list' approach. The legal list approach contrasts with the 'prudent investor' approach. Under the former, the state in its wisdom chooses a number of particular kinds of investments that may be made by trustees; these investments are supposed to be safe but yield a reasonable return. A trustee may not make an investment that is not on the list; if he does he will be in breach of trust. On the other hand, such a list makes things quite straightforward for trustees, especially non-professionals. So long as they choose investments from the list, they comply with their investment duties. Under the prudent investor approach, the trustees are not legally prohibited from making any particular kind of investment. They will be found in breach of trust, however, if they do not invest as a prudent investor would. The Trustee Act 2000, which now governs unless the trust instrument provides an investment clause, adopts the prudent investor approach; it thus (a) provides the trustee with a very broad power of investment, but (b) imposes a duty of care so as to ensure that the power is used prudently.

10.7 Section 3 of the Act provides a general power of investment by which

> a trustee may make any kind of investment that he could make if he were absolutely entitled to the assets of the trust.

That is, he may make any investment he could make if the funds were his own. However, the various properties, securities and so on he purchases for the trust must still count as 'investments'. What amounts to an investment is a matter of case law: it may be that certain sorts of financial products, such as derivatives or zero dividend preference shares, though perhaps useful for managing the risk and return of trust funds (especially in light of tax considerations), may not count, eg on the basis that they do not generate income (see Hicks 2001). For this reason, it is expected that settlors will, as was previously the norm, write trust instruments including bespoke investment clauses, rather than relying on the statutory provision. Section 8 provides the trustee with the power to acquire land, even if the land is not used to generate rental income, but is used to provide a place to live for a beneficiary or beneficiaries. This separate treatment of land is a holdover from past attitudes: in *Re Power* (1947), trustees were barred from buying a house for the beneficiaries to live in. Jenkins J said that such a purchase:

> ... is not necessarily an investment, for it is a purchase for some other purpose than the receipt of income.

10.8   Section 1 of the Act outlines a general duty of care applicable to trustees, and by Sch 1 this duty applies to the trustee when exercising any power of investment, either under the statute or conferred by the trust instrument (though the duty of care may be ousted by the trust instrument (Sch 7, s 7). By s 1, the trustee must exercise

> such care and skill as is reasonable in the circumstances, having regard in particular to (a) any special knowledge or experience that he has or holds himself out as having, and (b) if he acts in the course of a business or profession, to any special knowledge or experience that it is reasonable to expect of a person acting in the course of that kind of business or profession.

The act does not further elaborate upon the content of this duty of care, so recourse must be had to the case law to assess how the courts will apply the duty (**10.12** et seq).

10.9   Section 4 of the Act does, however, require the trustee when exercising any power of investment to have regard to 'standard investment criteria', and to review the investments from time to time with these criteria in mind. These criteria are (a) the suitability of particular kinds of investment for the trust, and (b) the need for diversification of the trust investments.

10.10 As regards diversification, investment strategy today is informed by 'modern portfolio theory', by which the risks of particular investments are balanced against the risks of others. Different investments are chosen which have offsetting risks; thus, for example, if natural gas sales rise at the expense of oil sales, investing in both offsets the risks of one against the other – if gas does well and gas shares rise, then oil shares will fall, and vice versa. Thus the overall risk of investing in both is less than the individual risk of either. The watchword, then, is 'diversification'; by diversifying the investment portfolio investments which singly pose substantial risks together provide a portfolio with a much more reasonable risk. Thus the modern prudent investor is to be judged not by the individual investment vehicles he chooses but on the overall portfolio. In *Nestlé v National Westminster Bank plc* (1988) Hoffmann J said:

> Modern trustees acting within their investment powers are entitled to be judged by the standards of current portfolio theory, which emphasises the risk of the entire portfolio rather than the risk attaching to each investment taken in isolation.

10.11 Section 5 of the Act also requires the trustee, before exercising any power of investment, to take advice from someone the trustee reasonably believes is able to provide proper advice of this kind by virtue of his ability and experience in such matters, unless it would be reasonable in the circumstances to forgo such advice. Such circumstances are not specified, but it would be reasonable not to seek advice in the case of a trust with very limited funds, such as the trust of the funds of an unincorporated association (**9.63** et seq) like a student law society, or a trust of short duration – the only sensible option in such cases might be to place the trust funds in a bank account.

The standard of prudence in making trust investments

10.12 A standard of prudence cannot be spelled out in terms of black and white rules: like many other standards in the law, it is a standard which depends on a reasonable appreciation of the purposes the standard is to serve and the circumstances in which it applies. In the leading case of *Speight v Gaunt* (1883), the trustee paid some £15,000 to a broker on the strength of a written 'bought note' which asserted that the broker had bought securities in that amount. The broker had never purchased the securities, and his fraud was not discovered before his subsequent bankruptcy, so all the money was lost. The trustee was not liable. The payment of funds to a broker in this way was in accord with the standard business practice of purchasing securities. Jessel MR said:

> [A] trustee is not bound because he is a trustee to conduct in other than the ordinary and usual way in which similar business is conducted by mankind in transactions of their own. It could never be reasonable to make a trustee adopt further and better precautions than an ordinary prudent man of business would adopt, or to conduct the business in any other way.

The judgment was affirmed in similar terms by the HL.

10.13   In *Re Whiteley* (1886) a trustee was found liable for imprudently investing £3,000 upon a mortgage of a brickworks. The land itself was not so valuable as to provide sufficient security for the mortgage – only if the brickworks operation continued as a going concern, which, in the event it did not, was the loan likely to be repaid. In the CA Lindley LJ framed the standard thus:

> The duty of a trustee is not to take such care only as a prudent man would take if he had only himself to consider; the duty rather is to take such care as an ordinary prudent man would take if he were minded to make an investment for the benefit of other people for whom he felt morally bound to provide.

In the HL (*Learoyd v Whiteley* (1887)) Lord Watson said:

> As a general rule the law requires of a trustee no higher degree of diligence in the execution of his office than a man of ordinary prudence would exercise in the management of his own private affairs. Yet he is not allowed the same discretion in investing the moneys of the trust as if he were a person sui juris dealing with his own estate. Businessmen of ordinary prudence may, and frequently do, select investments which are more or less of a speculative character; but it is the duty of a trustee to confine himself to the class of investments which are permitted by the trust, and likewise to avoid all investments of that class which are attended with hazard.

10.14   A trustee is not required to 'beat the market' or save the trust investments from declining in value due to general economic conditions. In *Re Chapman* (1896) Lindley LJ said:

> [A] trustee is not a surety, nor is he an insurer; he is only liable for some wrong done by himself, and loss of trust money is not per se proof of such wrong ... There is no rule of law which compels the court to hold that an honest trustee is liable to make good loss sustained by retaining an authorised security in a falling market, if he did so honestly and prudently, in the belief that it was the best course of action in the interest of all parties. Trustees acting honestly, with ordinary prudence and within the limits of their trust, are not liable for mere errors of judgement.

(See also *Nestlé v National Westminster Bank* (1994), **10.19 et seq.**)

10.15   Special considerations apply when the trust has a controlling shareholding in a company. In *Re Lucking's Will Trusts* (1967) a majority of shares in a family business was held on trust for the family members. One trustee, one of the family members, installed his friend as manager of the company, who proved most unsuitable, drawing large amounts of the company funds for his own use. The trustee failed to detect the manager's withdrawals until it was too late to recover them, and was held liable. Cross J said:

> Now what steps, if any, does a reasonably prudent man who finds himself a majority shareholder in a private company take with regard to the management of the company's affairs? He does not, I think, content himself with such information as to the management of the company's affairs as he is entitled to as shareholder, but ensures that he is represented on the board ... Alternatively, he may find someone who will act as his nominee on the board ... trustees holding a controlling interest ought to ensure so far as they can that they have such information as to the progress of the company's affairs as directors would have. If they sit back and allow the company to be run by the minority shareholders and receive no more information than shareholders are entitled to, they do so at their risk if things go wrong.

10.16   In *Bartlett v Barclays Bank Trust Co Ltd* (1980) almost all the assets of the trust consisted of private shares of a company which managed real property. The company embarked on a programme of hazardous and, as it turned out, disastrous property development, of which the trust company took little notice, implicitly trusting in the 'professional calibre' of the company board. The trust company was liable for the losses. Brightman J said:

> I do not understand Cross J [in Re Lucking's] to have been saying that in every case where trustees have a controlling interest in a company it is their duty to ensure that one of their number is a director or that they will have a nominee on the board ... He was merely outlining convenient methods by which a prudent man of business (as also a trustee) with a controlling interest in a private company, can place himself in a position to make an informed decision whether any action is appropriate to be taken for the protection of the asset. Other methods may be equally satisfactory and convenient, depending on the circumstances of the individual case. Alternatives which spring to mind are the receipt of the copies of the agenda and minutes of board meetings if regularly held, the receipt of monthly management accounts in the case of a trading concern, or quarterly reports.

A higher standard for paid trustees

10.17 As we have seen, the s 1 duty of care requires a trustee who holds himself out as having special expertise, or who has such expertise by virtue of his business or profession, to be judged accordingly. Although reference to such a higher standard was made *obiter* in several decisions prior to the Act (*Bartlett v Barclays Bank Trust Co Ltd* (1980) per Brightman J; *Re Waterman's Will Trusts* (1952) per Harman J; an obiter statement by Romer J in *Jobson v Palmer* (1893) denied such a higher standard), it does not seem as if any higher standard for professionals was ever applied as part of the *ratio decidendi* of a case, that is, a decision to hold a trustee liable or relieve him of liability has never turned on a higher standard for those with special expertise. There is, therefore, no real guidance to be gleaned from the case law as to the stringency or scope of the higher standard that is to apply to professional trustees.

10.18 It should also be borne in mind that paid trustees will invariably insist on exemption clauses before undertaking the trust (11.57 et seq), and such clauses provide that they will be liable only for their 'wilful default', not mere negligence, so any higher standard for paid trustees will likely be of zero practical importance.

10.19 In Nestlé a testamentary trust was created in 1922. When the holders of the life interests had all died, in 1986, the value of the capital was some £270,000 and the plaintiff remainderman claimed that the fund would have been worth well over £1m if it had been properly invested. The trustee had failed to understand the investment clause of the trust instrument, largely because it had failed to seek legal advice as to its meaning, and in consequence it believed that its investment options were much narrower than was the case and so failed to review the investments properly. Although it was clear that the real value of the fund fell dramatically, the CA was not convinced that the investment decisions the trustees actually made would have been in breach of trust even had they understood their investment powers and regularly reviewed the investments. In particular, the trustees' actions between 1922 and 1960 could not be judged by the standards of investment expertise of the post-1960 era, when modern portfolio theory favouring equity investment began to be generally applied. The CA accepted Hoffmann J's finding of fact that there was no provable loss to the fund given the advice of experts before the court on the standards of investment practice applicable over the history of the trust. It should not be assumed, however, that if a trust fund administered from the 1960s or later loses significant real value that will not indicate, at least *prima facie*, a failure to invest properly unless there are countervailing factors. Though that did happen to the trust in *Nestlé*, there were such factors.

10.20   Roughly, from the 1960s onwards the trustee adopted a policy of investing large proportions of the funds in investments which were tax exempt for foreign residents, as both the living life tenants lived abroad. This resulted in low capital growth, but also savings in estate duty. The court did not find that the trustee breached his duty of even-handedness between the life tenants and the remainderman in adopting such a policy, because the saving in estate duty accrued to the remainderman as well. Staughton LJ said this on even-handedness generally:

> At times it will not be easy to decide what is an equitable balance. A life tenant may be anxious to receive the highest possible income, whilst the remainderman will wish the real value of the trust fund to be preserved. If the life tenant is living in penury and the remainderman already has ample wealth, common sense suggests that a trustee should be able to take that into account, not necessarily by seeking the highest possible income at the expense of capital but by inclining in that direction. However, before adopting that course a trustee should, I think, require some verification of the facts.

10.21 There are two especially significant points to be taken from *Nestlé*: first, one cannot read the case without being impressed that the result very much turned on the defendant bank's winning the battle of the experts as to the investment expertise to be expected of a trustee, and this would seem to be an ineliminable element of adopting a prudent man approach. Secondly, while the bank was clearly 'in breach' to the extent that it woefully misunderstood the scope of the investment clause, it was not 'in breach' in so far as the investment decisions which it did make were held not to cause loss, because they *could have been justified* as valid investment decisions *had they known* their actual investment powers. In *Cowan v Scargill* (1985) Megarry VC stated this general principle as follows:

> If trustees make a decision on wholly wrong grounds, and yet it subsequently appears, from matters which they did not express or refer to, that there are in fact good and sufficient reasons for supporting their decision, then I do not think that they would incur any liability for having decided the matter on erroneous grounds; for the decision itself was right.

Quaere whether, the plaintiff having proven that the trustee bank had breached its duty by failing properly to understand the investment clause, the burden of proof ought not to have shifted to the bank to show that its breach of duty caused no loss.

'Social' or 'ethical' investing

10.22 Trustees must invest in order to preserve and if possible, enhance the value of the trust property. This obligation is so strict that in *Buttle v Saunders* (1950) trustees were held to have a duty to 'gazump', that is accept a higher offer for the purchase of land they were selling even though this involved the dishonourable conduct of reneging upon their acceptance 'subject to contract' of a previous offer. Before the advent of 'social investing', the main effect of this concentration on the financial interests of the beneficiaries was simply to rule out benefits in kind as proper trust income (unless of course the trust instrument provided otherwise) (See, eg *Re Power* (1947) (**10.7**)).

10.23 *Cowan v Scargill* (1985) concerned a dispute between the trustees of the National Coal Board pension fund for miners. The trustees appointed by the National Coal Board wished to approve an investment plan which included investment in overseas securities and in the oil and gas industries, industries in direct competition with the coal industry. The trustees appointed by the National Union of Mineworkers refused to consent to the plan. Megarry VC held that the NUM trustees' refusal to approve the scheme would be in breach of trust:

> When the purpose of the trust is to provide financial benefits for the beneficiaries, as is usually the case, the best interests of the beneficiaries are normally their best financial interests.

10.24 The fact that the NUM strategy might benefit present miners by perhaps assisting the health of the coal industry, which was by no means certain, would be of no benefit at all to retired miners who depended upon the financial performance of the investments to fund their current pensions, so the NUM strategy might also be regarded as not even-handed. Megarry VC continued:

> In considering what investments to make trustees must put to one side their own personal interests and views. Trustees may have strongly held social or political views. They may be firmly opposed to any investment in South Africa or other countries, or they may object to any form of investment in companies concerned with alcohol, tobacco, armaments or many other things. In the conduct of their own affairs, of course, they are free to abstain from making any such investments. Yet under a trust, if investments of this type would be more beneficial to the beneficiaries than other investments, the trustees must not refrain from making the investments by reason of the views that they hold.

10.25 However, Megarry VC also said:

> [I]f the only actual beneficiaries or potential beneficiaries of a trust are all adults with very strict views on moral and social matters, condemning all forms of alcohol, tobacco and popular entertainment, as well as armaments, I can well understand that it might not be for the 'benefit' of such beneficiaries to know that they are obtaining rather larger financial returns under the trust by reason of investments in those activities ...

To the extent this last passage is taken to suggest that a trustee might make 'ethical' investment decisions in such circumstances, Megarry VC's words should be disregarded. If all the actual and potential beneficiaries are adults, then a trustee intending such a policy should present it to them in advance and get their consent, in which case the investment will not be in breach of trust. Otherwise it is a breach of trust, since trustees should not have the power to determine by their own lights what constitutes an 'ethical' or 'moral' benefit to their beneficiaries as a whole.

10.26 In *Evans v London Co-operative Society* (1976) trustees had regularly loaned the whole of a pension fund to the employer at below market interest rates. Although such loans were authorised by the trust instrument the trustees were liable for breach for not adequately exercising their discretion in properly negotiating an interest rate. However, Brightman J said that the trustees could

> ... give the parent financial concern accommodation on preferential terms if the trustees consider that the security of the employment of their members may otherwise be imperilled.

10.27 In the Scottish case *Martin v City of Edinburgh District Council* (1989) the local authority's policy to disinvest in companies with South African interests was found to be a breach of trust, because the decision was taken without considering the best financial interests of the beneficiaries.

10.28 Charities raise particular issues. In *Harries v Church Comrs for England* (1993) the Bishop of Oxford sought a declaration that the Church Commissioners should use their assets with the objective in mind of promoting the Christian faith, and were not entitled to act in a manner inconsistent with that object; he thus proposed an active investment policy of seeking out investments to forward Christian objects. The court disagreed. As with any other trust, the normal duty of charitable trustees is to seek the maximum return while investing prudently. While the Commissioners' policy of excluding certain investments, armaments, gambling, tobacco, newspapers, and companies with interests in South Africa was considered acceptable, a more restrictive policy of requiring them generally to invest on the basis of non-commercial considerations would create too great a risk to the trust.

10.29 It thus seems that charity trustees may rightly choose not to invest in activities which directly contradict the purposes of the trust, so a charity for cancer research may rightly not invest in the tobacco industry, for it is assumed that such restrictions will leave the charity with an adequate range of investments to diversify a portfolio. Secondly charities may refuse to invest in otherwise sound investments if by so investing they would alienate those who give to the charity, thus reducing its overall financial position. But charities may not adopt a policy of accepting lower returns by treating their investments as a means of carrying out their charitable purpose. As Nobles (1992) points out, however, charities generally *give* their money away in pursuit of their purposes. Why should one mode of 'giving', ie investing in activities which may earn below-market returns, be disallowed, if it serves the charity's purpose? They are not, after all, trying to preserve and enhance the value of a sum of money for private beneficiaries. They should, therefore, be able to 'ethically' invest so long as the particular ethical investment furthers their *particular* charitable purpose. Note that while this licence may provide much latitude for charities such as churches, where 'Christian purposes' could be read very broadly, it would provide almost no latitude at all to, say, Dogs for the Blind.

10.30 Recently, Lord Nicholls (1995) speaking extra-judicially has suggested that:

> The range of sound investments available to trustees is so extensive that very frequently there is scope for trustees to give effect to moral considerations ... without thereby prejudicing beneficiaries' financial interests. In practice, the inclusion or exclusion of particular investments or types of investment will often be possible without incurring the risk of a lower rate of return or reducing the desirable spread of investments. When this is so, there is no reason in principle why trustees should not have regard to moral and ethical considerations, vague and uncertain though these are. The trustees would not be departing from the purpose of the trust or hindering its fulfilment.

This suggestion should be firmly resisted. In the first place, regardless of the actual financial returns to the beneficiaries, trustees should never be entitled to take into account their own moral and ethical considerations in exercising any of their trust powers. Trustees are instruments of the trust. If they were ever to act on their own views in this way, they would act in breach of their fiduciary obligation never to exercise a discretion in a way that puts themselves in conflict with the purpose of the trust; applying their ethical attitudes to investment decisions gives rise to such a conflict because the trustee's ethical views are extraneous to the consideration of serving the beneficiaries' interests.

313

Lord Nicholls does not say that the trustees must implement the *beneficiaries'* moral or ethical views, but presumably, may act on their own. There is no warrant whatsoever to give trustees who are placed in a position of power and who are generally paid the right to engage their ethical preferences when investing so long as the beneficiaries cannot prove (see *Nestlé*, 10.21) that they have caused the trust loss by doing so. Who trusts the 'ethical' perspective of a bank or trust company anyway?

10.31 Secondly, it is wrong to think that the range of investments is so great that a few ethical investment choices here and there will not affect the financial performance of the trust. As Langbein and Posner (1980) make clear, a decrease in the range of investments is not determined by the *number* of individual securities one does not invest in, but the percentage value of the investment market those securities represent:

> In 1979, Corporate Data Exchange, Inc identified ninety-nine companies that a socially responsible investor should avoid. The aggregate market value of the stocks of these companies was $342 billion. Yet the only criteria for exclusion were whether the company was predominantly non-unionised, had a poor record in occupational health and safety, failed to meet equal employment opportunity guidelines, or was a major investor or lender in South Africa. Although this is an arbitrarily limited set of criteria, it results in excluding such a large fraction (weighting numbers by market value) of listed equities as to create a degree of sampling error and sampling bias inconsistent with adequate diversification of the portfolio.

In other words, if a trustee refuses to invest in 'just two things', but those two happen to be cars and alcohol, he is unlikely to adequately diversify the trust portfolio because the car and drinks industries represent such a major fraction of the overall economy. It is irrelevant that there are, in terms of numbers, thousands of other companies or securities to invest in. The resulting inadequate diversification will entail a riskier investment of the trust funds.

The delegation of trustee functions

10.32 Before 1926, unless specifically authorised by the trust instrument to do so, trustees could not delegate their administrative functions unless doing so was reasonably necessary for their administration of the trust to the standard of a prudent man of business (*Speight v Gaunt* (1883); *Learoyd v Whiteley* (1887)). Furthermore, the general rule was that trustees could not delegate any of their discretions, the idea being, first, that the settlor, by conferring discretions upon his trustees, reposed in them specifically the trust to exercise them responsibly, and, second, that by undertaking the trust, the trustees undertook to use their own judgment where judgment was called for, and had no right to shift the job to others. Outside specific provision in the trust instrument, trustee's powers to delegate were governed by the Trustee Act 1925, ss 23 and 25. The Trustee Act 2000 introduced a new regime of delegation.

10.33 Under s 11(1) and (2) of the Trustee Act 2000, trustees may collectively delegate any of their functions to an agent to perform, except:

(a) any function relating to whether or in what way any assets of the trust should be distributed,

(b) any power to decide whether any fees or other payment due to be made out of the trust funds should be made out of income or capital,

(c) any power to appoint a person to be a trustee of the trust, or

(d) any power conferred by any other enactment or the trust instrument which permits the trustees to delegate any of their functions or to appoint a person to act as a nominee or custodian.

10.34 The trustees may delegate tasks to one of themselves (s 12(1)), though not to any trustee who is also a beneficiary (s 12(2)). By s 15, where the agent is to carry out any 'asset management functions', eg investment, the trustees must first provide a written 'policy statement' to guide the agent's exercise of his powers in the best interests of the trust, eg so that the investments provide sufficient income to meet the level of provision the trustees intend for the income beneficiaries. By s 22 the trustees are required periodically to review any delegation arrangements, and to consider whether the 'policy statement' needs to be revised. By Sch 1, art 3 the section 1 duty of care (**10.8**) applies to the trustees' appointment of agents and their review of them under s 22.

10.35 By s 25 of the Trustee Act 1925 (as amended by the Trustee Delegation Act 1999, s 5) any individual trustee may, by power of attorney, delegate any or all of his duties, powers, or discretions, whether administrative or dispositive, for up to 12 months. Under s 25(4), the trustee must inform in writing any person entitled to appoint new trustees under the trust (see **10.55** et seq) and all the other trustees, which will allow them to consider whether the delegating trustee should be replaced. The trustee is liable under s 25(7) for all acts and defaults of his delegate by power of attorney as if they were his own acts or defaults.

The power of maintenance

10.36 The power of maintenance enables a trustee to spend income, but not capital, for the benefit of infant beneficiaries, ie those under 18. A settlor may specifically confer upon or deny the trustee this power, directing instead that the income should be spent on someone else or accumulated. In any other case, where property is held on trust for an infant, the Trustee Act 1925, s 31 confers on the trustee a power to apply, in their sole discretion income for the infant's maintenance. The section applies whether the infant's interest is vested, eg '10,000 shares of XYZ plc on trust for my son Benjamin absolutely' or contingent, 'Blackacre to Bertram if he obtains the age of 25'. Once the beneficiary of a vested interest turns 18 then of course he is entitled to any income arising on the property, but under s 31(1)(ii) trustees must pay the income to a beneficiary even of a contingent interest upon his turning 18.

10.37 During his infancy, the trustees may pay such portions of the income for his maintenance as 'may, in all the circumstances, be reasonable', and must accumulate the rest. Unless, therefore, s 31 is excluded, even a beneficiary of an absolute interest will receive only such income as is required, in the trustee's discretion, for his maintenance. The trustees must have regard to 'the age of the infant and his requirements and generally to the circumstances of his case, and in particular to what other income, if any, is available for the same purposes' (s 31(1)). In *Wilson v Turner* (1883) the trustees paid the income to the infant beneficiary's father automatically without enquiring as to the beneficiary's actual needs, and the father's estate was required to repay the money.

10.38 Under s 31(2), income which is accumulated instead of being spent on maintenance in one year may be spent for the beneficiary's maintenance in later years. Thus income accumulated in the beneficiaries' 10th and 11th years may be spent in his 17th when his expenses are greater. Also under s 31(2), where a beneficiary has a vested interest or an interest which vests upon his turning 18, when he turns 18 any income that instead of being spent for his maintenance was accumulated will then be held on trust for him absolutely – he can demand the immediate payment of it. This rule does not apply, however, where the vested interest is a conditional interest in land or an interest in personalty that may in any way be defeated, eg by the exercise of a power of appointment (see *Re Sharp's Settlement Trusts* (1973)). In that case, and in any case where the beneficiary's interest in the property does not vest until later, eg where his interest is contingent upon his turning 25, these pre-18 accumulations are held on the same trust as is the capital. Thus they will likewise be susceptible to the same contingency as is his interest in the capital. Therefore if his interest in the capital vests only when he reaches 25, then his interest in the pre-18 accumulations only vests when he reaches 25. In view of this, the trustees should consider making a final payment of past accumulated income shortly before the beneficiary's 18th birthday; after that, he will have no recourse to this money until his capital interest vests.

10.39   The income available for maintenance payments is only that income which arises on the property to which the minor beneficiary is, or will be, entitled. This is straightforward in the case of a beneficiary with a present vested interest. All of the income (ie dividends) on the shares in XYZ plc will be available to make maintenance payments to Benjamin in the example above. In the case of contingent or future interests, however, only income from property held on trust which 'carries the intermediate income' is available. This is best explained by example. If a testator gives Barbara a contingent pecuniary legacy, say £20,000 conditional upon her attaining the age of 25, it will be paid in due course out of the testator's residuary estate when she turns 25; Barbara will not receive any accrued income or interest since no property was set aside for her on a special account. The gift, therefore, carries no intermediate income for maintenance payments if Barbara is a minor. The same will occur with a *future* pecuniary legacy, eg of £20,000 to Barbara on the death of her father. By contrast, in the case of any *inter vivos* trust, there is no 'residuary estate'; each gift has specific property allocated to it and therefore a contingent gift will be of specific property, and so until it vests it will carry the income that accrues on it and when the gift vests the beneficiary is entitled to that income. During the beneficiary's minority such income will therefore be available for maintenance payments. In all cases, however, any contrary indication in the terms of the trust will upset these rules, for example, a direction that the income should go to a different beneficiary.

10.40 By the operation of s 175 of the Law of Property Act 1925 and a number of cases which we shall not discuss, the following rules apply to different kinds of testamentary gift to determine whether they carry the intermediate income, assuming that there is no contrary intention. A testamentary gift, whether of personalty or realty, and whether contingent or future, whether of specific property or residuary property, carries the intermediate income unless the gift is:

(1) a residuary bequest (ie a gift of residuary personalty), whether vested or contingent, which is postponed to a future date (see *Re McGeorge* (1963));

(2) a contingent or future pecuniary legacy; but such a gift *will* carry the intermediate income where:
   (i) it appears that the testator intended to maintain the beneficiary; or
   (ii) the legacy has been set aside as a separate fund from the outset; or
   (iii) the legacy is contingent upon the beneficiary's attaining the age of majority, and the testator was his parent or stood *in loco parentis* to him, and there are no other funds available for the minor's maintenance.

The power of advancement

10.41 The power of advancement is the power to expend *capital* of the trust fund to benefit a beneficiary who has only a future or contingent interest in it. Thus if Betty is entitled to the trust property for life, and Barney in remainder, Barney has a vested future interest. If he is advanced capital before Betty dies, then he receives the benefit of the capital early. If Beatrix is given trust property conditional upon her attaining the age of 30, and she is advanced property at the age of 22, not only does she receive the benefit early, but if she dies at 28, she receives property she would not have received at all but for the advancement – there is no 'clawback' of advanced property if it turns out that at the end of the day the beneficiary does not meet the conditions entitling him to the contingent interest. An advancement is traditionally a significant sum intended to 'advance', or establish, a beneficiary in life (**9.35**), although 'benefit' is now interpreted much more broadly (**10.44**), and 'to advance' therefore generally simply means 'to advance' or bring forward, a beneficiary's capital interest, though this does not mean that the beneficiary will actually receive the benefit of the property sooner, since the capital may be brought forward and then re-settled on trusts which actually delay the vesting of a beneficiary's interest (**10.44**).

10.42 A power to apply the capital of the trust to any object may be expressly given, but s 32 of the Trustee Act 1925 empowers trustees to advance capital to beneficiaries of future or contingent interests in the capital unless expressly excluded by the trust terms. Section 32 empowers trustees to advance a beneficiary up to one half by value of the capital interest he ultimately expects, his 'presumptive share', and the value of the advancement must be taken into account when his final share is paid out. Subsequent advancements may be made over time so long as the beneficiary has not been paid out sums amounting to half of his presumptive share, but the traditional method of accounting for past money advances used in practice can be 'monstrously unjust' (Law Reform Committee (1982), paras 4.43-4.47; see Oakley (2003), 696 for an example of the calculations), and so alternative bases have been proposed (Hayton (2003), 544-45). If, based on the calculation of the fund at the present time, a beneficiary is advanced an amount which, taking account of past advancements, gives him his full presumptive share in his capital interest, he may no longer be advanced any funds (*Re Abergavenny's Estate Act Trusts* (1981)), regardless of how much the value of the capital increases in future years.

10.43 In certain cases the trustees will need the prior consent of one beneficiary to advance money to another. Consider a trust of shares 'to A for life and then to B'. B has a future interest in the shares and is a candidate for advancement. But clearly, any advancement to B will reduce the capital in the trust, ie the number of shares, so A's income which comes from the dividends on the shares will decline. Section 32(1)(c) provides that the trustees may only make an advancement to B if A, who is said to have a 'prior' interest, is *sui juris* and consents to the advancement in writing.

319

10.44 What counts as an 'advancement' under s 32 is very wide indeed: in *Pilkington v IRC* (1964) Viscount Radcliffe said, 'It means any use of the money which will improve the material situation of the beneficiary', and in that case the HL would, but for the rules against perpetuity, have approved a proposed advancement which would have re-settled a five-year-old's expected interest when she attained 21 upon a new trust which would delay the vesting of her interest in the capital until she reached the age of 30, in order to avoid the effects of death duty. In *Re Clore's Settlement Trusts* (1966) the court approved an advancement to a rich beneficiary allowing him to make a charitable donation he felt morally obliged to make; it was a material, though not decisive, consideration that by the advancement of capital the beneficiary could make the donation with much less severe tax consequences than if he did so out of his income.

10.45 Trustees have an obligation to see that the money advanced actually goes to benefit the beneficiary. In *Re Pauling's Settlement Trusts* (1964) it was held that trustees could not advance money:

... without any responsibility ... even to inquire as to its application.

There large sums were advanced which the trustees were aware were being spent by the beneficiaries' father on the family's living expenses; the advancements were therefore in breach of trust and the trustees were required to repay the money thus frittered away.

10.46 In *Pilkington* the HL decided that an advancement on re-settlement was permissable under s 32. This raises the possibility that funds advanced may be settled on discretionary trusts. A question arises as to whether an advancement under s 32 can be validly made which creates a trust under which the advanced beneficiary is, or may become (as under a protective trust), a discretionary beneficiary. The trustees under the new trust will have a discretion to benefit the beneficiary, and the general rule is that a trustee cannot delegate his discretion (**10.32**); by making an advancement on these terms it appears that that is just what he is doing. On the other hand, as pointed out by Oakley (2003, 703-04), all agree that the re-settlement itself might contain a power of advancement, and this confers a clear discretion on the new trustee. More to the point however, it would seem such a settlement should be judged by whether or not it confers a real 'benefit' on the beneficiary. Given his circumstances, it might appear that a protective trust in his favour might do that. This should be the over-riding consideration, and given that the benefit in *Clore* was acceptable, it seems possible that so might being a beneficiary under a discretionary trust. The delegation point, although raised in *Pilkington*, was not considered in any detail. Any express power of advancement can, of course, be framed to permit its exercise to re-settle part of the beneficiary's presumptive share on discretionary trust.

10.47 *Pilkington* also decided that for purposes of the rule against perpetuities, a power of advancement is to be treated as a special power of appointment, and therefore an advancement on re-settlement is subject to the time limitations of the original trust of the property (**3.36**). Where the re-settlement contains provisions void for perpetuity these will be void, of course, but the main trust for the beneficiary in whose favour the advancement is made will not fail, unless the failure of the void provisions significantly alters the benefit the advancement was intended to achieve (*Re Abraham's Will Trusts* (1969)).

Appointment, retirement and removal of trustees

10.48 Over the course of any trust, old trustees may retire and occasionally trustees must be removed, and in both cases, depending upon how many trustees remain, new trustees may need to be appointed. Trustees may be individual persons or trust corporations, companies which specialise in acting as trustees.

10.49 Any number of persons may be co-trustees of a trust where the corpus is made up entirely of personalty. There are restrictions upon any trust which contains interests in land: The Trustee Act 1925, s 34 sets a maximum of four (there are exceptions for charitable and other public purpose trusts); the Act also effectively sets a minimum of two trustees – while a sole trustee, ie a lone human trustee (not a trust corporation) of land is not prohibited, s 14(2) provides that a sole trustee cannot give a valid receipt for the purchase money to a purchaser of the land, and so no purchaser will knowingly deal with a sole trustee of land.

10.50 Trustees invariably hold property as joint tenants, so if one dies the survivor(s) alone continue(s) as trustee(s) (**1.19**). Only if a sole trustee dies does the legal title to the trust property pass to his personal representative, who in that case becomes a trustee. In the case of a trust created by will where all the intended trustees have predeceased the testator, the testator's personal representatives will be trustees until new trustees can be appointed, who may, of course, be themselves.

10.51 A trust will not fail for want of a trustee, but neither will anyone unwilling be forced to serve as a trustee. Thus if a testator by his will transfers property to Tom on trust for Beatrix, Tom may refuse to accept the role of trustee; the court, however, will ensure that someone undertakes the trust. If there is no one else willing, as a last resort the court may appoint the Public Trustee. The office of the Public Trustee was created by the Public Trustee Act 1906, largely to ensure the administration of trusts where no other person was willing to do so. While the Public Trustee may refuse to undertake a trust, he may not do so only because of its small value (Public Trustee Act 1906, s 2(3)). The Public Trustee is entitled to charge for his administration of the trust. Alternatively, the court may appoint a trust corporation, authorising it to charge for its services (Trustee Act 1925, s 42).

10.52 In the first instance, trustees are appointed by the settlor when the trust is created (by the testator by his will in the case of a testamentary trust), and he can choose whomever he wants. Once the trust is constituted, the trust terms themselves become operative, and these may give some individual(s), typically the settlor and the trustees for the time being, the power to appoint new trustees. However, such provisions are typically supplementary to the powers to appoint provided by s 36 of the Trustee Act 1925, which are generally regarded as adequate.

10.53 The basic purpose of s 36 is to ensure that there will be someone who can appoint trustees so that a court appointment is not required. It provides that where a trustee:

- has died (which includes the case of a trustee named in a will who has predeceased the testator (s 36(8)); or

- has remained outside the UK for over a year; or

- wishes to retire from the trust; or

- refuses to act, ie disclaims the role of trustee at the outset; or

- is unfit to act, eg bankrupt; or

- is incapable of acting, ie has a personal incapacity such as mental or physical infirmity; or

- is an infant; or

- has been removed by the exercise of a power in the trust instrument (s 36(2)),

then a new appointment may be made, first, by anyone nominated to do so in the trust instrument, and failing that, by the trustees for the time being, and failing that because they have all died, by the personal representatives of the last surviving trustee. By s 36(8), refusing or retiring trustees are considered trustees for the time being so as to enable them to appoint their successors. It has been held (*Re Coates to Parsons* (1886)) that where some trustees intend to undertake the trust or continue as trustees, but some refuse or intend to retire, respectively, the appointment of new trustees by the continuing trustees without the concurrence of a refusing or retiring trustee will make the appointment invalid if it is shown that the latter was competent and willing to act. It is therefore advisable that all trustees for the time being participate in any appointment. Section 36(6) permits the appointment of additional trustees up to a maximum of four trustees in total. An appointment must be made in writing, though a last surviving trustee may not appoint a successor by will (*Re Parker* (1894)). An appointment is usually made by deed in order to vest the property in, ie transfer the legal title to, the new trustees at the same time (**10.56**). Nevertheless, s 37(7) provides that a new trustee becomes fully liable as a trustee as soon as he is appointed, even if the vesting of the property occurs sometime later. Even if a purported appointment is void, a new trustee who deals with the property as a trustee will be liable as one (**11.75**).

10.54   Section 19 of the Trusts of Land and Appointment of Trustees Act 1996 gives beneficiaries what amounts to a power to both remove and appoint trustees, although the power can be excluded by the settlor. If all are *sui juris*, the beneficiaries may unanimously direct any trustee to retire from the trust, or direct the trustees to use their power to appoint new trustees in favour of any person they choose (reversing *Re Brockbank* (**3.27**) on this point).

10.55 Although the court has the power to appoint trustees under its inherent jurisdiction over trusts, s 41 provides that the court may appoint trustees where it is found 'inexpedient, difficult, or impracticable to do so without the assistance of the court', and in particular to replace a trustee who is mentally incompetent, bankrupt, or where a corporate trustee is in liquidation or has been dissolved. Clearly, then, this power is regarded as a long-stop provision where no one empowered by the instrument or s 36 may practicably appoint. The court has also appointed where, for example, all the trustees nominated by will predeceased the testator (*Re Smirthwaite's Trusts* (1871)), where an elderly trustee was physically and mentally incapable of carrying on (*Re Lemann's Trusts* (1883)), and where a trustee had permanently left the UK (*Re Bignold's Settlement Trusts* (1872)). In appointing trustees the court will be guided by criteria stated by the CA in *Re Tempest* (1866): (1) the wishes of the settlor, (2) the interests of all the beneficiaries, and (3) the efficient execution of the trust. Following the enactment of s 19 of the 1996 Act, recourse to the court should be rare.

10.56 Except in the case of managing/custodian trustees (**10.58**), the trust property must be vested in the new body of trustees when a new trustee is appointed. Section 40 of the Trustee Act 1925 allows a deed of appointment of new trustees to serve also as a vesting instrument, which vests the legal title in the new body of trustees. In the case of registered land, the Registrar must give effect to such an instrument by revising the registered title accordingly. Some property cannot be vested in this way: the most important example of this is company shares. The shares must be transferred into the names of the new trustees in the normal way so that the new trustees are registered as owners in the company's books.

10.57 A person may disclaim the role of trustee from the outset, may retire from the trust, or may be removed. Although one should disclaim by deed, a disclaimer may be expressed in or implied from words or conduct. Once a person has accepted a trust, which in general is found whenever he exercises any function of a trustee in respect of the trust, he cannot disclaim – he may then only retire from the trust. Under s 36 of the Trustee Act 1925 a trustee may retire from the trust on the appointment of a replacement; under s 39, a trustee may retire by deed if there remain at least two individuals or a trust company as trustee(s), and he obtains the consent of the other trustees and anyone else entitled to appoint new trustees. The beneficiaries may now direct a trustee to retire, which is tantamount to removing him, and the court under s 41 may remove one trustee to replace him with another. The court may also remove a trustee in exercise of its inherent jurisdiction without necessarily appointing a replacement, though the grounds for doing so are not well defined. Clearly, any trustee in breach of trust or otherwise in dereliction of his fiduciary duties is a suitable candidate for removal; in *Letterstedt v Broers* (1884) the PC refused to lay down any rule governing the exercise of the power, except to say that the general interest of the beneficiaries should guide any decision.

Custodian, nominee, managing, and judicial trustees

10.58 A few particular kinds of trustee should be mentioned. 'Custodian trustees' hold the trust property as legal owners, but the management of the trust, ie all the trust decisions, are taken by different persons, called 'managing trustees', which the custodian trustee executes in so far as a disposition of the legal title to the property is required. It is as if the custodian trustee were a bare trustee, but one who complies with the orders, not of the bare beneficiary, but of the managing trustees. (A custodian trustee, while essentially a bare trustee, may differ from a bare trustee in some respects for particular purposes: see *IRC v Silverts Ltd* (1951).) The main advantage of a custodian trustee is that once the property is vested in him, the managing trustees may retire or be removed and new managing trustees appointed, without having to revest the property each time. A 'nominee' trustee, or just 'nominee', is essentially identical to a custodian trustee, though 'nominee' tends to be used of trustees who hold assets of the trust for specific purposes or transactions, while 'custodian' tends to be used of a trustee intended to hold all of the assets of a trust on an ongoing basis. Under ss 16-18 of the Trustee Act 2000, trustees are empowered to appoint nominees and custodian trustees. Section 19 provides that trust corporations, corporations controlled by the trustees, or persons who carry on the business of acting as nominee or custodian, may be appointed.

10.59 A 'judicial trustee' is appointed by the court (Judicial Trustees Act 1896) in cases where some continuing court supervision is required because the administration of the trust has broken down; the court may give such directions as to the administration of the trust as it thinks fit.

Beneficiaries' rights to information

10.60 In *Armitage v Nurse* (1998) Millett LJ stated:

> If the beneficiaries have no rights enforceable against the trustees, there are no trusts.

Remember that the settlor has no power to enforce the trust; it is the beneficiaries alone who are entitled to call the trustee to account in respect of his stewardship of the trust property. But the beneficiaries cannot enforce such a right if they have no information as to how the trustee has carried out the trust.

The right to be informed one is a beneficiary

10.61 Beneficiaries of vested interests (certainly absolute vested interests) have a right to be informed of their interest (*Hawkesley v May* (1956)), and it is within the court's discretion in an appropriate case (viz where it is reasonable to assume that such beneficiary has a genuine likelihood or expectation that a dispositive discretion might be exercised in his favour) to require settlors to provide the names and addresses of trustees even to a discretionary beneficiary (*Re Murphy's Settlement* (1998)).

The right to see the trust accounts and other trust documents

10.62 The PC in *Schmidt v Rosewood Trust* (2003) recently reviewed the rights of objects of trusts to have access to the trust accounts and other trust documents, such as the minutes of trustees' meetings. Prior to that decision it was generally accepted that beneficiaries, whether of a fixed or discretionary interest (*Chaine-Nickson v Bank of Ireland* (1976), *Spellson v George* (1987)), perhaps even of a contingent interest (*Armitage* per Millett LJ), ie objects of a trustee's dispositive *duty* to distribute the trust property, were entitled to copies (made at their own expense) of the trust accounts and all trust documents.

10.63 However, the basis for these rights was not clearly established. From one perspective, the trust documents being trust property, the beneficiaries had a proprietary right to them, as they were the ultimate owners in equity of the trust property (*O'Rourke v Darbishire* (1920); *Re Londonderry's Settlement* (1965)). This is clearly misguided, for whether trust documents form part of the trust property or not, beneficiaries have no rights of access to the trust property itself; they merely have rights to whatever benefits of the trust property the trust terms dictate. The better view is that these rights flow from the beneficiaries' right to make the trustee account for his stewardship of the trust (*Hartigan Nominees Pty. Ltd v Rydge* (1992); *Re Rabaiotti's 1989 Settlement* (2000)). 'The beneficiaries' rights to inspect trust documents are now seen to be better based not on equitable proprietary rights but on the beneficiaries' rights to make the trustees account for their trusteeship' (*Re Rabaiotti's 1989 Settlement*, quoting Hayton).

10.64   *Schmidt* concerned a claim for rights to information, not from a beneficiary with a defined interest under the trust, but from an object of a mere power of appointment. Lord Walker, delivering the judgment of the PC, firmly adopted the view that the beneficiary's right to information flowed from the inherent jurisdiction of the court to ensure that trusts were properly supervised and enforced, and that, depending on the circumstances, in some cases an object of a power of appointment appropriately had such a right. In the exercise of its inherent jurisdiction, the court might refuse, in certain cases, a claim by an object for information, where, for example, issues arise as to personal or commercial confidentiality:

> Disclosure may have to be limited and safeguards put in place. Evaluation of the claims of a beneficiary (and especially of a discretionary object) may be an important part of the balancing exercise which the court has to perform on the materials placed before it. In many cases the court may have no difficulty in concluding that an applicant with no more than a theoretical possibility of benefit ought not to be granted relief.

10.65   The result in *Schmidt* can be questioned (see Pollard (2003); Smith (2003)). The decision seems to create a good measure of uncertainty in this area, and it may be difficult for trustees to decide what information they ought properly to reveal to objects without applying first to the court, which will create an expense for the trust. It might also suggest an unfortunate antagonistic attitude between trustee and beneficiary. On this latter point, Hayton has made a plea 'for more openness between trustees and beneficiaries. The more one tries to hide things from people the more suspicious they become: no one likes being treated like a mushroom, being kept in the dark and fed you know what.'

Variation of trusts

10.66 In general, a settlor may set whatever terms on a trust he desires. Because trusts generally last for some years, it is not uncommon for terms which seemed reasonable at the outset to cause problems or inconvenience later, eg terms which limit the trustee's power of investment, or modes of distribution of the assets which give rise to unforeseen tax liability. Furthermore, the beneficiaries may, even from the outset, be unhappy with the distribution of their particular beneficial interests. If the beneficiaries are all ascertained and *sui juris*, they may at any time combine to exercise their *Saunders v Vautier* rights to collapse the trust or vary its terms. Where this is not the case the assistance of the court must be sought.

10.67 The court has always had an inherent jurisdiction to vary trusts, though the scope of this jurisdiction is limited to variations which permit the trustees greater administrative or management powers, and then only in cases of 'emergency' (*Re New* (1901)); the court will not rearrange the beneficial interests (*Chapman v Chapman* (1954)). The only true exception to this rule is that the court will empower the trustees to apply income to maintain a settlor's minor children even where he directed the income to be accumulated. A court has also always been able to sanction a 'compromise' between beneficiaries' rights where they are the subject of doubt or dispute, but this is better seen as the court's settling what the beneficial interests are, not its remoulding of the beneficial interests.

10.68 Section 57 of the Trustee Act 1925 extends the court's jurisdiction to enhance the trustee's administrative powers to cases of expediency, ie to more than emergency situations. It clearly contemplates increasing the power of trustees to deal in particular ways with the trust property, not a wholesale re-writing of the trust, nor the remoulding of the beneficial interests (*Chapman v Chapman* (1954)).

10.69 An application to extend the trustee's investment powers provides a nice example of a variation under s 57. In *Trustees of the British Museum v A-G* (1984) Megarry VC refused to follow the 1961 decision in *Re Kolb's Will Trusts* which held that an extension of trust powers was to be approved only in special circumstances. He held that there should be a general power to widen investment powers based on a number of factors including: (1) the standing of trustees and their administrative plan for obtaining advice and controlling investments; (2) the size of the fund; and (3) the object of the fund (here capital growth was needed for the museum to be able to have an endowment for additions to the museum collection). In *Steel v Wellcome Custodian Trustees Ltd* (1988) Hoffmann J approved an extension of investment powers on similar principles.

10.70   The Variation of Trusts Act 1958 allows the variation of beneficial interests under trusts in cases where the beneficiaries are not in the position to do so by exercising their *Saunders v Vautier* rights. Essentially the Act allows the court to approve a variation on behalf of under-age beneficiaries and potential beneficiaries as yet unascertained. The variation is, therefore, effected by the unanimous exercise of the beneficiaries exercising their *Saunders v Vautier* rights – those who are *sui juris* and ascertained consent for themselves, and the court consents on behalf of those who are not; the Act does not give the court a general discretionary power to vary trusts at the application of an interested party (*Re Holt's Settlement* (1969); *IRC v Holmden* (1968); *Goulding v James* (1997)). For this reason, recourse to the 1958 Act should be made only when the beneficial interests are to be varied. Variations are to be treated as 'new trusts', and the varying parties as settlors of the new trusts, such that the new trusts are subject to whatever statutory provisions apply at the time of variation (*Re Holt's Settlement*). The mere extension of trustee powers, like the power of investment, should be sought under s 57 of the 1925 Act; in such a case the trustee is the proper applicant, not the beneficiaries, and since no need for the consent of all beneficiaries is required the s 57 application will be less costly (*Anker-Petersen v Anker-Petersen* (1991)).

10.71   The court will not consent on behalf of beneficiaries of full age even if their interests are contingent and extremely unlikely to vest in interest, and even if obtaining their consent will be very inconvenient, as in *Knocker v Youle* (1986) where there were several dozen contingent *sui juris* beneficiaries, a goodly number in Australia, who were almost certain never to take under the trust. Should Parliament amend the Act to allow the court to consent on behalf of such beneficiaries? Is a court dealing with a *McPhail*-type trust able to do this in substance already, given its power to 'implement a scheme of distribution' proposed by a representative group of beneficiaries in order to enforce such a trust (**3.50**)?

329

10.72 By s 1(1) of the Act the court may only approve an arrangement on behalf of a beneficiary if it would be to his 'benefit', unless (s 1(1)(d)) the beneficiary is an object of a discretionary 'trust over' following the determination of the life interest under a protective trust (**3.61**) in which case no 'benefit' need be shown. 'Benefit' has been construed broadly to include not only financial but moral and social benefits (*Re Holt's Settlement*). In *Re Weston's Settlements* (1969) Lord Denning MR refused to allow the export of a trust to Jersey where the settlor and the beneficiaries had recently moved to minimise tax liability. Considering social and educational benefits he said:

> I do not believe it is for the benefit of children to be uprooted from England and transported to another country simply to avoid tax.

10.73 The court will not require an absolute certainty of benefit – where subsequent events might make the variation disadvantageous to the beneficiaries on whose behalf the court consents, the scheme will still be approved if the more likely result is an advantage to them; the court should undertake on the beneficiaries' behalf the same sort of risks which an adult would be prepared to take (*Re Cohen's Will Trusts* (1959); *Re Holt's Settlement*). However, where the effect of a variation might lead to a possible beneficiary under the old trust, even an as yet unborn individual, being excluded from the new trust entirely, the variation will not be approved because if such a person is born the variation would be wholly disadvantageous to him (*Re Cohen's Settlement Trusts* (1965)).

10.74 In *Re Steed's Will Trusts* (1960) the CA gave the testator's intentions significant weight where a life tenant under a protective trust applied for a variation to give her an absolute interest. The essence of the settlor's concern in creating the protective trust for his former housekeeper was that if absolutely entitled to the property she would be 'sponged upon by one of her brothers'. The CA refused to consent to the variation on behalf of the possible objects of the discretionary trust over, ie those who would take if the primary trust was forfeited. This decision seems quite out of line with the obvious import of the Act, which, if anything, should favour the variation of protective trusts to give the determinable life-interest holder an absolute interest: s 1 specifically provides that the court may approve a variation on behalf of the beneficiaries of the discretionary trust arising on the forfeiture of a protective trust even if the variation is of no benefit to them. In *Re*

Remnant's Settlement Trusts (1970) an arrangement which overthrew the settlor's clear intentions was approved in the interest of family harmony and marital choice (a condition defeated a trust gift for objects marrying a Roman Catholic). Recently, in *Goulding v James* (1997), the CA made it clear that the settlor's intentions are only relevant in so far as they contribute to assessing whether the proposed variation is of benefit to the class on whose behalf the court consents. The *sui juris* beneficiaries, like any other beneficiaries exercising their *Saunders v Vautier* rights, may propose an arrangement which directly contradicts the settlor's wishes *for them*. Although *Re Steed* was not in terms disapproved, it was largely confined to its particular facts.

10.75 By contrast, in other jurisdictions, the *Saunders v Vautier* principle has been significantly cut down by judicial decisions and legislation, such that any proposed variation, even if consented to by all the beneficiaries, is prohibited to the extent that it would detract from a 'material purpose' of the settlor in creating the trust. (See, eg American Law Institute (1959), ss 337-339; Bahamas Trustee Act 1998, s 87.)

10.76 The 1958 Act empowers the court to consent to '*any* arrangement … varying or revoking *all or any* of the trusts' (my italics). Given the breadth of this language, and furthermore the court's interpretation that variations of trusts are to be understood as the exercise of *Saunders v Vautier* rights, it would seem that the court should happily countenance the complete revocation of the old trust and re-settlement of the property under a new one. Yet in *Re T's Settlement Trusts* (1964) Wilberforce J refused to approve a 'complete new resettlement' on the grounds that the Act was restricted to variations. However, in *Re Ball's Settlement* (1968) Megarry J said:

> But it does not follow that merely because an arrangement can correctly be described as effecting a revocation and resettlement, it cannot also be correctly described as effecting a variation of the trusts.

10.77 The most oft-quoted passage from the case is this, in which Megarry J quotes Martin J of the Supreme Court of Victoria in *Re Dyer* (1935):

> If an arrangement changes the whole substratum of the trust, then it may well be that it cannot be regarded merely as varying that trust. But if an

arrangement, while leaving the substratum, effectuates the purpose of the original trust by other means, it may still be possible to regard that arrangement as merely varying the original trusts, even though the means employed are wholly different and even though the form is completely changed.

With respect, this is just so much verbiage. The original trust has no 'purpose' besides distributing the beneficial interests in the way it does. Any change in that changes its 'purpose', even if it does so for good reasons, eg to avoid tax. If something like the settlor's wishes is what 'purpose' means, it is clear that the statement is just wrong, since variations may freely defeat those (**10.74**). What *should* be quoted from Megarry J's decision is the following, which comes a couple of lines later:

The jurisdiction of the Act is a beneficial one and, in my judgment, the court should construe it widely and not be astute to confine its beneficent operation. I must remember that in essence the court is merely contributing on behalf of infants and unborn and unascertained persons the binding assents to the arrangement which they, unlike an adult beneficiary, cannot give. So far as is proper, the power of the court to give that assent should be assimilated to the wide powers which the ascertained adults have.

Precisely.

Further reading

Goodhart (1996); Law Reform Committee (1982); Law Commission (1999); Langbein (1994); Langbein and Posner (1980); Nicholls (1995); Brownbill (1992-1995); Hicks (2001); Smith (2003a); Pollard (2003)

Must read legislation and cases: Trustee Act 2000, Parts I-IV, Sch 1; *Speight v Gaunt* (1883); *Learoyd v Whitely* (1887); *Nestlé v National Westminster Bank plc* (1994); *Bartlett v Barclays Bank Trust Co Ltd* (1979); *Cowan v Scargill* (1984); *Re Holt's Settlement* (1969); *Pilkington v IRC* (1962); *Re Pauling's Settlement Trusts* (1963); *Schmidt v Rosewood Trust Ltd* (2003); *Goulding v James* (1997); *Re Ball's Settlement Trusts* (1986).

Self-test questions

1. The trustees of the substantial funds of the London Ecumenical Christian Church are given by the trust instrument a power to invest in any investments they see fit, subject only 'to their legal duty of prudent investment'. For 15 years they have left half the funds in a building society account, earning a low rate of interest. The remainder has been invested in shares of two companies. The share price of one of the companies has recently dropped by 30% in line with a general collapse in the stock market. The trust has a holding of 55% in the second company. The company has recently gone into receivership following the failure of a speculative venture. The trustees had not known about the venture, and generally took no interest in the company's activities.
   (a) Advise the trustees whether they have committed a breach of their duty of prudent investment; and
   (b) Consider to what extent, if at all, the trustees are subject to a duty to ensure that trust funds are not invested in 'unchristian business activities'.

2. What limitations are there on a trustee's power to delegate his functions? In what circumstances will he be liable for the defaults of his appointed agents?

3. Bill, 14, and Bob, 23 are beneficiaries of a testamentary trust under which they are each entitled to a sum of £25,000 contingent upon their attaining the age of 25, and to a half share of a large share portfolio contingent on their attaining the age of 30. To what extent may the trustees use their statutory powers of maintenance and advancement in Bill and Bob's favour?

4. What differences are there between the rules which govern the variation of trusts (i) to modify the administrative powers of the trustees, and (ii) to alter the beneficial interests?

5. What powers have (i) the trustees, (ii) the beneficiaries, and (iii) the court, to appoint and remove trustees?

6. What are the strengths and weaknesses of the law governing a beneficiary's right to information from his trustee?

333

CHAPTER ELEVEN

Breach of Trust

SUMMARY

The array of claims that can arise when a breach of trust occurs

The difference between breach of trust and breach of fiduciary obligation

The trustee's liability to account: personal claims against the trustee

Liability of trustees *inter se*

Beneficiaries' consent to a breach of trust

Trustees' relief from liability under s 61 Trustee Act 1925, trustee exemption clauses, and the ouster of trustee duties

De facto trusteeship, or trusteeship *de son tort*

Liability for procuring or assisting in a breach of trust

Proprietary liability following the misapplication of trust property

Tracing

Proprietary claims to traceable proceeds: charges and equitable ownership

Subrogation claims reliant on tracing

Tracing 'at common law' and the quest for a fiduciary relationship

> **Personal claims against recipients of trust property or its traceable proceeds**
>
> **The restitutionary analysis of recipient liability**
>
> **Limitation of actions**

The array of claims that can arise when a breach of trust occurs

11.1 It is an easy thing to write a breach of trust question for an examination paper. Consider the following: Tim, the trustee of the Smith family trust, breaches the trust by giving £50,000 to Robert, his brother, telling him the money is a gift to help him with his business. Angelica, the branch manager at the bank where the trust's bank account is held, arranges for the payment from the trust account. The money is paid into Robert's business's current account, erasing his overdraft and bringing the balance to £20,000. Robert raises the balance to £25,000 by paying other funds into the account, and then he writes a cheque on the account for £30,000 to pay for new equipment.

11.2 This is clearly a case of breach of trust. The question actually tells you that Tim breached the trust. What are you supposed to say about it? Of course you would first say that Tim is liable for the breach of trust. Indeed, he is *strictly* liable, in the same way that a contracting party is strictly liable for breach of contract. In general the law does not inquire into why, or with what mental state, you breached your contract – whether you did so intentionally, or negligently, or perfectly innocently, trying your best to perform your obligation. And the same is generally true of the trustee in breach. If, for whatever reason or with whatever mental state, the trustee misappropriates trust property, ie takes property from the trust and deals with it in a way that is inconsistent with the trust terms (notice that as legal owner of the property he does not have to do anything to acquire legal title to it – as a trustee he already has that), a court of equity will require him to return it to the trust, ie hold it again as a trustee for the beneficiaries. Indeed, using a certain kind of terminology to which equity lawyers are occasionally prone, (usually with poor results for the law's clarity and coherence) 'equity will not *hear*' the trustee say that he misappropriated trust property; it will treat him as if he never committed the misappropriation, as if held the property properly for the beneficiaries all along. Where a trustee disposes of trust property in breach of trust so that the property is lost, or deals with the trust property in breach of trust so as to cause a loss of value to the trust fund, for example by making an unauthorised, losing, investment, the trustee will be strictly personally liable to restore the value of the trust, ie will be strictly liable to dig into his own pocket to pay into the trust the money value of the loss he caused. So whatever else you can say about this fact situation, you can certainly say that Tim will be strictly liable to repay the £50,000 out of his own pocket with interest.

11.3   But, alas, there is a lot more to be said. In many cases, Tim will be bankrupt or have disappeared, so the beneficiaries will have little hope of restoring the trust by pursuing him, and we must consider what rights the beneficiaries might have against third parties who may be somehow involved in the breach. One right they have is trivially easy to see: the beneficiaries are, after all, together the owners of the trust property in the eyes of equity, and as with all rights to property, third parties who come into possession of the property of others will be liable to the beneficiaries' claim, 'that's ours', and be liable return it to the beneficiaries. This is a conceptual 'base-line' truth about property rights: they bind everyone, more or less. As we have seen, the title the beneficiaries have in the trust property binds everyone except the bona fide purchaser (**2.35** et seq). So if, for example, Tim had given Robert a trust painting as a birthday present, the beneficiaries could simply say to Robert, 'that's ours' and demand its return. In doing so, the beneficiaries are said to *follow* their property into Robert's hands.

11.4   But the law allows them to do more than this: it also allows them to *trace* the value of their property through substitutions of one kind of property right for another (**2.46**). The best way to think about tracing is to see how it allows the beneficiaries to continue to have property rights even when their property comes into the hands of a bona fide purchaser for value. Imagine Robert were to sell the trust painting to a dealer who gives £10,000 for the painting innocent of the fact that it came to Robert in breach of trust. As a bona fide purchaser, the dealer takes the painting free of the beneficiaries' equitable title. So the beneficiaries cannot follow their trust property, the painting, into the dealer's hands. The dealer's purchase extinguishes their equitable title to the painting. But the law allows them to trace the value of the painting into the £10,000 that the dealer gave Simon for it – they can point to the £10,000 and say to

Simon, 'that is ours' – and the law will give effect to their claim just as if the £10,000 was money that was originally in the trust. And the beneficiaries can trace from one substitution into another ad infinitum, as long as the evidence permits, or until the value is expended but not in exchange for property, eg if Simon were to spend the £10,000 on a world cruise. So the first point to take away about the relationship of following and tracing is this – one can follow trust property up to the point it is exchanged for something else with a bona fide purchaser. When you run up against the bona fide purchaser, you must 'double back', as it were, bouncing your claim from the trust property back onto the proceeds of the exchange.

11.5 It is important to realise just how valuable to beneficiaries tracing has become given the world of property in which we now live. Very few modern trusts contain large amounts of tangible property, such as land or chattels like paintings, or hold money in specie, ie in cash. What they hold are various kinds of financial instruments, such as shares and bonds and bank accounts. These days it is unlikely that beneficiaries are able to follow their property very far, if at all. If it were not for the right to trace, their property rights would be extinguished, often immediately. Consider the opening question. Angelica the bank manager arranges for the payment from the trust account to Robert's business's current account, let us assume by a BACS (Banker's Automated Credit System) transfer, which is the way most employees' money gets into their bank accounts when their employers pay them each month. In such a case, Robert never really receives any trust property at all; there is *nothing* for the beneficiaries to follow. What happens (the truth is slightly more complicated) is that under its banking account contract with the trust, the trust's bank agrees to pay Simon's bank £30,000 to credit Simon's account, and is entitled to reduce the trust's bank balance by the same amount; that is, the trust agrees that the trust's bank now owes the trust £30,000 less than it did before (the relationship of banker to account holder is essentially just that of debtor and creditor). In short, then, the transaction is a contractual one where the trust's right against its bank is diminished in order that the trust's bank will buy a new contractual right from Robert's bank for Robert, ie the enhanced balance in Robert's business's current account at his bank. No title in any property of the trust passes to Robert at all. Therefore, if there were no right to trace value, the beneficiaries' equitable proprietary rights would be immediately extinguished by the very form of the breach.

11.6   The situation is not much better if Tim had written a cheque for £30,000 on the trust account payable to Robert. The cheque is trust property, so if before Robert deposits the cheque, the beneficiaries catch up with him, they can follow this trust property into his hands and claim back the cheque as theirs. But as soon as Robert deposits it, Robert's bank will enforce the cheque against the trust's bank, receiving money which it will immediately take as its own, and will credit Robert's account with the same amount. By crediting Robert's account, ie giving Robert a new or enhanced bank balance in his favour, Robert's bank creates a new or enhanced right for Robert – in doing so it gives good value for what it received from the trust's bank by enforcing the cheque, and so the bank is a bona fide purchaser. The beneficiaries must now trace the value into Robert's enhanced account balance. Thus if you think about how many breaches of trust must involve transfers of money by cheque or through the banking system, you will see how important tracing is.

11.7   In the facts of the question, the trust money pulls Robert's account out of overdraft, and he then draws on the account to buy equipment, putting it into overdraft again. As we will see, tracing into and out of bank accounts raises special problems: where did the money that paid off his overdraft 'go'? As the payment and subsequent transactions with the account 'mix' Robert's money and the trust money, how do we decide which of the them owns what? Whose money, or if both their moneys, in what shares, went to pay for the new equipment?

11.8   So far we have looked at Robert in terms of his *proprietary* liability. That is, we have looked at following and tracing to see when beneficiaries can make a 'that's ours' claim against him. But Robert may also be *personally* liable to restore the trust, that is, Robert may be liable to dig into his own pocket to pay back the value of what he received from the trust, even though he no longer has any of the trust property or its traceable proceeds – he might have blown all the trust money on a world cruise. Under certain circumstances, Robert will be liable to pay back what he received, under other circumstances not. This kind of personal liability was traditionally know as liability for 'knowing receipt or dealing', and as the name indicates, the traditional rule is that Robert will be personally liable only if he has a certain level of knowledge that the property he received came to him in breach of trust. But we will see that many commentators and judges have expressed deep misgivings about this

339

approach to the personal liability of a recipient of trust property or its traceable proceeds.

11.9 Now what about Angelica? As you can imagine, she is not mentioned just to add some colour. Angelica carries out the transaction that breaches the trust, and in certain circumstances she may be personally liable to restore the trust on the basis that she is an accessory to the breach. Recent decisions have made it clear that accessories will only be liable for assisting a breach of trust if they do so dishonestly; unfortunately, the courts have found that what counts as dishonesty harder to pin down.

11.10 So Tom's straightforward little breach of trust, described in a few lines, has led to all of this, all of which you must deal with if you are faced with such an exam question. So, before beginning to look at all of this in detail, keep a couple of points in mind. Dealing with breach of trust almost always involves working through, one by one, the array of remedies the beneficiaries may pursue. It is absolutely vital to keep these separate claims separate. Secondly, as we shall see, there is unfortunately no judicial or academic consensus about the right way to explain and justify the array of claims the beneficiaries may have. In what follows, the emphasis will be on explaining the traditional understanding in this area, but frequent reference will be made to alternative ways of thinking about the law. However trying it might be, these days even a trust student must have some understanding of the 'theoretical' battles which rage around the remedies available when there is a breach of trust.

11.11 Given that this is a large and complex area of the law of trusts, it is best to provide a bit of a roadmap for the rest of this chapter. We will first deal with the trustee's personal liability for breach of trust. A trustee can breach the trust in two basic ways. By far the most important sort of breach of trust occurs where a trustee *misapplies the trust property*. That is, the trustee gives the property away to someone who is not a proper object of the trust, as in the transfer to Robert in the opening question, or enters into a contract involving the trust property which is not allowed by the trust terms, say by investing in an unauthorised investment. Second, there are breaches by the trustee of his duty to act with care and skill in the administration of the trust which cause the trust loss, eg the claim made in *Nestlé* (**10.19**). Following an examination in detail of the trustee's personal liability, we will look at the various ways in which a trustee may be relieved of liability, such as by the insertion in the trust terms of an exemption clause.

11.12 We shall then consider the case where a third party dishonestly assists in the breach of trust. Such a 'stranger to the trust' (ie a third party, like Robert or Angelica in the question, who is neither a trustee nor a beneficiary) will be jointly and severally liable with the trustee for any loss to the trust caused by the breach. 'Joint and several' liability means that the beneficiary will be entitled to sue either the trustee or the dishonest assistant for the full amount of the loss; if he sues just one of them, that defendant must pay the full amount and is left to bring an action for 'contribution' against the other wrongdoer to recoup a money share from him. From the opening question we can see that Angelica is a candidate for this liability, though it is unclear on the facts whether she has acted dishonestly.

11.13 This is as far as we can go in discussing the array of claims that can arise on a breach of trust without, at last, looking at tracing in detail. So that is what we shall then do. Following that, we can look at the proprietary claims that the beneficiaries can make against the trustee, and those they can make against strangers to the trust who receive trust property, like Robert, and then look at the personal liability of third parties for 'knowing receipt'. Finally, with all of this 'law' in hand, we will briefly survey the judicial and academic debate surrounding this area of law.

Wrongs equivalent to breaches of trust and equity's 'concurrent' jurisdiction

11.14 Some of the cases which apply equity's principles for dealing with breach of trust occur in cases where there is not, strictly speaking, a breach of trust. The most common example is the case where a non-trustee fiduciary, such as an agent or company director, wrongfully deals with his principal's property, say where a company director embezzles his company's funds. In this case equity will treat the company director as a trustee in breach, and give the company the same sort of remedies as it would to a wronged beneficiary (eg *John v Dodwell & Co* (1918); *Re Duckwari* (1999); *JJ Harrison (Properties) Ltd v Harrison* (2002)). As a consequence, we will see cases that elaborate the principles of liability for breach of trust but which do not involve trustees at all, but rather, defaulting fiduciaries.

11.15 Moreover, equity will sometimes apply its principles in areas where neither trustees nor fiduciaries are involved. Equity developed what is called a 'concurrent' jurisdiction, whereby it would give plaintiffs the aid of equitable remedies even though the particular wrong was not an *equitable* wrong, not a wrong, that is, which breached a relationship that equity developed and took care of, such as the trust relationship or the fiduciary relationship. The most important example is the case of fraud. Frauds typically involve the breach of a contract, or the abuse of contracts. A company employee, whether he is a fiduciary to the company or not, obviously breaches his employment contract and commits a fraud if he embezzles funds from the company by altering the name on company cheques so as to pay them into his own bank account. Similarly, whether I am a fiduciary to you or not, I defraud you of your money if I sell you a car to which I have no title because, for example, I stole it. I use, and abuse, the legal relationship of contract in order to defraud you of your money. In certain cases equity will provide remedies to the defrauded party which it would give to wronged beneficiaries (eg *Collings v Lee* (2001); *Agip (Africa) Ltd v Jackson* (1990); *Dubai Aluminium v Salaam* (2003); *Papamichael v NatWest Bank* (2003); *Westdeutsche Landesbank v Islington LBC* (1996) per Lord Browne-Wilkinson; but see *Shalson v Russo* (2003)); in particular it may allow the wronged party to trace into the proceeds the fraudster may acquire with the property he defrauded the rightful owner of. Thus, as we shall see, some decisions which elaborate the rules of tracing are made in cases where there was no breach of trust, but only a fraud.

The difference between breach of trust and breach of fiduciary obligation

11.16 If you are able to grasp this difference and bear it in mind when you consider the cases, count yourself as an intellectual of the subject, because far too often judges and commentators make a mess of this. A trustee is strictly liable for breaches of trust, and it does not matter *why* he misapplies the trust property or neglects to invest it properly, whether because he favoured his own interests over the beneficiaries, or because of his incompetence, or for any other reason. As you will recall (**2.10**–**2.14**) and as we shall examine in detail in the next chapter, the fiduciary obligation is a very particular and precise obligation imposed upon people who have to use their discretion in making decisions for other people. They breach their fiduciary obligations when they act in conflict of interest in the course of exercising their discretions under their trust or agency or directorship of a company. The point is that if it were not for the fiduciary obligation, their actions would be perfectly correct. For example, a trustee may have the power to invest the trust property in shares. He does not breach the trust if he sells his own shares to the trust, for the trust terms allow him to invest in shares. What he breaches is his fiduciary obligation, for obviously he will be in a conflict of interest in trying to set a price for the shares – as a trustee he must try to get the shares at the lowest price possible, but as the owner of the shares himself he will try to sell them at the highest price possible. Notice, then, how the fiduciary obligation works – *it turns what would otherwise be a perfectly proper act of the trustee*, this investment in shares, *into a wrong*, because he undertakes it in conflict of interest. In short, a breach of a fiduciary obligation turns a rightful act into a wrongful one because of the existence of a conflict of interest. Therefore there is no point in referring to any fiduciary obligation if the act was a wrongful one in any event, as for example where the trustee in this case was not allowed to invest in shares at all. There is no *need*, and no *room*, for willy-nilly treating breaches of trust as breaches of fiduciary obligation where the breach is a breach of trust *simpliciter*. Judges and commentators often make this mistake because, as trustees are generally fiduciaries, they tend to use the words 'trustee' and 'fiduciary' interchangeably, and then go on to call any breach of trust a breach of a fiduciary obligation. As we shall see in the next chapter, judges such as Lord Millett have now begun to clamp down on this loose usage. *NB:* In 11.14 above we saw that equity will treat cases where a fiduciary transfers his principal's property wrongfully as cases of breach of trust; these cases do *not* turn on breaches of any fiduciary obligation. These, just as much as other cases of breach of trust, turn on the fiduciary doing something that is wrong anyway, for example a company director embezzling his company's funds. But because fiduciaries are creatures of equity, equity will treat these wrongful dispositions of the principal's property as equivalent to breaches of trust. True breaches of fiduciary obligation, by trustees and others, will be examined in detail in the next chapter.

The trustee's liability to account: personal claims against the trustee

11.17   The trustee's 'liability to account' is the starting point for understanding the beneficiary's remedies for breach of trust. This liability flows from the very nature of the trust relationship. The principal task of the trustee is to keep the trust property separate from his own and dispose of it according to the terms of the trust. In carrying out this task, he must keep track of what he does with the trust property; this is called 'keeping the trust account(s)', and, as you would imagine, normally involves keeping the documents concerning transactions with the trust property in good order. When a beneficiary suspects that something has gone wrong with the administration of the trust, this is normally because he does not accept the trustee's account (recall **10.60–10.65**), ie his record of what he has done with the trust property, and the beneficiary's primary legal right is to bring the trustee to the court of chancery and have 'the account taken', ie reviewed. If it appears that there has been a breach of trust, the beneficiary is entitled to 'falsify' or 'surcharge' the account, as Millett LJ, speaking extra-judicially, explains (1998):

> The primary obligation of a trustee is to account for his stewardship [of the trust]. The primary remedy of the beneficiary ... is to have the account taken, to surcharge and falsify the account, and to require the trustee to restore to the trust estate any deficiency which may appear when the account is taken. The liability is strict ... If the beneficiary is dissatisfied with the way in which the trustee has carried out his trust – if, for example, he considers that the trustee has negligently failed to obtain all that he should have done for the benefit of the trust estate, then he may surcharge the account.   ... The trustee is made to account, not only for what he has in fact received, but also for what he might with due diligence have received ... Where the beneficiary complains that the trustee has misapplied trust money, he falsifies the account, that is to say, he asks for the disbursement to be disallowed. If, for example, the trustee lays out trust money in an unauthorised investment which falls in value, the beneficiary will falsify the account by asking the court to disallow both the disbursement and the corresponding asset on the other side of the account. The unauthorised investment will then be treated as having been bought with the trustee's own money and on his own behalf. He will be required to account to the trust estate for the full amount of the disbursement – *not* for the amount of the loss. That is what is meant by saying that the trustee is liable to restore the trust property; and why common law rules of damage and remoteness are out of place.

11.18 Thus there are two remedial functions taking an account may serve. When the account is 'surcharged', a trustee is made liable for a breach of trust which does not involve a misapplication of trust property, such as his negligence in making investments, or his failure to insure trust property as he should; the trustee must pay into the trust fund, out of his own pocket, to compensate the trust fund to the value of any losses his breach caused. When the account is 'falsified', the trustee must 'restore' the trust, which will require one of two things. If possible, the trustee will be required to restore the trust '*in specie*'. That is, he must return the very property, or the same kind of property, to the trust. Thus if the trustee has wrongfully transferred unique property out of the trust, like land or a chattel like a valuable painting, the trustee should first try to get that property back. As you can imagine, however, many breaches will involve the trustee's having wrongfully sold the trust property to a bona fide purchaser (**2.35** et seq), and so it may be unlikely he can restore the trust *in specie*. In the cases of fungible property, such as shares, the trustee will most likely be unable to get back the very shares he wrongfully transferred, but he can go into the market and purchase a like number of the same shares, and if he does this he is regarded as restoring the trust *in specie*. Where the trustee cannot restore the trust *in specie*, he must restore the trust in money, obviously to the value of the misapplied trust property.

11.19 The beneficiary need not falsify the account if the trustee enters into a *profitable* unauthorised transaction; Millett LJ again:

> If the unauthorised investment has appreciated in value, then the beneficiary will be content with it. He is not obliged to falsify the account which the trustee renders; he can always accept it. (It goes without saying that the trustee cannot simply 'borrow' the trust money to make a profitable investment for his own account and then rely on the fact that the investment was unauthorised to avoid bringing the transaction into account.) Where the beneficiary accepts the unauthorised investment, he is often said to affirm or adopt the transaction. That is not wholly accurate. The beneficiary has a right to elect, but it is really a right to decide whether to complain or not.

11.20 The PC in *Tang Man Sit v Capacious Investments Ltd* (1996) reviewed the law governing a plaintiff's election of alternative remedies, and Lord Nicholls stated:

> The basic principle governing when a plaintiff must make his choice is simple and clear. He is required to choose when, but not before, judgment is given in his favour and the judge is asked to make orders against the

345

defendant. ... In the ordinary course, by the time the trial is concluded the plaintiff will know which remedy is more advantageous to him ... Occasionally, this may not be so ... A plaintiff may not know how much money the defendant has made from the wrongful use of his property. It may be unreasonable to require the plaintiff to make his choice without further information. To meet this difficulty, the court may make discovery and other orders designed to give the plaintiff the information he needs, and which in fairness he ought to have, before deciding upon his remedy.

11.21 The requirement of election is clearly to prevent the beneficiary from having it both ways – he cannot both 'adopt' the trustee's act which turns out to be profitable, and also claim damages for a loss on the footing that he wishes to disallow the transaction. Where he elects to falsify the account, the trustee must restore the trust to the position in which it would have been, but for the breach, at the time the court gives its judgment (*Re Bell's Indenture* (1980)).

11.22 Each beneficiary is entitled to individually elect whether to falsify the account or adopt the unauthorised transaction in respect of the loss or gain to his own interest under the trust. (In the case of minor beneficiaries, counsel for them or their representative in the action, called a 'guardian *ad litem*' or 'litigation friend', elects for them.) For example, where an unauthorised transaction benefits the life tenant but harms the capital beneficiary, the capital beneficiary can choose to falsify the account and make the trustee liable for the loss to the value of the capital interest (*Dimes v Scott* (1828), **11.33**). However, beneficiaries have no individual right to allow the trustee to *continue* keeping the property in a state which is in breach of trust, say in investments not allowed by the trust terms. The trustee's primary duty is to carry out the terms of the trust, and so when a breach comes to light, unless the beneficiaries are all *sui juris* and consent to the unauthorised investment, the trustee must 'realise' it, ie dispose of it and apply the money to an authorised investment. (*Wright v Morgan* (1926); *Re Jenkins and Randall & Co.'s Contract* (1903)). Otherwise, as Swinfen-Eady J pointed out in *Re Jenkins*, a trustee could never remedy a breach of trust by disposing of an unauthorised asset and replacing it with an authorised one unless he got the consent of all the beneficiaries, and he could never do that where any were minors, for minors cannot give valid consent. (See also **10.66** (variation of trusts) and **11.47-50** (beneficiary consent in advance to a breach of trust).

The personal liability of the trustee when the account is surcharged or falsified

11.23 Throughout this chapter, we will have to distinguish between a person's personal and proprietary liability. A person is personally liable for a wrong when he must pay money out of his own pocket to compensate for a loss. A person is proprietarily liable when the beneficiary can claim a property interest in something that party has; the most obvious case is that of a third party who receives trust property but is not a bona fide purchaser. The beneficiary can claim that property, because in the eyes of equity the property remains the beneficiary's. It is absolutely vital to see that where a trust is surcharged or falsified, the trustee's liability is *personal*. It can be nothing else where the account is surcharged, because the trustee can have no property in his hands that the beneficiaries can claim as their own if the loss does not involve a misapplication of trust property. One typically surcharges the account where the trustee *failed* to do something, like invest the trust funds with care, or insure the trust property, and this failure causes loss. The only way the trustee can make up the loss is by digging into his own funds; he thus has a *personal* obligation to pay some of his own money. But the same kind of liability arises when the account is falsified. The particular transfer of trust property is falsified, and the trustee has either a personal obligation to pay money or by some other means to get the trust property back in order to restore the trust *in specie*, or a personal obligation to pay money out of his own pocket to restore the value of the misapplied property. So in no case does surcharging or falsifying the account give rise to any proprietary liability against anyone. It is only when the beneficiary 'adopts' the trustee's misapplication of the trust property in some form or other that any proprietary liability arises, as we shall see.

'Equitable compensation'

11.24 Unfortunately, a confusing terminology has grown up to describe the case where equity makes someone personally liable to compensate someone for a loss. In cases of surcharging or falsifying the account, traditionally it was simply said that a trustee's personal liability was his 'liability to account'. However, sometimes the trustee would not have to pay money directly into the trust funds (often, following a breach, this would mean his having to pay money to a new trustee who replaced him, for trustees who misapply trust property or are negligent with the trust funds are often replaced). In certain cases, the trustee would have to pay money directly to the beneficiaries, as there was no point in reconstituting the trust fund itself. An example, which you will recall from **9.47**, is the case of the bare trust with mandate under which a solicitor holds funds prior to the completion of a purchase of land. Imagine such a solicitor pays those funds away in breach of trust. The beneficiary, the would-be purchaser whose money has not gone to buy the land as he intended, will obviously falsify the account. The solicitor will be liable to dig into his own pocket to replace the money paid away, but there is usually no point in his paying money back into his client trust account for the beneficiary, for at this stage the land purchase transaction will probably be irredeemably compromised by the solicitor's breach, and the beneficiary would be unlikely to want this solicitor to complete the land purchase in any event. The beneficiary will simply want the return of the funds to him directly. A similar sort of case would arise where the trustee, before misapplying the property, ought to have paid the entirety of the trust funds to the beneficiaries, if for example, where the trust was for A for life and then to B absolutely, and A has died. The trustee would then hold the funds for B absolutely. Again, then, there is no point in the trustee's reconstituting the trust with a money payment; rather, he should pay B directly. In cases where a trustee pays his beneficiaries directly to make up for his default, he has been said to make 'equitable compensation' to the beneficiaries. The idea is that the beneficiaries are compensated directly for the loss of their interest under the trust. Similarly, in certain cases a fiduciary who has breached his fiduciary obligations will be liable directly to his principal for causing him loss (**12.92–12.95**). An example would be where a solicitor, in conflict of interest, advises his client to make an investment that falls in value. The solicitor will be made to compensate his client directly, and again, this is called equitable compensation. Nevertheless, whether a trustee or fiduciary must pay his beneficiary or principal directly, or a trustee is personally liable to restore a trust fund, in all cases we are looking at equity's imposition of a personal liability to compensate for a loss. Therefore, the modern trend in terminology is to call all cases where equity imposes such a liability as 'equitable compensation', as Millett LJ does in the next paragraph. You, however, should not worry overmuch about applying this terminology. What you need to grasp is those circumstances in which equity imposes a personal liability to compensate, and the rules that apply in those circumstances. No trust examiner should pick nits with you about whether you call a trustee's personal liability to restore a trust 'his liability to account' or his 'duty to make equitable compensation', but your author felt obliged to mention all of this to you, largely so that you can better make sense of academic and judicial writings which may bandy around the term 'equitable compensation' without telling you that it means different things to different people.

The measure of liability in cases where the account is surcharged

11.25   In *Bristol and West Building Society v Mothew* (1998), Millett LJ said:

> Equitable compensation for breach of the duty of skill and care resembles common law damages in that it is awarded by way of compensation to the plaintiff for his loss. There is no reason in principle why the common law rules of causation, remoteness of damage and measure of damages should not be applied by analogy in such a case. *It should not be confused with equitable compensation for breach of fiduciary duty which may be awarded in lieu of rescission* [ie instead of a contract being set aside for self dealing **(12.59** et seq)] *or specific restitution [ie instead of an order to return specific property taken from the trust, where for example, the property is no longer in existence.]* (my italics)

Note the italicised portion of this quotation. In the case of a trustee's negligence, in principle he should be liable for the loss due to his negligence, in exactly the same way any person committing the tort of negligence is liable for money 'damages' to his victim. There is no reason why any special 'equitable' rules of causation ought to apply, for the wrong is the same as the tort of negligence at common law. Negligence is negligence. But, as we shall see (**11.27** et seq), some very particular (and in certain cases, arguably unjust) rules of causation, ie the rules which establish whether a particular loss should be attributed to the defendant's breach of duty, apply when the court determines a person's liability to restore the trust in cases of falsifying the account, and Millett LJ is rightly warning not to confuse the two situations.

11.26   Where an investment loss is caused by the trustee's negligence, the problem is to determine what the trust property would have been worth if it had not been for his negligence. In *Nestlé* (**10.19**), the plaintiff beneficiary failed to prove that the trust company's negligent misunderstanding of the trust instrument caused any loss; had she done so, however, Dillon LJ said *obiter* that the trustee would have to pay 'fair' compensation, ie an amount sufficient to restore the trust fund to a value it would have achieved if a proper investment policy had been followed, 'not just the minimum that might just have got by without challenge'.

The measure of liability where the account is falsified

11.27 Where trust money is misapplied in breach of trust, in principle the calculation of loss is easy, for the loss is simply the value of the trust property misapplied. If the trustee cannot restore the actual trust property *in specie*, what he must pay is simply the value of that property plus interest. The issue becomes complicated, however, where a breach of trust happened sometime before the beneficiaries realised a breach had occurred and took action against the trustees.

11.28 Here the rules of causation appear to make the trustee liable for all risks that attend the ownership of the property involved in the unauthorised transaction. In *Clough v Bond* (1838) Cottenham LC put it this way:

> It will be found to be the result of all the best authorities on the subject, that, although a [trustee], acting strictly within the line of his duty, and exercising reasonable care and diligence, will not be responsible for the failure or depreciation of the fund... yet if that line of duty not be strictly pursued, and any part of the property be invested by such [trustee] in funds or upon securities not authorised, or be put within the control of persons who ought not to be instructed with it, and loss be thereby eventually sustained, such personal representative will be liable to make it good, however unexpected the result, however little likely to arise from the course adopted, and however free such conduct may have been from any improper motive.

11.29 So, for example, if, in breach of trust, the trustee spends trust money on a painting, the beneficiaries can elect either to falsify the account or adopt the purchase of the painting. If the painting is stolen, then obviously they will falsify the account and demand that the trustee restore the money wrongfully spent on the painting. This makes perfect sense, for the trustee created the risk of the theft by purchasing a chattel that could be stolen.

11.30 But consider a case where the trustee sells one of a trust's collection of paintings, and shortly thereafter all of the trust's paintings are stolen through no fault of the trustee's. The loss of all these paintings will be a loss to the trust, but the trustee will not be liable for the loss occurred through no fault of his. (Normally, of course, in a case like this the paintings would be insured against theft, but ignore that for the moment). The beneficiaries now discover the breach. Now if the trustee has made a *good* bargain on the sale of the painting, they will of course adopt the transaction and require the trustee to hold the proceeds of the sale as trust money. But what if the trustee made a bad bargain, or the painting has risen in value, so that the present value of the painting is, say, £100,000, while the proceeds were only £50,000? The beneficiaries will falsify the account, impugning the trustee's sale of the trust painting, and demanding he restore its full value to the trust. (In 'accounting' terms, the £50,000 proceeds of sale will be treated as the trustee's own, and he will be required to pay £100,000 as the value of the painting; In practical terms, then, the trustee will have to add £50,000 in new money in addition to the £50,000 proceeds of the sale which he accounted for to the trust at the time of sale.) But notice that this falsification claim states, in theoretical or accounting terms, that the trustee never sold the painting; the beneficiaries 'falsify' the sale of the painting. So why, then, cannot the trustee, using the rules of causation which would normally apply at common law, argue that he need pay nothing in compensation, for had he left the painting in the trust, it would have been stolen with all the others? In other words, if the beneficiaries choose to falsify the sale, must they then not accept all the logical consequences of that? In short, why should not the trustee argue that the trust lost nothing because of his breach; indeed the trust is £50,000 better off than it would have been, because the trust at least has the proceeds of the sale? Unfortunately, the cases do not all speak with one voice, but it is unlikely that this argument will be accepted. When the beneficiaries falsify the account, the court will regard the trustee as having the painting in his possession, which he must either restore *in specie* or pay the full value of; subsequent events like the theft will not be taken into account to reduce his liability.

11.31   It is this sort of reasoning which gives rise to the general view that the principles for causation of loss in equity differ from those which apply in tort or contract cases at common law. But it is important to remember that these principles relate specifically to the risks and subsequent events concerning what happens to property and its value for the purpose of determining its 'replacement cost', ie the amount of money a trustee must pay to restore the trust when it is falsified. That is why Lord Millett points out that these special equitable principles are not relevant in the same way to cases of surcharging the account, for these cases do not involve the misapplication of trust property and the risks that flow from it.

11.32 The 19th century cases waver about what ought to be done where a trustee, instead of investing the trust property as he should, wrongly transfers the property to a third party on the terms of a loan, or holds onto property instead of investing it. In *Watts v Girdlestone* (1843) the trustees leant the money to a beneficiary instead of properly investing it in real property or government stock. The court held that they were liable to restore the trust as if they had invested the property in the most favourable investment they could have made. They therefore had to pay the difference between what they received back on the loan from the beneficiary and what they would have earned investing in government stock. By contrast, in *Shepard v Mouls* (1845), the trustees wrongfully allowed one trustee to personally take the trust funds on payment of interest. Some of the beneficiaries complained, and argued, as in *Watts*, that the trustees should be charged with the difference between the interest they were paid and what they would have earned if they had made the most favourable investment they were authorised to make. Here, however, the court decided against the beneficiaries, arguing that the trustees, having a discretion in how they might invest the funds, could not be charged with the returns they would have earned on any particular investment. One can see how allowing beneficiaries to charge the trustees in this way might be unfair in certain circumstances. It would not be fair to trustees who were allowed to invest in shares, but did not, to allow the beneficiaries to say, with the full benefit of hindsight, that they should have invested in shares of some company that had done spectacularly well in the meantime. On the other hand, however, it is a principle of the law that a wrongdoer should not benefit from uncertainties, whether of evidence or causation, ie of what might have been, which are due to his own wrong-doing (see, eg, *Armory v Delamirie* (1722), **11.103**). Today, it is most likely that the courts would follow the approach stated by Dillon LJ in *Nestle* (11.26); the courts should try fairly to assess what the trustees might reasonably have earned by properly investing.

11.33 A different issue arose in *Dimes v Scott* (1828). The trustees, in breach of trust, held onto an unauthorised investment in an East India

Company bond for 10 years, which paid 10% interest per annum on its face value, whereas they should have invested the money in 3% Consols, government securities which paid 3% interest per annum on their face value. At the end of the ten year period the trustees did what they ought to have done in the first place, and sold the East India bond and purchased 3% Consols. The trust was for a life tenant, who received the interest on the trust investments, and one remainderman, who had the interest in the capital (**3.19**). The remainderman falsified the account, for at first glance it seemed obvious that the life tenant had benefited from the breach at the remainderman's expense, receiving a rate of 10% interest on the unauthorised investment, whereas if the trust had been properly carried out, she would have received only 3% interest on the authorised investment, and normally this would have indicated that the East India bond was a poorer capital investment. The claim against the trustees, therefore, was that they should be liable to restore what the trustees had wrongly paid out to the life tenant, ie the difference between what she was actually paid in interest on the East India bond and what she would have received from the 3% Consols. However, as it turned out, when the trustees actually converted the East India bond into Consols, albeit ten years late, the price of Consols was much lower than it was ten years earlier, and so they were able to buy more Consols with the same amount of money. Thus the unauthorised investment turned out to be good for all concerned: the life tenant benefited for 10 years from the higher rate of interest payments, and the remainderman ended up with more Consols as the capital of the trust than he would have done if the trustees had converted the investment when they ought to have done. Nevertheless, when this was discovered, the remainderman maintained his claim. He argued that the trustees should still be liable for the over-payments to the life tenant (had the investment been properly converted 10 years earlier the life tenant would have received about £1000 less), and should not be able to take any credit for the 'accidental' increase in value of the capital fund owing to their mistake. The trustees argued, quite reasonably, that the remainderman could not have it both ways; he should not both 'adopt' the failure to convert in order to get the benefit of the mistake in terms of the increased capital value while at the same time falsify the account to recoup the overpayment to the life tenant. The Lord Chancellor Lord Lyndhurst decided in favour of the remainderman, and the trustees were required to pay into the trust the £1000 the life tenant was 'overpaid'. This case is generally regarded as harsh, and points out how the equitable rules of causation for loss arguably do not properly take into account the actual facts, or indeed, the logic of the beneficiaries' electing to falsify or adopt an unauthorised transaction.

11.34 It is perhaps fair to say that the 19th century authorities do not provide a consistent guide (see Mowbray et all (2000), 39-03, 39-27, 39-28), and may not be followed today. This should be borne in mind as we turn to the recent decision of the HL reviewing the principles of liability to restore the trust.

11.35 In *Target Holdings Ltd v Redferns* (1996), a solicitor of the firm Redferns acted both for Target Holdings, a mortgage lender, and Crowngate, a prospective purchaser of land (a standard bare trust with mandate (**9.47**)). Unbeknownst to Target, Crowngate was the final purchaser in a fraudulent land transfer scheme calculated to make the land appear much more valuable than it actually was: land purchased for £775,000 by one intermediary company was to be sold to another intermediary for £1.25m, which would then be sold to Crowngate for £2m. The solicitor was apparently fully aware of this series of transactions. Target agreed to lend Crowngate £1.5m for the final purchase in return for a mortgage over the land. Target transferred the loan money to Redferns in advance of completion on instruction to pay the money to Crowngate for the purchase in return for an execution of a charge over the land in Target's favour. In breach of this instruction, the solicitor transferred the money to the two intermediary companies in furtherance of the series of purchases. However, the final sale to Crowngate was eventually completed and the charge in Target's favour secured. Crowngate became insolvent, and as mortgagee Target sold the land; it fetched only £500,000. Target sued Redferns for breach of trust for paying away the loan money in breach of its instructions. In the CA, Target successfully won summary judgment against Redferns for the entire £1.5m paid away less the £500,000 realised on the sale, even though, despite the breach, Target was in the same position it would have been in had the money been paid according to its instructions, since Target did receive a charge on the correct land for their loan advance of £1.5m. The reasoning advanced by the CA was that, having paid away the £1.5m in breach of trust, there was then an immediate loss to the trust of that amount, which Redferns became immediately liable, and remained liable, to make good.

11.36 The HL reversed the decision of the CA. Lord Browne-Wilkinson, with whose opinion all their Lordships agreed, stated that both at common law and in equity the principles of compensation for loss are fundamentally the same – a plaintiff may only recover for a loss caused by a defendant's wrongful act, and the compensation is calculated to put the plaintiff in the position he would have been in but for the defendant's wrong. However, he further stated that the rules governing causation of loss and remoteness of damage differ between the common law claim for damages and a claim for equitable compensation.

> Even if the immediate cause of the loss is the dishonesty or failure of a third party, the trustee is liable to make good that loss to the trust estate if, but for the breach, such loss would not have occurred ... Thus the common law rules of remoteness of damage and causation do not apply. However there does have to be some causal connection between the breach of trust and the loss to the trust estate for which compensation is recoverable, viz the fact that the loss would not have occurred but for the breach ... Equitable compensation for breach of trust is designed to achieve exactly what the word compensation suggests: to make good a loss in fact suffered by the beneficiaries and which, using hindsight and common sense, can be seen to have been caused by the breach.

11.37 On these principles, Target obtained exactly what it would have obtained had there been no breach of trust, and so was entitled to no compensation. Target was, of course, entitled to pursue its claim that the solicitor had fraudulently procured the transaction by failing to inform Target of the deceitful series of sales; if that claim were successful Target would be able to claim the full value of the money paid away minus the money it received in the sale of the property, because, but for *that* wrong, ie the fraud, it would never have entered into the transaction at all. The HL restored the original order of the first instance judge that gave Redferns leave to defend against this claim only on the payment of £1m into court.

11.38 The decision can be criticised. In the first place, the court assumed that the rules of compensation for 'equitable compensation' generally applied in all cases where equity holds a defendant personally liable to compensate someone for a loss. But while this might be the right approach at a high level of generality, the court did not discuss in any detail the 19th century cases (**11.27-34**) which give rise to the various principles of causation that apply where trust property is misapplied. Furthermore, the court seems to have misunderstood the nature of restoration for misapplication of trust property, as Millett LJ speaking extra-judicially points out:

The solicitor held the plaintiff's money in trust for the plaintiff but with its authority to lay it out in exchange for an executed mortgage and the documents of title. He paid it away without obtaining these documents. This was an unauthorised application of trust money which entitled the plaintiff to falsify the account. The disbursement must be disallowed and the solicitor treated as accountable as if the money were still in his client account and available to be laid out in the manner directed. It was later so laid out. The plaintiff cannot object to the acquisition of the mortgage or the disbursement by which it was obtained; it was an authorised application of what must be treated as trust money. To put the point another way; the trustee's obligation to restore the trust property is not an obligation to restore it in the very form in which he disbursed it, but an obligation to restore it in any form authorised by the trust.

11.39 On Millett LJ's view, then, there was no loss not because the rules of causation indicated there was none, but because the misapplication was fully corrected when the trust was properly restored according to its terms, and this seems right. Given these criticisms, the HL's remarks on causation for loss must be treated with some care.

Setting an unauthorised gain against an unauthorised loss

11.40 What should happen where a trustee enters into two different unauthorised transactions, one of which causes a loss, but the other creates a gain for the trust. Can the beneficiary falsify only the loss-causing transaction, and adopt the successful one? In general, the answer is yes, if the transactions are distinct. (*Wiles v Gresham* (1854); *Dimes v Scott* (1828)). This seems right, for the trustee should not be exonerated of particular breaches because he can say, 'overall, the trust is in good shape'. However, where the losing and gaining unauthorised transactions form part of one composite transaction, the transactions must be falsified together or not at all (*Fletcher v Green* (1864)). For example, in *Bartlett* (**10.16**), the court held that the disastrous investment in one property development project was part of a larger investment policy favouring land development. In taking the account, then, this decision required the beneficiary to 'falsify' both the winning and losing projects as one invalid investment, with a resulting reduction in the amount of compensation. (Note: 'falsify' here is placed in quotation marks, as *Bartlett* was not a falsification case. Recall the facts in Bartlett. The trustee was liable for not preventing the company whose shares the trust held from embarking on property developments. Thus the case was one of negligence, and the beneficiaries surcharged the account. But the principles of causation for loss in falsification cases were relevant because the transactions the company entered into were essentially ones which, had the company been the trustee, would have been misapplications of trust property, and so it was appropriate to think in terms of falsification when assessing the loss to the trust.)

A personal claim where the account is not falsified

11.41 Where the beneficiaries choose not to falsify the account, the trustee must, of course, treat the property he holds as a result of the unauthorised transaction as trust property, and account for it to the trust. But as Millett points out above (**11.19**), a trustee cannot 'borrow' the trust funds but treat the profits he derives from the trust money as his own. If the trustee uses trust money in his own business, it will usually, however, be impossible to trace the money into any particular property the trustee holds which the beneficiaries could adopt as trust assets. Rather, the beneficiaries will usually be in the position of having to elect whether or not to adopt the trustee's 'loan' of the trust funds. If they do so, they then have a further choice: they can elect either for an accounting of the trustee's business profits which are attributable to the use of the beneficiaries' money, or for compound interest on the 'loan' (*Docker v Soames* (1834); *Westdeutsche Landesbank Girozentrale v Islington LBC* (1996)). Of course the beneficiaries will falsify the account if the authorised transaction the trustee ought to have made would have been more profitable than his business profits or compound interest.

Confusions between cases of negligence, misapplication of trust property, and breach of fiduciary obligation

11.42 There is no point in developing a precise terminology which distinguishes one kind of wrong from another if you fail to take advantage of it. When you are looking at a case where a trustee commits a wrong, you must *always* ask yourself whether the wrong is (1) negligence or a failure to act in some way, for which a beneficiary may surcharge the account; (2) a misapplication of trust property, for which the account can be falsified; or (3) a breach of fiduciary obligation. It is a failure of analysis simply to say the trustee committed a 'breach of trust' as if this term were precise enough to explain either what went wrong or what remedy is appropriate. Two cases where a precise analysis was necessary will show the importance of this.

11.43 *Bristol and West Building Society v Mothew* (1998) concerned a claim by a building society against a solicitor who had acted both for it and the borrower, holding the funds on trust prior to completion of the purchase of land, a bare trust with mandate (**9.47**). The solicitor negligently failed to include facts pertinent to assessing the creditworthiness of the borrower in filling out a standard form report to the society prior to the release of the mortgage loan. Though he had been aware of the facts, he had forgotten or overlooked them when making the report. The lender claimed that the solicitor both breached the trust and breached his fiduciary obligation. Millett LJ, writing the opinion of the CA, carefully considered the nature of the solicitor's wrong, disapproving the indiscriminate use of the labels 'breach of trust' and 'breach of fiduciary obligation', in particular the latter. He held that while the solicitor's paying out the money for the purchase was certainly a payment of *trust* money (it was clearly held by him on trust), his action in paying it was not a misapplication of trust money, for the solicitor was at that time complying with his standing instructions as to how the trust money should be applied. Neither was there a breach of fiduciary duty for there was no breach of loyalty or good faith, for the solicitor was not acting in conflict of interest in paying the money away. Rather, the solicitor was guilty of negligence in failing to take care in the preparation of the report, which probably also constituted a breach of his contract with the lender.

11.44 The recent decision of the Australian High Court (the supreme appellate court in Australia) in *Alexander v Perpetual Trustees WA Ltd* (2004) shows, in contrast, a disappointing failure of analysis. In this case a solicitor acted under a bare trust with mandate (**9.47**) to use the beneficiary's funds to make a certain kind of investment. The solicitor trustee paid the money to purchase the investments, but failed to acquire certain documents which provided security for the investments. At the same time, the beneficiary was also careless in failing to take notice of the fact that these security documents were never acquired, and continued to invest more sums regardless. As a result, all the money invested was lost. The main issue was whether a *beneficiary* could be partly liable for a breach of trust. (Note, the issue is not about whether a beneficiary can consent to a breach of trust (**11.47**); consent to an act is not the same thing as committing that act oneself). Now, if the case is one where the trust property is misapplied, then it would seem impossible for a beneficiary to be liable, for only a trustee can commit the acts, eg transfer the property and so on, which misapply the trust property. As we have already briefly discussed, (**11.9, 11.12**), agents of the trustee like his banker or his solicitor can participate in a misapplication of trust property, and if they do so dishonestly they will be liable for the loss. But a beneficiary does not usually act as an agent of the trustee, and did not in this case; it was the trustee alone who carried out all the steps in the transactions with the trust money. On the other hand, a negligent breach of trust is a very different case. Consider the case of a bare trust with mandate, as in *Motthew*. In these kinds of trust the trustee basically follows the directions of the beneficiary, and one can easily imagine a situation where both the lender and the solicitor carelessly contributed to the application of the trust property causing loss, say where the lender and the solicitor both carelessly failed to appreciate some facts showing the mortgagor/borrower's credit unworthiness. There would appear to be nothing in principle which would prevent the negligent solicitor from claiming that the lender was contributorily negligent, and should shoulder part of the loss. In *Alexander* itself, the trial judge said that if the case turned on negligence, the solicitor trustee was 60% liable, the beneficiary investor 40% liable, for the resulting loss. Unfortunately, none of the judges of the High Court specified what kind of breach of trust took place, that is whether the solicitor misapplied the trust funds in purchasing the investments without obtaining the security documents, for which the account could be falsified and the solicitor made strictly liable to restore all the funds paid away, or whether the money was properly paid under the mandate for the investments, but done negligently in the sense that the documents of security were never obtained. As Millett LJ made clear in *Motthew*, this is the crucial issue, for there is all the difference in the world between a trustee who carries out the trust terms by applying the money according to his mandate, but whose negligence gives rise to loss, and one who misapplies the money in breach of his mandate. What the court failed to analyse was whether the solicitor's purchase of the investment without acquiring the security documents was a misapplication of the trust money, akin to a solicitor's paying away a mortgage lender's money on completion of a house purchase without obtaining a charge on the property (the mortgage lender's mandate is to use its money to 'buy' a charge over the property), or whether the purchase of the investments was a perfectly proper application of the money according to the mandate, the failure to get the security documents being a collateral matter owing to the solicitor's, and, as the trial judge found, the beneficiary's, negligence. Having failed to analyse the facts and explicitly render a finding on this, it is no surprise that the High Court split 3:3.

Liability of trustees *inter se*

11.45 The general equitable rule is that individual trustees are only liable for their own breaches of trust, not for the breaches committed by their co-trustees. However, equity does not recognise a 'sleeping' or 'passive' trustee, ie a trustee who does not fully participate in the administration of a trust. As Cotton LJ stated in *Bahin v Hughes* (1886):

> [I]t would be laying down a wrong rule that where one trustee acts honestly, though erroneously, the other trustee is to be held entitled to an indemnity who by doing nothing neglects his duty more than the acting trustee.

On this basis a trustee would be liable for breaches of their co-trustees to the extent that they were negligent or fell below the standard of prudence in monitoring their co-trustees' behaviour.

11.46 Where two or more trustees are each liable for a breach of trust, they are 'jointly and severally' liable (**11.12**). Between themselves trustees may rely upon the Civil Liability (Contribution) Act 1978, which gives the court a discretion to apportion the share of liability each defendant trustee will bear, according to their relative individual responsibilities for the loss. In certain cases a trustee, though himself liable for breach of trust, may demand that his co-trustee indemnify him for any compensation he must pay – the effect of this, where that co-trustee is solvent, is to make him alone pay for the loss. Two such circumstances were stated in *Bahin v Hughes*. The first is:

> [W]here one trustee has got the money into his own hands, and made use of it, he will be liable to his co-trustee to give him an indemnity.

Second, a trustee may claim an indemnity against a co-trustee who is a solicitor if, but only if, that solicitor-trustee exercised a controlling influence over the conduct of a trust (*Head v Gould* (1898)). A third circumstance occurs when a breaching co-trustee is also a beneficiary under the trust, special considerations apply because of this dual status (**11.50**).

Beneficiaries' consent to a breach of trust

11.47 An adult beneficiary who freely consents to, or participates in, a breach of trust, may not sue the trustee to make good any loss caused by the breach. In *Re Pauling's Settlement Trusts* (1961) the trustee of a family settlement succumbed to the pressure of one beneficiary, the father, to make 'advancements' to his children, which in reality were not advancements at all: the money was not intended to benefit the individual children, but to defray the family's extravagant living expenses, including the cost of purchasing family homes. The children, though of full age, were not taken to have consented because, though they were aware of the true purposes of the advancements, the court held that their approval was procured by the undue influence of their father. The fact that several children received benefits to themselves from the advancements did not bar them from claiming against the trustee for breach of trust, though they did have to offset these benefits against their claim for compensation.

11.48 To truly consent a beneficiary must be fully aware of the facts, though not necessarily of his legal rights. Wilberforce J described the court's general approach in *Re Pauling's Settlement Trusts*:

> [T]he court has to consider all the circumstances ... with a view to seeing whether it is fair and equitable that, having given his concurrence, he should afterwards turn round and sue the trustees ... it is not necessary that he should know that what he is concurring in is a breach of trust, provided that he fully understands what he is concurring in, and that it is not necessary that he should himself have directly benefited by the breach of trust.

These principles were adopted in *Holder v Holder* (1968). The plaintiff sued to set aside the purchase of trust property by his brother who had technically acquired the status of an executor, for breach of the 'self-dealing' rule (**12.59** et seq); the plaintiff was held to have acquiesced in the sale though unaware at the time of the legal position. He had subsequently received part of the purchase price as a beneficiary under the will, and throughout had full knowledge of all the facts concerning the sale. Besides considering these facts which go to determining actual consent, in *Holder* the 'fair and equitable' requirement for allowing the beneficiary now to 'turn round and sue' was applied. Although it was clear that the plaintiff did not know his legal rights to block or set aside the sale until afterwards, the court felt that his conduct throughout, which appeared to be motivated largely by animosity towards his brother, and the fact that in failing to discover the brother's technical breach, he and his brother stood on an equal footing as both were legally advised, made it inequitable for him now to have the sale set aside.

11.49   The court has an inherent power to 'impound' the beneficial interest of a beneficiary who has requested, instigated, or consented to a breach of trust. By 'impoundment' is meant that the beneficiary's interest will be applied, to the full extent of the interest, to compensating the trust for the loss incurred by the breach. The result of this is that a beneficiary whose interest is impounded is not only prevented from suing the trustee for the breach, but is, in effect, made to indemnify the trustee for the latter's participation in it. It seems from *Chillingworth v Chambers* (1896) that where the beneficiary merely consents to a breach initiated by the trustee, ie in circumstances where the beneficiary has not instigated or requested the breach, his interest may only be impounded if he had consented in order to benefit from the breach himself. Section 62 of the Trustee Act 1925 now supplements the inherent jurisdiction, allowing the court to impound a beneficiary's interest if he consented to a breach irrespective of any benefit to himself, so long as his consent is made in writing.

11.50   Where the beneficiary is also a trustee, two rules come into operation. Normally a trustee may claim a contribution from his co-trustees for a share of the compensation to be paid (**11.46**). In the case of a beneficiary-trustee, the rule in *Chillingworth v Chambers* applies: where a beneficiary-trustee and his co-trustee are liable for a breach of trust from which the beneficiary-trustee alone has benefited, then the beneficiary-trustee's beneficial interest is impounded to its full extent, and only if his interest is insufficient to cover the loss will he be able to claim contribution from his co-trustee. Under the rule in *Re Dacre* (1916), whether his interest is impounded or not, the trustee-beneficiary is not entitled to receive any part of his beneficial interest until his breach *qua* trustee is remedied, nor is any assignee of his equitable interest.

Trustees' relief from liability under s 61 Trustee Act 1925, trustee exemption clauses, and ouster of trustee duties

11.51 Lord Cottenham LC once said that a person who accepted the office of trustee a second time was fit only for a lunatic asylum (Stebbings (2002), 26). This reflected the common 19th century view that the office of trustee, which was at the time only rarely remunerated, was a burdensome and thankless task, and that the liability of trustees for breach of trust could seem very onerous, given the altruistic character of the office. It was at this time that legislative attempts were first made to empower the court to limit a trustee's liability in cases of breach. A second way to address the problem was for the settlor to include a clause in the trust instrument limiting a trustee's liability for breach of trust. Take note: these limitations on liability, whether statutory or in the trust instrument, do not authorise or validate breaches of trust – to the extent that a trustee can remedy a breach, say by restoring a misapplication of trust property *in specie*, he must do so. What these limitations on liability do is remove or reduce a trustee's liability to pay out of his pocket to compensate the trust for a loss. Finally, a settlor might exclude certain duties in the trust instrument that might be inclined to give rise to liability.

Trustee Act 1925, s 61

11.52 Section 61 of the Trustee Act 1925 relieves trustees of liability for breach of trust in certain circumstances. It reads:

> If it appears to the court that a trustee, whether appointed by the court or otherwise, is or may be personally liable for any breach of trust ... but has acted honestly and reasonably, and ought fairly to be excused for the breach of trust and for omitting to obtain the directions of the court in the matter in which he committed such breach, then the court may relieve him either wholly or partly from personal liability for the same.

The court's exercise of the power is not governed by hard and fast rules. In *Re Pauling's Settlement Trusts* Upjohn LJ said:

> Section 61 is purely discretionary, and its application necessarily depends on the particular facts of each case.

11.53 Relief under s 61 was sought in three cases we have already considered. In *Re Pauling's Settlement Trusts* the sole trustee was a bank. Wilmer LJ opined that:

> Where a banker undertakes to act as a paid trustee of a settlement created by a customer, and so deliberately places itself in a position where its duty as trustee conflicts with its interest as a banker, we think that the court should be very slow to relieve a trustee under [s 61].

Relief was refused with respect to an advancement which benefited the bank because it was used to reduce the mother's overdraft with it. This suggests that any breach carried out by a trustee acting in clear conflict of interest, though not in terms dishonest, cannot be reasonable. With respect to another transaction the court held that the bank's relying upon the consent of the children, though over 21, when clearly it was obtained by their father's undue influence, was unreasonable, and so relief under s 61 was unavailable. The court did afford the bank relief in respect of one advancement where the bank-trustee's solicitors and the solicitor who separately advised the sons were largely at fault.

11.54 The trustees also sought relief under s 61 in *Bartlett* **(10.16)**. Brightman J tersely dismissed the plea, though covering each of the three criteria of the section:

> There is no doubt that the bank acted honestly. I do not think it acted reasonably. Nor do I think it would be fair to excuse the bank at the expense of the beneficiaries.

11.55 In *Re Mulligan* (1998) **(10.3)** a trust company and the testator's widow were trustees of a testamentary trust of which the widow was also the life tenant. They invested in fixed-interest securities which paid a high income to the widow but resulted in severe capital depreciation. Following the death of the widow the capital beneficiaries successfully sued the trust company and the widow's estate for the decline in the capital value arising from this breach of the even-handedness rule. Applying s 73 of the New Zealand Trustee Act 1956, which is in relevant respects identical to s 61, the court held that the trust company did not act reasonably because though it realised the danger of capital depreciation, it basically accepted the widow's insistence that they invest as she desired. Relief was also denied to the widow; a person of some business acumen, she could not claim that she did not appreciate the significance of the course of investment; furthermore, she failed as a trustee to exercise an independent judgment, clearly favouring her own interests above those of the other beneficiaries; she therefore did not act reasonably as a trustee.

11.56 The section was successfully pleaded in *Re Evans* (1999) by a lay administrator of her deceased father's estate, who distributed the property to herself in the reasonable belief that her brother, who she had not heard of in years, was dead; she took out a 'missing beneficiary' insurance policy, which when her brother later turned up, only partly compensated him for what he would have received. The court excused the daughter under s 61 from having to pay over the difference, except in the case of the deceased's house which she retained – her brother was entitled to his share in that.

Trustee exemption clauses

11.57 In *Armitage v Nurse* (1998) the CA held that an exemption clause in an instrument protecting the trustees from any loss or damage 'unless such loss or damage shall be caused by his own actual fraud' was valid. The effect of this is that trustees may be relieved of liability for any loss caused by their own negligence, even gross negligence. Millett LJ pointed out that such a clause does not purport to exclude, and does not exclude, a trustee's liability for breach of fiduciary duty. Thus it would not prevent a beneficiary setting aside a sale of trust property to a trustee, for that would not involve relieving a trustee for liability *for a loss*; neither, on such a view, would such a clause prevent a trustee from being stripped of an unauthorised profit, nor presumably, from liability for misapplications of trust property where the trustee acted in conflict of interest for in both those cases the trustee would be in breach of his fiduciary duty of loyalty.

11.58 Millett LJ accepted:

> ... that there is an irreducible core of obligations owed by the trustees to the beneficiaries and enforceable by them which is fundamental to the concept of a trust. If the beneficiaries have no rights enforceable against the trustees there are no trusts. But I do not accept the further submission that these core obligations include the duties of skill and care, prudence and diligence. The duty of trustees to perform the trusts honestly and in good faith for the benefit of the beneficiaries is the

minimum necessary to give substance to the trusts, but in my opinion it is sufficient ... [A] trustee who relied on the presence of a trustee exemption clause to justify what he proposed to do would thereby lose its protection: he would be acting recklessly in the proper sense of the term.

11.59 In his opinion, therefore, there was no basis in authority for saying that an exemption clause which relieved a trustee of liability for his gross negligence was 'repugnant' ie conceptually inconsistent with there being a trust. In his focus on conscious disloyalty Millett LJ went so far as to say that an exemption clause would relieve a trustee of liability even for a deliberate breach of trust if undertaken in the honest belief that it was for the best interests of the beneficiaries. This dictum was doubted by a subsequent CA in *Walker v Stones* (2001), who held that a solicitor–trustee could not rely upon an exemption clause where his 'perception of the interests of the beneficiaries was so unreasonable that no reasonable solicitor-trustee could have held such belief'.

11.60 Millett LJ examined the pleadings in the case and found that none clearly alleged dishonesty, but at most, negligence, and therefore the trustees were not liable. The trust arose as a variation of a previous trust under which both the plaintiff daughter and her mother were beneficiaries. Under the new trust, the plaintiff was the sole beneficiary. However, the trust largely consisted of a holding of farmland, and the trustees appointed a company controlled by her mother and grandmother to farm it, which also farmed the mother's own land. In essence the claim was that the trustees had managed the trust property with the interests of the family in mind, not the plaintiff, though the plaintiff was the only object of the trust. Millett LJ did not find in the pleadings sufficient particular allegations to sustain this charge, but allowed the plaintiff to re-amend her pleadings, adding:

> I express no view on whether there is material which would justify counsel in advising such a course; and I would not wish to encourage it. They will no doubt bear in mind that at the material time the trustees of the settlement consisted of one professional man and two distant relatives; and that a charge of fraud against independent professional trustees is, in the absence of some financial or other incentive, inherently implausible.

11.61 This narrow focus on fraud, however, seems to undercut Millett

LJ's previous point that such a clause would not relieve the trustee of any breach of fiduciary duty. Consider in particular the duty of even-handedness. In *Nestlé* (**10.19**) the CA did not consider the trustee to have breached this duty by tailoring its investments to benefit the current life tenants, because the court's appreciation of the duty gave the trustee a very wide discretion, but one can imagine another court taking a somewhat narrower view. The trustee did not, apparently, give much thought to its duty of even-handedness, as the investments favouring the life tenant seemed to have been made simply in response to the hectoring of one of the life tenants. In any case, the duty of even-handedness must be regarded as one of the core trustee fiduciary obligations for only by being even-handed between the beneficiaries does a trustee meet his obligation of good faith and loyalty to *all* the beneficiaries. Indeed, the duty of even-handedness is just a specification of the duty of loyalty and good faith where there is more than one beneficiary. Therefore, an exemption clause cannot relieve a trustee from his liability to a beneficiary for failing to be even-handed towards him. If the plaintiff's claims were made out, *Armitage* is clearly *a fortiori* to *Nestlé*, since the allegation was that the trustees were loyal to the interests of the plaintiff's mother, who was not a beneficiary at all.

11.62 Consider also *Re Pauling's Settlement Trusts*. There the trustee bank acted solely at the instigation of one beneficiary of the settlement, the father. It was apparently the forcefulness of his personality which largely led it to ignore the children's interests and make the advancements it did. In neither *Nestlé* or *Re Pauling's Settlement Trusts* did the professional trustees stand to gain significantly from the alleged breaches of trust; they did so in the absence of any 'financial incentive' and it is not clear what 'other incentive' they had beyond making their lives easier in the administration of the trust. (See also *Wilson v Turner*, **10.37**; *Re Mulligan*, **10.3**, **11.55**) So, although Millett LJ is right to suspect that any charge of actual fraud may be inherently implausible where the professional trustee gains no benefit by it, an allegation of a breach of the duty of even-handedness may be more plausible.

11.63 In *Armitage v Nurse* Millett LJ suggested that statutory reform of the general law on the valid scope of exemption clauses was appropriate. The Law Commission of England and Wales (2002; see also Scottish Law Commission (2003)) has taken up the suggestion, producing a consultation paper on the question. (See also Matthews (1989), for the suggestion that clauses should be capable of excluding a trustee's liability for negligence, but not gross negligence; Ontario Law Reform Commission (1984), arguing against the validity of exemption clauses generally in view of the court's power to relieve trustees of liability, as under s 61).

11.64 We can categorise the way in which trustees may breach their duties according to different criteria:

(1) According to the way in which the breach displays the fault of the trustee, for example, whether a breach is committed intentionally, dishonestly, or negligently;

(2) According to the particular sort of duty which is breached, in particular distinguishing breaches of trust duties, for example the duty to invest, the duty to keep the trust accounts, the duty to pay income as it arises in a timely fashion to the life tenant(s), etc, and breaches of fiduciary obligation, eg where a trustee invests the trust funds in conflict of interest or invests in a non-even-handed way.

11.65 As traditionally written, trustee exemption clauses seem clearly written to relieve trustees of liability according to the fault the breach displays, that is, according to the categorisation of breaches of trusts in (1). This seems to be the perspective Millett LJ takes in *Armitage,* and particularly in his characterisation of the 'irreducible core' of obligations without which a trust ceases to exist, ie an enforceable duty of loyalty and honesty. If this is correct, then an exemption clause can relieve a trustee of liability for any breach of trust, from not only failing to invest the trust property properly or failing to manage the trust property well, as in *Armitage*, to paying the trust property away to wrong beneficiaries, committing frauds on powers, to failing to maintain the trust accounts or failing to keep the property separate from his own or using the trust property for his own benefit, so long as the breach is not committed dishonestly.

11.66 With respect, it would seem that this perspective, whereby the usual envisaged breach is one of failing to manage the trust property well or invest it properly, loses much of its intuitive force when other sorts of breaches are envisaged. What if one examines the effect of trustee exemption clauses according to the type of breach as in (2). An initial distinction within this category could be between administrative and dispositive breaches. It would seem that the perspective in (1) most appropriately applies to administrative breaches, such as the breach of a duty to invest or manage the trust property, rather than to dispositive breaches, such as paying away the money to non-beneficiaries, or to committing frauds on powers. It is submitted that from this type-duty perspective, one might arrive at a different set of 'core obligations' in the absence of which a trust cannot be said truly to exist.

11.67 For example, it seems that if there is no enforceable duty to keep the trust accounts and to keep the trust property separate from the trustee's own, there cannot be a trust purely on equitable property principles, for the trust can only attach to specific property kept separate as a fund, where the various substitutions of one item of property for another from time to time in the fund are properly kept track of or accounted for. In other words, besides the core duties of loyalty and honestly, there are core duties to keep the trust property separate and keep the trust accounts which are just as much core duties in the absence of which there is simply no trust. A court might well not look favourably on an exemption clause employed to relieve trustees of liability for failure to keep the trust property separate from his own or for failure to keep the trust accounts. While at first glance it might be thought that such breaches would in every case reveal dishonesty or disloyalty as well, this is clearly not the case. Consider the case of a large corporate trustee whose property dealings and record keeping fall into disarray because of negligent management, eg the failure to properly train trust officers. It would not seem appropriate to allow an exemption clause to relieve the trustee of liability for this breach, for if the trust could not be restored by a proprietary claim against the trustee because, in the event, the property was untraceable, the entire value of the trust could be lost in such a way as to benefit the trustee or its creditors. The effect of a breach in such a case is, after all, essentially a taking of the beneficiaries' property by the trustee, and can be committed negligently. It would not seem at all just for an exemption clause in whatever terms to relieve the trustee of such a liability, for in such a case the relief from liability would not only save the trustee from having to restore the trust or to compensate the beneficiaries for their loss, but because of the nature of the breach would essentially sanction the trustee's inadvertent 'theft' (see Penner (2002)).

11.68 It might be contended that the trustee in such a case might be liable under two heads, firstly, to restore the trust or render equitable compensation to the beneficiaries, but secondly, under the law of restitution or unjust enrichment, to repay the value it acquired by its mixing of the trust property with its own so as to make it untraceable, in order to prevent its unjust enrichment at the beneficiaries' expense. If so, then whilst a trustee exemption clause could afford the trustee relief from the first liability to restore or compensate the trust, it might arguably be regarded as ineffective against the second, restitutionary, claim. However, it would be unwise to think that a court would rely upon what might appear a rather scholastic distinction in the way a case might be framed, and might rather seek to modify or embroider upon Millett's 'core obligation' thesis to find an exemption clause ineffective to discharge the trustee of such a liability, on the basis that keeping the trust accounts and the trust property separate from one's own is one of the 'core' duties of the trustee.

11.69 As to breaches of fiduciary obligations, since the breach of fiduciary obligations can be framed as a breach of one of the core obligations Millett LJ recognises, to act in good faith in the best interests of the beneficiaries, at first glance it might seem that no exemption clause can relieve a trustee of liability for breach of fiduciary obligation. The problem is simply that fiduciary breaches can be committed innocently, without negligence, and in good faith with the best interests of beneficiaries in mind. None of the defendants in *Nestle* or *Re Pauling's ST*, or *Re Mulligan* or *Armitage* were accused of acting in conscious bad faith (see also *Boardman v Phipps* (1967), **12.5** et seq). If the 'fault' test of (1) is applied, such non-fraudulent breaches would necessarily be relieved by any clause such as the one found in *Armitage*, and which Millett found valid. On the other hand, fiduciary obligations might well be regarded as 'core' trust obligations, and, thus once again, the decision in *Armitage* does not give certain guidance as to the effect of exemption clauses in these circumstances.

11.70 The Law Commission proposes that exemption clauses should not be effective to relieve professional trustees of liability, but should continue to operate in the case of lay trustees. They also propose that trustees should be indemnified from the trust fund for the cost of liability insurance. It is clear that the Commission prefers the fairness of the 'insurance solution' (each pay a little so that no one, because of a harm that befalls him, pays a lot (see further Ham (1995)) to a case by case development of the boundaries of 'core obligations' to embroider upon the law begun in *Armitage*.

The ouster of trustee duties

11.71   A settlor may, by a provision in the trust instrument, oust, ie remove, a duty that trustees would otherwise have under the general law of trusts (*Wilkins v Hogg* (1861) (duty to see to the application of money by co-trustee); *Hayim v Citibank* (1987) (duty to deal with a specific asset, a house lived in by the settlor's siblings, as a regular trust asset prior to their death)). For example, it is nowadays common for trustees to be relieved of the duty to monitor the affairs of a company in which the trust has a substantial shareholding, reversing the general rule described in *Bartlett* (1980) (**10.16**). Fiduciary obligations can also be ousted, and where a trust instrument puts someone in a situation of conflict of interest this will serve to authorise good faith exercises of discretions or powers even though taken in a situation of conflict (*Sergeant v National Westminster Bank* (1990); *Re Z Trust* (1997)).

11.72   There is a possible problem with the ouster of duties, or the use of similar 'power-extending' clauses, which permit what would otherwise be denied by a general trust duty, (eg a power 'to speculate freely with the trust assets as if the assets were entirely unneeded to provide for the beneficiaries in any way whatsoever such that the entire value of the fund might be lost with no adverse consequences to the beneficiaries whatsoever'). As Millett LJ made clear in *Armitage v Nurse* (**11.58**) a trust requires a minimum of duties owed by the trustee to the beneficiary and enforceable by them, otherwise there is no trust. If an ouster of a duty or duties is untoward or excessive, which can only be judged in the context of the particular trust, the 'trust' may not actually be valid as a trust, leading to the rather drastic result that either the 'trustee' is regarded as the beneficial owner of the property, or that the whole trust fails, as not being an effective disposition on trust.

11.73   The Law Commission (2002) in its consultation paper on trustee exemption clauses reasoned that the ouster of a particular duty does not *pro tanto* oust a general duty to take care, nor does the extension of a power, and neither would they *pro tanto* oust the fiduciary duties of loyalty to the beneficiaries. Thus, depending very much on the nature of the particular trust, such provisions in the trust instrument may not provide protection from a failure to fulfil the over-arching duties that is normally provided by an exemption clause. The Law Commission saw no sensible way of generally limiting the ability of trustees and settlors to oust duties and extend powers; whether an ouster or extension was judged to be effective could only be determined in the context of the particular trust, and the validity of such a provision could only be assessed in light of whether the actions of the trustee taking advantage of the provision was consistent with the purposes of the trust and reasonable in the circumstances. In consequence, the Law Commission proposed that the court should have the power to disapply such provisions where this was not the case. It is not clear whether such a statutory power is even needed, given the general background position of equity that powers may not be exercised for purposes for which they were not intended and that a minimum duty to the beneficiaries is a core requirement for a valid trust. It is unlikely that a court would treat a clause ousting entirely any duty to take care in the administration of a trust as an effective provision of a valid trust.

11.74 Take note: it must always be remembered that it is one thing to relieve a trustee of liability for the breach of a trust duty, and quite another to remove a duty altogether. Whatever the trustee's liability for breach, where there is a duty, a breach of it can be enjoined by a beneficiary taking the trustee to court, so that, for example, a dangerously risky investment can be prevented. Similarly, a co-trustee can make reference to such a duty in thwarting the injudicious proposals of his co-trustees. And where there is a duty, there can be an advertent or reckless breach of a duty, which an exemption clause can not protect against. Finally, whether there is exemption clause relief or not, a breach of trust may be grounds for removal of a trustee. By contrast, where a trustee is entirely relieved of a duty, there can be no breach of it, and so no possible liability for breach. Ouster and extension clauses should be regarded as bespoke provisions providing the right latitude for action for a trustee given the general purposes and features of the particular trust. They are not equivalent, much less ideal substitutes for, valid exemption clauses.

De facto trusteeship, or trusteeship de son tort

11.75 Where an individual who is not a trustee 'intermeddles' with the trust affairs, though innocently, he may become liable as a trustee for any misapplication of trust property or other loss caused to the trust (*Mara v Browne* (1896)); such a person is known as a trustee *de son tort* (a trustee 'by his own wrong'), although Lord Millett (*Dubai Aluminium v Salaam* (2003)) would put it otherwise:

> Substituting dog Latin for bastard French, we would be better to describe such persons today as *de facto* trustees. In their relations with the beneficiaries they are treated in every respect as if they had been duly appointed. They are true trustees and are fully subject to fiduciary obligations. Their liability is strict; it does not depend on dishonesty.

Such a person is typically, though not necessarily, an agent of the trust who takes it upon himself to exercise trustee functions over the property beyond the scope of his agency.

Liability for procuring or assisting in a breach of trust

Liability for procuring a breach of trust

11.76   In *Eaves v Hickson* (1861) the father of five children forged a marriage certificate in order to make it appear that his five children were legitimate, and presented the forged document to the trustee of the trust, who paid each of the children the shares of the estate to which they would be entitled had they been legitimate. Now, in a case such as this, where someone procures or induces the trustee to misapply the trust property, two principles regarding a trustee's liability come into conflict. The first is that a trustee is strictly liable for the misapplication of the trust property – the other beneficiaries should have the right to falsify the trust account and make the trustee personally liable to restore the property wrongfully paid away to these five children. The second principle, however, is that a trustee is not to be held liable for the loss or theft of the trust property through no fault of his own (*Morley v Morley* (1678)); he is not an insurer of the trust property (*Speight v Gaunt; Learoyd v Whiteley; Re Chapman* (**10.12(1)–10.14**)). Here the trustee was defrauded of the trust funds through no fault of his own. Normally, of course, if the trustee is defrauded of trust funds, the second principle alone will apply, for most frauds do not involve the misapplication of trust property. Consider the case of a trustee entitled under the terms of the trust to buy works of art, and who purchases a painting from an apparently reputable dealer. If this dealer sells the trustee a stolen painting, the trust will not receive good title to the painting, and the dealer will have defrauded the trustee of the purchase money. The trustee, not being at fault, will not be personally liable for this loss, because the purchase of the painting was not a misapplication of the trust money, for the trustee was entitled to invest in art. He was defrauded in the course of *properly* applying the trust funds. But in *Eaves,* the fraud induced a *misapplication* of the funds, for which the trustee would normally be strictly liable. In *Eaves,* the court gave weight to both principles in the form of its order: the illegitimate children were liable to repay what they received with interest; and to the extent they could not repay the whole, then their fraudster father must pay the balance; only to the extent that there was then any deficiency, would the trustee be liable.

Liability for assisting a breach of trust

11.77　The principles governing liability for assisting, or being an 'accessory' to, a breach of trust were reviewed by the PC in *Royal Brunei Airlines Sdn Bhd v Tan* (1995). Mr Tan was the principal shareholder and director of BLT, a company which was Royal Brunei Airlines' general travel agent in certain locations. Under the airline's agreement with BLT, the proceeds of ticket sales were to be held on trust for the airline. The proceeds, however, were never paid into a separate trust account, but into BLT's current account, and the money was used for BLT's general business purposes. The PC denied that an accessory could only be liable if the trustee was engaged in a dishonest or fraudulent design himself. That view derived from Lord Selborne LC's statement in *Barnes v Addy* (1874) that an accessory was not liable 'unless they assist with knowledge in a dishonest and fraudulent design on the part of the trustees'. The PC decided that the accessory's liability should turn on his own dishonest participation in the breach, whether the trustee committing the breach did so dishonestly or not.

11.78　What does 'dishonesty' mean? Lord Nicholls said that though honesty has a strong subjective element, the standard of liability was objective:

> Honesty is not an optional scale, with higher or lower values according to the moral standards of each individual ... Unless there is a very good

and compelling reason, an honest person does not participate in a transaction if he knows it involves a misapplication of trust assets to the detriment of beneficiaries. Nor does an honest person in such a case deliberately close his eyes and ears, or deliberately not ask questions, lest he learn something he would rather not know, and then proceed regardless. ...

Acting in reckless disregard of others' rights or possible rights can be a tell-tale sign of dishonesty. An honest person would have regard to the circumstances known to him, including the nature and importance of the proposed transaction, the nature and importance of his role, the ordinary course of business, the degree of doubt, the practicability of the trustee or the third party proceeding otherwise and the seriousness of the adverse consequences to the beneficiaries. The circumstances will dictate which one or more of the possible courses should be taken by an honest person. He might, for instance, flatly decline to become involved. He might ask further questions. He might seek advice, or insist on further advice being obtained. He might advise the trustee of the risks but then proceed with his role in the transaction. He might do many things. Ultimately, in most cases, an honest person should have little difficulty in knowing whether a proposed transaction, or his participation in it, would offend the normally accepted standards of honest conduct. Likewise, when called upon to decide whether a person was acting honestly, a court will look at all the circumstances known to the third party at the time. The court will also have regard to personal attributes of the third party such as his experience and intelligence, and the reason why he acted as he did.

11.79 The PC found Mr Tan liable. He had assisted in the breach of trust by 'causing or permitting' BLT to undertake the transactions in breach of trust in full knowledge that the moneys were to be held on trust, and that amounted to dishonest conduct. BLT was also dishonest, since Mr Tan's state of mind as its director was to be imputed to the company.

11.80 In *Bank of Credit and Commercial International (Overseas) Ltd v Akindele* (1999; affd 2001, CA) the defendant, a Nigerian businessman, was found not liable for dishonest assistance for entering into a share purchase agreement with BCCI (which was part of a scheme by which directors of BCCI defrauded it) simply because the agreement was in some respects unusual or artificial and he benefited from a high rate of interest on the transaction.

11.81 The *Royal Brunei* dishonesty standard was interpreted by the HL in *Twinsectra* (2002) (**7.28, 9.58**). Was a solicitor who had 'shut his eyes' to the transaction which gave rise to a vague *Quistclose* trust, liable for assisting the breach of that trust when, following the payment of the loan moneys into his solicitor's client account, he disbursed the money as his client demanded but in breach of the *Quistclose* trust purpose? Potter LJ, writing for a unanimous CA, overturned the trial judge. He found the solicitor liable and said:

> [I]n the case of a solicitor, the scope for variation in the applicable standard of honesty or necessity for inquiry is more narrowly confined than in the case of, say, a businessman less versed in the nuances of legal obligation and professional propriety.

11.82 The HL, by a 4:1 margin, reversed the CA, Lord Hutton giving the leading speech. Emphasising that it was unusual for a CA to reverse a trial judge in his finding of fact on an issue of a defendant's dishonesty, he proposed a 'combined' objective/subjective test of dishonesty: not only must the defendant have acted in a way which reasonable persons would regard as dishonest; he must himself have understood that to act in such a way was dishonest. While the trial judge accepted that the solicitor had 'shut his eyes' to the facts of the transaction, this did not, in the circumstances, amount to dishonesty on his part. In a vigorous dissent, Lord Millett argued that the test proposed by Lord Nicholls in *Royal Brunei* was an objective one, and that a finding by the trial judge that the solicitor had 'shut his eyes' to the pertinent facts ought to have been sufficient to make him dishonest for the purpose of accessory liability.

11.83 Third parties or agents to the trust are, however, not liable as accessories when they negligently, but not dishonestly, fail to discover that the transaction in which they participate is a breach of trust:

> [B]eneficiaries cannot reasonably expect that all the world dealing with their trustees should owe them a duty to take care lest the trustees are behaving dishonestly. (Lord Nicholls, *Royal Brunei*)

11.84 In *Agip (Africa) Ltd v Jackson* (1990; affd CA 1991) the test of 'dishonesty' was applied to a solicitor and an agent who managed companies set up entirely for the purpose of receiving moneys obtained by fraud and then passing them on to unknown others. The only purpose of the companies was to make it difficult to detect the fraud and to follow the money that had been fraudulently obtained. With respect to finding a third party dishonest, Millett J said:

> It is essentially a jury question. If a man does not draw the obvious inferences or make the obvious inquiries, the question is: why not? If it is because, however foolishly, he did not suspect wrongdoing or, having suspected it, had his suspicions allayed, however unreasonably, that is one thing. But if he did suspect wrongdoing yet failed to make inquiries because 'he did not want to know' ... or because he regarded it as 'none of his business' ... that is quite another. Such conduct is dishonest, and those who are guilty of it cannot complain if, for the purpose of civil liability, they are treated as if they had actual knowledge.

11.85 In *Agip*, there was evidence that the defendants might have believed that they were assisting in a scheme, not to defraud a company, but to avoid the currency exchange controls of Tunisia. Millett J said:

> [I]t is no answer for a man charged with having knowingly assisted in a fraudulent and dishonest scheme to say that he thought that it was 'only' a breach of exchange control or 'only' a case of tax evasion. It is not necessary that he should have been aware of the precise nature of the fraud or even the identity of its victim.

11.86 This perspective was not adopted by Rimer J in *Brinks Ltd v Abu-Saleh* (1995). He found a woman not liable as an accessory for knowingly assisting her husband in a dishonest scheme, because she believed she was participating in a tax evasion exercise, which was false, rather than helping to transfer the proceeds of a robbery from England to the continent, which was what was really going on. It is unlikely this sympathetic treatment will be extended to other accessories.

11.87 In the CA decision in *Lipkin Gorman v Karpnale Ltd* (1992 – the case went to the HL, but the decision on accessory liability did not form part of the appeal), a law firm sought to hold its banker liable because it allowed a partner of the firm, one Mr Cass, who was addicted to gambling, to withdraw money from the firm's client account for that purpose. The CA decided that given the contract between the banker and its client, the bank could not be liable unless it was in breach of its contract to its client to operate and monitor the account properly. In this case Cass's withdrawals were perfectly valid within the terms of their contract with their customers – Cass had full authority to draw on the client's account.

And although the bank manager knew that Cass was a gambler, this was not a sufficient reason to suspect that he was looting the client account, and the CA held that it would impose an excessive burden on bankers to monitor all of their accounts to pick up suspicious withdrawals.

11.88   In *Finers v Miro* (1991) a firm of solicitors sought directions from the court concerning assets it held on trust for a client. The solicitors suspected that some portion of the assets represented the proceeds of a fraud the client allegedly committed by unlawfully transferring assets from a US company, now in liquidation. The CA directed the solicitors to inform the liquidator of the US company that they held assets which might be assets of the company. But for the strong suspicion of fraud, informing the liquidator would amount to a breach of their fiduciary duty of confidence to their client. The CA based its decision in part on the fact that the knowledge of the solicitors was now such that should they dispose of any of the property to the defendant they might well be liable as accessories to a breach of trust, following *Agip*. Banks are now subject to a wealth of legislation which requires them to take action where they are suspicious that a customer is laundering the proceeds of crime, including rules which make it an offence to 'tip-off' a customer who is or might be under investigation, and so banks must act very carefully in such circumstances. (See, eg, *Bank of Scotland v A Ltd* (2001); for an overview, see Gleeson (1995)).

Proprietary remedies for the misapplication of trust property

11.89   Recall that in most circumstances, the trust property is a fund (**2.32**). It is therefore a normal part of the life of the trust that a trustee exchanges one item of trust property for another, so that the constituent properties of the trust change from time to time. The trust will also of course 'capture' any funds arising from its ownership of any particular trust property, eg dividends paid on shares owned by the trust. Because of this, where the beneficiaries adopt, or as Millett LJ puts it (**11.19**), decide not to complain about, an unauthorised transaction, the resulting property forms part of the trust fund just as would the proceeds from any authorised transaction. Therefore, where the trustee breaches the trust by making an unauthorised investment, the beneficiaries need do nothing. The trustee will hold the investment as property in the trust fund, and that is that. In one sense the beneficiaries can be said to 'trace' (**2.46**, **11.96** et seq) the trust funds into the unauthorised investment and claim it as their own. But this right to trace against the trustee is nothing more than the recognition that the trust is a fund, and so the proceeds of any transactions with trust funds are automatically captured by the trust unless, because of a breach, the beneficiaries exercise their right to falsify the account.

11.90　A trustee who turns out to be a rogue typically commits two different wrongs when he breaches the trust; not only does he misapply the trust property, but he treats the proceeds of that misapplication as his own, as for example when a trustee uses trust funds to buy himself a new car. He should not have used the trust funds to buy a car, and his breach is compounded by his using the car as his own, that is, by failing to keep the trust property separate from his own and dealing with it properly under the trust. But these are distinct wrongs, and a trustee can commit one without committing the other. An honest trustee may misapply the trust property, as where he mistakenly makes an unauthorised investment, yet hold that investment properly as part of the trust fund. In contrast, a trustee may treat the trust property as his own without misapplying the trust property, eg, where a trustee takes a trust painting to hang in his office. The painting remains an authorised trust property, but the trustee still acts in breach of trust, and should he fail to return the trust property to where it should properly be kept, the beneficiaries can get a court of equity to make him do so.

11.91　By doing so, they are, in a sense, making a proprietary claim against the trustee, claiming 'that painting is ours'. But this suit does not *establish* their equitable ownership of the painting. That is taken as a given; it forms the basis of their right to make the claim they do. What they are actually claiming is not equitable ownership of the painting, but *specific performance* of the trust by the trustee. They are suing to make him carry out his trust duties properly, which in this case is to treat trust property as trust property, not as his own. In this case there is no question of either falsifying the account or adopting a misapplication of trust property, for the simple reason that 'misapplication of trust property' refers not to this sort of case, but to a case where the trustee *transfers title* to the property in breach of trust (or creates some other sort of interest in trust property, say, by mortgaging it). Although in both cases one might frame the beneficiaries' demand as 'that property is ours!', do not be confused. Demanding that the trustee deal with the trust property properly is not the same thing as 'adopting' an unauthorised transaction, although in the typical case of a breach by a rogue trustee, beneficiaries who want to make a proprietary claim against the trustee will both 'adopt' the trustee's misapplication of the proceeds so as to claim them for the trust and, of course, ask the court of equity to order the trustee to deal with those proceeds as trust property. In the case of a rogue trustee, this will almost always mean he will be ordered to transfer title to new trustees replacing him.

11.92   The more difficult cases arise when the trustee misapplies the trust property and mixes the trust funds with his own, where for example the trustee draws cash from the trust's bank account, and then banks the cash in his own personal account. This is where the rules of 'tracing' against a trustee come into play (**11.96** et seq). But wherever the tracing leads, the same basic principles apply – the beneficiaries can either adopt the transaction which produces the proceeds in one form or other, claiming the proceeds as 'theirs', or they can falsify the account so as to make the trustee personally liable to restore the trust.

Third party recipients of trust property

11.93   Where trust property is misapplied, someone obviously receives it. The beneficiary has the right to claim the property back from a subsequent recipient, for he retains equitable title to the property unless the recipient is a bona fide purchaser for value of a legal title to the property without notice. Besides merely 'following' the trust property into the hands of third party recipients, aka 'strangers' to the trust, the beneficiary may trace the value of the property into the proceeds of exchanges. If the beneficiary can trace the value of the trust property, he may be able to make an equitable proprietary claim to those proceeds. Finally, the beneficiary may have a *personal* claim against recipients of trust property or its traceable proceeds for its value. We will discuss this in detail below, but a few things should be said now so as to clearly distinguish the claims against third parties.

11.94   The plaintiff will be able to rely only upon a personal claim against the recipient of trust property or its proceeds (if such a claim is available, **11.164** et seq) if the recipient has destroyed or dissipated the trust property or proceeds, as no proprietary claim can be made. Obviously this personal claim will be significantly valuable only if the recipient is solvent. By contrast, a proprietary claim is most valuable in the case of the recipient's insolvency, for if the beneficiary can establish a proprietary right to property held by the recipient, that property does not form part of the recipient's estate in bankruptcy.

11.95   The preceding personal claim must be distinguished from personal liability for being an accessory to a breach of trust (**11.77** et seq), although the recipient of trust property might also be an accessory. Therefore, against a stranger to the trust, the beneficiary may have three claims in respect of the misapplication of trust property. One, a proprietary claim for the actual trust property or traceable proceeds that the stranger retains; two, a personal claim to restore the value, ie pay over money, for the value of the trust property or traceable proceeds he received; and three, a personal claim for his being an accessory to the breach. Notice in particular the different basis and scope of liability between liability for 'knowing assistance' and liability for 'knowing receipt'. The former is a kind of 'secondary liability', under which the defendant is liable for participating in another's breach of duty – the assistant cannot breach the trust, only the trustee can, but is rather liable for assisting the trustee in doing so. This can be a very extensive liability indeed, making the assistant liable for much more than the value of any trust property he might have received (if he received any at all), since the scheme of misapplication in which he assisted may have sent large amounts of trust property to others besides himself. The latter is not a kind of secondary liability at all; if a recipient of trust property knows that he receives it in breach of trust, or later finds this out, but uses the property for his own benefit in violation of the beneficiary's interest anyway, then he himself breaches the trust; he knowingly breaches the constructive custodian trustee relationship imposed upon him by law, and only he can breach the trust in this way, for only he has title to the trust property which he ought to hold on behalf of the beneficiaries. We now turn to consider in detail the rules of tracing. Remember throughout that the tracing of value through different transactions may serve two purposes: (1) to allow the beneficiary to establish a *proprietary* claim to property still in the defendant's hands; and/or (2) to allow the beneficiary to say that his property or his value was received by the defendant, in order to establish the defendant's *personal* recipient liability to restore to the trust the value of the trust property he received.

381

Tracing

11.96 It is obviously easiest to trace value through direct substitutions of one item of property for another. If the trustee gives an antique chair which belongs to the trust to A who sells it for £500, then the beneficiary can claim that the £500 is the traceable proceeds of the chair. Almost all of the difficulty in tracing arises when the misapplied trust property is money, or once the value is traced into money, for what people tend to do with money is bank it. The reason why banking money causes problems is that bank accounts are typically *mixtures* of value, and tracing through mixtures of value raises a host of problems.

11.97 If A takes the £500 traceable proceeds and deposits them in his bank account, which has a balance of £1,000, raising the balance to £1,500, what does this new balance of £1,500 amount to in law? One view is that a bank account is a series of individual debts which add up to the current balance. Here the bank owes A at least two debts, one for £500, and as many further debts as correspond to the deposits which made up the previous balance of £1,000. The alternative view is that A and the bank agree under their contract that the Bank will, in exchange for the title to the £500, replace A's right against the bank to be paid his current balance of £1,000, for a new right against the bank to be paid £1,500: in essence A exchanges the £500 plus one debt owed him by the Bank for a new, more valuable debt owed him by the Bank. Thus the old balance is fully replaced by a new balance, and a bank account balance at any one time is a simple whole or 'monolith', which is not made up of a series of debts. On either view it is clear that the bank is a purchaser of the £500 for value (Gleeson 1995). The bank, either on the 'series of debts' or the 'monolithic debt' analysis, raises A's balance to £1,500, and thereby valuably enhances A's rights. Unless the bank has notice that the money is paid into the account in breach of trust, the bank is a bona fide purchaser for value of the £500 in cash, or of the rights represented in a cheque worth £500 if that is what A deposited. The beneficiary must trace the cash or cheque into the proceeds that the trustee acquires under this further exchange transaction with the bank, that is, into the new debt the bank owes him, either into the new debt of £500 on the 'series of debts' view, or into the new debt of £1,500 on the 'monolith' view. Of course a withdrawal is just the opposite of a deposit, and is just as much a purchase for value. The customer, in return for cash, or in the case of a cheque, in return for the bank's complying with his order to pay a third party, gives value since under his contract with the bank the debt the bank owes him is extinguished in whole or in part to the value of the withdrawal.

The 'first in, first out' rule

11.98 The 'series of debts' view is the common law view of bank accounts for the purposes of regulating the relations between banker and customer. When a customer withdraws money from the bank account, he extinguishes one or more of the debts the bank owes him. So for example, assume A's account has had only two transactions so far, one deposit of £1,000 and one deposit of £500. If A withdraws £400, the bank in providing him with those funds has extinguished one of these debts by that amount. Either the £1,000 debt is reduced to £600, leaving debts of £600 and £500, or the £500 debt is reduced, leaving debts of £1,000 and £100. Which debt is it? At common law *Clayton's Case* (1816) decides that, where the intentions of the parties do not determine the issue, a 'first in, first out' rule applies. The first debt is paid off first, as if the debts stood in a queue waiting for extinction. So here the result of A's withdrawal is that the £1,000 debt is reduced to £600, and the £500 debt is untouched. If A had withdrawn £1,200, that would have first fully extinguished the £1,000 debt, and then reduced the £500 debt to £300.

11.99 *Clayton's Case* establishes the rule between A and the bank as to the disposition of their serial transactions on the 'series of debts' view – should it also regulate the relations between A, if he is a trustee, and the beneficiary, for the purposes of tracing withdrawals which follow the deposit of trust money? Assume in the example above that the £1,000 deposit was A's own money, but the subsequent £500 deposit was an unauthorised deposit of trust money. If *Clayton's Case* is followed, then the £1,000 credit against the bank would be A's value alone, and so the beneficiary could not trace into that; his value went into creating the £500 credit. Under the 'first in first out' rule of *Clayton's Case*, then, A's subsequent withdrawals up to the value of £1,000 would all be withdrawals of his value alone, and only withdrawals after that would represent value into which the beneficiary's value can be traced, for only they would be substitutions for the debt in which his value lies. Obviously, it matters what rule is adopted, for it often matters which withdrawals

383

represent trust money and which the trustee's own. For instance , if the trustee buys a valuable painting with one withdrawal, but then withdraws all the rest of the money to spend on riotous living (giving rise to no assets one can trace into), the beneficiaries will obviously hope that the first withdrawal, to buy the painting, can be shown to have been made with their money, rather than the money that was dissipated.

11.100 The question arose in *Pennell v Deffell* (1853), and then again in *Re Hallett's Estate* (1880). Both were cases in which a trustee paid trust money into his own account. In *Pennell* the 'first in, first out' rule in *Clayton's Case* was applied by the CA in Chancery, to the detriment of the beneficiaries under the trust; *Clayton's Case* was considered to have settled what the correct approach to bank accounts was. The CA reconsidered this in *Re Hallett's*. There the trustee paid trust funds into his bank account first, and then added money of his own; he then made withdrawals of money which he dissipated. Under the 'first in, first out' rule, the trust money went into the dissipated withdrawals. The CA decided that the 'first in, first out' rule should not be applied; rather a presumption of honesty should be attributed to the trustee, so that he was taken to have withdrawn his own value from the account first.

11.101 Thesiger LJ dissented:

> Equity has gone very far in aid of trust creditors [ie beneficiaries] when it holds that they may follow and obtain in priority to general creditors moneys paid to a banker, and, therefore, no longer existing in specie as moneys numbered and earmarked, but converted into debt, and it may be that the distinguished judges [in *Pennell v Deffell*] may have thought that equity had gone far enough, and that in the absence of express appropriation the general rule of appropriation of payments in and out of a bank account should apply to that debt when forming part of a larger debt made up as to the rest of moneys not trust moneys paid into the bank.

It is always worth remembering in respect of tracing that, the more favourable the rules are to trust beneficiaries, the less favourable they are not only to the trustee, but also to his creditors.

11.102 In *Re Oatway* (1903), the trustee purchased shares with money from a bank account in which trust money and other money (treated as his own by the court) had been combined. When the shares were purchased, there was enough value so that the value of the trust money was not needed for the purchase, so if the *Re Hallett's* presumption that the trustee spends his own money first applied, the shares would be his own. The remaining funds, however, were later all withdrawn and dissipated. Joyce J refused to apply the presumption:

> [W]hen any of the money drawn out has been invested, and the investment remains in the name or under the control of the trustee, the rest of the balance having been afterwards dissipated by him, he cannot maintain that the investment which remains represents his own money alone, and that what has been spent and can no longer be traced and recovered was the money of the trust ... the trustee must be debited with all the sums that have been withdrawn and applied to his own use so as to be no longer recoverable, and the trust money in like manner be debited with any sums taken out and duly invested in the names of the proper trustees. The order of priority in which the various withdrawals and investments have been respectively made is wholly immaterial.

11.103   The result of these decisions together is apparently to give the beneficiary the right to control the book-keeping of the bank account to his advantage, claiming his value went into any profitable investment and denying it went into any untraceable expenditure. However Martin ((2001), 694-95) argues that *Re Tilley's Will Trusts* (**11.135**) suggests that the *Re Hallett's* presumption is to be applied first, so that where the remaining bank balance is sufficient to cover the beneficiary's value, the beneficiaries may only trace into that balance. Oakley (2003, 827) reads *Re Halletts's* as also indicating that the beneficiaries should look first to the balance of the fund, and approves of this on the basis of simplicity and consistency. There is no clear English authority, but the better view is put by Smith (1997, 158, 183 et seq), that the beneficiary may trace into such withdrawals as he pleases (within the arithmetic limits of what he and the trustee contributed), on the principle that all reasonable inferences will be made against a wrongdoer whose own act gave rise to the factual difficulty (*Armory v Delamirie* (1722)). In this case, the wrongdoing trustee created the problem by mixing the trust funds with his own, so as he 'unmixes' the funds by making various withdrawals, the beneficiary, not him, can choose which 'unmixing' withdrawal belongs to him. If this is right, then the beneficiary may 'cherry-pick' the profitable expenditures, treating them as trust investments, even though there remain ample funds in the account to restore the trust.

The 'lowest intermediate balance' rule

11.104 The extent of this right to control the book-keeping of the account extends, however, only to withdrawals. Subsequent *deposits* by the wrongdoing trustee to the bank account are not presumed to be repayments to replace any trust moneys that have been withdrawn and dissipated (*James Roscoe (Bolton) Ltd v Winder* (1915)); this makes obvious sense, for if the trustee wished to make good his breach and restore the trust, it hardly seems likely that he would do so by adding money to his own bank account. This decision leads to the 'lowest intermediate balance' rule of tracing into bank accounts. Beneficiaries cannot trace in an arithmetically impossible way. If for example, the trustee paid £500 of trust money into his account with £500 of his own, and then £900 is withdrawn, at least £400 of trust money must have been withdrawn. A subsequent addition of the trustee's own money cannot create a new source of funds into which the beneficiaries can trace.

Tracing amongst innocents

11.105 Different rules apply to tracing through bank accounts when the value that the trustee mixes in one bank account comes from different trusts, or when an innocent volunteer receives trust value and adds it to his own bank account. This makes obvious sense, for there no presumptions, justified by a party's wrongdoing, should lie against equally innocent parties; the rules must be neutral. Note, the wrongdoer/innocent distinction is *not* equivalent to the distinction between the trustee and third party recipients. Of course, a trustee who misapplies trust property is always treated as a wrongdoer, however 'innocent' he is; that is, his state of mind is irrelevant. But the state of mind of third parties is relevant; if they have sufficient knowledge that the property they received came to them in breach of trust (a tricky question, dealt with below, **11.164** et seq), then they will be treated just like a defaulting trustee, and will be subject to all the presumptions against a wrongdoer in the tracing exercise. In a case where none of a wrongdoer's money is involved, say where a trustee wrongfully mixed the funds of two trusts together, the general rule that apparently applies to tracing in and out of such a mixture is the 'first in first out' rule of *Clayton's Case*. The application of the rule here has been criticised (see, eg Smith (1997), 193-194), and it is suggested that the innocents should be able to trace into all the withdrawals and into any value that remains in shares proportionate to the amounts of value that they contributed. Such a solution would be in line with the common law rule governing 'fluid' mixtures, ie mixtures of goods like oil where the separate identity of the mixed parts cannot be ascertained – the innocent owners of the mixed goods co-own the whole in proportion to the amounts they contributed. (See Birks (1992); *The Ypatianna* (1988)).

11.106 The applicability of the rule in *Clayton's Case* to these situations was, however, reluctantly affirmed by the CA in *Barlow Clowes International Ltd v Vaughan* (1992). The case concerned the proper means of allocating the remaining value in a pooled investment scheme amongst the contributing investors. All three judges, however, held that the authorities indicated that the rule was not to be applied blindly in all circumstances. In this case, because the investment scheme involved the pooling of investment funds, the contributors could be presumed to intend that their interests in the fund were proportionate to their contributions, so they were entitled to be traced as co-owners into the remaining funds in proportionate shares. Leggatt LJ's dissatisfaction with the rule in *Clayton's Case* was most apparent, saying it had 'nothing to do with tracing'. Most recently, in *Russell-Cooke Trust Co v Prentis* (2003), Lindsay J also refused to apply the rule in *Clayton's Case* to the remaining funds of another investment scheme where it was clear to the investors that purchased securities would not be allocated on a strict first come, first served basis when their payments were received; as in *Barlow Clowes*, the 'proportionate shares' or pari passu solution was adopted. Thus although the rule in *Clayton's Case* remains the general rule, it seems that it is easily departed from, and most likely will be in most cases.

11.107 The mode of tracing between innocents Leggatt LJ preferred is called the 'rolling charge' or 'North American' solution (as it is applied in Canada and the US; see eg *Re Ontario Securities Commission and Greymac Credit Corpn* (1986)). The value contributed by innocents is traced into mixtures so that they become proportionate co-owners of the whole, but the 'lowest intermediate balance' rule is properly taken account of, as are the *Re Hallett's* and *Re Oatway* rules as between the trustee and the beneficiaries as co-owners of the trust value. Assume a rogue trustee, T, pays into his account £500 of beneficiary A's, and then £500 of beneficiary B's, which already contains £500 of his own, raising the balance to £1,500. Now assume T withdraws £750 and dissipates the money. By *Re Hallett's*, T will be presumed to spend his own £500 first and so only £250 of the trust money. As co-owners in proportionate shares, A and B will suffer the loss equally, each now tracing into a half share of £750. Now T adds £500 from beneficiary C. Under the principle of the lowest intermediate balance, it must be the case that A and B can only trace into the £750, which is all the trust money that remains when C's money is added, not into C's contribution. From now on, however, the mixing means that C's fate is linked with A's and B's as proportionate co-owners of the entirety of their traceable value: A and B each have a $(1/2 \times £750)/£1250 = 3/10$ share, and C a 4/10 share of the whole of £1,250 of trust value.

11.108 Under the same scenario, the rule in Clayton's case delivers the following result: The £250 trust money attributed to T's withdrawal of £750 will, under the 'first in first out' rule of *Clayton's Case*, be £250 from A's contribution alone, so if that is the end of the story, A will receive only £250, while B will receive his full £500 back. Assume now that T adds £500 of C's, who is also an innocent. T then withdraws £500. This withdrawal will wipe out A's remaining traceable value of £250, will reduce by £250 B's value, and leave C's value untouched. If the money the trustee withdraws is dissipated, and the story ends there, then the timing of the deposits will mean that though each contributed £500, A can trace into nothing, B into £250 in the account, and C his full value into £500 in the account.

11.109 Notice that both the 'rolling charge' mode and the 'first in first out' rule will require a careful examination of the transactions over the history of the account, which will be expensive, expenses which will, in an insolvency, reduce the total amount of funds available for distribution. This was the case in *Barlow Clowes*, and this was one consideration against applying the 'rolling charge' solution, though it is the most fair. Note that while the typical effect of the rule in *Clayton's Case* is to prejudice early contributors, the proportionate co-ownership solution adopted in *Barlow Clowes* prejudices late contributors. Given that we are concerned with tracing the actual value of contributors, the lowest intermediate balance rule ought to apply. But the proportionate shares solution ignores this rule, putting the contributor who paid in money long ago on the same footing as one who contributed last week, even though it is almost certain that on any realistic examination of the past account withdrawals, a significant proportion of the early contributor's value was withdrawn.

Tracing with respect to overdrawn accounts and backwards tracing

11.110   One 'backwards traces' when one traces value into property purchased by the recipient _before_ he receives the value which is traced. If a rogue trustee buys an antique table worth £3,000 _on credit_, by taking a loan from a bank, or by using his overdraft facility, or with his credit card, and then later pays off the debt incurred with trust money, logically it is clear that the value of the trust money now resides in the antique table. As Smith ((1997), 146) says:

> Suppose that D buys a car from C with some money. If we were tracing the value inherent in ownership of the money, we could trace it into ownership of the car. Now change the facts slightly, so that D buys the car on credit; he takes ownership of the car, but he is C's debtor in respect of the purchase price. A day later, D pays the debt with the money being traced. Can we trace from the money into the car as before? It is difficult to see why not. There is no substantial change in the transaction; the period of credit might be reduced to a minute or a second to better make this point. If that is right, then when money is used to pay a debt, it is traceable into what was acquired for the incurring of the debt.

Unfortunately, the law has not adopted this logical and compelling position, in part as a result of some confusion about tracing into overdrawn bank accounts, ie about the way in which a bank receives deposits.

11.111   Normally, when money is paid into a bank account, there is no difficulty determining the substitution that has occurred. The bank takes title to the money, and gives value in exchange in the form of the increased bank balance. The increased bank balance is, of course, the traceable proceeds of the payment in of the money. Where £500 is paid into an account which is £500 in overdraft, resulting in a balance of zero, what are the traceable proceeds? In exchange for the title to the money, the bank gives value in the form of the reduction of the debt it is owed by the customer to zero. No debt now exists between the bank and the customer, and therefore no rights between them which can be the traceable proceeds of the £500 payment. For this reason, it is generally but wrongly assumed that the payment of a debt is the end of the tracing exercise, since there just _are no proceeds_. While it is absolutely right to deny that anything of value _in the account_ is traceable by the plaintiff, for there is no existing right between the bank and customer, this does not mean that the tracing exercise must end when the rights between the bank and its customer 'run out'; if you stop there you have merely given up the tracing exercise prematurely; the tracing exercise has not come to a natural conclusion by itself. The overdraft was incurred, after all, by withdrawing funds, and the payment of the overdraft is therefore traceable into those funds, and into whatever those funds were spent upon.

11.112 Of course, tracing into the proceeds of an overdraft may be evidentially difficult, and therefore may often be impossible in practice, but that is no reason to deny this form of backwards tracing in principle, especially in clear cases where it is apparent that what was purchased on credit was subsequently paid off by trust funds. Consider the case of a trustee who uses trust money to pay off his credit card bill; all the card transactions are clearly recorded in his monthly statements and receipts, and it would seem preposterous for the court to refuse to trace into the television, antique table, and suit of clothes so manifestly acquired with the beneficiary's value.

11.113 It is clear that the courts have implicitly allowed backward tracing: in *Agip* the court allowed the plaintiff to treat a payment by Lloyds Bank in London to the defendant as the transfer of his value even though the payment from the plaintiff to Lloyds correspondent bank in New York was made *later*. Thus Lloyds had made the payment to the defendant before, and in expectation of, receiving a corresponding amount from the plaintiff via a New York bank. (See also the tracing through credit facilities in *El Ajou v Dollar Land Holdings plc* (1993)). Furthermore, backward tracing necessarily underlies the ability of equity to trace through bank cheque clearing systems generally, since the settlement between banks is not simultaneous with the crediting and debiting of accounts. It also provides a sensible interpretation to Lord Bridge's assimilation of the payment of purchase money and payment of mortgage instalments in trusts of the family home (**5.14**). The HL recently conducted a backwards tracing exercise in *Foskett v McKeown* (2001) without explicitly stating as much (see **11.128-131**) and, most recently, in *Law Society v Haider* (2003) Judge Richards QC allowed the claimant to trace from a payment discharging a mortgage into the house that was purchased with the mortgage loan, and thence into the proceeds of the sale of that house and into another house purchased with those proceeds. The decision is clearly inexplicable if not for backwards tracing.

11.114 The CA considered backward tracing in *Bishopsgate Investment Management Ltd v Homan* (1995). At first instance Vinelott J was willing to allow backward tracing in limited circumstances, ie:

> ... where an asset acquired by [the defendant] with moneys borrowed from an overdrawn or loan account and there was an inference that when the borrowing was incurred it was the intention that it should be repaid by misappropriation of [the plaintiff's] money. Another possibility was that moneys misappropriated from [the plaintiff] were paid into an overdrawn account of [the defendant] in order to reduce the overdraft and so make finance available within the overdraft limits for [the defendant] to purchase some particular asset.

Dillon LJ accepted this as correct, but Leggatt LJ found the contention utterly wrong on the basis that it was simply impossible for a claim to be made in respect of an asset acquired before the misappropriation took place. There is no majority decision on this point in the case, for the third judge, Henry LJ, simply agreed with both judgments, so it is not clear what the status of backward tracing of any kind in English law now is. Backwards tracing was inconclusively considered again by the CA in *Foskett v McKeown* (1998; see also *Boscawen v Bajwa* (1995); **11.139**).

11.115 As Smith (1995) points out, however, the basis for Vinelott J's version of backward tracing is deficient in any event. As to the first case he mentions, it seems to violate the general principle of tracing to require that the defendant *intends* to use the misappropriated trust property to purchase the asset. All that is generally required is that he acquire the asset with the plaintiff's value – his intention is entirely irrelevant. As to the second case, this is in violation of the rules of tracing, for if the payment of the overdraft is traced, it should be traced into the value for which the debt *was incurred*, not for any new purchases enabled by the reduction of the overdraft. While those purchases might not have been possible 'but for' the payment in of the plaintiff's value, the new overdraft facility allows the defendant to use the *bank's value* to make more purchases, not the plaintiff's. The plaintiff's value can only be traced via the overdraft into what was purchased so as to give rise to the overdraft debt. (For an exploration of applying 'but for' causation to develop a novel basis for tracing, see Evans (1999)).

Proprietary claims to traceable proceeds – charges and equitable ownership

11.116 Once the process or exercise of tracing succeeds in locating the beneficiary's value, he may then make a claim in respect of that value, whether against the trustee or a third party. (See *Boscawen v Bajwa* (1995) per Millett LJ.) Note however, that a wrongdoing trustee may at any stage do his duty and reinstate or restore the trust. If he does so, he must do so properly. As Millett LJ points out above (**11.19**), the trustee has no right to 'borrow' trust money for his own purposes and then just replace what he has borrowed. Thus if he uses £1,000 of trust money to buy shares now worth £2,000, he will only restore the trust if he then declares that he holds the shares on trust. If the shares fall in value to £500, he may only restore the trust by replacing the full £1,000 plus interest. If he uses £1,000 of trust value plus £1,000 of his own to buy shares for £2,000 now worth £5,000, he is likewise liable to hold half of the shares on trust. If the shares fall in value to £1,500, he must hold the shares as if charged by the trust to the value of £1,000 plus interest; only the remaining value counts as his own.

11.117 This example of the trustee restoring the trust should remind you of the basic terms in which equity allows the beneficiary to deal with a misapplication of trust property against a trustee. He may either falsify the account, in which case he denies any proprietary interest in the proceeds of that transaction in the beneficiary's hands, claiming instead that the misapplication never took place and looking to the trustee personally to restore the trust in specie or in money, *or* he may adopt the transaction *in any form most favourable to the beneficiary* (eg as a loan at interest, or an investment to acquire business profits (**11.41**)). Where the trustee misapplies the trust property so as to acquire a valuable asset, the beneficiary will adopt the transaction as an authorised purchase for the trust, ie claim that the trust owns the asset; in short he makes an equitable ownership claim.

11.118 Where, on the other hand, the asset acquired by the trustee is less valuable than the trust money misapplied to get it, there are two ways of framing the beneficiary's claim. Conventionally, it is said that the beneficiary can 'bring a personal claim against the trustee for breach of trust and enforce an equitable lien or charge on the proceeds to secure restoration of the trust fund' (*Foskett v McKeown* (2001) per Lord Millett).

But this seems wrong in principle; by bringing the personal claim for breach of trust, the beneficiary falsifies the account, and disowns any interest in the proceeds of the falsified transaction, and thus should have no right to claim a lien over them, or any other property of the trustee for that matter. When one falsifies the account, one denies the transaction, claiming that the trustee retains the original trust property. The better way to explain the beneficiary's right to a lien in these circumstances is as follows: a beneficiary can adopt the misapplication of trust funds in any form most valuable to him; here, he will adopt the transaction as a *secured loan to the trustee*; the beneficiary will authorise the misapplication of the trust money as a loan to the trustee, secured against the property he acquired with it. Thus the beneficiary claims an equitable lien or charge over the asset, which will in part satisfy his personal claim for repayment of the 'loan' by the trustee. To the extent the trustee fails to repay this 'loan', the beneficiary has the right, like any chargee or lien holder, to possess and sell the asset; the trustee, like any chargor or borrower giving security, is liable for the full amount of the loan, so if the sale of the asset does not generate enough money to pay back the full amount, the trustee will be personally liable to dig into his pocket to make up the shortfall.

11.119 It is sometimes suggested (eg Hayton (2003), 852; Elliott & Mitchell (2004)) that the beneficiary may claim both the ownership of an asset and that the trustee should personally make up any shortfall if the asset's value is less than the amount that was misapplied to acquire it. This view is based on *Re Lake* (1903), but this case is in conflict with earlier authority, *Thornton v Stokill* (1855) (see also Mowbray et al (2000), 618; Oakley (2003) 768 n.40), and seems wrong in principle: a beneficiary cannot logically adopt an asset as an authorised trust property and at the same time falsify the account so as to make the trustee personally liable. The beneficiary has an *election* either to adopt the transaction in any form he chooses, or falsify the account, but elect he must; he cannot have it both ways.

11.120 The same basic principles apply to the beneficiary's making a proprietary claim against a third party recipient of trust property, but you must think very carefully here, for explaining the treatment of third party recipients of trust property has shown to be one of the most difficult intellectual enterprises facing judges and academics. Start with the simplest case, following trust property into the hands of the stranger to the trust. In order to get to this point, of course, one might have engaged in a very complex tracing exercise against a wrongdoing trustee, but as a beneficiary may treat any traceable proceeds the trustee acquires as trust property itself – remember (**2.32**) that the trust property is a fund, and the trust fund captures any traceable proceeds of trust property – this poses no conceptual problem; any original trust property or traceable proceeds received by the stranger equally count as trust property received by him. Unless the stranger is a bona fide purchaser, the beneficiaries can claim against him, 'that's ours', and demand the return of the property.

11.121 Things get complicated, 'conceptually' or theoretically complicated, however, when the stranger exchanges the property he receives for traceable proceeds. As a matter of law, the beneficiary *can* claim for the trust any traceable proceeds the stranger acquires with the trust property he receives. But it is not immediately clear why the beneficiary should be able to do so. It is one thing to say that the original trustee, the 'express' trustee who took upon the trust voluntarily, must treat any traceable proceeds he acquires as trust property, for that is part of what it means to hold property on trust, ie he holds the property as a fund. But should the stranger, who is clearly not an express trustee, be treated in the same way? Why should we treat him as holding the trust property he receives as equivalently the holding of the property as a fund, so that the beneficiary may likewise claim from him any traceable proceeds he acquires as also trust property?

11.122 People who adopt a restitutionary analysis of this situation (to be discussed in detail below, **11.181** et seq) have an answer. They hold that the stranger is liable just as much to hold the proceeds he acquires as trust property because, if he were not, he would be unjustly enriched by getting the proceeds as his own, at the beneficiary's expense. We will discuss this explanation below; the only point we need to make here is that this cannot be the traditional theoretical basis in equity for this result, for the restitutionary analysis was essentially unknown to, or at the least entirely unacknowledged by, equity when this law was developed, and furthermore it 'proves too much' in the sense of entailing collateral consequences for equity's treatment of strangers who receive trust property which go beyond the law as it currently stands. Therefore before simply adopting the restitutionary analysis we must see if we can make sense of this result under the traditional attitude of equity to cases of breach of trust.

11.123   We can begin with two propositions: the first is that the stranger recipient is not an express trustee; the way we characterised him before (**5.4**) is as a 'constructive trustee of an express trust interest', ie as someone whose trusteeship arises by operation of law, although the property he receives is only trust property because of the express trust that was created, the property of which was misapplied by the express trustee. Second, we have seen that the right way to understand the way in which a beneficiary brings a proprietary claim against the trustee for trust property or traceable proceeds in his hands is to adopt the original misapplication of trust property in the form most favourable to the beneficiary. So the question is, how does the beneficiary adopt his express trustee's transferring the trust property to the stranger? It is submitted that the beneficiary 'adopts' this misapplication as the express trustee's placing the trust property with a 'custodian' trustee (**10.58**), ie as a bare trustee holding the trust property or its traceable proceeds for the express trust under the directions of the express trustee. Under this form of adoption, as we shall later see, the beneficiary is more restricted in the sort of claims he can make against the third party recipient. For the time being, however, the main point is that as a custodian trustee the stranger is not a constructive trustee in the sense of a replacement trustee (**10.48** et seq), who like an express trustee is meant to carry out the trust for the beneficiary. Rather, he is bound by the trust only in the sense of holding property to the order of the managing trustee. Nevertheless, *as a trustee*, the stranger still holds the property he receives as trust property, ie property subject to the basic rule of a fund that the property interest of the beneficiary captures any traceable proceeds. I must make it plain that this analysis of the beneficiary's right to trace into the proceeds acquired by the stranger with trust property is, in a sense, novel. What I am trying to do is explain how the traditional basis for equity's making a third party liable to the beneficiary when a breach of trust has occurred works. Smith (1999) describes the traditional attitude of equity as follows:

> [Why the beneficiary pleads his case the way he does] appears to lie in the logic of the trust. Prima facie, the beneficiary of the trust cannot sue anyone but his trustee. This is part of the package of legal incidents which is delivered when parties choose to use the trust institution to order their affairs; in other words, when they choose to entrust assets to their trustee.

It is submitted that the best strategy for explaining the traditional perspective on third party liability is to pay close attention to the basic election the beneficiary has either to falsify the account or 'adopt' the misapplication of trust property. Only by paying close attention to the *form* in which the beneficiary adopts a misapplication of trust property can we explain third party claims in the shape that they have, ie as claims against persons equity will treat as trustees liable to the beneficiary. And only by getting a sense of this traditional explanation can we later assess the recent, revolutionary, restitutionary analysis.

Claiming followed property, 'clean' traceable proceeds, and 'mixed' traceable proceeds

11.124 Where there have been no substitutions of trust property requiring tracing to locate the value taken from the trust, ie where the beneficiary is able simply to follow the trust property into the hands of the trustee (eg the case of the trustee who takes a trust painting for his office, **11.90–11.91**) or a third party (not a bona fide purchaser for value), the beneficiary simply specifically enforces the trust. The trustee will be required to hold the property on trust again as he should, and the court will order any third party to deliver it up or assign the legal title back to the trustee (typically a replacement trustee). By specifically enforcing the trust, the beneficiary merely 'vindicates' his continuing equitable title in the trust property.

11.125 In the case of 'clean' substitutions, ie where the original trust property is spent to acquire traceable proceeds, but only trust property is spent – there are no mixtures of the trust value with the trustee's or a third party's – then, in the case of a trustee or a stranger who receives the trust property knowing it came to him in breach of trust,   the beneficiary can adopt the misapplication either as the purchase of the proceeds for the trust, or as a secured loan of the trust funds to the wrongdoer (see, eg *Re Hallett's* per Jessel MR). Where the proceeds are of equal or greater value to the property misapplied, the beneficiary will elect for the former, claiming equitable ownership of the proceeds, ie claiming that the proceeds are trust property. And, just as in the case of following trust property, the beneficiary will specifically enforce the trust, requiring a trustee to hold the proceeds as trust property, or the wrongdoer to deliver up or assign the legal title to the property to the trustee. Where the proceeds are of lower value than the misapplied trust property, the beneficiary will make the latter claim, ie a personal claim for the return of the value of the trust property, secured with a lien on the proceeds.

11.126 In the case of an innocent third party, the beneficiary can follow any trust property or its traceable proceeds into the third party's hands, and adopt this as the placement of trust property with a custodian. He can then specifically enforce the trust against this third party. Where the innocent third party then himself makes a clean substitution of the property in his hands, the beneficiary can likewise trace into this, but he can only adopt this transaction in order to make an ownership claim of the proceeds. So for example, if a trustee writes a cheque on the trusts' bank account in favour of his nephew, telling him it is a birthday present, and the nephew spends this money on a motorbike which is now worth less than the trust money he paid for it, the beneficiary cannot adopt the nephew's purchase of the motorbike as a secured loan of the trust money, and claim a lien on the motorbike as security for the repayment by the nephew of the full amount. The beneficiary is restricted to claiming the motorbike as trust property, whatever its value. (Of course the beneficiary will be happy with this result if the proceeds are more valuable than the trust money spent for them, but the risk of the value being lower lies with the beneficiary too.)

11.127 This follows from the logic of adopting the transfer of the trust property to the innocent third party as the placement of trust property with a custodian trustee (**11.121-123**). A custodian trustee is a bare trustee, and so is not liable for any misapplication of trust property unless he is aware of the terms of the trust – a custodian basically follows the orders of the managing trustee, here the wrongdoing trustee uncle that paid him the cheque. Hence a custodian trustee does not have anything like the freedom of action in dealing with trust property as does a managing trustee, and so the beneficiary cannot adopt the innocent third party's purchase of the motorbike in any form he chooses. By presenting the money as a gift, the wrongdoing trustee essentially directs the innocent third party to use the property *as his own*, ie as the beneficial legal owner thereof. Thus, since one cannot borrow one's own property from oneself, much less make a secured loan against oneself, but can only exchange one's own property for other property, the beneficiary can only adopt the transaction as an exchange of trust property for its proceeds, and claim ownership of the proceeds for the trust. To put this in terms of the more traditional formulation, an innocent custodian trustee cannot be liable for breach of trust, ie the beneficiary cannot falsify the account against him to make him personally liable to restore the trust, a liability 'secured' by a lien over the proceeds of his misapplication; the most the beneficiary can do is adopt any transaction in the only form of transaction the innocent recipient can undertake, ie as an exchange of one trust property for another. (See also 11.134.) Take note: if, *after* receiving the trust property, the innocent third party *learns* that the property came to him in breach of trust, and subsequently enters into any transaction with the trust property, he will be liable as a wrongdoer in respect of any proceeds, for a custodian trustee is liable for breach of trust if he knows that his action does so, for example where he carries out an order of the managing trustee knowing it breaches the trust terms, or intentionally misapplies the trust property even in the absence of any order from the managing trustee.

11.128 Where a trustee or other wrongdoer has purchased property with a mixture of his own and trust money, the beneficiary, in accordance with the case of a clean substitution, is entitled to a lien over the proceeds, or a proportionate equitable co-ownership interest in the proceeds. This was recently made clear by Lord Millett in *Foskett v McKeown* (2000):

> Where a trustee wrongfully uses trust money to provide part of the cost of acquiring an asset, the beneficiary is entitled *at his option* either to claim a proportionate share of the asset or to enforce a lien upon it to secure his personal claim against the trustee for the amount of the misapplied money. It does not matter whether the trustee mixed the money with his own in a single fund before using it to acquire the asset, or made separate payments (whether simultaneously or sequentially) out of the differently owned funds to acquire a single asset.

11.129 In *Foskett* a trustee used his own funds to purchase the first two premiums, then trust funds to pay two later premiums, on a life insurance policy in favour of his wife and children. The beneficiaries claimed that they were entitled to a share of the proceeds of the policy which were paid when the trustee committed suicide, a share proportionate to the value of the premiums paid with trust money. The HL, by a 3:2 decision, reversing the CA (1998), agreed. In the leading judgment, Lord Millett held that the insurance company's contractual duty to pay the £1m payout on death was a single 'chose in action' (ie a contractual right to be paid a certain sum which is regarded as a property right) which was purchased in instalments. The complicating fact which obscured this analysis is that, unlike in typical purchase agreements, the number of instalment payments and thus the total price to be paid for the insurance policy cannot be known at the outset; indeed, the total purchase price is only known immediately prior to the end of the contract, ie when the insured dies and the insurer must forthwith pay the £1m (at which point the contract is at an end). Thus the beneficiaries could rightly trace from the instalment payments made with the trust moneys into the contractual right to the payoff on the assured's death, and claim a proportionate share of the proceeds.

11.130 Lords Hope and Steyn, who would have affirmed the majority decision of the CA, adopted a different analysis: the contract of insurance was to be seen as the outright purchase of a piece of property, the contractual right to the payoff on the assured's death, with the first premium. However that property right is subject to defeasance: the policy (the contract) and the right to be paid £1m on death (the property) will lapse if further premiums were not paid. An analogy here might be with the purchase of a long residential lease, of a flat in London, say, for £250,000, but with a requirement in the lease to pay £2,000 pa in 'ground rent'. One is full owner of the leasehold interest with the first payment, though one might lose the lease for failure to pay the annual ground rent (assuming the failure to do so would entitle the landlord to re-enter the premises and forfeit the lease). But paying the ground rent does not constitute making a purchase payment instalment, by which one acquires a greater ownership share in the lease. Because of a wrinkle in the contract, it was the case that had the premiums paid with the trust money not been paid at all, the policy would have stayed on foot. (Each premium had a savings element in it, and if a premium was missed the savings element of prior premiums was automatically employed to make up the missed premiums to keep the insurance element of the contract on foot; enough premiums had been paid before the trust money was used to cover those premiums even if they had not been made.) Therefore, the premiums paid with trust money did not even save the policy from lapse, and so even had they not been made, the wife and children would have received the proceeds on death. Lords Hope and Steyn would, therefore, have denied the beneficiaries a proportionate share.

11.131 Notice that Lord Millett's analysis depends, albeit implicitly, upon the legitimacy of backwards tracing. To transfer property in return for being paid in instalments is to advance credit, and in paying for a property right in instalments one discharges one's debt to the transferor; thus to trace the later trust money premiums into the right to the payoff is to trace backwards through the discharge of a debt into the property acquired by incurring the debt.

11.132 As in the case of a clean substitution, in the case of a mixed substitution the beneficiary's election of a co-ownership share or a lien will turn on whether the value of the proceeds has increased or declined. If £5,000 of trust value and £5000 of the trustee's value went into the purchase of shares now worth £20,000, the beneficiary will claim a 50% co-ownership of the shares. If they fall in value to £7,000, he will claim a lien over the shares, ie over *all* the shares, for the £5,000 value that went into them plus interest. Notice that in this case the lien extends to the whole of the property, not just that fraction of the property which represents the appropriate proportionate share. In essence, then, in this case the form in which the beneficiary adopts the misapplication is equivalent to the typical case of a mortgage lender; although the borrower usually puts in some money of his own, ie his 'down payment', the mortgagee's loan is secured against the whole of the property purchased with a mixture of their money.

11.133 Hayton ((2001b), 866, fn 88) takes this logic one step further. He argues that where the trustee buys an asset with both trust money and some of his own, but the facts indicate that *but for the use of the trust money he would not have been able to acquire the asset at all*, then if the asset rises in value the beneficiary should be able to claim ownership of the whole asset subject to a charge in favour of the trustee for the value he put in. For example, if the trustee because of his credit record is unable to borrow money to buy a house, puts in £40,000 of trust money with £10,000 of his own to buy a house now worth £100,000, why, Hayton asks, should the beneficiaries be restricted to a co-ownership share of four-fifths, ie £80,000? Should they not be able to claim the whole subject to a charge in favour of the trustee for the return of his £10,000 plus interest? According to this analysis, the form in which the beneficiary adopts the misapplication of trust funds is a purchase of trust property which is assisted by a secured loan from the trustee. While at first glance this seems perfectly acceptable in principle, remember that a beneficiary most relies upon proprietary rights against a recipient of trust property where the latter is insolvent, and so that if the ability to elect the form in which an unauthorised transaction is adopted is too generous (why not say that the trustee assisted the trust's purchase of the house by *giving* the trust £10,000 of his own?) it will be his creditors who will be harmed. Therefore, there might be sound policy considerations which limit the beneficiary to the standard forms of claiming co-ownership share or personal repayment secured by a lien on the traceable proceeds. There might also be a principled objection to Hayton's analysis, akin to the *James Roscoe (Bolton)* rule (11.104), which is that while the beneficiary can elect to adopt the transaction in different forms, he cannot do so in a way which presents the trustee as altruistic, ie lending or giving his property to the trust, for that seems to belie the fact that the trustee was, not only not altruistic in breaching the trust, but was actually taking advantage of it.

11.134 In keeping with the preceding analysis of the claims that can be made by a beneficiary against an innocent recipient (11.121-123, 11.127), where (1) an innocent third party recipient purchases an asset with trust money and some value of his own, or (2) property is purchased by a trustee or other wrongdoer with a mixture of money from several trusts, each innocent party is entitled to a proportionate equitable co-ownership share in the proceeds. In neither case would a personal claim for the value contributed secured by a lien on the proceeds be appropriate, for this claim puts one party at an advantage as against the other party (or parties), and as the parties are equally innocent, there is no basis for choosing between them so as to give one such an advantage.

11.135 Hayton (1990, 2001b, 877), however, argues that there might be a case of two innocents where there is a justified departure from the co-ownership share result, based on the decision in *Re Tilley's Will Trusts* (1967), in which the beneficiaries were *restricted* to a claim for a lien over assets purchased with trust money which had risen in value. The widow of a testator was trustee of his testamentary trust, and thoroughly confused the trust moneys with her own funds. She made several profitable property investments, but Ungoed-Thomas J decided that because the trustee (1) did not deliberately use the trust moneys, and (2) she had ample overdraft facilities to make the property purchases she did, and so did not *rely* on any of the trust value to fund her purchases, the beneficiaries were entitled at most to a lien over the acquired property. It seems wrong in principle to allow this argument to be made by an 'innocent' *trustee*, since trustees are strictly liable for their misappropriations of trust property, and should be susceptible to all the normal equitable claims regardless of their intentions or innocence. But, suggests Hayton, this decision might be justifiable in the case of an innocent volunteer recipient of trust funds who innocently mixed trust money with his own. Given his ample funds, he could argue that the beneficiary should not benefit from his investment expertise he had exploited for his own benefit, and so a beneficiary should be *restricted* to a personal claim for repayment of their money, secured by a lien or charge on the property.

11.136 While this argument draws upon a certain sense of fairness, it seems to prove too much. If the innocent mixer *could* have purchased the asset with all of his own funds, why should a beneficiary have any property right in the asset at all, ie even a lien, as opposed merely to a personal claim that he repays them an equivalent amount to what he received from the trust? The logic of this position seems to be that the innocent recipient was merely unjustly enriched by the receipt of the trust property, ie that following the breach he was merely more wealthy than he was before, and should return a similar amount of wealth, *not* that he was in possession of the beneficiary's property. But the logic of falsifying the account or adopting a misapplication, and of following and tracing, turns on the idea that a recipient *is* in possession of the beneficiary's property, and we can trace that property into whatever proceeds it contributes to the acquisition of. As Smith makes clear in the debate over backwards tracing (**11.115**), the intentions of the party who acquires the proceeds are irrelevant, and so, presumably, should they be here, as should any other facts about his general financial position.

The multiplication of claims and the 'exchange product theory' and 'power in rem' theories of claiming

11.137 It is perfectly possible for a beneficiary to be able to trace the trust value into a multiplying track of substitutions. Consider the case where the trustee sells a trust asset, say an antique clock, to X, who is not a bona fide purchaser for value, for £2,000. The beneficiary can trace into the proceeds of that exchange, the £2,000, but at the same time can claim an ongoing equitable title in the clock. If X sells the clock to Y for £3,000, and Y is also not a bona fide purchaser, then the beneficiary's array of claims expands again, since he can trace into the £2,000, the £3,000, and still claim he retains title in the clock. This process can go on indefinitely in principle. But, following the logic of falsifying the account or adopting the misapplying transaction at each step, the beneficiary must elect a path to one of the properties, whether he claims for an equitable charge or equitable (co-)ownership against the trustee, X, or Y. It is a difficult theoretical issue whether (1) the beneficiary has all of these property claims at once, but is only allowed to enforce one because, like all claimants, he is limited by the principle of double (or multiple) recovery, ie as soon as the beneficiary has recovered property or money to account for all the trust value misapplied, he should be barred from bringing any further claims; or (2), his rights against these different defendants and their property are 'inchoate', in suspense, until he elects which party he will pursue, at which point his property right 'crystallises' as a fully-fledged property right in the asset that party holds. We can refer to (1) as the 'exchange product' theory of claiming: the beneficiary is entitled to make a proprietary claim to the proceeds because the proceeds immediately become his, ie he gets an immediate equitable title to them, when they are received in exchange for the trust property; in a sense, they are automatically 'captured' by trust just like any property the trustee receives when he carries out an authorised transaction with the trust property. The election that the beneficiary may in some cases be able to make (ie against trustees and wrongdoing recipients) exists because it is part and parcel of the beneficiary's equitable interest in the trust fund that he may elect to treat items of the fund acquired by a trustee or wrongdoer in breach of the trust terms (ie via a misapplication of trust property) as security for a loan to the trustee or wrongdoing recipient, ie in a form most favourable to him. We can refer to (2) as the 'power *in rem*' theory, for this theory says that the beneficiary has a power **(2.6)** to vest himself with the equitable interest (either an ownership share or a lien) he elects, a power he exercises when he brings a claim against a recipient. The former view has been endorsed by Lord Millett in *Foskett*:

> A beneficiary of a trust is entitled to a continuing beneficial interest not merely in the trust property but in its traceable proceeds also, and his interest binds every one who takes the property or its traceable proceeds except a bona fide purchaser for value without notice.

On this view, when a beneficiary elects to pursue one of several possible defendants, the property rights against the others are either extinguished, or at a minimum, are unenforceable, so that their possession of these assets becomes legally secure.

Subrogation claims reliant upon tracing

11.138 Subrogation is the acquisition of another person's rights against a third party upon the making of a payment: very roughly, by making a payment the plaintiff 'purchases' those rights. The classic example occurs in the insurance context – if I am insured against injuries caused by the negligence of others, my insurance company, upon paying me an insurance award compensating me for my loss, is entitled to sue the tortfeasor, ie the negligent injurer, in my name for damages. Thus acquiring my right to sue, the insurance company is said to be 'subrogated' to my claim against the tortfeasor. A different sort of subrogation is relevant here. In certain circumstances, if X pays off Y's debt to Z, X will, by operation of law, be subrogated to Z's right as a creditor. In other words, by paying off Z, X will in effect 'purchase' Z's right to the payment of the debt against Y. Notice that in the insurance example, the insurer takes over rights which the insured continues to have against his tortfeasor. The case is different where X pays off Y's debt to Z. By paying off Y's debt, X *extinguishes* the debt and thus Z's right as a creditor. The right against Y that X acquires by subrogation is a new right that arises by operation of law; in essence Y's debt is *revived* in favour of X, and in consequence this is known as a case of 'reviving' subrogation (Mitchell (1994), 4).

11.139 In *Boscawen v Bajwa* (1995), Bajwa intended to sell his mortgaged land for a price roughly equal to what he owed under the mortgage to the Halifax Building Society. On the sale Bajwa would be required to use the purchase money to pay off the mortgage, which would leave him with little if any proceeds for himself. The purchasers raised £140,000 on a mortgage loan from Abbey National, and the money was transferred to solicitors in advance of the completion of the sale. In breach of trust the money was advanced before completion and was applied to pay off the mortgage loan to Halifax. The sale never occurred, and as a result Bajwa ended up with an unmortgaged property, while Abbey National had advanced funds and received no mortgage on the property in return. The CA held that Abbey National was entitled to be subrogated to Halifax's mortgage on the land, thus entitling them to priority over a charge on the land which had been subsequently granted by the court to judgment creditors of Bajwa. The court clearly distinguished between the process of tracing, which allowed Abbey National to show that its value was received by Bajwa, and the claim to be subrogated.

11.140   Millett LJ said:

> If the plaintiff succeeds in tracing his property, whether in its original or in some changed form, into the hands of the defendant and overcomes any defences which are put forward on the defendant's behalf, he is entitled to a remedy. The remedy will be fashioned to the circumstances … If the plaintiff's money has been applied by the defendant, for example, not in the acquisition of a landed property but in its improvement, then the court may treat the land as charged with the payment to the plaintiff of a sum representing the amount by which the value of the defendant's land has been enhanced by the use of the plaintiff's money. And if the plaintiff's money has been used to discharge a mortgage on the defendant's land, then the court may achieve a similar result by treating the land as subject to a charge by way of subrogation in favour of the plaintiff … Tracing was the process by which the Abbey National sought to establish that its money was applied in the discharge of the Halifax's charge; subrogation was the remedy which it sought in order to deprive Mr Bajwa   … of the unjust enrichment which he would otherwise obtain at the Abbey National's expense.

(For a HL decision applying these principles to a more complicated set of facts, see *Banque Financière de la Cité v Parc (Battersea) Ltd* (1999).)

11.141   The result in this case can be doubted. Note first that subrogation, while achieving a similar result in the case of a secured loan, is the opposite of backwards tracing. In backwards tracing, one traces into items purchased with the borrowed funds. In contrast, a subrogation claim allows the beneficiary plaintiff to stand in the shoes of the lender; in the case of an unsecured debt, for example a credit card debt which is paid off with trust money, the beneficiary will acquire by subrogation nothing more than a *personal* claim for money against the defendant, for that is all the credit card company had. In the case of a mortgage, however, subrogation provides a result similar to backwards tracing. A backwards tracing claim would allow the beneficiary to trace his value into the property purchased with the credit given, and in the case of a mortgage of land, that will be the land itself, of course. The beneficiary might then claim a proportionate share of the value of the land or, if the recipient is a trustee or wrongdoer, elect to take a charge on it. By subrogation, the plaintiff will necessarily acquire a proprietary right in the land too, since the loan was a secured one, and the charge forms part of the right to which he is subrogated. But the plaintiff cannot acquire by subrogation an ownership or co-ownership share. So the first thing to note is that, if backwards tracing had been authoritatively recognised and applied in this case, the issue of subrogation would never have arisen, for a claim based on backwards tracing would have been superior.

11.142 There is a further 'fishy' aspect to this decision. As Millett LJ made abundantly clear in the case, the beneficiary's right to be subrogated arises by operation of law as a *restitutionary* remedy, to reverse the unjust enrichment the defendant would otherwise retain.   Now, as we shall see further on (**11.181** et seq), many commentators, including judges speaking extra-judicially and *obiter* in cases (Lord Millett amongst them), have argued that a stranger's proprietary and personal liability alike for receipt of trust property should be analysed as a liability arising in the law of restitution for unjust enrichment. But this is in conflict with the traditional understanding of the law, which treats the beneficiary's proprietary claim against a recipient of trust property or its proceeds as a matter of his equitable title, and any personal liability of the recipient as a matter of his wrong-doing, ie it is a fault-based liability. In view of this, *Boscawen* counts *either* as a revolutionary case in which the restitutionary nature of the beneficiary's claim against third party recipients was recently recognised, *or* a case which mistakenly imports restitutionary principles into the property- and fault-based rules governing liability for receipt of trust property.

11.143 You might think that this is all just a matter of theory; after all, how much difference in practice will it make whether the beneficiary (1) is entitled to be subrogated to a charge over the property or instead (2) has the right to elect either an ownership claim or a lien following backwards tracing? Of course the latter right to elect is itself a valuable right, but since both (1) and (2) establish proprietary rights, why should we be troubled whether the rights acquired are restitutionary, or arise by electing how to deal with the asset as the proceeds of an application of trust property in the traditional way? There is a significant difference, however, when we consider the case of an innocent recipient of trust property. Why? Well, notice that the subrogation claim does not turn on the fact that the debt that was paid off with trust money was a *secured* debt. The right to be subrogated applies to the payment of any debt the recipient makes with trust property. Of course, this right to be subrogated to the payment of an unsecured debt will only give the beneficiary a personal right against the recipient to repay the money expended on the debt, and where the recipient is a trustee this will be a pointless, additional right, for the trustee is strictly personally liable to restore the trust anyway (**11.17** et seq); the same applies to the case of a third party recipient who knows that the property in his hands is trust property; he will be strictly personally liable as well; but an innocent recipient, whilst he is liable to hold the trust property or traceable proceeds in his hands as trust property – ie the beneficiary can specifically enforce the trust over this property against him – is *not* personally liable to dig into his own pocket to restore the trust (**11.164** et seq). But if the subrogation claim is available, then it is likely that the innocent recipient will be personally liable to restore the trust to a large extent, for if you think of the way people spend money, they almost always do so in the discharge of debts. Except for gifts and over-the-counter shop sales (see Penner (1996a)), most expenditures of money pay off contractually-incurred debts of one kind or another. When you pay your restaurant bill at the end of dinner, you pay off a contractual debt incurred when you ordered the meal; when you pay for your vacation, you pay off the debt incurred when you booked the holiday. Everything you ever buy on a credit card, ie on credit, creates a debt which you must ultimately discharge. Thus if a beneficiary can be subrogated to the rights of all the debtors who a recipient pays off with trust money, and, as we have just seen, most payments a person makes discharge debts, then the beneficiary is subrogated to an array of personal claims against this innocent recipient, with the result that, contrary to what the traditional law teaches us, the innocent recipient *is* largely personally liable to restore the trust out of his own pocket. Although those in favour of a restitutionary analysis of liability for receipt of trust property would be happy with, perhaps exult in, this result, it cannot be the case that this general right of subrogation can stand alongside the conventional law under which an innocent recipient of trust property is *not* personally liable to restore the value of any trust property or traceable proceeds he receives.

11.144   One final note about the case: in the quoted passage Millett LJ considers that a beneficiary is entitled to a charge over land which has been improved with traceable value. In *Re Diplock* (1948) such a charge was denied beneficiaries under a will where the innocent recipient was a charity who was mistakenly paid by the executor, on the ground that a charge, being enforceable by sale, might require the charity to sell the property, and therefore the consequences of imposing a charge would do more than merely restore the plaintiff's value, but cause the charity a significant actual loss. The question is a difficult one because such a case is not equivalent to the usual case of an innocent recipient 'mixing' trust property or proceeds with his own; the usual case of 'mixing' is combining money in one bank account and drawing upon money from this mixed fund to buy a new asset. Spending money to make an improvement is not equivalent to 'purchasing' a share of an asset; it is paying for a service (and, usually, some materials) the performance of which does not consist in the acquisition of any new item of property, but which may raise the value of something already owned. It seems simplistic to say that a beneficiary should simply be able to trace his value into the money spent on the improvement service and materials and thence into the improved property regardless of the extent to which the property increased in value or the inconvenience to the innocent improver of charging the property. We await a rigorous examination by the courts.

Tracing at common law and the quest for a fiduciary relationship

11.145 For various complicated historical reasons, plaintiffs who held full beneficial legal title to property have been largely unable to claim legal title to property acquired in exchange for their property, ie to the traceable proceeds. For example, if a fraudster gets you to transfer your watch to him, say in exchange for a forged and worthless cheque, and the fraudster sells the watch for £100, which he banks in his own current account, and then draws upon the account to purchase a car, the position at common law appeared to be, roughly, that you had no right to claim any share of the car as your legal property. The supposed reason for this result was that the common law rules of tracing were much less sophisticated than those of equity. In particular, the legal owner of property had a much harder time claiming any rights in traceable proceeds once his value had been added to a bank account, because, it was believed, the common law could not trace through mixtures of value.

11.146 The idea that the common law was mentally deficient in this respect is clearly belied by the fact that the common law developed principles to deal with the mixing of goods, as where a quantity of one individual's oil was mixed with that of another (**11.105**), or the rule in

Clayton's Case, whereby a bank balance is treated as a series of individual debts. The real issue becomes clear when we pay attention to the distinction between tracing and claiming. The common law, no less than equity, was and is capable of tracing value through the proceeds of exchanges; but unlike equity, the common law resists giving the legal owner a new legal entitlement to proceeds (see Smith (1997), 321-339).

11.147   Recall the two different theoretical bases for the beneficiary's right to claim the proceeds of trust property following the tracing exercise (11.137), the 'exchange product' theory and the 'power *in rem*' theory. The authority for the 'exchange-product' theory In respect of legal title, ie that a legal owner may claim legal title to the proceeds acquired in exchange for his property, is frail. The foundational cases in favour of the theory are *Taylor v Plumer* (1815) and *Banque Belge pour l'Etranger v Hambrouck* (1921), but it is now generally accepted that the former case was decided on *equitable*, not common law, principles (see Smith (1995), Kurshid & Matthews (1979); Matthews (1995b)), and the latter case is unsatisfactory, first, because two judges in the CA based their decision on *Taylor,* and the other on equitable principles, and secondly, because the case is better explained in terms of a power *in rem* (see, eg Khurshid & Matthews (1979)), ie a power of the plaintiff to acquire title in the proceeds, not on the basis that he automatically acquires title to the proceeds on exchange.

11.148   The issue came up for consideration in *Lipkin Gorman v Karpnale* (1991). A solicitor of the firm of Lipkin Gorman, Cass, used his signing authority to withdraw funds from the firm's client account which he then lost gambling. The firm sued Karpnale Ltd, which owned the Playboy Club in Mayfair where Cass gambled away the money. The money was clearly trust money, and Cass clearly stood in a fiduciary position with respect to the use of the money, if not as a trustee himself, so there was no question that had the case been argued on equitable principles, the trust money might have been traced, if the transactional links could be shown, into the hands of the Club. The case, however was argued only on common law principles of restitution. The HL decided that despite the fact that Cass became the legal owner of the money he withdrew from the client account, the firm retained a sufficient legal interest in the money to claim that the Club received the firm's value at common law. Since the firm clearly did not intend the money to go to the Club, indeed the firm was ignorant of the transfer of the money, the Club would be unjustly enriched unless it was a bona fide purchaser of it. Because however, the Club acquired title to the money by wagering contracts the court reasoned (almost certainly incorrectly) that as such contracts are unenforceable, the Club did not in the eyes of the law give valuable consideration for the money, and therefore the Club was held liable to a restitutionary claim.

11.149   Lord Goff said the following:

> It is well-established that a legal owner is entitled to trace his property into its product, provided that the latter is indeed identifiable as the product of his property. Thus in *Taylor v Plumer* ... , where Sir Thomas Plumer gave a draft to a stockbroker for the purpose of buying exchequer bills, and the stockbroker instead used the draft for buying American securities and doubloons for his own purposes, Sir Thomas was able to trace his property into the securities and doubloons in the hands of the stockbroker, and so defeat a claim made to them by the stockbroker's assignees in bankruptcy. Of course, 'tracing' or 'following' property into its product *involves a decision by the owner of the original property to assert his title to the product in place of his original property. This is sometimes referred to as a ratification. I myself would not so describe it; but it has, in my opinion, at least one feature in common with ratification, that it cannot be relied upon so as to render an innocent recipient a wrongdoer.* (My italics)

11.150   There are two things to note about this description of common law claims to traceable products. It undermines the 'exchange-product theory', since it depends upon the owner's assertion of his title to the proceeds. Second, the legal interest in the proceeds cannot 'be relied upon to render an innocent recipient a wrongdoer'. This means that the Club, which received the money innocently, was not deprived of the change of position defence (below, **11.186-187**), which can only be relied upon by defendants to restitutionary claims who are innocent. It also means that a third party who innocently received the proceeds could not be liable for the tort of 'converting' the proceeds, ie the tort of interfering with someone's title, which is committed, for example, by a thief who steals your bicycle (below **11.182**), for that is a wrong. Thus the legal interest in the product the legal owner gets is a distinctly peculiar one (see also Birks (1991); Smith (1997), 325-339). Unfortunately for our understanding of the law, the Club conceded (somewhat inexplicably) that if it was shown that the firm had a legal interest in the money in

410

Cass's hands, his mixing of the firm's money with his own would not prevent the firm's tracing the money into that received by the Club, so the HL did not have to deal with the possibility that the identity of the firm's value might have been untraceable given that it is commonly held that the common law would not trace through mixtures of value.

11.151   But things get curiouser and curiouser, as Alice might have said: subsequent to the difficult to understand decision in *Lipkin Gorman*, Millett LJ treated us to an even more challenging decision in *FC Jones & Sons (Trustee in Bankruptcy) v Jones* (1997). Following an act of bankruptcy by a partnership, which made it unlawful for any of the partners to draw on a partnership account, one of the partners drew cheques in favour of his wife, Mrs Jones, who banked them into her account with a commodities broker, and used them to speculate on the potato futures market, making a large profit. The profits were paid into her account with the brokers, and the trustee in bankruptcy of the firm claimed them. Millett LJ held that the wife was not a trustee of the cheques or her account balance at the brokers; she did not receive the money in a fiduciary capacity. So far so good. But Millett LJ went on to say that she did not obtain *any title at all*, legal or equitable, to the cheques or the account balance at her brokers; the title remained throughout with the trustee in bankruptcy, who took over all the partnership's assets following the act of bankruptcy:

> ...as from the date of the act of bankruptcy the money in the bankrupts' joint account...belonged to the trustee [in bankruptcy]. The account holders had no title to it at law or in equity. The cheques which they drew in favour of the defendant... were incapable of passing any legal or equitable title. They were not, however, without legal effect, for the bank honoured them. The result was to affect the identity of the debtor but not the creditor [ie the creditor, the trustee in bankruptcy, now had a claim against the brokers into the account in which Mrs. Jones banked the cheques, not the partnership's bank where the partnership's account was, and on which the cheques were drawn] and to put the defendant in possession of funds to which she had no title. A debt formally owed by [the partnership's bank] to the [partners] ultimately became a debt owed by the brokers apparently to the defendant but in reality to the trustee.

11.152   As both Birks (1997) and Smith (1997, 328 et seq) have pointed out, this is very difficult to reconcile with the orthodox law of property.

When Millett LJ says that Mrs Jones was put 'in possession' of the funds, he seems to be making an analogy with the case of a misappropriated chattel. As we know (**2.41**), legal title to chattels is very robust. A thief acquires no title to what he steals, and he cannot pass good title to a purchaser, however innocent he is. The idea at work in this passage appears to be that Mrs Jones never acquired any title to the cheques (this is probably true, as the cheques themselves were chattels), but also acquired no title of any kind to her account balance at her brokers. But an account balance is the sort of property known as a *chose in action* or 'thing in action', a personal right to be paid a certain sum. One cannot merely 'possess' such a right without having 'title' to that right, for the right is all there is. Either Mrs Jones had a right to be paid the balance of her account at the brokers or she did not. She could not have that right but not have that right at the same time, ie have the right without having 'title' to it. In short, there is no possible conceptual distinction between 'title' and 'possession' which can make the analogy with the chattel work.

11.153 It should also be noted that if Millett's analysis is right, the position of banks and other account holders like Mrs Jones becomes impossible, for if the true title to the bank balance belongs to someone like a trustee in bankruptcy rather than the person who opens the account, the bank will commit a wrong if it pays the account holder. But how is the bank to know that someone else 'really' has title to the bank balance? Thus, if Millett LJ is right, then banks are placed under an enormous risk they can do nothing to prevent every time their customers pay funds into their accounts (see further Matthews (1995b); Smith (1997), 329-330).

11.154 Millett LJ might better have made an analogy with the legal device of the 'power of attorney', whereby one person is empowered to deal with the legal title of another person. Such an analogy does not provide a workable interpretation of Millett LJ's views as stated, though, since Millett LJ does not allow that Mrs Jones had any power of any kind over the property here. Birks (1997) argues that nevertheless the case should be understood along the 'power *in rem*' analysis following *Lipkin Gorman*.

11.155 On the positive side, in this case Millett LJ, emphasising the difference between tracing and claiming, argued that the tracing rules should be the same at both common law and equity: 'There is no merit in having distinct and different tracing rules at law and in equity, given that tracing is neither a right nor a remedy but merely the process by which the plaintiff establishes what has happened to his property and makes good his claim that the assets which he claims can properly be regarded as representing his property'.

11.156 Because of the supposedly superior tracing process recognised in equity, and because equitable remedial rights in the form of an equitable charge or an equitable co-ownership claim are available to the plaintiff who can establish an equitable claim to traceable proceeds, the law of England has been coloured by plaintiffs arguing that the original misapplication of their property involved a breach of fiduciary duty. Like trustees, fiduciaries such as agents or company directors who misapply their principals' property are liable to account for the misapplication (**11.14**), and principals may trace the value of the property transferred using equitable tracing rules and avail themselves of equitable claims to the proceeds. These proprietary claims are, of course, most valuable in the case where the defendant is insolvent. The high watermark of this development occurred in *Chase Manhattan Bank v Israel-British Bank* (1981) (**4.58**), in which Goulding J appeared to manufacture a fiduciary relationship out of thin air so as to allow a bank which mistakenly paid $2m to another bank to trace into the proceeds remaining in the recipient banks hands.

11.157 In *Westdeutsche Landesbank Girozentrale v Islington London Borough Council* (1996) the HL held this reasoning to be wrong. (As we have seen, the HL also rejected the Birks/Chambers theory of the resulting trust which would have justified the decision (**4.59**).) However, Lord Browne-Wilkinson did state, *obiter*, that the result in *Chase Manhattan* could be justified on the basis that when the recipient bank learned of the mistaken payment, its conscience was affected, at which point equity would impose a *constructive* trust over the money received. This justification seems quite wrong, and as a mere *obiter dictum* should not be followed; the constructive trust seems to be raised on nothing more than the recipient's awareness that he owes the plaintiff a certain sum, ie that he must repay an equivalent amount to that which he received. This is just a normal everyday recognition of a legal liability to pay a debt, no different in principle than a recognition of any other kind of debt, such as a debt to pay one's credit card bill. The mere realisation that one is indebted does not turn one into a trustee, or a fiduciary, or a wrongdoer in equity, and therefore there is no basis for the imposition of a constructive trust here. The better view is simply that *Chase Manhattan* was wrongly decided (see Millett (1998)).

Tracing from legal title to secure an equitable interest

11.158   To review where we've got to in 'tracing at common law' so far: although there seems no good reason why the rules of tracing value through exchanges, whether through mixed bank accounts or not, should differ in common law from equity, there may be good reasons not to allow legal owners to acquire by operation of law legal title in the traceable proceeds that derive from exchanges with their legal title, for reasons which become apparent, as we have just seen, in the case of banks if Millett LJ's analysis in *FC Jones* is correct. The most that seems reasonable is to allow such claimants to assert their title in proceeds via the somewhat strange 'power *in rem*' devised in *Lipkin Gorman*. As Smith (1997, 330) argues:

> [C]ommon law rights... serve as a baseline. They can be transferred at will by the one who holds them. If it is necessary to change the result, one looks to equity, which can encumber legal rights in various ways. ... It is true that equitable proprietary rights may be hidden, but for this very reason, they are fragile, always destroyed where a bona fide purchaser acquires a legal interest for value without notice of the equitable rights.

(See also Matthews (1995b).)

11.159   For this sort of reason it has been suggested that a legal owner should be able to trace into the proceeds acquired in exchange for property he owned, not so as to acquire *legal* title in the proceeds, but rather an *equitable* one. As we have seen (**11.14–11.15**), in cases of property transferred in breach of fiduciary obligation, and in some cases of fraud, equity will allow the wronged party to trace into the proceeds acquired with the property to which he had legal title. But so far the law has not recognised a general principle allowing a legal owner to claim equitable title to proceeds that result from exchanges with what is, or was, his legal property, particularly in cases of fraud (for a recent consideration of the question, see *Shalson v Russo* (2003)). The difficulty of formulating a general principle of this kind can be shown by considering an *obiter dictum* of Lord Browne-Wilkinson in *Westdeutche Landesbank*.

11.160 Lord Browne-Wilkinson opined that money that is stolen is traceable in equity, because the thief will immediately hold the money under a constructive trust. Strictly speaking, this makes no sense at all, for the thief does not acquire any legal title to stolen property upon which any such trust could 'bite'. Presumably what his Lordship meant was that any proceeds to which the thief acquires legal title in exchange for the stolen property are held on trust for his victim.

11.161 But with respect, his Lordship expressed this view without considering the surrounding law dealing with such a case. Where do you think the *proceeds* come from? Well, obviously from someone who purchased the stolen goods from the thief. Now, as we know, money is negotiable (**2.40**), so if the thief steals your money and buys, say, a car with it, then the seller of the car gets good title to the money. If you acquire an equitable title to the car, as the proceeds of the thief's use of his money, this does not adversely affect the seller, who as we have seen, is entitled to keep the stolen money. But consider the case of the thief who steals your car and then sells it. By doing this, he defrauds the buyer (makes a fraudulent misrepresentation to the buyer, ie that he has title to the car, to induce him to part with his money in exchange for it). Now, according to Lord Browne-Wilkinson, you immediately get an equitable interest in the money proceeds; notice also, because a thief cannot pass good title, you retain title to your car, so you can also sue the buyer of it for its full value – the action under which you claim against him is called 'conversion', for you claim damages for his 'converting' of your goods to his use, essentially for interfering with your title to the goods (see now Torts (Interference with Goods) Act 1977). But is it correct that you have a right both to claim the proceeds and to claim damages against the buyer for conversion? Contracts that are induced by a fraudulent misrepresentation are typically voidable. That means, that upon discovery of the fraud, the victim, here the buyer of your car, can rescind the transaction, and the normal result of rescission is to re-vest in the victim the legal title to the property he transferred.

11.162 Now we see the obvious complication. If your trust over the proceeds arises by operation of law upon the sale, then it effectively extinguishes any right of the buyer's to rescind the transaction, for what's the use of the buyer's rescinding and regaining legal title if it is bound by your trust over it? And is this a fair result? You, remember, retain your title to the car; why should the law deny the buyer's right to revest his title in the money, which was, after all, *his* property to begin with?

11.163 One might say of course, that none of this matters practically, for if you assert title in the substitute, the proceeds, then you must be taken to 'adopt' or 'ratify' the sale of your car by the thief, so that the buyer is no longer liable for conversion. But what if the proceeds increase in value? Say the thief sells your car to the buyer for £10,000, which he then invests in shares now worth £15,000. Both the owner and the buyer will wish to have an interest in these proceeds. How should we decide which of the two has a better claim? By not thinking through the possible consequences of his remarks, Lord Browne-Wilkinson's *obiter dictum* cannot be treated as authoritative, and has been recently criticised, and not followed, by Rimer J in *Shalson v Russo* (2003). (See also Matthews (1995b))

Personal claims against recipients of trust property or its traceable proceeds

Knowing receipt and knowing dealing

11.164 A recipient of trust property or its traceable proceeds may be personally liable to repay money equal to the value he has received. That is, he will be liable to dig into his own pocket and pay the value of the trust property he received irrespective of whether he *retains* any traceable value of the beneficiary, in respect of which the beneficiary may make a proprietary claim of some kind. There are two sorts of case: the first occurs when a person receives trust property or its traceable proceeds *knowing* that it was transferred in breach of trust; clearly he should have held the property for the benefit of the trust – normally, this would involve returning the property to the trustees, unless it was clear that the trustees had fraudulently breached the trust, in which case the defendant should apply to the court for directions. If he acts properly in this way, the recipient will not be personally liable. If, however, he acts otherwise, treating the property as his own or in any other way inconsistent with the rights of the beneficiary, then he will be personally liable to restore the value of the property to the extent that the beneficiary cannot make a proprietary claim for any property or proceeds he retains. In essence, then, this *knowing* recipient will be treated as if he is a custodian trustee (**11.121-23, 11.127**) of the property who knows that he is: he has no obligations to carry out the terms of the trust himself, but must hold the property to the order of the rightful trustees of the trust, and if he acts otherwise, will be personally liable for his breach of that trust. In view of this, we can understand why the knowing recipient is traditionally called a 'constructive trustee'. He is not an express trustee, of course, because it is not at all relevant whether he actually agreed to hold the property on trust when he received it; rather, equity imposes upon him the duty of custodian trusteeship.

11.165   The second case is a minor variation. Where a person receives trust property or its proceeds ignorant of the breach of trust by which it came to him, but then later learns of the breach of trust, then at that point he will be treated the same as the knowing recipient. He will not be liable for any untraceable dissipations of the trust property he makes up to that point, but thereafter he is personally liable to restore the trust for any further dissipations of the trust property. Similarly, where a person receives funds perfectly properly as an agent of the trust, but then knowingly deals with the property inconsistently with the trust, he will be personally liable for any loss. A classic case is *Lee v Sankey* (1872). Solicitors received the proceeds of the sale of trust property and held it for further investment, and this was perfectly correct under the terms of the trust. However, knowing this was a breach of trust they transferred part of the funds to only one of the trustees, who dissipated the whole amount. The solicitors were personally liable for the loss. Because the constructive trusteeship arises not on the receipt of the trust property or its proceeds, but when the recipient only later learns of the trust, this liability is traditionally called liability for 'knowing dealing'.

11.166   A similar but distinct case is *Andrews v Bousfield* (1847). The case involved a debtor to a marriage settlement, ie someone who had received a loan of the settlement funds. Inconsistently with the terms of the trust, the borrower paid moneys to the trustees, which was lost. He was liable to repay the loan again, this time properly. The case is not really one of knowing dealing, for the money he paid to the trustees was not trust property. The correct way to view the case is that a debtor cannot effectively discharge his debt to the trust if he knowingly pays the trustees in circumstances where the payment would not be consistent with the trust terms. He is treated as making a payment to the trustees personally for their own benefit, not a payment to them *as trustees* which discharges his debt to the trust.

11.167 Finally, a stranger can only be liable for the receipt of trust property if it is transferred *in breach of trust*. If the property is not misapplied, but transferred by the trustee to a person according to terms of the trust, as for example when the trustee properly pays income to the income beneficiary, or properly spends money on an authorised investment, then there is, of course, no breach of trust, and the recipient cannot possibly be liable. Although this is obviously true, if not truistic, it can at times be difficult to apply to certain fact situations. Consider *Brown v Bennett* (1999): the plaintiffs, shareholders in a company, Pinecord, alleged that the defendant directors used their powers as directors to drive Pinecord into receivership despite the company's underlying value both in terms of its goodwill and as a properly-managed going concern. The business of Pinecord was sold by the receiver to Oasis, a company in which the defendants were directors, and Pinecord went into liquidation. There was no question that the receiver's sale was a perfectly proper transaction by it for the best obtainable offer. However, the plaintiffs claimed that Oasis was fixed with the knowledge of their directors, ie of the defendants, and therefore knew of the defendants' breach of their fiduciary obligations to Pinecord which led to its going into receivership; therefore, the plaintiffs claimed, Oasis was liable for the knowing receipt of assets (the business of Pinecord) which were transferred as a result of their breach of fiduciary obligation. The judge at first instance struck out the plaintiffs' claim against Oasis, and the CA dismissed the plaintiffs' appeal. Morritt LJ said:

> The matter, I think, can be tested in this way. Let us assume a mansion house vested in trustees. The trustees fail to perform their fiduciary duties and allow it to fall into appalling disrepair. They are then replaced by other trustees who decide that the matter has gone too far and decide to sell the property. They sell the property to a next-door neighbour, who for the previous 40 years has watched the mansion house falling into disrepair. The sale by the new trustees to the neighbour is entirely proper, at a proper price. The neighbour unquestionably has notice of the previous breaches of duty, because he watched them happen, but the breaches of duty did not give rise to any receipt by the neighbour; the neighbour was not in any way responsible for them and he paid the full value for what he received from the new trustees when he bought. I can see no reason why in those circumstances there should be any constructive trust liability imposed upon the neighbour merely because he watched the house fall into disrepair before he was enabled to buy it.

11.168 Thus the plaintiffs' claim failed on the fundamental point that no property subject to any trust was passed to Oasis. A past breach of fiduciary duty *in relation* to a person's stewardship of trust property (or, in the company case, to company property in respect of which a fiduciary has stewardship) does not impress that property with a trust in favour of the beneficiaries. The beneficiaries or principals have a *personal* claim against the trustee or fiduciary, of course, but that personal claim does not attach itself to the trust property turning it into a *proprietary* claim, either during the time the property is held on trust by the trustee or, *a fortiori*, following any proper transfer of it out of the trust. Therefore knowledge of any breach of fiduciary obligation in relation to the property makes no difference to a transferee if the property is properly transferred to him under the trust terms. Liability for knowing receipt can only arise for a recipient when the transfer of the property itself is in breach of trust or in breach of fiduciary obligation.

The current standard of knowledge

11.169   In preceding paragraphs we referred to *knowing* receipt and dealing. What does the recipient need to know to be fixed with liability? The law governing the knowledge required is extraordinarily confused, largely because in a series of cases the courts did not appear to distinguish between liability for assisting a breach of trust, liability for knowing receipt or dealing, and the knowledge or notice which would prevent someone from being a bona fide purchaser of trust property, ie the knowledge which would make a purchaser for value *proprietarily* liable to the beneficiaries as a holder of trust property (see Harpum (1986)). Secondly, the issue has not reached the HL in a long time, and there are conflicting opinions in the CA.   In the recent case of *BCCI v Akindele* (2000), which we will look at in some detail (**11.175**), the CA tried to start afresh from first principles, but the decision is unsatisfying. First we will undertake a brief review of the law leading up to *Akindele*.

11.170   In *Baden v Société Générale* (1992) Peter Gibson J distinguished five categories of knowledge:

> ... (i) actual knowledge; (ii) wilfully shutting one's eyes to the obvious; (iii) wilfully and recklessly failing to make such inquiries as an honest and reasonable man would make; (iv) knowledge of circumstances which would indicate the facts to an honest and reasonable man; (v) knowledge of circumstances which would put an honest and reasonable man on inquiry.

Knowledge in all of these categories is sufficient to fix the defendant with 'notice', the standard of cognisance which applies in determining whether a person has 'notice' of a breach of trust or the beneficiary's rights. Category (i), actual knowledge is narrower than 'actual notice' (recall **2.43** et seq), but actual notice might cover categories (i), (ii) and (iv), as covering facts which would be apparent if all available information were taken into account. The 'constructive' knowledge described in (iii) and (iv) appears to be equivalent to a narrower version of constructive notice, with (iii) adding an element of dishonesty or 'want of probity', as it is sometimes put. Categories (i) to (iii) together might be regarded as 'dishonest' knowledge showing a want of probity, whereas knowledge in (iv) and (v) would not, for the defendant may fail to draw the right inferences or inquire appropriately because he was foolish or otherwise unreasonable, but not actually dishonest (see *Agip* per Millett J, above **11.84**).

11.171 The authorities do not indicate a uniform standard of cognisance that will fix a recipient of trust property or its proceeds with personal liability. In *Re Montagu's Settlement Trusts* (1987) Megarry VC was unwilling to fix a volunteer recipient of chattels in breach of a family trust, who later sold them, with personal liability to repay their value. He held that even if the recipient had once known that the chattels were property of the trust, he would not be personally liable where he had honestly forgotten that they were. Megarry VC clearly distinguished between notice and knowledge; only the latter was sufficient for acquiring personal liability for receipt of trust property. Megarry clearly regarded personal liability for receipt as liability to account 'as a constructive trustee', ie on the traditional formulation we have set out above (**11.121-23, 11.127, 11.164-65**), ie on the basis that the recipient himself breaches his custodian trusteeship. Where the recipient is innocent, then he cannot be liable for breach of trust because he does not act inconsistently with the orders of the managing trustee, and commits no breach of trust as far as he knows.

11.172 In *Agip* and *El Ajou v Dollar Land Holdings plc* (1993) Millett J appeared to hold that something less than actual knowledge is sufficient. Comparing his view with that of Vinelott J's in *Eagle Trust plc v SBC Securities Ltd* (1992) he said:

> Vinelott J based liability firmly on inferred knowledge and not on constructive notice. For my own part, I agree that even where the plaintiff's

claim is a proprietary one, and the defendant raises the defence of bona fide purchaser for value without notice, there is no room for the doctrine of constructive notice in the strict conveyancing sense in a factual situation where it is not the custom and practice to make inquiry. But it does not follow that there is no room for an analogous doctrine in a situation in which any honest and reasonable man would have made inquiry ... I am content to assume, without deciding, that dishonesty or want of probity involving actual knowledge (whether proved or inferred) is not a precondition of liability; but that a recipient is not expected to be unduly suspicious and is not to be held liable unless he went ahead without further inquiry in circumstances in which an honest and reasonable man would have realised that the money was probably trust money and was being misapplied ... Moreover, I do not see how it would be possible to develop any logical and coherent system of restitution if there were different requirements in respect of knowledge for the common law claim for money had and received, the personal claim for an account in equity against a knowing recipient and the equitable proprietary claim. In the present case, for example, it would be illogical and undesirable to require the plaintiff to assert a proprietary claim he does not need in order to avoid the burden of having to prove dishonesty or ask the court to infer it.

11.173   There are several things to notice about this paragraph. While Millett J seems to adopt a lower requirement for knowledge than does Megarry VC, he still applies a 'fault' standard, in that to be liable the recipient must fall below the standard of conduct of an honest and reasonable person. Secondly, the sort of inquiry such a person should undertake must be adapted to the particular circumstances of dealing; notice, as it applies to land transfers because of the standard practices of inquiry, should not apply to transactions for which there is no such practice. However he clearly seems keen to bring together the common law restitutionary claim for money had and received with the recipient's personal and proprietary liability to form 'a logical and coherent system of restitution'. Thus we have an early indication of Millett J's view that the stranger's liability of any kind for receipt of trust property attracts restitutionary reasoning. As regards the standard of knowledge for a *volunteer* recipient, though Millett J cited the view of Megarry VC in *Re Montagu's*, he regarded this issue as controversial, implicitly doubting whether Megarry VC got it right. Nevertheless, in *Westdeutsche Landesbank*, Lord Browne-Wilkinson specifically approved *Re Montagu's* (in support of the passage quoted below, **11.192**).

11.174 In three recent decisions of the CA, *Houghton v Fayers* (2000), *Bank of Credit and Commerce International v Akindele* (2000), and *Brown v Bennett* (1999) a requirement of some kind of knowledge was applied. All courts cited Hoffmann LJ's formulation in *El Ajou v Dollar Land Holdings plc* (1994):

> [T]he plaintiff must show, first, a disposal of his assets in breach of fiduciary duty; secondly, the beneficial receipt by the defendant of assets which are traceable as representing the assets of the plaintiff; and thirdly, knowledge on the part of the defendant that the assets received are traceable to a breach of fiduciary duty.

This passage would appear to indicate that the defendant must have some actual or 'naughty' knowledge of the offending transaction, but in *Houghton* Nourse LJ, delivering the judgment of the court, went on to say (citing *Belmont Finance Corpn v Williams Furniture Ltd (No 2)* (1980)) that the defendant would be personally liable for receipt if he knew or *ought to have known* the money was paid in breach of fiduciary duty, thus adopting a standard of constructive knowledge.

11.175 In *Akindele* Nourse LJ, again writing for the court, undertook a review of the authorities governing the requisite degree and character of knowledge necessary to fix a recipient with personal liability to restore the value of the assets received. Nourse LJ's decision is significant in two respects. The first is that he held that, while a defendant need not be found to have acted dishonestly in receiving the trust property, he must have known something about the breach of trust to be liable; however, he expressed 'grave doubts' about the usefulness of the *Baden* categories of knowledge in determining personal liability for receipt. He said:

> What then, in the context of knowing receipt, is the purpose to be served by a categorisation of knowledge? It can only be to enable the court to determine whether, in the words of Buckley LJ in *Belmont (No 2)*, the recipient can 'conscientiously retain [the] funds against the company' or, in the words of Megarry VC in *Re Montagu's Settlement Trusts*, '[the recipient's] conscience is sufficiently affected for it to be right to bind him by the obligations of a constructive trustee'. But if that is the purpose, there is no need for categorisation. All that is necessary is that the recipient's state of knowledge should be such as to make it unconscionable for him to retain the benefit of the receipt.
>
> For these reasons I have come to the view that, just as there is now a single test of dishonesty for knowing assistance, so ought there to be

a single test of knowledge for knowing receipt. The recipient's state of knowledge must be such as to make it unconscionable for him to retain the benefit of the receipt. A test in that form, though it cannot, any more than any other, avoid difficulties of application, ought to avoid those of definition and allocation to which the previous categorisations have led.

11.176 With respect, this is really very unsatisfactory. The term 'unconscionable', like 'unfair' or 'unjust', gives absolutely no guidance to a court trying properly to characterise the sorts of facts which must be in place for personal recipient liability to arise. A defendant's behaviour must be unconscionable, unfair, or unjust *according to law*. The whole point of paying attention to the facts and decisions in the past cases is to acquire some understanding of what 'unconscionable' receipt amounts to. The end of the exercise cannot be the declaration of a standard — that the receipt must be 'unconscionable'— which assumes a prior grasp of the result this exercise was intended to provide; this is to beg the whole question. The *Baden* scale is not by any means perfect, but it does fulfill the useful function of pointing out some of the different ways and extents to which a defendant might have acquired knowledge of a breach of trust, and therefore requires a judge to appreciate that the question whether the defendant's awareness in the case before him is sufficient to make his receipt 'unconscionable' will often require a fairly subtle and nuanced appreciation of the particular facts in their surrounding context.

11.177 Nourse LJ is further mistaken to think that his declaration of a single test of knowledge for knowing receipt by reference to unconscionability is a proper parallel to Lord Nicholls's adoption of a standard of dishonesty for knowing assistance. 'Dishonest', unlike 'unconscionable', is much less a legal term of art, and it was to a common, member-of-a-jury, understanding of dishonesty that Lord Nicholls appealed. Even so, as we have seen (11.78), he then went on to elaborate in some detail what should count as dishonest; Nourse LJ here undertakes no similar effort with a term which is much less likely to have any commonly well-grasped sense.

11.178 The second significant feature of Nourse LJ's judgment is that Lord Nicholls's extra-judicially expressed view that liability for receipt of trust property should be strict, subject to a change of position defence, was referred to in argument before the CA, although no argument on the precise suggestion made by Lord Nicholls was made, presumably because it would have been, in the words of Nourse LJ, a 'fruitless exercise', the CA being bound by its previous decisions so as to make a radical departure of this kind unavailable to it. Nevertheless, Nourse LJ had this to say:

> I beg leave to doubt whether strict liability coupled with a change of position defence would be preferable to fault-based liability in many commercial transactions, for example where, as here, the receipt is of a company's funds which have been misapplied by its directors. Without having heard argument it is unwise to be dogmatic, but in such a case it would appear to be commercially unworkable ... that, simply on proof of an internal misapplication of the company's funds, the burden should shift to the recipient to defend the receipt either by change of position or perhaps in some other way.

11.179 The point Nourse LJ makes about the shifting of the burden of proof is an important one. As Smith (2000) points out:

> The strict liability approach would contemplate that a plaintiff need only allege that a bank received trust property, not that the bank knew of or should have known of the trust; with no more than that, the bank would be required to prove its good faith as a defence, or to account for what it had done with this money. In other words, there is no procedure which a bank, be it ever so honest, can adopt in order to ensure that it is not prima facie liable for the receipt of trust funds.

11.180 In summary, it is probably fair to say that as things stand at the moment, a recipient who has given value for trust property will fail to be a bona fide purchaser if he has notice of the breach of trust, but the standard of notice will vary according to the normal practice of inquiry which attends the specific kind of transaction in issue, ie whether he purchases land, securities, chattels, and so on. Where he is fixed with notice, so that the beneficiary can claim equitable title to the trust property or make some other proprietary claim to the proceeds if the recipient still retains them, it is not clear if the recipient is thereby also immediately personally liable because of his notice. Despite the recent CA decision in *Akindele*, it is probably wisest to make reference to the range of views expressed by different judges that we have seen (11.170-74), as even if Nourse LJ's 'unconscionability' test prevails in name, much will have to be done to sort out exactly how knowledge and/or notice are relevant to its application.

The restitutionary analysis of recipient liability

The impulse towards fusion

11.181 The way third party recipients of trust property or its traceable proceeds, with its combination of proprietary liability and fault-based personal liability for knowing assistance, is a unique battery of remedies devised by equity. It does not match up with the way that recipients of another's property can be made liable at common law. At common law, a person who receives the property of another in flawed circumstances will be liable either for the tort of conversion, and be required to pay compensation for loss, or will be liable to make restitution for unjust enrichment. For many commentators, this difference in treatment suggests that like cases are not being treated alike, and thus that the current law does not provide a workable, coherent, justice. The most forceful arguments that have been made have come from restitution lawyers, who argue that liability for receipt of trust property should be analysed in harmony with common law liability for unjust enrichment. While, as we have seen, it is not currently the law that equity approaches the liability of third party recipients of trust property from a restitutionary perspective, there is a distinct chance that following a review of the area by the HL this perspective might be adopted, so it is necessary to assess this perspective in some detail. The basic question which must be asked is whether the case of receipt of trust property is really a case sufficiently like the traditional cases of restitution, such that their assimilation really makes sense in terms of coherence and justice.

Conversion and restitution

11.182 A person is strictly liable for 'converting' an owner's chattel 'to his own use', ie possessing the owner's chattel to the exclusion of the owner. Conversion is a tort, defined as the interference with the right to possession. While the tort arose at common law, it now has a statutory basis in the Torts (Interference with Goods) Act 1977. A convertor is personally liable to pay the owner damages equivalent to the value of the chattel for his conversion, whether or not he retains the chattel. If A's toaster is stolen by B who sells it to C, then C, even if he buys from B in complete good faith, ignorant of B's theft, is strictly liable for the value of the toaster to A, even if he has sold it on to D. C is left to recoup his loss by in turn bringing an action against B. C's knowledge or ignorance of A's title is irrelevant. Liability for conversion, because framed in terms of the wrong of interference, therefore covers past interferences as well as currently ongoing ones, so C who has sold the toaster is still liable. Furthermore, in most cases the true owner, A, does not have the right to the return of his chattel. He must be satisfied with the payment of money damages. While it has been said that equity's treatment of the recipient of trust property is an equitable version of conversion, the disanalogies are clear. First, in equity, and unlike in common law conversion, the beneficiary has the right to get the trust property or its traceable proceeds back – he is not limited to a claim for compensation for loss. Furthermore, the recipient's personal liability is not strict. To the extent that he no longer retains any trust property or its traceable proceeds, then only if he is at fault, ie has some degree of knowledge that the property is trust property and deals with it as his own anyway, will he be personally liable. While one might achieve fusion by either modifying equitable liability for receipt of trust property so that it matches up with common law conversion, or vice versa, or modify each to split the difference in some way, as far as I know no commentator presently advocates such a course.

11.183 From the restitutionary perspective, the recipient of trust property is liable simply because he has received value to which he is not entitled, so he must give it back. Otherwise he would be unjustly enriched. This claim then, is not for compensation for a wrong as in conversion, but restitutionary, ie the recipient must give up the gain he received. The analogy here is with common law restitutionary actions, such as the action traditionally called the action 'for money had and received': for example, where A mistakenly pays his gas bill of £50 a second time, forgetting his earlier payment, then the gas company will be strictly liable to repay this unjust enrichment of £50 to A. As with the standard of knowledge applicable to conversion, the gas company's knowledge about A's mistake is irrelevant.

11.184 The now largely-accepted formula for determining whether a person is liable to a restitutionary claim is framed in a series of questions:

(1) Has the defendant been enriched?

(2) Was the enrichment at the claimant's expense?

(3) Was the enrichment unjust?

(4) Does the defendant have any defence to the claim?

11.185   To review A's mistaken payment of his gas bill under this formula, we can see that (1) the gas company was enriched by receiving £50, (2) it came from A, and (3) the enrichment is unjust because of the 'unjust factor' of A's paying the money by mistake. Under the English law of restitution, the plaintiff must prove that the enrichment of the defendant is compromised by an unjust factor. The classic unjust factor is that of mistake, but enrichments tainted by unconscionability, duress, etc, also give rise to restitutionary claims. As we shall see (**11.199-11.201**), one of the problematic aspects of treating liability for the receipt of trust property under a restitutionary analysis is that of determining the unjust factor. Now, to question (4). The most wide-ranging defence available to a defendant otherwise liable to make restitution is the defence of 'change of position'.

The defence of change of position

11.186   This defence was firmly established as part of English law only recently, in the HL decision in *Lipkin Gorman* (**11.148-50**). The Playboy Club was able to reduce its liability on the basis that it had innocently 'changed its position' in response to its receipt of the money from Cass, by paying him significant amounts on his winning wagers. Lord Goff said:

> Where an innocent defendant's position is so changed that he will suffer an injustice if called upon to repay or to repay in full, the injustice of requiring him so to repay outweighs the injustice of denying the plaintiff restitution. If the plaintiff pays money to the defendant under a mistake of fact, and the defendant then, acting in good faith, pays the money or part of it to charity, it is unjust to require the defendant to make restitution to the extent that he has so changed his position ... I am most anxious that, in recognising this defence to actions of restitution, nothing should be said at this stage to inhibit the development of the defence on a case by case basis, in the usual way.

11.187   The law has indeed since developed on a case by case basis, and it is beyond the scope of this book to examine the law in detail – if the HL goes 'restitutionary' in analysing liability for the receipt of trust property, trusts students will then be responsible for knowing the law in detail (see, eg, Burrows (2002), 510 et seq), but until such time you should merely be aware of it in outline. The main points to be aware of are, first, that the defence arises on the basis that the defendant has made an extraordinary expenditure on the faith of his greater wealth due to the enrichment, or has suffered an extraordinary loss because of it. Lord Goff gives the example of a person who celebrates his new found wealth by making a gift to charity he would not otherwise have made. Other stock examples are organising a more lavish wedding for one's child, or taking a world cruise. The defence applies because the recipient can argue that had he not received the money, he would not have spent it on these things, and it would now be unjust to require the full amount back, for that would leave him in a worse position than if he had never received the money at all. The change of position defence does not arise when one merely spends in the normal way – paying one's rent is an expense one would have had to meet anyway, so there is no change of position that flows from the enrichment. A example of a successful invocation of the defence is *Philip Collins Ltd v Davis* (2000). Two backing band musicians were mistakenly overpaid, but they successfully reduced their liability to make restitution by establishing that their general economic philosophy was to raise their expenditure based on their income. Second, this limb of the defence is only available to innocent recipients. A person who realises that he has been unjustly enriched and will have to return his newly acquired wealth has no justification for making any extraordinary expenditures. Finally, as to the notion of extraordinary loss, consider this case: you receive a mistaken payment of cash of £1000, and on the way to bank it you are robbed. The receipt of this much cash exposed you to an extraordinary risk of theft, and it may not be just to require you to pay it back if the risk materialises.

Judicial support for the restitutionary analysis

11.188 There have been a number of obiter and extra-judicial statements by judges which argue for treating liability for the receipt of trust property as liability for unjust enrichment leading to a claim for restitution. In *Royal Brunei Airlines*, for instance, Lord Nicholls sharply distinguished accessory liability and recipient liability:

> Different considerations apply to the two heads of liability. Recipient liability is restitution-based, accessory liability is not.

In *El Ajou v Dollar Land Holdings plc* (1993) Millett J said:

[Knowing receipt] is the counterpart in equity of the common law action for money had and received. Both can be classified as receipt-based restitutionary claims.

n *Lipkin Gorman* Lord Goff said the following:

[T]he recognition of the [change of position] defence should be doubly beneficial. It will enable a more generous approach to be taken to the recognition of the right to restitution, in the knowledge that the defence is, in appropriate cases, available; and, while recognising the different functions of property at law and in equity, there may also in due course develop a more consistent approach to tracing claims, in which common defences are recognised as available to such claims, whether advanced at law or in equity.

11.189 In respect of the final sentiment, Millett LJ in *Boscawen*, dealing with the claims of an owner in equity for recipient liability against a defendant into whose hands he has traced his value, made it clear that the change of position defence should apply. Moreover, he said:

The introduction of the defence not only provides the court with a means of doing justice in future, but allows a re-examination of many decisions in which the absence of the defence may have led judges to distort basic principles in order to avoid injustice to the defendant.

11.190 Writing extra-judicially, Lord Nicholls (1998) takes *Lipkin Gorman* to be a catalyst in the development of the law, and has argued vis-a-vis recipient liability:

In this respect equity should now follow the law. Restitutionary liability, applicable regardless of fault but subject to a defence of change of position, would be a better-tailored response to the underlying mischief of misapplied property than personal liability which is exclusively fault-based. Personal liability would flow from having received the property of another, from having been unjustly enriched at the expense of another. It would be triggered by the mere fact of receipt, thus recognising the endurance of property rights. But fairness would be ensured by the need to identify a gain, and by making change of position available as a defence in suitable cases when, for instance, the recipient had changed his position in reliance on the receipt.

Most recently, in obiter remarks in *Criterion Properties v Stratford UK Properties* (2004), Lord Nicholls criticised the reasoning of the CA in

Akindele and re-asserted the restitutionary analysis in cases of knowing receipt.

11.191 Finally, some support in authority for this position is provided by *Re Diplock* (1948, CA; affirmed by the HL sub nom *Ministry of Health v Simpson* (1950)). In that case the executors of a will distributed a large sum of money to various charities. It was discovered that the charitable gift was void for uncertainty, and so the money ought to have gone to the next of kin. The CA, exercising its equity jurisdiction, found the charities strictly liable to the personal claims of the next of kin for the value they received, subject, however, to the next of kin first exhausting their personal claim against the executors for misapplying the funds. However, while the similarities between the circumstance of a legatee whose personal representative had paid the money to the wrong person and the beneficiary whose trustee misapplies trust property to the wrong person are patent, it seems that the *Re Diplock* claim is quite an anomalous remedy, 'mired in its own rather complex history' (Harpum, 1994) involving equity's assumption of the ecclesiastical court's jurisdiction over wills. The case certainly reveals that equity is not constitutively averse to awarding a personal restitutionary liability, but it seems a frail basis for revolutionising the law of knowing receipt.

11.192 The move toward a restitutionary analysis has not been unanimous, of course. In *Westdeutsche Landesbank Girozentrale v Islington London Borough Council* (1996) Lord Browne-Wilkinson quite clearly affirmed, *obiter*, the traditional formulation:

> Even if the third party [recipient of trust property], X, is not aware that what he has received is trust property B [the beneficiary] is entitled to assert his title in that property. If X has the necessary degree of knowledge, X may himself become a constructive trustee for B on the basis of knowing receipt. But unless he has the requisite degree of knowledge he is not personally liable to account as trustee.

However, viewed in its context, the statement may be taken to be directed only to the question whether the third party recipient should, without knowledge, be regarded as having a trustee's duties and liabilities such as the liability to account (the answer being 'no'), leaving entirely open whether the third party recipient might have personal liabilities arising

430

on a different basis, ie on the basis of his unjust enrichment or his interference with the beneficiary's proprietary rights.

1.193 We have also seen that Nourse LJ in *Akindele* (11.178) strongly doubted whether knowing receipt should be reframed along restitutionary lines; though in *Grupo Torras v Al Sabah* (2001) the CA appeared to leave the question more open.

1.194 Originally it was argued by restitution lawyers that liability under the 'knowing receipt' label was not truly fault-based, but was an unrealised form of liability for unjust enrichment, and this appears to have been the view of judges found in most of the preceding quotes. The currently favoured view (see, eg Birks 2002b) is that there is concurrent liability, both fault-based liability for knowing receipt, and strict restitutionary liability for unjust enrichment. This is the view advanced *obiter* by Lord Millett in *Dubai Aluminium v Salaam* (2003):

> Dishonest receipt gives rise to concurrent liability, since the claim can be based on the defendant's dishonesty, treating the receipt itself as incidental, being merely the particular form taken by the defendant's participation in the breach of fiduciary duty; but it can also be based simply on the receipt, treating it as a restitutionary claim independent of any wrongdoing... .

1.195 In terms of authority, however, this more recent view seems no more plausible than the former view. As Smith (2000) puts it:

> It has been said that the claim in knowing receipt belongs to the law of unjust enrichment, and since claims in unjust enrichment do not depend on fault, therefore it cannot be right that the knowing receipt claim should depend on fault. The startling consequence is that not some but all of the cases on the subject are wrong. More recently, another line has been taken, to the effect that even if the claim in knowing receipt is based on wrongdoing rather than unjust enrichment, nonetheless there is no reason that a plaintiff cannot put to one side the claim based on wrongdoing, and sue instead in unust enrichment. The consequences of this view are only slightly less startling: the cases may be right, but all of the lawyers and judges involved failed to notice that there was another claim available to the plaintiff, and moreover one which renders otiose any inquiry into cognition. That of course is the inquiry with which the cases are most concerned. It is important to stress that no defendant

appears ever to have been made strictly liable for the receipt of trust property/

The recipient's enrichment

11.196 As we have seen, in order for a claimant to establish the restitutionary liability of the defendant, he must first show that he has been enriched at the expense of the plaintiff, and then point to an unjust factor which makes the defendant's enrichment unjust. We will deal with each point in turn.

11.197 There is a long-running dispute amongst commentators on the law of restitution as to whether someone in the position of the recipient of trust funds is enriched. As we know, unless the recipient is a bona fide purchaser, the beneficiary retains equitable title in the property he receives. In view of this, it seems impossible to say that the recipient is enriched, for the beneficiary retains his beneficial title and the recipient acquires no beneficial title. This contrasts sharply with the case of the typical mistaken payment. If you pay your gas bill a second time, the gas company acquires beneficial legal title to your money, since you transferred it with the intention that title should pass. The gas company is clearly enriched because it now has beneficial title to money which was once yours, and at your expense since you have beneficial title no more. But the very opposite is the case with the third party recipient of trust property. Traditionally, if a third party is in possession of property that is beneficially yours, one brings a 'title' claim, not a restitutionary claim, eg a claim for damages for interference with your beneficial title if the property is a chattel, a claim to be put into possession if the property is land, a claim to specifically enforce the trust against a recipient of trust property (11.90-11.91, 11.124). From a traditional perspective, there would not seem to be room for a restitutionary claim in these circumstances, and this distinction between title claims and restitutionary claims appeared to be endorsed by Lord Millett in *Foskett v McKeown*.

11.198 In reply to this argument, Birks (1997) argues that 'enrichment' encompasses more than 'legal' enrichment of this kind. 'Factual' enrichment also counts: merely being in possession of the trust property should count as an enrichment sufficient to generate a restitutionary claim. (For a response, see, eg Grantham & Rickett (2001)). It is beyond the scope of this outline of the law to examine this dispute in detail.

raise it here simply to point out an apparent disanalogy between the typical case of restitution at common law and the case of the recipient of trust property.

The unjust factor

11.199   What is the unjust factor making the receipt by the third party of trust property unjust? The problem here is that the trustee, in transferring the property in breach of trust, does not make a mistake, nor does the recipient (at least in the vast majority of cases) acquire the property by acting unconscionably or by putting the trustee under duress (and if he did, the trustee would simply have a common law claim for restitution against the third party which he would be bound to pursue on behalf of the trust). Birks (1985) claims that the unjust factor is 'ignorance': the beneficiary's property is transferred away from the trust and he does not even know about it. This, argues Birks, is clearly a stronger case of injustice than that of the mistaken payor who pays his gas bill twice, for here the beneficiary could do nothing to prevent the transfer; his ignorance of the transfer makes the stranger's receipt of the trust property unjust.

11.200   There is, however, a glaring problem with this argument, which is simply that the beneficiary is typically ignorant of all the dispositions of the trust property the trustee makes, whether unauthorised or authorised (except, of course, payments to that beneficiary himself under the terms of the trust, and sometimes not even those). The argument therefore proves too much. If the beneficiary was entitled to reverse any disposition of the trust property of which he was ignorant, he could reverse any transaction a trustee undertook, whether it was authorised or not. The beneficiary's 'ignorance' of the trustee's dealing is simply part and parcel of the way trusts work, of the fact that it is the trustee who has all the legal powers to deal with the trust property and is expected to use them according to the terms of the trust, not according to the beneficiary's instructions. (See also Swadling (1996), Grantham & Rickett (1996), Bant (1998).) One might reply that in the case of authorised transactions, the 'ignorance' factor is displaced by the beneficiary's implicit 'consent' to authorised transactions, ie transactions within the terms of the trust – to the extent that the beneficiary claims any benefit under the trust at all, it is only to such a benefit as is within its terms, and therefore he must consent to any transaction within the terms. But this argument revises the unjust factor to 'unauthorised or wrongful transactions of which the beneficiary is innocent', and this does not describe the cases. A breach is a breach of trust whether the beneficiary is ignorant of or knows about it (a beneficiary's mere knowledge does not amount to consent (11.47-11.50)), so clearly the operative factor here is that the transaction is wrongful; the beneficiary's knowledge or ignorance is irrelevant. Thus the only unjust factor that would appear to operate is the trustee's wrong in carrying out the unauthorised transaction. But if this is the unjust factor, then it would seem the appropriate analogy to the common law is liability for conversion (11.182), not liability for unjust enrichment. As we have seen, at common law liability for interfering with another's title is strict, and so differs from knowing receipt, which depends upon fault. But in view of the battery of claims that a beneficiary can make in cases of breach (he always has a strict liability claim against the trustee, may have a claim for knowing assistance against a third party, etc), it may make sense that the 'conversion' claim in equity is fault-based (see further 11.203 et seq).

11.201 A similar point is put by Smith (2000):

Writing on this subject, [Lord Nicholls (1998)] deploys the following example. A defendant innocently receives some money, trust property, as a gift from the trustee. He spends it on something which he would have bought anyway, and which leaves no traceable product. If fault is required, there is no claim; if fault is not, then there probably is, because the facts are intended to imply that the defendant cannot use the defence of change of position. Lord Nicholls takes the view that this defendant should repay; he has been made better off out of the plaintiff's trust fund, and if the defendant is required to repay, he will only be back to where he started. But of course the fact that someone is only back to where he started does not justify liability. Otherwise all gifts would be recoverable, subject only to a defence of change of position. Presumably Lord Nicholls would say, this is not a gift; the plaintiff never intended the defendant to be enriched. But in another sense, it was a gift; it was a gift from the trustee. Ignoring that amounts to ignoring that there is a trust. This defendant might reasonably ask why he should be required to account in court for what he has done over the preceding several years with money that was legally his own (subject only to the [plaintiff's] undiscoverable equitable interest), failing which he will have to dig into his pocket to repay. He might ask why the plaintiff should not instead look for relief to his trustee, the one whom the money was entrusted in the first place. But the argument for strict liability consistently ignores the essential fact that there is a trust, and seeks to treat the trust beneficiary like a legal owner.

Untraceable expenditure of the trust property

11.202 The preceding considerations would seem to undercut the idea that a third party recipient of trust property should be strictly personally liable to transfer an equivalent amount of value to the beneficiary on the basis that he was unjustly enriched at the beneficiary's expense. They would seem to suggest that the present law, whereby the beneficiary can enforce the trust against the recipient in respect of any trust property or traceable proceeds in his hands is both sufficient and just. However, what if the recipient dissipates the trust property or proceeds, ie spends it on something which does not generate any traceable proceeds in exchange, say blowing it all on a holiday? Cannot the restitutionary lawyer intervene at this stage? For by spending the money in this way, the beneficiary's title is extinguished (the holiday agent is a bona fide purchaser) in a way that legally, not just factually, benefits the recipient, for he acquires the contractual right to the performance of the holiday agent, which he benefits from when he takes the holiday.

11.203 The problem again comes down to the unjust factor: there is no mistake, duress, unconscionability, and as we have seen, 'ignorance' does not work either. The transaction is not 'vitiated' in any way on any of these bases. What has happened here is simply that the recipient has bought his holiday with trust money – that is, he has interfered with the beneficiary's equitable title in that property. So if the recipient should be liable, he would be primarily liable for committing this wrong, not for being unjustly enriched at the beneficiary's expense. Now, someone who interferes with one's title at common law can also be liable in certain circumstance to 'disgorge', ie give up, a profit earned from the wrong, eg where a thief steals your car and sells it at a handsome profit (see, eg, Burrows (2002b), 455 et seq), and so by analogy we might wish to strip the recipient of the benefit or gain he received from the holiday which arose because he committed a wrong in interfering with the beneficiary's title. But coming to this conclusion depends upon saying that the innocent recipient of trust property commits a wrong when he spends the trust property, ie commits a wrong in the eyes of equity. But this is precisely what the cases do not say. Smith (2000) again:

The argument that suggests that personal claims based on receipt of trust property must line up with the strict liability in *Lipkin Gorman v Karpnale* seems to ignore a very basic truth: a beneficiary's interest under a trust is not legal ownership. Equitable proprietary rights are not protected in the same way as legal ones. In general, they are protected less well. They are always subject to destruction by bona fide purchase of a legal interest or overreaching, and wrongful interference with them is dependent on fault. ... The argument for strict liability would make the most sense as part of an agenda which sought the abolition of the trust, and the return to a regime in which only one person can claim to be the owner of a given asset. That would be an odd agenda to pursue, when civilian systems all over the world, aware of the flexibility which the trust device offers, are introducing it in various forms. Certainly as the law is now, the beneficiary's interest under a trust attracts different incidents from legal ownership. It is not clear that it would make sense to abolish some of the characteristics of equitable property rights while leaving others intact. If liability for receiving trust property is strict, why should equitable interests be subject to destruction by the defence of bona fide purchase of a legal interest?

The trustee is (usually) the legal owner. If he makes, for example, a mistaken payment, or is defrauded..., he will have at his disposal all of the strict liability claims which protect his legal title and protect him from defective transfers. On the other hand, he might not have a claim; he might have given the trust money away in breach of trust. But it does not follow from this that we must give the beneficiaries the same rights that the trustee would have had, had he acted properly. It is in the nature of the trust institution that beneficiaries are vulnerable to breaches of trust, in ways which they would not be if they were the legal owners of the trust property. To complain about this is to complain about the incidents of the institution of the trust.

11.204 The contrast with the typical two party case of restitution at common law, eg where you pay your gas bill twice, and the situation of breach of trust, can be further sharpened, by pointing out that in the case of breach of trust, the beneficiary has, besides the recipient, a defendant who is always strictly liable for the entire loss to the trust, with no change of position defence, that is, the trustee. So while the beneficiary's remedial protection can look weaker from a restitutionary point of view, this is so only if one focuses only on the third party recipient. Recall the array of claims that can arise in a case of breach of trust (11.1 et seq).

11.205 Another point to consider is that it seems fair that beneficiaries should take the bad with the good regarding the fact that their property interest in equity is an interest in a fund. It is only because equity conceives of the beneficiary's property interest as an interest in a fund, and treats the third party recipient as a custodian trustee of the fund, that the beneficiary has the right to the enhanced proprietary claims he can make following the tracing process. This is an advantage of one's property interest being treated as an interest in the fund, not in the individual items of property in that fund. But there is a corresponding disadvantage. One cannot treat the recipient's transaction with one of the items in the fund as the disposition of one's title in that property, as if one were the legal owner of it, equivalent to conversion. In order to make the recipient personally liable for such a transaction, it must be shown to have been a breach of trust by him, and as we have seen (**11.121-23, 11.127, 11.164-11.65**), by treating the recipient as a custodian trustee equity will not regard the transaction in this way unless the recipient knowingly breaches the trust, for custodian trustees, unlike managing trustees, are not responsible for carrying out the terms of the trust. This brings us to the final issue concerning restitutionary analyses in this area of law.

Tracing and restitution

11.206   At first glance, there appears to be a very strong argument for saying that only by relying upon a restitutionary analysis can one explain a fundamental aspect of the law governing breach of trusts, and that is that the process of tracing and claiming can only be explained as the application of restitutionary principles. The argument concerns the nature of funds. The restitution lawyer asks, why does the property that is the proceeds of a transaction with trust property become in turn the property of the trust. After all, a trustee does not have to declare a new trust over any property he buys with money from the trust fund. The trust over the proceeds arises by operation of law. And, reasons the restitution lawyer, whenever a new interest in property arises by operation of law, the law must have a reason in justice for awarding it, and the most obvious reason is that otherwise the trustee would be unjustly enriched, for he would acquire an unencumbered legal title to property purchased with trust money. So the law imposes a trust over the proceeds. The same reasoning goes a fortiori in the case of tracing through substitutions made by a third party recipient of the trust funds.

11.207   This characterisation of tracing was rejected by the HL in *Foskett v McKeown*, most forcefully by Lord Millett who said:

The transmission of a claimant's property rights from one asset to its traceable proceeds is party of our law of property, not of the law of unjust enrichment. There is no 'unjust factor' to justify restitution (unless 'want of title' be one, which makes the point). The claimant succeeds if at all by virtue of his own title, not to reverse unjust enrichment.

11.208 Unfortunately, Lord Millett presents the picture too simply. As we have seen, tracing per se is merely a process of following value. The rules of tracing should be equivalent in all branches of law. What matters with respect to following one's value is what sort of claim one can make following the tracing process. The restitution lawyer's argument is that the claim one makes is justified because getting a property right in the proceeds of tracing reverses unjust enrichment. Lord Millett does not indicate what it is about the beneficiary's entitlement to trust property that justifies his being able to claim the traceable proceeds.

11.209 Thus, in order to counter the restitution lawyer's argument, and defend Lord Millett's view that the right to claim traceable proceeds flows from the rules of the law of property, one must focus on the nature of the beneficiary's title. As we have seen, Smith points out why the nature of legal title, as a baseline property right, counsels against a legal title-holder's being entitled to claim a legal title in the traceable proceeds of his original property (**11.158**). Similarly, we notice that the rather odd 'power in rem' to claim traceable proceeds described in *Lipkin Gorman* is shaped largely in consideration of its effects on third parties, a classic property or title concern, for the essence of property rights is that they bind third parties, or 'all the world', as it is sometime put. We have already looked at similar points about why certain kinds of property are negotiable, ie subject to a bona fide purchaser rule (**2.35** et seq), and some not. Negotiability and non-negotiability are incidents of title of different kinds of property. If we keep in mind the different 'incidents of title' that various kinds of property can have, we can see that the beneficiary's right to claim traceable proceeds flows from the fact that the beneficiary's title is a title to a fund. It follows from the kind of property interest an interest in a fund is that the fund captures substitutions of one item in a fund for another. And in the eyes of equity, this is true as much for the third party recipient, who the beneficiary, by electing to adopt the wrongful transfer to him by the trustee, is able to treat as a custodian trustee, as it is for the express trustee himself.

11.210 As a matter of policy, you may think that equity goes too far in allowing the beneficiary, when there is a breach of trust, to elect to treat a third party recipient of trust property as a kind of trustee (a custodian) himself. Under the rules of the Hague Trust Convention, which lays out basic rules of trusts which are meant to provide a basic structure that might work both in common law and civilian legal systems, it is not considered a necessary incident of the beneficiary's title that he should be able to trace against third party recipients in this way. This is rightly viewed as a matter of legal policy, taking into consideration the way that such a property interest interacts with other rules of private law. But, it is submitted, it is a matter of policy concerning the incidents of title, not a matter to be explained as the application of the law of restitution in every instance of tracing.

Limitation of actions

11.211   The Limitation Act 1980 provides:

> **21.** (1) No period of limitation prescribed by this Act shall apply to an action by a beneficiary under a trust, being an action —
> (a) in respect of any fraud or fraudulent breach of trust to which the trustee was a party or privy; or
> (b) to recover from the trustee trust property or the proceeds of trust property in the possession of the trustee, or previously received by him and converted to his use.

11.212   The scope of this section has been recently rather emphatically clarified by Millett LJ in *Paragon Finance plc v Thakerar & Co* (1999). These sections, which set no period of limitation on actions for breach of trust, properly apply only to cases where a person who has in a lawful transaction undertaken fiduciary obligations to the plaintiff, or can be implied to have put himself in a position where he owes such obligations, *then* goes on to breach those obligations by wrongfully obtaining his principal's property or converting his principal's property to his own use.

11.213   This clearly covers the case of an express trustee who misappropriates trust property, or a company director who misappropriates company property, for in both of these cases the fiduciary obligation arises independently of, and prior to, the wrong of misappropriating the principal's property. However, since the company

439

director is not a trustee, since he holds no legal title for his principal, the company, following his misappropriation of company property he will hold that property on constructive trust for the company, and therefore can be regarded as a constructive trustee. Thus, the section will apply to him, and no period of limitation runs in his favour and against the company seeking to sue him. So the section does apply to certain 'constructive' trustees.

11.214 However, the section does not apply to persons sometimes called 'constructive trustees' or held 'liable to account as a constructive trustee', because they commit a wrong (**11.15**) or receive trust property (**11.164**) or are otherwise subject to the remedial jurisdiction of equity (eg **11.14**). In such cases, Millett LJ said,

> the expressions 'constructive trust' and 'constructive trustee' are misleading, for there is no trust and usually no possibility of a proprietary remedy; they are 'nothing more than a formula for equitable relief' (quoting Ungoed-Thomas J in *Selangor United Rubber Estates v Cradock* (1968)).

In these cases, equity will apply by analogy the limitation periods under the statute which apply to corresponding actions at common law. Thus, a fraudster who is liable in equity for dishonest assistance will have the benefit of the same limitation period (six years) as would apply to one committing a fraud actionable at common law. Millett LJ's approach has since been followed in *JJ Harrison (Properties) Ltd v Harrison* (2002) and *Gwembe Valley Development Co Ltd v Koshy* (2004), and re-iterated by himself in *Dubai Aluminium v Salaam* (2003).

11.215 Cases which fit into the above exceptions, where no statutory limitation periods apply, are however subject to the equitable doctrine of laches, or delay. A suit may not succeed in equity if by reason of the plaintiff's delay the defendant would be unfairly disadvantaged. *Paragon Finance* concerned a claim by a mortgage company, Paragon, against a solicitor who it claimed had breached its fiduciary duty to it. The solicitors received funds from Paragon on a bare trust with mandate (**9.47**) to complete a sale of land. The funds were so paid, but Paragon claimed that by doing so the solicitors had knowingly participated in a scheme to defraud it. In finding that the limitation period of six years in the case of fraud applied, Millett LJ said that, while it was true that the solicitors held the money pending sale on trust for Paragon, Paragon could not establish a breach of this trust, for that trust was merely to pay the money to the purchaser on the sale. The 'trust' upon which Paragon had to rely was a 'constructive' trust of the kind which arose in equity in response to the solicitors' alleged fraud, ie the solicitors would be liable in equity as dishonest accessories to the fraud and would be liable to account for the proceeds of their fraud to Paragon.

Further reading

Birks (1991, 1992, 1995, 1996a); Harpum (1994); Millett (1998); Smith (1994, 1997, 2000); Swadling (1994, 1996b, 1997, 1998); Brownbill (1993, Part VI); Trust Law Committee (1999, 'Trustee Exemption Clauses'); Penner (2002); Mitchell (2002); Law Commission (2002); Birks and Pretto (2002); Matthews (1995b); Elliott & Mitchell (2004); Grantham & Rickett (2001); Worthington (2003, 159-76)

Must read cases: *Re Pauling's Settlement Trusts* (1963); *Armitage v Nurse* (1997); *Target Holdings v Redferns* (1995); *Bristol & West Building Society v Mothew* (1996); *Royal Brunei Airlines v Tan* (1995); *Agip (Africa) Ltd v Jackson* (1989); *Lipkin Gorman v Karpnale Ltd* (1991); *Re Hallett's Estate* (1880); *Re Oatway* (1903); *Russell-Cooke Trust Co. v Prentis* (2003); *Boscawen v Bajwa* (1995); *Foskett v McKeown* (2000); *Westdeutsche Landesbank v Islington London Borough Council* (1996); *Re Montagu's Settlement Trusts* (1987); *Twinsectra v Yardley* (2002)

Self-test questions

. What does it mean for a beneficiary to (a) 'falsify the account'; and (b) 'surcharge the account'? How are these ways of dealing with breaches of trust related to the concept of 'equitable compensation'? Give examples from actual cases where these terms can be employed to explain the decisions.

. '[I]t must be acknowledged that the view is widely held that these clauses have gone too far, and that trustees who charge for their services and who, as professional men, would not dream of excluding liability for ordinary professional negligence, should not be able to rely on a trustee exemption clause excluding liability for gross negligence.' (Millett LJ in *Armitage v Nurse* (1997)) Discuss.

3. Tom is the trustee of the Higgins family trust. He misappropriates £30,000 which he pays into his bank account raising the balance to £40,000. He makes the following payments from his account. He buys shares for £5,000, which are now worth £10,000. He uses £20,000 to pay off the mortgage on his flat. He then adds £10,000 of his own to the account, raising the balance to £25,000. He gives £10,000 to his son, Ted, who is ignorant of the source of the money. Ted uses it to buy ten cases of vintage wine; he drinks up five of the cases and lays down the rest. Tom dissipates the remaining funds in the account.

   With the knowledge of Harry Higgins, one of the beneficiaries, Tom misappropriates another £10,000 which they together spend on a world cruise.

   Discuss the liability of Tom, Harry, and Ted.

4. What insights, if any, arise from a restitutionary analysis of the liability of a third party recipient of trust property or its traceable proceeds?

5 In 1990, Pavlos, a solicitor, received £40,000 from Nicos on discretionary trusts for Nicos's relations. He paid the money into a separate bank account, and in each of 1990, 1991, and 1992 drew £1,000 a year from the account to pay premiums on a life insurance policy on his own life. Having fallen in love with Nicos's daughter in 1991, he exercised his discretion under the trust to make large payments to her. In 1993 he exercised a power of appointment under the trust in favour of Christos, one of the proper objects of the power, giving him £2000 on condition Christos and he split the money 50 50. In late 1993 Nicos realised that he did not much like his relations anymore, and exercised his power under the trust to revoke the trust, telling Pavlos to hold the remaining money in the account to his order. Instead of doing that, Pavlos immediately withdrew the money from the account and dissipated it gambling. Early in 2000, Nicos demanded the transfer of the funds from Pavlos, who committed suicide in response. Advise Nicos.

6. In breach of trust Max ordered his broker Bob, to invest £50,000 of the Simpson family trust in junk bonds. Bob complied with the order although he was surprised that a trust fund would permit such

hazardous investment. The bonds are defaulted upon almost immediately, becoming worthless. Max then transferred £100,000 from the trust account into his own bank account, raising the balance to £150,000, immediately using £120,000 to buy a London flat. Six months later he sold the flat for £180,000 and spent the entire amount at auction for a painting which has been independently appraised to be worth only £100,000. Of the remaining £30,000 in his account, Max, (a) used £10,000 to clear a gambling debt with Horatio, (b) used £10,000 to make a support payment to his ex-wife, Fran, which was in arrears, and (c) gave £10,000 to his son, Philip, who used the money to pay off his credit card bill, the charges on which he had mostly incurred in taking holidays over the past several years. Max is now bankrupt. Advise the beneficiaries.

CHAPTER TWELVE

The Law Governing Fiduciaries

SUMMARY

The 'no conflict' rule

Authorised profits

Unauthorised profits and the liability to account for them

The self-dealing and fair-dealing rules

The proprietary and personal nature of the liability to account

Equitable compensation for breach of fiduciary obligation

Secondary liability for breach of fiduciary obligation

The scope of fiduciary obligations

12.1 To begin with, review the description of fiduciary obligations at **2.9-2.14**, and **11.14-11.16**. It is essential to realise, as Millett LJ makes clear in his review of the nature and scope of fiduciary duties in *Bristol and West Building Society v Mothew* (1998), that just because A stands as a fiduciary to B, that does not mean that every duty he owes B is a fiduciary duty:

> The expression 'fiduciary duty' is properly confined to those duties which are peculiar to fiduciaries and the breach of which attracts legal consequences differing from those consequent upon the breach of other duties. Unless the expression is so limited it is lacking in practical utility. In this sense it is obvious that not every breach of duty by a fiduciary is a breach of fiduciary duty ... It is ... inappropriate to apply the expression to the obligation of a trustee or other fiduciary to use proper skill and care in the discharge of his duties ... A fiduciary is someone who has

445

undertaken to act for or on behalf of another in a particular matter in circumstances which give rise to a relationship of trust and confidence. The distinguishing obligation of a fiduciary is the obligation of loyalty. The principal is entitled to the single-minded loyalty of his fiduciary. This core liability has several facets. A fiduciary must act in good faith; he must not make a profit out of his trust; he must not place himself in a position where his duty and his interest may conflict; he may not act for his own benefit or the benefit of a third person without the informed consent of his principal ... [Where] the fiduciary deals with his principal ... he must prove affirmatively that the transaction is fair and that in the course of the negotiations he made full disclosure of all facts material to the transaction. Even inadvertent failure to disclose will entitle the principal to rescind the transaction ... The nature of the obligation determines the nature of the breach. The various obligations of a fiduciary merely reflect different aspects of his core duties of loyalty and fidelity. Breach of fiduciary obligation, therefore, connotes disloyalty or infidelity. Mere incompetence is not enough. A servant who does his incompetent best for his master is not unfaithful and is not guilty of a breach of fiduciary duty.

As Millett LJ points out, the duty of loyalty has been elaborated in the form of a number of more particular duties, concerning profits from the trust, conflicts of interest, and transactions with the trust property. We shall examine each in turn.

The 'no conflict' rule

12.2   The 'no conflict' rule is the basic rule governing fiduciaries. A fiduciary must not place himself in a position where his own interests might conflict with those of his principal. As we shall see, the no conflict rule underlies all the more specific rules governing fiduciaries. Under the 'no conflict' rule, a fiduciary is liable to account for any profit he obtains in circumstances where his interests *may* conflict with his duty to his principal. The rule is exceptionally stringent, in that it is framed – '*may* conflict' – in terms of the possibility of conflict, not in terms of there being an actual conflict of interest.

12.3   Perhaps the most extreme example of the no conflict rule is *Keech v Sandford* (1726). A trustee held a lease for a minor beneficiary, which he sought to renew. The lessor refused to renew the lease in favour of the minor. The trustee took the new lease for his own benefit. King LC required the trustee to hold the lease on trust for the beneficiary, even though his interest when he acquired it could not, strictly speaking, be in conflict with his duty to the beneficiary, since the lessor absolutely refused to renew to a minor. Lord King accepted that the consequence of the rule's application was that:

> ... the trustee is the only person of all mankind who might not have the lease; but it is very proper that the rule should be strictly pursued, and not in the least relaxed; for it is very obvious what would be the consequences of letting trustees have the lease, on refusal to renew to the cestui que trust.

12.4 In *Protheroe v Protheroe* (1968) the CA, without a review of the relevant authorities, held that the rule in *Keech* applied to a trustee's purchase of the reversion upon a lease held by the trust so that it was automatically to be held on trust for the beneficiary. While on the authorities this would be a clear extension of the rule, Hayton ((1996), 342) argues that the decision is right on a strict application of the no conflict rule, because the trustee would, as landlord, have interests in conflict with his role as fiduciary holder of the lease, or 'trustee-lessee', for the beneficiary.

12.5 The leading modern case is *Boardman v Phipps* (1967). The defendants were Boardman, the solicitor to the Phipps family trust, and Tom Phipps, one of the beneficiaries. The trust held a significant holding in a private company which was ailing. Boardman and Phipps decided that with new and effective management the company could generate significant profits for the shareholders. With the informed consent of the two active trustees (a third trustee was the settlor's widow who was senile), Boardman and Phipps, as proxy holders of the trust shares, tried to get Phipps elected to the board, and failed. They also failed to negotiate a splitting up of the business between the Phipps holding and the other major block of shareholders. The two active trustees made it clear that they would not buy any more shares of the company for the trust. Finally, Boardman and Phipps purchased sufficient shares with their own money to enable them, with the support of the trustees, to take control of the company. As a result, they were able to sell off certain of the company assets, paying out large dividends while at the same time maintaining a high share price. Tom's brother, John Phipps, another beneficiary under the family trust, then sued Boardman and Tom Phipps, calling upon them

447

to account for the profits they had earned on the shares they had purchased, as profits acquired in breach of their fiduciary duties, because acquired in conflict of interest with 'the trust'. The HL, by a 3:2 margin, found Boardman and Phipps liable to account for the profits they earned.

12.6 Clearly Boardman stood in a fiduciary position as solicitor to the trustees; but there is no position of 'solicitor to the trust', and it was an unfortunate aspect of the case that the court did not specify clearly how or when Boardman came under a fiduciary obligation to John Phipps. The case was also argued and decided on the basis that Tom Phipps should be treated equally with Boardman whatever the outcome, though Tom Phipps, as a beneficiary under the trust, obviously did not stand in the same fiduciary capacity. Lord Guest's finding that Boardman was liable was straightforward:

> In the present case the knowledge and information obtained by Mr Boardman was obtained in the course of the fiduciary position in which he had placed himself. The only defence available to a person in such a fiduciary position is that he made the profits with the knowledge and assent of the trustees. It is not suggested that the trustees had such knowledge or gave such consent.

12.7 Thus because the information was acquired in the course of his dealings with the trust, and he was a fiduciary 'to the trust', any profits made from using that information would be profits arising from his fiduciary office; unless authorised, they must be accounted for. Simple. Two points should be noted. First, this simple equation of liability with Boardman's having profited from information acquired in his conduct of the trust would not have led to the liability of Tom Phipps, for as a beneficiary under the trust he could well argue that he obtained any information in that capacity, not as a fiduciary to the trust. Second, Lord Guest speaks of the consent of the *trustees*. (There was no informed consent by *all* the trustees, since the third, senile, trustee, was not informed at all.) This poses something of a puzzle. Normally, the consent of the beneficiaries is required to authorise any act which would otherwise be a breach of trust. Where a trustee employs a fiduciary agent, the agent owes his duties to the trustee, and the trustee may then authorise what would otherwise be a breach of that agent's fiduciary duty. But, if the trustee does so for insufficient reasons, then he would be liable to the beneficiaries for a breach of trust, ie for failing himself to carry out his duties properly. However in this case Boardman was liable to the beneficiaries directly, so it can only be the case that because of his close relationship with the trustees and the beneficiaries he owed a fiduciary duty directly to them.

12.8 Lord Hodson took a similar line to that of Lord Guest. Pointing out that in *Keech* the beneficiary could not have acquired the disputed assets himself, it was irrelevant that the trustees had decided not to purchase further shares in the company. Any profit obtained by a fiduciary made possible by his fiduciary position was to be accounted for unless consented to, although Lord Hodson made it clear that the consent required was that of the complaining beneficiary.

12.9 Unlike Lords Guest and Hodson, Lord Cohen did not wholly rely upon the *Keech* rule, as if any use of information acquired in the course of dealing with the trust to generate a profit for the fiduciary automatically entailed that the profit was to be accounted for. He stated:

> [I]n my opinion, Mr Boardman would not have been able to give unprejudiced advice if he had been consulted by the trustees [about acquiring further shares for the trust] and was at the same time negotiating for the purchase of the shares on behalf of himself and Mr Tom Phipps. In other words, there was, in my opinion, at the crucial date ... a possibility of a conflict between his interest and his duty.

12.10 Lord Cohen's opinion thus has the virtue of specifying the precise way in which Boardman's purchase of the shares for himself can be interpreted as an act undertaken in conflict of interest, for given Boardman's personal intention to acquire the shares, counselling the trust to acquire the rest of the shares would conflict with his own interests.

12.11 Lord Upjohn dissented and said:

> The phrase 'possibly may conflict' requires consideration. In my view it means that the reasonable man looking at the relevant facts and circumstances of the particular case would think that there was a real sensible possibility of conflict; not that you could imagine some situation arising which might, in some conceivable possibility in events not contemplated as real sensible possibilities by any reasonable person, result in a conflict ... it has been assumed that it has necessarily followed that any profit made by [a fiduciary] renders him accountable to the trustees. This is not so.

In Lord Upjohn's opinion the 'no conflict' rule was not to be applied automatically, for that would only lead to the harsh and inequitable consequences of the majority decision. In order for a fiduciary to be accountable, he reasoned, the fiduciary must have made a profit (1) earned within 'the scope and ambit of his duty', and (2) in circumstances where he had placed himself in a position where there was a 'real sensible possibility of conflict' between his duty and his interest.

12.12 Viscount Dilhorne also dissented. He reasoned that when the trustees firmly insisted they would purchase no further shares, the trustees no longer sought to rely upon Boardman as an advisor as to the shares' value, and so on, but rather from that time forward Boardman and Phipps and the trustees acted in a sort of joint venture to get the value out of the company. Viscount Dilhorne's reasoning is plausible on the facts, and delivers the same result Lord Upjohn preferred without watering down the 'no conflict' rule, requiring the court to engage in a inquiry as to whether a conflict arose in the eyes of a 'reasonable' person. The essence of Viscount Dilhorne's argument is that a fiduciary can be released from his fiduciary role by his principal(s) (ie the acting trustees) if done in full knowledge of the circumstances, as was the case here; thenceforward the principal is no longer relying on the fiduciary to make his decisions for him, or rely on his advice. The former principal and fiduciary are now free to act as partners or joint venturers, who while they have fiduciary obligations as business partners to eachother (**2.14**), do not have the fiduciary obligations of advisor to advisee.

12.13 The majority decision in *Boardman* can certainly be criticised for what appears to be an unjustifiably harsh result. Although Boardman and Tom Phipps were allowed remuneration for their efforts on a liberal scale, they were stripped of all their profits from investing their own money in an endeavour which hugely profited the trust beneficiaries.

12.14 What should a fiduciary do who finds himself in a position of conflict of interest? In *Public Trustee v Cooper* (2001) Hart J laid out three ways in which a conflict might 'in theory, successfully be managed'; Hart J speaks only of trustees, but one presumes his views apply *mutates mutandis* to other fiduciaries:

> One is for the trustee concerned to resign. This will not always provide a practical or sensible solution. The trustee concerned may represent

an important source of information or advice to his co-trustees or have a significant relationship to some or all of the beneficiaries such that his or her departure as a trustee will be potentially harmful to the interests of the trust estate or its beneficiaries.

Secondly, the nature of the conflict may be so pervasive throughout the trustee body that they, as a body, have no alternative but to surrender their discretion to the court.

Thirdly, the trustees may honestly and reasonably believe that, notwithstanding a conflict affecting one or more of their number, they are nevertheless able fairly and reasonably to take the decision. In this third case, it will usually be prudent, if time allows, for the trustees to allow their proposed exercise of discretion to be scrutinised in advance by the court, in proceedings in which any opposing beneficial interests are properly represented, and for them not to proceed until the court has authorised them to do so. If they do not do so, they run the risk of having to justify the exercise of their discretion in subsequent hostile litigation and then satisfy the court that their decision was not only one which any reasonable body of trustees might have taken but was also one that had not in fact been influenced by the conflict.

The 'no conflict' rule and company directors

12.15 The leading case applying the 'no conflict' rule to company directors is *Regal (Hastings) Ltd v Gulliver* (1942). The defendants were directors of a company, Regal, which owned and operated a cinema. Two other local cinemas were available for lease, and the directors decided to create a subsidiary company which would acquire leases to these cinemas, and that Regal would then sell its holding in all three cinemas as a going concern. The landlord of the two cinemas was not prepared to grant the leases to the subsidiary unless either a personal guarantee was given by the directors, or the subsidiary had paid-up capital of £5,000. The directors were reluctant to provide personal guarantees, so the second route was chosen. However, the directors decided that Regal could not put up more than £2,000 of the required £5,000. Four directors then each subscribed for shares worth £500, as did the solicitor to Regal at the request of the directors; one director also acquired £500 worth of shares for third parties. With £5,000 paid-up capital the subsidiary acquired the leases. As it turned out, Regal did not sell its interest in the three-cinema business; rather, the shareholders of Regal and the subsidiary sold their shares to a purchaser. The directors who had put up part of the capital for the subsidiary company received a handsome profit for their investment. The purchaser installed a new board of directors, and Regal, now under their control, launched this action against the former directors, calling for them to account for the profits they had made on their sale of the subsidiary shares. Regal succeeded in the HL. In the lower courts the directors successfully defended the claim, by arguing the decision they made for Regal to invest no more than £2,000 in the subsidiary was *bona fide* – indeed it might have been a breach of trust to have risked more of Regal's money; therefore, the directors putting up their own money *secured* a benefit for Regal which it could not otherwise have obtained, and so there was no basis for holding them liable to account for the profits they had personally made.

12.16   The HL unanimously rejected this interpretation of the case, applying the rule in *Keech* in its full rigour. Lord Russell said:

> The rule of equity which insists on those, who by use of a fiduciary position make a profit, being liable to account for that profit, in no way depends on fraud, or absence of *bona fides*; or upon such questions or considerations as whether the profit would or should otherwise have gone to the plaintiff, or whether the profiteer was under a duty to obtain the source of the profit for the plaintiff, or whether he took a risk or acted as he did for the benefit of the plaintiff, or whether the plaintiff has in fact been damaged or benefited by his action. The liability arises from the mere fact of a profit having, in the stated circumstances, been made. The profiteer, however honest or well intentioned, cannot escape the risk of being called to account.

12.17   None of the non-director subscribers of shares in the subsidiary, including the solicitor, were accountable, for none were fiduciaries subject to the rule. The solicitor took up his shares at the request of the company (a request made, of course, through its directors), and Lord Russell said:

> I know of no principle or authority which would justify a decision that a solicitor must account for profit resulting from a transaction which he has entered into on his own behalf, not merely with the consent, but at the request of his client.

12.18   Note that the effect of the decision was to give the new purchasers of the company and subsidiary shares a windfall, for they were, by this action by Regal, able to secure the return of part of their purchase price to Regal's coffers – had the company itself just sold the cinema business, the purchasers would not have been able to make such a claim, for the 'injured company' which suffered by the directors' breach would not have been in their hands. Recognising this, Lord Porter said:

> This, it seems, may be an unexpected windfall, but whether it be so or not, the principle that a person occupying a fiduciary relationship shall not make a profit by reason thereof is of such vital importance that the possible consequence in the present case is in fact as it is in law an immaterial consideration.

12.19 Lord Russell suggested that the directors' liability might easily have been avoided. Their decision to take up shares in the subsidiary could have been approved by the vote of a general meeting of the company, ie a general shareholders' meeting, and being in control of the company, they doubtless would have controlled the voting to ensure the result they desired. Such approval in the case of a company is equivalent to the informed consent of the beneficiaries under a trust. But as pointed out by Lowry (1997), the fact that company directors are typically able to control the voting at a general meeting makes the court's ringing endorsement of the application of the rule in *Keech* somewhat hollow, for if Lord Russell's suggestion is correct then any well-advised company directors who control by proxy a sufficient number of the company's shares may, by ensuring the approval of a general meeting, engage in profit-taking of this kind as they please. However, this view seems to conflict with the PC decision in *Cook v Deeks* (1916), where such a resolution was held to be ineffective.

12.20 The *Regal Hastings* principle was applied in *Industrial Development Consultants Ltd v Cooley* (1972). Cooley was the former chief architect of the West Midlands Gas Board. He joined IDC as their managing director, principally in order to procure work in the gas industry. He was approached by representatives of the Eastern Gas Board with respect to some large contracts for work to be done in the near future. The evidence indicated that the Eastern Gas Board would not have entered into contracts with IDC, as they disagreed in principle with 'the set-up' of IDC; the Board was willing, however, to enter into contracts with Cooley personally. Cooley secured his release from his position at IDC by lying to them that he was seriously ill, and secured the lucrative contracts for himself. Roskill J found that Cooley had clearly placed himself in actual conflict with IDC; it was his fiduciary duty to inform IDC of the Eastern Gas Board's plans and not to keep secret his dealings with the Board to his own advantage; the court declared that he held the profits of the contracts on trust for IDC. Roskill J realised that his decision secured for IDC a profit which it would never would have obtained if Cooley had complied with his fiduciary duty, but he accepted that:

> ... [i]t is an over-riding principle of equity that a man must not be allowed to put himself in a position in which his fiduciary duty and his interests conflict.

12.21 In the middle of the last century North American courts began to take the view that a genuinely good faith decision by a board of directors not to take up a corporate opportunity frees individual directors or other company fiduciaries to take up such opportunities themselves. For example, in *Peso Silver Mines v Cropper* [1966] SCR 673 the Supreme Court of Canada held that a director was not liable to his company for acquiring mining properties and profitably exploiting them when they had previously been offered to the company and the board of directors had *bona fide* decided not to take up the offer. It is noteworthy that in *Peso* the court clearly approved the following statement of Lord Greene, MR, from his judgment in the Court of Appeal in *Regal Hastings*:

> To say that the Company was entitled to claim the benefit of those shares would involve this proposition: Where a Board of Directors considers an investment which is offered to their company and bona fide comes to the conclusion that it is not an investment which their Company ought to make, any Director, after that Resolution is come to and bona fide come to, who chooses to put up the money for that investment himself must be treated as having done it on behalf of the Company, so that the Company can claim any profit that results to him from it. That is a proposition for which no particle of authority was cited; and goes, as it seems to me, far beyond anything that has ever been suggested as to the duty of directors, agents, or persons in a position of that kind.

12.22 In *Canadian Aero Services v O'Malley* (1971), Laskin J reviewed the English, Commonwealth, and US authorities, and said:

> In holding that ... there was a breach of fiduciary duty by [officers of a company for pursuing and capturing a contract for surveying work which their company was actively seeking to acquire itself, even though the officers had resigned their offices prior to the award of the contract] I

am not to be taken as laying down any rule of liability to be read as if it were a statute. The general standards of loyalty, good faith and avoidance of a conflict of duty and self-interest to which the conduct of a director or senior officer must conform, must be tested in each case by many factors which it would be reckless to attempt to enumerate exhaustively. Among them are the factor of position or office held, the nature of the corporate opportunity, its ripeness, its specificness and the director's or managerial officer's relation to it, the amount of knowledge possessed, the circumstances in which it was obtained and whether it was special or, indeed, even private, the factor of time in the continuation of fiduciary duty where the alleged breach occurs after termination of the relationship with the company, and the circumstances under which the relationship was terminated, that is whether by retirement or resignation or discharge.

12.23 Notice the effect of this ruling: henceforth the bright line 'prophylactic' strictness of the rule, as enunciated in *Keech*, is replaced by the very inquiry into a number of factors to determine the good faith and reasonableness of the fiduciary which a strict rule is meant to avoid. One of the main reasons for applying the rule stringently is so as not to make the rule turn on difficult inferences from facts difficult to establish, lest the fiduciary obligations of directors be weakened, in practice, as a result. One might argue that the substantial compensation which directors and senior officers of companies receive partly reflects the fact that they are denied the right to exploit corporate opportunities, even ones the company itself decides to refuse; thus they are compensated for the stringent application of the rule.

12.24 In the US the courts have similarly developed a 'corporate opportunity doctrine', the purpose of which is to determine which opportunities for profit 'belong' to a company, from which directors may not personally profit (*Guth v Loft Inc* (1939); *Broz v Cellular Information Systems Inc* (1996)).

12.25 There are signs that the inflexibility of the *Regal Hastings* approach may no longer be so acceptable to English judges either. The PC, in an appeal from Australia, *Queensland Mines Ltd v Hudson* (1978), decided that Hudson, a former managing director of a company who had resigned from the board to take up mining licences personally which the company had decided, due to its financial difficulties, not to pursue itself, was not liable to account to the company for the profits he earned. The court reasoned that although the opportunity came Hudson's way in his role as a fiduciary to the company, the company board knew of his interest and had given their fully informed consent. This decision directly contradicts both *Regal Hastings* and the received wisdom generally, since it is not the directors but the shareholders in a general meeting who are capable of giving such consent. The PC also decided that the good faith rejection of the opportunity placed the opportunity 'outside' the scope of Hudson's fiduciary duty.

12.26 However, as Sullivan (1979) points out:

> This [ground for the decision] enables the directors when exercising their managerial prerogative to reject corporate opportunities to thereby remove those opportunities from the restrictions imposed by their fiduciary duties ... The orthodoxy is that the director's legal powers of management are subject to the equitable obligations imposed by their fiduciary role; *Queensland* stands this on its head in allowing a managerial decision to delineate the scope of a fiduciary duty.

This aspect of the decision is particularly significant, since if it represents the law, a board's rejection of an opportunity may now be challenged only on the basis that it was not in good faith, raising all the difficulties of proof which such a charge may entail.

12.27 Two more recent first instance English cases are also of relevance. It is, as you might imagine, a rule that a trustee may not operate a business in competition with the trust (*Re Thomson* (1930)), and this applies to other fiduciaries vis-à-vis their principals as well. However, in *Island Export Finance Ltd v Umunna* (1986) Hutchison J decided that, while a director's fiduciary obligations did not cease utterly upon the termination of his post, the mere fact that he entered into competition with his former company following his departure did not make him liable, so long as he did not capture a 'maturing business opportunity' of the company. (The phrase comes from *Canadian Aero Services*.) Hutchinson J said:

> In this context counsel for the defendants rightly stresses the fundamental principles relating to contracts in restraint of trade. It would, it seems to me, be surprising to find that directors alone, because of the fiduciary nature of their relationship with the company, were restrained from exploiting after they ceased to be such any opportunity of which they had acquired knowledge while directors. Directors, no less than other

employees, acquire a general fund of knowledge and expertise in the course of their work, and it is plainly in the public interest that they should be free to exploit it in a new position.

12.28 Similarly, in *Balston Ltd v Headline Filters Ltd* (1987), Falconer J stated:

> [A]n intention by a director of a company to set up business in competition with the company after his directorship has ceased is not to be regarded as a conflicting interest within the context of the principle, having regard to the rules of public policy as to restraint of trade, nor is the taking of any preliminary steps to investigate or forward that intention so long as there is no actual competitive activity, such as, for instance, competitive tendering or actual trading, while he remains a director.

12.29 Recently, in *Plus Group Ltd. v Pyke* (2002), the CA took a firm line on conflicts of interest in respect of individuals who serve as a director of different companies whose businesses compete. Sedley LJ said:

> [T]he fiduciary must not only not place himself in a position (of conflict of interest); if, even accidentally, he finds himself in such a position he must regularise it [ie get the consent of his principal(s)] or abandon it. … [It is not the case that] a director can go cheerfully to the brink so long as he does not fall over the edge. [I]f he finds himself in a position of conflict he must resolve it openly or extract himself from it.

12.30 The CA also affirmed that every decision on the principle governing conflict of interest is fact-specific. In *Plus Group* a director was not found to have been liable for acting in conflict of interest for engaging in business with a client of the company of which he was formerly a director, where his dealings with the client began six months after he had been effectively expelled from the management of the company.

12.31 As the US case law reveals (see in particular *Broz v Cellular Systems Inc* (1996)), and Lowry and Edmonds point out (1997, 1998), the common law rules are likely to have little influence in the vast majority of cases simply because (subject to the reservation in reference to *Cook v Deeks*, **12.19**) the directors, if agreeing that all or some or one of them may exploit a corporate opportunity, will be able to secure the ratification of their decision at a general meeting. In many cases even a single director, because of his influence over the board and control of general meetings, may secure the ratification of exploits undertaken entirely for his own benefit. This leaves the common law to deal with the infrequent *Cooley* situation where the fiduciary will undoubtedly be liable under any regime of accountability because of his subterfuge and bad faith. The problem of ensuring the safety of shareholders from the illegitimate capture of corporate opportunities by directors is only likely to be achieved by changes in company law.

Authorised profits

12.32 Most trusts are today undertaken by professional trustees, so it is clear that there is no rule of equity which prevents a trustee from profiting from his position as trustee. The rule is that a trustee may not obtain any *unauthorised* profits. Most trusts contain express remuneration clauses in the trust instrument. Formerly if there was no such provision the trustee was not entitled to any remuneration whatsoever; however under s 29 of the Trustee Act 2000, where the trust instrument is silent on this point a professional trustee or trust company, though not a lay trustee such as a family friend, is entitled to 'reasonable remuneration' for services provided. All trustees are, however, entitled to the reimbursement of their out-of-pocket expenses incurred in carrying out the trust terms, such as the costs of employing solicitors or brokers, or to pay those expenses directly from the trust funds (s 31 Trustee Act 2000).

The rule in Cradock v Piper

12.33 The only true exception to the rule disallowing unauthorised profits is the rule in *Cradock v Piper* (1850). Just like any other trustee, unless authorised by the trust instrument a solicitor trustee cannot charge for any professional legal work done for the trust. Nor may he retain his own firm to do any such work, for he will indirectly benefit from the firm's revenue (*Christophers v White* (1847)), though he may employ a partner of his firm on the basis that he will receive no share of the profits (*Clack v Carlon* (1861)). Under the rule in *Cradock v Piper*, a solicitor trustee is allowed his usual charges for litigation work done for the body of trustees, which include himself, so long as his being one of the parties has not added to the expense of the litigation. This limited exception for litigious work is illogical and has not been extended to other cases.

The rule is of limited practical importance since any competent solicitor undertaking a trust will insist that the instrument contain an appropriate provision allowing him to charge for his professional services.

The inherent jurisdiction to authorise remuneration

12.34 The court has inherent jurisdiction to authorise remuneration for trustees and other fiduciaries, and to increase the remuneration beyond that provided in the trust terms. The general principles were examined in the leading case, *Re Duke of Norfolk's Settlement Trusts* (1982). In this case a trust's charging clause provided a level of payment well below the current market standard; furthermore, due to changes in the nature of the trust holdings, the work required by the trustee had increased significantly. The CA decided that the inherent jurisdiction covered not only the power to allow remuneration for past services, and to allow remuneration for future services upon the appointment of a trustee, but to increase the level of remuneration beyond that fixed in the trust instrument.

12.35 Two arguments stood in the way of the court's increasing the trustee's remuneration: first, if one regards the remuneration provision as a contract between the settlor and the trustee, then the trustee should, on contractual principles, live with the bargain he has made. Second, it was argued that by increasing the level of remuneration the court would in effect vary the beneficial interests under the trust because less would then go to the beneficiaries, and the court had no inherent jurisdiction to vary beneficial interests (**10.66** et seq). The CA rejected both arguments.

12.36 Fox LJ said this of the contractual analysis:

It might have some appearance of reality in relation to a trustee who, at the request of the settlor, agrees to act before the settlement is executed and approves the terms of the settlement. But very frequently executors and trustees of wills know nothing of the terms of the will until the testator is dead ... It is difficult to see with whom, in such cases, the trustees are to be taken as contracting. The appointment of a trustee by the court also gives rise to problems as to the identity of the contracting party. The position, it seems to me, is this. Trust property is held by the trustee upon the trusts and subject to the powers conferred by the trust instrument and the law. One of those powers is the power given to the trustee to charge remuneration ... [I]t seems to me to be quite unreal to regard them as contractual. So far as they derive from any order of the court they simply arise from the court's jurisdiction and so far as they derive from the trust instrument itself they derive from the settlor's power to direct how his property should be dealt with.

12.37 Brightman LJ said:

[The contractual conception] also seems to me, in the context of the present debate, to give little weight to the fact that a trustee, whether paid or unpaid, is under no obligation, contractual or otherwise, to provide future services to the trust. He can at any time express his desire to be discharged from the trust and in that case a new trustee will in due course be appointed ... The practical effect therefore of increasing the remuneration of the trustee (if the contractual conception is correct) will merely be to amend for the future, in favour of a trustee, the terms of a contract which the trustee has a unilateral right to determine.

12.38 In so far as these reasons are intended to justify the court's power to increase a trustee's remuneration, they are inadequate. Although Fox LJ emphasises that a trustee may have no say in determining the particulars of a remuneration clause, still, trust obligations are always voluntarily undertaken (no one is forced to become a trustee of any particular trust), and when a trustee does undertake a trust with an express remuneration clause, he must be assumed to accept the clause as adequate. In this respect his agreement to take on the trust is very like his agreeing to enter into a contract. The voluntariness of the trustee's undertaking is made clear by Brightman LJ's observation that a trustee has an escape route, retirement, if he later feels underpaid. Therefore the court should be slow to upset the 'bargain' represented by the remuneration clause, because, especially in the case of a professional trustee, his voluntary acceptance of the trusts is very close to contractual. The court should not exercise its inherent jurisdiction simply to allow him to escape from a bad bargain, ie an agreement to undertake a trust which later turns out not to be as profitable as expected. If he wishes to retire, so be it, and if a new trustee will only undertake the trust on better remuneration terms, it may be better to consider increasing the remuneration for him, not for the original trustee. Such an approach would prevent a trustee from being in the position, by reason of his incumbency, to hold the trust to ransom.

12.39 With regard to the second argument, the CA held, quite rightly, that in authorising a trustee's remuneration the court was exercising its jurisdiction to ensure the adequate administration of the trust. In doing so the court did not concern itself with the beneficial interests as such, and so cannot be regarded as varying them.

12.40 When considering increasing the remuneration of an incumbent trustee, Fox LJ said this:

> [T]he court has to balance two influences which are to some extent in conflict. The first is that the office of trustee is, as such, gratuitous; the court will accordingly be careful to protect the interests of the beneficiaries against claims by the trustees. The second is that it is of great importance to the beneficiaries that the trust should be well administered. If therefore the court concludes, having regard to the nature of the trust, the experience and skill of a particular trustee and to the amounts which he seeks to charge when compared with what other trustees might require to be paid for their services and to all the other circumstances of the case, that it would be in the interests of the beneficiaries to increase the remuneration, then the court may properly do so.

12.41 In his opinion Brightman LJ referred to the court's 'power to increase *or otherwise vary* the future remuneration of a trustee who has already accepted office' (my italics). It would be interesting to see in what circumstances the court will exercise its inherent jurisdiction to *reduce* the remuneration provided by the trust instrument, and whether a trustee opposing such an application would fare any better with the contractual argument, insisting that a bargain is a bargain.

12.42 Finally, although it has been said that the jurisdiction 'should only be exercised sparingly, and in exceptional cases' (*Re Worthington* (1954) per Upjohn J), Fox LJ in his reasons said that he and Brightman LJ were both of the impression that orders authorising increases in remuneration had been made in chambers since the 1950s, which might suggest that the exercise was not, in practice, all that exceptional.

12.43 These principles were applied recently in *Foster v Spencer* (1996) in which trustees of a cricket club were awarded remuneration for having tackled various problems 'vigorously and unremittingly' over the course of 20 years to enable the club to sell its ground. The court disagreed with the proposition that it could only allow remuneration, whether for past or future service, in order to engage or retain the services of the particular trustees for the future, ie to obtain the future services of trustees who would not act unless remunerated.

> Where, as in this case, there were no funds out of which to pay remuneration at the time of their appointment, nor was a true appreciation of the extent of the task possible, a prospective application would be impracticable, if not impossible. The refusal of remuneration ... would result in the beneficiaries being unjustly enriched at the expense of the trustees. The right of a trustee to remuneration for his past services cannot depend upon the circumstance that at the time he seeks it, his services are further required so that he is in a position to demand remuneration for the past as a condition of continuing in office.

12.44 Here one trustee was awarded a retrospective annual fee, and another a percentage of the sale price of the ground which took into account his successful effort in obtaining planning permission for the development of the site.

12.45 Take note: a trustee seeking remuneration, or an increase in remuneration, is clearly not in a situation where his interest and duty *may* conflict; they definitely are in *actual* conflict. The court, therefore, must be astute to assess the trustee's claims that he 'requires' such and such a level of remuneration. In the case of an increase of remuneration, taking a strict *Keech* approach would mean that the only person who could not benefit from the trustee's advice to the court that the remuneration of the trust was insufficient would be that trustee himself, because of the 'very obvious consequences' which would ensue if a trustee were able to argue for an increase in remuneration which would be to his own benefit; thus a court would only accept a trustee's argument that the proper administration of the trust required an increase on the basis that a new trustee who would take advantage of the increased remuneration would be appointed. To state this is not to argue that the court should adopt such a rule, but only to question whether the court's strict and automatic application of the 'no conflict' rule is justifiable when *Re Norfolk's Settlement Trusts* shows that the court thinks itself fit to determine an appropriate division of benefits between the beneficiary and the trustee in a clear situation of actual conflict of interest.

12.46 Finally, the court may even award unauthorised remuneration to trustees or fiduciaries in breach of their fiduciary duties. In *Boardman* *v Phipps* (1967), fiduciaries who acted in breach of the no conflict rule, though they did so honestly and in so doing created a large profit for the trust, received remuneration on a 'liberal scale', and in *O'Sullivan v Management Agency and Music Ltd* (1985) remuneration including a profit element was allowed for management and production companies which had procured a contract from an artist through undue influence, but whose efforts were clearly in part responsible for the artist's financial success.

12.47   In *Guinness plc v Saunders* (1990) a director who had negotiated on behalf of a company in a takeover bid sought an allowance from the court for his efforts. The HL questioned whether the court should ever authorise exceptional remuneration to a director, since the company articles specifically provided for the payment of directors – the exercise of the inherent jurisdiction:

> ... may be said to involve interference by the court in the administration of a company's affairs when the company is not being wound up. (per Lord Goff)

The court would definitely not do so in this case where the director had plainly put himself in a position of conflict of interest by agreeing to provide his negotiation services for a fee the size of which depended on the price his company would pay in the takeover.

Unauthorised profits and the liability to account for them

12.48   The rule regarding unauthorised profits is boldly framed in the oft-quoted statement of Lord Herschell in *Bray v Ford* (1896):

> It is an inflexible rule of the court of equity that a person in a fiduciary position ... is not, unless otherwise expressly provided, entitled to make a profit; he is not allowed to put himself in a position where his interest and duty conflict. It does not appear to me that this rule is, as has been said, founded on the principles of morality. I regard it rather as based on the consideration that, human nature being what it is, there is danger, in such circumstances, of the person holding the fiduciary position being swayed by interest rather than by duty, and thus prejudicing those whom he was bound to protect.

12.49   It is clear from this statement that the prohibition on unauthorised profits arises to avoid conflicts of interest. If a trustee were entitled to profit from the trust as he saw fit, his own interests would be in conflict with his fiduciary duty to act solely in the interests of the beneficiaries.

12.50 You will recall (**11.17** et seq) that the primary duty of a trustee is to 'account' for his stewardship of the trust, ie reveal his dealings with the trust property and so afford a beneficiary a right to surcharge or falsify the account. Normally, it is said that a fiduciary is 'liable to account' for any unauthorised profits which he receives as a result of his fiduciary position. The difficult question which this formulation of the fiduciary's liability raises is whether the principal's right to make his fiduciary account for an unauthorised profit is personal or proprietary. Does the fiduciary merely have an obligation to pay the value of the unauthorised profit to his principal, or does the fiduciary hold the unauthorised profit on trust for the beneficiary from the moment he receives it, as in *Keech* with respect to the lease which the trustee obtained? Clearly, if the fiduciary is insolvent, only the trust will ensure that the principal receives the value of the property; furthermore, if the property rises in value, a right to the property itself will be superior to a merely personal claim against the trustee that he pay the value of the property at the time he received it. We will consider the issue in detail at **12.68** et seq.

Incidental profits

12.51 A typical example of an incidental unauthorised profit is a commission a trustee receives by directing the trust business to a particular company. In *Williams v Barton* (1927) a trustee had a contract with a brokerage firm under which he received a commission on work for clients which he had introduced to them; he was accountable to the trust for the commission he earned by directing trust business to the firm. In *Swain v Law Society* (1981), CA; revsd (1983), HL, a solicitor claimed that the Law Society was acting as a fiduciary vis-à-vis solicitors when it procured liability insurance for the profession, and so it held its share of a broker's commission on trust for the members of the Society. The argument succeeded in the CA, but it was decided in the HL that the Law Society was acting under a statutory duty to secure insurance cover and not as a fiduciary for the members; there was, however, no doubt that had the Society been acting as a fiduciary the commission would have been an incidental profit for which it would have been accountable to the members.

12.52   Another example is directors' fees. Trustees must safeguard the trust investments and it will be appropriate and sometimes necessary for a trustee to be appointed to the board of directors of a company in which the trust has a large shareholding (**10.15-16**). The general rule is that their directors' fees are incidental profits of their position for which they must account to the trust (*Re Macadam* (1946)), unless of course their retention of the fees is authorised. The decision in *Re Dover Coalfield Extension Ltd* (1907) is problematic. In that case two directors of the Dover company were appointed to the board of the Kent company, in which Dover held shares. In order for the appointments to be effective, the directors were required to hold a certain minimum number of shares in Kent. Sufficient shares were transferred from Dover into their names as trustees for Dover; though the beneficial interest remained with Dover, their legal title to the shares was sufficient to qualify them as directors. The CA held that the directors were not liable to account for their directors' fees. The basis of the decision is unclear, although the judgments seem to rest on two grounds; first, since they became directors of Kent at Dover's request, this amounted to an authorisation from Dover to retain their fees; secondly, because the appointment to Kent was obtained before they acquired Dover's shares in Kent, and the fact that 'they did the work' as directors, the contract between the directors and Kent was a bona fide agreement for their services, ie so that they were not on the board simply as trustee-monitors of Dover's interests.

12.53   In *Re Gee* (1948) Harman J, after reviewing the authorities explained the law as follows:

> [A] trustee who either uses a power vested in him as such to obtain a benefit (as in *Re Macadam*) or who (as in *Williams v Barton*) procures his co-trustees to give him, or those associated with him, remunerative employment must account for the benefit obtained. Further, it appears to me that a trustee who has the power, by the use of trust votes, to control his own appointment to a remunerative position, and refrains from using them with the result that he is elected to a position of profit, would also be accountable. On the other hand, it appears not to be the law that every man who becomes a trustee holding as such shares in a limited company is made ipso facto accountable for remuneration received from that company independently of any use by him of the trust

holding, whether by voting or refraining from so doing. For instance, A who holds the majority of shares in a limited company becomes the trustee of the estate of B, a holder of a minority interest; this cannot, I think, disentitle A to use his own shares to procure his appointment as an officer of the company, nor compel him to disgorge the remuneration he so receives, for he cannot be disentitled to the use of his own voting powers, nor could the use of the trust votes in a contrary sense prevent the majority prevailing.

12.54 In *Re Gee* the trustee-director was not liable to account for his remuneration as a director because the company resolutions to appoint and pay him were unanimously voted by the shareholders, and since there was only a minority of shares held on trust, the resolutions did not turn on the voting of the trust shares – even if the trust shares had been voted against the resolutions, that would not have changed the result.

Secret profits

12.55 One important subset of incidental profits are what are sometimes called 'secret' profits; while the term might be regarded simply as a synonym for unauthorised commission or profits, including, for example, the commission in *Williams v Barton*, it is useful to restrict the term to bribes and hidden commissions which the trustee knowingly obtains in breach of his fiduciary position.

12.56 In *A-G for Hong Kong v Reid* (1994), Reid, the acting Director of Public Prosecutions, accepted bribes to obstruct the prosecution of criminals. Reid was liable to account for the bribe money to the Crown in right of Hong Kong. Lord Templeman said:

> Where bribes are accepted by a trustee, servant, agent, or other fiduciary, loss and damage are caused to the beneficiaries, master, or principal whose interests have been betrayed. The amount of loss or damage resulting from the acceptance of a bribe may or may not be quantifiable. In the present case the amount of harm caused to the administration of justice in Hong Kong by Mr Reid in return for bribes cannot be quantified.

12.57 Note that the fiduciary is accountable for the money to the principal whether or not the principal has himself suffered loss; the effect of the rule is to strip the fiduciary of his profits, not compensate the fiduciary for any loss.

12.58 In *Islamic Republic of Iran Shipping Lines v Denby* (1987) a solicitor accepted a 'commission' of $200,000 from the opposite side for securing the settlement of a legal action brought by his client. Legatt J said, 'What he received was, quite simply, a bribe', and he was liable to pay the sum to his client.

The self-dealing and fair dealing rules

12.59 The self-dealing and fair-dealing rules apply to all fiduciaries, but they are most easily explained in the case of the trustee-beneficiary fiduciary relationship, so we will deal with that case first, and then elaborate the rules briefly in respect of other fiduciaries.

The self-dealing rule

12.60 The self-dealing rule makes voidable any transaction in which a trustee purchases the trust property or, more unusually, sells his own property to the trust, unless the transaction is specifically authorised, and explicit authorisations are strictly construed (*Wright v Morgan* (1926)). The rationale, as explained by Lord Eldon in *Ex p Lacey* (1802) (see also *Ex p Bennet* (1805)), is that because the trustee acts both as vendor for the beneficiaries and purchaser or *vice versa*, he places himself in an obvious conflict of interest and it is impossible to determine whether he has served the beneficiaries' interests properly in securing the best price for them. In consequence, if a trustee sells trust property to himself, the sale may be set aside, ie is voidable, at the insistence of any beneficiary, regardless of how fair the transaction is. The principle in all its rigour was affirmed and applied in *Re Thompson's Settlement* (1986) to a trustee-landlord's consent to the assignment of a lease; the principle essentially applies to all trust property transactions.

12.61 *Holder v Holder* (1968) is an exceptional case where the purchaser from a testator's estate, though not proving the will, admitted at trial that by having performed certain minor acts in the administration of the estate he had become an executor, and therefore a fiduciary. Innocent of his fiduciary status, he purchased the property at fair value at a public auction. The CA refused to set aside the sale, and in this respect the case appears to be an extention from previous authority where sales were not set aside where a purchaser had retired from the trust 12 years prior to the sale (*Re Boles and British Land Company's Contract* (1902)), or where a purchaser was entitled to but did not take up the office of trustee (*Clark v Clark* (1884)). Harman LJ argued that the purpose of the rule was to prevent any sale by a person acting as both vendor and purchaser, but here the property was prepared for sale by the two proving executors of the will with no input from the purchaser:

> I feel the force of the judge's reasoning that if the [purchaser] remained an executor he is within the rule, but in a case where the reasons behind the rule do not exist I do not feel bound to apply it.

12.62   Danckwerts and Sacks LJJ both went further and questioned whether the rule should ever be applied automatically, doubting that it was beyond the court to determine whether the trustee had taken unfair advantage of his position. Vinelott J in *Re Thompson's Settlement* clearly preferred the traditional approach. Note that the problems of determining a trustee's good faith in the face of an actual conflict are just the same here as they were in *Regal Hastings*, where the court refused to mitigate the severity of the rule on evidence that the director's decision that Regal could invest no more than £2,000 in the subsidiary was *bona fide*.

The fair-dealing rule

12.63   The fair-dealing rule applies to purchases not of the trust property itself, but of a beneficiary's interest in the trust property. So, the rule comes into play when, eg, a capital beneficiary assigns (**2.28-29**) his capital interest under the trust to his trustee. The rule is less harsh, for the simple reason that the danger here is less: since there are two real parties to the transaction with their own interests at stake, not a trustee selling to himself, the bargain is much more likely to be a real one. Therefore if a trustee purchases the beneficial interest of a beneficiary the transaction may not be set aside automatically at the beneficiary's insistence, but only if the trustee cannot show (and the onus is on him to do so) that he has taken no advantage of his position, has fully disclosed all relevant information to the beneficiary, that the beneficiary did not rely solely on his advice, and that the price was fair. (See, eg the characterisation of Megarry V-C in *Tito v Waddell (No 2)* (1977), cited in *Re Thompson's Settlement*; *Edwards v Meyrick* (1842).)

The application of the self-dealing and fair-dealing rules to other fiduciaries

12.64   The rules apply to other fiduciaries who, like trustees, have the discretion or power to enter into property sales or other contracts on behalf of their principals. So, for example, the self-dealing rule applies to a company director who enters into a contract to buy goods for his company from another company in which he is interested (see, eg *Aberdeen Rlwy Co v Blaikie Bros* (1854)). The rule also applies where someone close to the director, eg his spouse, has an interest in the second company. The fair-dealing rule would apply where the director enters into a contract between himself and the company, so long as the company is represented by some other person or persons, eg where the director sells land for development he owns to a company by negotiating the contract with the board of directors. Because it is not uncommon for company directors to have outside interests of various kinds, company law and company articles generally provide for a director to escape liability for breach of these rules by making full disclosure of his interests under such a transaction (see Lowry & Dignam (2003), 317 et seq).

12.65   The self-dealing rule applies to all contracts, not just contracts for the sale of property. If your literary agent signs a book contract for you with a publisher in which he has an interest, this breaches the self-dealing rule. The fair-dealing rule typically applies only to property transactions. Thus, if your agent negotiates to buy the movie rights for the book from you, unless he can discharge the onus of showing that the deal was fair, he will breach the fair-dealing rule. The reason why the fair-dealing rule usually applies only to property transactions is that in other cases, the principal will typically be negotiating with the fiduciary to perform a further service for the principal, and this will not usually involve a transaction involving the existing fiduciary relationship, but will be a contract establishing a new one. On the other hand, in certain circumstances one can imagine the fair-dealing rule applying; where an agent's contract is renewed, for example, it is easy to conceive a court setting aside the new contract if the agent failed to disclose that he had breached the prior contract in significant ways, ways difficult for the principal to detect.

12.66   If a fiduciary attempts to circumvent the application of either the self-dealing or the fair- dealing rules by collusively selling to a third party, the sale is liable to be set aside as if the fiduciary were a party himself. In *Re Postlethwaite* (1888) the court did not set aside a sale to a third party just because the trustee entertained a hope of purchasing the property himself from him. Sales to family members or spouses will be viewed suspiciously, and a trustee will not be entitled to avoid the application of the rule by retiring from the trust in order to purchase trust property (*Re Boles and British Land Co's Contract* (1902)).

12.67 Where a sale is liable to be set aside, the transaction is voidable, not void at the outset, so an innocent third party purchaser of the property from the fiduciary before a principal acts will take a good title; in these circumstances the fiduciary will be liable to account for any profits made on the resale, or if it is shown that the resale was at an undervalue, the difference between the sale price and the true value. Where the transaction is avoided while the property is still in the hands of the fiduciary, the principal may require the return of the property in return for the purchase price received, or may require a re-sale of the property on the open market – if the property fetches more on the open market than the price paid by the fiduciary the difference is the principal's, of course (see *Holder v Holder* (1968); Conaglen (2003)).

The proprietary and personal nature of the liability to account

12.68 Where a trustee is liable to account for an unauthorised profit, one might understand this as a claim that the trustee has failed to bring trust property into the account. That is, his liability to account is simply a recognition of the fact that the property is trust property in his hands which he has not properly accounted for, ie included in the trust accounts as an addition to the trust funds, and thus the beneficiaries' claim amounts to a claim to specifically enforce the trust over that property (**11.90-11.91, 11.124**). It would follow from this analysis that the particular profit, as trust property, is held on trust for the beneficiary from the moment the trustee receives it – as the beneficiary's interest in the trust is an interest in a fund, the interest will comprise all those items of property which from time to time are 'captured' by the trust.

12.69 It is important to realise that on this view, the property should be regarded as being held under an *express* trust, the express trust under which all of the other trust property is held. Such a profit would stand on the same footing as would the proceeds of the sale of any of the trust property, or the income from trust property, which a trustee might wilfully or inadvertently have paid into his own bank account. Such property, just like capital proceeds or income, is captured by and is within the terms of the express trust. On this view, then, there is no question of the court's *imposing* a constructive trust on the particular profits or the income earned on it, and of course the profit can be traced into the proceeds of substitutions. The trustee will, of course, also be personally liable to the trust for the value of the property if it has disappeared or cannot be traced, for that will be how he will satisfy the account if he cannot do so with the actual property itself or its traceable proceeds.

12.70   But this perspective cannot apply easily to all fiduciaries, for as I have rather pounded into the reader's head, not all fiduciaries are trustees. They do not hold property on trust for their principals, and so their principals have no proprietary right in any of the property the fiduciary owns the way a beneficiary does in his trustee's property. As we have seen, of course, in certain cases equity does tend to treat fiduciaries who are not trustees as if they were (**11.14**), and one might do so here, arguing that a non-trustee fiduciary who receives an unauthorised profit should hold it on trust for the principal, in this case the court imposing a constructive trust in order to provide parity of treatment with the trustee fiduciary. But this perspective, which seems to be espoused by Lord Millett (**12.76**), assumes the correctness of the view that the fiduciary's liability to account should be modelled on that of the express trustee, whose liability to account flows from his stewardship of the beneficiary's property. But as we know, the essence of the fiduciary obligation does not lie in the stewardship of property – it lies In the fiduciary's discretionary powers to alter his principal's legal position. And so, in determining whether the fiduciary holds any unauthorised profit on trust, or is rather personally liable to pay over the value of such a profit, we should look to the basic rationale of the fiduciary's liability for unauthorised profits. We will return to this following a review of the way that the courts have dealt with the issue.

12.71   In *Williams v Barton*, Russel J decided that the trustee held the commission as a 'constructive trustee' and 'was liable to account' as if this meant much the same thing. In *Boardman*, when the HL affirmed the order of Wilberforce J at first instance, they affirmed that the shares were held on trust, though apart from Lord Guest all of their Lordships spoke only of the defendant's liability to account. Similarly, in *Industrial*

Development Consultants Ltd v Cooley, the court declared that Cooley was a trustee of the profits he earned from his contracts, and liable to account for those profits plus interest.

12.72 It does appear that whenever judges refer to the trust over a fiduciary's profits, even in the case of an express trustee, they always speak of a *constructive* trust, but the use of 'constructive' in these circumstances may be little more than a judicial tic – it may be that the court has a tendency, when it must decide the entitlement in equity to a piece of property which the legal owner disputes belongs in equity to another, and it finds against him, to say that he holds it on 'constructive' trust. For example, if the trustee himself appropriates property which clearly belongs to the trust, any profits or income on the property are clearly trust property, ie property under the express trust, for as we have seen (**11.89** et seq), if beneficiaries wish to claim property acquired in breach of trust they 'adopt' the transaction giving rise to it, thereby capturing the property as trust property. Yet, it is typically said that such profits are held on 'constructive' trust (eg Martin (2001), 624).

12.73 In *Lister & Co v Stubbs* (1890) the CA clearly regarded the fiduciary's liability to account for a bribe to be personal, not proprietary. Stubbs was a purchaser for Lister & Co, who received large secret commissions from one of Lister's suppliers, Varley & Co, for ordering goods from them. Stubbs had invested part of the commission money in land, and Lister sought an interlocutory injunction restraining Stubbs from dealing with the land, arguing that the land, as an investment purchased with the commission money, belonged in equity to it. The CA refused. Here is the famous passage from Lindley LJ's judgment:

> Then comes the question, as between Lister & Co and Stubbs, whether Stubbs can keep the money he has received without accounting for it? Obviously not. I apprehend that he is liable to account for it the moment he gets it. It is an obligation to pay and account to Messrs. Lister & Co, with or without interest, as the case may be. I say nothing at all about that. But the relation between them is that of debtor and creditor; it is not that of trustee and *cestui que trust*. We are asked to hold that it is – which would involve conseqences which, I confess, startle me. One consequence, of course, would be that, if Stubbs were to become bankrupt, this property acquired by him with the money paid to him by Messrs Varley would be withdrawn from the mass of creditors and be handed over bodily to Lister & Co. Can that be right? Another

consequence would be that, if the Appellants are right, Lister & Co could compel Stubbs to account to them, not only for the money with interest, but for all the profits which he might have made by embarking in trade with it. Can that be right? It appears to me that these consequences show that there is some flaw in the argument. If by logical reasoning from the premises conclusions are arrived at which are opposed to good sense, it is necessary to go back and look again at the premises and see if they are sound. I am satisfied that they are not sound – the unsoundness consisting in confusing ownership with obligation.

12.74 Thus Stubbs's liability to account was treated as a purely personal obligation to pay over the value of the commission, or bribe – he was in the position of debtor to his principal for that amount, not trustee of the bribe money for him. Thus his obligation to pay over the bribe, though a fiduciary obligation, was nevertheless still only an obligation – he did not become a trustee of, or in other words, Lister did not get equitable ownership of, the bribe money the moment it was received. While Lindley LJ was absolutely right to insist upon the distinction between ownership and obligation, he did not himself explain why, in this circumstance, Stubbs only had the obligation to pay over the value of the bribe, and not the obligation to hold the bribe money on trust as soon as he received it. For those reasons one must consider Cotton LJ's judgment.

12.75 Cotton LJ appeared to decide that, if Lister had proceeded to set aside the contract with Varley, then any moneys paid by Lister to Varley and which were then paid by Varley to Stubbs as a bribe might be regarded as Lister's in equity. He also distinguished cases where the fiduciary or trustee had in his possession funds actually withdrawn from the trust. Thus the CA appeared to decide that the false fiduciary would only hold property in his possession on trust for his principal where the funds were previously funds of the trust; or rather, funds which prior to his defalcation *were already* trust property, and so remained trust property though wrongly dealt with by the trustee. Presumably the court would also have agreed that dividends payable on shares owned by the trust and paid to the trustee would be trust property the moment they were received, so that if a trustee put them into his own pocket rather than into the trust's bank account he would hold them on trust the moment he received them. Although not property of the trust prior to their receipt by the trustee, such income is payable by virtue of the ownership of the capital, and the beneficiaries are the beneficial owners of that, and so as proceeds of trust property dividends are captured by the trust fund the moment the trustee receives them.

12.76 In 1994, however, the PC in *A-G for Hong Kong v Reid* (1994) decided that the recipient of a bribe held it on trust for his principal. There were two bases for the decision. On one hand, Lord Templeman quoted with approval the words of Sir Peter Millett, speaking extra-judicially:

> [The fiduciary] must not place himself in a position where his interest may conflict with his duty. If he has done so, equity insists on treating him as having acted in accordance with his duty; he will not be allowed to say that he preferred his own interest to that of his principal. He must not obtain a profit for himself out of his fiduciary position. If he has done so, equity insists on treating him as having obtained it for his principal; he will not be allowed to say that he obtains it for himself. He must not accept a bribe. If he has done so, equity insists on treating it as a legitimate payment intended for the benefit of the principal; he will not be allowed to say it was a bribe.

12.77 This analysis, of course, leads to a finding that the bribe is held as trust property from the outset, under an express trust, just as much as any other trust 'income', like the dividends on shares, would be. On this reckoning, the liability to account is a proprietary liability *per se*, as considered in **12.68-72** above, and *Lister* must be wrong because it is conceptually in error – there is just no such thing as a liability to account which means that the fiduciary has only a personal obligation to pay over the value of the property in question.

12.78 But Lord Templeman *also* stated that the fiduciary was subject primarily only to an equitable obligation to pay the money over to the principal, ie was a 'debtor in equity', not a trustee of the bribe money at all. But he further reasoned:

> Equity considers as done that which ought to have been done. As soon as the bribe was received, whether in cash or in kind, the false fiduciary held the bribe on constructive trust for the person injured.

12.79 The application of this maxim in these circumstances is nonsensical, (see Crilley (1994)), for as Swadling (1997) points out, the maxim does not work in the case of a debt:

[T]hat debt can be satisfied by the payment of money belonging to the fiduciary taken from any source. It is not only discharged by the handing over of the very money received. And since there is no duty to pay over the bribe *in specie*, the application of the maxim 'equity considers as done that which ought to have been done' cannot give rise to any proprietary rights over those moneys, for the payment over of the bribe itself is not that 'which ought to have been done'.

12.80 The judgment is certainly subject to criticism for depending upon two apparently incompatible grounds for the decision, but furthermore, the PC was not, as was the court in *Lister*, willing to distinguish between situations where unauthorised profits are held on trust by the fiduciary from the outset, and those in which they are not. Rather, the PC appears to suggest that in line with the general application of the 'no conflict' rule, any and all such profits will be held on trust from the outset. The constructive trust in *Boardman*, for example (assuming one *was* actually imposed), was cited with apparent approval, and Lord Templeman cited *Sugden v Crossland* (1856) with approval for:

... dispos[ing] succinctly of the argument ... that there is a distinction between a profit which a trustee takes out of a trust and a profit such as a bribe which a trustee receives from a third party. If in law a trustee who in breach of trust invests trust moneys in his own name holds the investment as trust property, it is difficult to see why a trustee who in breach of trust receives and invests a bribe in his own name does not hold those investments also as trust property.

12.81 In short, the decision pretty much abolishes the merely personal liability to account for an unauthorised profit – it is essentially proprietary in all cases. While the PC's decisions are technically only of persuasive authority in England and Wales, no one doubts that *Reid* will be given great weight here, although given the broad terms of its expression and the difficulties of its reasoning, its ambit has yet to be precisely settled.

12.82 In *Halifax Building Society v Thomas* (1996) the CA refused to hold that the profit a fraudster had acquired as the result of purchasing land with a fraudulently acquired mortgage was held by him on constructive trust for the mortgagee, though the court accepted that he was liable to pay the value of the profit to the mortgagee. There are clear parallels between this sort of case and that of a person who profits from a bribe, and yet *Reid* was not applied.

12.83 Although the CA in *Lister* did not provide a complete set of principles for differentiating between a trustee's personal and proprietary liability to account, it is submitted that it is essential to do so, and that *Reid* must be faulted on this score. *Pace* Lord Templeman, it is one thing for equity to require a fiduciary to hold on trust a profit acquired by misappropriating the trust property itself, or the income arising on it, but quite another thing to do the same for any property acquired in breach of any of his fiduciary duties.

12.84 What, after all, is the rationale for stripping the fiduciary of his unauthorised profit? It cannot be to *compensate* the principal for a loss, for in most cases (there are exceptions which we shall consider in a moment) the principal does not suffer any loss when his fiduciary acquires an unauthorised profit, earning a commission or director's fees or taking a bribe: the rule applies across the board to all unauthorised profits. Rather, the rationale is to *strip* the fiduciary of any *gain* he earns *in conflict of interest*: this is typically called a 'disgorgement' remedy, and its purpose is to ensure that the fiduciary who places himself in situation of conflict of interest cannot benefit thereby. It is a rule put in place to keep fiduciaries up to the mark, not to generate any extra resources for the principal. The goal of the rule is that fiduciaries *never* earn profits of this kind in the first place, *not* to create a new source of revenue for their principals when they do. Understanding this quasi-punitive nature of the rule explains why it is often questioned why the principal should have the right to the profit anyway – should it not be forfeited to the state, as proceeds of a wrong? Why shouldn't the Attorney-General have the right to claim the profit? The most compelling justification for according the right to the principal is simply that as a matter of private law rights, he is the only appropriate plaintiff, for he has been wronged by the fiduciary's act, and though the principal suffered no loss, if given the incentive of claiming the profit, he will be likely to enforce the claim and strip the fiduciary of the profit. Understood this way, the rationale for stripping the fiduciary's profit follows the maxim 'no one should profit from his own wrong', and the principal's claim is one for 'disgorgement' or 'restitution' for a profit acquired in the commission of a wrong. This topic is, therefore, typically discussed in restitution texts under the heading 'restitution for wrongs' (see, eg Burrows (2002), 455 et seq.)

12.85 In view of this, it seems clear that the primary remedy against the fiduciary should be personal, not proprietary. Consider the consequences in the context of insolvency (**2.57** et seq). If B has the obligation to pay A money, and B goes bankrupt, then A is an unsecured creditor; if B has breached his fiduciary obligations to A and has earned a profit in so doing, but not because his breach was one where he appropriated any of A's property (in equity), our goal should be to ensure that B does not profit from his wrong against A, ie B's breach of fiduciary duty. . In order to accomplish that there is no need for A *to acquire* a proprietary interest in those profits, for that simply allows A to gain a priority over B's other creditors when B, *ex hypothesi*, has not appropriated or interfered with A's property. Where a trust is automatically imposed on B's unauthorised profit however innocently it was acquired, as in *Boardman*, A gains an unjustified advantage merely because the obligation that was breached was a fiduciary one; it is difficult to say that John Phipps's right to Boardman's profits is any more compelling than C's common law right to be paid by Boardman for the property C has provided him under a contract, for C has thereby increased the value of Boardman's estate, or D's common law right to be compensated for Boardman's running him down with his car, for in this case Boardman's wrong has caused D to suffer an actual (monetarily-quantifiable) loss at Boardman's hands. C and D have no proprietary claim, of course.

12.86 Because of these considerations, restitution lawyers typically argue that, except in cases where the fiduciary's profit can be treated as in some way a misappropriation of his principal's property, the remedy should be personal, not proprietary (see, eg Burrows (2002), 499 et seq). Is a trust over property in the breaching fiduciary's hands which is not originally property of the trust, or its traceable proceeds, or income of that property, ever justified? A trust over some unauthorised profits may be justified. If the bribe in *Lister* can be regarded as a payment which was really part of the consideration in the contract between Lister and Varley, then the money, this 'rebate' on the purchase price of Varley's supplies, should have gone back to Lister in the first place. On this view, the trust over the bribe prevents an unjustified distinction between a case of embezzlement and fraudulent conversion: one should not allow the trustee to avoid holding the property on trust from the outset simply because he embezzled it (ie prevented property that should have gone into the trust from getting there by treating it as his own) rather than fraudulently converted it (ie appropriated the existing trust property to his own benefit); both are equally examples of theft. The argument is that this 'rebate' is akin to the income on property, like dividends on shares. The agent 'intercepts' this payment to his principal, treating it as his own (ie embezzling it) rather than paying it over to his principal.

12.87 In *Mahesan v Malaysia Government Officers' Co-operative Housing Society Ltd* (1979) an agent of the housing society took a one-quarter share of an overvalue of $488,000 on a price of $944,000 paid for a piece of land the agent purchased for the society from the briber. The bribe of $122,000 clearly represented the agent's 'cut' of the overvalue. The housing society sued the agent for its loss on the purchase, $443,000, which was the amount of the overvalue minus certain costs. Having elected for that remedy, the society was unable also to claim the value of the bribe, since the value of the bribe clearly formed part of the total overvalue. In other words, both the bribe and the rest of the overpayment element of purchase price were equally treated, quite rightly, as different kinds of appropriations by the fiduciary resulting in loss to his principal.

12.88 But there are bribes and bribes. Certainly the A-G for Hong Kong could hardly claim that it should have received the profits from Reid's suborning of the judicial process. In that sort of case, the principal, by having a claim against the fiduciary, is really just stripping him of the profits of his wrong, not demanding property which was his from the outset, or was a payment made to him intercepted by his fiduciary. A useful thought experiment is always to ask what should happen if the 'unauthorised profit' or bribe is stolen before the principal has a chance to claim it. If the money is really trust money, then the principal's claim should lapse with the theft, for the theft was of *his* property; if you think the principal should be able to sue the false fiduciary for the value of the bribe regardless, then it was the taking of value which was the wrong, not any 'theft' or 'misappropriation' of any particular 'trust asset'. (And note, you cannot have it both ways.) In *Boardman*, Boardman did not appropriate any property of the beneficiaries, unless the use of the information was itself an acquisition of trust property. While Lords Hodson and Guest treated the information as trust 'property', the majority did not, and there is little to recommend that view (see Lord Upjohn's dissent on the point). In such a case it would be right to strip Boardman of his profits (assuming the case was rightly decided), but the profits should not be regarded as trust property from the outset.

12.89 There is, finally the case of what Goode (1991, 1998) has called 'deemed agency gains', where, as for example in *Cooley* (**12.20**), the fiduciary acquires for himself what he ought to have acquired, if he acquired it at all, for his principal; in such circumstances again a trust would seem appropriate, for in such a case the acquisition was one which should have gone to his principal, should, in that sense, have been brought under the fiduciary's 'express trust' towards his principal.

12.90 Most recently, in *Daraydan Holdings v Solland International* (2004), Collins J said that he would follow *Reid* in preference to *Lister*, but held that the case was one in which the fiduciary's profit, a secret commission on a contract he arranged for his principal, was to be analysed as an overpayment under the contract misappropriated from his principal, so that a constructive trust was justified even on the principles enunciated in *Lister*.

12.91 A last point: one of the concerns which seems to motivate the imposition of the trust is that if the trustee invests his ill-gotten gains, perhaps earning substantial profits, and he is only personally liable to account, he will only be liable for the value of his initial receipt plus interest. Thus he will not be stripped of all the profits of his wrong. But there is no reason why the account should be rendered in this way. A personal liability to account might also include a liability to pay over the value of all profits obtained by investment of the money. Such an accounting of profits is a remedy available for patent infringement, though the remedy is personal, not proprietary, ie no constructive trust is declared over the profits (Cornish (1996), pp 63-64).

Equitable compensation for breach of fiduciary obligation

12.92 As we have seen in respect of the no conflict rule, the standard response of equity is to strip the defendant of any profit earned by participating in a transaction in conflict of interest. In the case of the self-dealing and fair-dealing rules, the court will reverse the transaction, if possible, and if not, again will strip the false fiduciary of any profit. However in certain circumstances the breach of fiduciary obligation will not give rise to any profit to the false fiduciary, or not only do that, but may actually give rise to a loss on the part of the fiduciary's principal. In such a case the fiduciary must compensate his principal for the loss, and this compensation for loss is styled *equitable compensation*, which we have already encountered (**11.24**). The leading modern case which establishes the jurisdiction of equity to award equitable compensation for breach of fiduciary obligation is *Nocton v Lord Ashburton* (1914). Nocton, a solicitor, advised Lord Ashburton to advance £60,000 on a mortgage as part of a scheme to develop land. Nocton derived personal advantages under the scheme of which he did not inform Ashburton. Later Nocton advised Lord Ashburton to release a property from the mortgage, which made the mortgage loan less secure, and which again unbeknownst to Lord Ashburton benefited Nocton. The scheme failed to be profitable, and the value of the property securing the mortgage fell far short of what Lord Ashburton had advanced. The House of Lords unanimously decided that, though Nocton had not intended to defraud Lord Ashburton, he was in breach of his fiduciary obligations to him in advising him to act so as to benefit Nocton, and the court affirmed the lower court's direction to inquire into the amount of Lord Ashburton's losses.

12.93   The principles underlying equitable compensation for breach of fiduciary duty were considered, as we have seen, by Lord Browne-Wilkinson, in *Target Holdings* (1996) (**11.35** et seq), although in the context of the measure of liability to restore the trust when the account is falsified, so you should review what he said there now. These principles were considered by the CA in *Swindle v Harrison* (1997). Mrs Harrison, at the instigation of her son, mortgaged her house to provide capital to purchase the Aylesford Hotel, in order that together they could operate a family restaurant business. She contracted to buy the hotel and paid a £44,000 deposit, which would have been forfeited if she did not pay the remainder of the sale price and complete the purchase. Unfortunately, by the date of completion, she and her son were unable to obtain sufficient money to complete the purchase. Her solicitor, the engagingly named Mr Swindle, arranged for his firm to provide a bridging loan so that she could complete. In breach of fiduciary duty, Mr Swindle failed to inform her of certain pertinent facts, in particular his firm's profit on the loan. It was clear that but for the bridging loan, Mrs Harrison would not have been able to purchase the restaurant, and she would have lost her £44,000 deposit. The restaurant business turned out to be a disaster, resulting in the loss of the entire sum she had raised on the equity in her home. Because the solicitor failed to disclose material facts to her in breach of his fiduciary duty, she was clearly entitled to rescind the bridging loan agreement; indeed, by the time of trial, that loan agreement had been rescinded by agreement. It was argued that the solicitors' firm was liable for any losses which would not have resulted 'but for the loan', ie all the losses resulting from the restaurant business.

12.94   The CA unanimously found against Mrs Harrison. Unfortunately, all three judges in the CA gave extensive judgements which used different terminology and provided different rationales for doing so. Essentially, however, all three agreed that the particular breach in question, the failure to inform Mrs Harrison of the profit Mr Swindle's firm was taking on the loan, did not lead to the losses caused by her entering the restaurant business.

12.95   Another recent example is *Gwembe Valley Development v Koshy* (2004); in conflict of interest, a director made a massive profit on currency transactions contracts he arranged for his company. While we was liable, of course, to disgorge those unauthorised profits, the court held that these contracts had not contributed to the ultimate failure of the development venture, so he was not liable to compensate the company for the resultant losses.

Secondary liability for breach of fiduciary obligation

12.96   As we have seen (11.14), where a fiduciary misappropriates his principal's property, say where a company director fraudulently draws a cheque from the company bank account in his own favour, equity regards this as equivalent to a breach of trust and the normal breach of trust remedies against third parties, ie for knowing receipt or knowing assistance, will apply. Making third parties liable in the case of a true breach of fiduciary obligation is, however, a more vexed question (see Mitchell (2002)). There are, of course, some breaches of fiduciary obligation which necessarily involve misapplications of the principal's property, ie breaches of the self-dealing and fair-dealing rules, and there would seem to be no objections in principle to making third parties who dishonestly assist such breaches, or receive property via them, to be held liable. The same might be said for those cases in which a fiduciary is properly held to hold an unauthorised profit on constructive trust for his principal, ie those in which the unauthorised profit can fairly be said to be a misappropriation of the principal's property (12.84-12.89). In these cases the analogy with knowing receipt and knowing assistance is straightforward.

12.97   For example, in *CMS Dolphin Ltd v Simonet* (2001) Collins J treated a director's exploitation for himself of a maturing business opportunity 'as appropriating for himself [the property of his company]'. The new company he formed which took the benefit of the opportunity (and which was deemed to have his knowledge) was liable either as a 'participant' in a breach of trust, or alternatively as a knowing recipient of trust property transferred in breach of trust (see also *Comax Secure Business Services v Wilson* (2001)). While the reasoning that a maturing business opportunity is a company's 'property' is questionable (**12.21** et seq), the principle upon which the company was found liable seems a straightforward application by analogy of the rules governing secondary liability for breach of trust.

12.98   Nevertheless, the cases do not speak with one voice. In *Satnam Investments Ltd v Dunlop Heywood & Co Ltd* (1999) the plaintiff's competitor was assisted in its purchase of a site for development, a site in which the plaintiff was also interested, by the unauthorised release of confidential information by the plaintiff's agent, which the court treated as a breach of its fiduciary obligation. The CA refused to hold that the competitor held the site on constructive trust for the plaintiff. Distinguishing *Boardman* on the basis that there the defendants had placed themselves in a fiduciary position vis-a-vis the beneficiaries, the court said that it would be contrary to commercial good sense to hold a competitor, who of course had no prior fiduciary duty to the plaintiff, liable as a fiduciary for taking advantage of the plaintiff's agent's breach and stripping it of the asset it had acquired. This case seems to suggest that merely knowingly receiving a benefit which would not have come to one but for another's breach of fiduciary obligation is insufficient to render one liable to the wronged principal. Notice one can analyse this case on the 'deemed agency gain' basis (**12.89**), such that the acquisition of the site for development could be regarded as something that its agent should have acquired for its principal if for anyone; there seems little doubt that had the agent acquired the site itself, it would have been liable to hold it on trust for the principal. Thus, as a case equivalent to a 'misappropriation of trust property' case, it seems directly to conflict with *CMS Dolphin*.

12.99   It seems doubtful that a third party could be held liable in a case where the unauthorised profit does not represent in any way a 'taking' from a principal, as in *Reid* (**12.76** et seq), which one might call a 'pure' gain-stripping case. For presumably only the person acquiring the profit in breach of obligation can be justly stripped of the gain. A third party who participates in a transaction in which the fiduciary acts in conflict of interest, but who acquires no gain himself, has no gain to be stripped of. And where he does acquire a gain, but does not himself owe any fiduciary obligations, there seems to be no reason to strip him of the gain. This reasoning may justify the result vis-à-vis the third parties in *Regal Hastings* (**12.15** et seq); recall that besides the directors, the company's solicitor subscribed for shares, and one director subscribed for shares for third parties. Neither the solicitor nor the third party were stripped of their profits, though, on the facts, it could hardly be clearer that the solicitor knowingly participated in and benefited from the scheme, and the third party benefited from the scheme. Neither was the director who subscribed for others liable secondarily for those others' gains. This was so even though all of them knowingly participated in a scheme which would not have come off but for their participation, and which they were in a position to realise, if they had thought about it, was a scheme reflecting a conflict of interest.

The scope of fiduciary obligations

12.100 Trustees, agents, and company directors are the classic cases of those who owe fiduciary duties, but the concept has been stretched to cover other cases, sometimes appropriately, sometimes not. A sensible extension of the concept brings the solicitor and client relationship (see, eg, *Longstaff v Birtles* (2002)), and similar cases of authoritative advice-giving, into the fold. While a solicitor does not usually have true legal powers to affect his client (he does not typically act as the client's agent, strictly speaking), the solicitor does advise his client how to deal with third parties in circumstances where the client essentially follows the solicitor's advice, and so in that sense the solicitor has strong practical powers to affect his client's legal position vis-à-vis those third parties. Clearly if a solicitor advised a client to settle an action against a company, not because that was what the client's legal position indicated, but because the solicitor was interested in the company, this would be a breach of loyalty and good faith which is essentially equivalent to the trustee's or agent's breach of fiduciary obligations.

12.101 However, various inappropriate extensions of the concept have been made, typically in cases where the person named as a 'fiduciary' has committed a legal wrong, a legal wrong which is not just wrong, but can be characterised as one which shows an abuse of loyalty or good faith. Perhaps the oddest extension of the concept is found in the decision of the Canadian Supreme Court in *M (K) v M (H)* (1992); see also *Norberg v Wynrib* (1992)). In *M (K)* the plaintiff was sexually abused by her father, the defendant, from the age of 8 until she was 16 and left the family home. She suffered various psychological problems, and it was only following psychological therapy, at the age of 28, that she brought an action against her father for damages for the tort of assault. A jury found for her and awarded $10,000 general damages and $40,000 punitive damages. The trial judge, however, set aside the award and dismissed the action on the basis that the claim was barred by the Ontario Limitations Act. On appeal to the Supreme Court of Canada, the plaintiff/appellant claimed that for various reasons the Limitation Act should not apply to bar her claim in tort, and her appeal on this ground succeeded. But she also claimed that her father's incestuous assault also constituted a breach of fiduciary obligation; in view of the fact that there was no statutory limitation period in respect of breach of a fiduciary obligation, if she succeeded on this ground she would have been in a much better position to avoid any bar based upon the lapse of time between the assaults and her launching her action against her father. The court accepted her argument that her father had breached a fiduciary obligation in assaulting her.

12.102 Reread **12.1** where Millett LJ in *Mothew* describes the nature and scope of fiduciary obligations, and the facts of *Mothew* at **11.43**. There Millett LJ emphasised the particular nature of fiduciary obligations to distinguish them clearly from a duty to take care. His separate treatment of breach of trust also indicated that he does not regard all breaches of trust as breaches of fiduciary obligation. In view of this, how do you think Millett would approach the question whether the father in *M(K)* breached a fiduciary obligation? Both in *Mothew* and in *M(K)* we appear to have plaintiffs who have resorted to a claim for breach of fiduciary obligation, rather than for a tort (negligence or assault), because of a perceived difficulty in proceeding under that description of the claim. However, Millett LJ in *Motthew*, unlike the court in *M(K)*, strongly disapproved of resorting to equity in this way.

12.103 Child abuse is of course a terrible wrong, and is also, in a sense, a dreadful breach of loyalty and good faith when committed by a parent or guardian, and it seems that the latter consideration is what drove the court to accept the abuse as a breach of fiduciary obligation (see Flannigan

(2000)). But child abuse is a crime and a civil wrong. No one has a legal power or discretion to commit child abuse, one which should be exercised in good faith or not at all. Fiduciary obligations are intended to ensure that a fiduciary takes decisions *which he is otherwise legally empowered or obliged to undertake in one way or another under his trust or agency or retainer* in a manner which best serves the interests of his principal. In view of a fiduciary's fiduciary obligations, an otherwise *legitimate* use of a *legitimate* power or discretion may be *turned into* a wrong, because it reveals a breach of loyalty or good faith. A breach of any old obligation, whether the commission of a tort like assault or child abuse, or a breach of contract, does not become a breach of a fiduciary obligation simply because, besides being wrong in its own right, it *also* reveals self-interested disloyalty or bad faith; those acts are not within the range of decisions which make up the extent of the fiduciary's discretion, to which, and only to which, the fiduciary's fiduciary obligations apply. As Lord Millett has said in another context (*Dubai Aluminium v Salaam* (2003)): 'Sexually assaulting a boy is not an improper mode of looking after him. It is an independent act in itself, not an improper mode of doing something else.' Thus if your trustee favours his own interests over yours by beating you up or slandering you or stealing your bicycle he certainly commits a wrong, but does not breach his fiduciary obligations to you. Nevertheless, as in *M (K) v M (H)*, courts appear to have occasionally stretched the concept of 'fiduciary' in just this way as a means more effectively to deal with a wrongdoer.

12.104   To put this another way, the existence of a fiduciary obligation *turns something one would otherwise be perfectly allowed to do into a wrong* because it is done in conflict of interest. If this is so, things that are already straightforwardly wrongs are not within the scope of a fiduciary obligation, because they are wrongs already. Just because a wrong manifests, in addition to its wrongness *per se*, a breach of loyalty, doesn't turn it into a breach of fiduciary obligation. On this view, the parent in *M(K) v M(H)* did not commit a breach of fiduciary obligation, because the act of sexual assault is straightforwardly a wrong whoever does it. It *aggravates* the wrong that it is committed by a parent, a person one should be able to trust; but that doesn't turn it into a different sort of wrong, a breach of fiduciary obligation, because it is not a case of a person using a power or discretion in conflict of interest, for no one has the power or discretion to commit a sexual assault against anyone. Indeed, from this point of view, it *belittles* the gravity of the wrong to say that the essence of the wrong is its manifestation of a 'conflict of interest' – what's wrong about sexual assault is the heinous violation of the victim's bodily integrity, not any 'breach of loyalty'. The essence of a breach of fiduciary obligation is that the fiduciary is the wrong party to take part in the transaction – he is an unsuitable contracting party with his principal, for in contracting with his principal he places himself in a conflict of interest. But the wrong of sexual assault is not wrong because it was the *wrong person* who carried out the assault. It is a wrong because assault itself is wrong, whoever does it.

12.105 Another example of a case where the fiduciary relationship was distorted to achieve a particular result is *Reading v A-G* (1951). A sergeant in the British Army stationed in Egypt assisted smugglers by riding in their lorries wearing his uniform so that they would not be stopped at check points. The British authorities seized £20,000 of the money he was paid for these services. In an action to recover the money Reading argued that while he had obtained it wrongfully, the Crown had no right to retain it; the HL held that as a non-commissioned officer he stood in a fiduciary relationship to the Crown and therefore he was liable to account to the Crown for any profits he obtained by the misuse of his position. Only on the very strained rationale that Reading, by wearing his uniform had the practical power to affect the Crown's practical interests, by affecting the reputation of the Crown in Egypt, could Reading be regarded as a fiduciary.

12.106 Much the better explanation is simply that the terminology of fiduciary was fictitiously applied to Reading in order to provide a basis for stripping him of his ill-gotten gain, ie to treat it as an 'unauthorised profit'(**12.48** et seq); the case would better have been dealt with openly as one in which the principles of the law of unjust enrichment applied to deny Reading the gain he made by committing a wrong (see Jones (1968); **11.203**). The point to take away here is that there are many ways in which a person who is not a fiduciary to someone may harm someone in some way and make a profit by doing so. A security guard may have no legal right to admit anyone to the building on his shift, but if he is bribed to let in some thieves, we should surely wish to strip him of that profit; but just because we wish to strip him of his profit is no reason retroactively to characterise him as a fiduciary. He should be stripped of his bribe because otherwise he would be unjustly enriched by his wrong, not because he breached any fiduciary obligation, for he had none.

12.107 The case of bare trusts raises an interesting question regarding the scope and nature of fiduciary obligations. Recall that for fiduciary obligations to arise, there must be some scope for discretion or leeway in the fiduciary's performance of his duties. No such discretion or leeway arises in the case of the bare trust, for in such cases the trustee is only to follow his beneficiary's instructions exactly. If the bare trustee breaches the trust in some way, he will certainly be liable for breach of trust, but as we know (**12.1**), not all breaches of trust are breaches of fiduciary obligation. For example, a bare trustee might mistakenly do something he was not directed to do like paying trust money away to the wrong person; that would not constitute a breach of fiduciary obligation, because it would not be a consequence of the trustee favouring his own self-interests over those of his beneficiary. Now here's the tricky issue: since a bare trustee is not empowered to take decisions off his own bat which legally bind his beneficiary, *any* decision he takes off his own bat will be a wrong *per se*, a clear breach of trust, for in that case he will not be following his beneficiary's instructions. And as we have just seen, the mere commission of a wrong does not become a breach of fiduciary obligation because it shows that the wrongdoer favoured his own interest over that of the person he wronged. Thus, can one argue that, because the bare trustee never undertook to act as a decision-maker for his beneficiary, he cannot be a fiduciary to him, and so cannot commit a breach of fiduciary obligation? In other words, since there are no decisions which he could *legitimately* take off his own bat, is it not correct to maintain that, while he can commit various wrongs (breaches of trust), there is nothing that he can do which could amount to a breach of fiduciary obligation?

12.108 While this line of reason is appealing, and seems to flow from a cogent characterisation of the rationale behind the imposition of fiduciary obligations outlined above, it was not accepted by Cross J in *Re Brooke Bond & Co Ltd's Trust Deed* (1963). The case concerned a *custodian trustee* (**10.58**), a bare trustee who takes directions from a *managing trustee* rather than from the beneficiaries. Clearly the managing trustee had fiduciary obligations to the beneficiaries, but did the custodian trustee? In this case the custodian trustee was an insurance company, and the managing trustee decided that the trust should take out a policy of insurance to protect the beneficiaries' interests in the trust fund. The managing trustee decided to take out the trust policy with the custodian trustee in its capacity as an insurance company. Now if the custodian trustee was a regular trustee with fiduciary obligations, taking out an insurance policy for the trust with itself would have been prohibited, because there would have been a clear conflict of interest, and a violation of the self-dealing rule. But was such a transaction prohibited here, given that the managing trustee had made the decision, the custodian trustee having no discretion to make the policy with itself? Cross J held that it was, though the reasons he gave for his decision do not go to the root of the matter in any detailed way. Rather, he seems to have just felt that as a trustee of whatever kind, the custodian trustee would be obliged to undertake any dealings with the trust with the best interests of the beneficiaries in mind, and so must not put itself in any position of conflict of interest (Cf Hayton (2003), 668).

12.109 Despite the insufficient reasoning, the case seems to indicate that in all cases of trusts, the trustee will be characterised as a fiduciary regardless of whether the trustee has undertaken to take discretionary decisions in the beneficiaries' best interests. Thus even in the case of a bare trust, a wrong committed by a trustee which reveals the trustee favouring his own interests over the beneficiary may be regarded as a breach of fiduciary obligation. Indeed, some rationale for this may lie in the simple fact that a trustee, unlike other fiduciaries, holds legal title to the beneficiaries' property. Being in charge of someone else's property gives a trustee such scope for doing wrong, and provides such a temptation to commit a wrong for one's own benefit, that a court may think it right to treat any wrong he commits in respect of his stewardship of the property that reveals a preference for his own interests over those of his beneficiaries to be regarded as a breach of fiduciary obligation and, in general, to apply the conflict of interest rules to him as they were applied to the custodian trustee in *Brooke Bond*.

12.110 Recall, however, *Paragon Finance* (11.211 et seq): there, a clearly wrongful act by a fiduciary, indeed a trustee, who dealt with the trust property held under a bare trust with mandate in a way which (if the allegations of fraud are correct) clearly manifested his acting in his own best interests in total disregard of those of his beneficiary, was not regarded as a breach of any fiduciary obligation under the trust. As it appears the obligations the solicitors had with respect to the trust property were limited to carrying out the terms of the land purchase trust, which gave them no discretion as to how to deal with the trust money, this decision seems to affirm the view that there can be no breach of a fiduciary obligation except where a person acts to favour his own self-interest within the scope of a discretion undertaken to permit him to serve the interests of another. Since the solicitors had no discretions to exercise over the trust money, they therefore had no fiduciary obligations in respect of it, and therefore their fraudulent disposition of the money could not be a breach of any fiduciary obligation in respect of it — rather, it was just a fraud. Their being solicitor-trustees just put them in a good position to carry it out.

Further reading

Swadling (1997); Crilley (1994); Birks (ed.) (1994, Vol II, Part IV); Lowry (1997); Lowry and Edmonds (1998); Millett (1998); Brownbill (1993, Part VI); Birks (ed.) (1997); Ho (1998); Smith (2003b)

Must read cases: *Re Duke of Norfolk's Settlement Trusts* (1981); *Keech v Sandford* (1776); *Re Gee* (1948); *Boardman v Phipps* (1966); *Regal (Hastings) Ltd v Gulliver* (1942); *Lister & Co v Stubbs* (1890); *Holder v Holder* (1968); *A-G for Hong Kong v Reid* (1993).

Self-test questions

1. Discuss the scope and rationale for the conflict of interest rule as it governs a fiduciary's personal profits, and the remedies available to a principal or beneficiary where the fiduciary is liable under the rule.

2. Andrew is a farmer, who farms his own land and also manages and farms the land of Frank. Andrew recently purchased a load of seed cheaply, and now realises it is more than he can use on his own farm. He plants a ton of the seed on Frank's land, and charges Frank the going price, making a profit of £600. An agent of Superseeds Ltd rings up Andrew at his manager's office on Frank's farm and asks whether Frank will grow a new genetically-modified tomato Superseeds has developed. Frank has a policy against growing genetically-modified crops, and Andrew offers to grow the tomato on his own farm. The crop does spectacularly well, earning Andrew a profit of £20,000. Finally, Andrew offers to purchase half of Frank's acreage. He provides Frank with the accounts of his management of Frank's farm; they are in such disarray that it is impossible to determine how profitable the

operation is, but Frank sells anyway. Discuss Andrew's liability to Frank.

3. In what circumstances, if any, should a fiduciary hold any unauthorised profit on constructive trust for his principal?

4. Arthur is the director and chief operating officer of Smartco, a clothing manufacturer. In 2003 he purchased, on behalf of the company, £15,000 worth of fabric from a company in which both he and his wife have a major shareholding. Later in the same year he moved the head office of Smartco to Guildford, in Surrey, where he lives, so as to reduce his need to commute. The move cost the company approximately £150,000. The company's solicitor, Derek, carried out the necessary conveyancing work, earning a fee of £20,000. In early 2004, Smartco acquired a controlling interest in Splash Ltd, a swimwear manufacturer, and Arthur used the Smartco shares in Splash to vote himself on to Splash's board of directors, taking £10,000 director's fees. As a director of Splash, Arthur discovered it was under-valued, and purchased the remaining shares of Splash for himself. Following a reorganisation of Splash largely brought about through Arthur's efforts, its shares have increased in value by 50%. Advise Smartco.

CHAPTER THIRTEEN

Charitable Trusts

SUMMARY

The charitable character of public purpose trusts

Trusts for the relief of poverty

Trusts for the advancement of education

Trusts for the advancement of religion

Trusts for other purposes beneficial to the community

The public benefit requirement

A charity must be for exclusively charitable purposes

Preservation from failure: cy près

Reform

13.1 Charity has no essential connection with the law of trusts, as Matthews (1996) explains:

> [Charity] derived from the ecclesiastical jurisdiction, not from that of the Chancery. Charity did not need to be performed through the medium of the trust. It was not so in English law at the outset, and even today it need not be. It could, for example, be carried out through a company. And many legal systems have well developed laws of charity without recourse to, indeed without any knowledge of, trusts. It is a historical accident that the Court of Chancery hijacked the charitable gift and squeezed it (with some difficulty) into the pre-existing framework of the trust.

While there are some particular features of charitable trusts which concern their nature as trusts *per se* (eg the cy près doctrine, 13.41 et seq), this topic largely comprises particular aspects of the law of charities. Be warned, therefore, that what you learn here will, for the most part, have only marginal relevance to what else you have learned in this book, which is why it is at the end. The topic is, however, invariably covered in trusts courses, most likely because it is easy, providing at least one exam question on which all should do well. It also makes a welcome change for those who hate studying trusts, or more likely, for those who hate teaching it.

13.2 Charitable trusts are (1) trusts for purposes which benefit the public, which (2) on the authority of statute and common law are 'charitable'. Not all publicly beneficial purposes are considered by the law to be charitable. What counts as a charitable purpose is the source of a never-ending supply of case law, and has been the subject of many reform proposals (**13.52** et seq).

13.3 Charitable trusts are not subject to the beneficiary principle (**9.2**) Charitable trusts are valid purpose trusts which are enforced, not by beneficiaries, but by the Attorney-General, or more recently, by the Charities Commissioners (who also have other duties, such as registering charitable trusts, monitoring the accounts of charitable trusts, investigating the running of charities to check abuses, and advising charitable trustees) Charitable trusts can last forever, and on that score are not subject to the rule against perpetuities (**3.31**). (Charitable gifts which are determinable or made upon condition subsequent, are however, subject to the rule as it applies to gifts of that kind.)

Fiscal benefits

13.4 Charities are generally exempt from income tax, capital gains tax corporation tax, inheritance tax, and stamp duty, although they do have to pay VAT on the goods and services they purchase. They are also able to claim an 80% rebate on council tax for the land they hold, and local councils may refund the remaining 20% on a discretionary basis. Relief from inheritance tax, capital gains tax, and income tax is also available for donors who give to charities. Charities are not taxed on the profits they earn from trading so long as the profits are applied to charitable purposes and the trading carries out the purpose of the charity Finally, charities may also reclaim income tax paid by donors on money given to charity; thus a charity will be able to claim £220 from the Inland revenue it if receives a gift of £1000 from a donor who pays income tax at the basic rate of 22%.

The conditions for charitable status

13.5   In order for a purpose trust to be charitable:

• the *character* of the purposes must be charitable;

• the purposes must, on balance, be beneficial rather than detrimental;

• the trust must benefit a section of the public, not a collection of private individuals;

• the purposes must be *exclusively* charitable, and in particular, the purposes must not be political; and

• the trust must not be profit-distributing.

The charitable character of public purpose trusts

13.6   Charitable purposes are those which may be found amongst those listed in the preamble to the Charitable Uses Act 1601, or purposes which are analogous to those in the preamble and are within its 'spirit and intendment'. The relevant section of the preamble is as follows:

> ... some [property given] for relief of aged, impotent and poor people, some for the maintenance of sick and maimed soldiers and mariners, schools of learning, free schools, and scholars in universities; some for repair of bridges, ports, havens, causeways, churches, sea banks and highways; some for education and preferment of orphans; some for or towards the relief, stock, or maintenance of houses of correction; some for marriages of poor maids; some for supporting, aid and help of young tradesmen, handicraftsmen and persons decayed; and others for relief or redemption of prisoners or captives, and for aid or ease of any poor inhabitants concerning payment of fifteens, setting out of soldiers and other taxes ...

t seems that in 1601 this list consisted almost totally of purposes which would directly work a public benefit by lowering the local rates, since he persons and projects named would otherwise have been financially supported by the parish; thus an individual who devoted his funds to such purposes provided a very tangible public benefit indeed. There is a school of thought which holds that even today tax relief afforded to charities can only be justified to the extent that these charities provide services which would otherwise require the allocation of state funds.

13.7 Basing himself on the guidance the preamble provided, in *Income Tax Special Purposes Comrs v Pemsel* (1891) Lord Macnaghten produced his famous four-fold characterisation of what is charitable:

> Charity in its legal sense comprises four principle divisions: trusts for the relief of poverty; trusts for the advancement of education; trusts for the advancement of religion; and trusts for other purposes beneficial to the community, not falling under any of the preceding heads.

13.8 In *Scottish Burial Reform and Cremation Society Ltd v Glasgow Corpn* (1968) the HL decided that the Scottish Burial Reform Society, a non-profit making company whose main object was the inexpensive, sanitary disposal of the dead, particularly by cremation, was a charity. Lord Reid stated:

> [The] benefit [must be] of a kind within the spirit and intendment of the [Charitable Uses Act 1601]. The preamble specifies a number of objects which were then recognised as charitable. But in more recent times a wide variety of other objects have come to be recognised as also being charitable. The courts appear to have proceeded first by seeking some analogy between an object mentioned in the preamble and the object with regard to which they had to reach a decision. Then they appear to have gone further, and to have been satisfied if they could find an analogy between an object already held to be charitable and the new object claimed to be charitable.

13.9 In *Incorporated Council of Law Reporting for England and Wales v A-G* ((1972) CA) Sachs and Buckley LJJ held that the Council, which produces the Law Reports, was a valid charity under the education head, and if not charitable under that head, under the fourth head of purposes beneficial to the community. Russell LJ felt that the Council was a valid charity under the fourth head only, but he also argued that proceeding by analogy from the preamble with respect to the fourth head was unnecessary; he argued that the court should just make a determination of whether the charity carries out a purpose beneficial to the public.

494

This 'first principles' approach has since been doubted by Dillon J at first instance in *Re South Place Ethical Society* (1980), and clearly differs from the HL affirmation of the analogy approach in the *Scottish Burial Society* case.

13.10 The history of this expansion by analogy is not a particularly honourable one. Worries about testators disinheriting their families through gifts to the Church and to charities led to the Mortmain and Charitable Uses Act, 1736 (now repealed) which made most gifts of land on trust to charities void. In order to bring about the failure of as many gifts as possible under the Act, the boundaries of what counted as charitable slowly expanded. In particular, the wide scope for what counts as religion can be explained in part by the fact that a wide definition ensured that gifts of land to all sects were equally struck down. In the famous case of *Thornton v Howe* (1862), a trust to publish the writings of Joanna Southcott, 'an ignorant and foolish woman' who nonetheless believed herself with child by the Holy Spirit and about to give birth to the new Messiah, was held charitable, therefore void under the Act.

13.11 The *Charity Commissioners Annual Report* (1987, para 24ff) outlines the Charity Commissioners' approach to analogy. Although bound to follow the route of precedent and analogy, they try to do so 'constructively and imaginatively'.

Trusts for the relief of poverty

13.12 Poverty does not mean destitution; trusts for poverty are for those who would otherwise have to 'go short' (*Re Coulthurst* (1951)), so trusts for 'ladies of limited means' (*Re Gardom* (1914)) and for 'decayed actors' (*Spiller v Maude* (1881)) were valid. The charity can be limited to particular classes so long as it does not name individuals, nor include those who might not be poor. So trusts for poor employees (*Dingle v Turner* (1972)), or an individual's poor relations (*Re Scarisbrick* (1951); *Re Segelman* (1996)) are good, but a trust benefiting the working classes was not because being a member of the working class did not necessarily imply poverty (*Re Sanders' Will Trusts* (1954)). In *Re Niyazi's Will Trusts* (1978) a trust for a working man's hostel in Famagusta, Cyprus, where there was a grave housing shortage, was upheld as charitable, though Megarry VC opined that the trust was 'desperately near the border-line'.

Trusts for the advancement of education

13.13 This head obviously includes conventional education and training: thus trusts for schools, colleges, universities and other institutions of learning are valid. But this head extends to cover research, artistic and aesthetic education *(Royal Choral Society v IRC* (1943)), museums *(British Museum Trustees v White* (1826)), sport facilities provided for the young at school *(Re Mariette* (1915)), student unions *(London Hospital Medical College v IRC* (1976)), and professional bodies so long as they advance education *(Royal College of Surgeons of England v National Provincial Bank Ltd* (1952)). However, courts are careful to ensure that this head is not used to provide charitable status for political purposes masquerading as education or research.

13.14 Education of the young must be taken in a broader sense than mere classroom learning. In *IRC v McMullen* (1981) a trust for the provision of facilities to play association football or other sports in schools or universities was held valid. In *Baldry v Feintuck* (1972) the charitable status of student unions was affirmed as part of the educational enterprise, but the devotion of funds to political campaigns by student unions was not, and could be restrained by injunction (see also *Webb v O'Doherty* (1991)). However, the fact that a student union provides facilities to political clubs does not invalidate its charitable status.

13.15 The education head also covers the dissemination of useful knowledge. It was upon this basis that the CA decided that the production of the Law Reports was charitable in *Incorporated Council of Law Reporting v A-G*. It also covers the promotion of culture; in *Re Delius* (1957) a charity to promote the music of Delius was good.

13.16 Carrying out useful research is charitable under the education head as well, but the limits of charitable research are not entirely clear: in *Re Shaw* (1957) George Bernard Shaw's testamentary gift to be devoted to research into a 40-letter alphabet for English and the translation of one of his works into the new alphabet was held to be not charitable; this was probably a narrow decision, based on the idea that the gift did not contemplate education or teaching. In contrast, in *Re Hopkins' Will Trusts* (1965) a gift to the Francis Bacon Society 'to be earmarked and applied towards finding the Bacon-Shakespeare manuscripts', ie to finding evidence that Francis Bacon wrote the works attributed to Shakespeare, was valid under the education head, on the basis that such a discovery would be of immense importance. In *McGovern v A-G* (1982), Slade J summarised the principles:

> (1) A trust for research will ordinarily qualify as a charitable trust if, but only if (a) the subject matter of the proposed research is a useful subject of study; and (b) it is contemplated that knowledge acquired [thereby] will be disseminated to others; and (c) the trust is for the benefit of the public, or a sufficiently important section of the public. (2) In the absence of a contrary context, however, the court will [readily construe] a trust for research as importing subsequent dissemination of the results thereof. (3) Furthermore, if a trust for research is to constitute a valid trust for the advancement of education, it is not necessary either (a) that a teacher/pupil relationship should be in contemplation or (b) that the persons to benefit from the knowledge to be acquired should be [students] in the conventional sense. (4) ... [the court] must pay due regard to any admissable extrinsic evidence which is available to explain the wording of the will in question or the circumstances in which it was made.

13.17 The production of mere propaganda is not the advancement of education. *Re Hopkinson* (1949) is one of several cases in which trusts for educating adults in the principles of particular political parties were held invalid, in which the oft-cited words of Vaisey J appear: 'political propaganda ... masquerading as education is not education within the statute of Elizabeth'. *Re Koeppler Will Trusts* (1986) concerned a trust for carrying on the work of the 'Wilton Park' Institution, which ran conferences for representatives of member nations of major western organisations to exchange views on political, economic, and social issues; though political figures participated, the conferences did not further any particular political viewpoint, and the trust was charitable under the education head.

Trusts for the advancement of religion

13.18 In general the law of charities assumes that any religion is better than none, but as between religions, stands neutral (*Neville Estates Ltd v Madden* (1962) per Cross J). Religion, however, requires a spiritual belief or faith in some higher unseen power. Trusts promoting morality or particular ethical ways of life are not religious. In *Re South Place Ethical Society* (1980) Dillon J said: 'Religion is concerned with man's relations with God, and ethics are concerned with man's relations with man'. The trust in question, one for the study and dissemination of ethical principles and the cultivation of a rational religious sentiment was not charitable under the religion head, but was as a trust for the advancement of education, as well as under the fourth head as contributing to mental or moral improvement. In *R v Registrar General, ex p Segerdal* (1970), the 'Church' of Scientology, based upon the American L Ron Hubbard's theory of 'dianetics', was held to be a philosophy of existence, not a religion, so not a charity. In the Australian case, *Church of the New Faith v Comr for Pay-roll Tax* (1983), scientology was held charitable under the religion head: the court considered any 'belief in a supernatural Being, Thing, or Principle' to be sufficient so long as that belief was combined with canons of conduct giving effect to that belief.

Trusts for other purposes beneficial to the community

13.19 For obvious reasons this is the most difficult category for which to define what counts as charitable, and the 'growth by analogy' approach is most evident here. Perhaps the easiest case is a gift to a locality, such as a village or town (eg *Re Allen* (1905)), or even England (*Re Smith* (1932)) which will be treated as a gift for charitable purposes unless non-charitable purposes for the gift are clearly specified (*A-G Cayman Islands v Wahr-Hansen* (2001)). In *Williams' Trustees v IRC* (1947) there was a gift on trust to establish and maintain an institute, to be known as the 'London Welsh Association', the purposes of which included maintaining an institute for the benefit of Welsh people in London, and promoting their language and culture. The various activities of the institute included lectures, dances, games, and provision of facilities for clubs. These purposes and activities not being exclusively charitable, the trust failed. Lord Simonds quoted Viscount Cave LC in *A-G v National Provincial and Union Bank of England* (1924):

> ... it is not enough to say that the trust in question is for public purposes beneficial to the community; you must also show it to be a charitable trust;

Nor did the gift count as a gift to a locality. Lord Simonds said:

> If the purposes are not charitable *per se*, the localisation of them will not make them charitable.

Thus for a purpose under the fourth head to be charitable, it must be one of those in the Preamble, or one which has already been decided to be analogous to one in the Preamble, or one which the courts are prepared to hold for the first time is analogous to one of those. Simply because the gift is beneficial to a particular community is entirely insufficient.

13.20   The preamble specifically mentions the 'relief of aged, impotent and poor people'. This passage is construed disjunctively, so trusts for the provision of housing for the aged are charitable (*Joseph Rowntree Memorial Trust Housing Association Ltd v A-G* (1983)), as are trusts for blind children (*Re Lewis* (1955)), the seriously ill or wounded (*Re Hillier* (1944)), the permanently disabled (*Re Fraser* (1883)), and trusts for hospitals, even if they charge fees to patients, so long as they are not profit-distributing (*Re Resch's Will Trusts* (1969)). (The same reasoning applies to make independent schools which charge fees charitable.) Trusts for the relief of victims of disasters are charitable (*Re North Devon and West Somerset Relief Fund Trusts* (1953)), but only in so far as they provide relief from poverty, or in the case of sickness or disability, the class is a public one. The Charity Commissioners advise a restriction to those in need under the poverty head, for if the victims are a specific and identifiable group, it may lack public benefit vis-à-vis the relief of sickness or disability.

13.21   Certain public services and facilities are charitable under the fourth head, such as the production of the Law Reports (*Incorporated Council of Law Reporting v A-G*, above) and the work of the National Trust (*Re Verrall* (1916)).

13.22   Although apparently far from the concerns evident in the Preamble, trusts for animal welfare such as the Society for the Prevention of Cruelty to Animals (*Tatham v Drummond* (1864)) and the preservation of wildlife through animal sanctuaries (*Re Wedgwood* (1915) (Wild Fowl Trusts)) are charitable. However, in *Re Grove-Grady* (1929) the CA held that a gift for an animal sanctuary which specifically excluded humans so that the animals would not be molested, was not charitable, for such a gift produced no public benefit. In the New South Wales case of *A-G for New South Wales v Sawtell* (1978) the court reasoned that there has been a general change in public opinion, which now recognises the intrinsic value of the preservation of wildlife, and held such a gift charitable. *Re Grove-Grady* should not be regarded as casting doubt on the ability to create wildlife sanctuaries, but rather suggests that such purposes be expressed in terms of education or environmental protection rather than as a trust purely to benefit the wild animals themselves.

13.23 Trusts for sport or recreation have had a difficult time. In *Re Nottage* (1895) trusts for mere sport, here yacht racing, were held not to be charitable purposes. On the other hand, the provision of land for a recreation ground for public use by the community at large is charitable (*Re Hadden* (1932)). In a Canadian case, *Re Laidlaw Foundation* (1985), it was held that amateur sports institutions would generally be regarded as charitable; the court reasoned that in contrast to the time of *Nottage*, when most people got exercise from manual labour and it was generally the rich who engaged in recreational activities like yacht racing, in these sedentary times amateur sport should be looked upon as promoting health. This approach was not followed by the Charity Commissioners in the case of the Birchfield Harriers (CC Annual Report, 1989, paras 48-55). They decided that the Birchfield Harriers, an amateur athletic club which trained prospective top athletes including many Olympians, and was therefore not available as a facility for the public generally, was not a charitable institution. The Commissioners felt that *Re Nottage* was still the law in England. Similarly, in *IRC v City of Glasgow Police Athletic Association* (1953), the HL accepted that trusts which promote the efficiency of the police or the armed forces are charitable, but held that a trust for the purpose of promoting athletic sports and general pastimes for the Glasgow police was not, being more in the nature of a private trust for the advantage of the members.

13.24 In *IRC v Baddeley* (1955) a trust to be administered by Methodist leaders for the promotion of religious, social and physical well-being of persons resident in West Ham and Leyton, by the provision of facilities for religious services and instruction and for the social and physical training and recreation of persons, who for the time being were or were likely to become members of the Methodist Church who had insufficient means to otherwise enjoy these advantages, was held not charitable by the HL. These recreational purposes were not charitable because there was insufficient public benefit. The public benefit requirement was considered particularly important in the case of charities under the fourth head. Viscount Simonds said that one must observe the distinction

> ... between a form of relief accorded to the whole community yet by its
> very nature advantageous only to the few, and a form of relief accorded

to a selected few out of a larger number equally willing and able to take advantage of it ... I should in the present case conclude that a trust cannot qualify as a charity within the fourth class ... if the beneficiaries are a class of persons not only confined to a particular area but selected within it by reference to a particular creed. The Master of the Rolls in his judgement cites a rhetorical question asked by [counsel] ...: 'Who has ever heard of a bridge to be crossed only by impecunious Methodists?' The reductio ad absurdum is sometimes a cogent form of argument, and this illustration serves to show the danger of conceding the quality of charity to a purpose which is not a public purpose.

The Recreational Charities Act 1958

13.25 Lord Reid dissented in *Baddeley*, and the law was felt to be in some confusion. In response the Recreational Charities Act 1958 was passed. Section 1 states:

1. (1) Subject to the provisions of this Act, it shall be and be deemed always to have been charitable to provide, or assist in the provision of, facilities for recreation or other leisure-time occupation, if the facilities are provided in the interests of social welfare:

Provided that nothing in this section shall be taken to derogate from the principle that a trust or institution to be charitable must be for the public benefit.

(2) The requirement in the foregoing section that the facilities are provided in the interests of social welfare shall not be treated as satisfied unless –
(a) the facilities are provided with the object of improving the conditions of life for the persons for whom the facilities are primarily intended; and
(b) either –
   (i) those persons have need of such facilities as aforesaid by reason of youth, age, infirmity or disablement, poverty or social and economic circumstances; or
   (ii) the facilities are to be available to the members or female members of the public at large.

The act does not define its own public benefit requirement, and so it is not clear that it does much more than restate the law, except in so far as s 1(2)(b) allows facilities restricted to a class on the basis of social and economic circumstances which do not, apparently, simply mean poverty; the other restrictions appear to define classes which have an independent status in the law of charities: gifts for the poor, aged and impotent are good anyway, and recreational facilities for youth are generally treated as charitable as advancing education. The Act does not seem to overturn *Williams v IRC, Baddeley,* or the *Glasgow Police* cases.

13.26   In *IRC v McMullen* (13.14) the HL decided that the gift for sports fell under the education head, and so did not consider the Recreational Charities Act, but in its 1979 decision in the case the CA did; the majority held that the gift was not 'provided in the interests of social welfare', because it did not merely provide facilities for those deprived; second, it was not intended to 'improve the conditions of life of those for whom the facilities were primarily intended', for it was intended as a gift for pupils generally, but would only benefit those who played, irrespective of their conditions in life. Bridge LJ dissented from this 'deprived class' view, saying, 'Hyde Park improves the conditions in life for residents in Mayfair and Belgravia as much as for those in Pimlico or the Portobello Road'. His dissent won the day in the HL in *Guild v IRC* (1992) where a gift for a public sports centre was held to be charitable.

The public benefit requirement

13.27   There are two aspects to the public benefit requirement. The first is that the purpose must be *beneficial* to the public, not detrimental. The second is that the purpose must be of benefit to a section of the public. This aspect of the requirement varies from category to category. Trusts for the relief of poverty are regarded as benefiting the public *per se;* In the case of trusts for the advancement of religion it seems to have been reduced almost to the vanishing point, while for the fourth *Pemsel* category, it appears to be of the essence of charitable status. A charity which operates abroad satisfies the public benefit test if its activities would be charitable if carried out in England (*Re Carapiet's Trust* (2002)).

A detrimental purpose cannot be charitable

13.28   Though a purpose is public in nature, it must be to the public benefit, not to its detriment, to be charitable. Occasionally the courts seem willing, or perhaps feel they are forced, to make decisions about the ultimate benefits of certain purposes. In *National Anti-Vivisection Society v IRC* (1948) the HL decided to weigh the conflicting moral and material utilities of, on one hand, the advancement of morals and education which would result from a suppression of vivisection, and on the other, the benefits to medical science and research vivisection afforded. It decided that on balance the suppression of vivisection was not beneficial to the public. It departed from the earlier case of *Re Foveaux* (1895), which held that the court stood neutral on the public benefit of abolishing vivisection. In *Re Hummeltenberg* (1923) a gift for the training of spiritual mediums was held to provide no public benefit, and in the course of his decision in *Re Pinion* (1965) Harman J gave the illustration of schools for prostitutes or pickpockets as purposes which would not be charitable on this score. In *McGovern v A-G* (**13.36**) the court considered the possible detriment that Amnesty International's activities might have in the conduct of foreign affairs by the government.

13.29 In the case of religion the court appears to allow charities which it regards as having no benefit whatsoever, as in the case of *Thornton v Howe* (**13.10**). With respect to detrimental religious purposes, the Church of Scientology was held to be not charitable (**13.18**), and this may in part have reflected the pronouncements of judges in other cases not concerning scientology's charitable status; in *Hubbard v Vosper* (1972) Lord Denning said that scientology was 'dangerous material', and it was described by Goff J as 'pernicious nonsense' in *Church of Scientology v Kaufman* (1973). In the government white paper, *Charities: A Framework for the Future* (1989, ch 2) the government considered the anxieties of those frightened by religions or cults which insist on members breaking ties with their families, or whose practices were regarded as tantamount to brainwashing. The paper sensibly held that no one had yet devised a definition of 'public benefit' which was workable to distinguish particular religions as actually detrimental, and said it was, in general, the *conduct* of some groups which was not in the public interest, not their religious objects *per se*. Any conduct which was detrimental was more properly addressed by the general criminal and civil law, not by the law of charities.

The requirement that a section of the public must benefit

13.30 In the case of trusts for the advancement of religion, the requirement that a section of the public benefit is minimal, though not non-existent. In *Gilmour v Coats* (1949) the HL held that a gift to a contemplative order of nuns was not charitable, reasoning that intercessory prayer on behalf of members of the public was not a sufficient public benefit; there must be some engagement with the public. In *Neville Estates Ltd v Madden* (1962) a gift to the Catford synagogue was good, for the court:

> ... is entitled to assume that some benefit accrues to the public from the attendance at places of worship of persons who live in this world and mix with their fellow citizens.

In *Re Hetherington* (1990), a gift for the saying of masses for the repose of the donor's husband and relations was charitable on the basis that the masses were said in public.

13.31 The public benefit requirement is more crucial in the case of trusts for the advancement of education. While independent schools are charitable though the benefits directly accrue only to those who are able to pay fees, the case of scholarships restricted to particular classes has caused problems. Trusts for the education of residents of particular localities, or for the children of members of various professions are valid. In *Oppenheim v Tobacco Securities Trust Co Ltd* (1951) a trust for the education of children of employees or former employees of the British-American Tobacco Company, whose employees numbered over 110,000, was held to be not charitable by the HL, on the ground of insufficient public benefit, employing what has been called the 'personal nexus' test: if a class is defined by a personal nexus to someone, and in this case the children's connection with their parent's employer stands on the same footing as one's connection with a relation, then that class is not a section of the public. Lord MacDermott dissented, asking whether there should there be a difference between a trust for the children of coalminers before all the pits were nationalised, which would be charitable, and one for the same children afterward, which would fail since they would all be joined by the employment nexus to the National Coal Board. He rejected the test and said that the court must consider all the circumstances of the case, and would have held the gift charitable. In *Dingle v Turner* (1972) Lord MacDermott's criticism of the personal nexus test was accepted by the HL, though this was *obiter*, as the gift in that case was a gift to relieve poverty, in respect of which there are no similar tests on the extent of the class.

13.32 Indeed, in respect of trusts to relieve poverty, it appears that the public benefit test means no more than that the trusts cannot be for named individuals; a gift for one's poor relations is perfectly valid (*Re*

Scarisbrick (1951)). *Dingle v Turner* (1972) concerned a trust to pay pensions to poor employees. Being restricted to the poor, the trust was valid, but in the course of his judgment Lord Cross rejected the personal nexus test in favour of determining a trust's validity on the basis of all the circumstances of the case. This view was unanimous, but three of the five Law Lords refused to follow him when he said that the fiscal benefits of charitable status were relevant to the determination of charitable status:

> [T]he courts – as I see it – cannot avoid having regard to the fiscal privileges accorded to charities ... [T]hey enjoy immunity from the rules against perpetuity and uncertainty and although individual potential beneficiaries cannot sue to enforce them the public interest arising under them is protected by the Attorney-General. If this was all there would be no reason for the courts not to look favourably on the claim of any 'purpose' trust to be considered a charity if it seemed calculated to confer some real benefit on those intended to benefit by it whoever they might be and if it would fail if not held to be a charity. But that is not all. Charities automatically enjoy fiscal privileges which with the increased burden of taxation have become more and more important and in deciding that such and such a trust is a charitable trust the court is endowing it with a substantial annual subsidy at the expense of the taxpayer ... It is, of course, unfortunate that the recognition of any trust as a valid charitable trust should automatically attract fiscal privileges, for the question whether a trust to further some purpose is so little likely to benefit the public that it ought to be declared invalid and the question whether it is likely to confer such great benefits on the public that it should enjoy fiscal immunity are really two quite different questions.

In particular, he said that certain schemes like the educational scheme in *Oppenheim*, perhaps, were akin to fringe benefits for employees which should not be subsidised by the taxpayer.

13.33 The 'fringe benefit' appeared to be central in two cases which concerned the preferential treatment of a private class in educational trusts. *Re Koettgen's Will Trusts* (1954) concerned a trust for the promotion of commercial education for members of the public who could not afford it, which, however, contained a provision stating that a preference should be given to the families of employees of a named company of up to 75% of the total fund; it was held charitable, though it is clearly very close to the line, if not incompatible with *Oppenheim*. The more recent CA decision in *IRC v Educational Grants Association Ltd*

(1967) may better reflect the current judicial thinking. Here there was a fund devoted to the advancement of education in general terms, which was therefore charitable; the fund was maintained by payments from the Metal Box Company; in one year, however, when the claim was made for tax relief, between 76% and 85% of the income was paid for the education of children of persons connected with the company; the tax relief was denied, because it was held that it was not spent for charitable purposes only – the non-charitable payments were *ultra vires*.

13.34 The public benefit requirement is very much of the essence in respect of trusts under the fourth head. In particular, trusts will fail if the benefit appears to be unnecessarily or artificially restricted, as in *Baddeley*, or restricted to what amounts to a class of private individuals, as in *Glasgow Police*. Such a gift is not bad on this count because the benefits are restricted to residents of a particular community, nor for the reason that only those able to pay fees may take advantage, as in *Re Resch's Will Trusts*. Nor does the trust's being restricted to victims of a disaster create an invalid class (*Re North Devon and West Somerset Relief Fund Trusts*), though being the victim of a disaster does not alone make one an object of charity – only if, and to the extent that, one is thereby impoverished, or disabled, etc. So if a millionaire loses his rose garden in a flood, he is not the proper object of a disaster relief charity.

A charity must be for exclusively charitable purposes

13.35 Trusts have failed for being expressed to be for more than charitable purposes. A classic example is *Morice v Bishop of Durham* (1805), where a trust for 'charitable or benevolent' purposes failed, since not every benevolent purpose would count as a charity under the law. However, charitable trusts may engage in subsidiary purposes or activities which are not themselves charitable, such as fund-raising, which contribute to the fulfillment of their main purposes. It is, however, the issue of charities engaging in political activity which has raised some of the thorniest issues. In general, political purposes are not charitable. The orthodox rationale for this was explained by Lord Simonds in the *National Anti-Vivisection Society* case:

> [Quoting Tyssen on Charitable Bequests:] 'However desirable the change may really be, the law could not stultify itself by holding that it was for the public benefit that the law itself should be changed. Each

court in deciding on the validity of a gift must decide on the principle that the law is right as it stands.' ... Lord Parker [in *Bowman v Secular Society* (1917)] uses slightly different language, but means the same thing, when he says that the court has no means of judging whether a proposed change in the law will or will not be for the public benefit. It is not for the court to judge and the court has no means of judging.

Furthermore, Lord Simonds pointed out that the Attorney-General must supervise and enforce charities, and in some cases, formulate a scheme for their execution, and he should not be put in the position of forwarding a purpose which he and his government might feel to be quite against the interests of the general welfare.

13.36 *McGovern v A-G* (1982) concerned a trust set up by Amnesty International for those of its purposes which it felt were charitable. The relevant purposes were to secure the release of prisoners of conscience, to procure the abolition of torture and other cruel, inhumane or degrading treatment of prisoners, to undertake research into the maintenance and observation of human rights and to disseminate the same. Slade J held that where the political purpose was one of a change in the laws of a foreign country, there was no danger of the court 'stultifying' itself by having to regard a law which it was bound to apply as both right and needing to be changed, since the law was a foreign one. But such a trust would still fail the public benefit test for the court would in such a case have even less means of judging whether the proposed change in the law was of benefit to the local inhabitants. Furthermore, the court would have to take into account the substantial risk that such activity by a UK charity would prejudice the foreign relations of the UK with that country. Precisely the same dangers would apply to changing the administrative practice of a foreign government if the purpose could be achieved by that end. Therefore trusts whose central purposes involved a change in the law, government policy, or administrative practice either in the UK or abroad were political and thus not charitable.

13.37 On the requirement that trust purposes must be wholly and exclusive charitable, Slade J said:

> [Each] and every object or purpose designated must be of a charitable nature. Otherwise, there are no means of discriminating what part of the trust property is intended for charitable purposes and what part for non-charitable purposes and uncertainty in this respect invalidates the

whole trust. Nevertheless, ... a distinction of critical importance has to be drawn between (a) the designated purposes of the trust, (b) the designated means of carrying out these purposes and (c) the consequences of carrying them out. Trust purposes of an otherwise charitable nature do not lose it merely because, as an incidental consequence of the trustees' activities, there may enure to private individuals benefits of a non-charitable nature. Thus, for example, in *Incorporated Council of Law Reporting* the Court of Appeal rejected contentions that the Council of Law Reporting was a non-charitable body merely because publication of the law reports supplied members of the legal profession with the tools of their trade. Similarly, trust purposes of an otherwise charitable nature do not lose it merely because the trustees, by way of furtherance of their purpose, have incidental powers to carry on activities which are not themselves charitable ... The distinction is ... one between (a) those non-charitable activities authorised by the trust instrument and which are merely subsidiary or incidental to a charitable purpose, and (b) those non-charitable activities so authorised which in themselves form part of the trust purpose. In the latter but not the former case, the reference to non-charitable activities will deprive the trust of its charitable status.

13.38 Slade J found that both securing the release of prisoners of conscience and securing the abolition of torture and other degrading or inhuman punishments were not charitable purposes. As to the former, the purpose:

> ... must be regarded as being the procurement of the reversal of the relevant decisions of governments and governmental authorities in those countries where such authorities have decided to detain prisoners of conscience, whether or not in accordance with local law. The procurement of the reversal of such decisions cannot, I think, be regarded as one possible method of giving effect to the purposes ... it is the principal purpose itself.

Making reference to the Amnesty International statutes, Slade J construed the latter purpose as including the abolition of capital and corporal punishment, and found as its main object:

> ... to procure the passing of the appropriate reforming legislation for the purpose of abolishing inhuman or degrading punishments by process of law, including capital and corporal punishment ...

Had research into human rights and dissemination of the result thereof been the only purpose, Slade J would have found the trust charitable, but given that the other purposes were not, it fell with the rest. The general orientation of Slade J's approach has continued in the recent CA decision in *Southwood v A-G* (2000) (see Garton 2000).

13.39 The Charity Commissioners produce guidelines from time to time on ancillary political activities by charities, eg *Political Activities and Campaigning by Charities* (Charity Commission, 1999). In summary, it advises charitable trustees that they may engage in political activity if there is a reasonable expectation that the activity concerned will further the charitable purpose, to an extent justified by the resources spent on the activity, and if the views expressed are 'based on a well-founded and reasoned case and are expressed in a responsible way'. Charities may express views of this kind by making representations to national or local government or individual politicians, but must not participate in party political demonstrations nor support any political party. In the government white paper, *Charities: A Framework for the Future* (1989, paras 2.37-2.46), the government suggested that the law in this area 'commands general agreement', and expressed no intention to reform it.

A charity must be non-profit-distributing

13.40 Charitable trusts may engage in activities to raise funds, including charging fees for their services (*Re Resch's Will Trusts* (1969)), though they must not distribute profits. This goes for charitable companies as well as charitable trusts, obviously. As for earning profits, in *Oxfam v Birmingham City District Council* (1976) the HL held that a charity shop was not entitled as a charity to relief from rates, because it was used for the purpose of fund-raising and was not directed to the charitable purposes themselves. The general rule, therefore, is that the profit-earning activities of charities are liable to the same rates and taxes, such as VAT, as are any other businesses, though various exceptions exist. For example, The Rating (Charity Shops) Act 1976 overturned the *Oxfam* ruling in respect of those shops which are used solely or mainly for the sale of donated goods, the proceeds of which are used solely for charitable purposes.

Preservation from failure: the cy près doctrine

13.41 Where a charitable purpose would fail because the means chosen by a testator for its implementation are either impractical or

509

impossible to carry out, the cy près doctrine, and more recently, ss 13 and 14 of the Charities Act 1993 can be applied so that it will not fail. 'Cy près' is law French, originally meaning something like 'as near as possible'. The cy près power of the courts allows the court to direct that the trust property be applied to a purpose as close as possible to the one intended by the settlor. Cy près can save charitable trusts from failure at the outset, or from subsequent failure when carrying out the purpose becomes impossible or impractical.

Preservation from failure at the outset

13.42 The cy près doctrine can save a charitable trust from failure at the outset because the charitable purpose is impractical or impossible to carry out. NB: The doctrine only applies to a purpose which already counts as a charitable purpose, ie to relieve poverty, or advance education, or some other charitable purpose. Students regularly make the mistake on exams of thinking that the court can use the cy-près doctrine to turn a non-charitable purpose into a charitable one – the court cannot. In order for the court to re-direct trust money intended for a charitable purpose which fails by applying the cy près doctrine, the court must find that the donor manifested a 'general' or 'paramount' charitable intention, ie an intention to give the money to charitable purposes of which the particular gift was but a specification; if the intention was to give only to the specific charity or charitable purpose, and the charity is defunct or the purpose impossible to carry out, then the gift fails.

13.43 What is a general charitable intention? In *Re Lysaght* (1966) Buckley J said:

> A general charitable intention ... may be said to be a paramount intention on the part of a donor to effect some charitable purpose which the court can find a method of putting into operation, notwithstanding that it is impracticable to give effect to some direction by the donor which is not an essential part of his true intention – not, that is to say, part of his paramount intention. In contrast, a particular charitable intention exists where the donor means his charitable disposition to take effect if, but only if, it can be carried into effect in a particular specified way, for example, in connection with a particular school to be established at a particular place, *Re Wilson* (1913), or by establishing a home in a particular house: *Re Packe* (1918).

3.44 The courts have employed cy près effectively to strike out conditions on trusts for scholarships. In *Re Lysaght* (1966) an endowment of medical studentships at the Royal College of Surgeons was to be restricted to recipients not of the Jewish or Roman Catholic faith; the College would not accept the gift because the condition was 'so invidious and so alien to the spirit of the college's work as to make the gift inoperable in that form'. In *Re Woodhams* (1981), music scholarships were restricted to boys from two particular groups of orphans' homes. In both cases the condition was regarded as an inessential element of the testator's bequest, specifying particular means of carrying out his general charitable intention to fund the said scholarships, and the conditions were deleted. It is said (Hayton (2001b), 578; Martin (2001), 448) that these cases are an exception to the rule that a trust will not fail for want of a trustee, since it was considered essential to the gift that the scholarships were at the named institutions. Despite the words of the judges in the cases, however, this betrays a misunderstanding. While the *participation* of the named institution was essential for the gifts, so that had they refused to allow their students to take up the scholarships the charitable purpose would indeed have failed, this has nothing to do with who held the funds on trust. The gifts would have failed even if the money was to be paid by another trustee to students nominated by the institutions. A trust never fails for want of a trustee, but a charitable purpose may fail if carrying it out requires the participation of a particular individual or institution and that individual or institution refuses.

3.45 Many cases in which charitable gifts are saved from failure at the outset concern testamentary gifts to charitable institutions or bodies which operated when the testator made his will but have since been amalgamated with others or have gone defunct. Three cases must be distinguished. The first concerns gifts to particular named charities which no longer exist in their own right, but whose purposes are continued by other charities. In *Re Faraker* (1912) there was a testamentary gift to 'Mrs Bayley's Charity, Rotherhithe' which had, with other local charities, been consolidated into a trust for the poor in Rotherhithe. The CA held that the gift should go to the consolidated charity because it continued the named charity. This is not an example of cy près, for the gift is regarded as being successfully made to the intended charity. This is so even in the circumstances where, as in *Faraker*, the continuing charity has substantially different overall purposes; the original charity was for poor widows, and the consolidated charity was for the poor generally, so that there was no guarantee that any of the gift actually went to poor widows.

13.46   Second, where the particular charitable institution named to be the recipient of the gift no longer exists, the gift will not fail if on a true construction of the testator's intentions he intended to create a charitable purpose trust and merely indicated this institution to serve as the trustee. Since a trust will not fail for want of a trustee, the court will find another trustee to carry out the charitable purpose. This construction is much more likely in the case of a gift to an unincorporated charitable body than an incorporated one, for the following reasons given by Buckley J in *Re Vernon's Will Trusts* (1972):

> Every bequest to an unincorporated charity by name without more must take effect as a gift for a charitable purpose. No individual or aggregate of individuals could claim to take such a bequest beneficially. If the gift is to be permitted to take effect at all, it must be as a bequest for a purpose, viz., that charitable purpose which the named charity exists to serve. A bequest which is in terms made for a charitable purpose will not fail for lack of a trustee ... A bequest to a named unincorporated charity, however, may on its true interpretation show that the testator's intention to make the gift at all was dependent upon the named charitable organisation being available at the time when the gift takes effect to serve as the instrument for applying the subject matter of the gift to the charitable purpose for which it is by inference given. If so and the named charity ceases to exist in the lifetime of the testator, the gift fails: *In re Ovey* (1885). A bequest to a corporate body, on the other hand, takes effect simply as a gift to that body beneficially, unless there are circumstances which show that the recipient is to take the gift as a trustee. There is no need in such a case to infer a trust for any particular purpose ... the natural construction is that the bequest is made to the corporate body as part of its general funds, that is to say, beneficially and without the imposition of any trust. That the testator's motive in making the bequest may have undoubtedly been to assist the work of the incorporated body would be insufficient to create a trust.

13.47   This reasoning is inventive but unpersuasive. Surely most testators do not know whether the institutions to which they give are unincorporated or not, and second, most probably do not register a distinction between a gift to a charitable body as an accretion to its funds or a gift for the charitable purposes it carries out; how then, can such a distinction be used to discern the testator's intentions? Nevertheless the distinction is accepted as good law; it was applied in *Re Finger's Will Trusts* (1972), so that a gift to a now defunct unincorporated association was valid as a purpose trust, whereas a gift to a defunct incorporated body failed, though the latter was saved by applying the money cy près. Re *Vernon* and Re *Finger* were both cited with apparent approval by the CA in Re *Koeppler Will Trusts* (1986). Such a purpose trust is a trust for that specific purpose only; a particular charitable institution serving as trustee must not treat the gift as a general accretion to its funds, but must apply it only to the specific purpose (Re *Spence* (1979)). In contrast, testamentary gifts to an incorporated charity which took effect following a court order that it be wound up, but before its actual dissolution were, on the same principles, held by Neuberger J not to be gifts on trust for a charitable purpose, but gifts in accretion to the corporation's funds; the gifts went into the general assets of the charitable corporation for distribution to its creditors (Re *ARMS (Multiple Sclerosis Research) Ltd* (1997)).

13.48 True cases of cy près only occur where the intended charitable gift actually fails, as in the gift to the incorporated body in Re *Finger's Will Trusts* above. In Re *Rymer* (1895) the testator gave money to a particular seminary, which at the time of the testator's death has ceased to exist, although its current students were transferred to another seminary. The gift could only be saved by application of the cy près doctrine, but since the court found that the gift was to the particular seminary only, there was no general charitable intention, so cy près could not be applied.

13.49 Re *Harwood* (1936) established something of a general rule that a gift to a particular charity that once existed but is now defunct, is interpreted, unless there are indications to the contrary, as a gift intended for that body alone, disclosing no general charitable intention, whereas in the case of a gift to a named charity which never existed it is much easier to find a general charitable intention. In Re *Spence* Megarry VC extended the principle to the case where the testator has selected a particular charitable purpose, here the purpose of benefiting the residents of a particular old folks home which at the testatrix's death ceased to exist. He explained the rule's rationale as follows:

> I do not think that the reasoning of the In re *Harwood* line of cases is directed to any feature of institutions as distinct from purposes. Instead, I think the essence of the distinction is in the difference between particularity and generality. If a particular institution or purpose is specified, then it is that institution or purpose, and no other, that is to be the object of the benefaction. It is difficult to envisage a testator as

being suffused with a general glow of broad charity when he is labouring, and labouring successfully, to identify some particular specified institution or purpose as the object of his bounty. The specific displaces the general. It is otherwise where the testator has been unable to specify any particular charitable institution or practicable purpose, and so, although his intention of charity can be seen, he has failed to provide any way of giving effect to it. There, the absence of the specific leaves the general undisturbed. It follows that in my view in the case before me, where the testatrix has clearly specified a particular charitable purpose which before her death became impossible to carry out, [there is] that level of great difficulty in demonstrating the existence of a general charitable intention which was indicated by *In re Harwood*.

13.50 Section 14 of the Charities Act 1993 usefully provides that where collections are on public appeal for a charitable purpose, eg purchasing a work of art for the National Gallery so that it remains within the UK, which fails at the outset, eg not enough money is raised for the purpose, the money will be applicable cy près as if given for charitable purposes generally.

Preservation from subsequent failure

13.51 When a charitable trust has been effectively carried out for a time, but then its purposes become impossible or impractical to carry out, the court may modify the purposes, on the basis that they are giving effect to the settlor's intention to give property 'out and out' to charity. Up to the turn of the century, the cy près power to modify the terms of a trust was narrowly construed, and only if the original terms were actually impossible or impractical to carry out would the court intervene. So, as Martin ((2001), 446) remarks, cumbersome, uneconomical, and inconvenient trusts for 'the distribution of loaves to the poor or of stockings for poor maidservants' continued well into this century. S 13 of the Charities Act 1993 has expanded the scope for the doctrine, in particular providing that a cy près modification may occur where the original purposes have been adequately provided by other means, which encompasses statutory services in a welfare state. Section 13, though often used by the Charities Commissioners, has not been frequently litigated. In *Re JW Laing Trust* (1984), it was held that s 13 applied only to permit alterations in the purposes of a trust, not variations of settlor's directions which were merely administrative, though in this case, such a direction, that the capital and income be fully distributed within a short time period, was deleted under the court's inherent jurisdiction (**10.73**)

Varsani v Jesani (1999) is an interesting recent case. The court employed its power under s 13 to divide the assets of a religious sect between two rival factions following a fundamental disagreement over the true tenets of the faith.

Reform

13.52 In 2002 the Cabinet Office's Strategy Unit published *Private Action, Public Benefit* (Cabinet Office, 2002). While the report is written in the ugly sloganeering, bullet-point style beloved of the only functionally literate, it contains some useful information on the 'non-profit sector'. It also suggests several reforms, the most important of which have been accepted by the Government (with some modification, following its own consultation) in *Charities and Not-for-Profits: A Modern Legal Framework* (Home Office, 2003).

A statutory definition based on a list of charitable purposes

13.53 A new statutory definition of charity is proposed, as follows

A charity is an organisation which provides public benefit and which has one or more of the following purposes:
1. The prevention and relief of poverty;
2. The advancement of education;
3. The advancement of religion;
4. The advancement of health (including the prevention and relief of sickness, disease, or of human suffering);
5. Social and community advancement (including the care, support and protection of the aged, people with a disability, children and young people);
6. The advancement of culture, arts, heritage, and science;
7. The advancement of amateur sport;
8. The promotion of human rights, conflict resolution and reconciliation;
9. The advancement of environmental protection and improvement;
10. The promotion of animal welfare;
11. The provision of social housing;
12. Other purposes beneficial to the community.

3. 54 The proposed reform is clearly anything but radical; save for the advancement of amateur sport, the new list of purposes merely makes 'accessible to the layman' what was already charitable under the old case law, a 'rebranding' exercise, if you will. The stated purpose is not to produce a definition which would render uncharitable anything which is now charitable under the law.

13.55 It should be noted in particular that the proposals confirm the charitable status of the advancement of religion, and indeed would widen the definition of religion in any legislation to ensure that 'faiths that are multi-deity (such as Hinduism) or *non-deity* (such as some types of Buddhism) should also qualify' (Cabinet Office, 2002, para 4.34, my italics). But can the public recognition of charitable status (and whatever fiscal benefits flow from that) be justified in regard to any 'religious' activities, much less all of them? We may be living in a new age of faith, but as has been said before, the problem with the death of God is not that people believe in nothing, but that people will believe in anything, crystals, dolphins, the summer solstice, heaven only knows what nonsense. It will be interesting, perhaps appalling, to see what 'non-deity' faiths might now be registered as charities.

The 'public character' of charities – ongoing 'checks'

13.56 Under the proposals, all charities would be subject to ongoing checks to affirm that they were really operating in the public benefit, and no charitable purpose, in particular the purpose of advancing religion, would be regarded as automatically conferring public benefit, although the proposals seem to accept the case law view (**13.29**) that the public celebration of a religious rite provides a public benefit. Finally, can we admit the charitable status of religions while at the same time drawing a line around unacceptable conduct which may be the direct result of religious belief? Can one support the belief without indirectly and culpably, supporting the conduct to which it leads? Should charitable status turn on the conduct of adherents acting upon their beliefs? For example, should religious organisations whose adherents support, or worse undertake, acts of violence, be de-registered?

13.57 These ongoing checks also threaten the status of organisations which charge high fees for their services, such as fee-charging hospitals and independent schools. Such organisations, to ensure they retain a public character, must show that they provide access for those who would be excluded by their high fees, for example scholarships in independent schools or some public access to their facilities.

Dissociating validity from exemption from taxation

13.58 The new proposals do not consider the tax reliefs accorded to all charities, but the issue remains a live one. Are the taxation exemptions that automatically follow from charitable status the real cause of worry about which purposes are charitable, as Lord Cross appeared to think in *Dingle*? The new proposals seem to side-step the issue by apparently assuming that all charities, to be charitable, must be for the public benefit. But is that a defensible provision? Is the practice of religious rites or the education provided by public schools as beneficial to the public as the support of medical research or cultural institutions such as the National Gallery? The idea is sometimes mooted that the state ought to give money directly to those 'true' charities (eg Chesterman (1999)). If that were to be done on a fair and transparent basis, however, it would simply require a new definition of, or graded scale for, 'public benefit'. If the government of the day was able to subsidise whichever charities in whatever amounts it liked, then one is faced with the concern that the independence of charities to pursue public goals which might be politically unpopular would be discouraged, leading some charities at least to tailor their purposes for political reasons; furthermore, smaller charities which could not muster the political support to lobby for a state subsidy would be unfairly disadvantaged.

Further reading

Gravells (1977); Moffat (1999), ch 18; Cabinet Office (2002); Home Office (2003); Charity Commissioners (1999); Economist (1995); Chesterman (1999); Mitchell (1999a,b)

Must read cases: *McGovern v A-G* (1981); *Re Lysaght* (1965); *Incorporated Council of Law Reporting for England and Wales v A-G* (1972); *IRC v McMullen* (1981); *IRC v Baddeley* (1955); *Oppenheim v Tobacco Securities Trust* (1951); *Dingle v Turner* (1972); *Re Faraker* (1912); *Re Vernon's Will Trusts* (1960); *Re Finger's Will Trusts* (1971); *Re Spence* (1978).

Self-test questions

1. Are the following purposes charitable? If not, should they be?
   • to set up an amateur sporting institute, for the better training of Great Britain's most promising young amateur athletes;
   • to provide birth control to students in schools in London;
   • to provide tennis rackets to the unemployed of Manchester;
   • to provide a national health service in a poor third world country where the predominant religion prohibits blood transfusions;
   • to further the activities of a religious sect which counsels its adherents to withdraw from the world and live in remote communes;
   • to provide scholarships to assist students to learn ballroom dancing while at university, with the condition that the trustees may, in applying up to 75% of the income of the trust, give preference to children of employees of Y Ltd.;
   • to provide funds to the Sisters of 2001, an association of Roman Catholic nuns whose sole activity is to persuade the Vatican to allow the ordination of women priests.

2. What is the public benefit requirement, and how does it operate with respect to the different categories of charity?

3. How does the law operate to save charitable trusts from initial failure? Describe and critically assess the law governing the court's finding of a 'general charitable intention'.

4. 'The Government's recent proposals to 'reform' charities law represent a missed opportunity'. Discuss.

Select bibliography

American Law Institute (1959), *Restatement of Trusts, 2d* (American Law Institute: St. Paul, Minn., 1959)

Baker, J (1990) *An Introduction to Legal History*, 3rd edn (London: Butterworths)

Bant, E (1998) ' "Ignorance" As a Ground of Restitution – Can It Survive?' [1998] LMCLQ 18

Bell, A (1989) *Modern Law of Personal Property* (London: Butterworths)

Birks, P (1989) 'Misdirected funds: restitution from the recipient' [1989] LMCLQ 296

Birks, P (1991) 'The English recognition of unjust enrichment' [1991] LMCLQ 473

Birks, P (1992) 'Mixing and Tracing' 45(2) *Current Legal Problems* 69

Birks, P (1992) 'Restitution and Resulting Trusts' in Goldstein, *Equity and Contemporary Legal Developments* (Oxford, Oxford University Press)

Birks, P (1993) 'Persistent Problems in Misdirected Money: A Quintet' [1993] LMCLQ 218

Birks, P (1994) '*In rem* or *in personam? Webb v Webb*' 8 TLI 99

Birks, P (1996a) 'Inconsistency between Compensation and Restitution' 112 LQR 375

Birks, P (1996b) 'Equity in the Modern Law: An Exercise in Taxonomy' 26 University of Western Australia Law Review 1

Birks, P (1997) 'On taking seriously the difference between tracing and claiming' 11 TLI 2

Birks, P (2000a) *English Private Law* (Oxford: Oxford University Press)

Birks, P (2000b) 'Rights, Wrongs, and Remedies' 20 Oxford J Leg Stud 1

Birks, P (2002a) 'Rights, Wrongs, and Remedies' 20 OJLS 1

Birks, P (2002b) 'Receipt' in Birks & Pretto (2002), 213

Birks, P (2002c) 'The Content of Fiduciary Obligations' 16 TLI 34

Birks, P and Pretto, A (eds) (2002) *Breach of Trust* (Oxford: Hart)

Birks, P, (ed) (1994) *The Frontiers of Liability, Volumes I and II* (Oxford: Oxford University Press)

Birks, P, (ed) (1995) *Laundering and Tracing* (Oxford: Clarendon Press)

Birks, P, (ed) (1997) *Privacy and Loyalty* (Oxford: Clarendon Press)

Brownbill, D, 'Anatomy of a Trust Deed' Parts I-III: (1992) 1 Journal of International Planning 35, 100, 165; Parts IV-VI: (1993) 2 Journal of International Trust and Corporate Planning 49, 103, 164; Parts VII-VIII (1994) 3 Journal of International Trust and Corporate Planning 50, 166; Part IX (1995) 4 Journal of International Trust and Corporate Planning 51.

Burn, E (1994) *Cheshire and Burn's Modern Law of Real Property*, 15th edn (London: Butterworths)

Burrows, A (2001) 'Proprietary Restitution: Unmasking Unjust Enrichment' 117 LQR 412

Burrows, A (2002a) 'We Do This At Common Law But That In Equity' 22 OJLS 1

Burrows, A (2002b) *The Law of Restitution* 2d Ed (London: Butterworths)

Cabinet Office (2002) Number 10 Strategy Unit Report: *Private Action, Public Benefit: A Review of Charities and the Wider Not-For-Profit Sector* http://www.number-10.gov.uk/su/voluntary/report/index.htm

Chambers, R (1997) *Resulting Trusts* (Oxford: Clarendon Press)

Chambers, R (2001) Comment on *Lohia v Lohia*, 15 TLI 26

Chambers, R (2001-02) 'Constructive Trusts in Canada', 15 TLI 214 and 16 TLI 2

Charity Commission (1999) 'Political Activities and Campaigning by Charities' http://www.charity-commission.gov.uk/publications/cc9.asp

Charity Commissioners (1995) 'Political Activities and Campaigning by Charities'

Chesterman, M (1999) 'Foundations of Charity Law in the New Welfare State' 62 MLR 333

Conaglen, M (2003) 'Equitable Compensation for Breach of Fiduciary Dealing Rules' 119 LQR 246

Cornish, W (1996) *Intellectual Property* 3rd edn (London: Sweet & Maxwell)

Crilley, D (1994) 'A Case of Proprietary Overkill' [1994] Restitution Law Review 57

Cullity, M (1975) 'Judicial Control of Trustees' Discretions' 25 University of Toronto Law Journal 99

Cullity, M (1985) 'Liability of Beneficiaries: A Rejoinder' 7 Estates and Trusts Quarterly 35

Cullity, M (1986) 'Liability of Beneficiaries: A Further Rejoinder to Mr Flannigan' 8 Estates and Trusts Quarterly 130

Economist (1995) 'Not as deserving as they seem' (15 July 1995) The Economist 22

Elliot, D (1960) 'The Power of Trustees to Enforce Covenants in Favour of Volunteers' 76 LQR 100

Elliott, S & Mitchell, C (2004) 'Remedies for Dishonest Assistance' 67 MLR 16

Emery, C (1982) 'The Most Hallowed Principle – Certainty of Beneficiaries of Trusts and Powers of Appointment' 98 LQR 551

Endicott, T (1997) 'Vagueness and Legal Theory' 3 Legal Theory 37

Evans, S (1999) 'Rethinking Tracing and the Law of Restitution' 115 LQR 469

Flannigan, R (1984) 'Beneficiary Liability in Business Trusts' 6 Estates and Trusts Quarterly 278

Flannigan, R (1986) 'The Control Test of Principal Status Applied to Business Trusts' 8 Estates and Trusts Quarterly 37

Flannigan, R (2000) 'Fiduciary Regulation of Sexual Exploitation' 79 Canadian Bar Review 301

Ford, H, and I Hardingham (1987) 'Trading Trusts: Rights and Liabilities of Beneficiaries' in Finn, P *Equity and Commercial Relationships* (Sydney: The Law Book Co.). 48-88.

Gardner, S (1993) 'Rethinking Family Property' 109 LQR 263

Gardner, S (1998) 'A detail in the construction of gifts to unincorporated associations' [1998] *The Conveyancer* 8

Garton, J (2000) Comment on *Southwood v A-G*, 14 TLI 233

Garton, J (2003) 'The Role of the Trust Mechanism in the Rule in *Re Rose*' [2003] Conveyancer 364

Gleeson, S (1995) 'The Involuntary Launderer: The Banker's Liability for Deposits of the Proceeds of Crime' in P Birks (ed) *Laundering and Tracing* (Oxford: Clarendon), 115.

Glister, J (2002) '*Twinsectra v Yardley*: trusts, powers, and contractual obligations' 16 TLI 223

Glister, J (2004a) 'Trusts as Quasi-Securities? The Law Commission's Proposals for the Registration of Security Interests' LMCLQ forthcoming

Glister, J (2004b) 'The Nature of Quistclose Trusts: Classification and Reconciliation' CLJ forthcoming

Goode, R (1991) 'Property and Unjust Enrichment' in Burrows, A (ed) *Essays on the Law of Restitution* (Oxford: Clarendon Press), 215

Goode, R (1998) 'Proprietary Restitutionary Gains' in Cornish et al (eds) *Restitution: Past, Present, and Future* (Oxford: Hart, 1998), 63

Goodhart, W (1996) 'Trust Law for the Twenty-first Century' in Oakley AJ (ed) *Trends in Contemporary Trust Law* (Oxford: OUP, 1996), 257

Grantham, R & Rickett, C (1996) 'Restitution, Property and Ignorance - A Reply to Mr Swadling' [1996] LMCLQ 463

Grantham, R & Rickett, C (1998) 'Trust Money as an Unjust Enrichment A Misconception' [1988] LMCLQ 514

Grantham, R & Rickett, C (2001) 'On the Subsidiarity of Unjust Enrichment' 117 LQR 273

Gravells, N (1977) 'Public Purpose Trusts' 40 MLR 397

Grbich, Y (1974) 'Baden: Awakening the Conceptually Moribund Trust' 37 MLR 643

Green, B (1980) 'The Dissolution of Unincorporated Non-Profit Associations' 43 MLR 626

Green, B (1984) 'Grey, Oughtred, and Vandervell – A Contextual Reappraisal' 47 MLR 385

Grubb, A (1982) 'Powers, Trusts and Classes of Objects' [1982] Conveyancer 432

Hackney, J (1987) *Understanding Equity and Trusts* (London: Fontana)

Halliwell,M (1992) [1992] *Conveyancer* 124 on bona fide purchaser defence to restitutionary claim

Ham, R (1995) 'Trustees' liability' 9 TLI 21

Harpum, C (1986) 'The Stranger as Constructive Trustee' 102 LQR 114 267 – double article

Harpum, C (1990) 'Overreaching, Trustee's Powers, and the Reform of the 1925 Legislation' 49 Cambridge LJ 277

Harpum, C (1994) 'The Basis of Equitable Liability' in Birks, P (ed) *The Frontiers of Liability, Volume I* (Oxford: Oxford University Press), 9

Harris, J (1971) 'Trust, Power, or Duty' 87 LQR 31.

Haskett, T 'The Medieval English Court of Chancery' (1996) 14 Law and History Review 245

Hayton, D (1990) 'Developing the Law of Trusts for the Twenty-first Century' 106 LQR 87

Hayton, D (1994) 'Uncertainty of Subject-Matter of Trusts' 110 LQR 335

Hayton, D (1996) 'The Irreducible Core Content of Trusteeship' in Oakley, A (ed) *Trends in Contemporary Trust Law* (Oxford: Oxford University Press), 47

Hayton, D (1999) 'English Fiduciary Standards and Trust Law' 32 Vanderbilt Journal of Transnational Law 555

Hayton, D (2001a) 'Developing the Obligation Characteristic of the Trust' 117 LQR 96

Hayton, D (2001b) *Hayton and Marshall: Commentary and Cases on the Law of Trusts and Equitable Remedies* 11th edn (London: Sweet & Maxwell)

Hayton, D (2003) *Underhill and Hayton: Law of Trusts and Trustees* 16th ed. (London: Butterworths)

Hicks, A (2001) 'The Trustee Act 2000 and the modern meaning of "investment"' 15 TLI 203

Ho, L (1998) 'Attributing losses to a breach of fiduciary duty' 12 TLI 66

Hodge, D (1980) 'Secret Trusts: The Fraud Theory Revisited' [1980] Conveyancer 341

Home Office (2003) 'Charities and Not-for-Profits: A Modern Legal Framework' http://www.homeoffice.gov.uk/docs3/charitiesnotforprofit.eng.pdf

Hopkins, J (1971) 'Certain Uncertainties of Trusts and Powers' [1971] CLJ 68

Hornby, J (1962) 'Covenants in Favour of Volunteers' 78 LQR 228

Jones, G (1959) 'Delegation By Trustees: A Reappraisal' 22 MLR 381

Jones, G (1968) 'Unjust Enrichment and the Fiduciary's Duty of Loyalty' 84 LQR 472

Khurshid, S and Matthews, P 'Tracing Confusion' (1979) 95 LQR 78

Kodilinye, G (1982) 'A Fresh Look at the Rule in Strong v Bird' [1982] Conveyancer 14

Langbein, J (1994) 'The new American trust-investment Act' 8 TLI 123

Langbein, J and Posner, R (1980) 'Social Investing and the Law of Trusts' 79 Michigan Law Review 72

Law Commission (1999) *Report: Trustees' Powers and Duties* Law Com No 262

Law Commission (2003) 'Registration of Security Interests: Company Charges and Property other than Land (Consultation Paper 164) http://www.lawcom.gov.uk/239.htm#lccp164

Law Commission for England and Wales (2002), 'Trustee Exemption Clauses; Consultation Paper No. 171' (Law Commission, 2002) http://www.lawcom.gov.uk/files/cp171.pdf

Law Reform Committee (1982) *23rd Report: The Powers and Duties of Trustees*, Cmnd 8733

Lewin on Trusts – see Mowbray et al (2000)

Lowry, J & A Dignam (2003) *Company Law 2d.Ed* (London: Butterworths)

Lowry, J (1994) '*Regal (Hastings)* Fifty Years On: Breaking the Bonds of the *Ancien Régime*' 45 Northern Ireland Legal Quarterly 1

Lowry, J (1997) 'Directorial Self-Dealing; Constructing a Regime of Accountability' 48 Northern Ireland Legal Quarterly 211

Lowry, J and Edmonds, R (1998) 'The Corporate Opportunity Doctrine: The Shifting Boundaries of the Duty and its Remedies' 61 MLR 515

Macnair, M (1988) 'Equity and Volunteers' 8 Legal Studies 172

Maitland, FW (1909) Equity; also the forms of action at common law: two courses of lectures

Martin, J (2001) Hanbury and Martin's Modern Equity 16th edn (London Sweet & Maxwell)

Matthews, P (1979) 'The True Basis of the Half-Secret Trust?' [1979] Conveyancer 360

Matthews, P (1989) 'The Efficacy of Trustee Exemption Clauses in English Law' [1989] Conveyancer 42

Matthews, P (1995a) 'A problem in the construction of gifts to unincorporated associations' [1995] Conveyancer 302

Matthews, P (1995b) 'The Legal and Moral Limits of Common Law Tracing' in Birks (ed.) (1995), 23

Matthews, P (1996) 'The New Trust: Obligations without Rights?' in Oakley AJ (ed) Trends in Contemporary Trust Law (Oxford: Oxford University Press), 1

McKay, L 'Re Baden and the Third Class of Uncertainty' (1974) 38 Conveyancer 269

McKnight, A (2004) 'Review of Swadling, (ed.) The Quistclose Trust' (2004 TLI (forthcoming)

Millett, P (1985) 'The Quistclose Trust – Who Can Enforce it?' 101 LQR 269

Millett, P (1998) 'Equity's Place in the Law of Commerce; Restitution and Constructive Trusts' 114 LQR 214, 399

Millett, P (2000) 'Pension schemes and the law of trusts: the tail wagging the dog?' 14 TLI 66

Mitchell, C (1994) The Law of Subrogation (Oxford: OUP)

Mitchell, C (1999a) 'Redefining Charity in English Law' 13 TLI 21

Mitchell, C (1999b) 'Charity taxation under review' 13 TLI 107

Mitchell, C (2002) 'Assistance' in Birks & Pretto (2002), 139

Moffat, G (1999) Trusts Law: Text and Materials 3rd edn (London Butterworths)

Mowbray, J et al (2000) Lewin on Trusts 17th Ed. (London: Sweet & Maxwell)

Murphy, W (1991) 'The Oldest Social Science? The Epistemic Properties of the Common Law Tradition' 54 MLR 182

Nicholls, Lord (1995) 'Trustees and their broader community: where duty, morality, and ethics converge' 9 TLI 71

Nicholls, Lord (1998) 'Knowing Receipt: the Need for a New Landmark' in Cornish, W et al (eds) *Restitution: Past, Present and Future* (Oxford: Hart)

Nobles, R (1992) 'Charities and Ethical Investment' [1992] Conveyancer 115

Nobles, R (1992) 'The Exercise Of Trustees' Discretion Under A Pension Scheme' [1992] Journal of Business Law 261

Nolan, R (1995) 'Change of Position' in Birks, P (ed) *Laundering and Tracing* (Oxford: Clarendon Press), 135

Nolan, R (2002) '*Vandervell v IRC*: A Case of Overreaching' 61 Cambridge LJ 169

Nolan, R (2004) 'Property in a Fund' 120 LQR 108

O'Sullivan, D (2002) '*The Rule in* Philips v Philips' 118 LQR 296

Oakley, A (2003) *Parker and Mellows Modern Law of Trusts* 8th ed. (London: Sweet & Maxwell)

Parkinson, P (2002) 'Reconceptualising the Express Trust' 61 CLJ 657

Penner, JE (1996a) 'Voluntary Obligations and the Scope of the Law of Contract' 2 Legal Theory 325

Penner, JE (1996b) 'The 'Bundle of Rights' Picture of Property' 43 UCLA Law Review 711

Penner, JE (1997) *The Idea of Property in Law* (Oxford: Clarendon Press)

Penner, JE (2000) Review of Baxendale-Walker, *Purpose Trusts* (London: Butterworths, 1999), 14 TLI 118

Penner, JE (2002) 'Exemptions' in Birks & Pretto (2002), 241

Penner, JE (2004) 'Lord Millett's Analysis' in Swadling (2004), 41

Perrins, B (1985) 'Secret Trusts: The Key to the *Dehors*' [1985] Conveyancer 248

Pollard, D (2003) 'Case note: *Schmidt v Rosewood Trust*' 17 TLI 90

Rickett, C (1980) 'Unincorporated Associations and their Dissolution' 39 CLJ 88

Rickett, C (1999) 'The Classification of Trusts' 18 *New Zealand Universities Law Review* 305

Rickett, C (2001) 'Completely Constituting an *Inter Vivos* Trust: Property Rules?' [2001] Conveyancer 515

Rose, F (1996), 'Gratuitous Transfers and Illegal Purposes' 112 LQR 386

Scott, A (1917) 'The Nature of the Rights of the Cestui Que Trust' 17 Columbia Law Review 269

Scottish Law Commission (2003) 'Discussion Paper on Breach of Trust; Discussion Paper No. 123' (Scottish Law Commission, 2003) http://www.scotlawcom.gov.uk/downloads/dp123_breach_of_trust.pdf

Sealy L (1962) 'Fiduciary Relationships' [1962] CLJ 69

Sheridan, L (1951) 'English and Irish Secret Trusts' 67 LQR 314

Simpson, A (1986) A History of the Land Law, 2nd edn (Oxford: Clarendon Press)

Smith L (2003b) 'The Motive, Not the Deed' in Getzler et al (eds) Rationalizing Property, Equity and Trusts (London: Butterworths, 2003)

Smith, L (1994) 'Tracing, 'swollen assets' and the lowest intermediate balance: Bishopsgate Investment Management Ltd v Homan' 8 TLI 102

Smith, L (1995) 'Tracing in Taylor v Plumer: Equity in the Court of King's Bench' [1995] LMCLQ 240

Smith, L (1997) The Law of Tracing (Oxford: Clarendon Press)

Smith, L (1998) 'W(h)ither Knowing Receipt?' 114 LQR 394

Smith, L (1999) 'Constructive Trusts and Constructive Trustees' 58 Cambridge LJ 294

Smith, L (2000) 'Unjust Enrichment, Property, and the Structure of Trusts' 116 LQR 412

Smith, L (2003a) 'Access to Information: Schmidt v Rosewood Trust Ltd' 23 Estates, Trusts & Pensions J 1

Smith, L (2003b) 'The Motive, Not the Deed' in Getzler et al (eds) Rationalising Property, Equity, and Trusts (London: Butterworths), 53

Smith, L (2004) 'Understanding the Power' in Swadling (2004), 67.

Stebbings, C (2002) The Private Trustee in Victorian England (Cambridge: Cambridge University Press)

Sullivan, G (1979) 'Going it Alone – Queensland Mines v Hudson' 42 MLR 711

Swadling, W (1987) 'The Conveyancer's Revenge' [1987] Conveyancer 451

Swadling, W (1994) 'Some Lessons from the Law of Torts' in Birks, P (ed) The Frontiers of Liability, Volume I (Oxford: Oxford University Press), 41

Swadling, W (1995) 'The Nature of Ministerial Receipt' in Birks, P (ed) Laundering and Tracing (Oxford: Clarendon Press), 243

Swadling, W (1996) 'A Claim in Restitution?' [1996] LMCLQ 63

Swadling, W (1996a) 'A new role for resulting trusts?' 16 Legal Studies 110

Swadling, W (1996b) 'A Claim in Restitution?' [1996] LMCLQ 63

Swadling, W (1997) 'Property and Unjust Enrichment' in JW Harris (ed) Property Problems: From Genes to Pension Funds (London: Kluwer), 130

Swadling, W (1998) 'Property and Conscience' 12 TLI 228

Swadling, W (2000) 'Property: General Principles' in Birks (2000), 203-384

Swadling, W (2004) *The Quistclose Trust* (Oxford: Hart)

Treitel, G (2003) *The Law of Contract* 11th edn (London: Sweet & Maxwell)

Trust Law Committee (1997) *Rights of Creditors Against Trustees and Trust Funds; A Consultation Paper*

Trust Law Committee (1999) *Report and Consulation Papers: Report on Rights of Creditors Against Trustees and Trust Funds; Consultation Papers on Capital and Income of Trusts, Trustee Exemption Clauses*

Underhill & Hayton *Law of Trusts and Trustees* – see Hayton (2003)

Waters, D (1967) 'The Nature of the Trust Beneficiary's Interest' XLV Canadian Bar Review 219

Waters, D (1996) 'The Protector: New wine in Old Bottles?' in Oakley, A (ed) *Trends in Contemporary Trust Law* (Oxford: Clarendon Press), 63.

Watkin, T (1981) 'Cloaking a Contravention' [1981] Conveyancer 335

Weinrib, E (1975) 'The Fiduciary Obligation' 25 University of Toronto Law Journal 1

White Paper (1989) 'Charities: A Framework for the Future' Cmnd 694

Willoughby, P (1999) *Misplaced Trust* (Saffron Walden: Gostick Hall)

Worthington, S (1996) *Proprietary Interests in Commercial Transactions* (Oxford: Clarendon Press)

Worthington, S (1999a) 'Reconsidering Disgorgement for Wrongs' 62 MLR 218

Worthington,S (1999b) 'Fiduciaries: When is Self-Denial Obligatory?' 58 CLJ 500

Worthington, S (2000) 'Corporate Governance: Remedying and Ratifying Directors' Breaches' 116 LQR 638

Worthington, S (2003) *Equity* (Oxford: Clarendon Press)

Wright, D (1999) 'The Rise of Non-Consensual Subrogation' [1999] Conveyancer 113

Youdan, T (1984) 'Formalities for Trusts of Land, and the Doctrine in *Rochefoucauld v Boustead*' 43 CLJ 306

Index

The Law of Trusts

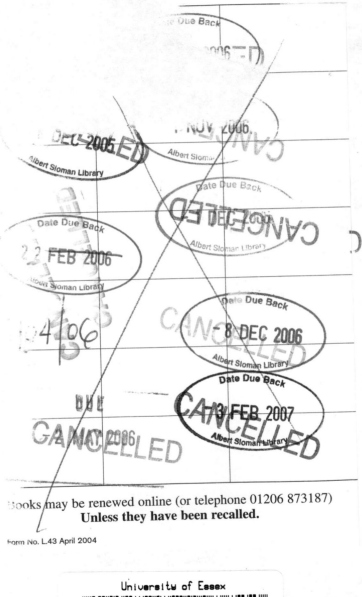

Books may be renewed online (or telephone 01206 873187)
Unless they have been recalled.

Form No. L.43 April 2004